STATE AND SOCIETY

THIRD EDITION

edited by Alain-G. Gagnon

broadview press

National Library of Canada Cataloguing in Publication

Québec : state and society / edited by Alain-G. Gagnon. — 3rd ed.

Includes bibliographical references and index.
ISBN 1-55111-579-4

1. Québec (Province)—Politics and government—1960- 2. Québec (Province)—Social conditions—1960-1991. 3. Québec (Province)—Social conditions—1991- I. Gagnon, Alain-G. (Alain-Gustave), 1954-

FC2926.Q42 2003   971.4'04   C2003-906288-0

Broadview Press, Ltd. is an independent, international publishing house, incorporated in 1985.

North America
Post Office Box 1243,
Peterborough, Ontario,
Canada K9J 7H5
Tel: (705) 743-8990
Fax: (705) 743-8353

3576 California Road,
Orchard Park, New York
USA 14127

UK, Ireland, and Continental Europe
NBN Plymbridge
Estover Road
Plymouth PL6 7PY UK
Tel: 44 (0) 1752 202301
Fax: 44 (0) 1752 202331
Fax Order Line: 44 (0) 1752 202333
Customer Service:
    cserv@nbnplymbridge.com
Orders: orders@nbnplymbridge.com

Australia and New Zealand
UNIREPS
University of
New South Wales
Sydney, NSW, 2052
Tel: + 61 2 96640999
Fax: + 61 2 96645420
info.press@unsw.edu.au

Broadview believes in shared ownership, both with its employees and with the general public; since the year 2000 Broadview shares have traded publicly on the Toronto Venture Exchange under the symbol BDP.

We welcome any comments and suggestions regarding any aspect of our publications — please feel free to contact us at the addresses below, or at broadview@broadviewpress.com / customerservice@broadviewpress.com / www.broadviewpress.com

Broadview Press Ltd. gratefully acknowledges the financial support of the Government of Canada through the Book Publishing Industry Development Program for our publishing activities.

Eco-Logo Certified.
30% Post.

Cover design and typeset by Zack Taylor Design, www.zacktaylor.com.

This book is printed on acid-free paper containing 30% post-consumer fibre.

Printed in Canada

Québec

Québec

Contents

Part II Governance

Part III Political Parties and Social Movements

Part IV Education, Language, and Immigration

Part V Territoriality, Globalization, and International Relations

Acknowledgements

Carrying out a project of this magnitude requires the intervention of several contributors. To begin, I would like to thank the authors of the texts, who have submitted contributions that are both original and rich in substance to this new edition. Moreover, most of the authors participated in a preparatory conference at McGill University, within the framework of activities surrounding the *Summit of the Americas* held in Québec and in Montréal in March 2001, and were subsequently asked to revise their texts following some critical commentary by their peers. The assistance of Stéphan Gervais, assistant to the Director of the Québec Studies Program at McGill University, was particularly valuable during the tenure of the conference.

I would also like to thank all of the translators who have allowed the present studies to become accessible in English, Spanish, French, Portuguese, particularly Roberto Breña and Zila Bernd, who supervised the Spanish and Portuguese translations.

Several other people have also assisted in this project. I am thinking of Jean-Guy Côté, a student in the Québec Studies Program of McGill University, whose follow-ups ensured that the authors' deadlines were met in the final preparatory stages of the manuscript. The new contributors, including Peter Graefe (McMaster University), Raffaele Iacovino (McGill University), Jocelyn Maclure (University of Southampton), Éric Montpetit (Université de Montréal), and Luc Turgeon (University of Toronto), have contributed important considerations with a view to developing new aspects to the present edition and I gladly thank them.

One dimension that should not be neglected here is the necessity for financial aid in the preparation of a book published in four languages. I would like to take this occasion to express my gratitude to the Mouvement Desjardins for its generous contribution to the Québec Studies Program and to the Office of the Vice-Principal (teaching) of McGill University. The financial contributions of the International Association of Québec Studies (AIEQ) and of the Fonds de solidarité du Québec must also be emphasized. On the governmental side, this project has benefited from the support of the Ministry of State for International Relations, the Ministry of State for the Economy and Finances, the Ministry of Canadian Intergovernmental Affairs, the Ministry of State for Education and Youth, as well as the Ministry of Research, Science and Technology and the Ministry of Relations with Citizens and Immigration of the Government of Québec.

I am especially grateful for the support received from Raymond Bachand, Claude Béland, Louise Beaudoin, Jean-Pierre Beaudry, Gretta Chambers, Gilles Charland, Michel Chevrier, Jacques Joli-Coeur, Alban D'Amour, Fernand Daoust, Joseph Facal, Claude Girard, Emmanuel Kattan, Naim Kattan, Ingo Kolboom, Robert Laliberté, Ginette Lamontagne, Bernard Landry, Daniel Legault, François Legault, Jacques Léonard, Chantal Létourneau, Louiselle Lévesque, Nicole McKinnon, Patrick Muzzi, Gabriel Polisois, Michel Robitaille, Jean Rochon, Michel Sarra-Bournet, Sylvain Simard, Jacques Vallée, and Luc Vinet.

I wish to deeply thank Hugh Segal and his team at the Institute for Research on Public Policy where I spent the first eight months of 2002. While I was there, I found a professional environment that was very stimulating, contributing greatly to the progression of the present project.

Finally, sincere thanks to the staff of Broadview Press who supported me throughout the project, especially Michael Harrison, and to Laurna Tallman for her editing.

Alain-G. Gagnon

Introduction

It has already been 20 years since I invited over 20 political scientists, sociologists, and specialists in the history of ideas, from diverse schools of thought, to provide their perspective on the question of Québec. The first French language edition, published by Québec Amérique in 1994, went on to receive the Richard-Arès Book Prize in 1995. The book is now available in its second edition in French and its third in English. One particularly interesting development is that, as of 2003, *Québec: State and Society* will be available in the four principal languages of the Americas, as Portuguese and Spanish versions, under the respective supervision of Zila Bernd and Roberto Breña will be released by the Universidade Federal do Rio do Sul de Porto Alegre and the Universidad de Guadalajara (Centro Universitario de Ciencias Sociales y Humanidades).

This book has become required reading for those who wish to grasp the political life of Québec; it is used in the majority of Canadian and Québec universities, and in most of the foreign research centres on the study of Québec where it has become essential reading for students and researchers alike.

Québec: State and Society mirrors a society that continues to transform itself, one that adjusts to changes taking place on the international scene, while providing an understanding of its unique experience across the world.

The present edition distinguishes itself from the preceding ones by proposing five main themes of the Québec condition. In the first section, Jacques Beauchemin, Jocelyn Maclure, Luc Turgeon, Dimitrios Karmis, and Daniel Salée proceed respectively with analyses that centre on Québec's sense of being, identitive narratives and counter-narratives, the main historiographical paths, national identities, and the Aboriginal question. Québec is taken as a vast laboratory of primary significance that allows us to identify, among others, some major challenges confronted by small nations within advanced liberal democracies, including memory, identities, and pluralism.[1]

In the second section, the theme of governance is examined from several angles. On the one hand, Alain-G. Gagnon and Andrée Lajoie undertake a study of constitutional debates, assessing Québec-Canada relations from the English conquest to the enactment of the *Clarity Bill*, which followed the publication of the Ruling by the Supreme Court of Canada with regards to the Reference case on the right of Québec to secede. On the other, Éric Montpetit, Christian Rouillard, Luc Bernier, and Francis Garon meticulously examine the functioning of neo-corporatist networks, central agencies, and the sociétés d'État in Québec in light of the challenges brought about by globalization and the centralizing tendencies of Canadian federalism as they are exacerbated by the neoliberal movement across the Americas.[2]

The third section of the volume discusses a series of fundamental questions on the role played by the various elements of civil society in Québec, ranging from the relevance of political parties to the diversity of social movements including the anti-globalization movement, the trade-union movement, and the women's movement. Brian Tanguay, Marc Lemire, Jean Charest, and Chantal Maillé assess the mechanics of the Québec state, the links established with representatives of civil society as agents of legitimacy, and examine the main political families that compete for Québec's political space.[3]

In the fourth section, education, language, and immigration are at the forefront of the researchers' interests.[4] Marie Mc Andrew opens this section with an analysis of the links that need to be constructed between immigration, pluralism, and education in order to endow Québec with the tools for development in light of new challenges. Garth Stevenson proposes an informed reading of the political history of anglophones in Québec by emphasizing their behaviour as a minority group, even though they were over-represented in Québec institutions until the middle of the 1970s. Elisabeth Gidengil, André Blais, Neil Nevitte, and Richard Nadeau continue on this subject by re-assessing the question of cultural insecurity among francophone Quebecers and the evolution of public policies in Québec. Alain-G. Gagnon and Raffaele Iacovino conclude this section with a study of Québec's model of interculturalism as a novel means for establishing a citizenship model that is more conducive to Québec's societal project.

In the final section, the authors look at some significant contemporary questions and propose a vast program for research in areas that include nationalism, territoriality, globalization, and international relations. Researchers present a critical look at modern Québec. Michael Keating and François Rocher propose a rich and insightful reading of Québec's insertion into the globalized continentalized economic system. Peter Graefe examines the capacity of the Québec nationalist movement to confront globalization while maintaining its basic progressive characteristics. Louis Balthazar concludes this section with an exhaustive portrait of the development of policies targeted towards increasing Québec state's presence in international relations.[5]

Notes

1. Two collective works can be consulted: Jocelyn Maclure and Alain-G. Gagnon, eds., *Repères en mutation. Identité et citoyenneté dans le Québec contemporain*, "Débats" series (Montréal: Québec Amérique, 2001) and Michel Venne, ed., *Penser la nation québécoise*, "Débats" series (Montréal: Québec Amérique, 2000).

2. On the centralist tendencies of the Canadian federal system, see the analyses by eight specialists on the Canadian Social Union project in Alain-G. Gagnon and Hugh Segal, eds., *The Canadian Social Union Without Québec* (Montréal: Institute for Research on Public Policy, 2000) as well as the volume edited by Alain-G. Gagnon, Montserrat Guibernau, and François Rocher, *The Conditions of Diversity in Multinational Democracies* (Montréal: Institute for Research on Public Policy, 2003).

3. The reader can pursue this topic by consulting Alain-G. Gagnon and Alain Noël, eds., *L'espace québécois* (Montréal: Québec Amérique, 1995).

4. Marie Mc Andrew, *Immigration et diversité à l'école: le débat québécois dans une perspective comparative* (Montréal: Les Presses de l'Université de Montréal, 2001) and Marc Levine, *The Reconquest of Montréal* (Philadelphia: Temple University Press, 1990).

5. See also Alain Dieckhoff, *La nation dans tous ses états. Les identités nationales en mouvements* (Paris: Flammarion, 2000); Alain-G. Gagnon and James Tully, *Multinational Democracies* (Cambridge: Cambridge University Press, 2001); Michael Keating, *Plurinational Democracy: Stateless Nations in a Post-Sovereignty Era* (Oxford: Oxford University Press, 2001).

PART I
Québec Today: Memory, Identity, and Pluralism

1

What Does It Mean to be a Quebecer?
Between Self-Preservation and Openness to the Other

JACQUES BEAUCHEMIN*

The most important theoretical and political issue concerning what is usually called the Québec question resides in the definition of the political subject, and of the political community in which the subject emerges as a totalizing figure of society.

This debate, in which many intellectuals in Québec are engaged, revolves around the different forms of these essential definitions. The contrast that characterizes the debate between ethnic and civic nationalism postulates a distinction between a community of shared memory and belonging and one that defines a group of citizens around rights from the standpoint of formal equality.[1] In political sociology, transformation in the conception of the "collective we," which has progressively abandoned the concept of culture for the concept of identity, again distinguishes between *identity* as "substantive" and *society* as constructed dialogically through an openness towards Otherness, the crossbreeding of identities, and in the experience of pluralism.[2] The promulgation of law C-20, which concerns the constitutionality of a possible referendum on Québec sovereignty, raised a debate in the same vein because C-20 opposed a communitarian conception of society whereas the sovereignty proposal's legitimacy resides in the recognition of a specific collective experience. Law C-20 also opposed a liberal conception, namely, that the definition of the political subject can only rely on a procedural framework of regulation that is blind to the assertions of communitarians.

* Translated from French into English by Michael Darroch.

We find the basis of this debate most clearly formulated in the writings of Fernand Dumont. Dumont distinguishes the "French nation"—Quebecers of French-Canadian descent with those who have been assimilated into this group—from the Québec "political community."[3] This latter corresponds to the symbolic and institutional sphere where the diverse components of Québec society converge. Thus, according to Dumont, the political community represents the normative framework within which identity issues are developed, among them the "French nation," which is postulated to be rooted in history and thus to have a certain permanence. From this viewpoint, the Québec nation does not exist and the goals the sovereignty proposal pursues can only correspond to a desire to fulfill the French-Canadian destiny. Such a proposal should, therefore, integrate minority groups within a Québec political community that is governed by the francophone majority. This distinction has incited rather severe criticism, insofar as it has been seen to bear features of a potentially ethnic conception of the Québec nation.[4] The problem is even more complex if one considers that within the definition proposed by Dumont, the political community only unites the three "traditional" national groups that make up Québec society. In recent years, a broader concept of political community has established itself in which Québec society welcomes identity claims by diverse groups. Alongside the protagonists—the francophone, anglophone, and Aboriginal communities—new identity groups (women, youth, or even visible minorities) have now emerged with their own demands, who reject the symbolic and political hegemony of the totalizing political subject of the nation.[5]

The emotions that Dumont's thesis stirs up would lead us to believe that his argument parts the waters, separating on one hand those who advocate a nationalism open to the fundamental pluralism of society and, on the other hand, adherents to a nationalism still associated with French-Canadian history and, as such, exclusivist. The Dumontian distinction not only serves to raise an interesting theoretical problem; it also locates the problem by questioning the definitions of the Québec political community and the political subject who claims to represent it. In other words, the Dumontian distinction asks: what does it mean to be a Quebecer? More precisely, the question at the centre of the debate on the future of Québec is threefold: it consists in the definition of the Québec political subject, the definition of the political community capable of producing this subject, and, ultimately, it addresses the legitimacy of the sovereignty proposal.

In the pages that follow, I will examine competing concepts of the Québec political subject. It is not my intention to establish which one best corresponds to the political scene. Rather, I wish to reveal the ambiguity on which current attempts to restructure the political community have floundered. The argument behind this illustration is as follows: though not usually recognized as such, there is a tension stretching throughout political thought in Québec, between an ideal of citizenship in which the locus is constituted as a specific definition of nation, and another definition, in accordance with which a goal of complete openness towards the diversity of political identity concomitantly is pursued. In other words, fully recognizing the pluralism of the political community unsaddles the Québec political-national subject (of which Quebecers of French-Canadian descent make up the majority community sharing a common history), whose consistency and historical permanence we wish, in fact, to assert. On a more directly political level, this sometimes explicit, but most often implicit, desire to promote what Dumont calls the "French nation" simultaneously with a nation whose "political community" has been reconstituted and whose plural character is immediately recognizable, leads to an ungrounded affirmation of francophone nationalism, one that does not tend to include other identities. Furthermore, it leads to the affirmation of what Laurent-Michel Vacher has called "sovereignism without nationalism."

Before examining several concepts of the Québec subject and political community as found in the field of political sociology, we must return to some fundamental questions pertaining to notions of the political subject and the political community.

Unity of Politics in Modern Society

Historically, the unity of the political field has been defined with reference to three constituent dimensions: (1) the existence of different communities of shared history and memory within one social-historical sphere; (2) a dimension transcending the diversity in the image of a political subject that the nation produces, that is, where the nation subsumes diverse affiliations to different cultural underpinnings and particularistic identities; and (3) democracy as a formal framework for debate. The unity of the political field thus combines the existence of a shared history, a political sphere within which the legitimacy of decisions that derive from democratic debate is recognized—the nation—and a political structure of debate—democracy—within which ethical orientations to communal life are debated and the conflicting claims stemming from various historical communities are organized. The political subject (which, in the history of modernity, is generally a national subject according to which social actors recognize themselves as, for example, French, German, American, or Québécois) is always related to a certain definition of common interests and the legitimacy of orientations adopted in the name of these interests. The political subject is commonly defined in relation to a majority community of shared history that always strives to invest the subject with the memory of its particular historical path. This shared history constitutes the empirical-historical substratum of the political subject; it always strives to assert itself through a subject as if he or she were the sole representative of the nation. It is crucial to note that conflict is by no means absent from the definition of the political subject.

Its claim to universalism is always questionable and its monopoly of identity always contested. In effect, communities of shared history or groups assembled on a peer basis in social movements, united by alternative practices, or even members of cultural minorities—groups marginalized within a universalizing movement having a dominant shared history that establishes itself already adorned with characteristics of the universal—will denounce this fallacious universalism asserted in the unity of the national political subject. For this reason, one can say that the affirmation of a national political subject that claims to unify opposing interests within a political community, in which a conflict of identities nevertheless prevails, always constitutes an act of power.[6] This also explains why national minorities have been marginalized in the historical development of great nations. Furthermore, in the name of the common good certain demands have been made outside of the law, claims whose legitimacy we now consider unquestionable, such as the right to strike or women's right to vote.

Nevertheless, if the political community constitutes, by definition, the place of conflict, it is also the place where conflict is managed. For this reason, politics defines itself more precisely as the management of an ethical-political project. This implies that, for the individual, the exercise of citizenship depends at once on his capacity to register dissidence in discussion led under the protection of democratic debate within the political community, as well as on his support for a specific definition of the totalizing political subject and the ethical project of communal life that it entails.[7] The protection of the three dimensions that form the unity of politics is essential to the simultaneous pursuit of freedoms and the ethical project of managing conflicts engendered by this very distribution of freedoms. Citizenship in early modernity thus bound the exercise of citizenship to an ethical-political project supported by the integrity of the national political subject and the respect for democracy.

In what way has modernity attempted to protect the integrity of the three dimensions of the political field? It succeeded, until very recently, by affirming the unity of the political subject to which this goal was linked, by bringing the legitimacy of the ethical and political choices undertaken in its name to the national sphere, and by defending the integrity of the formal framework of debate in a defence of democracy. Citizenship was thus defined, at the dawn of modernity, in a vertical relationship to the transcendent whole of the political subject and its sphere, as well as in respect for the rules of democracy.[8] It is crucial to observe that current attempts to redefine citizenship in western societies seem to be undertaken within a mode of politicization relatively free both of the question of the integrity of the political subject and the question of the social-historical sphere in which its project is carried forward. In this light, that is, from the perspective of the fragmented political subject, I would now like to examine the characteristics of a new type of citizenship.

Contemporary citizenship has redefined itself through the recognition of identities. This occurs in the dynamic of politicizing social relationships that can be described as political identities.[9] In other words, the new citizenship represents a goal of political inclusion, embracing all categories of actors within the scope of a dynamic where all are recognized by all.[10] In this perspective, the exercise of genuine citizenship is based on three conditions. The first requires that we recognize who is laying the claim to political identity. The second requires that we recognize the political character of the demands made by social actors who claim this identity as their own. The third calls for establishing, from the perspective of social equality, an evaluation of this claim in the scope of political identity. The conditions associated to this new definition of citizenship are at the origin of a transformation according to which exercising citizenship is no longer based on the simple respect of basic rights. Rather, the exercise of citizenship implies acquiring new rights, to the extent that new identity groups coalesce—groups that are capable of asserting the specificity of their situation in the light of universal egalitarianism. More than ever before, citizenship corresponds, to use Arendt's words, to the right to have rights. It is no coincidence that this new reasoning for the claim to citizenship expresses a failure to observe these three rules as a denial of citizenship. The common sphere has progressively gained in significance, in accordance with which it no longer suffices to have conventional civic rights in order to be a citizen. Not receiving a reasonable minimum income, being a victim of discrimination at the workplace, or not being able to make oneself heard in the public sphere all would constitute denials of citizenship in the eyes of an underlying politics of equality.

Henceforth, this new image will no longer situate the citizen in relation to a centrally defined political subject and to the ethical-political project with which the subject is associated. The question of citizenship now arises in the context of the fragmentation of the unitary political subject claiming universality; a subject that at one time was represented by the nation. Indeed, social actors no longer emerge into the political arena with the age-old status deriving from the simple fact of being a citizen of the nation. They now lay claim to respect for their rights under the banner of a much more narrowly defined identity. This renewal of citizenship, sought to a great extent by actors of civil society and promoted by the Charter of Rights, is essentially based on the notions of fragmented identity and pluralism. It is now a matter of endorsing such pluralism rather than fighting against it.[11] Up to a certain point, the new form of citizenship establishes itself in opposition to its previous form. It puts forward particularist claims stemming from identity pluralism against an imperium political subject that overshadows such distinctive characteristics and decrees, in the name of the universal, a normalcy to which everyone is supposed to submit for the sake of the public good or general interests. With the disappearance of the image of a unitary political subject, a reconstitution of the political community asserts itself. Groups of citizens no longer assert democratic claims under the banner of the nation, but rather in the name of the very groups to which they are associated through their specific affinities. Clearly, we can favourably welcome this transformation in politics, recognizing in it the continuation of the dynamic of political emancipation that modernity introduced by accepting pluralism. Nevertheless, this transformation is certainly at the origin of competing definitions of the Québec political community, of a distinct ambiguity in the definition of the political subject, and of the ideal of citizenship, which now deserve further consideration.

Québec Citizenship in a National Pluralistic Framework

The present government of Québec would like Québec citizenship to be fashioned so that a well-defined policy framework finally may be achieved. More precisely, it is a matter of incorporating the Québec definition of citizenship into a political community clearly organized around the political subject of a sovereign Québec.[12] The Québec government thus believes that the revitalization of citizenship will meet with the pitfalls represented by the double allegiance that the Québec-Canada duality engenders. A citizen of Québec can effectively define himself as Canadian or Quebecer, or he can call simultaneously upon these twin allegiances. What seems to "confuse the exercise of citizenship" consists in the citizen's capacity to play one affiliation against another or even enter into one model of integration or another. In ideal circumstances, Québec citizenship would stand in relation to a Québec political community in full possession of the means necessary for its self-assertion. From this perspective, citizenship is defined by its relation to the totalizing subject of the nation. It thus implies a vertically defined allegiance between a national political subject and the citizen who accepts the former act as for the public good or for a general interest that is defined nationally.

The first definition does not fit well into the second, which the government nevertheless praises, and which consists in the recognition of all by all, that is, in welcoming the multiple claims to political recognition that are now expressed from all directions. In the latter case, citizenship is defined horizontally: multiple groups of actors meet at the centre of the political arena, progressing under the auspices of equality and laying claim to recognition and rights, both necessary, in their eyes, to achieve an ideal of citizenship. Now, this redefinition of citizenship, where we may hope to renew the pursuit of particularist rights on the horizontal plane, would seem to oppose a notion of citizenship founded on the allegiance to a political subject that is the focus of a desire to live together. One could evidently retranslate this antagonism in terms of two opposing visions of citizenship: between the republican and Jacobin vision, as it emerged from the French experience, and the vision that emerged from the American experience, in which the separation of powers and the importance of community life within a dynamic civil society constitute the foundations of citizenship. It is clear enough that this second sense of citizenship has asserted itself definitively as our societies opened up to identity pluralism. However, in a society such as Québec where a national question persists, the adherence to an ideal of citizenship founded on the acceptance of pluralism and on the recognition of diverse identities raises two problems. The first problem is that the assertion of a citizenship open to particularist claims and recognizing the fragmentation of the political community questions the legitimacy of a nationalist project that is based on a specific shared history. The second problem is that this openness to pluralism does not eliminate to any extent the need to base the legitimacy of political action on the image of a political subject capable of symbolically transcending competition between particularisms when members of these identity groups lay their claims as a condition of fully achieving citizenship. For this reason, state rhetoric revolving around the revitalization of citizenship urges the expression of pluralism and, simultaneously, attempts to limit the corrosive effects of these demands for recognition on the integrity of the social connection by invoking a necessary convergence around a Québec political subject that sovereignty would sanction.

Québec is not the only society grappling with this dilemma that would see citizenship reconstituted at once through the liberation of distinct identities, and through a unified and totalizing political subject embodying a specific relation to the public good. Certainly, the national question in Québec makes this contradiction more apparent, a contradiction intimately connected to new forms of politicizing social relations in contemporary societies. At the same time, the particular circumstances in Québec best allow us to understand this dynamic. Here, rather contradictory assertions of citizenship from strong, diverse voices in civil society coexist with the necessary assertion of a totalizing reference point, which contains the centripetal forces of the demands for recognition.

I will now examine three relatively contradictory archetypal positions that appear among the most important contributions to the political analysis of Québec society. In roughly sketching their orientations, I will attempt to demonstrate that these positions may be grouped in relation to three images of the political subject: monologic, ambivalent, and dialogic.

The Monologic Subject of the Nation

The first concept of political community, and the political subject that would represent this community in its entirety, presents the subject as a relatively unified one. From this viewpoint, the figure of a colonized and alienated subject is discernible in the French-Canadian destiny, a figure that must be liberated and allowed to come into its own.[13] Numerous interpretations of the political subject can be found in works of political sociology since the 1960s. Nevertheless, it is true that these positions became increasingly scarce as the new definition of the subject emerged, and thus the form of citizenship that locates this definition within the sphere of pluralism.

This theoretical political position offers a clear and unambiguous understanding of the Québec political subject, the nature of the political community that fosters it, and of the goal that it should pursue.[14] This position is embodied in the French-Canadian who became a Quebecer after the Quiet Revolution, an image to which all those who wanted to follow the same path have progressively attached themselves. Alongside the majority community of French-Canadian heritage, the political community brings together minority groups receiving the same political treatment that all democratic societies provide for minorities: respect for basic rights and, in the case of Québec, the protection of a certain number of acquired rights. We expect these minority communities to assimilate into the majority or, at the very least, that they will not impede the majority's broader project. It follows naturally from this position that the French-Canadian majority community should uphold the idea of its political independence to the extent that this project constitutes the means for decolonization.

From this perspective, advocates of a national and unitary political ideal have risen up against current efforts to establish a more open definition of this subject and the form of citizenship that it calls for. They see it as a theoretical ploy laced with political treachery.[15] Theoretically, positions based on a concept of civic nationalism would evade the otherwise inescapable reality of the communitarian foundation of social existence. Laurent-Michel Vacher finds it strange that Québec intellectuals who are in complete support of sovereignty also challenge nationalism on the grounds of the potentially exclusivist attitude that it harbours.[16] On the political plane, definitions inspired by pluralism and openness to others would make Québec sovereignty a "strategy without content, a means without purpose, a project without memory."[17] Serge Cantin is perhaps the most eloquent representative of this perspective. He denounces theoretical positions that, from this point of view, constitute a dangerous form of resignation that opposes the duty to preserve the memory of and the protection of French-Canadian culture. He is not alone in upholding this opinion; many others think that these positions entail an obstinate attachment to the past, entirely devoted to protecting the buried treasure of the French-Canadian historical legacy. Did not Jean Bouthillette, also concerned about the future of the French-Canadian people, affirm as early as 1971 that "our people will first be conquered by the extreme fatigue, the deceitful temptation of death"?[18]

A republican model of citizenship corresponds to this definition of the political subject. Nevertheless, to shed this challenge and promote a unitary political subject belongs less and less to the current temper of the times. Similarly, the dream of achieving national sovereignty through the simple determination of a people finally fulfilling its destiny does not seem to take into account that the political dynamic, which I referred to earlier as identity politics, is not an epiphenomenon arising from a specific historical context, but constitutes rather the most important phenomenon as far as the feasibility and legitimacy of the sovereignist proposal is concerned. Ancient nations formed themselves "from top down." They asserted a political subject connected to a form of citizenship that was henceforth associated to the nation. Modern nations—those that wish to emerge within a pre-existing national framework—must build themselves "from bottom up" by organizing diverse identity interests. Such is the contemporary definition of the political community and its corresponding form of citizenship. By no means does this definition entirely contradict the sovereignist proposal, but the effects of this political dynamic require us to reflect upon its feasibility.

It is nonetheless vital to observe that advocates of a national and unitary political subject (which may also be considered republican) do not level unfounded criticism at the devotees of a civic nationalism open to the expression of identity. This does not imply that one line of reasoning is superior to the other, but rather that the argument for pluralism and difference, by promoting diversity and recognizing rights in the range of identities, accords an ambiguous place to a community of shared history.

The Ambivalent Subject of the Nation

In contrast to the self-assured definition that clearly delineates the figure of the monologic political subject, others have posited a fundamentally ambivalent subject, or in another sense, a subject whose identity markers are not limited to the nation. This point of view assumes that the political community is irremediably plural and divided.[19] Moreover, this essential division indicates that a new democratic experience is taking root. From this perspective, the sovereignist project does not bear the same urgency, and constitutes but one emancipatory claim among many others.

Jocelyn Létourneau has sought to answer the difficult question of how intellectuals can contribute to producing the historical consciousness of the Québec nation by taking into account or, more to the point, by affirming the nation's fundamental and insurmountable deficiency of identity.[20] Létourneau finds the response to this question in two intellectual positions that he places under the theme "remembering where we are coming from" (*se souvenir d'où l'on s'en va*) and in the belief that "the future is open and is not subject to any teleological purpose." For this reason, we must take the calculated risk of a future bound to ambivalence. Létourneau believes the stagnation of Québec identity is due to an "ambivalence of being." Above all, he sees the paralysis in the permanence of this movement among Québec intellectuals, a movement that, ever since Parent and Garneau, brings them to the rescue of a nation coming to understand itself while being incapable of developing politically. Ambivalence and a mission of redemption—for Létourneau, these are the constants of the broad dialogue that the country carries on, along with those whose job is to interpret it.

For Létourneau, Dumont's nationalism, furthered by Cantin's version, is representative of this position. In effect, Létourneau finds in Dumont the most eminent spokesperson for all those who persist obstinately in constructing the historical consciousness of the French-Canadian and, since the 1960s, the Québec nation. One could say, therefore, that the obstinacy and constantly renewed disenchantment evoked by Létourneau correspond to the urgency of providing the nation with new insight into itself, or to the old sorrow of not seeing the nation come into being, a nation which is nevertheless aware of its existence. It is evident that this position challenges the voluntarism by virtue of which the Québec political subject would absolutely have to be identified and assigned the task of realizing itself through sovereignty. This political subject is ambivalent with respect to its self-definition, but we should not seek to suppress the political community in which contradictory definitions intersect. Intellectuals who watch over the subject as if it required curing of its eternal indecisiveness should accept its ambivalence.

Nevertheless, in admitting that intellectuals always harbour the desire to lead the nation to truth, does it not remain necessary for all society, as Dumont claims, to base its ethical-political project on a sense of belonging to the world, on the image of a shared world of experience in the name of which this project finds meaning? Suppose we admit a need for this common world: could the image that social actors form of such a common world (in Hannah Arendt's sense) be constructed solely on the serene acceptance of an ambivalent identity? Could it be constructed on this availability of identity despite the possibilities that the future holds, including the possibility that their identity may disappear?

One can undoubtedly maintain that the sovereignty proposal does not correspond to the fundamental ambivalence of the Québec political subject. Nevertheless, does it not matter whether the issues concerning the subject are defined politically in one way or another? The continuity of the community of shared history formed by "Quebecers of French-Canadian descent" is an issue that has been questioned historically and that continues to be addressed today. This collective had to live on throughout Canadian history to be able to express its desire for recognition and be granted all the political prerogatives pertaining to this recognition, and in order that the problem that this collective raises within Canadian federalism can still be made the object of colloquiums and books today. Now, this persistence is not only a result of the calm and reticent stubbornness of those French Canadians who, from the heart of their campaign and their minority status, continue to speak French and remain attached to their traditions. This community of shared history has not been wiped from Canadian history, because it was able, at an opportune time, to establish claims to recognition through political means. Within the Union, it is impossible to govern a United Canada without duplicating all of the important functions, because French Canadians will not accept representation by members of the "other nationality." At the time of Confederation, they demanded the formation of provinces, against the wishes of MacDonald who sought a centralized union.[21] In this way, they believed they would be able to defend their institutions. The unfolding of events has clearly proved them right. The political institution that the provinces represent has enabled the community to reproduce itself. If it is still possible today to discuss French-Canadian heritage, to see it renewed within the sphere of francophonie, or even to contemplate its North American-ness, it is without doubt owing to the fact that the means were adopted to form this historical community into a political subject, admittedly ambivalent, but sufficiently consistent to be able to gain recognition and initiate its own project.

Although the identity of Quebecers of French-Canadian descent is faring well, should we expect a miraculous continuity to this heritage now intersected with other identities?

The Dialogic Subject of the Nation

Gérard Bouchard has posited the need to "open up the circle of the nation," thus locating the political community within the pluralism that comprises it without challenging the underlying memory of French-Canadian culture.[22] This implies integrating diverse affiliations and identities into the framework of the "political community." Defining the political subject and its ensuing (civic) citizenship in this manner raises additional theoretical and political questions. On the theoretical plane, such a conception of the political community diminishes the need to see the community overshadowed by the totalizing political subject. From this perspective, the subject need not be defined culturally or ethnically: the pursuit of a goal aimed at developing a North American francophonie already circumscribes the definition of the subject, and is sufficient to assign an objective to it. It would thus be a matter of breaking with the substantialist definition of community, preferring instead the image of a more fluid "collective-we" that joins heritages and influences. This subject would henceforth be formed through a dialogic process that would enable a future identity open to all possibilities to emerge.

This position does not formally turn its back on the cultural foundations of the historical French-Canadian community. Bouchard has frequently reiterated the fact that his proposals for reconstituting the political community are not directed at redefining the Québec political subject to a degree of "zero ethnicity." The fragility of his argument resides in the tension instigated by the goal of an identity attained through openness and heritage. Can the ideal of a "North American francophonie" sufficiently allow elements of long-standing French-Canadian culture to live on, elements that remain active in Québec identity today, in order to gain the support of all those who continue to imagine the political subject with regard to a community of shared history that still bears a concrete memory of national oppression? Both the idea of a French-Canadian race, and the later notion of a Québec culture that emerged in the 1960s, imply a certain centrality to the French-Canadian collective. Fernand Dumont has demonstrated well that the paradigm of a French-Canadian race was produced in the course of the nineteenth century through particular socio-historic decisions prompted by the fear of assimilation.[23] Certainly, it is not a question of deploring this substantialist definition of the French-Canadian community, whose exclusivist potential and retrograde character have been the urgent subject of many analyses. At the same time, however, the concept of Québec identity, which now acts as a substitute for the two broad designations for community, the notions of culture and race, is working towards dispelling the image of Québec culture in terms of belonging.

The problem seems to reside in the fact that acknowledging a Québec identity that is at once plural or fragmented and for which the nation no longer constitutes the sole horizon contributes to the erosion of favourable arguments for the political liberation of a historically positioned community. Nevertheless, for the majority of writers who take this approach, analyses conducted from the perspective of hybrid identity and civic nationalism most frequently draw the theoretical and political conclusion that sovereignty is a necessity. Meanwhile, the appeal to representing a composite identity seems to contradict the notion of a sovereignty proposal that would affect only one component of this nebulous identity. On the political plane, the defence of sovereignty appears artificial, insofar as the encouraged mixing of identities and belongings can take place without sovereignty. We could ask ourselves whether promoting a Québec identity that fully takes up a cultural dialogue through which the political subject is constructed does not impede nationalist claims put forward by Franco-Quebecers.

Thus, the definition of a new Québec political subject that is able to define itself only in terms of the goal of achieving a North-American francophonie maintains an ambiguous relationship to politics in two ways. First, sovereignty is not a necessary vehicle to realize a North-American francophonie. Second, this ideal anticipates a not-yet attainable goal politically, since it could only be carried out by diminishing the importance of the shared memory of the French-Canadian community, the principal element backing the sovereignist proposal.

Conclusion

The coexistence of several potentially contradictory concepts of the Québec political subject raises a question that extends beyond the case of Québec. One could argue that the broader goal of emancipation based on recognizing all groups of actors who are able to demonstrate a lack of recognition related to their distinctive identities should be achieved without reference to a unitary political subject that is more or less directly associated with one particular community's culture and history. This is, for example, what Habermas's proposal of a "constitutional patriotism" embraces, one of the most important issues confronting contemporary political theory. The question is, effectively, to know whether it is possible to ensure the legitimacy of an ethical-political project without linking it to a subject that would be its guarantor and ultimate purpose.[24] In early modernity, the representation of the public good with respect to the national subject was preserved in three ways by the project to master the unruly forces that modernity freed: (1) by entrusting the division of matters to the laws of the market, (2) by offering individuals the possibility of pursuing their own interests, and (3) by establishing the right to own property. The search to demarcate the forces of emancipation meant recognizing that allowing these forces to develop freely would not always serve the objectives of a good life; it meant anticipating that the free market sometimes conflicts with social solidarity and that fraternity can only come about through the will to make society a human world despite the development of these forces. We must assess the challenge created by the fragmentation of the political subject and the difficulty of imagining a project for solidarity that would be backed alone by the forces of liberating political identity.

No one will challenge the determination that is universally present to comply with demands, forwarded through politics, to recognize identities. We will not return to the form of politicization of liberal modernity in which only the actors who are structured by their labour in society—for example, the working class—could establish themselves as political subjects through the related denunciation of the false political unity of the people. Who would deny today the democratic advances that represent the emergence of women as a political subject, or the recognition of the Aboriginal identity and the rights that accompany it? Is it necessary to criticize progressive initiatives issuing from civil society? Do they not defend minority or marginal conditions left to the side by a universalist principle, a rule that we know better serves the interests of those who hide behind it in order to ignore the persistence of inequality and exploitation? Nevertheless, the power of identity, to use the terms of Manuel Castells, and the will for liberation that it carries forward, should associate this will to an ethical project in accordance with which identities could be asserted both as a political and an ethical issue. The progression of identities should be able to claim its roots in an ethical-political project of mastering the forces that the fragmentation of society has freed—a project capable of opposing an idea of solidarity to the rise of particularisms. We could formulate in a different way the ethical vacuity to which claims to recognition lead, claims that are limited to the single dimension of their demands. Since identities frequently do not advance their claim to recognition in an ethical project of living together—or, rather, because they assume that communal life will follow from the accumulation of good causes, or even that everyone will arrive in unison at the finishing line on the course towards equality—identities maintain a passive indifference towards each other. This indifference results from the fact that in a society of multiple identities, social actors do not appear to each other to be enlisted in an ethical-political project capable of organizing them in any other way than by their common course to exerting rights. Modern society is founded on politics as a means of managing social conflict and on common ethics capable of curbing the desocializing forces that this very openness to a diversity of interests has implicated. The political subject was the agent through whom society achieved this project, a subject connected to endorsing the value of practice and a subject through which it was possible to examine practice in the light of common goals. This is what might lead us to support, in Québec, the assertion of a political subject around which a consensus regarding broad ethical orientations to communal life in Québec could be reached.

Québec finds itself at a crossroads of identity. It has neither eliminated the memory of French-Canada, nor does this memory completely reflect the contemporary Québec. The issue confronting Québec society resides in arranging the intersection of conflicting identities in the framework of law, tolerance, and openness to pluralism. We already know that to be a Quebecer in 100 years will mean something else entirely from what it does today. Québec identity is open to the four winds, and Quebecers of French-Canadian heritage must welcome the profound transformations that this identity will undergo by accepting the fact that, in 100 years, little of what they legitimately defend today will remain. For the present time, however, those who are preoccupied with reconstructing the Québec political subject must not ignore the fact that, behind the undeniable willingness to accept others, a clear desire to fulfill French-Canadian history is smouldering among many Franco-Quebecers. While we must respect this memory, we must equally make this story, great in itself, receptive to any Quebecers who wish to join it.

Notes

1. This dichotomy is found in many recent contributions to the debate revolving around the national question. See, in particular, J.-P. Derriennic, *Nationalisme et démocratie: réflexion sur les illusions des indépendantistes québécois* (Montréal: Boréal, 1995); Gérard Bouchard, *La nation québécoise au futur et au passé* (Montréal: VLB éditeur, 1999); Michel Seymour, *La nation en question* (Montréal: L'Hexagone, 1999); Claude Bariteau, *Québec 18 septembre 2001* (Montréal: Éditions Québec Amérique, 1998); Michel Venne, ed., *Vive Québec! New Thinking and New Approaches to the Québec Nation* (Montréal: James Lorimer, 2001).

2. For a discussion, removed from the Québec context, of "ethnic" and "civic" nationalisms and more specifically of the phenomenon of the ethnicization of nationalism that worries a number of European intellectuals, one can refer to Alain Touraine, "Le nationalisme contre la nation," in Pierre Birnbaum, ed., *Sociologie des nationalismes* (Paris: Presses universitaires de France, 1997) 401-23 and in the same collection, Jean-Marc Ferry, "Quel patriotisme au-delà des nationalismes? Réflexion sur les fondements motivationnels d'une citoyenneté européenne," 424-62.

3. Fernand Dumont, *Genèse de la société québécoise* (Montréal: Boréal, 1993) and *Raisons communes* (Montréal: Boréal, 1995).

4. These types of reservations are expressed clearly in Bouchard, *La nation québécoise*, 47-50.

5. This viewpoint is found in particular in Jocelyn Maclure, *Récits identitaires. Le Québec à l'épreuve du pluralisme* (Montréal: Québec-Amérique, 2000) and in Diane Lamoureux, *L'amère patrie. Féminisme et nationalisme dans le Québec contemporain* (Montréal: les Éditions du remue-ménage, 2001).

6. Daniel Salée has attempted a critique of this act of power. See Daniel Salée, "La mondialisation et la construction de l'identité au Québec," in Mikhael Elbaz, Andrée Fortin, and Guy Laforest, eds., *Les frontières de l'identité* (Québec: Les Presses de l'université Laval, 1996),105-25, and his review of the collection *Penser la nation québécoise* in *Globe* 3, 2 (2000): 212-13.

7. Daniel Jacques has very clearly demonstrated the complex relations that unite nation, freedom, and the project of communal life in *Nationalité et modernité* (Montréal: Boréal, 1998). To gain further insight on this same question, read Michael Keating, *Les défis du nationalisme moderne. Québec, Catalogne, Écosse* (Montréal: Les Presses de l'Université de Montréal, 1997).

8. A description of the architectonics of politics in modernity that is rather close to this one may be found in Jean-François Thuot, *La fin de la représentation et les formes contemporaines de la démocratie*, (Montréal: Éditions Nota Bene, 1998).

9. I draw my inspiration here from a number of works concerning the question of claims to identity foundations and to the social, historical, and political dynamic that has witnessed their development. See in particular Charles Taylor, *Multiculturalism: Examining the Politics of Recognition* (Princeton, NJ: Princeton University Press, 1994); *Sources of the Self* (Cambridge: Harvard University Press, 1989); Gilles Bourque and Jules Duchastel, *L'identité fragmentée* (Montréal: Fides, 1996); Manuel Castells, *Le pouvoir de l'identité. L'ère de l'information* (Paris: Fayard, 1999); Axel Honneth, *La lutte pour la reconnaissance* (Paris: Cerf, 2000).

10. The women's movement and feminist sociology have substantially contributed to the assertion of this new citizenship. See on this subject Diane Lamoureux, "La démocratie avec les femmes," *Globe. Revue internationale d'études québécoises*, 3,2 (2000): 23-42 and in the same issue Chantal Maillé, "Féminisme et mouvement des femmes au Québec, un bilan complexe," 87-105 and Yolande Cohen, "Chronologie d'une émancipation. Questions féministes sur la citoyenneté des femmes," 43-64.

11. Contemporary political thought is largely mobilized by the question of pluralism and the political modes of its arrangement. See in particular Salvator Veca, *Éthique et politique* (Paris: Presses universitaires de France, 1989); Michael Walzer, *Pluralisme et démocratie* (Paris: Éditions Esprit, 1997); Michael J. Sandel, *Democracy's Discontent. America In Search of a Public Philosophy* (Harvard: Harvard University Press, 1998).

12. This is, at any rate, one of the objectives outlined by the *Ministère des Relations avec le citoyen et de l'Immigration (MRCI)* in the consultation paper entitled *La citoyenneté québécoise*, made public during the *Forum national sur la citoyenneté et l'intégration*, which was held in September 2000 in Québec City.

13. This position was supported by successive generations of sovereignists from 1960 until the mid-1980s, while political regulation based on respect for the Charters of Rights was established and the dynamic of political identity became widespread.

14. For an analysis of this definition of the political subject as it was established in particular during the *Estates general of French Canada* in 1967, see Charles Bellerose and Jacques Beauchemin, "Communauté nationale et définition du sujet politique québécois: analyse de deux grandes consultations populaires au Québec 1967-1995," *Québec studies* 28 (Autumn 1999-Winter 2000): 27-55.

15. Serge Cantin, "J'impense, donc j'écris. Réplique à Jocelyn Létourneau," *Arguments* 1, 2 (1999): 139-42 and Laurent-Michel Vacher, *Une triste histoire et autres petits écrits politiques* (Montréal: Liber, 2001): 70-71.

16. Laurent-Michel Vacher, *Une triste histoire et autres écrits politiques* (Montréal: Liber, 2001): 70-71.

17. Serge Cantin, "Cinq ans de bouchardisme," *Le Devoir* 20 Jan. 2001.

18. Jean Bouthillette, *Le Canadien francais et son double* (Montréal: L'Hexagone, 1972).

19. Jocelyn Létourneau is the most eloquent representative of this position. An enlightening synthesis of his work on this question may be found in Jocelyn Létourneau, *Passer à l'avenir* (Montréal: Boréal, 2000). For a different standpoint, but one still focused on the theme of ambivalence, see Yvan Lamonde, *Trajectoires de l'histoire du Québec* (Montréal: Éditions Fides, 2001) and *Allégeance et dépendances. Histoire d'une ambivalence identitaire* (Montréal: Nota Bene, 2001).

20. Jocelyn Létourneau, "Impenser le pays mais toujours l'aimer," *Cahiers internationaux de sociologie* 105 (1998): 361-81.

21. For more on this, consult the work of Stanley Ryerson, *The Founding of Canada: Beginnings to 1815* (Toronto: Progress Books, 1963) and *Unequal Union: Confederation and the Roots of Conflict in the Canadas 1815-1873* (Toronto: Progress Books, 1968).

22. Bouchard, *La nation québécoise*.

23. Fernand Dumont, *Genèse de la société québécoise*.

24. On this question and for a more general perspective on the notion of constitutional patriotism, see Frédérick-Guillaume Dufour, *Patriotisme constitutionnel et nationalisme. Sur Jurgen Habermas* (Montréal: Liber, 2001).

2

Narratives and Counter-Narratives of Identity in Québec

JOCELYN MACLURE*

The nation cannot be separated from its narration. It does not exist *in itself*, but is rather disclosed in the representation that its members make of it. To be sure, the nation rests on a certain number of "objective" elements, such as, *inter alia*, a spatio-temporal inscription, one or several languages and one or several religious traditions. But the nation only exists truly once it is *named* by subjects who claim to be of common belonging. Hence it is difficult to invalidate Benedict Anderson's claim that the nation is an "imagined community."[1] As I will attempt to show, this common denomination does not, however, presuppose consensus on the substance of the shared identity.[2]

The narration of the historical experience of a nation is fundamental. Indeed, it is impossible, as Fernand Dumont pointed out, "to grasp the nature of a nation by bracketing the ongoing work of interpretation of its existence by its members."[3] Representations of identity and social practices are interwoven in the configuration of collective identities. Consequently, any understanding of national identities takes place at the levels both of the imaginary and of praxis. In this essay, I will explore, in a synthetic fashion, the main narratives and counter-narratives of identity that have powered the collective self-awareness of Quebecers since the years that preceded the Quiet Revolution.[4] Discussions of Québec identity, I will argue, are dominated by the perennial opposition between melancholic nationalism and liberal

* Translated from French into English by Edouard Vo-Quang. The author wishes to thank Chantal Maillé for her very helpful comments and suggestions.

and cosmopolitan anti-nationalism. Despite its ongoing hegemony, the confrontation between these two paradigmatic categories of identity has proven to be a hermeneutical terrain sufficiently fertile for the emergence of alternative self-interpretations and political projects. Transformations of identity, especially with respect to collective belongings, rarely proceed from a clean slate. Only out of pre-existing narratives is it possible to imagine new figures, to become other, or, to use Michel Foucault's apposite expression, to "free ourselves from ourselves." Certain problems, as Ludwig Wittgenstein has suggested, stem from our "bewitchment" — from our being held captive by a particular picture. A shifting of perspectives is required in order to free ourselves from this bewitchment. But this shifting of perspective is more a question of re-arranging that which has long been known than of the production of new knowledge.[5]

Melancholic Nationalism and the Fetishism of Refoundations

The nationalist discourse in contemporary Québec is plurivocal. There are, in fact, several nationalist discourses. The nationalism that one can characterize as "melancholic" probably is the one that has dominated the history of French Canada and has served as the main reference point for the Québécois neo-nationalism that emerged in the early 1960s. Melancholic nationalism is grounded in a "tragic" relation to the past, or in what Daniel Jacques has called a "traumatic memory." These traumas, which have been shared by a spectrum of narrators from different generations, do not, however, entail a state of permanent dejection and passivity. Instead, this troubled relationship with the past has given rise to a kind of activism and political voluntarism that, in principle at least, would enable the resolution of the problems inherited from the Conquest.[6] Concretely, this political voluntarism has almost always cast itself as an apologetic discourse in favour of the independence of Québec, which independence was seen as the necessary path to a long-awaited re-birth. A bruised memory and an ardent desire for a political re-founding constitute the pillars of melancholic nationalism. A third force, according to melancholic nationalists, is necessary in order to ensure the passage from an entrapment in history to a repossession of the self, namely the "healing" of the unhappy consciousness of the francophone Quebecers.

According to the melancholic historical narrative, which often takes the form of litany, the history of Québec is a long series of failures, set-backs, and humiliations. First, came the defeat of the Plains of Abraham in 1759, then the abandonment of New France by the motherland and its surrender to England in 1763. Next, the domination of the conqueror and the persistent threat of assimilation (of which the Durham Report and the Act of Union (1841) were the most obvious instances) were followed by the hanging of Louis Riel and the crisis of conscription. Repeated failures of the re-founding of the country (1837-1838, 1867, 1980, 1995) culminated finally in the constitutional "humiliations" suffered by Québec in 1982 (the unilateral patriation of the constitution), 1990 (the failure of the Meech Lake Accord), and 1999 (the Clarity Act). All these were events that confirmed and aggravated the alienation of a small, colonized, and minority francophone nation.

Since the end of the 1940s, the group of thinkers known as the Montréal historians, constituted mainly of Guy Frégault, Maurice Séguin, and Michel Brunet, tried to show that "Quebecers had never entirely recovered from the [English] Conquest" of 1760.[7] The Conquest, as a cataclysmic event in the history of Québec, was, according to the followers of the Groulx canon, the event that structured the future being of francophones in Canada. It was an event the repercussions of which were still being felt in the Québec of the 1950s and 1960s. The most striking example of the traumatic memory of certain nationalist thinkers may be found in the apocalyptic words of Séguin:

> it is possible to consider the anglo-american conquest and the change
> of empires as a major disaster in the history of French Canada. It was
> a disaster that tore this young colony from its protective milieu and
> affected it in its very organization as a society and as a young nation,
> condemning it to annexation, to political and economic subordina-
> tion....[8]

The verdict is unequivocal: New-France was a society on the verge of crossing the threshold of political, economic, and cultural normalcy. But annexation to the British Empire was the beginning of a long process of disorganization and de-structuring of French Canada. The Canadian people, according to Frégault, was then "broken."[9] By uniting their efforts, Brunet, Fégault, and Séguin painted the portrait of a French-Canadian society made in the image of other colonial societies in America. According to Frégault, "up until 1760, the prospects for French America were similar to those of British America."[10] Only the seism provoked by the Conquest could derail a people that was progressively making its way towards political normalcy. As opposed to the historians of the Université Laval, who, as we will see, placed the responsibility for French-Canadian society's cultural, economic, and political anomie upon the francophones themselves, the neo-nationalists of Montréal placed the "blame ... on others, most notably the English speakers who had conquered Québec in the eighteenth century and whose descendents still dominated the scene."[11]

The Conquest, according to the neo-nationalists, had the effect of a caesura in the history of Québec. And it is from this break that the long purgatory known as *survivance* emerged. Indeed, since economic, cultural, and political emancipation was structurally fettered by English occupation, French Canadians could hope only for survival—that is, they had to cling, for better or worse, to certain practices and institutions inherited from the French regime, and try to stave off the threat of assimilation. The alternatives were clear: survive or perish. According to the Montréal historians, the tragic existence of francophones is embodied in this perpetual dilemma between *survivance* and assimilation.

Several observers agree that the source of Québécois neo-nationalism can be found in the works of the Montréal historians. Having broken with the more conservative and clerical nationalism of Lionel Groulx, thinkers of the Brunet, Frégault, and Séguin variety laid the foundations of an affirmationism that has, ever since, been constantly renewed.[12] What is clear is that the historians from the Université de Montréal have considerably shaped the imagination of a whole generation of Québécois nationalists who, like Séguin, ask themselves how they could "set two centuries of history straight."[13] Convinced of the abnormality of the past and present Franco-Quebecer identity, the heirs of the Université of Montréal historians consider the "correction" of our past to be the most important challenge of our history. And the path that such correction must take is clear: we must come face to face with our status as a conquered and dominated people and begin a process of *decolonization* that, two centuries later, has yet to materialize.

Hubert Aquin has attempted to understand the psychological consequences of the colonization of French Canadians. According to Aquin, the francophone collectivity, having been a minority for 200 years, developed a series of pathological traits that are generally found in individuals who suffer from serious inferiority complexes and low self-esteem. From a tranquil and persistent alienation—an alienation symptomatic of the inertia of a whole culture—emerged what Aquin calls the "cultural fatigue of French Canada."

> Need I evoke all the psychological corollaries that follow from the awareness of this minority status: self-punishment, masochism, self-deprecation, "depression," the lack of enthusiasm and vigor, all implicit attitudes of dispossession that anthropologists have identified as "cultural fatigue." French Canada is in a state of cultural fatigue and, because it is invariably tired, it becomes tiring.[14]

Like other melancholic thinkers, Aquin believes that we can transpose to the study of collectivities certain categories that were developed for the analysis of the individual psyche (to use a pleonasm). This congenital, atavistic, and inhibiting fatigue is, according to Aquin, the main obstacle to the mutation of the collective consciousness of the francophones of Québec. Thus arose the desire to subject this *petit peuple* to a vast collective psychoanalysis that alone could trigger the necessary process of national "disalienation."[15]

Melancholic nationalism has doubtless been spoken about by a whole gamut of persons who were able to *name*, with force and eloquence, a sensibility, a way of living and of feeling "Québecness" (*la québécité*), that was widely shared in pre-Quiet Revolution Québec—such intellectuals and poets as Gaston Miron, Michèle Lalonde, André D'Allemagne, Marcel Rioux, and Pierre Vadeboncoeur. Fernand Dumont remains, however, the narrator to whom we owe the most subtle and nuanced articulation of melancholic nationalism as both a narrative of identity and a political project. Because the consequences of the conquest, according to Dumont, were never identified, assumed, and sublimated, therefore the exploration and auscultation of the Quebecer collective subconscious became one of the most important tasks for the contemporary intellectual in Québec. In a way, Dumont wanted to draw from the soul of Quebecers the origins of their historical *mal d'être*.

The birth of the French-Canadian society, in the Dumontian historical narrative, takes the form of a "still-birth," a "failure," a "rupture," or some form of "traumatism." In the chasm separating the European Utopia of a *New* France free from the defects of the old, and the reality of a weak and clearly inadequate colonization, is a wound that never really healed. According to Dumont, "a breach occurred too soon in the projection of the European dream upon New-France, such that our *origin* appears to us more as a still-birth than a beginning."[16] Even before Conquest, French-Canadian society was disrupted, injured in its representation of self and world, deprived of its illusions and ambitions. It was a society already traumatized and cowering in the soft wadding of Utopia that the English came to occupy. This "traumatism of infancy" was then constantly evaded by the projection into a Utopian future, or, to use Dumont's terms, by the "compensatory work of the imagination."[17]

Thus, even if the Conquest is no longer interpreted as the foundational breach, it was, nevertheless a determinative stage in the establishment of a troubled, ambiguous, and negative self-concept. In his interpretation of the genesis of Franco-Quebecer identity, Dumont focuses on the effects on long-term memory and self-concept of the original failure and annexation. He claims that the internalization of the paternalistic yet scornful glance of the other is the most important consequence of anglophone colonization on the self-representation of francophones. Without fully realizing it, francophones have constantly observed, scrutinized, interpreted and narrated themselves through the eyes of the conqueror. Self-concept and presence of the other, according to this argument, have become intermingled.[18]

In their determining moments French Canadians, according to Dumont, constantly fall back upon the solid ground that is constituted by the glance of the other in order not only to fight against ethnocide, but also to draw from it "the most solid representation of their identity."[19] The appropriation of the image reflected by the other is, consequently, understood as being responsible for the contempt and hatred of the self that, according to Dumont, has animated francophones from Québec since their origin. The price of *survivance* resides in the atavistic and congenital sentiment of inferiority that is lived and felt by every new generation of Quebecer.[20] This low self-esteem is, then, one of the distinguishing features of the French-Canadian people. Dumont concedes that some authors tried, for the most part in the 1960s, to exhibit and explain this self-referential contempt upon which Franco-Quebecer identity was erected. Thus, according to Dumont, some of these thinkers were able to

> draw out what we had had so much trouble admitting throughout our history: the contempt for ourselves. We had, without a doubt, appropriated the glance of the conqueror—a glance that oscillated between pity for our backwardness and fondness for our folkloric ways.... Given that the sentiment of inferiority was one of our distinguishing features, we maintained it with care as a way of carrying out *survivance*. Are we yet cured of this ailment?[21]

According to Dumont, even despite knowledge of the quasi-hegemonic and regulative character of self-contempt in the social imaginary of the francophone Quebecers, it is not at all obvious that this sentiment of chronic inferiority really ever left the *ethos* of the francophone Quebecers—that we are cured of this historic ailment. Indeed, since an open and trusting relationship with difference requires a healthy self-esteem, "the difficulty to deal with other cultures" arises out of this negative self-awareness.[22]

One need not search long and hard in Dumont's work to see that, without claiming that Québec society has been immobile while the backdrop of history has changed, he nevertheless considers that our contemporary malaises of identity are rooted in attitudes and ways of being that we have inherited from the past. Dumont writes: "The genesis of our society has left us, a century later, with problems that have not yet been solved, with reflexes that resemble repetitions." Dumont's diagnostic is clear: despite the Quiet Revolution and the emergence of a Québécois affirmationism, the "underlying situation has not changed." Since both "our mental colonization [and] our exile into representations that are not really ours have not ended," our escape into the compensatory work of Utopia will always characterize us.[23] In trying to free themselves of the shackles of their past, the Quiet Revolutionaries in fact renewed the sources of their subjugation: "I am tempted to think that, in trying to free ourselves from ourselves, we have in fact taken the same old path of colonialism that has been ours since the origins of our collectivity."[24] In other words, the Quiet Revolution did not actually occur. Or, more specifically, it did occur, but it only shifted the ailment from one place to another.

The persistent and inexorable mental colonization that was diagnosed by Dumont manifests itself in the ambiguity that is characteristic of the Franco-Quebecer people. Like the other melancholic authors, this ambiguity is equated with abnormality, with a congenital stain, with a problem that must be solved in order to pass on to the next stage (maturity) of our collective becoming. In the works of Dumont, the analysis of the contemporary ambiguity of identity must start with the French-Canadian condition of the nineteenth century, wherein the protection of French specificity (*survivance*) coexisted with the assertion of the political freedoms inherent in British parliamentarianism (constitutional struggles) in the heart of the French-Canadian identity. This contradiction, according to Dumont, "was never to be overcome."[25]

Thus, our identity is, according to Dumont, "problematic" and "confused." Passing through the various stages of a birth that took the form of a "still-birth," conquest, a multi-dimensional subjugation, a slow but progressive assimilation of the degrading glance of the other, the constitution of a self-awareness grounded on the sediments of contempt and shame, and, finally, political ambiguity, and pusillanimity, contemporary Québécois identity could not be seen by Dumont but as heavy-footed, procrastinating, agonizing, and, especially, saddening. In the same spirit as his contemporaries and heirs, Dumont thought that a rupture and a political new beginning, taking the form of independence, could be the source of a mutation of the self-representation of the French-Canadian nation. While taking exception to the globalizing rhetoric of a certain separatist discourse, Dumont believed nevertheless that upon attaining sovereignty, certain struggles resulting from conquest finally would come to an end.[26] According to Dumont, independence had the potential to act as the foundation for a new discourse, a new vocabulary of identity and a new point of reference to which Québécois could turn in the definition of their collective identity. Thus we find both hope and regret in the following passage by Dumont: "There are peoples who can look back to some great foundational act — a revolution, a declaration of independence, a spectacular turn of events — that preserves in them the certainty of their greatness. In the genesis of Québec society, nothing of the sort. Only a long resistance."[27]

The fetishism of (re)foundation haunts the imagination of such intellectuals of a new generation as Daniel Jacques and Marc Chevrier, who have continued the search for the conditions of a "successful foundation."[28] In the meantime, melancholic nationalist thinkers call for and anticipate the day when the Franco-Quebecers finally will bring the "courage for freedom" to the "stubborn patience of yesteryear." Only then will history again move forward and Quebecers come out of their long, heart-breaking "hibernation."[29]

Antinationalism and Cosmopolitanism in Québécois Thought

The melancholic language-game was, at least until the referendum of 1980, predominant in the social discourse on the Québec nation. Indeed, Jocelyn Létourneau has claimed that melancholy "constitutes one of the fundamental matrices of the literary and scientific production—if not of the historical and memorial episteme—of Québec in the past and present."[30] I argue, Létourneau is correct in making of melancholic nationalism one of the foundational matrices of the literary and scientific production of Québec in the past (mostly) and present (a little less so). I hesitate, however, to associate this matrix with an episteme, that is, a partially subconscious structure that orders the worldview of the francophone collectivity in Québec. This melancholic nationalist interpretation has always had to deal with individualist and often vigorously antinationalist thought. Very few intellectuals denied that, for the period spanning from World War II to the beginning of the Quiet Revolution, Québec found itself in a position of "inferiority" and "backwardness." However, the historians from the Université Laval, in response to the historians of the Université de Montréal, claimed that the francophones had no one but themselves to blame for their stagnation. Consequently, they claimed that openness to the universal unfolding of reason could well bring this small nation back on track to progress. This is very different from the long and detailed archaeological work that Dumont hoped would lift the sediments of colonization deposited on the self-consciousness of French Canadians. Historians such as Marcel Trudel, Jean Hamelin, and Fernand Ouellet have laboured ceaselessly to minimize the impact of the Conquest upon the development of French-Canadian society.[31]

Pierre Elliot Trudeau was undeniably the most influential spokesperson of this alternative vision of French Canada and Québec. He refused to see in the Conquest an injury powerful enough to anesthetize the will of French Canadians. The annexation of French Canadians to the British Empire in 1763 did not change the fact that francophones, by virtue of the division of powers defined in the British North America Act of 1867, had the means to face the challenges of political modernity:

> Whether or not the Conquest was the cause of all our woes, whether or not "les Anglais" ... were the most perfidious occupying power in the history of mankind, it was all still true that the French-Canadian community held in its hands *hic et nunc* the essential instruments of its regeneration: by means of the Canadian Constitution, the Québec

State could exercise far-reaching power over the soul of French Canadians and over the territory which they occupied — the richest and largest of all Canadian provinces.[32]

The position taken by Trudeau and his colleagues of the journal *Cité libre* was not to negate the humiliations suffered by French Canadians, but rather to raise consciousness and "to bring French Canadians to accept their own responsibilities."[33] It was more important for the *citélibristes*, according to Trudeau, to participate in the modernization of the State, of democracy and of the economy of Québec than to add verses to the melancholic song that seemed to them interminable. Similarly, before quarrelling with Ottawa for more powers, French Canadians had better learn to use, to their optimal level, the powers and resources they already had. Thus, French Canadian neo-nationalism was expending the very energy that was needed for the modernization of Québec. In a transvaluation of settled ideas, Trudeau claimed that this supposedly emancipatory nationalism was, in fact, a source of alienation. Nationalism "misdirected into struggles against 'les Autres' the very forces that were needed a thousand times over to stand up to the people ultimately responsible for our own utter poverty: our so-called elites."[34] Trudeau did not have problems only with French-Canadian or Québécois nationalisms. He believed that nationalism as a way of relating to the self and to others, and as a medium of political expression, was an aberration. Deeply rooted in the heritage of the Enlightenment, Trudeau thought that the house of man was not the nation, but rather reason. *Prima facie*, the nationalism that Trudeau felt was but a notch in the unfolding of reason in history wasn't just "a mere feeling of belonging to the nation," but rather the necessary fusion of nation and state.[35] But it is relatively easy to see that Trudeau's dissatisfaction ran deeper and was not restricted to the idea of the nation-state. Trudeau's now notorious diatribe against Québec's nationalist intelligentsia of the early 1960s is a good example of the kind of slippage that occurs in his political thought. In his "New Treason of the Intellectuals," Trudeau writes that "[i]t is not the idea of *nation* that is retrograde; it is the idea that the nation must necessarily be sovereign."[36] A little further, through a subtle semantic slip, Trudeau abandons the nation-state, and expresses annoyance at the idea of the *nation*: "a concept of nation that pays so little honour to science and culture obviously can find no room above itself in its scale of values for truth, liberty, and life itself. It is a concept that corrupts all...."[37] Others of his writings confirm this profound dissatisfaction with the concepts of nation and nationalism. As a product of the Enlightenment, Trudeau's thought is powered by the ideals of individual freedom, autonomy, justice, and equality (understood as universal values that are always identical to themselves). In the eyes of this once *citélibriste*, nationalism is no less than a ruse of reason. Indeed, nationalism lays traps against the great unfolding of reason in history. The association of nationalism with irrationality is nowhere more patent in Trudeau's writing than in the article eloquently titled "Federalism, Nationalism, and Reason." There is no doubt in Trudeau's mind that when the peoples of the world are sufficiently mature and enlightened, nationalism, as a worldview, will die and be heaped up with the already bountiful residues of history:

> And just like clannishness, tribalism, and even feudalism, national-
> ism will probably fade away by itself at whatever time in history the
> nation has outworn its utility: that is to say, when the particular values
> protected by the idea of nation are no longer counted as important,
> or when those values no longer need to be embodied in a nation to
> survive.[38]

In the same vein, Trudeau hopes that "in advanced societies, the glue of nation-alism will become as obsolete as the divine right of kings."[39] In short, in Trudeau's linear, yet tortuous philosophy of History, nationalism loses ground just as Reason progresses, unfolds and actualizes itself. Whereas federalism rests upon a rational foundation, nationalism draws its powers of attraction from the immaturity, inse-curity and emotivity of individuals. The enlightened intellectual's task, therefore, is to demystify the role of the nation and nationalism in the formation of personal identity.

What Trudeau calls "cold reason" must thus be opposed to the mystifying powers of nationalism. The "rise of reason in politics" constitutes for Trudeau an "advance of law." Indeed, law is "an attempt to regulate the conduct of men in society rationally rather than emotionally."[40] Coming from the perspective of clas-sical political liberalism, Trudeau is here referring only to individual rights. The individual, being rational, needs but "negative" freedom (i.e., the guarantee that his/her rights and freedoms will not be arbitrarily infringed) in order to emancipate and fully actualize him/her self as a human agent.[41] Only the weak, according to Trudeau, need collective rights. Hence Trudeau's opposition to the granting of any special status to Québec within the Canadian federation—an opposition that he maintained and affirmed throughout his life. In the first place, he believes that there is an antinomy between the definition of special status for Québec and the applica-tion of a universal and undifferentiated citizenship. Second, he alleges that the demand for special status or for collective rights for Québec is in fact symptomatic of the survival of the old inferiority complex of French Canadians. Thus, Trudeau refuses to "insult" Quebecers by claiming that Québec requires special treatment if it is to progress within the confederation.[42] Québec does not need "crutches" in order to insert itself within a political and economic modernity of multiple tribulations.[43]

The repatriation of the Constitution in 1982 and the entrenchment of the Canadian Charter of Rights and Freedoms are in this respect the consecration and the completion of Trudeau's political thought and career. If, before 1982, some could still see in the Canadian federation a multinational entity founded upon a contract between the founding nations of Canada, this conception nevertheless died with the unilateral action of the federal government and the other provinces and the erection of a Charter that could, at any moment, invalidate provincial laws. Trudeau himself admitted that "the Canadian Charter was a new beginning for the Canadian nation: it sought to strengthen the country's unity by basing the sovereignty of the Canadian people on a set of values common to all, and in particular on the notion of equality among all Canadians."[44] Trudeau here confirms Dumont's diagnosis of the events of 1982 as the origins of a "second foundation" of Canada.[45]

The Opening towards New Possibilities: The Rise of Alternative Voices

From the often acrimonious debate between *Cité libre* and *Partis pris*, through the controversy raised in the summer of 1996 by the publication of Marc Angenot's articles in *Le Devoir* to the epistolary exchanges between ministers Stephane Dion and Joseph Facal, the confrontation between melancholic nationalism and anti-nationalism seems to occupy a preponderant position in the history of thought in Québec since the 1950s. These two antagonistic and paradigmatic positions, however, never completely monopolized the narrative possibilities and the intellectual field in Québec. In what follows, I will discuss but a few of the breaches opened up in the debate over the boundaries of Québec identity.

Between the Paradigm of Normalcy and the Critique of Nationalism: Nationalism as Affirmationism

In his classic study of nationalism, Ernest Gellner argues that in the modern period, a nation without a state is abnormal.[46] He concludes, therefore, that nationalism is a movement that seeks to unite the nation and the state. But recent scholarship on nationalism seems to point to the end of the paradigm that holds that a "normal" nation must necessarily constitute itself as a (nation-) state.[47] We see in this scholarship a disjunction between state and nation. In an era where the "territorialist epistemology" of the nation-state is radically contested by transnational and intranational forces, the destiny of those nations that are not completely sovereign is increasingly less likely to pass through the desire to duplicate the nation-state model.[48] But this deflationist vision of nationalism has existed for quite some time in the universe of thought in Québec. André Laurendeau, a contemporary and critic of the debate between the secessionist nationalism of *Partis pris* and the anti-nationalism of the central figures of *Cité libre*, obstinately defended an affirmationist nationalism that did not see political independence as the normal and necessary conclusion—indeed, as the apotheosis of—the collective emancipation of Québec. Laurendeau's thought was often discredited by his contemporaries. On the one hand, melancholic-nationalist thinkers, who believed (and still believe) that the ambivalence of Quebecer identity, as well as the political ambivalence of the Franco-Quebecer people, was a chronic pathological condition, could not but reject the bilingual and bicultural vision of Canada that the then editor-in-chief of *Le Devoir* so cherished. On the other hand, Trudeau and the other partisans of a uninational Canada founded on the premise of the primacy of individual rights were even more disconcerted by the non-secessionist nationalism of Laurendeau than by *Parti pris*'s struggle for liberation. Thus, Guy Laforest writes that "in the domain of ideas, it is [Laurendeau], even more than René Lévesque, who was the true adversary of Pierre Trudeau."[49]

The equality of the founding nations of Canada should become, according to Laurendeau, the *idée-force* of Canadian federalism. Indeed, the Canadian federal arrangement should not, according to his recommendations, be addressed solely to individuals who are equal before the law. Instead, it should recognize collective rights: "it is not cultural growth and development at the individual level which is at stake, but the degree of *self-determination* which one society can exercise in relation to another."[50] Laurendeau believed—and this is increasingly recognized today—that the individual equality promoted by political liberalism "could only really exist if every community everywhere has the means of progressing in its culture and of expressing it."[51] Such cultural equality was, according to Laurendeau, far from existing in the Canada of the late 1960s. French was not recognized as an official language, Francophone communities of Canada were not represented in official institutions and, most importantly, these communities enjoyed but a low level of self-determination. Moreover, the bicultural character of Canada was, more often than not, denied by the anglophone majority.[52]

Laurendeau was far from being an unconditional supporter of Canadian federalism. However, the independence of Québec, although he took it seriously, was not the political option that he preferred for his native land.[53] Resistance to American hegemony is the motive most often invoked by commentators when trying to justify Laurendeau's reticence to support the separatist movement in Québec. According to Laurendeau, it is only by uniting that Québec and Canada could resist being swept up by the winds of homogenization that were blowing from the United States.[54] But important alterations needed to be made to the Canadian federation if Québec and Canada were to join forces. The establishment of an asymmetrical federalism capable of recognizing Québec as a "distinct society" and respectful of provincial prerogatives, was, therefore, Laurendeau's aim. On the plane of ideas, the importance of Laurendeau's thought resides in the fact that he was one of those who ferociously resisted being enrolled in the dichotomistic thought that held that one *had* to choose between secessionist nationalism and anti-nationalism.[55] Today, such authors as Guy Laforest and Jocelyn Létourneau have been inspired, each in their own way, by this interpretive tradition in their attempts to understand contemporary Québec while avoiding the pitfalls that plague both melancholic nationalism and anti-nationalism.[56] This third option opened the door, without crossing the threshold, to a new and in-depth conceptualization of the process of pluralization of identities that is inherent in the radicalization of modernity.

Feminism, Nationalism and the Pluralization of the Markers of Identity

Beyond being an interpretive position, nationalism is also clearly a social movement. As Micheline de Sève and Diane Lamoureux point out, nationalism and feminism are the social movements that were the most influential in the "detraditionalization" of Québec since the 1960s.[57] According to de Sève, in the early 1960s "the context was favorable for the rapprochement of the nationalist and feminist identity movements on the terrain of the search for the optimal conditions of freedom and access to equality in the future Québécois society."[58] The construction of the Welfare State in Québec, which was to power the process of "autonomization" that was sought by both nationalists and feminists, proved to be a rallying point for both movements.[59] The State was, of course, going to serve different ends—the blurring of the public/private distinction for feminists; the taking control of the socio-economic development of Québec and the promotion of its distinct national identity for the nationalists—but its construction nevertheless occasioned an intermingling of the nationalist and the feminist struggles. As Lamoureux points out, the slogan "no Québec without the liberation of women, no liberation of women without a free Québec" shows the "interdependence of the processes of liberation of the [respective] assigned identities."[60]

The materialization of this partial alliance nevertheless created some friction. The introduction of feminine and feminist preoccupations, visions, and, most importantly, world views was bound to run up against certain male-centred aspects of nationalist thought (the propensity, for example, to make maternity the essence of feminine identity). According to de Sève, the conflict between nationalism and feminism went beyond punctual divergences with respect to specific issues (such as, for example, abortion), "since it [this conflict] brought out into the open the consequences of the arrival, in active political life, of a new category of actors—i.e., women—with its own approach and priorities."[61] Even though the allegiance to the feminist cause could sometimes be nicely reconciled with the struggle for national autonomy, the asperity of political militancy was such that these two emancipatory movements would, at times, clash in radical ways.

This polemic association with nationalism, along with the internal heterogeneity of feminine identity, forced feminists to rethink the requirements and the boundaries of their being together. In order to avoid the "trap of sorority," feminists have had to learn to think about feminine identity without in so doing postulating some homogenous or consensual nature.[62] Like other identity signifiers, feminism has had to struggle with what Foucault has called the "end of the heroism of political identity." Thus, Chantal Maillé writes, "gender becomes one point of reference of identity among many, and the experience of gender is no longer the central political rallying point, since other referents come to be added to the de-centered process of identity definition."[63] In late modernity, marked, among other things, by an acute awareness of the plural and labile nature of identities, communities, be they national, ethnic, sexual, generational, spiritual, gender, class, or some other, can no longer be thought of as sites of synthesis and reconciliation wherein difference etiolates. An irreducible trace of otherness is always present in the heart of identity.[64] Communities, in other words, are plurivocal, and consequently dissensual, sites of conversation. In addition to being encouraged by feminist thinkers, this process of re-signification of *belonging*, in the context of globalization, is also stimulated by "migrant" thinkers who problematize and redefine the meaning of Québec "national" literature,[65] by theorists and activists who reflect on the possibilities and limits of sexual identity,[66] by those who try to render, in all their complexity, the processes of hybridization and of re-composition of cultural identities,[67] by Aboriginal intellectuals who stress the undeniable *multinational* nature of Québec society,[68] and so on. These voices that come, more often than not, from the margins, are all *counter-narratives* of identity that participate, more and more, in the reconfiguration of the sites of identity and politics in Québec.

Conclusion

Nationalism is the kind of belonging that resists most obstinately this redefinition of identity. The nation, which in a way succeeded without really eradicating the great religions, proved to be the most powerful modern source of collective identification. In spite of this, there is an ongoing attempt, in Québec as elsewhere, to imagine conceptions of national identity that are not erected on the negation of the contemporary dissemination of identity. Thinkers from different perspectives, such as Guy Laforest, Alain-G. Gagnon, François Rocher, Michel Seymour, and Gérard Bouchard, seem to me to share this new regulative ideal of the nation. Certain nationalist intellectuals, like Nicole Gagnon, have nevertheless been open about their discontent with this project.[69] Taking a more nuanced approach,

Jacques Beauchemin wonders if the price to pay for stripping the nation of its status as transcendent political subject is too high.[70] Others still, such as Daniel Salée, believe that since the institution of the nation rests on a set of relations of power and domination that *de facto* eliminate any possibility of convergence and mutual respect between the heterogeneous parts of the nation, then the exercise of imagining conceptions of national identity that do justice to the dissemination of identity is but a vain formalism that is subject to the danger of dissimulating the relations of power that exist between communities.[71] Although it is not my purpose to position myself vis-à-vis these various perspectives that are based on divergent normative foundations,[72] the effervescence of this plural discursivity corroborates, I believe, the thesis that Québec is a community of plurivocal and dissensual conversation.

Notes

1. Benedict Anderson, *Imagined Communities: Reflections on the Origin and Spread of Nationalism* (London: Verso, 1991).

2. Homi Babha, *The Location of Culture* (London: Routledge, 1991) 139-70; Jocelyn Maclure "Between Nation and Dissemination: Reappraising the Tension Between Nation and Diversity," in Alain-G. Gagnon, Montserrat Guibernau, and François Rocher, eds., *Conditions of Diversity in Multinational Democracies* (Montréal: Institute for Research on Public Policy, 2003).

3. Fernand Dumont, *Genèse de la société québécoise* (Montréal: Boréal, 1996) 15.

4. For a more complete discussion, see Jocelyn Maclure, *Récits identitaires. Le Québec à l'épreuve du pluralisme* (Montréal: Québec Amérique, 2000). A translation of this book is forthcoming from McGill-Queen's University Press.

5. Ludwig Wittgenstein, *Philosophical Investigations*, 2nd ed., trans. G.E.M. Anscombe (Oxford: Blackwell, 1953) paras. 109, 115.

6. Fernand Dumont, *Raisons communes* (Montréal: Boréal, 1995), 25.

7. Ronald Rudin, *Making History in Twentieth-Century Québec* (Toronto: University of Toronto Press, 1997), 93.

8. Maurice Séguin, *Une histoire du Québec. Vision d'un prophète* (Montréal: Guérin, 1995), 15.

9. As Jean Lamarre puts it, "according to the holders of the neo-nationalist faith—a strand of thought that was developed and incarnated by the Montréal historians—the economic inferiority of the French Canadians, the backwardness of their institutions, the disproportionate influence exercised by the clergy in their society, as well as national *survivance* are but the various consequences of the rupture provoked by English Conquest in the becoming of the French Canadian nation." Jean Lamarre, *Le devenir de la nation québécoise selon Maurice Séguin, Guy Frégault et Michel Brunet (1944-1969)* (Sainte Foy, QC: Septentrion, 1993), 19.

10. Guy Frégault, *La guerre de la conquête* (Montréal: Fides, 1954), 100.

11. Rudin, *Making History*, 153.

12. See Denis Vaugeois in Séguin, *Une histoire du Québec*, Part V, and Rudin, *Making History*, 118.

13. Séguin, *Une histoire du Québec*, 210.

14. Hubert Aquin, "La fatigue culturelle du Canada-français," in *Blocs erratiques* (Montréal: Typo, 1998), 99, 100.

15. Consider, for example, the shift from the practice of psychiatry to politics of the former PQ minister Dr. Camil Laurin. For others, however, the reflective and psychoanalytic articulation of the neurosis of identity of the francophones was not enough. Those who rallied around the journal *Parti pris*, trained in the schools of Marxism and anti-colonialism, also felt the need to articulate a praxis that was capable of freeing Québec from the shackles of socio-economic (not just cultural) alienation. The classic text in this regard is, no doubt, Pierre Vallières's *White Niggers of America*, trans. J. Pinkham (Toronto: McClelland & Stewart, 1971).

16. Dumont, *Genèse de la société québécoise*, 55.

17. Ibid., 57.

18. Ibid., 133.

19. Dumont, *Genèse de la société québécoise*, 138.

20. Ibid., 236.

21. Fernand Dumont, *Récit d'une emigration* (Montréal: Boréal, 1997), 129.

22. Fernand Dumont, *Genèse de la société québécoise*, 324. This is what Gaston Miron has called the "French-Canadian neurosis with respect to the Other," in his *L'homme rapaillé* (Montréal: Typo, 1998), 221.

23. Fernand Dumont, *Le sort de la culture* (Montréal: Hexagone, 1987), 242.

24. Fernand Dumont, *Raisons communes*, 79.

25. Ibid., 151.

26. Ibid., 27.

27. Fernand Dumont, *Genèse de la société québécoise*, 331.

28. See Daniel Jacques, "From 'Winning Conditions' to 'Meaningful Conditions,'" and Marc Chevrier, "Our Republic in America," in M. Venne, ed., *Vive le Québec! New thinking and new approaches to the Québec nation*, trans. R. Chodos and L. Blair (Toronto: James Lorimer, 2001).

29. Dumont, *Genèse de la société québécoise*, 336.

30. Jocelyn Létourneau, "'Impenser' le pays et toujours l'aimer," in *Cahiers internationaux de sociologie*, 105 (1998), 363. Elsewhere, Létourneau goes further and claims that "this sad, indeed dejected interpretation of the past is an interpretation that the great French-Canadian and Franco-Québécois intellectuals, from Garneau to Dumont, have erected fairly and in good faith—although this has been of varying degrees of modulation, subtlety, and complexity." *Passer à l'avenir: Histoire, mémoire, identité dans le Québec d'aujourd'hui* (Montréal: Boréal, 2000), 116.

31. Rudin, *Making History*, 129-70.

32. Pierre Elliott Trudeau, "Nationalist Alienation," in G. Pelletier, ed., *Against the Current: Selected Writings 1939-1996* (Toronto: McClelland & Stewart, 1996), 143.

33. Ibid., 144.

34. Ibid., 145.

35. Pierre Elliott Trudeau, "Federalism, Nationalism, and Reason," in Pelletier, ed., *Against the Current*, 191.

36. Trudeau, "New Treason of the Intellectuals," in Pelletier, ed., *Against the Current*, 151.

37. Ibid., 157.

38. Trudeau, "Federalism, Nationalism, and Reason," 190.

39. Ibid., 197. Similarly, Trudeau suggests that with the progression of reason, "nationalism will have to be discarded like a rustic and clumsy tool." Ibid., 204.

40. Ibid., 197.

41. For a critique of this conception of freedom, see Charles Taylor, "Qu'est-ce qui ne tourne pas rond dans la liberté negative?" in *La liberté des modernes* (Paris: Presses universitaires de France, 1997), 255-84.

42. Pierre Elliott Trudeau, "Le Québec et le problème constitutionnel," in *Fédéralisme et la société canadienne-française* (Montréal: HMH, 1967), 40.

43. "And that's why I groan when I hear calls for special status, as though we need crutches because we're not bright enough or can't protect our own language. Well, you can't have crutches against the world. You have to go out and fight." Pierre Elliott Trudeau, *The Essential Trudeau*, R. Graham, ed. (Toronto: McClelland & Stewart, 1998), 160. His position relative to the Aboriginal peoples of Canada is in every respect identical. See ibid. For a discussion of this aspect of Trudeau's thought, see Guy Laforest, "Des béquilles et des droits," in *De la prudence* (Montréal: Boréal, 1993), 173-94.

44. Pierre Elliott Trudeau, *The Essential Trudeau*, 78, 79.

45. For a discussion of the nexus between Trudeau's political thought and his political action, see Guy Laforest, *Trudeau and the End of a Canadian Dream*, trans. P.L. Browne and M. Weinroth (Montréal: McGill-Queen's University Press, 1995). In *Récits identitaires*, 151-80, I show how such thinkers as Jean-Pierre Derriennic, Marc Angenot, and Régine Robin have enriched Québécois anti-nationalist thought.

46. Ernest Gellner, *Nations and Nationalism* (Ithaca: Cornell University Press, 1983).

47. For different perspectives on the critique of the paradigm of "normalcy," see the essays by Michael Keating and Alain Dieckhoff in J. Maclure and A.-G. Gagnon, eds., *Repères en mutation: identité et citoyenneté dans le Québec contemporain* (Montréal: Québec Amérique, 2001).

48. Geneviève Nootens, "Identité, citoyenneté, territoire: la fin d'un paradigme?" in Maclure and Gagnon, *Repères en mutation*.

49. Guy Laforest, "La tradition d'une situation," in *De l'urgence: Textes politiques 1994-1995* (Montréal: Boréal, 1995), 155.

50. Canada, *Report of the Royal Commission on Bilingualism and Biculturalism* 1 (Ottawa: Queen's Printer, 1967), xlv. [emphasis in original].

51. Ibid., at xxxiv. This insight was later taken up and rearticulated by Will Kymlicka in his *Liberalism, Community, and Culture* (Oxford: Clarendon Press, 1989). Alain-G. Gagnon discusses this aspect of Laurendeau's thought in "La pensée politique d'André Laurendeau: communauté, égalité et liberté," in *Les cahiers d'histoire du Québec au xxe siècle*, 10 (2000): 31-44.

52. According to Laurendeau, this negation was enough to make francophones "furious." "À la base du canadianisme: une foi trop volontariste et un objet trop flou…," in *Ces choses qui nous arrivent* (Montréal: HMH, 1970), 145.

53. See André Laurendeau, "Indépendance? Non: un Québec fort dans un fédéralisme neuf," ibid., 31-34.

54. Pierre Bellefeuille, "André Laurendeau face au séparatisme des années 60," in Robert Comeau and Lucille Beaudry, eds., *André Laurendeau: Un intellectuel d'ici* (Québec: Les Presses de l'Université du Québec, 1990), 158.

55. Charles Taylor is the other great pillar of this intermediate interpretive tradition. See Guy Laforest, ed., *Reconciling the Solitudes* (Montréal: McGill-Queen's University Press, 1993).

56. For a more in-depth discussion of the work of Laforest and Létourneau, see J. Maclure, *Récits identitaires*, 111-32.

57. Micheline de Sève, "Les féministes québécoises et leur identité civique," in D. Lamoureux, C. Maillé, and M. de Sève, eds., *Malaises identitaires* (Montréal: Remue-ménage, 1999), 167; Diane Lamoureux, *L'amère patrie* (Montréal: Remue-ménage, 2001), chs.4 and 6. It is important to note that neither de Sève nor Lamoureux claim that Québec went from *Gemeinschaft* to *Gesellschaft* in the short period of time marked by the Quiet Revolution. For a critique of the tradition-modernity thesis, see L. Cardinal, C. Couture, and C. Denis, "La révolution tranquille à l'épreuve de la 'nouvelle' historiographie et de l'approche post-coloniale," *Globe* 2 (1999): 75.

58. Micheline de Sève, *Les féministes québécoise*, 169.

59. Diane Lamoureux, *L'amère patrie*, 145.

60. Ibid., 163.

61. Micheline de Sève, *Les féministes québécoise*, 170.

62. Ibid., 174. See also D. Lamoureux, *Malaises identitaires*, 164; C, Maillé, "Matériaux pour penser un Québec féministe postmoderne," *Malaise identitaires*, 155.

63. Ibid., 148.

64. I argue this perspective in *Récits identitaires*, 182-203. See also J. Derrida, *L'autre cap* (Paris: Les Éditions de Minuit, 1991).

65. See Pierre Nepveu, *L'écologie du réel. Mort et naissance de la littérature québécoise contemporaine* (Montréal: Boréal, 1998); Simon Harel, *Le Voleur de parcours. Identité et cosmopolitisme dans la littérature québécoise contemporaine* (Montréal: Le Préambule, 1989).

66. See Ross Higgins, "Identité construite, communautés essentielles. De la liberation gaie à la théorie *queer*"; Robert Schwartzwald, "Y a-t-il un sujet *queer*? Aporie d'un débat actuel," in D. Lamoureux, ed., *Les limites de l'identité sexuelle* (Montréal: Les éditions du remue-ménage, 1998).

67. See Sherry Simon, *Hybridité culturelle* (Montréal: L'île de la tortue, 1999). The works on the *américanité* of Québec are also worth noting here. See Gérard Bouchard, *Genèse des nations et cultures du nouveau monde* (Montréal: Boréal, 2000).

68. For two points of view on this issue that are both different and complementary, see Taiaiake Alfred, "Sur le rétablissement du respect entre les peuples kanien'kehaka et québécois" 2, 31 *Argument* (2000): and Georges Sioui, "Québécois et Canadiens dans l'ordre historique amérindien," in Maclure and Gagnon, *Repères en mutation*.

69. Nicole Gagnon, "Comment peut-on être Québécois? Note critique," *Recherches sociologiques*, 41, 3 (2000): 545. In her essay, Gagnon takes issue with the various attempts to dilute the Québécois national identity. Instead, she expresses a preference for a "counter-norm: assimilation as the normal and necessary destiny of the majority of the children or grandchildren of immigrants." Ibid., 563.

70. Jacques Beauchemin, "Défense et illustration d'une nation écartelée," in *Penser la nation Québécoise*, 259; "Le sujet politique québécois: l'indicible 'nous,'" Maclure and Gagnon, *Repères en mutation*.

71. Daniel Salée, "De l'avenir de l'identité nationale québécoise," Maclure and Gagnon *Repères en mutation*.

72. Which I do in the conclusion to *Récits identitaires*, 204-15.

3

Interpreting Québec's Historical Trajectories: Between *La Société Globale* and the Regional Space[1]

LUC TURGEON*

In the last 40 years, Québec has been variously described as a province like all others, as a distinct society, as the principal centre of the French-Canadian culture, as a nation, as a multinational society, or as a country in the making. In many respects, the conceptualization of the Québécois community has become a political issue in itself.[2] In concert with this investigation into the socio-political model most able to capture contemporary Québec, Québécois themselves have reflected on the origins, evolution, and future of their culture. Is Québec culture unique or an extension of French culture, or even a francophone variant of North American culture?

These interrogations, taking place across the political and social spectra, have found an echo in the work of social scientists studying Québec. These specialists have certainly been influenced by reflection within Québec society and conversely have contributed to the process. Historians, sociologists, and political scientists function within a particular society and hence are not immune from debates that command society's attention. As Marcel Fournier pertinently reminds us in his analysis of the evolution of Québec sociology, the intellectual participates in the transformation of national identities to the extent that he develops cognitive categories that permit the collectivity to imagine (or re-imagine) its identity.[3]

That being said, we must avoid limiting the explanation of changing interpretations of Québec society to socio-political transformations taking place within the

* Translated from French into English by Sarah Lyons.

province. Social scientists who examine Québec society do so in an intellectual atmosphere that transcends Québec's frontiers. Their work is influenced by intellectual production outside of Québec and more generally by those methodological advances and theoretical currents that shape their discipline at any given time. Additionally, the intellectual field in Québec has greatly benefited from work done by foreign academics, such as André Siegfried from France and Michael Keating from Scotland, who have contributed to our understanding of Québec in a comparative perspective.

In this chapter, I explore how the historical evolution of Québec has been interpreted and conceptualized by past and contemporary analysts of Québec society. This text does not attempt to provide an exhaustive presentation of all concepts and theories used to describe contemporary Québec, but rather seeks to familiarize the reader with the principal meta-narrative categories (and narrations) that have been used to interpret the historical trajectory of Québec. In particular, I will demonstrate how intellectual production, particularly in the fields of sociology and history, has traditionally been characterized by a dichotomy between those viewing the historical experience of Québec as unique and those viewing Québec as a society influenced by the socio-economic forces and ideologies common to North America as a whole. In my opinion, these two positions can be conceptually defined as an interpretation of Québec as an all encompassing society evolving according to its own internal logic, what is referred in French as *une société globale*, on the one hand, and an interpretation of Québec as a regional space within North America on the other. In the last section, I argue that new comparative approaches advanced in the past few years move beyond this opposition between regional space and *une société globale*. Recent comparative work has brought new interpretative categories, such as Québec as a new collectivity, and Québec as a small nation and region-state, that allow for the simultaneous understanding of the unique and shared characteristics of Québec's historical trajectories.

Québec as Une Société Globale in North America

The unique character of the French-Canadian, and later the Québécois, experience on the North American continent has been reflected on by a considerable number of thinkers, representing many different intellectual fields and working from sometimes opposing theoretical perspectives. For example, historians associated either with the Montréal or the Québec school of history did not agree on the effects of the Conquest and on the causes of the economic inferiority of French Canadians. They nonetheless almost unanimously took for granted that the trajectory of Québec in North America was largely different from that of the rest of Canada and the United States. Also, they agreed that this society was organized and directed by actors (the clergy), principles (Catholicism and nationalism), and an infrastructure (the parish) that made it *une société globale*, that is to say a society evolving largely according to its own internal dynamics.[4]

The conceptualization of Québec as a unique entity in North America finds its historical beginning in interpretations of the response of French Canadians to the failure of the Patriot Rebellion at the end of the 1830s. The rebellion was intellectually rooted, for the most part, in the principles of liberalism, which were spreading across the Americas at the time, and its failure lead, according to a generation of historians and sociologists, to the withdrawal of French Canadians into a logic of survival (*la survivance*). As the late Marcel Rioux, sociologist, suggested in the wake of the defeat of the Patriots and following the Durham report which advocated assimilation: "the Québécois were no longer forming a nation which would one day achieve independence but rather an ethnic group with a particular culture (religion, language, customs). From then on the task was to preserve this culture like a sacred heritage."[5]

According to Rioux, this survivalist ideology marks a tragic retreat. Directed by a clerical elite that opposed liberalism and capitalism and that promoted fidelity to the land and tradition, French Canadians throughout the country became progressively alienated from the socio-economic forces and ideologies sweeping the continent. While modernity, liberalism, and industrial capitalism were flourishing in North America, French-Canadian thinking privileged agriculturalism, anti-statism, and messianism.[6] Journalist Jean-Paul Tardivel, at the beginning of the twentieth century, expressed as follows the foundations of this ideology, which he thought to be unique to the French-Canadian people:

> It is unnecessary for us to possess industry and money. We would no longer be French-Canadian but Americans, similar to all the others. Our mission is to possess the land and sow ideas. Attaching ourselves to the soil, raising large families, entertaining the intellectual and spiritual aspects of life, this must be our role in the Americas.[7]

It would be an over-statement to say that analysts viewing Québec *as une société globale* viewed it as plainly isolated. Most analysts point to the disruptions caused by industrialization and rapid urbanization, occurring in Québec as elsewhere during the first half of the twentieth century. Many, however, emphasize the fact that the French-Canadian mentality was incapable of adapting to the new socio-economic conditions. Fernand Dumont makes this point as follows:

> In the face of industrialization, in the face of the crisis, only nostalgic responses were proposed! And yet we were perhaps too harsh on our

own traditional nationalism, our Social Weeks (*les Semaines sociales*), on the *École social populaire*, and many doctrines that now appear old fashioned. These were, as always, ideologies of the poor. Intellectuals, as much as the population, were helpless in the face of new situations. They drew their inspiration from the same pool of traditional attitudes and thoughts. They were considered, with reason, to be out of touch. But we (French-Canadians) were not involved in any major historical movements. How might we have learned the great currents and complex mechanisms of history?[8]

This particularity of French-Canadian society during the period of urbanization and industrialization (presented as a lapse in the evolution of the superstructure and the infrastructure) became the subject of a considerable amount of theorizing by social scientists during the first half of the century.[9] It was through the notion of traditional society or the concept of "folk society" that the specificity of Québec was approached. In his analysis of French-Canadian society, American sociologist Everett Hughes described thus the unique experience of this rural society facing the powers of the industrial revolution:

> The arrival of new industries represents an invasion by actors armed with capital and techniques from the more established financial and industrial centres of Great Britain and the United States. These managers and technicians are strangers to the French-Canadian cultural milieu. Language and temperament and often religion define them as outsiders. On the other hand, the industrial workforce, which constitutes the bulk of the emerging cities, is indigenous in the sense that it is made up of French-Canadians attached by sentiment, tradition, and parental ties to the surrounding countryside.[10]

This process of modernization would lead nonetheless to the Quiet Revolution, a defining moment marking the entry of French Canadians into modernity and their transformation into real Québécois, as the territorial dimension progressively triumphed over ethnic membership in the national imagination. Those working from within *une société globale* paradigm during the 1960s and 1970s present the coming of the Quiet Revolution as a play in three acts. First, the French-Canadian society of the "pre-revolutionary" period, described alternately as the Great Darkness or the long Québécois winter, is characterized, as we discussed earlier, by a disconnection between changes in the social structure caused by industrialization and urbanization, and a traditional world view promoted by the clergy. This contradiction contributes, in the second period, to a slowdown, to the development of an industrial and democratic society, resulting in Québec's backwardness in "almost all the domains of human activity."[11] Examples of this backwardness include: the slow evolution of urbanism and industrialization, low levels of schooling, weak worker unions and a weak women's movement, and limited state intervention in the social domain.[12] In the final stage, this archaic system falls apart with the Quiet Revolution, symbol of Québec's accession to modernity. Seizing control of the state, a new social and political elite—the new middle class—adopts the goal of catching up to other occidental societies. The population, in turn, buys into this ideology of change.

As a period of liberation, the Quiet Revolution allowed the French-Canadian collectivity to open itself up to North American culture, to invest in sectors long reserved for anglophones, to incorporate ideologies of the time (decolonization, Marxism, liberalism) into political debates and, by renewing itself as a territorially based collectivity, to mark a new beginning. Through this same process, Québec opens itself up to the long-resisted fundamental forces and values of modernity: capitalism, liberalism, progress, change, autonomy, and the search for authenticity. With the Quiet Revolution, Guy Rocher argues, "the old traditional, clerical and closed society collapsed and gave way to a new post-industrial, secular society, integrated into North American civilisation."[13] This idea of a leap from a traditional society to a post-industrial society is taken up by Jacques Lazure, who argues that it is "as if, newly emerging from traditional society, we light-heartedly leaped over industrial society to jump headlong into the vast fields of post-industrialism and fervently began exploring its horizons and virtues."[14]

The Québec that emerged from the Quiet Revolution, while finally in step with the rest of North America, remains, however, *une société globale* to be studied as an independent unit of analysis. Marcel Fournier notes that the change from French-Canadian society to Québécois society was reflected in the titles chosen for works written by Québec sociologists of the 1960s and 1970s. For example, in 1964, Rioux and Yves Martin published a collection of essays called *French Canadian Society*. By the end of the 1970s, the object of analysis for Rioux has changed as he publishes *La Question du Québec* (1969) and later *Les Québécois* (1977).[15] Still, the distinctiveness of the Québécois collectivity continues to be emphasized. The focus shifts from the study of Québec as an inwardly focused group in North America to a group that, now conscious of its inferior historical state, was attempting to establish its economic and political independence. The national struggle, while taking on new forms, (independence replacing "la survivance") is still portrayed as the basis of Québec's unique history and trajectory in North America.

In approaching Québec as *une société globale*, these authors insisted on the dominance of the Catholic Church, as a pillar of the community, in Québec history. They have read the Quiet Revolution as a redirection of Québec's trajectory, and insisted on Québec's ambiguous and often conflicting relationship with the Other (be they Canadians or Anglo-Québecers). This version of Québec's history has remained the most popular amongst the Québécois, even though an alternative paradigm for understanding Québec society emerged in the late 1970s.

Québec as a Regional Space within North America

At the end of the 1970s, a new generation of social scientists began to question the idea of Québec as a society that had lived in isolation from the socio-economic and ideological trends that had shaped the rest of the North American continent. This emerging problematization can be associated with two relatively distinct, but complementary, currents of thought: political scientists and sociologists working out of the paradigm of regional space, and historians associated with historical revisionism.

The former questioned the primacy of the national question and asserted the importance of re-situating Québec in its Canadian and North American environment. In his Introduction to the seminal *Espace Régional et Nation*, Daniel Salée questions the tendency of social scientists in the 1960s and 1970s, "obsessed with the national question," to consider Québec "within strict socio-geographic limits that were taken for granted, as if its national specificity could be defined outside the social and institutional materiality of the Canadian State."[16] Since social contradictions are not limited to ethnic antagonisms, the Québec question cannot therefore be one of a particular group struggling for independence and autonomy. Rather, analysts must dwell on the social relationships that exist within the regional space, as well as on socio-economic conditions that strongly affect them. In sum, it is impossible to understand Québec without referring to the development of North American capitalism, to the functioning of the federal Canadian state, and to the pluralism of interests and experiences within its territory.

While sociologists and political scientists working through the lens of a regional space analysis created the basis for a conceptual renewal of the study of Québec, historical revisionists were proposing a new narrative of Québec history. Historical revisionism is often misunderstood and at this point some explanation is necessary. First of all, it should be noted that historical revisionism is not a "negation of history," which is to say a refusal of well-known and documented historical facts. Rather, it is a re-interpretation of the meaning previously given to the actions and discourses of certain actors, an interrogation into the validity of certain foundational concepts in Québec historiography, and a questioning of the relative weight accorded to certain events over others in Québec's collective narration. It should also be noted that historical revisionism is not unique to Québec, being equally present in many other societies, particularly in political entities that have been strongly influenced by Roman Catholicism, such as Ireland and Spain. Like Québec, these societies have long been considered traditional, primarily in comparison to Anglo-Saxon countries, which have been viewed as the true models of modernity. Many social scientists who work on these societies, some taking inspiration from post-colonialism, remind us that there are multiple ways to experience modernity. The latter is a non-linear process of progressive institutionalization of the political and the economic, as opposed to a single defined path to the complete realization of the subject.[17] Liah Greenfield elaborates this point well:

> To claim that one nation—say an economically successful, liberal, democratic one is more modern than another (economically unsuccessful and a dictatorship) is as little justified as to insist that a university professor, for instance, is more human than an illiterate farmer or a new born-infant. Modernity—like humanity—is a qualitative, not a quantitative concept; it denotes a species of social being, heterogeneous as most species are and radically different from others.[18]

What historical revisionists are proposing is essentially a new interpretation of the Québécois subject and his/her spatial-temporal positioning. Instead of placing emphasis on the unique character of the Québec experience, they argue that on the whole, the Québec's historical trajectory is very similar to that of other North American societies. In light of his work on French-Canadian entrepreneurship since the beginning of the nineteenth century, Gilles Paquet argues that "we did not live, before 1960, in a world of oppression, of paralysing conservatism and illiberalism, but rather in a world that closely resembled what was to be found elsewhere in Canada."[19]

These analysts are looking not simply at the history of French-Canadian society but more accurately at the history of the totality of people living in Québec. Paul-André Linteau and his collaborators describe their objectives in the introduction of their influential synthesis of the history of Québec, so as to assert that they are not simply presenting the history of a specific ethnic group, but that of all men and women who inhabit Québec's geographic space, "whether their ancestors came from the north west thousands of years ago, from France during the time of Jean Talon, whether they are Scottish and crossed the Atlantic in 1780, Irish fleeing the Great Famine, Jews trying to escape persecution in some countries of Eastern Europe or even Italians wanting to leave a Mezzogiorno that had little to offer them."[20] Additionally, this approach rejects the conceptual dichotomy between a traditional Québec before 1960 and a modern Québec emerging from the reforms of the Quiet Revolution:

For us, there is no clear distinction between a society that would be declared old and traditional and one that would be labelled as new and modern. Modernisation is seen as a process, made up simultaneously of continuities and ruptures, of adaptations to the challenges faced by each generation, to pressures from technological changes, to the arrival of foreign men and women, ideas and capital.[21]

Sociologists Gilles Bourque, Jules Duchastel, and Jacques Beauchemin, in a controversial work on liberal Duplessist society,[22] also reject the dichotomization of tradition and modernity, insisting instead on the notion that modernity is made up both of freedom and of the need for stability and order. From this perspective, the discourse of the Duplessis government is typically modern in the sense that it tries simultaneously to promote ideals of modernity like progress, law, and justice, and to limit its outbursts by constantly asserting the importance of tradition, order, and authority. The authors argue in conclusion: "A regime of great fear much more than of great darkness, this regional political force created, through its discourse, a timid society that was propelled by the promise of universal access to the consumer world and mass culture, but in which everyone was under a constant state of surveillance, right down to the most ordinary details of life."[23] In this analysis, pre-Quiet Revolution Québec is already modern and the Revolution does not mark the entry of Québec into a liberating modernity but rather the rise of the welfare state, with the establishment of large scale social programs, as was simultaneously occurring in the majority of occidental societies.[24]

Not only does Québec not exist in a different space and time from the rest of North America, and most especially the United States, it also embraces similar ideas and shares the same path of socio-economic development. For revisionists, the importance of Québec's Americanness in explaining its historical trajectory is demonstrated by the now famous equation created by Yvan Lamonde: $Q = Fr + GB + (USA)^2 - R$.[25] Schematically, for Lamonde, Québec's history and identity (Q) are made up of less France (F) than we believe, more Great Britain (GB) than we want to admit, a much larger American (USA) influence than we think, and much less input from Rome (R) and the clergy than thought. According to Lamonde, Québec has always been a site of convergence of many cultures:

In a sense, Québécois identity did not need to wait until post-modernity to be multiple and traversed by the Other: it was transformed very early, confronted by difference and the task of integrating its elements. This variety of influences did not cause decomposition, fragmentation, or explosion; it produced a process of integrating multiple aspects of the French, British, American and Roman cultures.[26]

According to many historians, because of the influence of English and American thought, the Québécois embraced certain liberal principles well before the 1960s. Additionally, their relationship with Catholicism was not simply one of passive observation of the social doctrine of the Church. Finally, the processes of urbanization and industrialization in Québec were similar to those in the rest of North America. First, Fernande Roy has outlined the influence of liberalism on francophone commerce at the end of the nineteenth century. In her view, understanding the influence of liberalism helps to explain the individualist tone of francophone entrepreneurs, dominated by the values of progress, harmony, and liberty. According to the historian, French-Canadian entrepreneurs, "because they want to be modern and future-oriented, ... refused to allow heritage and old traditions to impose themselves on the present."[27] Second, in a fascinating work titled *La norme et les déviantes*, Andrée Lévesque demonstrates how the conservative discourse of the clerical elite during the inter-war period was in part a reaction to the "deviant" (abortion, contraception, prostitution) behaviour of Québec women. Lévesque concludes her work by arguing that "twenty years of social and economic transformations inspired a discourse and normative practices that tried desperately to put the brakes on social change and to reinforce the traditional image and role of women. Twenty years during which women, who were being defined as deviant, were immersing themselves in their activities and adopting behaviours which were in fact much more accepted than we admitted."[28] Finally, as a regional space in North America, Québec has been influenced throughout its history by the same socio-economic forces as the rest of the continent: industrialization, urbanization, immigration, emigration, and mass consumption. As Jacques Rouillard has shown, the pace of urbanization and industrialization, both for Québec as a whole and for the Franco-Québécois population in particular, has been similar and sometimes more rapid than in the rest of Canada.[29] Over the past two decades, sociologists and historians have thus presented us with a portrait of a pluralist society, open to the world and evolving at the same pace as the rest of North America.

Comparative Perspectives on Québec: New Collectivity, Small Nation, and Region-state

The revisionist perspective presented in the last section has been the subject of a number of critiques in recent years. Credit for having launched the debate on historical revisionism goes to Ronald Rudin, author of the book *Making History in Twentieth Century Québec*.[30] Rudin, in a series of texts published at the beginning of the 1990s, challenged the tendency of revisionists to promote a version of Québec history that lacks uniqueness and specificity.[31] According to Rudin, "revisionists have ignored most of the behaviours which cannot be explained by universal social and economic forces." He characterizes historical revisionists as attempting to "demonstrate the extent to which the modern and liberal Québécois was a rational being."[32]

It should be noted that Rudin is not nostalgic for pre-revisionist historiography or sociology. He clearly states, "maintaining that Québec was a retrograde society, lead by priests, in which the state did nothing, francophone businessmen were almost non-existent and class conflict evaporated in favour of ethnic and linguistic battles, was clearly a distortion of reality."[33] This being said, he denounces the fact that in demonstrating the comparability of Québec history with the socio-economic development of other collectivities, the revisionists were incapable of "admitting to a history that includes episodes of xenophobia, the slow development of a modern and urban society, the presence of a considerably influential clergy, and a popular fear of consenting to a powerful state."[34]

Thus, Rudin promotes a post-revisionism, a political rather than social approach to history that grants a greater importance to ethnic conflicts and to ideas and actors than to material forces as explanations of change in Québec. Clearly, the parameters of a post-revisionist narration, a synthesis or even methodological approach are hazy. In many respects, Rudin does not propose much beyond what Jean-Marie Fecteau has correctly described as "equilibrium therapy":[35] the desire to reassert the distinctiveness of Québec without seeking to establish new interpretive schemas or methodologies. All this being said, I suggest it is only through adopting an explicitly comparative approach, that what is and what is not unique about Québec will be distinguished. Québec social scientists have consistently neglected the comparative approach, describing, in at most a paragraph, differences in the economic and social development of Québec and that of Ontario, or France, or the United States. It is only recently that analysts of Québec society have made systematic comparisons of Québec with other Western societies. In the next section I briefly present two of these analyses.

Québec as a New Collectivity

Comparison, as Gérard Bouchard argues in his impressive volume *Genèse des nations et cultures du nouveau monde*, "presents itself like a ruse which invites us, in a somewhat paradoxical manner, to discover in the mirror of the Other, a more real image of ourselves." It gives the analyst an opportunity to "give a universal resonance to the singular."[36] In his comparative study of New World collectivities (Québec, Canada, United States, Latin America, Australia, and New Zealand), Bouchard attempts to trace both the universality and the specificity of Québec's historical trajectory.

In an earlier work, Bouchard had already shown how the demographic, economic, and cultural development of the Saguenay region, a rural French-Canadian society, had been, in many respects, similar to that of Anglo-Canadian provinces and American states.[37] It is to an entirely different question, however, that he turns in his recent work. Coming from a cultural and macro-historical perspective, he discusses primarily how new collectivities have adapted culturally to their new territory (in day-to-day life), have negotiated their relationship with the motherland (in the intellectual sphere), and have developed a specific integration model (in particular at the national level). Gérard Bouchard invites us, therefore, to reflect not on the way Québec has been influenced by being on the North American continent (as in the regional space perspective) but rather on the way the Québécois have historically thought about, modelled, and interpreted their place in the New World.

According to Bouchard, new collectivities have evolved following either a model of continuity, or a model of rupture, with the motherland. Following this dichotomy, the historian analyzes, from a comparative perspective, the historical trajectory of Québec, in his words an "old new country."[38] While in his earlier work he focused on the similarities of Québec's socio-economic evolution with the rest of North America, in this work he turns to the specificity of Québec's cultural identity and its evolution. The popular classes in Québec, as in other new collectivities, developed strategies for adapting to their new circumstances that became imbedded in popular culture and henceforth integral to social and cultural life. Because they were uncertain of their national identity, new collectivities often developed a notion of an outside threat against their collective survival (Yellow Peril in Australia and New Zealand, fear of American influence in English Canada, fear of immigration in American history). Additionally, ruralism has occupied a central place in the representation of the nation, particularly in Australia where the national imagination has drawn from the legends of the outback.[39] Bouchard demonstrates, thus, that a number of cultural and ideological traits thought to be unique to Québec, were in fact present in numerous other societies that were also engaged in the process of forging new identities. Nonetheless, Québec does distinguish itself in certain respects from other new collectivities.

First of all, Québec, like Puerto Rico, is one of the few collectivities of the New World not to have achieved political sovereignty. Second, Québec is unique in that it draws influence from several outside powers (France, the Vatican, the United States, Canada, Great Britain). Québec is most distinguished, however, by the persistence of an ideology of continuity, and an idealisation of the pre-revolutionary French motherland. If, before the failure of the Patriot Rebellion, an ideology of radical change persisted, afterwards, the idea of continuity became dominant, for example in the notion of the French-Canadian race having a civilizing role in the Americas. What we see, therefore, are essentially "models of the Old World transposed or adapted to the American continent much more than true reconstruction plans breaking with the heritage of the motherland."[40] For Bouchard, the predominance of cultural continuity over rupture is partially explained by the fact that amongst new collectivities, the cultural elite in Québec, which primarily produced collective ideals and national projects, was the slowest at adapting to the reality of the new continent, and additionally was the most culturally distant from the popular classes.[41] As such, it was not until after 1960 that Québec experienced a real cultural break with France. This break, according to Bouchard, is still not complete, since the cultural elites have been hesitant to adhere to the American Dream embraced by the middle class.[42] With his use of the concept of new collectivities, Bouchard re-introduces the notions of representations and ideologies into the study of Québec society. He demonstrates, in particular, that while the popular classes in Québec generally evolved at the same pace as elsewhere in North America, the elites developed ideals that set them apart.

Québec as a Small Nation and a Region-State

The presence of a strong nationalist sentiment is a constant in Québec history. However, this nationalism has undergone radical transformation since the Quiet Revolution. The ethnic conception of Québécois identity and the conservative defence of the constitutional status quo dominant prior to the 1960's were replaced, under a new elite, with a more civic, territorially-based nationalism, more assertive in its demands for a reformed Canadian federation or alternatively an independent country.[43]

As we have been reminded by a good number of analysts, parallel transformations occurred in certain small nations of the "Old World," like Catalonia and Scotland.[44] In the period after World War II, these societies saw the emergence not only of organizations seeking guarantees of autonomy and of cultural survival, but also social and political movements. Such movements were engaged in a redefinition of the cultural boundaries of their communities, of the values guiding their evolution, and, principally, of the relationship with the central state. Scotland, for example, was historically distinguished from Great Britain through the Presbyterian Church, and unique university and judicial systems. The nationalist renewal of the 1980s and 1990s, however, was largely associated with more collective social orientation emerging in response to the Thatcher government's conservatism. As in Québec, threats against the welfare state became a central factor in nationalist mobilization.[45] The nationalist mobilization was not simply elite driven, but engaged all of civil society, allowing a plurality of voices and opinions into the project and reinforcing its civic character.

Scottish political scientist Micheal Keating is without a doubt the analyst who has made the largest contribution to our comprehension of the rising political prominence of small nations since World War II. For Keating, the rise of nationalist movements in Québec, Scotland, and Catalonia, while rooted in a long history of struggle for survival, is primarily related to two contemporary phenomena: the decline in legitimacy of central states, resulting from their incapacity to adapt to new socio-economic problems (in particular the crisis of the welfare state), and the reconfiguration of political space resulting from continental integration and globalization.[46]

In particular, the globalization of economic exchange and its correlate, free trade, have reduced the economic dependence of small nations on the rest of Canada, Great Britain, and Spain. Since nation-states are unable to adequately control economic instability, these small nations have tried to re-negotiate the terms of their participation in multinational entities in order to be able to face new challenges emerging from the rising interdependence of countries and global regions. Keating argues that this new reality "gives a new meaning both to the idea of the nation and to the nationalist project. Nationalist discourse is modernist and concerned with development and adaptation rather than antiquarianism and looking to the past. It accepts the limits of sovereignty and searches for new ways in which self-government may be made effective and a project for nation-assertion mounted, in the absence of the classical nation-state."[47] The nationalist movements in the three small nations in question are, indeed, fervent partisans of economic integration on their respective continents.

Québécois nationalism distinguishes itself however from Catalan and Scottish nationalism in several respects. First, political independence as an option has received much more support in Québec than in Catalonia or in Scotland. Second, Québec has had the most trouble, according to Keating, in developing a truly civic conception of the nation, anglophones and Aboriginals having been historically excluded from representations of the nation.[48] Scotland has avoided this problem in the sense that its identity has been linked to civil society institutions more than to cultural traits like language. Similarly, Catalonia has benefited from a cooperative effort among elites, after the death of Franco and the establishment of the autonomous communities, to advance a civic conception of the nation. Third, among the three nations, Québec, without a doubt, has the most political power at its disposal. These powers have lead, reciprocally, to an exceptional level of control over local economic and industrial resources. Paradoxically, while Québec is the small nation possessing the most control over its destiny, it has not succeeded in finding recognition for its distinct character, something which has been obtained, to some extent, by Scotland in Great Britain and by Catalonia and the Basque Country in Spain.[49] This institutional power, in combination with a lack of recognition by other partners in the Canadian federation, explains in large part the sourness of the constitutional struggles of the last 40 years and the lack of resolution, in the eyes of many analysts, of the Québec question.

Working from an analytically different perspective, but agreeing with Keating, Alain-G. Gagnon affirms that these small nations have had, and will continue to have, an increasing tendency to construct themselves as region-states. Gagnon focuses mostly on the future of Québec's trajectory. Region-states distinguish themselves from other political units (such as other Canadian provinces) by having their own international profile, and by being the site of strong cohesion between political authorities and local social and economic stakeholders. Additionally, they develop their own citizenship regime, or a model of social integration (like inter-culturalism in Québec), different from that proposed by the central state.[50] According to Gagnon, conceiving of Québec as a region-state does not deny its national dimension (in the sense that it is precisely this national dimension which has facilitated the differentiation in the first place), but instead admits to the range of possibility open to it:

> With an emphasis on solidarity, the region-state allows its constitutive groups to assert themselves by offering innovative avenues for their insertion. On another level, it reduces the inevitability of secession being the only means to achieve national realisation, citizens being free actors able to dispose of themselves as they wish.[51]

In sum, these small nations are evolving in the context of international dynamics over which they have very little direct control. Far from being immobilized, however, they develop innovative strategies that accentuate their originality and their distinctive character in the context of their respective continents.

Conclusion

New analyses of Québec's historical trajectories have emerged at an accelerated pace in the past few years. Confronted by new economic and social realities, social scientists have turned once again to the past to investigate different events that their predecessors had not fully explored. This exploration has sometimes given rise to veritable re-interpretations of Québec history. Like Québec society itself, the intellectual landscape in Québec is home to many voices and narratives. New interpretations have been dissected, analyzed, and criticized. Others, not looking to totally reject new paradigms in sociology, political science, and history, have tried to nuance certain propositions.

The Québécois have undoubtedly benefited from their historical trajectory being put in perspective with that of other collectivities. The comparative approach, despite its limits, brings a more accurate comprehension of Québec history. Views advanced by analysts coming from other parts of the world have been equally helpful. This is not to say that only an outsider, or "objective," perspective can accurately portray a society but simply that analysts from outside Québec have asked questions and developed theoretical models that have sometimes led Québécois to view old problems from new angles. The question of Québec continues, then, to arouse an abundant literature. The recent creation and relative success of the International Association of Québec Studies shows the extent to which the Québécois reality continues to stimulate and fascinate social scientists here and abroad.

Notes

1. This text has greatly benefited from discussions over the past few years with Alain-G. Gagnon, David Cameron, Linda Cardinal, and Brian Young on interpretations of Québec history. I would like to point equally to the priceless help of Louiselle Lévesque and the constant support of my colleagues in the Department of Political Science at the University of Toronto. Finally, I acknowledge the financial support of the Québec Fund for Research on Society and Technology (formerly the FCAR fund).

2. For example, the insistence of Québec Premier Bernard Landry on referring as often as possible to the Québec nation and the similar insistence of Prime Minister Jean Chrétien on refuting the existence of this nation, preferring to speak of the Canadian nation or even the French-Canadian nation.

3. Marcel Fournier, "Québec Sociology and Québec Society: The Construction of a Collective Identity," *The Canadian Journal of Sociology*, 26, 3, (2001): 334.

4. For a critique of the concept of *société globale*, see Gilles Bourque, Jules Duchastel, and Jacques Beauchemin, *La société libérale duplessiste* (Montréal: Les Presses de l'Université de Montréal, 1994), 19-26.

5. Marcel Rioux, *La Question du Québec* (Montréal: L'Hexagone, 1987), 86.

6. Michel Brunet, "Trois dominantes de la pensée canadienne-française l'agriculturisme, l'anti-étatisme et le messianisme," in Michel Brunet, *La présence anglaise et les Canadiens*, (Montréal, Beauchemin, 1964), 113-66.

7. Cited in M. Brunet, "Trois dominantes de la pensée canadienne-française," 163.

8. Fernand Dumont, *La Vigile du Québec*, (Montréal: Bibliothèque Québécoise, 2001), 37.

9. On this effect see Claude Couture, "Discours sur la modernisation sociale au Canada français: effets pervers et transmission de la culture anglo-américaine," *Études canadiennes*, 41 (1996): 129-44.

10. Everett C. Hughes, *Rencontre entre deux mondes* (Montréal: Les éditions du Boréal Express, 1972), 20.

11. Marcel Rioux, "Sur l'évolution des idéologies au Québec," reproduced in Gérard Boismenu, Laurent Mailhot, and Jacques Rouillard, eds., *Le Québec en texte, 1940-1980* (Montréal: Boréal Express, 1980), 132.

12. Fernand Ouellet, "La révolution tranquille, un tournant révolutionnaire?," in Thomas S. Axworthy and Pierre Elliot Trudeau, eds., *Les années Trudeau: la recherche d'une société juste* (Montréal: Le Jour, 1990), 336-62.

13. Guy Rocher, *Le Québec en mutation* (Montréal: Hurtubise HMH, 1973), 11.

14. Jacques Lazure, "Les affinités du Québec avec la nouvelle culture," in C. Houle and J. Lafontaine, eds., *Écrivains québécois de la nouvelle culture* (Montréal, Bibliothèque Nationale, 1975), XXV. Cited in Daniel Latouche, *Une société de l'ambiguïté* (Montréal: Boréal Express, 1979), 113.

15. Marcel Fournier, "Québec Sociology and Québec Society," 340.

16. Daniel Salée, (L'analyse socio-politique de la société québécoise: bilan et perspectives," in Gérard Boismenu et al., *Espace régional et nation. Pour un nouveau débat sur le Québec* (Montréal: Boréal Express, 1983), 37.

17. For a "post-colonialist" and revisionist critique of the use of the traditional-modern dichotomy in the study of Québec see Linda Cardinal, Claude Couture, and Claude Denis, "La Révolution tranquille à l'épreuve de la 'nouvelle' historiographie et de l'approche post-coloniale. Une démarche exploratoire," *Globe* 2, 2 (1999): 75-95.

18. Liah Greenfeld, "Nationalism and Modernity," *Social Research*, 63, 1 (1996): 33-34.

19. Gilles Paquet, *Oublier la Révolution tranquille* (Montréal: Liber, 1999), 13.

20. Paul-André Linteau et al, *Histoire du Québec contemporain*, II (Montréal: Boréal, 1989), 5.

21. Ibid., 6.

22. See the debate on the work of Bourque, Duchastel, and Beauchemin in Alain-G. Gagnon and Michel Sarra-Bournet, eds., *Duplessis: Entre la Grande Noirceur et la société libérale* (Montréal: Québec Amérique, collection "Débats," 1997).

23. G. Bourque et al., *La société libérale duplessiste*, 331.

24. For a similar interpretation see Luc Turgeon, "La grande absente. La société civile au coeur des changements de la Révolution tranquille," *Globe*, 2, 1 (1999): 35-56.

25. See Yvan Lamonde, *Allégeances et dépendances. Histoire d'une ambivalence identitaire* (Montréal: Nota bene, 2001).

26. Yvan Lamonde, *Ni avec eux ni sans eux: le Québec et les États-Unis* (Montréal: Nuit Blanche Éditeur, 1996), 9. Trans. Lyons.

27. Fernande Roy, *Progrès, Harmonie, Liberté. Le libéralisme des milieux d'affaires francophones à Montréal au tournant du siècle* (Montréal: Boréal, 1988), 275.

28. Andrée Lévesque, *La norme et les déviantes: Des femmes au Québec pendant l'entre-deux-guerres* (Montréal: Les éditions du remue-ménage, 1989), 167.

29. Jacques Rouillard, "La Révolution tranquille: Rupture ou tournant?," *Revue d'études canadiennes*, 32, 4 (1998): 23-51.

30. As Rudin is critical of the limited attention given to ethnic conflict and the overemphasis on material conditions in explaining the behaviour of actors, his criticism could be levelled equally against sociologists and political scientists working from a regional space perspective. See Ronald Rudin, *Making History in Twentieth Century Quebec* (Toronto: University of Toronto Press, 1997).

31. These citations come from a collage of texts by Rudin in "L'éclipse du national dans la nouvelle histoire du Québec," in Michel Sarra-Bournet, eds. *Les nationalismes au Québec du XIXe au XXIe siècle* (Sillery: Presses de l'Université Laval, 2001), 277-305.

32. Ibid., p. 298.

33. Ibid., p. 282.

34. Ibid., p. 294.

35. Jean-Marie Fecteau, "La quête d'une histoire normale: réflexion sur les limites épisté-mologiques du 'révisionnisme' au Québec," *Bulletin d'histoire politique*, 4, 2, (1996): 31.

36. Gérard Bouchard, *Genèse des nations et cultures du nouveau monde* (Montréal: Boréal, 2000): 74.

37. Gérard Bouchard, *Quelques Arpents d'Amérique. Population, économie, famille au Saguenay, 1838-1971* (Montréal: Boréal, 1996).

38. For a critique of the position advanced by Bouchard see Jocelyn Létourneau, *Passer à l'avenir* (Montréal: Boréal, 2000), 43-78.

39. Bouchard, *Genèse des nations et cultures du nouveau monde*, 55.

40. Gérard Bouchard, *L'histoire comparée des collectivités neuves* (Montréal: Université McGill, Programme d'études sur le Québec, 1999), 24-25.

41. Bouchard, *Genèse des nations et cultures du nouveau monde*, 60.

42. Ibid., 180.

43. On the subject of this transformation see Louis Balthazar, *Bilan du nationalisme québé-cois* (Montréal: l'Hexagone, 1986) and Michael Behiels, *Prelude to Quebec's Quiet Revolution: Liberalism Versus Neo-nationalism, 1946-1960* (Montréal and Kingston: McGill-Queen's University Press, 1985).

44. The comparison of Québec and Northern Ireland or the Basque Country is usual fodder for academics investigating inter-ethnic tensions or nationalist terrorist movements. On this subject see Katherine O'Sullivan, *First World Nationalisms: Class and Ethnic Politics in Northern Ireland and Québec* (Chicago: The University of Chicago Press, 1986).

45. On this topic see the comparative work of Nicola McEwen, "The Nation-Building Role of State Welfare in the United Kingdom and Canada," in Trevor C. Slamon and Michael Keating, eds., *The Dynamics of Decentralization* (Kingston: School of Policy Studies, Queen's University, 2001), 85-105. Also on Scotland, see Jonathan Hearn, *Claiming Scotland : National Identity and Liberal Culture* (Edinburgh: Polygon, 2000) and for Québec, Alain-G. Gagnon and Guy Lachapelle, "Québec Confronts Canada: Two Competing Societal Projects Searching for Legitimacy," *Publius*, 26, 3 (1996): 177-91.

46. See Michael Keating, *Nations against the State* (New York: St-Martin's Press, 1996) and *Plurinational Democracy* (Oxford: Oxford University Press, 2001). For a similar perspective see Stéphane Paquin, *La revanche des petites nations* (Montréal: VLB éditeur, 2001).

47. M. Keating, *Nations against the State*, 53.

48. Ibid., 218.

49. Nicola McEwen and Luc Turgeon, "Leçons écossaises pour le Québec," *Le Devoir*, 8 June 2000, A8.

50. See Alain-G. Gagnon and Raffaele Iacovino, "Framing Citizenship Status in an Age of Polyethnicity: Quebec's Model of Interculturalism," in Harvey Lazar and Hamish Telford, eds., *The State of the Federation 2001*, (Kingston: Institute of Intergovernmental Relations, 2001), 313-42; Jane Jenson, "Fated to Live in Interesting Times: Canada's Changing Citizenship Regimes," *Revue canadienne de science politique*, 30, 4 (1997): 627-44.

51. Alain-G. Gagnon, "Le Québec, une nation inscrite au sein d'une démocratie étriquée," in Jocelyn Maclure et Alain-G. Gagnon, eds., *Repères en mutation: Identité et citoyenneté dans le Québec contemporain*, (Montréal: Québec Amérique, collection Débats, 2001), 54.

4

Pluralism and National Identity(ies) in Contemporary Québec: Conceptual Clarifications, Typology, and Discourse Analysis[1]

DIMITRIOS KARMIS*

At the end of the 1970s, John Dunn ironically wrote, "we are all democrats today."[2] According to him, democratic discourse had become the moral Esperanto of our times, "the name for the good intentions of states or perhaps the good intentions which their rulers would like us to believe that they possess."[3] Dunn was calling for analytical prudence. It was no longer possible to speak of "democracy" without defining it. Some 20 years later, the problem has many more complexities. Not only is auto-proclaimed democracy more present than at any other period in time, but in the most advanced democracies, it has turned into auto-proclaimed pluralist democracy. Without being as unanimous as auto-proclaimed democracy, auto-proclaimed pluralist democracy is rising and its polysemy calls for analytic prudence.

Québec—as well as Canada—claims to be among the most pluralist polities of the world. Is that really the case? What does pluralism mean? What are its main variants? How much of a pluralist society is contemporary Québec? This chapter suggests a three-time reflection. First, I will offer a certain number of conceptual clarifications: a distinction between de facto pluralism and normative pluralism; a presentation of the links between pluralism, national identity, and citizenship; a list of three criteria to evaluate the degree of pluralism of conceptions of national identity. Second, on the basis of these three identified criteria, I will make a critical

* Translated from French into English by Mélanie Maisonneuve.

presentation of the two classical conceptions of national identity (civic nationalism and ethnic nationalism) and of four more recent conceptions that pretend to be more pluralistic (multinationalism, multiculturalism, integration nationalism and interculturalism). Finally, I will evaluate the pluralistic character of the conceptions of national identity that have marked Québec since the Quiet Revolution. I will argue that the general picture is far more nuanced than what is usually recognized. For the last 40 years, Québec has not been dominated by an ethnic nationalism or by a purely civic nationalism.[4] Contemporary Québec is mostly defined by a strong competition between three conceptions of national identity. These conceptions are characterized by various degrees of pluralism.

What is pluralism?

In contemporary political and academic debates, the term pluralism is used to refer both to a sociological fact and to a political ideology. In its descriptive meaning, pluralism refers to the fact that contemporary states are characterized by a growing diversity of collective identities and by a growing political expression of that diversity.[5] In its normative sense, pluralism refers to an ideology (more precisely, a family of ideologies) claiming that definitions of citizenship should be sensitive to sociological pluralism. Historically, we could say that sociological pluralism came first. Most modern states were built on identity differences (nation, ethnicity, language, gender, religion, etc.) which the majority or the strongest groups tried to exclude, assimilate, or even exterminate. These differences never totally disappeared and they gradually led to demands of inclusion, tolerance, and differentiated citizenship that we can see as the first expressions of normative pluralism. In the last 40 years, various phenomena contributed to an unprecedented increase in normative pluralism, particularly in the West. Let's just mention the increase in number and diversity of the migrant populations, the revolution in communication technologies and the rise of new social movements. The 1968 movements definitely represent a crucial step in what Charles Taylor called "the politics of recognition."[6] In other words, sociological pluralism and normative pluralism emerged and continue to intertwine in a dialectical relation.

A distinction too often forgotten must be reiterated. The principal bone of contention in the contemporary debates on pluralism does not concern the presence or absence of sociological pluralism. Even such authors as Bhikhu Parekh and Brian Barry, in profound disagreement on normative pluralism, agree on the existence of sociological pluralism. However, they argue that the passage from sociological pluralism to normative pluralism is not inevitable and that both have to be distinguished conceptually.[7] The heart of the matter is the nature of sociological pluralism and the type of normative response it should receive. To what extent are modern democracies shaped by sociological pluralism? Should they review their conceptions of citizenship because of such pluralism? What are the different variants of normative pluralism and how can we evaluate them?

Citizenship is more than the image that is most often portrayed. It is not limited to the legal status conferred by a passport. As Joseph Carens mentions, citizenship has three distinct but closely related dimensions: a legal dimension, a psychological dimension, and a political dimension.[8] The legal dimension refers to the rights and duties attached to membership in a state. The psychological or identity dimension refers to everything that concerns identification with that state. Finally, the political dimension refers both to political virtues and to the effective participation to the state's political life. In the case of federal systems, we have to consider these three dimensions with regard to a plurality of states sharing sovereignty.[9] This is the first objection that normative pluralism can make to the dominant modern conception of citizenship: citizenship is not necessarily one and indivisible. Here is how Carens summarizes the dominant modern conception of citizenship:

> In the modern world, talk about citizenship sometimes presupposes, as a background assumption, an idealized (and misleading) conception of the nation-state as an administratively centralized, culturally homogeneous form of political community in which citizenship is treated primarily as a legal status that is universal, equal and democratic. In this idealized conception, the nation-state is the only locus of political community that matters and citizenship just means membership in a nation-state.[10]

More generally, normative pluralism is opposed to monistic citizenship because states are marked by a plurality of communities of identity. What normative pluralism suggests is a plural and differentiated citizenship in its legal, psychological, and political dimensions. This chapter focuses primarily on the pluralist claims related to the identity dimension of citizenship, or what we most often call, rightly or wrongly, a national identity.[11] Obviously, demands for a pluralistic revision of national identity often lead to a revision of the legal and political dimensions of citizenship. Multiculturalism policies and processes of federalization are examples of the impact of pluralist claims related to the identity dimension of citizenship.

The contemporary problem of national identity is well explained by what Parekh calls the paradox of national identity. According to Parekh, national identity is both necessary and dangerous. It can be an indispensable instrument of inclusion and unity for states marked by de facto pluralism as much as a cause of exclusion and fragmentation of the diversity characterizing these states. On the one hand, writes Parekh,

[l]ike any other community, a political community needs to, and as a rule tends to develop some idea of the kind of community it is, what it stands for, how it differs from others, how it has come to be what it is, and so forth; in short a view of its collective or national identity.... Its shared conception of its identity serves several purposes.... The political community includes millions of people whom one has never seen and might never see [what Benedict Anderson calls an "imagined community" (Benedict Anderson, *Imagined Communities* [London: Verso, 1991], 6)] but for whose sake one is expected to pay taxes, make sacrifices, and even give up one's life. It also spans countless past and future generations to whom again one is bound by common ties of affection, interests and obligations. Its sense of national identity bonds these individuals and generations, and articulates and explains why they all form part of a single community.... It also inspires them to live up to a certain collective self-image and cultivate the relevant virtues, facilitates the community's self-reproduction and intergenerational continuity, fosters common loyalties, and orders their moral and political life.[12]

On the other hand, because each definition of national identity is selective and is also the object of power relations between groups within the political community, it necessarily tends to favour certain values, conceptions of the good life and interpretations of history of certain groups.[13] As Eamonn Callan mentions, the example of public education speaks well of this situation: "since the creation of state-sponsored schooling on a mass scale in the nineteenth century, the problem of creating a cohesive society in the midst of pluralism has typically been addressed by imposing a conception of common education that expresses the culture and advances the interests of politically dominant groups."[14] In short, national identity can be monistic, exclusive, and discriminatory as much as it can be pluralistic, inclusive, and egalitarian. Normative pluralism is a response to monistic, exclusive and discriminatory conceptions of national identity.

What are the criteria for evaluating the degree of pluralism in conceptions of national identity? Three general criteria appear to be particularly important. These criteria correspond to three levels of pluralism on a rising scale. At the first level, the conception of national identity put forward by the state and the principal political actors and institutions must make inclusion possible for all citizens. In other words, no criteria of the essentialist type should be used in the definition of national identity. This eliminates such criteria as race, social class, sex, and ethnicity, without eliminating totally criteria such as language and culture. This may be called the criterion of *possible inclusion*. On a second level, the conception of national identity put forward should be inclusive in the sense that it reflects and asserts the practices, the institutions, and the memory of all the cultural communities that inhabit a state. Such a level of pluralism implies, for example, a revision of national history as it has been conceived and taught for the past two centuries, that is to say, as the history of the majorities, by the majorities, and for the majorities. This is what I call the criterion of *symbolic inclusion*. On a third level, the conception of national identity must be compatible with the plurality and complexity of citizens' identities, including national identities. As Parekh points out, "there is no reason why one cannot be both Scottish and British, Québécois and Canadian, Basque and Spanish, Breton and French, and Hindu or Sikh and American."[15] This is what I call *deep inclusion*. Such pluralism implies that minority communities may participate fairly in the definition and redefinition of national identity. Deep inclusion requires a reform of democracy and, more specifically, a reform of what we have called the legal and political dimensions of citizenship. On the basis of these three criteria, we may evaluate the main types of national identities that have characterized the modern period.

Two Monistic Conceptions of National Identity and Four Variants of Pluralism

Contemporary pluralism is largely a response to two monistic conceptions of national identity that constitute the paradigmatic typology of conceptions of national identity: civic nationalism and ethnic (or genealogical) nationalism.[16] After a critical presentation of these two types of nationalism, I will evaluate the level of pluralism of four conceptions of national identity that have been presented as alternative solutions.

The idea of a purely civic nationalism was inspired by classical republicanism and initially took shape throughout the American and French revolutions. In spite of the differences between the American and French republican traditions, supporters of the civic model generally present a similar understanding of national identity. In the civic model, national identity rests on four elements: a historical territory; a community of laws and political institutions; the principle of equal political and civil rights for all citizens; the socialization to a common civic culture that ensures a rational adherence to the institutions, practices, and principles that constitute the national identity.[17] In this perspective, a national identity is first and foremost characterized by its openness, its cultural neutrality, its individualism, and its voluntarism. Anyone may adhere to universal political principles. There are no impassable barriers to inclusion and adherence. Everything is a matter of individual and rational choice.[18] In this way, there is no doubt that the civic model meets the first criterion of pluralism, the criterion of possible inclusion. However, the pluralism of the civic model stops at this first level. The idea of a purely civic national identity is one that is particularly vulnerable to two closely related criticisms.

First of all, from a sociological perspective, the civic model relies on a poor understanding of national identity. Collective identity, whatever it is, may never be a simple and rational individual choice of universally valid political principles. Every collective identity has an important *cultural* and *linguistic* dimension because every collective identity is the result of power struggles between a plurality of possible interpretations—and of languages in which such interpretations are expressed—of the past and future of a given community. In other words, every interpretation of collective identity is historically and culturally located and has a language to express itself. The Gadamerian idea of a "fusion of horizons" well exemplifies the interpretive process that shapes national identity. Simply put, Hans-Georg Gadamer breaks down the hermeneutic situation into three horizons of meaning: the historical and cultural horizon in which the interpreters are located; the horizon of the past phenomenon that the interpreters wish to understand (vertical interpretation); the extra-cultural horizon with which the interpreters interact (horizontal interpretation). According to such a perspective, a given national identity transforms itself through interactions between the nation's present horizon of meaning and its historic and extra-cultural horizons. As Bernard Yack mentions, "the idea of the civic nation, with its portrayal of community as a shared and rational choice of universally valid principles, is itself a cultural inheritance in nations like France and the United States. One aspect of distinctly French and American ideologies is to portray their own cultural inheritance as a universally valid object of rational choice."[19]

The sociological deficiencies of the civic model are all the more obvious since no nation can claim that its unity is guaranteed by the sharing of common values. As Wayne Norman points out, if such a definition of identity was sociologically valid, we would probably witness the emergence of a willingness to join Canada in certain northeastern American states. It may be argued that the dominant values of these states are closer to Canadian dominant values than to the values of most states of the south of the United States. Similarly, states with converging values such as Sweden and Denmark would consider merging.[20] So far, nothing indicates such trends. As for Jeremy Webber, he argues that in countries such as Canada and the United States, many political and social values that are considered typical—for example equality—are far from making consensus, even when constitutionalized.[21]

Second, from a political point of view, this sociological negation of the cultural dimension of national identity has a major implication. Whether it is voluntary or not, defending a supposedly neutral conception of national identity is to defend a monistic conception of national identity that de facto favours the cultural and linguistic majority. More precisely, because every set of political principles is inextricably linked to a culture, history, and language, to argue that a national identity may be expressed exclusively by a universal set of principles is equivalent to imposing the culture, history, and language of the group that promotes these principles. This group is generally the majority group or the strongest group. In the United States, as in France, the history of republicanism very well exemplifies the monism of the civic model. In the United States, despite geographical and social conditions particularly favourable to the foundation of a new nation on purely contractual and civic bases, the WASP culture and the English language came to dominate political institutions and public education and became an integral part of the American identity. Moreover, in spite of a federal political structure, which in theory is favourable to a plural sense of national belonging, American nationalism has never accepted multiple national allegiances. It has constantly tried to *subordinate* regional identities to a hegemonic national allegiance, instead of trying to *coordinate* them. This monism has generated a pluralist reaction that has never ceased to gain strength since 1945. In France, engaged in a long struggle with monarchism, Jacobinism turned out to be particularly monistic and even repressive against any collective identity susceptible to weakening the growing French republican allegiance. An important distinction must be made here. While American culture has often been imposed under cover of the principle of the neutrality of the state (this is what we might call *neutralist* civic nationalism), Jacobinism has openly advocated assimilation to a culture and language that pretend to universality and cannot be separated from French republicanism.[22] This assimilating monism does not only target immigration. Jacobinism has also built the French republic upon the persecution and repression of regional cultures and languages. This is why Yack argues that civic nationalism can be as much exclusive and repressive as ethnic nationalism is.[23] In short, the civic model hides a cultural and linguistic component that favours the majority. The civic model is pluralist only in the sense that it makes inclusion possible. Inclusion is achieved through assimilation and cannot reflect and express the practices, institutions, and memory of the communities that inhabit a given state, any more than it can be compatible with the plurality and complexity of the identities of its citizens.

The exclusive and monistic character of ethnic nationalism is much less subject to debate than that of civic nationalism. Historically, ethnic nationalism is in fact a reaction to the alleged universalism of the civic model. The ethnic "we" is monistic and exclusive by definition. In the perspective of ethnic nationalism, it is the more or less admitted presumption of a community of descent that is the determining criterion of belonging. Behind ethnic nationalism, there is the presumption "that there existed in some hazy, pre-recorded era a [national] Adam and Eve, and that the couple's progeny has evolved in essentially unadulterated form down to the present."[24] In other words, in the ethnic model, national belonging is based on criteria that are considered to be objective. For example, the name, the genealogy, and certain physical characteristics (the colour of the skin, the height, etc.) are used to determine the national belonging of individuals. Of course, the ethnic model cannot do without a recurrent insistence on the language, culture, and religion of the nation. They give reality, meaning, and value to the nation. However, in this model, they are the equivalent of natural attributes given at birth. They set national belonging for life. An individual cannot really know and identify with more than a single language and a single culture, and these are his/her maternal language and culture. Even the assimilated individual who has a strong mastery of the national language, without any accent, cannot be considered as a full member of the nation. Therefore, the ethnic model puts insurmountable obstacles to inclusion and does not meet even the first criterion of pluralism. Such a conception of national identity usually leads to more or less discriminatory citizenship policies against those who cannot claim to be part of the ethnic "we." It goes from an inferior legal status to segregation, deportation, or, in the most extreme cases, genocide.

Since the 1960s, several conceptions of national identity have been put forward as pluralist alternatives to the ethnic and civic models. Four of these conceptions have been particularly present in recent political and academic debates: multinationalism; multiculturalism; integration nationalism; interculturalism. These forms of pluralism propose a more or less profound revision of the monism of the ethnic and civic models. Their capacity to meet the three criteria of pluralism varies greatly.

Multinationalism is a normative conception that is generally based on three interrelated observations. First, as Will Kymlicka points out, "there are few examples this century of national minorities—that is, national groups who share a state with larger national groups—voluntarily assimilating into the larger society."[25] Second, as Connor already advocated in a study of 1971, "a prime fact about the world is that it is *not* largely composed of nation-states."[26] In fact, most states—and this is even more so after the fall of the Soviet empire and the resurgence and reinforcement of many nationalist movements—are (de facto) multinational states, that is to say, states in which more than one community use what Craig Calhoun calls the language of nationalism.[27] Third, the transformation of these multinational states into nation-states is not conceivable on a large scale, meaning that the reality of multinational states is here to stay. On the one hand, a number of minority nations are too small or too dispersed to constitute viable nation-states, or they just do not want to do so for various reasons. On the other hand, even in the cases where secession is desired and potentially viable, it is unlikely that the newly created state will be mononational. For example, a sovereign Québec would undoubtedly have to deal with national demands from Aboriginal peoples and the anglophone community, as is already the case within the Canadian federation.

Based on these three observations indicating a de facto national plurality in most contemporary states, multinationalism advocates a redefinition of national identity that is more sensitive to national plurality. In other words, multinationalism proposes to redefine national identity as being multinational. Such a redefinition first means that the new multinational national identity makes inclusion possible for members of national minorities. It also implies that the new identity reflects and expresses the practices, institutions and memory of every national community living in a given country. Finally, the new identity must be compatible with the plurality and complexity of citizens' national allegiances. Furthermore, because the use of the language of nationalism usually expresses a desire for governmental autonomy on a so-called national territory, recognizing the plurality of national allegiances is also opening the door to federal arrangements, and such arrangements raise again the question of the redefinition of national identity at the level of federate states. For instance, in the Canadian federation, it is not only the central state that should redefine its identity in the terms of multinationalism, but also the federate states.

The type of pluralism advocated by multinationalism is limited in many respects. First, multinationalism does not go beyond the recognition of the plurality of national communities. It does not propose anything for cultural communities that are not defined as nations, notably communities from recent immigration. Second, multinationalism does not propose a profound revision of the civic and ethnic models. In the cases where nations are defined in civic terms, national communities are the only ones that may escape assimilation. Moreover, even national minorities adopt policies of assimilation when they get political autonomy. In the cases where nations are defined in ethnic terms, national communities are the only ones that may escape exclusion, and even national minorities generate exclusion when they obtain political autonomy. Third, multinationalism tends to conceive multinational identity more as *juxtaposition* than as *coordination* of various national identities. Therefore, mulinationalism is an obstacle to the expression and development of plural and complex identities insofar as it assumes and favours partition and competition between national allegiances. This is why multinationalism involves the risk of making the multinational identity instrumental and subordinated.

Multiculturalism proposes a significantly different form of pluralism than multinationalism, but it has important limitations as well. Prior to any discussion of multiculturalism, we must say something about its numerous definitions. As Seyla Benhabib mentions, the term multiculturalism has been used indiscriminately to refer to various forms of pluralism.[28] It has even been used as a synonym for the generic term pluralism. In this chapter, multiculturalism refers to one of its major definitions, one that is dominant in Canada. Multiculturalism is a form of pluralism advocating the state recognition of the various ethnocultural communities on its territory, without any distinction between the communities who claim to be nations and those who do not. Multiculturalism does not distinguish between the identity and political claims of nations and those of ethnocultural communities from recent immigration. However, there is a world of difference between claiming national political autonomy on ancestral land and claiming a fair political integration for individuals.[29]

Multiculturalism, like multinationalism, is a normative conception based on the recognition of the sociological pluralism of contemporary states. However, contrarily to multinationalism, multiculturalism talks about ethnocultural communities in general, without any distinction. Proponents of multiculturalism contend that most ethnocultural communities—including those from recent immigration—have resisted assimilation. They also maintain that the vast majority of contemporary states are multicultural states rather than nation-states or multinational states. Finally, they assert that the increasing level of external and internal migrations in the last century has made the transformation of multicultural states into nation-states or multinational states impracticable, dangerous, and unjust.

On the basis of these remarks, multiculturalism proposes a multicultural national identity. At the first level of pluralism, this means that national identity should be defined in a way that makes inclusion possible for everyone inhabiting a state. At the second level, it implies that national identity should reflect and express the practices, institutions, and memory of every ethnocultural community established in a state. Finally, at the third level, national identity should welcome shared allegiances, including the allegiances of immigrants who will never fully give up their former identity.[30]

As a form of pluralism, multiculturalism is not less limited than multinationalism. First, multiculturalism denies the distinct character of the identity and claims of the communities speaking the language of nationalism. By neglecting the differences between nations and other ethnocultural communities, multiculturalism does not fully meet the second and third criteria of pluralism. Multiculturalism makes inclusion possible for the members of minority nations, but it makes it incompatible with the recognition of the national character of their practices, institutions, memory, and allegiances. Second, multiculturalism, as it has been defined, is not inclusive of cultural identities based on lifestyle (gay identity, punk identity, etc.) or an alternative conception of the world (ecologist identity, feminist identity, etc.), notably cultural identities expressed in new social movements. Multiculturalism conceives ethnocultural communities as monolithic blocs rather than communities shaped by plural identities. Third, multiculturalism tends to conceive multicultural national identity as a *juxtaposition* of ethnocultural identities. In a way similar to multinationalism, multiculturalism assumes and favours partition and competition between identities. Such a tendency is detrimental to the expression and development of plural and complex identities. It is also stronger when ethnocultural communities define themselves in ethnic terms rather than in cultural or linguistic terms. Thus, multiculturalism involves the risk of making the multicultural national identity instrumental and subordinated.

Integration or convergence nationalism is a combination of civic nationalism with linguistic and cultural nationalism. It also includes a good measure of multiculturalism and some elements of multinationalism. This third type of pluralism can be seen both as an alternative to civic and ethnic nationalism and as a response to the deficiencies of multinationalism and multiculturalism.

Integration nationalism agrees with multiculturalism regarding the ethnocultural pluralism of contemporary states. It also agrees with multinationalism on the multinational reality of most contemporary states. In other words, integration nationalism establishes a clear distinction between nations and ethnocultural communities. Integration nationalism is a form of normative pluralism that emphasizes the integrative role of a common civic culture, but also the integrative role of the culture and language of the majority nation itself.[31] The culture and language of the majority nation are conceived as the rallying point for the various communities established on a territory. This form of nationalism easily meets the first criterion of pluralism. The culture and language of the majority are not used as markers of exclusion but as instruments of inclusion that must be easily accessible to everyone through the public system of education. This is a question of justice. The integrationist model is also pluralist because it does not support *assimilation*; it proposes *integration* to the majority nation. Finally, it is pluralist in the sense that the allegiance to the integrative nation does not have to be exclusive.

This third form of pluralism also has its limitations. First, it is usually reluctant to fully recognize and express the practices, institutions, and memory of minority communities that use the language of nationalism. This language tends to be perceived as an obstacle to integration and the communities using it tend to be perceived as competitors that threaten the ascendancy of the integrative majority nation. Second, although it accepts the reality of plural identities, integration nationalism is still prisoner of the monistic paradigm of the competition and subordination between collective identities. It clearly seeks to make dominant the allegiance to the integrative majority nation. Furthermore, in the case of multinational federations, it tends to intensify the competition and subordination between federate integrative nations and the central integrative nation.

Interculturalism is, without any doubt, the most advanced form of pluralism today. Moreover, it is important to emphasize that this model of pluralism is not dominant in any country. Interculturalism combines the observations of both multiculturalism and multinationalism regarding the sociological pluralism of contemporary states. However, interculturalism is based on three additional and closely interrelated observations. First, according to interculturalism, de facto pluralism is not limited to ethnocultural communities and nations. It also concerns cultures related to lifestyles and conceptions of the world. Second, cultural communities are intertwined rather than simply being juxtaposed. Third, interculturalism breaks with the monistic paradigm of competition and subordination between collective identities. On the one hand, it asserts that most individuals have multiple identities. On the other hand, it maintains that none of these identities is dominant enough to subordinate the others.

Interculturalism surpasses the pluralism of the other models in many ways. First, it is the only model advocating a fair conception of national identity. Interculturalism recognizes and expresses the practices, institutions, and memory of every cultural community in its own terms. That includes nations, ethnocultural groups, and non-ethnic cultural groups. From an intercultural perspective, no cultural community should be excluded from national identity or be assimilated to another type of cultural community. Second, interculturalism contends that a fair conception of national identity can emerge only on the basis of an egalitarian—and necessarily political and democratic—intercultural dialogue between all the various communities of a state. Therefore, national identity should be the result of a constant process of dialogue guided by two principles: a principle of *openness* that favours encounters and exchanges between cultural communities and a principle of *asymmetry* that ensures that encounters and exchanges take place in fair conditions. Finally, interculturalism is not only open to the plurality and complexity of allegiances, but it also tries to favour them. According to Tzvetan Todorov, intercultural relations may both "enrich the self"[32] and transform his/her relationship with others through what Northrop Frye called "transvaluation," that is, through the "looking back on oneself with a glance informed by contact with others."[33] On the one hand, by providing new sets of perspectives, reference points and preoccupations, intercultural dialogue may fuel the minimal requirements of critical judgement and freedom of choice that are necessary to identity pluralization. As Todorov argues, "the choice is possible only when one has been informed of the existence of such a choice."[34] On the other hand, intercultural dialogue may generate identity pluralization. The ongoing and mutual process of transvaluation may come to transform one's self-definition and one's perception of the other in ways that make room for identification with both a pre-existing intra-cultural community of conversation and a new intercultural one. In other terms, through transvaluation, the intercultural conversation may come to be valued for itself, for the enrichment and pride of peacefully building a society on differences as well as commonalities. For the intercultural self, both communities of conversation take categorical importance, although one may be more important than the other. They both are constitutive of *inter*-culturalism, that is to say, the encounter of distinct communities of conversation. That being said, interculturalism involves a greater measure of indeterminacy than the other models in the sense that it focuses on the process leading to the formation of national identity rather than on the result of such process. Moreover, interculturalism is characterized by an optimism that seems hardly justifiable in numerous cases of conflicts in which resentment is so high that it makes almost impossible the mere beginning of a dialogue, for example cases of genocide or prolonged wars. Proponents of interculturalism have still a lot of work to achieve on the conditions of a minimally fruitful intercultural dialogue in such cases.

To sum up, these six conceptions of national identity do not constitute an exhaustive list. They are merely ideal-types closely interrelated in the sense that they respond to each other as well as sometimes borrowing elements from one another. However, this typology is a useful instrument of analysis because it presents the principal monistic and pluralist conceptions that shape the contemporary debates on national identity. It makes possible the break with the classical and simplistic typology that reduces debates on national identity to a simple opposition between civic and ethnic nationalism. This is absolutely necessary to understand the complexity of contemporary debates on national identity in Québec.

The Case of Contemporary Québec: A Nuanced Interpretation[35]

Since the Quiet Revolution, Québec has been the place of uninterrupted debates on its collective identity. Artists, writers, academics, politicians, and journalists all have been major actors in these debates. From a comparative point of view, there are not many places in the world where there have been so many innovative reflections about the politics of identity. Unfortunately, the growing variety and richness of these reflections is often hidden by the omnipresence of the civic nationalism/ethnic nationalism dichotomy and by its partisan use. As the debate on the political future of Québec has persisted and become embittered, especially since the 1995 referendum, opponents of sovereignty or even special constitutional status for Québec have been increasingly quick to accuse Québec nationalism of being "ethnic." In the face of these accusations, Québec nationalists generally have adopted a defensive position and argued that their nationalism is purely "civic" or "territorial." However, for the past 40 years, Québec has been dominated neither by ethnic nationalism nor by a purely civic nationalism. The picture of the dominant conceptions of national identity is much more complex and nuanced than that. In this final section, I will argue that contemporary Québec is characterized by the ongoing battle between three different conceptions of national identity and pluralism: (1) Trudeauism, which is a mix of civic nationalism and Canadian multiculturalism opposed to the redefinition of Québec as a nation; (2) Québec nationalism of the Jacobin style; (3) Québec nationalism of the integrationist type. I will maintain that, contrarily to what Trudeauists often imply, the history of the PQ has been marked by a debate between the proponents of assimilation and those of integration rather than by the remnants of ethnic nationalism.

From a Gadamerian perspective, we might say that national identity changes in concert with the interplay between the present horizon of meaning of a nation and its historical and extra-cultural horizons. In other words, the question of collective identity is not always a matter of public discussion and debate. For it to become so, the society in question must come under the influence of more than one tradition of thought, or a dominant tradition must be beset with deeply conflicting interpretations. Pre-World War II Québec was not the monistic exception that many observers have pictured since the Quiet Revolution. As revisionist historiography has shown in the past years, French-Canadian nationalism was characterized by severe tensions between conservative and liberal currents. Furthermore, Québec was far from being the only conservative place in Canada and Northern America.[36] What really changed after World War II and even more so with the Quiet Revolution, is that the critics of traditional nationalism and anti-statism that dominated the Duplessis era became more numerous, more visible, and more profound. In the wake of the *Refus Global* manifesto, several groups of intellectuals became increasingly active and influential. While they shared similar criticisms of traditional nationalism and anti-statism, these groups made common cause until the 1960 electoral victory of the Québec Liberal Party (QLP) led by Jean Lesage. In a way, this is the transition from the opposition to Duplessis's regime to the debates about the alternative to Duplessisism that led to a direct confrontation on the issue of national identity. This is where Québec contemporary debate on national identity really begins.

We often divide the critics of Duplessisism in two camps. On the one hand, there is a group of intellectuals gathered around the periodical *Cité libre*, who generally define themselves as anti-nationalists and who put emphasis on Canadian identity. On the other hand, there is a group of neo-nationalist intellectuals gathered around *Le Devoir*, who try to transform the French-Canadian ethnic nationalism into a *québécois* nationalism of the Jacobin type. This neo-nationalism is based on the idea that the Québec state should be a "normal" state and, therefore, should assimilate immigrants to the language and culture of the francophone majority. As the link between the new interventionism of the Québec state and the construction of a *québécois* identity became clearer, most of the *citélibristes* turned to the federal government and engaged in the task of building a Pan-Canadian national identity. This is what became Trudeauism. After a critical presentation of these two founding trends of the contemporary debate on national identity in Québec, I will examine Québec integration nationalism.

Trudeauism is a combination of civic nationalism and multiculturalism originating largely from the *citélibristes*' ideas. The anti-nationalism of the *citélibristes* was directed against the nation-state model, without any distinction. By ignorance or by political calculation, the *citélibristes* did not distinguish between nation-states based on ethnic nationalism—which are not pluralist in any way—and nation-states based on Jacobin nationalism—which meet the first criterion of pluralism. As soon as they saw a link between the policies of the new interventionist Québec state and the construction of a *québécois* identity based on the culture and language of the majority, the *citélibristes* started to draw unfair parallels between Québec neo-nationalism and traditional French-Canadian nationalism.[37] Furthermore, they saw the autonomist neo-nationalism of the Lesage government as nothing less than the first step towards the creation of a new nation-state. The rejection of the nation-state model is a driving force behind Pierre Trudeau's conception of national identity in the aftermath of the Duplessis era. A few words about Trudeau's thinking will help to better understand his opposition to Québec nationalism and his preference for a pan-Canadian national identity that combines the civic and the multicultural models.

In line with the civic model, Trudeau's thinking is based on a universalizing and rationalizing individualist liberalism. In the early 1960s, faced with the simultaneous challenges of autonomist and secessionist neo-nationalisms in Québec, Trudeau contrasted "sociological nation," emotion, particularism, and the nation-state paradigm on the reactionary side, with "juridical nation," reason, universalism, and the federal model on the progressive side. In this perspective, he writes that, "the history of civilization is a chronicle of the subordination of tribal 'nationalism' to wider interests."[38] For Trudeau, the principle of the nation-state slowed down the process of civilization. Recognizing the existence of the nation in a sociological sense, he considers that it produces an emotive and particularistic attachment contrary to human reconciliation. As the foundation of the state, the sociological nation is said to lead to fragmentation and never-ending wars.[39] Trudeau considers that the openness to "universal values" is threatened by Québec neo-nationalism,[40] because any sociological nationalism is the first step towards secessionist movements based on the nation-state model. As an alternative, Trudeau proposes the idea of a "juridical nation" or civic nation—a political entity founded on reason—as the basis for reconciliation, unity, and peace. And for him, federation represented the most accomplished form of the juridical nation and embodies the exercise of reason in politics.[41]

Unlike the supporters of a purely civic model, Trudeau combines his pan-Canadian civic nationalism with bilingualism and multiculturalism. Trudeau argues that his pan-Canadian nationalism is founded on potentially universal values. Such values would find expression in a purely civic identity of juridical type. They appeared in the LPC platform for the 1968 election under the slogan of the "just society": individual liberty and the equality of opportunity required for its exercise.[42] The "just society" program came out against the recognition of any particular collective status founded on historical, cultural, or territorial claims. It addressed solely individuals and attempted to shift the priority of their allegiances towards the Canadian "juridical nation." Linguistic and cultural rights were seen as compatible with liberal values only to the extent that they were given to individuals and justified as necessary for their equality and autonomy. It is on this basis that the Trudeau government justified its 1969 policy of bilingualism and its 1971 policy of multiculturalism. When he unveiled the latter, Trudeau clearly establishes the links between the pan-Canadian civic nationalism of the "just society" and multiculturalism:

> Il ne peut y avoir une politique culturelle pour les Canadiens d'origine française et britannique, une autre pour les autochtones et encore une pour tous les autres. Car, bien qu'il y ait deux langues officielles, il n'y a pas de culture officielle, et aucun groupe ethnique n'a la préséance. Il n'y a pas un citoyen, pas un groupe de citoyens qui soit autre que canadien, et tous doivent être traités équitablement.... Tout homme verrait sa liberté entravée s'il se trouvait enfermé dans un compartiment culturel déterminé uniquement par sa naissance ou sa langue. Il est donc essentiel que tout canadien, quelle que soit son origine ethnique, puisse apprendre au moins l'une des deux langues dans lesquelles le pays conduit les affaires publiques. Le multiculturalisme dans un cadre bilingue apparaît au gouvernement comme le meilleur moyen de préserver la liberté culturelle des Canadiens. Une politique de ce genre devrait permettre de réduire la discrimination et la jalousie qu'engendrent les différences de culture. Pour que l'unité nationale ait une portée personnelle profonde, il faut qu'elle repose sur le sens que chacun doit avoir de sa propre identité; c'est ainsi que peuvent naître le respect pour les autres, et le désir de partager des idées, des façons de voir. Une politique dynamique de multiculturalisme nous aidera à créer cette confiance en soi qui pourrait être le fondement d'une société où régnerait une même justice pour tous....[43]

It goes without saying that the Trudeauist choice of combining civic nationalism and multiculturalism meets only very partially the second and third criteria of pluralism. As a matter of fact, this choice was motivated partly by a strong opposition to the option of biculturalism—which meant binationalism—proposed in 1965 by the preliminary report of the Royal Commission on Bilingualism and Biculturalism (B&B Commission).[44] As Gilles Bourque and Jules Duchastel remark, the point here is not to argue that the federal policy of multiculturalism is purely a matter of political opportunism. It is simply to recognize "the fact that the constitutionalization of multiculturalism is part of a larger debate on the nature of the Canadian political community that implies the negation of the existence of the Québec nation."[45] The same remark might be made about Aboriginal nations. For example, Aboriginal peoples had to fight in order to get a very reluctant recognition of their rights in the Constitution Act of 1982.[46] Moreover, Trudeau admitted later that his government had never had the intention of granting territorial political rights to specific sociological groups like the Aboriginal nations.[47] In other words, the multicultural and civic nationalism of the Trudeauists does not recognize the distinct character of the identity and political claims of the nations of Canada. Trudeauism excludes all forms of multinationalism. There is one nation in Canada and it is the Canadian nation. For Trudeauists, the first collective allegiance of all Canadians must be towards this nation because, as Trudeau said in 1971, "there is not one citizen, not one group of citizens that is anything else but Canadian."

No matter how we evaluate this pan-Canadian nationalism, there is no doubt that it has had a significant effect on the sense of belonging of many Canadians. Trudeauism reached several of its most important objectives. For instance, today, it is a truism to say that many Canadians feel a strong attachment to the Canadian Charter of Rights and Freedoms.[48] However, Trudeauism also has led to unexpected divisive effects.[49] In Québec, if we exclude a significant part of the anglophone and allophone communities, the Trudeauist policies have not had the expected impact. They certainly have contributed to reinforce civic identification for the francophone majority, but not necessarily with the Canadian nation. As Simon Langlois points out, the homogenizing pressure of the identity policies of the federal government have served to reinforce and accelerate the sense that Québec itself forms a "global society." This sense took off during the Quiet Revolution and increasingly became a reality when the Québec government began building a network of social and political institutions parallel to that of the federal government.[50] Moreover, this development of Québec citizenship—achieved both in an autonomist federalist perspective under the QLP and in a sovereignist perspective under the PQ—is closely linked with the culture and language of the majority. This combination of civic nationalism with Québec's cultural and linguistic nationalism is characteristic of the other two major players in the contemporary debate on national identity in Québec: Jacobin nationalism and integration nationalism.

As already mentioned, Québec Jacobinism originates from a post-war neo-nationalist movement that contested Duplessisism with as much vigor as did the *citélibristes*. Under the influence of French ideas, the neo-nationalists had in mind a North American version of the French republican identity. Initially, neo-nationalist policy proposals were limited to the abandonment of monarchy and the creation of a Canadian binational republic. After 1960, however, following many disappointments, they choose the path of the "Québecization" of their identity and of their struggle for the preservation and flourishing of francophone way of life in North America. The political objective became the constitution of a francophone global society in Québec, whether through the autonomist way of the QLP or the sovereignist path of the PQ. The francophones of Québec gradually abandon the struggles of the French Canadians and redefined themselves as a majority in Québec, capable of assimilating immigrants to its culture and language through Québec state and citizenship. A major difference between this Jacobinism and the French model is that the assimilating majority is also a small minority in North America. Moreover, we may even argue that Québec Jacobinism sometimes has difficulty breaking from the defensive mentality and the ideology of *la survivance* that characterized French-Canadian clerical nationalism. The writing of Jean-Marc Léger, a long-time militant for Québec independence and former journalist at *Le Devoir*, offers a good example of Québec Jacobinism.

Based on the precariousness of the majority's situation and on the French conception of the nation-state,[51] Léger recommends vigorous policies supporting a rising birth rate and a careful selection of immigrants based on their potential for assimilation to the majority. In Léger's view, the ideal immigrant family is one whose children have become "perfect *Québécois*, that is to say, *Franco-Québécois* whose accent and behaviour reveal nothing of their foreign origins."[52] Even if this assimilationism is less drastically opposed to the recognition of the national status of the Aboriginal and anglophone minorities than before, this is never a priority and is always grudgingly regarded as a concession. For example, according to Léger, the urgent problem in Québec is the cultural survival of the French-speaking majority rather than the respect for minority rights.[53]

Despite the multinationalization and multiculturalization of states discussed in the second part of this chapter, Québec Jacobinism continues to support the monistic model of the nation-state by using the rhetoric of "normality." For example, Nicole Gagnon recently proposed "assimilation as the normal and necessary destiny for the majority of children or grandchildren of immigrants."[54] However, in the last years, this model has seemed to be increasingly outdistanced by Québec integration nationalism.

Integration nationalism has become dominant more recently, in the middle ground between Trudeauism and Jacobinism. Its emergence paralleled Québec's reconfiguration as a "global society" and represents a reaction to the failure of the deficiencies of the other two models: the incapacity of Trudeauism to take into account the multinational character of Canada and the failure of Jacobinism to take into account the multinational and multicultural character of Québec. Integration nationalism is a combination of civic identity with cultural and linguistic identity of the integrationist type. It tries to break with the defensive mentality that often characterizes Québec Jacobinism. Portraying francophone Quebecers as an increasingly strong linguistic and cultural majority rather than as a fragile appendage of a greater French cultural universe and positing pluralist liberal democratic citizenship as a shared good of this majority, it looks upon Québec as a land open to all cultures and seeks the integration rather than the assimilation of immigrants. Moreover, it emphasizes the importance of guaranteeing certain collective rights to Québec national minorities, the English-speaking community and Aboriginal peoples. In this perspective, the language and culture of the majority are seen as common goods to be preserved and promoted, but not at the cost of discouraging plural allegiances and sealing off the majority culture from other cultural influences. The language and culture of the majority represent distinctive features of Québec that need to be preserved for their own value, but also for their capacity to facilitate political deliberation and social solidarity in a diverse democracy. Therefore, the language and culture of the majority constitute a rallying point for the various nations and ethnocultural communities of Québec. According to the proponents of integration nationalism, this rallying point is a necessary condition of what they call Québec "interculturalism," as opposed to Canadian multiculturalism.[55]

Since the 1980s, this conception of national identity appears increasingly in Québec public discourse. In 1990, the *Énoncé de politique en matière d'immigration et d'intégration* of the QLP government marks a turning point. It is the first governmental document that clearly supports and explains the perspective of integration nationalism. On the one hand, the document argues that "the unambiguous affirmation of the francophone collectivity and institutions as a pole of integration for immigrants represents an absolute necessity in order to guarantee the survival of the French fact in Quebec."[56] On the other hand, it asserts that Québec should be a "pluralist society open to multiple contributions within the limits imposed by the respect of fundamental democratic values and the necessity of intercommunal exchange."[57]

It is important to mention that this conception of Québec national identity has nothing to do with the interculturalism as defined in the second part of this chapter. If we take the example of the 1998 *Politique d'intégration scolaire et d'éducation interculturelle* of the PQ government, we see so clearly a predominance of the preoccupation for unity over the preoccupation for pluralism (diversity) that it becomes illegitimate to talk about interculturalism. There can be no fair intercultural dialogue when the majority's preoccupation for integration, cohesion, and unity seems to be everything that counts. The 1998 policy says practically nothing about Aboriginal peoples and non-ethnic cultural groups, it says nothing about the multinational character of Québec, and it tends to erase the otherness that constitutes interculturalism and its merits. It includes many references to social cohesion, common values, and a common sense of belonging.[58] It contains a lot less about the merits of recognition, diversity, and complexity. Furthermore, and this is a particularity of the integration nationalism of the PQ as opposed to that of the QLP, the 1998 statement says strictly nothing on Canada, whether it be on the intercultural relations between provinces or the specific characteristics of citizenship and pluralism in a federation. In fact, the terms "Canada" and "federation" do not even appear in the document. The PQ government's objective of sovereignty is perfectly legitimate, but, as long as Québec is part of the Canadian federation, this objective does not justify such a silence when the government speaks about pluralism.[59] And the 1998 document is not an exception. The 2000 consultation document presented by the PQ government at the Forum national sur la citoyenneté et l'intégration is still more insistent on the need for unity, consensus, and cohesion.[60] In fact, the vocabulary of the document is closer to that of Jacobinism than of integration nationalism.

In short, Québec integration nationalism is more pluralist than Québec Jacobinism, but not much more than Trudeauism. It is more pluralist than Jacobinism in the sense that it partially meets the second and third criteria of pluralism. On the one hand, its conception of national identity is not completely closed to the practices, institutions, and memory of ethnocultural communities; it integrates them to the majority culture. On the other hand, it allows the expression of three forms of allegiance to Québec: that of the allophones who express a double or triple allegiance; that of francophones and anglophones, who identify with both Canada and Québec; and, that of the sovereignists who identify exclusively with Québec. However, this pluralism is almost as limited as the Trudeauist pluralism in the sense that it only partially meets the second and third criteria of pluralism. It is more pluralist by distinguishing between nations and ethnocultural communities, but its recognition of both is seriously limited by its concern for the precedence of the language and culture of the majority. Whereas the Trudeauists' primary allegiance may be only to the Canadian nation, the primary allegiance of the proponents of Québec integration nationalism goes necessarily to Québec. Let us add that in the case of the PQ's version of integrationism, Canadian belonging is simply erased. All in all, neither Québec integrationism nor Trudeauism allow a fair participation to the definition and redefinition of national identity. In both cases, the dice are loaded.

However, it is important to be precise about the place of ethnic nationalism within the Québec independence movement. Contrary to what Trudeauists imply, the history of the PQ—the main independentist political organization since its creation in 1968—has been marked considerably more by a continuing debate between Jacobinists and integrationists than by ethnic nationalism. Furthermore, the integrationist tendency has often been dominant, especially in the last two decades. As Gérard Bergeron maintains, at the time of the PQ's foundation, "[René Lévesque] risked his political career over the principle of linguistic rights for the minority [anglophone] group."[61] With the PQ's first ascent to power in 1976, the two tendencies clashed over the question of Québec's language law. The initial version of Bill 101, adopted in 1977, represented a clear victory for the assimilationist view.[62] Four years later, in December 1981, shortly after the first referendum on Québec independence and one month after the decision to repatriate the Canadian Constitution without the consent of the Québec government, a PQ congress was held that was marked by radical speeches and resolutions sponsored by the party's assimilationist wing. Disturbed by an apparent resurgence of elements of the ethnic discourse, Lévesque once again laid his leadership of the party on the line and asked members to vote in favour of three fundamental principles that would serve to guide the party in the future. The resolution on the third principle was as follows: "[Be it resolved] that the party reaffirm its respect for and openness towards all Quebecers, whatever their ethnic or cultural origin, notably by the recognition of the right of the minority English-speaking community to its own essential institutions, educational or other."[63] The successful passage of this resolution seemed to boost the party's integrationist wing, which gained further strength by successfully pushing for a series of important amendments to the French Language Charter in 1983 (Bill 57).[64] Ten years later, in the spring of 1993, the PQ reaffirmed its commitment to the historic rights of Anglo-Quebecers in a policy paper insisting that Québec culture would never be monolithic and that it is enriched by the contribution of citizens of diverse ethnic and cultural traditions.[65] Then, at the party congress of August 1993, the battle between the two tendencies was renewed. The party leadership withdrew a modest proposal for allowing bilingualism on commercial signs in reaction to manifest discontent within the rank and file.[66] However, two days later, despite the opposition of one-quarter of the delegates, party leaders were able to pass a resolution stating that the rights of the anglophone community would be written down in the constitution of an independent Québec.[67]

In this context, how can we interpret the speech of Jacques Parizeau on the night of the very close 1995 referendum, or the more recent so-called "affaire Yves Michaud"? Is it a return to ethnic nationalism, or even a proof that integration nationalism and Jacobin nationalism were only illusions masking the ethnicism of the majority? The answer must be nuanced. From a pluralist perspective, we can see three different problematic elements in Parizeau's speech. First, and this is the only element that held the media's attention, Parizeau attributed the referendum defeat to "money and ethnic votes."[68] Second, he constantly used an exclusive "we":

> on va cesser de parler des francophones du Québec voulez-vous? On va parler de nous à 60%. On a voté pour. On s'est bien battu, et nous, on a quand même réussi à indiquer clairement ce qu'on voulait.... Alors ça veut dire que la prochaine fois, au lieu d'être 60 ou 61% à voter OUI on sera 63 ou 64% et ça suffira.... L'indépendance du Québec reste le ciment entre nous. Nous voulons un pays et nous l'aurons!... N'oubliez jamais les trois cinquièmes de ce que nous sommes ont voté OUI.[69]

Finally, his speech was given in an acrimonious tone that was not inviting at all for those excluded from the "we." As for the remarks of the old PQ militant and ex-parliamentarian Michaud, the problems are similar: the attribution of the referendum defeat to the "ethnic vote,"[70] the stigmatization of Jews in general, in particular, the stigmatization of the B'nai Brith as "anti-*Québécois* and anti-sovereignist,"[71] the acrimonious tone against the ethnocultural minorities who dare to vote No.

Such remarks are very far from pluralism, but they are closer to the fine line separating Jacobinism from ethnic nationalism than to a purely ethnic perspective. Contrary to ethnic nationalism, Parizeau and Michaud do not exclude non-francophones from the sovereignist project on the basis of essentialist motives. They exclude them from the "we" by resentment, because they refuse, in vast majority, to support a political position that has mainly been defined with the interests of the francophone majority in mind. In other words, Parizeau and Michaud are so imprisoned in the paradigm of the nation-state that they confuse Québec national identity with the sovereignist project, the complete realization of the former being possible only with sovereignty. The similarities with the behaviours of ethnic nationalism and the risks of the slippery slope are more obvious when Parizeau and Michaud blame minorities—namely Jews—for the referendum defeat, even if 40 per cent of francophones voted No. Such an ethnicist reading of reality may lead to rancor and to a more essentialist, radical, and permanent exclusion.

Since Parizeau's speech and following resignation, the PQ seems to have escaped the path of exclusion. Under the leadership of Lucien Bouchard, the PQ continued to be divided by struggles between Jacobinism and integration nationalism, but the latter most often prevailed. As a matter of fact, Bouchard himself was an active and convinced integrationist. On 11 March 1996, at the Centaur Theatre, in his famous reconciliation speech to the representatives of the anglophone community, there was a strong repudiation of the remarks of his predecessor:

> [a]s a sovereignist leader, I can tell you I find nothing surprising in the fact that a great number of anglophones would vote to remain in the federation where they have more friends and family, more economic ties, more shared history, a shared language, and a far keener sense of belonging than do most francophone Quebeckers. It was perfectly legitimate that they did so.... La tâche des souverainistes est d'augmenter le nombre d'anglophones souverainistes, sans condamner le choix des autres.[72]

In the same speech, Bouchard reaffirmed the "solemn commitment" of his government "to preserve the rights of the anglophone community, now and in a sovereign Québec," proposing to entrench such rights in the constitution of a sovereign Québec before holding the next referendum.[73] Furthermore, he proposed a resolution of mutual respect between sovereignists and federalists, especially regarding "each other's beliefs and values." Then, he apologized for having said in January 1996 that Canada was not a real country. He also reaffirmed that "that the Québec nationalism that we are building no longer defines itself as that of French-Canadians, but as that of all Quebecers; it no longer seeks homogeneity but it embraces diversity and pluralism."[74] Finally, Bouchard made reassuring remarks about the place of English and anglophones in Québec.[75] In the years following this effort to integrate, the influence of Bouchard was often decisive. For example, he repeatedly contributed to the defeat of the Jacobins who wanted a return to a tougher version of Bill 101. It is still too early to know whether Bouchard's resignation in the wake of the "affaire Michaud" will lead to a weakening of the integrationist tendency within the PQ.

Conclusion

In the first part of this chapter, I argued that pluralism is both a sociological fact and a political ideology that call for a redefinition of the identity dimension of citizenship. Pluralism is opposed to the two conceptions that constitute the classical typology of national identity: civic and ethnic nationalism. Then, I proposed three criteria for evaluating the level of pluralism in conceptions of national identity. These criteria correspond to three levels of pluralism on a rising scale: (1) possible inclusion; (2) symbolic inclusion, and (3) deep inclusion.

In the second part, on the basis of these three criteria, I assessed six ideal-typical conceptions of national identity. First, I argued that both civic and ethnic nationalism have mythical and monistic conceptions of national identity. Civic nationalism meets only the first of the three criteria of pluralism, whereas ethnic nationalism does not meet any of them. Then, I argued that the three most common pluralist alternatives (multinationalism, multiculturalism, and integration nationalism) fully meet the first and partially meet the second and third criteria of pluralism. Finally, I maintained that while it is by far the most advanced model of pluralism, interculturalism still has to respond to many practical questions in order to become a credible alternative.

In the third part, I argued that the picture of the dominant contemporary conceptions of national identity in Québec is more complex and nuanced than is often believed. During the past 40 years, Québec has not been dominated by ethnic nationalism or by a purely civic nationalism. Contemporary Québec is characterized by the ongoing battle between three different conceptions of national identity and pluralism: (1) Trudeauism, which is a mix of civic nationalism and Canadian multiculturalism opposed to the redefinition of Québec as a nation; (2) Québec nationalism of the Jacobin type; (3) Québec nationalism of the integrationist type. I also maintained that, contrary to what Trudeauists often imply, the history of the PQ has been marked by a debate between the proponents of assimilation and those of integration rather than by the remnants of ethnic nationalism. That being said, it is obvious that both Québec and Canada have considerable progress to make on the road to pluralism. Today, the intercultural model is not much more than a vision of intellectuals in the margins of democratic debates. A major step would be taken if we could free ourselves from the ideological yoke of the civic nationalism/ethnic nationalism dichotomy.

Notes

1. I wish to thank Linda Cardinal for her comments and suggestions on the first version of this chapter.

2. John Dunn, *Western Political Theory in the Face of the Future* (Cambridge: Cambridge University Press, 1979), 1.

3. Ibid., 12.

4. I will argue in the second part of the article that pure civic nationalism has never existed.

5. By definition, we should actually be speaking of "plurality" rather than "pluralism," but common usage refers to "pluralism."

6. Charles Taylor, "The Politics of Recognition," in Amy Gutmann, ed., *Multiculturalism and the "Politics of Recognition"* (Princeton: Princeton University Press, 1992), 25-73.

7. See Bhikhu Parekh, *Rethinking Multiculturalism: Cultural Diversity and Political Theory* (Cambridge, MA: Harvard University Press, 2000), 6; and Brian Barry, "Muddles of Multiculturalism," *New Left Review* 8 (2001): 50.

8. Joseph Carens, *Culture, Citizenship, and Community: A Contextual Exploration of Justice as Evenhandedness* (Oxford: Oxford University Press, 2000), 162.

9. Ibid., ch. 7.

10. Ibid., 161.

11. Within a pluralist perspective, the concept of national identity is problematic in itself. In fact, this concept is part of the heritage of the monistic language of the nation-state and is often perceived as incompatible with the plurality of nations—and of national identities—within multinational states such as Canada, Australia, Belgium, United Kingdom, Spain and, as mentions Walker Connor, most contemporary states. Walker Connor, *Ethnonationalism: The Quest for Understanding* (Princeton: Princeton University Press, 1994), 96. Nevertheless, most proponents of normative pluralism continue to use the concept of national identity when referring to what could also be labelled as a state, a political, a civic, or a multinational identity. This practice implies that a national identity can host other national identities and that we can speak of a nation of nations. For example, we may say that both Canada and Québec are nations of nations. This is the way I understand the concept of national identity in this chapter.

12. Parekh, *Rethinking Multiculturalism*, 230-31.

13. Ibid., 231.

14. Eamonn Callan, *Creating Citizens: Political Education and Liberal Democracy* (Oxford: Oxford University Press, 1997), 171.

15. Parekh, *Rethinking Multiculturalism*, 232. For a more detailed analysis of the question of the plurality and complexity of identities in modern states, especially in federal systems, see Dimitrios Karmis and Jocelyn Maclure, "Two Escape Routes From the Paradigm of Monistic Authenticity: Post-Imperialist and Federal Perspectives on Plural and Complex Identities," *Ethnic and Racial Studies* 24 (2001): 361-85.

16. For a conventional use of this classical typology, see Anthony D. Smith, *National Identity* (London: Penguin, 1991); and Michael Ignatieff, *Blood & Belonging: Journeys into the New Nationalism* (Toronto: Viking, 1993).

17. Smith, *National Identity*, 8-11.

18. It is important to point out that the concept of "equality" in the civic model cannot be separated from the dominant conceptions of the human being and social organization that have characterized the Western World over the last two centuries. On the exclusion of women and Blacks from full American citizenship, see Judith Shklar, *American Citizenship* (Cambridge, MA: Harvard University Press, 1991). On exclusion within republican France, see Pierre Rosanvallon, *Le sacre du citoyen*, (Paris: Gallimard, 1992).

19. Bernard Yack, "The Myth of the Civic Nation," in Ronald Beiner, ed., *Theorizing Nationalism* (Albany: State University of New York Press, 1999), 117.

20. Wayne Norman, "Unité, identité et nationalisme libéral," *Lekton* 3 (1993): 43.

21. Jeremy Webber, *Reimagining Canada: Language, Culture, Community, and the Canadian Constitution* (Montréal and Kingston: McGill-Queen's University Press, 1994), 186-88.

22. See Stanley Hoffmann, "Thoughts on the French Nation Today," *Daedalus* 122 (1993): 64.

23. Yack, "The Myth of the Civic Nation," 115-16.

24. Connor, *Ethnonationalism*, 94.

25. Will Kymlicka, *Politics in the Vernacular: Nationalism, Multiculturalism, and Citizenship* (Oxford: Oxford University Press, 2001), 242.

26. Connor, *Ethnonationalism*, 96.

27. Calhoun defines nationalism as a particular discursive formation, a particular perspective and rhetoric, a style of thinking and speaking about social solidarity, collective identity and related questions that relies on several characteristic ideas (the idea of boundaries, the idea of sovereignty or governmental autonomy, the idea of popular legitimacy, the idea of a common culture, the idea of common descent, etc.) and that makes possible to differentiate nations from other forms of human communities. As he emphasizes, "there is no perfect list; we are identifying a common pattern, not a precise definition of nation. The points listed can help us to develop an 'ideal type', but this is an aide to conceptualization, not an operational definition or an empirically testable description. The word 'nation' is used sensibly and commonly understood when it is applied to populations which have or claim most of the characteristics listed. Which six, or seven, or eight characteristics will be most important will vary from nation to nation. Recognition of nations works not by discerning the 'essence' of nationhood, but through what Ludwig Wittgenstein … called a pattern of 'family resemblance.' Some siblings may have the family nose without the family jaw, or the family's characteristic green eyes without its characteristic high forehead; none of the features is shared among all the members of the family without also being shared with others who are not part of the family. Yet we can see the pattern. National ideology in any one

setting may lack one or more of its characteristic features, or place greater or lesser emphasis on others. Recognition as a nation is not based on strict definition, but on a preponderance of this pattern" (Craig Calhoun *Nationalism* [Minneapolis: University of Minnesota Press, 1997], 5-6). In other words, a nation is a community imagined in the language of nationalism, it being understood that different uses of this language lead to different types of nations and nationalism.

28. Seyla Benhabib, "Introduction," in Seyla Benhabib, ed., *Democracy and Difference: Contesting the Boundaries of the Political* (Princeton: Princeton University Press, 1996), 17.

29. On the considerable differences between the claims of nations and those of ethnocultural groups, see Will Kymlicka, *Finding Our Way: Rethinking Ethnocultural Relations in Canada* (Toronto: Oxford University Press, 1998), 36-39.

30. For a good list of measures designed to promote a multicultural national identity, especially through public education, see Kymlicka, *Finding Our Way*, 36.

31. In the case of a multinational federation, integration nationalism may be put forward by different nations in the various states.

32. Tzvetan Todorov, *The Morals of History* (Minneapolis: University of Minnesota Press, 1995), 82.

33. Ibid., 79.

34. Ibid., 82.

35. Some passages of this section are drawn from Dimitrios Karmis "Interpréter l'identité québécoise," in Alain-G. Gagnon, ed., *Québec: État et société* (Montréal: Québec/Amérique, 1994), 305-27.

36. For a good example of revisionist interpretation, see Fernande Roy, *Histoire des idéologies au Québec aux XIXe et XXe siècles* (Montréal: Boréal, 1993).

37. It is difficult to believe that such parallels have nothing to do with ideological and political interests, especially after Trudeau, Pelletier and Marchand joined the Liberal Party of Canada (LPC).

38. Pierre Elliott Trudeau, *Federalism and the French-Canadians* (New York: St Martin's Press, 1968), 156.

39. Ibid., 151-59.

40. Pierre Elliott Trudeau, *Memoirs* (Montréal: McClelland & Stewart, 1993), 72.

41. Trudeau, *Federalism and the French Canadians*, 195-96.

42. Pierre Elliott Trudeau, "Des valeurs d'une société juste," in Thomas S. Axworthy and Pierre Elliott Trudeau eds. *Les Années Trudeau. La recherche d'une société juste* (Montréal: Le Jour, 1990), 381-82.

43. Trudeau cited in Claude Couture, *La loyauté d'un laïc. Pierre Elliott Trudeau et le libéralisme canadien* (Montréal: L'Harmattan, 1996), 125-26. It is not possible to have one political culture for the Canadians of French origin and British, another for the Native Canadians, another for all others. Because, although there are two official languages there is not an official culture, and no ethnic group has precedence. There is no citizen, nor group of citizens, who are other than Canadian, and all should be treated equally.... All persons will see their liberty hindered if they find themselves locked into a cultural compartment uniquely determined by birth or language. It is, therefore, essential that all Canadians, whatever their ethnic origins, be able to learn at least one of the two languages in which the country conducts its official business. Multiculturalism in a bilingual environment appears to the government to be the best means of preserving the cultural freedom of Canadians. A policy of this sort would permit the reduction of discrimination and the jealosy that breeds

cultural dissention. For national unity to have a profound personal impact it is necessary that it reside in the idea that each has to have one's own identity; thus can arise that respect for others, the desire to share ideas, ways of seeing. A dynamic politics of multiculturalism will help us to create that mutual confidence that can be the foundation for a society where the same justice for all prevails. (Trans. L. Tallman)

44. Michael Oliver, "Laurendeau et Trudeau: leurs opinions sur le Canada," in Raymond Hudon and Réjean Pelletier, eds., *L'engagement intellectuel. Mélanges en l'honneur de Léon Dion* (Sainte-Foy: Les Presses de l'Université Laval, 1991), 341-42.

45. Gilles Bourque and Jules Duchastel, "Multiculturalisme, pluralisme et communauté politique: le Canada et le Québec," in Michael Elbaz and Denise Helly, eds., *Mondialisation, citoyenneté et multiculturalisme* (Québec: Les Presses de l'Université Laval/L'Harmattan, 2000), 159.

46. David Hawkes and Bradford Morse, "Alternative Methods for Aboriginal Participation in Process of Constitutional Reform," in Ronald L. Watts and Douglas Brown, eds., *Options for a New Canada* (Toronto: University of Toronto Press, 1991), 164-65.

47. Trudeau, "Des valeurs d'une société juste," 389.

48. See Alan C. Cairns, *Disruptions: Constitutional Struggles, from the Charter to Meech Lake* (Toronto: McClelland & Stewart, 1991); and Charles Taylor, *Reconciling the Solitudes: Essays on Canadian Federalism and Nationalism* (Montréal and Kingston: McGill-Queen's University Press, 1993).

49. See Kenneth McRoberts, *Misconceiving Canada: The Struggle for National Unity* (Toronto: Oxford University Press, 1997) and Dimitrios Karmis and Alain-G. Gagnon, "Federalism, Federation and Collective Identities in Canada and Belgium," in Alain-G. Gagnon and James Tully, eds., *Multinational Democracies* (Cambridge: Cambridge University Press, 2001), 137-175.

50. Simon Langlois, "Le choc de deux sociétés globales" in Louis Balthazar, Guy Laforest and Vincent Lemieux, eds., *Le Québec et la restructuration du Canada 1980-1992: enjeux et perspectives* (Sillery: Septentrion, 1991), 93-108.

51. It is important to note that Léger relies on a highly idealized view of the French case. In the first place, contrary to what he believes, the Fifth French Republic has not successfully assimilated North African immigrants and has been witness to serious debate on the validity of the assimilationist model (see Hoffmann, "Thoughts on the French Nation Today," 65-69). Moreover, Léger seems to ignore the long and painful history of resistance mounted by national minorities in France. A nation that is "one and indivisible" does not come about painlessly, in France or elsewhere.

52. Jean-Marc Léger, *Vers l'indépendance? Le pays à portée de main* (Montréal: Leméac, 1993), 80.

53. Ibid., 68-69.

54. Nicole Gagnon, "Comment peut-on être Québécois? Note critique," *Recherches sociographiques* 41 (2000): 563.

55. It is important to note that Québec discourse on interculturalism has developed largely in reaction to the 1971 Canadian policy of multiculturalism. Generally speaking, it criticizes the policy of multiculturalism on two grounds: its failure to distinguish between ethnocultural group and nation; its tendency to be conducive to identity fragmentation rather than identity convergence. As we have seen, the first of these two criticisms is fully justified, while the second needs to be nuanced, especially since the end of the 1980s (see Danielle Juteau, Marie McAndrew, and Linda Pietrantonio, *"Multiculturalism à la Canadian*

and *Intégration à la Québécoise: Transcending their Limits,*" in R. Bauböck and J. Rundell, eds., *Blurred Boundaries: Migration, Ethnicity, Citizenship* [Vienna/Brookfield: European Centre Vienna/Ashgate Publishing, 23, 1998], 100-01; and Kymlicka, *Finding Our Way,* 2-3).

56. Gouvernement du Québec, Ministère des Communautés culturelles et de l'Immigration, *Au Québec. Pour bâtir ensemble. Énoncé de politique en matière d'immigration et d'intégration,* (Québec: Gouvernement du Québec, 1990), 16.

57. Ibid., 15.

58. Gouvernement du Québec, Ministère de l'Education, *Une école d'avenir. Politique d'intégration scolaire et d'éducation interculturelle* (Québec: Gouvernement du Québec, 1998), 1, 2, 5, 6, and 7.

59. More generally, it is important to emphasize that this is an abdication of the Arendtian principle of responsibility for the world. This principle states that it is the responsibility of the existing society to introduce children (and immigrants) to the world as it is, both because the existing society took part in the making of this world, because it knows it, and because it is the world into which newcomers must enter (see Hannah Arendt, *Between Past and Future* [New York: Penguin, 1968], 188-91).

60. Gouvernement du Québec, Ministère des Relations avec les citoyens et de l'Immigration, *Forum national sur la citoyenneté et l'intégration. Document de consultation* (Québec: Gouvernement du Québec, 2000), 19.

61. Gérard Bergeron, *Notre miroir à deux faces* (Montréal: Québec/Amérique, 1985), 164.

62. On the PQ's internal debates on the adoption of Bill 101, see Marc V. Levine, *The Reconquest of Montréal: Language Policy and Social Change in a Bilingual City* (Philadelphia: Temple University Press, 1990), 113-19.

63. Cited in Bergeron, *Notre miroir à deux faces,* 277.

64. See Levine, *The Reconquest of Montréal,* 130-31.

65. Parti Québécois, *Le Québec dans un monde nouveau* (Montréal: VLB éditeur, 1993), 57-60.

66. See Pierre O'Neill, "Congrès du PQ. La proposition sur l'affichage commercial est retirée," *Le Devoir,* 21 Aug. 1993, A1.

67. See Roger Bellefeuille, "Le PQ a frôlé le précipice," *Le Soleil,* 23 Aug. 1993, A1; and Martine Turenne, "Jacques Parizeau satisfait que les droits de la minorité anglophone aient été réglés," *Le Devoir,* 23 Aug. 1993, A1.

68. Jacques Parizeau, "Mes amis, on se crache dans les mains et on recommence," *Le Soleil,* 31 Oct. 1995, A14.

69. Ibid.

70. Yves Michaud, *Paroles d'un homme libre* (Montréal: VLB éditeur, 2000), 31-33.

71. Michaud cited in Kathleen Lévesque, "Le PQ au cœur de la tempête Michaud," *Le Devoir,* 21 Dec. 2000, electronic edition.

72. Lucien Bouchard, "Living Together Before, During, and After the Referendum," (Montréal: Gouvernement du Québec, 11 March 1996), 6.

73. Ibid., 7.

74. Ibid., 8-9.

75. Ibid., 11-13.

5

The Québec State and Indigenous Peoples

DANIEL SALÉE[*]

> This is perhaps the oldest paradox of North America. Although large
> scale projects such as the 1975 James Bay Agreement and the 1999
> creation of Nunavut have been implemented, fundamental problems
> remain unresolved. It is disconcerting that after so many years of
> interaction, Indigenous and non Indigenous peoples have not yet
> developed shared, let alone dialogical views.
>
> — Louis-Edmond Hamelin[1]

Introduction

Despite the good intentions of successive Québec governments towards Indigenous
peoples, despite economic and administrative measures aimed at improving their
lot[2] and despite socio-economic indicators that may suggest that the situation of
Indigenous peoples seems, comparatively speaking, less desperate in Québec than
in most other Canadian provinces,[3] the relationship between the Québec state and
Indigenous peoples has often been uneasy since the now infamous Oka Crisis of
1990. The last decade has been punctuated by intense moments, often marked by
brash stances and hostile or acrimonious declarations on the part of Indigenous

---

[*] Translated from French into English by Manon Tremblay.

leaders. One need only recall the unflinching political offensive launched by the Eeyou (Cree)[4] Nation on the international scene against the Great Whale River hydro-electric project. Closely covered by the media at the time, the actions of Eeyou leaders, especially at the United Nations, were largely successful in bringing the Québec government to abandon a project on which hinged many hopes for economic recovery for the province. One may also recall the caustic debates between representatives of the sovereignist Parti Québécois government and several Indigenous leaders during the 1995 referendum on Québec sovereignty, the former declaring that the Québec territory was indivisible while the latter proclaimed their inherent right to self-government and consequently, their right to exclude their ancestral lands from a sovereign Québec. There were as well direct accusations of racial discrimination, xenophobia, and colonialism levelled at the Québec government by Eeyou and Innu leaders on the international scene, in reaction to dissatisfying territorial negotiations, or due to disputes over the management of the James Bay and Northern Québec Agreement. Finally, the violent confrontations between government authorities, Mi'kmaq and the surrounding non-Indigenous population in the sawmill rights conflict that arose at Listuguj (Restigouche) in the summer of 1998 also come to mind.

The list could go on. Some might argue that these are incidents that were more or less serious, and that they resulted from the political tactics and posturing that are part of the inevitable and conflictual process between a politically active minority group out to maximize its gains, and a state that controls resources coveted by the minority group. The fact is, notwithstanding this tendency to minimize the divide between the state and Indigenous peoples in Québec, and notwithstanding as well some recent positive developments that seem to suggest the dawning of a new era in their relationship, the opposition between the Québec state and Indigenous peoples is very real and constitutes in itself a permanent, even inescapable dimension of the Québec political landscape. It raises fundamental questions that take us back to the very nature of democracy in Québec and to the parameters of its application: why, despite its spirit of inclusion and open-mindedness on Indigenous issues, does the Québec government still seem to elicit suspicion, and why do mutually satisfying solutions that would put an end to the rivalry with Indigenous peoples still seem to elude the Québec state?

This essay is an attempt to provide answers to these questions. After a brief overview of the evolution of the official policies of the Québec state regarding Indigenous peoples, three factors that may help in shedding some light will be examined in turn: the internal political workings of Québec society, especially with regard to the question of nationhood; the nature of political life in Indigenous communities; and the impact of the normative liberal and democratic framework of the Québec state and society.

The Policy of the Québec State Regarding Indigenous Peoples: Context and Evolution[5]

The elaboration of Québec's policy on Indigenous Peoples began in the early 1960s. Up to that point, the exclusive jurisdiction of the federal government in Indigenous affairs, in accordance with the provisions of the British North America Act, largely accounts for the Québec government's absence on this policy front. A growing interest in mining ventures in the North forced Québec to chart its territory and adopt regulations to control development in that particular region. The first attempts at policy-making, under the Lesage government, provided for the participation of the Inuit in local development projects, while paving the way for the Québec government to step into a jurisdiction it had hardly ever considered before. Interest in the development of hydro-electric projects in the James Bay drainage basin was what first incited the Québec government to become involved in Indigenous affairs. Its desire to benefit from the exploitation of hydro-electric resources confronted the Québec state with local Indigenous Nations (Inuit, Eeyouch, Naskapis) and with the stipulations of the 1912 Transfer Act, which annexed to the province of Québec all the territory north of the 53rd parallel. According to the provisions of the Transfer Act, the active presence of the Québec state could not take place without the prior, explicit consent of local Indigenous Nations to relinquish their territorial rights to the Québec government. As a result, and following a key 1973 ruling by Judge Albert Malouf of the Superior Court, Québec was forced to negotiate an agreement with Indigenous Nations before contemplating any kind of development project. Two agreements soon followed in co-operation with the Canadian government: the first was the James Bay and Northern Québec Agreement struck in 1975 with the Eeyouch and the Inuit, and the second, the Northeastern Québec Agreement was signed with the Naskapis three years later. With these agreements, the Indigenous peoples involved effectively transferred their territorial rights to Québec. In return, and as far as its jurisdictional competencies allowed, Québec recognized the right of Indigenous peoples to maintain traditional hunting, fishing, and trapping activities, the right to participate in land management, and the right to scrutinize any activity that might threaten the social and biophysical environment. The Québec state also granted $225 million in compensation.

The clinching of these two agreements was a turning point in the elaboration of Québec's official policy regarding Indigenous peoples. It constitutes a milestone in the history of the relationship between the Québec state and Indigenous peoples and would impact on the evolution of that relationship. As a former high-ranking official responsible for Indigenous affairs for the Québec government in the 1970s noted, these two agreements established two axioms that Québec could not, henceforth, ignore: "First, development projects should not be the sole determinant of Québec's interest in Indigenous populations; second, Québec cannot elaborate a sound Indigenous policy without it being the object of negotiated agreements,"[6] Indeed, in 1983, the Cabinet ratified the terms of reference which, two years later, would undergird the general framework in which the Québec state was to cast its future actions towards Indigenous peoples. A resolution passed on March 20, 1985 by the National Assembly, along with a complementary one passed in 1989, recognized the existence of 11 distinct Indigenous nations in Québec[7] and acknowledged their ancestral rights as well as those stipulated in the James Bay and Northern Québec Agreement and the Northeastern Québec Agreement. The 1985 resolution also stipulates that these two agreements as well as any other agreement of the kind were tantamount to treaties. The resolution stresses the importance of establishing a harmonious relationship with Indigenous peoples, founded on mutual trust and the respect of inherent rights. It encourages the government to conclude agreements with the Indigenous Nations who so wish (or with any of the communities that constitute them) to guarantee their right to autonomy in Québec, their right to preserve and express their culture, language, and traditions; their right to own and control land; and their right to hunt, fish, trap, harvest, and participate in wildlife resource management, in order to allow them to develop as distinct nations with their own identity and with the ability to exercise their rights in Québec. With this resolution the Québec state affirms its intention to protect, within Québec's fundamental and defining laws, Indigenous peoples' rights enshrined in any agreement signed with them. The resolution also suggests that a permanent parliamentary forum be established allowing Indigenous peoples to raise awareness of their rights, their aspirations, and their needs. Finally, the resolution spells out that Indigenous rights apply to women as well as men. The spirit of this resolution — the first of its kind to be passed by a Canadian government — provides the basic tenets that inform the Québec state's overall strategy towards Indigenous peoples. However, the permanent parliamentary forum was never implemented.

Then there was Oka. During the summer of 1990, a dispute broke out between the municipal authorities of Oka and Kanehsatake, the neighbouring Kanien'kehaka (Mohawk) community, over the proposed expansion of a municipal golf course which would have encroached on lands considered sacred by the Kanien'kehaka. The dispute resulted in the death of one man and 78 days of armed conflict, bitter confrontations, tense bargaining, and negotiations between Québec, Canada, the three surrounding Kanien'kehaka communities (Kanehsatake, Kahnawake, and Akwesasne), and the non-Indigenous population of the region.[8] Those 78 days left an indelible mark on the collective memory of the Indigenous and non-Indigenous populations.

Looking back, the Oka crisis was a launching pad of sorts for a decade that was troubled, but also full of promise for Indigenous peoples. Oka inspired the radicalization and political mobilization of other Indigenous communities across Canada. After Oka, there was, in 1995, the Gustafsen Lake standoff in British Columbia and the Ipperwash conflict in Ontario, where one man died also. There was, in 1998, a conflict at Listuguj in Québec and repeated confrontations at Esgenôôpetitj (Burnt Church) in New Brunswick in 2000 and 2001. All these place names are reminiscent of direct and violent clashes and they are a constant reminder to the state — and Canadian society in general — of the frustrations, the dissatisfaction, and the profound malaise of Indigenous peoples with respect to their socio-economic status. In Québec, as has already been mentioned, there were also public accusations from some Indigenous leaders against the Québec government; political actions on the international scene against hydro-electric projects; disputes around the illegal sale of tax-free tobacco products by some residents of Kanien'kehaka communities; attacks against the sovereignist goals of the Québec government; denial of the existence of the Québec people as a distinct nation; and accusations of racism and colonialism.

Pressed by events and a number of Supreme Court rulings that changed the order of things in the interface between the state and Indigenous peoples,[9] the Canadian and Québec governments were forced to awaken to what appeared during the 1990s to be the Indigenous "problem." They started to appreciate the importance of modifying the dynamics of the state's relationship with Indigenous peoples in a tangible fashion and in accordance with the moral and political imperatives of a society that purports to be liberal, democratic, pluralistic, and respectful of cultural differences. The federal government went on to set up the Royal Commission on Aboriginal Peoples whose voluminous final report, tabled in November 1996, spelled out 440 recommendations inviting the state to make important changes to the relationship between Indigenous and non-Indigenous populations, as well as between Indigenous peoples and Canadian governmental authorities.[10] In January 1998, the federal government responded to the Commission's final report with an action plan entitled *Gathering Strength*. In addition to acknowledging the injustices to which Indigenous peoples were subjected through history and establishing an Aboriginal Healing Fund of $350 million, *Gathering Strength* commits the state, among other things, to preserve and promote Indigenous languages; to include Indigenous partners in the creation, the elaboration, and the delivery of programs; to favour the development of Indigenous peoples' ability to negotiate and implement self-government; to facilitate their increasing financial autonomy; to improve the living conditions and the quality of social and sanitary installations in Indigenous communities; and to develop strategies for job creation, educational reform, and access to capital funds.[11]

The Québec government was not to be outdone. In the Spring of 1998, it unveiled its new policy framework on Indigenous peoples in a document entitled

Partnership, Development, Achievements. This new policy statement reaffirmed and updated the government's commitment to the March 20, 1985 resolution. It is set in an overall perspective of equity and expresses the concern of the Québec government that Indigenous and non-Indigenous populations in Québec have "equal access to the same living conditions, the same general development opportunities as well as access to their fair share of public wealth while allowing Indigenous peoples to preserve and develop their own identity."[12] This policy statement guides the Québec state's current approach to Indigenous populations. It binds the government:

- to encourage the participation of Indigenous peoples in economic development particularly by facilitating their access to certain key resources located off-reserve, by encouraging their participation in the exploitation of these resources, and by including them in the management of economic activities on targeted lands;

- to recognize Indigenous institutions and their legitimacy to oversee formal, contractual relationships through agreements that acknowledge Indigenous self-government within the jurisdiction of the Québec state;

- to ensure legislative and statutory flexibility by modifying, if need be, Québec's laws and regulations so as to keep in line with the terms of agreements for development and for transfer of responsibilities, and in order to ensure that Indigenous jurisdictional latitude be fully allowed to unfold;

- to develop a harmonious relationship with Indigenous peoples through information and awareness campaigns (revised history curriculum, valorization of Indigenous cultures, intercultural exchange initiatives) and an increase in networking between Indigenous groups and non-Indigenous local institutions by fostering partnerships between local Indigenous and non-Indigenous businesses and organizations in matters of business, community development, and public service;

- to maintain coherence and convergence of governmental actions within Indigenous communities.

The actions contemplated by the government in order to carry out this new position include the creation of a site for political debate, exchanges and consultations between elected officials from Indigenous governments and Québec; the signing of contextual and sectoral agreements (transfer of responsibilities and development agreements) that are meant to increase the autonomy of Indigenous communities and promote their economic development; the establishment of a five-year Indigenous development fund in order to support Indigenous economic development and resource management initiatives; and, finally, the conclusion of fiscal agreements allowing Indigenous governments to generate their own sources of revenue. The government intends to implement this action plan by adapting it according to whether it applies to Indigenous Nations who have not signed an agreement or who do not participate in a comprehensive claims process, to agreement signatories, to nations involved in overall land negotiations, or to Indigenous peoples living off-reserve.

Since the publication of its strategic plan, and in addition to participating in a large variety of initiatives likely to contribute to the socio-economic advancement of Indigenous peoples, the Québec government has already signed more than 50 general and sectoral agreements with several Indigenous communities. These agreements range from declarations of mutual respect to precise protocols of interaction and exchange on specific issues (forestry, community development, social and sanitary installations, etc.). Almost two-thirds of the Indigenous Development Fund's $125 million were used to sponsor over 80 economic development and community infrastructure projects.

Recently the government signed or proposed distinct comprehensive agreements with the Eeyouch, the Inuit, and the Innu. These significantly modify and are meant to improve Québec's relationship with these nations as they foster their administrative self-determination and seek to develop economic cooperation and partnerships. In February 2002, the government and the Grand Council of the Crees (Eeyou Istchee) signed a final agreement, called the "Paix des Braves," which commits the Québec government to pay the Eeyouch in excess of $3.5 billion over the next 50 years. In return, the Eeyouch promise to drop all outstanding legal proceedings, pledge not to initiate new court challenges in relation to past applications of the James Bay and Northern Québec Agreement, and agree not to oppose the Québec government's hydro-electric development projects in their region. Furthermore, the government promises to integrate the Eeyouch as active partners in the elaboration and implementation of local natural resources exploitation plans and to help the Eeyouch take charge of their own community and economic development. The Québec government proudly hailed this agreement as a model of reconciliation that "opens the way to a new era of collaboration and to a genuine nation-to-nation relationship between the Crees and Québec."[13] Two months after this agreement the Québec government signed another one, on April 9, 2002, with the Inuit of Nunavik. Similar in spirit and content to the "Paix des Braves," this agreement, known as "Sannarutik," comes with a commitment made by the state to pay the Inuit $360 million over the next 25 years. With it, the state also acknowledges the Inuit's capacity for self-management and control over their community and economic development. For their part, the Inuit agree to foster and facilitate the development of the hydroelectric, mining, and touristic potential of the region, as well as support and participate in the implementation of eventual hydroelectric projects initiated by Hydro-Québec on their territory. Finally, at the end of Spring 2002, the government announced an agreement in principle with four Innu communities of Lac Saint-Jean and Québec's North Shore (Mashteuiash, Essipit, Betsiamites, and Nutashkuan). Dubbed "Approche commune," the proposed agreement would double the surface of the territory under the full ownership of the Innu communities involved in the agreement, and bring under their direct management 14,000 additional square kilo-metres of park lands and patrimonial sites. The agreement also includes direct capital transfers totalling $377 million (275 from the federal government and 102 from Québec) in return for which the Innu promise to drop Betsiamites's $500 million legal suit against Hydro-Québec. The agreement recognizes the Innu's governmen-tal autonomy, and thus the power to make their own laws, and confirms as well the validity of their aboriginal title and ancestral rights. Despite significant opposition expressed by a variety of stakeholders from surrounding non-Aboriginal communi-ties in the ensuing months, the new Liberal government of Jean Charest, elected in April 2003, is on the record as being officially committed to signing and officializing this agreement in principle before the end of 2003.

The Dynamics of Québec-Indigenous Peoples' Relations

The preceding presentation of Québec's policy towards Indigenous peoples is in great part a reflection of the official views and perceptions of those who fashioned it. Inevitably, there is a positive tone to it, an impression of generosity and open-mindedness on the part of the state. Modern liberal states who do not initially strike a theoretical pose of benevolence and ideological generosity towards their constituents are rare. Admittedly, during the last two decades, the Québec state has often found itself in a leading position compared to other provincial administrations and even compared to the Canadian government, when it comes to its dealing with Indigenous issues. In time, Québec seems to have elaborated a policy that at least in appearance treats Indigenous peoples as equals and offers them the means to political and economic emancipation. Can we conclude, then, that the relationship between Québec and Indigenous peoples is finally peaceful, forever to be marked by harmony and good will? Are the protracted political disputes of the last dec-ades a thing of the past? Can we assume that the situation will only get better for Indigenous peoples? Will the Québec government's new action plan actually give Indigenous peoples the means to satisfy their cultural, community, and nationalist aspirations and equally suit Québec society as a whole?

While considering these questions, it is important, first, to understand that the apparent goodwill of any modern, liberal-democratic state, as authentic as it may be, is neither automatic nor inherent. It results from power struggles that inevitably occur between social actors. It develops through the resistance and opposition of society's outcasts, who never cease to demand that the state make amends and whose relentlessness eventually leads to the establishment of an ideological environment that is more open to the creation of a fairer socio-political balance between the majority and minority groups. A balance that remains, however, necessarily fragile and that is in constant need of being re-calibrated. If the Québec state seems generous today and better intentioned than ever in regard to Indigenous peoples, this munificence does not derive from its natural or innate penchant for virtue. Rather, the Québec state was forced in part to adopt this line of conduct: forced by the courts to negotiate the James Bay and Northern Québec Agreement and the Northeastern Québec Agreement, and to rethink its hydro-electric development plans with respect to the populations they would affect; forced to acknowledge the validity of ancestral rights recognized by the Supreme Court; forced to soften its political stance in the face of opposition movements that would not back down; forced, finally, by the very moral imperatives of its own political ethos, as the considerable gap in socio-economic conditions that exists between most Indigenous peoples and the rest of the population[14] is in itself an aberration that Québec, as a modern and affluent society priding itself on its liberal and democratic character, cannot tolerate indefinitely. In its most recent formulation, the Québec government's policy towards Indigenous peoples partakes of long-standing dynamics of power and resistance of which the outcome is neither fixed nor predictable. Also, even if the current policy towards Indigenous peoples seems to reflect the government's good side and a commendable will to do what is right — or, at least, to look good — the reality of practices in the field does not always match official views,[15] or satisfy Indigenous stakeholders. Neither can it be said that the Québec state's approach satisfies all Indigenous stakeholders in one broad sweep. In most liberal societies, the complexities inherent to the nature of the relationships between the majority and the minorities, between the dominant groups of society and the outcasts, cannot be transcended easily even by the most enlightened policies. It is important to keep this in mind in order to achieve a better understanding of the relationship between the Québec state and Indigenous peoples.

Indigenous Peoples and the Vagaries of Québec's National Question

During the last decade, particularly under the leadership of the Parti Québécois, the Québec state has deployed considerable efforts in order to transform Québec nationalism. The government and its supporters insist that political self-determination and Québec sovereignty must reflect the general will of the whole of the Québec people and not only that of its francophone majority, as has often been implicitly assumed in the past. Meant to be fundamentally inclusive, the new Québec nationalism rests on a vision that is essentially civic (as opposed to ethnic) and invites all Quebecers, regardless of their linguistic affiliation or ethnocultural origin, to work together to develop a common public culture founded on universal values to which everyone can readily adhere (democracy, open public participation, gender equality, free speech, socio-economic solidarity, etc.) and for which the French language acts as instrument of reproduction and transmission.[16] This new-style Québec nationalism is different from the ethnocentric nationalism of the 1960s and 1970s, which mainly articulated the nationalist aspirations of Québec's francophone majority.[17]

In spite of these conceptual changes, the ethnicist image of Québec nationalism and of the sovereignist project it supports dies hard, especially outside Québec and among Québecers who are opposed to it. Québec nationalists, regardless of what they say or do, are still largely perceived as people who are looking to impose the dominance of the Québec state — and by extension, the cultural and institutional logic of the francophone majority — on Québec's ethnocultural minorities.[18] This image takes an even more negative turn when it relates to Indigenous peoples, often portrayed as the quintessential victims of history: the Québec state then appears as moved by colonialist and racist ambitions. Such views have been expressed, for example, by many Eeyouch and Innu leaders, over the past several years on the national and international scene. On several occasions they have berated the Québec government for systematically minimizing, through its actions, the status of nation recognized to Indigenous peoples and for denying their rights guaranteed by treaties and by the Canadian Constitution.[19] In a brief presented to the Commission des Institutions of the National Assembly in February 2000, the Grand Council of the Cree claimed that the "Act respecting the exercise of the fundamental rights and prerogatives of the Québec people and the Québec state" (Bill 99, passed in December, 2000)[20] creates the all-encompassing and fictitious category of "Québec people," to which it attributes the right to self-government, and gives the Québec government and the National Assembly the power to control this right, but refuses by the same token to grant Indigenous peoples the possibility of self-government and self-identification. Through this Act the Québec state emerges as the sole representative of all persons residing on the Québec territory: the Eeyouch refute this assumption and consider it to be a violation of their human rights. Kanien'kehaka intellectual, Taiaiake Alfred, agrees and believes that the successive governments of the past three decades have always tried, with a view to consolidate the sovereignty of the Québec state, to impose their authority on Indigenous peoples and to further restrain the limited but hard won political and administrative autonomy acquired over the years. Alfred believes the Act to be unquestionably tantamount to a move towards re-colonization.[21]

Although improved and now more open to the "Other," the Québec nationalist platform continues to appear threatening, indeed unacceptable, to Indigenous peoples. In fact, it challenges their own nationalism, their own desire for sovereignty.[22] Originally, the modern concept of sovereignty and the idea of power that lies behind it, were foreign to Indigenous peoples' traditional and political philosophy, but inevitably they have penetrated their political world as a result of the compelling and inescapable influence of Western political thought. The *de facto* negation of Indigenous presence through repeated attempts on the part of non-Indigenous governments to appropriate ancestral lands and the fruits of their natural resources has brought most Indigenous peoples to react by proclaiming their own identity and their right to exist according to the political and cultural criteria that suit them — to use, in other words, the political grammar and the typical claims of nationalism. For example, although the first Eeyou mobilizations at the beginning of the 1970s simply attempted to prevent Hydro Québec from building dams, their fight has slowly transformed itself into a movement for political assertion that stems from a concept of identity based on a sense of belonging to a nation.[23] Insofar as Indigenous peoples today can perceive themselves as nations — and who could blame them in Québec since the government has already recognized this status — they expect to receive the same regard normally reserved to duly constituted nations. Any attack, real or symbolic, against the expression of their existence as nations, any practice that in the end would limit the full exercise of their status as nations, becomes highly reprehensible. Because they also use the same lexicon of the nation, Indigenous peoples' claims inevitably are on a collision course with nationalist aspirations — however civic they may be — of the Québec state, which covets the same territory and the same political space.

Within this context, even if the latest incarnation of the Québec state policy towards Indigenous peoples can appear to be imbued with open-mindedness, generosity, and a genuine desire to support their socio-economic development, many within Indigenous communities see it as problematic.[24] They deplore the fact that the policy remains within the confines of a structure of authority and administrative jurisdiction over which Indigenous peoples have no control and that rests within the exclusive domain of the Québec state. They point out that the policy was not devised in collaboration or in consultation with Indigenous peoples and that it did not receive the benefit of a negotiated agreement between equals. Despite the government's claims that it considers Indigenous peoples as partners, critics argue that the policy is founded on the unilateral imposition of the Québec state's jurisdictional authority and is predicated on the sovereignty and legislative and regulatory predominance of the National Assembly: this is absolutely unacceptable to Indigenous peoples, who do not wish to be subjugated or subordinated to a government that they did not choose and that is foreign to them. By failing to grant Indigenous peoples a distinct legal status the Québec state is, in a way, denying their nationhood and their right to self-determination. Furthermore, Québec's insistence on implementing bipartite agreements delegitimizes the historic link between Québec's Indigenous peoples and the federal government and curtails the right of Indigenous peoples to choose their political partners freely: Québec retains, in fact, effective control over the Indigenous peoples who live within its geographic boundaries. The Québec government is guilty, in their view, of a political double standard, its right to sovereignty, its fundamental right to choose its political future, and the indivisibility of its territory but fails to recognize the same rights for Indigenous peoples. For all these reasons, many believe that Québec's current policy towards Indigenous peoples does not constitute a satisfying foundation upon which an equal partnership can be built. Some will even go as far as to say that the Indigenous peoples will only be able to fully achieve their political potential outside the Euro-American parameters and models of governance, and by rekindling their own, time-honoured political philosophies.[25]

Although the clash between Indigenous and Québec nationalisms feeds on its own logic, the Canadian political framework is a contributing factor to this clash. Given the jurisdictional division of power and responsibilities provided by the Canadian Constitution, the relationship between Indigenous peoples and the Québec state is inescapably determined by a triangular system that inevitably includes the federal level of the Canadian state. Thus, the Québec state is not the only master on board and it cannot negotiate the terms of its relationship with the Indigenous peoples without taking into account the political imperatives of the Canadian state framework. Neither can Indigenous peoples put aside their historic legal and administrative ties to the federal government, as per the terms of the *Indian Act*. The fact is, the federal government imposes itself as a third party between the Québec state and the Indigenous peoples of Québec, a third party whose political and administrative powers set the tone of their relationship, playing one against the others, often to serve its own particular interests. For example, during the 1995 referendum on Québec sovereignty, as several Indigenous Nations unequivocally declared their refusal to join a sovereign Québec[26] — to the dismay of the Québec government who proclaimed the indivisibility of the Québec territory — the federal government hastened to sympathize with Indigenous peoples' self-government goals inasmuch as they seemed to emphasize the alleged inconsistencies of Québec's sovereignist rhetoric and intentions. How could Québec demand for itself a total territorial and political autonomy while refusing the same advantage to Indigenous Nations? If Canada is divisible in the eyes of Québec sovereignists, why is Québec not?[27] In debates on this question, some even went so far as to declare a moral superiority to Indigenous peoples' claims over the nationalist aspirations of the Québec people.[28]

For their part, Indigenous peoples are not necessarily happy with the federal government, either, for reasons largely based on their historically unequal relationship but also because for several decades, the federal government has tended gradually to off-load some of its responsibilities towards Indigenous peoples, especially its financial ones, onto provincial administrations, in order to reduce the federal deficit and the public debt.[29] The problem is, Indigenous peoples have long tried to exempt themselves from the application of certain provincial laws that limit the exercise of some of their ancestral rights such as hunting and fishing. Their appeals to the Supreme Court (*Sparrow* case, *Sioui* case, and others) are ample evidence of this fact. The idea, obviously, is for them to assert their right to self-government, but the voluntary decentralization of federal jurisdiction over Indigenous affairs to the provinces upsets them because it restricts their right to choose the level of government with which they want to transact and because it also forces them to work with an administrative framework that does not suit them and that in no way satisfies their desire for self-determination.

In short, regardless of the standpoint, the Canadian political and administrative system does not facilitate the dialogue between the Québec state and Indigenous peoples. The logic behind this system in the context of Québec politics does not help to make Québec's policy towards Indigenous peoples more palatable to them.

To many Indigenous peoples Québec's language policies figure as an additional irritant that only exacerbates their political distance from the Québec state. Language policies that maintain the primacy of the French language in all aspects of public life, sometimes amplify the tensions that oppose Indigenous peoples to the Québec state. Generally speaking, close to two-thirds of the Indigenous population masters the English language and prefers it over French.[30] The French language's official dominance can represent for many Indigenous peoples in Québec a source of aggravation that adds to their grievances and leads them to be wary of the Québec government. Québec's insistence on building a national political community based on the French language is perceived as the utmost ethnocentric manifestation of Québec nationalism, which, regardless of its underlying civic discourse, is seen as being focused on the preservation of the French language and culture over all others. Although language policies do not necessarily constitute a major stumbling block for all Indigenous peoples in Québec, they are perceived in many quarters as an obstacle to open dialogue between Indigenous peoples and the Québec state,[31] and can complicate the process of reconciliation the latter would like to see unfold.

The Challenges of Internal Community Dynamics

The Québec state, like most Western liberal states, has a tendency to reify the "Other," as if the people who are different from the majority are all the same and can be treated in the same manner. This process of reification is a product of the essentialization of difference. When it comes to Indigenous peoples in Canada, this essentialization stems from the legal, administrative, and regulatory framework of the Indian Act. The reserve system and band councils, as well as the administrative differentiation between "status Indians" (recognized by the Indian Register as people who have the right to live on a reserve and to benefit from services and advantages dispensed by the state) and "non-status Indians" (not recognized by the state as "real" Indigenous people, generally due to marriages with non-Indigenous individuals and therefore prohibited from living on a reserve and deprived of related advantages), are creations of the Canadian state; it defines Indigenous peoples as wards of the state.[32]

The mechanisms of governance that prevail in Indigenous reserves have been imposed by the Canadian state, in keeping with the principles of elected democracy, but to the detriment of local political systems and cultures that existed well before the forced westernization of Indigenous peoples. Traditional systems that are still alive and well continue to influence the management of social relationships in many Indigenous communities. It is not unusual for judicial and institutional frameworks and systems of governance steeped in ancestral practices to coexist within the same community,[33] or for these systems to be opposed to the political and administrative parameters set by the state. More often than not, traditionalists do not recognize the authority or even the legitimacy of the band council who speaks for them. In addition, the rivalries that are inherent to all human societies, between families, clans, individuals, or parties can, and will, in some cases, effectively paralyze the band council's actions and invalidate its representativeness. Whether it is justified or not, the delegitimizing of band councils poses a problem for the state (both at the federal and provincial levels) because the band council is the state's partner of choice, the principal outlet by which it can intervene within the communities. Usually, the state only transacts with Indigenous peoples who adhere to the rules and institutions that it has established.

It would be wrong to believe that because the state has elaborated a policy meant to be reformist or has signed agreements negotiated with the "official" Indigenous leadership, that outstanding disagreements that opposed Indigenous communities to the state are now settled. The attitude of the Eeyou chiefs who succeeded the signatories of the James Bay and Northern Québec Agreement is a perfect testimony to this fact. During the last two decades, Eeyou leaders have never stopped to question this accord, challenging its content, taking the Québec state to task, and blaming their predecessors for agreeing to the terms of the Agreement.[34] Even today, the latest agreement signed between the Grand Council of the Crees (Eeyou Istchee) and the Québec government in February 2002, which should theoretically put an end to the conflicts and disputes that have long opposed the two parties, is already the object of criticism on the part of some Eeyou leaders.[35]

This kind of internal process is not unique to the Eeyou. In the Mi'kmaq community of Listuguj confrontations took place in the summer of 1998 around the issue of sawmill rights. The band council, recognized by the Québec state, was then at odds with rival groups composed of traditionalists, who opposed the turn that negotiations were taking and deplored the government's will to deal only with the band council. Personal animosities, differing ideological positions, and particular, irreconcilable interests prevented the band council from imposing itself as the only voice of Listuguj, which greatly irked the government.[36] The Oka crisis is another, even more famous example of a situation where groups who operate outside the parameters of officially accredited local authorities managed to take control of the process of political mobilization and to impose themselves as negotiators, thus gaining the upper hand, in terms of internal legitimacy, over the band councils of all three Kanien'kehaka communities involved in the conflict. In fact, for the Kanien'kehaka, the Longhouse, as well as the normative framework and the traditional concepts of government associated with it, have long functioned as the parallel site of power and pole of social management, which, in reality, can sometimes marginalize the impact of the band council's interventions and reduce the scope of its authority.[37]

The fight led over the last several years by Indigenous women for the recognition of their human rights and their equal integration in Indigenous society has created quite a stir in some communities and constitutes another example of internal community turbulence. C-31, a 1985 amendment to the Indian Act, is a key issue for Indigenous women's organizations that have campaigned for years to right the wrongs generated by some of the perverse effects of the Indian Act. Enacted in the hope of satisfying the right to equity provided by section 15 of the 1982 Constitution, Bill C-31 was meant to correct the discriminatory dispositions (based on gender) of the Indian Act. Before 1985, the Indian Act granted Indian status to all male individuals with Indigenous blood who belonged to a particular band, to their children, and to any woman they legally married. However, this same status was denied to the Indigenous woman who married a non-Indigenous man or a non-status Indian and to her children. Bill C-31 restored status and the right to belong to a band to the people who had previously been denied or stripped of this privilege. Generally speaking, these were Indigenous women married to non-Indigenous men or non-status Indians and their offspring.[38] C-31 also gave bands the right to decide who they wished to add to their membership list or to implement rules governing band membership. This is the area where this new legislation hurt most since the return to the reserve of people who have reacquired their status put additional pressure on housing and other resources that were already insufficient in many communities. In reaction to the situation, some band councils imposed criteria which were difficult, even impossible, to fulfill for reintegration to the community (racial purity based on blood quantum, authorization to return given to the woman but not to her non-Indigenous husband or her children). This situation often gives rise to political tugs-of-war between Indigenous women and the Indigenous leadership at the local and even national level.[39] Although they do not question the right to self-government for Indigenous peoples, Indigenous women are increasingly reluctant to endorse the nationalist and autonomist agenda of the male-dominated Indigenous leadership as long as they will not have sufficient guarantee of their social, economic, and political integration within their own communities in accordance with the fundamental principles of social justice and respect for human rights.[40] In this sense, the particular claims of Indigenous women play a part in destabilizing the legitimacy of the political goals of recognized Indigenous leaders. To some within their communities, Indigenous women have become an important source of opposition and animosity, perhaps even more fundamental than others because they question traditional hierarchies, power struggles between men and women, prevailing mechanisms of governance, and even the nationalist aspirations of some Indigenous peoples. In so doing, they challenge the very foundations of the approaches favoured by Indigenous leaders in their dealings with the state.

Beyond internal community dynamics, the state must also contend with a polymorphous social and cultural reality that affects the Indigenous peoples of Québec. In some cases, the state cannot begin to appreciate the importance or the significance of particular situations and issues that tend to curtail, in the eyes of some, the legitimacy of policies that the state would like to implement across the board. For example, the very diversity of the Indigenous peoples who reside on the Québec territory implies the existence of a variety of many socio-economic issues, experienced or tackled in different ways, multiple and possibly contradictory political objectives and aspirations, and different ways of relating to non-Indigenous populations. The Assembly of First Nations of Québec and Labrador, like its counterparts in Ottawa (the Assembly of First Nations) and in the other provinces, only represents Indigenous people who live on reserve and who abide by the Indian Act. This represents only about one-quarter of the Indigenous population. Indigenous people living off reserve and non-status Indians who are not recognized by the Indian Register are not entitled to the same benefits and to the same government resources available to status Indians. Their issues are different and their needs are expressed in different ways. The official Indigenous organizations, with which the state prefers to interact, are not necessarily sensitive to the interests of these people.

In the absence of formal communication and resource distribution channels between the state and non-status or off-reserve people, the latter often feel neglected by the state. Not without reason: since they have practically no direct control over natural resources coveted by the state — a consequence of their geographical distance from the said resources and the unofficial character of their status — governments do not seem to feel the same obligations or show the same attentiveness towards them as they do towards Indigenous people who live on reserves. Furthermore, because their dispersal over the Québec territory the state does not feel any particular urgency to offer adapted and specific services and structures such as the ones implemented on reserves, where the concentration of the targeted population makes things easier. Also, non-status Indians and Indigenous people who live off reserve do not necessarily share the perception of their officially recognized peers on a host of Indigenous issues. The questions that are pressing for the former may be different from the ones confronting people who live on reserves and so, then, are their strategies for relating to the state.[41] Insofar as the state's general actions and policies regarding Indigenous peoples are articulated more on the basis of the needs of Indigenous people who live on reserve and enjoy official recognition, their repercussions on non-status and off-reserve people is weak. In this sense, the policies undertaken by the Québec state concerning Indigenous peoples reach only a part of the population they are targeting.

There is no real analysis of the internal political divisions in Québec's Indigenous communities. It is still difficult to grasp their nature and their extent. It is also difficult to assess adequately how they affect relationships between the Québec state and Indigenous peoples. One can safely surmise, however, that power struggles within Indigenous communities are not without consequence. Contrary to what bureaucratic and political personnel like to believe, the accords and agreements signed by the government with "accredited" Indigenous leaders do not necessarily reflect a consensus within the communities they represent. It should not be surprising then that policies and measures publicly announced by the government as proof of its goodwill and magnanimity towards Indigenous peoples do not always meet with the expected approval and are opposed instead.

Indigenous Issues and the Liberal Democratic Normative Framework

Even if the national question or identity politics did not factor in the relationship between Indigenous peoples and Québec, and even if all Indigenous communities and stakeholders were of one mind on every issue of mutual concern, the Indigenous question would not necessarily be less complex or easier to "manage." A liberal society such as Québec is undergirded by an ideological and political framework that, despite its apparent theoretical recognition of difference and respect for individual sovereignties, asserts as universal the normative values that inform it: in other words, liberal societies tend to homogenize. They pretend to protect minority rights and celebrate difference but only as long as these rights and manifestations of difference conform to the will of the majority and fall within the scope of the dominant political and judicial framework. The problem is, in an era when identity claims largely shape the political dynamics of multicultural societies, such as Québec, the dominant ethos hardly accepts that the demands of minorities be subsumed in a great universal and homogeneous whole. On the contrary, the apparent national consensus and traditions on which the liberal political community is based are deconstructed and exposed as the result of historic power struggles that operate to the disadvantage of minority groups.[42] The will to recognize identity claims is not necessarily incompatible with the eventual creation of parallel jurisdictional spaces, even separated from the central political unit. However, it blatantly contradicts the deeply set founding myth of liberal democratic societies that all, without distinction, must be rigorously considered and treated as equals. This points to a fundamental and yet unresolved social and political tension anchored at the very heart of modern societies.

Within the context of Indigenous politics in Québec, this tension manifests itself in at least two ways: through the direct relationships between non-Indigenous populations and Indigenous peoples and the understanding each has of the "privileges" supposedly enjoyed by the latter; and through more subtle and, in some ways, less transparent practices of the state in matters of concern to Indigenous peoples.

At Oka and more recently at Listuguj, the impatience and frustration of non-Indigenous populations regarding Indigenous claims and political actions were clear. As attempts at stoning Indigenous motorists leaving the Kahnawake reserve and torrents of racist abuse and incendiary denunciations on public radio hot lines bear witness, any existing capital of sympathy towards Indigenous causes can quickly dissolve as soon as Indigenous claims or actions make the non-Indigenous population uncomfortable, or are perceived to alter the balance of power between the two groups, or are thought to result in advantages that are not equally extended to members of the non-Indigenous population. As soon as Indigenous groups or communities seek to put into practice the rights that theoretically are guaranteed to them, or as soon as they are granted advantages that are not to benefit also the rest of the Canadian population, it is not unusual for its non-Indigenous citizens to mobilize and contest their legitimacy. One only has to think of the protest movement (and of the referendum) against the treaty that grants self-government to the Nisga'a of British Columbia on an important part of the province's territory, or of the steps undertaken by non-Indigenous fishermen in order to stop Esgenôôpetitj's Mi'kmaq from trapping lobster out of season in New Brunswick, or even the several different parapolitical associations or lobby groups across Canada who do their utmost to criticize what they perceive as Indigenous gains or unacceptable breach of the formal egalitarianism that should, in their opinion, preside over socio-economic relationships.[43] Similarly, there are intellectuals and other commentators who never hesitate to chastize publicly any government policy or measure that results in a differential treatment or that seems to be to the advantage of Indigenous peoples.[44]

In this clatter of non-Indigenous opposition to Indigenous claims, Quebecers may not be the most vocal, but they are not exactly silent. In Québec, there are also more or less organized groups who take exception to Indigenous claims and who publicly question their validity.[45] In fact, in Québec as everywhere else, most people who endorse the characteristic principles of formal liberal egalitarianism do not understand or readily accept the political legitimacy of other cultures or identities, or that the creation of differentiated spaces of citizenship for Indigenous peoples may be warranted. They do not tolerate the fact that the state is seemingly giving in to particular Indigenous claims, especially when it comes to land claims or the recognition of special rights and status. Given the intrinsically idiosyncratic nature of Indigenous demands (idiosyncratic, that is, within the context of a homogenizing liberal society), as long as this state of mind persists, the reconciliation between Indigenous peoples and non-Indigenous populations hoped for by some stakeholders is not likely to occur.

In fairness, the Québec state does not necessarily share the simplistic egalitarian vision that can emanate from popular perceptions. The recognition of Indigenous peoples as distinct nations, direct economic development aid for Indigenous communities, the implementation of certain exceptional fiscal measures, the bestowing of relative self-government (particularly in matters of public security, community health, and education) are policies that bear witness to the manifest will of the state to give Indigenous peoples in Québec the benefit of what is closely approaching special status. This being said, it does not mean that the Québec state is prepared to endorse fully the particularistic, identity-based logic that drives Indigenous claims for self-determination. Despite the apparent openness of its official positions, the Québec state welcomes these claims with a relative benevolence only so far as it can integrate them into the political, administrative, and institutional schemes it determines and controls.

Several studies have shown, as in the case of the James Bay and Northern Québec Agreement, that co-management of renewable natural resources between the state and concerned Indigenous populations often escalates into power struggles between the two parties. In the end, the state imposes its own management practices or standards and reduces the administrative and decision-making latitude guaranteed to Indigenous peoples by the Agreement.[46] In fact, a closer look at the Québec state's practices with respect to the Indigenous peoples of Québec brings out numerous examples of attempts, some more successful than others, to enclose Québec's Indigenous peoples within a frame of reference that hardly agrees with their core values or aspirations. For example, in 1996 the Québec state denied before

Supreme Court (*R. versus Côté*) that the Indigenous peoples of Québec had ever had any particular rights. Québec was trying to exempt itself from the application of Article 35 of the 1982 Constitution Act and, consequently, from its obligations to recognize the ancestral rights of Indigenous peoples. As well, the Parti Québécois' political platform includes Indigenous peoples under the heading of "historical minorities," lumping them together with the anglophone community and implying thus that Indigenous peoples are citizens of Québec and that they are just another constituency of the Québec people, implicitly denying at the same time their right to self-government and to a distinct identity outside of the institutional parameters of the Québec state. As stated above, the 1998 policy regarding Indigenous peoples is a clear indication of this situation as it imposes fundamental markers, presented as inescapable, outside of which the Québec state refuses to deal with Indigenous peoples: Québec's territorial integrity, the sovereignty of the National Assembly and the legislative and regulatory pre-eminence of the Québec state.[47]

In short, although the Québec state has demonstrated clearly enough a desire for open-mindedness and a will to improve the objective situation of the Indigenous peoples of Québec, there is no question that it wants to remain master of its own ship. (The latest important agreements signed with the Eeyouch and the Inuit are to the advantage of the government and finally give the green light to development projects it had hoped to achieve for quite some time.) The state may seem, at first glance, more enlightened in the wording of its public policies than certain popular sentiments towards Indigenous peoples would allow, but it also remains steeped in its typical liberal and homogenizing vision. Some Indigenous Nations could decide to make do with this. Others, like the Kanien'kehaka, the Eeyouch, and even the Innu, are lead by nationalist and affirmationist aspirations that likely never will be satisfied with the role of administrative appendix to which the state tends to confine them. Between the state's logic of univocal inclusion and the Indigenous logic of self-government, there is a considerable chasm that goodwill alone may not be able to bridge.

Conclusion

From Oka to the "Paix des Braves" and "Approche Commune," the Québec state may seem to some to have come a long way in a relatively short time, a sign, one could argue, of a rapid evolution of mentalities. The February 2002 agreement with the Eeyou of James Bay and the agreement, of the same nature, signed two months later with the Inuit seem at first to herald the dawn of a new era of equal relationships and partnerships between the Québec state and the Indigenous peoples of Québec. One can only hope that this is indeed the case. The preceding analysis suggests, however, a more prudent and less optimistic interpretation of reality. The latest successes of Québec diplomacy with respect to Indigenous issues can hardly conceal that there are a persistent number of grey zones, unresolved conflicts, latent and still unnamed problems, even practically indelible enmities that separate and estrange each party from the other, and could very well force everyone involved constantly back to the drawing board. As sociologist Jean-Jacques Simard noted, since Oka, "we are starting to realize that the Aboriginal question is part and parcel of the *ontological*, historical fiber of Canadian and Québec society, that it cannot be easily 'resolved,' that is, eliminated, but that it will always remain embedded in the constitutional dynamics of our country, subject to a permanent, contradictory and pluralist debate, and calling for practical makeshift repairs and institutional adjustments that will constantly need to be reassessed."[48]

There are several other factors that remain hard to fathom. In addition to those treated in this essay, we must remember that the rapid and essentially exogenous changes of the last few decades have disrupted traditional practices and seriously destabilized the customary dynamics behind the social relationships in many Indigenous communities. In many localities, widespread idleness, moral leadership crises, almost non-existent job opportunities, and excessively abnormal rates of suicide are the perverse effects of an uncontrolled access to a modernity that was not necessarily desired and that, in the majority of cases, was imposed from the outside.[49] The result is that collective claims are becoming more urgent, especially among youth who have everything to lose from the social hurdles faced by their communities. We should not be surprised if this segment of the Indigenous population becomes more radical with time; they were responsible, in part, for the opposition to the latest agreement between the Québec state and the Grand Council of the Cree.

By opening the door to the institutional and political recognition of Indigenous peoples, even with all the usual dampers, the Québec state has, in a way, offered them the tools to take over their own affairs. It set off for Indigenous peoples a greater desire for autonomy, the will to assume fully, without being dependent, their own development and reinforced, somewhat paradoxically, the ever deeply rooted conviction that they do not belong to Québec society. Theirs is a familiar reaction that distinguishes historically almost all human groups who have tried to free themselves from oppressive situations. If the Québec state and the whole of Québec society are not ready to accompany Indigenous peoples on this path of collective emancipation, with full knowledge of the facts and according to the latter's own terms, Indigenous resistance is not likely to fade away, and the efforts at reconciliation of the last few years may well fall flat in the end.

Notes

1. Louis-Edmond Hamelin, *Passer près d'une perdrix sans la voir ou attitudes à l'égard des autochtones*, Grande conférence Desjardins, Montréal, Programme d'études sur le Québec, McGill University, 1999, 5. Trans. Salée.

2. For the past 10 years or so the Québec government has been regularly signing administrative and sectoral agreements with most Indigenous reserves within its jurisdiction. Varying according to the communities, these agreements are generally aimed at developing the local economy (financing of enterprises or of recreational, cultural, social, or public health infrastructures), or at increasing the degree of autonomy of communities in the management of governmental programs and administrative structures. Since 1998, the government has created a Development Fund for Natives and has stepped up the signing of agreements of mutual respect. Those may be framework agreements or more specific agreements dealing with particular issues. For more details see the government web site: <http://www.mce.gouv.qc.ca/d/html/d0466001.html>.

3. According to a statistical study of the Department of Indian and Northern Affairs in which the human development index (HDI) developed by the United Nations has been applied to the situation of Indigenous peoples in Canada, Québec's HDI is among the least disastrous of all the Canadian provinces (Ontario and British Columbia are ahead). Life expectancy for Indigenous peoples is the highest in Québec (74.9 years, compared to 70.7 for all of the Indigenous peoples in Canada). The per capita income of Indigenous peoples is among the highest in Québec ($10,231 compared to $10,541 in Ontario and only $8,205 for Indigenous peoples in all of Canada). This does not mean that the situation of Indigenous peoples in Québec is good. While Canada's HDI ranks it among the best and most attractive countries in the world, Indigenous peoples in Canada rank, comparatively, among the least fortunate and least advantaged nations in the world. Indigenous peoples in Québec do not fare any better overall. However, in all the Canadian provinces, the gap between Indigenous peoples and non-Indigenous populations is the smallest in Québec. See Daniel Beavon and Martin Cooke, *Measuring the Well-Being of First Nation Peoples* (Ottawa: Department of Indian and Northern Affairs, 1998). See also Bradford Morse, "Comparative Assessment of the Position of Indigenous peoples in Québec, Canada and Abroad," a study prepared for the Commission d'étude des questions afférentes à l'accession du Québec à la souveraineté, rev. edn., (Québec: Ministère du Conseil exécutif, 2001).

4. The names usually adopted to identify Indigenous nations more often than not are derived from European appellations used after contact. In many cases those names do not correspond to the way by which the members of those nations designate themselves in their own language. In order to counteract the result of this social and cultural obliteration more and more Indigenous peoples identify themselves with the terms that are their own. In this chapter, whenever it is possible and suitable, the "self-designation" term is used rather than the colonialist appellation. It applies more specifically to three nations: Mohawks (Kanien'kehaka), Cree (Eeyou), and Montagnais (Innu).

5. This section draws from diverse sources: Pierre-Gerlier Forest, "Les relations politiques entre le Québec et les peuples autochtones depuis la Révolution tranquille," *Zeitschrift für Kanada-Studien*, 16, 29 (1996): 80-96; Eric Gourdeau, "Le Québec et la question autochtone," in A.-G. Gagnon, ed., *Québec: État et société* (Montréal: Québec-Amérique, 1994), 329-55; Eric Gourdeau, "Autochtones: un tour de force," *Le Devoir*, 14 July 2001; Sylvie Vincent, "La révélation d'une force politique: les Autochtones," in *Le*

Québec en jeu, Gérard Daigle, ed., with Guy Rocher (Montréal: Presses de l'Université de Montréal, 1992), 749-90; Sylvie Vincent, *Les relations entre le Québec et les Autochtones: brève analyse d'un récit gouvernemental* (Montréal: Programme d'études sur le Québec, McGill University, 1995).

6. Eric Gourdeau, "Autochtones: un tour de force," *Le Devoir*, 14 July 2001.

7. These nations are the Abenakis, the Algonquins, the Attikamekw, the Eeyouch (Cree), the Wendat (Hurons), the Mi'kmaq, the Kannien'kehaka (Mohawk), the Innus (Montagnais), the Naskapis, and the Inuit. The Maleseet were added to this list by the 30 May 1989 resolution of the National Assembly.

8. For a detailed history of events at Oka see Geoffrey York and Loreen Pindera, *People of the Pines: The Warriors and the Legacy of Oka* (Boston: Little Brown, 1991).

9. During the 1990s several cases bearing on the ancestral right to practice traditional and subsistence activities or on ownership rights of Indigenous peoples were brought before the Supreme Court of Canada. Among the most significant rulings are *Sioui* (1990), *Sparrow* (1990), *Van der Peet* (1996), *Côté* (1996), *Delgamuukw* (1997), and *Marshall* (1999). Together these rulings constitute a jurisprudence that establishes the predominance of Indigenous rights on a number of policies and legislation of Canada's various governmental jurisdictions. Concretely, this means that no government can force Indigenous peoples to surrender ancestral rights or terminate a treaty concluded several hundred years ago without the explicit consent of concerned Indigenous communities. Similarly, governments cannot undertake any development project or territorial modification without prior consultation with the Indigenous populations affected by it.

10. Major recommendations include the following: "legislation, including a new Royal Proclamation stating Canada's commitment to a new relationship and companion legislation setting out a treaty process and recognition of Aboriginal nations and governments; recognition of an Aboriginal order of government, subject to the *Charter of Rights and Freedoms*, with authority over matters related to the good government and welfare of Aboriginal peoples and their territories; replacement of the federal Department of Indian Affairs with two departments, one to implement the new relationship with Aboriginal nations and one to provide services for non-self-governing communities; creation of an Aboriginal parliament; expansion of the Aboriginal land and resource base; recognition of Métis self-government, provision of a land base, and recognition of Métis's rights to hunt and fish on Crown land; initiatives to address social, education, health, and housing needs, including the training of 10,000 health professionals over a 10-year period, the establishment of an Aboriginal peoples' university, and recognition of Aboriginal nations' authority over child welfare." See Mary C. Hurley and Jill Wherrett, *The Report of the Royal Commission on Aboriginal Peoples* (Ottawa: Library of Parliament, Parliamentary Research Branch, document PRB 99-24E, 1999), 2-3.

11. M.C. Hurley and J. Wherrett, *The Report of the Royal Commission on Aboriginal Peoples*, 3-4.

12. *Notes pour une allocution du ministre des Transports, ministre délégué aux Affaires autochtones et ministre responsable de la Faune et des Parcs, monsieur Guy Chevrette à l'occasion d'une mission en Europe portant sur les affaires autochtones, du 30 janvier au 10 février 2001.* Author's translation. Web site of the Secrétariat aux affaires autochtones du Québec, http://www.mce.gouv.qc.ca/d/html/d1162001.html. Consulted 30 March 2002.

13. *Notes pour une allocution du premier ministre du Québec, monsieur Bernard Landry à l'occasion de la signature de l'entente finale entre le gouvernement du Québec et le Grand*

Conseil des Cris du Québec, site web du Secrétariat aux affaires autochtones du Québec, http://www.mce.gouv.qc.ca/d/html/d2057013.html. Consulted 30 Mar. 2002.

14. According to the government's own data, the average Indigenous household income is 20 per cent lower than the average non-Indigenous household income, this, in spite of the fact that Indigenous households generally comprise twice as many persons as the average non-Indigenous household. Income derived from gainful employment accounts for 42 per cent of the average Indigenous household, while 77 per cent of the income of average non-Indigenous households derives from gainful employment. More than 40 per cent of Indigenous peoples living in Québec have no more than a grade 9 education, while 20 per cent of the non-Indigenous population finds itself in that situation. (Secrétariat aux affaires autochtones, *Partenariat, développement, actions*, [Québec: Secrétariat aux affaires autochtones, 1998] 9). Data from Statistics Canada indicate that the unemployment rate is often higher than 50 per cent in many Indigenous communities; in Québec, the unemployment rate for Indigenous peoples as a whole is more than 30 per cent. The rate of participation in the labour market is often lower than 50 per cent (it is at 62 per cent for Canada). Since 1980, the number of Indigenous recipients of welfare benefits has doubled. Sixty-five per cent of Québec's Indigenous peoples who are 15 years old and older have not completed their high school education (compared to 35 per cent in the non-Indigenous population). The personal income of Indigenous peoples in Québec is one-third lower than that of the general population. (Carole Lévesque and Nadine Trudeau, "Femmes autochtones et développement économique ou la rencontre des modernités," in *La tension tradition-modernité*, Andrea Martinez and Michèle Ollivier, eds., (Ottawa: Presses de l'Université d'Ottawa, 2001), 15.

15. The numerous complaints of the Eeyouch about the state management of the James Bay and Northern Québec Agreement bear witness to this dissatisfaction. For a full discussion of the stakes, difficulties, and conflicts involved in this question see Colin H. Scott, ed., *Aboriginal Autonomy and Development in Northern Québec and Labrador* (Vancouver: UBC Press, 2001). See also Marie-Anik Gagné, *A Nation Within a Nation. Dependency and the Cree* (Montréal: Black Rose Books, 1994) and Jean-Jacques Simard, "Développement et gouvernements autochtones: l'expérience de la Baie James," *Politique et sociétés*, 28 (1995): 71-86.

16. See Parti Québécois, *Le Québec dans un monde nouveau* (Montréal: VLB Éditeur, 1993); Parti Québécois, *La volonté de réussir* (Montréal: Parti Québécois, 1997), section B. See also Claude Bariteau, *Québec 18 septembre 2001* (Montréal: Québec-Amérique, 1998); Gérard Bouchard, *La nation québécoise au futur et au passé* (Montréal: VLB éditeur, 1999); Anne Légaré, "La souveraineté: nation ou raison," in *Québec: État et société*, Alain-G. Gagnon, ed., (Montréal: Québec-Amérique, 1994), 41-60; Michel Sarra-Bournet, ed., *Le pays de tous les Québécois* (Montréal: VLB éditeur. 1998); Michel Seymour, *La nation en question* (Montréal: L'Hexagone, 1999).

17. Louis Balthazar, "Les nombreux visages du nationalisme au Québec," in Alain-G. Gagnon ed., *Québec: État et société* (Montréal: Québec-Amérique, 1994), 23-40.

18. See Diane Francis, *Fighting for Canada* (Ottawa: Key Porter Books, 1996); William Johnson, *A Canadian Myth. Québec, Between Canada and the Illusion of Utopia* (Montréal: Robert Davies Publishing, 1994); Mordecai Richler, *Oh Canada! Oh Québec! Requiem for a Divided Country* (Toronto: Penguin, 1992).

19. See, for example, the speeches of Matthew Coon-Come, Grand Chief of Québec Cree delivered at the Harvard Center for International Affairs and at the Kennedy School of Government, 28 October 1996, and of Ted Moses, ambassador of the Grand Council of the

Québec Cree delivered at the United Nations, 20 April 1998, also at Harvard. The official position of Eeyouch is detailed in *Sovereign Injustice. Forcible Inclusion of the James Bay Cree and Cree Territory into a Sovereign Québec* (Nemaska: Grand Council of the Cree, 1995). In the summer of 1997, Innu representatives of Mamit Innuat went to Vancouver and Geneva to speak before the Working Group on Indigenous peoples of the United Nations' Human Rights Commission to denounce the neo-colonialist attitude of the Québec government in the negotiation process over land claims. Their position echoes that of the Eeyouch. See the Web site <http://www.innu.ca/innuat43.htm>. Consulted 25 Mar. 2002.

20. *Bill 99: A Sovereign Act of Dispossession, Dishonour and Disgrace. Brief of the Grand Council of the Crees (Eeyou Istchee) to the Québec National Assembly Committee on Institutions* available at <http://www.gcc.ca/Political-Issues/bill_99.htm>. Consulted 16 Mar. 2002.

21. Taiaiake Alfred, "Sur le rétablissement du respect entre les peuples kanien'kehaka et québécois," *Arguments*, 2, 2 (2000): 31-43.

22. Gerald R. Alfred, "Aboriginal Peoples and the Future of Québec," *Choice*, 1, 10 (1995): 1-18.

23. Martin Papillon, "Mouvements de protestation et représentation identitaire: l'émergence politique de la nation crie entre 1971 et 1995," *International Journal of Canadian Studies*, 20 (1999): 101-22.

24. See the annual report of the director of the Grand Council of the Cree, Bill Namagoose, August 1998, available at Web site <http://www.gcc.ca/Overview/entities/gccei/annual_report_1998.htm>. Consulted 16 Mar. 2002. See also Campbell Clark, "Kahnawake Dispute is a Turf War," *The Gazette*, 20 June 1998, A-1, A-15.

25. T. Alfred, "Sur le rétablissement du respect entre les peuples kanien'kehaka et québécois"; G.R. Alfred, "Les peuples autochtones et l'avenir du Québec," 7; Audra Simpson, "Paths Toward a Mohawk Nation: Narratives of Nationhood and Citizenship in Kahnawake," in *Political Theory and the Rights of Indigenous peoples*, Duncan Ivison, Paul Patton, and Will Sanders, eds., (Cambridge: Cambridge University Press, 2000), 113-36.

26. Through local referenda, particularly in Eeyou and Innu communities, people voted massively, often in excess of 95 per cent, to support the idea of "seceding" from Québec should the sovereignists win their own referendum on Québec sovereignty.

27. Jill Wherrett, *Aboriginal Peoples and the 1995 Québec Referendum: A Survey of the Issues*, BP-412E, (Ottawa: Library of Parliament, Parliamentary Research Branch, 1996) 8. See also "Irwin Guarantees Protection for Aboriginals," *Ottawa Citizen*, 28 Oct. 1995; "Québec Divisible, Chrétien says," *Globe and Mail*, 30 Jan. 1996; "Native Land, not Québec's, Irwin says," *Globe and Mail*, 14 Feb. 1996.

28. Reg Whitaker, "Québec's Self-Determination and Aboriginal Self-Government: Conflict and Reconciliation," in *Is Québec Nationalism Just?* Joseph Carens ed. (Montréal: McGill-Queen's University Press, 1995), 193-220.

29. Daniel Salée, "Autodétermination autochtone, souveraineté du Québec et fédéralisme canadien," in François Rocher, ed., *Bilan québécois du fédéralisme canadien* (Montréal: VLB Éditeur, 1992), especially 392-98; Radha Jhappan, "The Federal-Provincial Power-Grid and Aboriginal Self-Government," in *New Trends in Canadian Federalism*, François Rocher and Miriam Smith, eds., (Peterborough: Broadview Press, 1995), 155-84.

30. This is an approximation based on data on the demographic and linguistic situation of each Indigenous Nation. Except for the Huron-Wendat, the Maleseet, and the Abenaki (whose use of the ancestral language has disappeared and for whom French is now basically their mother tongue), the Innu and the Attikamekw (who have preserved their original

language, but readily adopt French as their main language of communication with non-Indigenous people), English is the language most commonly used by large numbers of Indigenous peoples in Québec. Such is the case in particular among Kanien'kehaka and Eeyouch, the largest and most politically active Indigenous populations of Québec, and among Inuit and Naskapi. The Kanien'kehaka have revived their ancestral language, largely spoken by the younger generation, but English remains the mother tongue and the language of socialization of the greatest number. The Eeyou and Inuit have fully preserved their ancestral language. In their communities English is used as a second language much more readily than French, which is almost nonexistent. Among the other Indigenous nations the use of French and English varies according to the communities and the individuals.

31. T. Alfred, "Sur le rétablissement du respect entre les peuples kanien'kehaka et québécois."

32. For a concise and clear description of the administrative and political framework within which Canada's Indigenous peoples have to operate, see Renée Dupuis, *La question indienne au Canada* (Montréal: Boréal, 1991), 42-58.

33. Andrée Lajoie, Henry Quillinan, Rod MacDonald, and Guy Rocher, "Pluralisme juridique à Kahnawake," *Les Cahiers de Droit* 39 (1998): 681-716.

34. See among others Ted Moses's intervention in Sylvie Vincent and Garry Bowers, eds., *Baie James et Nord québécois: dix ans après* (Montréal: Recherches amérindiennes au Québec, 1988). See also the proceedings of the conference on *Regard sur la Convention de la Baie-James et du Nord québécois* Montréal, 25-26 Oct. 2001. This conference was jointly organized by Makivik Corporation, the Grand Council of the Cree (Eeyou Astchee), the Québec and Canadian governments, Hydro-Québec, and McGill University's Programme d'études sur le Québec. Ted Moses had called for a boycott of this conference a few weeks before its opening because, in his view, the negotiations with the Québec government were not progressing fast enough. He changed his mind on 23 Oct. 2001 after the signing of the Accord in Principle which led to the 7 Feb. 2002 agreement between the Eeyouch and the Québec government.

35. It is not unlikely that before long this Agreement, which received significant support by the Eeyou population through referenda held in all the communities, might be called in question by the leaders of the next generations. Ashley Iserhoff, President of the James Bay Cree Youth Council, has openly denounced the Agreement, doubting the intentions of the government and Eeyou negotiators and arguing that the Agreement puts the physical and cultural health of Eeyou communities at risk. At least two other Chiefs, Vice Grand Chief Matthew Mukash and Nemaska's Vice Chief Josie Nimiken, have publicly echoed Iserhoff's sentiments. See the special dossier prepared by *Nation*, an Eeyou bi-weekly, on the web at <http://www.ottertooth.com/Reports/Rupert/News/nation.htm>. Consulted on 16 Mar. 2002.

36. Guy Chevrette, Minister responsible for Aboriginal affairs, declared: "We will only deal with the legally elected Mi'kmaq authorities. A society cannot negotiate on barricades." Trans. Salée. See André Pépin, "Blocus micmac: la population commence à s'impatienter," *La Presse*, 8 Aug. 1998, A1.

37. On this issue, see A. Lajoie et al. "Pluralisme juridique à Kahnawake?". See also Robert Vachon, "La nation mohawk et ses communautés," ch. 1 (Quelques données sociologiques majeures), *Interculture* 24, 4 (Fall 1991), booklet 113 and ch. 2 (Cultures politiques: occidentale et mohawk. Une mise en contraste), *Interculture* 25, 1 (Winter 1992), booklet 114.

38. The state imposes some limits on this recognition. For example, it is no longer possible to transfer the status of Indian after two successive generations of union between

Indigenous and non-indigenous or non-status individuals. This restriction applies both to women and to men. This means that it is no longer possible for Indigenous men to pass on their status to their spouse and children as the old provisions of the *Indian Act* allowed. The state has simply levelled off the status rights by putting everyone on the same footing, making sure that men would have no more rights than women (rather than extending to women the rights that men had). The perspective of status termination has been pushed back one generation. For more details on this question and the changes brought by C-31, see Jill Wherrett, *Indian Status and Band Membership Issues*, Ottawa, Library of Parliament, Parliamentary Research Branch, BP-410E, 1996; Harry Daniels, *Bill C-31: The Abocide Bill*, Web site of the Congress of Aboriginal Peoples available at <http://www.abo-peoples.org/programs/dnlsc-31.html>. Consulted 16 Mar. 2002.

39. The Association of Québec Indigenous Women (Association Femmes autochtones du Québec) has presented a lengthy list of claims and grievances against Indigenous leadership to the Department of Indian and Northern Affairs in a document titled *Changements proposés à la Loi sur les Indiens et à l'administration de la Loi sur les Indiens*, Montréal, Femmes autochtones du Québec, 29 Sept. 2000.

40. Edith Garneau, "Les femmes autochtones partagent-elles le même projet national que les hommes autochtones?" in Maryse Potvin, Bernard Fournier, and Yves Couture, eds., *L'individu et le citoyen dans la société moderne* (Montréal: Presses de l'Université de Montréal, 2000), 145-64; Edith Garneau, *Perspectives de femmes des Premières nations Québec sur les chevauchements identitaires: entre le genre et la nation*, doctoral thesis, Political Science, UQAM, 2002.

41. For a detailed picture of the situation and of the political orientations of non-status Indians or off reserve Indigenous people, see the Web site of the Congress of Aboriginal Peoples, <http://www-abo-peoples.org>, and of the Alliance autochtone du Québec, <http://www.allianceautochtone.com>.

42. Anna Yeatman, *Postmodern Revisionings of the Political* (New York: Routledge, 1994), 90.

43. The Ontario Federation for Individual Rights and Equality (ONF.I.R.E.) is an example of this, created in 1995 in the wake of the Ipperwash events in response to the frustration and dissatisfaction expressed by some over the way in which the Canadian and Ontario governments deal with the territorial claims of Indigenous nations. ONF.I.R.E. argues that Indigenous claims are exaggerated and that the state does not stand up firmly enough to Indigenous leadership. ONF.IR.E. supporters believe that anyone who lives within the boundaries of Canada enjoys equal rights guaranteed by the Canadian Constitution and nobody can benefit from rights that are not equally accessible to all. See the organization's Web site, <http://www.oxford.net/~onfire/Onfire.html>. Consulted 30 Mar. 2002. There are other organizations with similar views, such as the Ontario Federation of Anglers and Hunters who would like the state to terminate the fishing and hunting rights of Indigenous peoples, and the BC Real Estate Association.

44. See Tom Flanagan, *First Nations, Second Thoughts* (Montréal: McGill-Queen's University Press, 2000); Melvin H. Smith, *Our Home or Native Land? What Government's Aboriginal Policy is Doing to Canada* (Victoria: Crown Western, 1995).

45. One such example is the Mouvement estrien pour le français (MEF). This regional, independent organization is dedicated to the defence and promotion of French language and culture in Québec. Its Web site has a substantial section titled "Les Indiens," which contains over 60 short essays on a variety of Indigenous issues and a whole dossier on Oka

and its aftermath. Through these pieces, mostly written in a cynical and arrogant tone, MEF clearly indicates its exasperation at the "privileges" and the claims of Indigenous peoples, which it considers exaggerated and unfounded. MEF argues that all residents of Québec should be treated on the same footing, regardless of their creed, culture, origin, or ethnicity and opposes "racial privileges" based on "ethnic primacy." See MEF's Web site, http://www.mef.qc.ca/indiens.htm. Consulted 6 Apr. 2002.

46. Québec is not unique in this regard. This is a situation that occurs regularly all over Canada in state-Indigenous peoples relations. See Thierry Rodon, *En partenariat avec l'État. Les experiences de cogestion des Autochtones du Canada* (Québec: les Presses de l'Université Laval, 2003) 177-200, for a concise analysis of the co-management experience within the James Bay Agreement. See also Lorrain Brooke, *The James Bay and Northern Québec Agreement: Experiences of the Nunavik Inuit with Wildlife Management*, research report, Royal Commission on Aboriginal Peoples, 1995; Harvey Feit, "James Bay Cree Self-Governance and Land Management," in Edwin Wilmsen, ed., *We are Here: Politics of Aboriginal Land Tenure* (Berkeley: University of California Press, 1989); Ignatius LaRusic, *La négociation d'un mode de vie: la structure administrative découlant de la Convention de la Baie James. L'expérience initiale des Cris* (Ottawa: Department of Indian and Northern Affairs, 1983).

47. Paul Joffe, "Assessing the Delgamuukw Principles: National Implications and Potential Effects in Québec," *McGill Law Journal* 45 (2000): 155-208. See 190-203 in particular.

48. Jean-Jacques Simard, *Le problème autochtone*, updated study originally presented to the Commission d'étude des questions afférentes à l'accession du Québec à la souveraineté (Québec: 2001), 11. Trans. Salée.

49. Jean-Jacques Simard, *Tendances nordiques. Les changements sociaux, 1970-1990 chez les Cis et les Inuit du Québec. Une enquête statistique exploratoire* (Québec: Université Laval, GÉTIC, 1996).

PART II
Governance

6

Québec-Canada's Constitutional Dossier

ALAIN-G. GAGNON

To begin with, Québec is not a province like the others. Adequately accounting for such a political reality necessitates an adapted analytical focus. As such, we employ the notion of the Québec state as a political nation inscribed within a multinational whole and as a historic region in order to highlight Québec's specificity, rather than simply treating Québec as a province, a subordinate government or a political grouping. The latter expressions appear to us as misleading considering the manner in which a large majority of Quebecers perceive and define themselves.[1]

There are many ways to address Québec-Canada dynamics in the area of federal-provincial relations. Some researchers have opted for a legal approach (e.g., Andrée Lajoie, in this volume), while others have chosen to proceed with the study of fiscal federalism (e.g., the Séguin Commission on fiscal imbalance in Canada[2]). The present text will privilege the historical-institutional dimensions of federal-provincial relations with the aim of providing a more encompassing portrait, allowing for a perspective that more effectively accounts for the evolution of power relations between orders of government as well as within the partisan system. We will proceed in three periods: (1) the first period will consider the historical foundations and the establishment of the first constitutional order; (2) the second period is one of transition and covers the years from 1960 to 1982; and (3) the third period extends from 1982, the year of constitutional repatriation without the consent of Québec, to the present time, stressing the rupture with the established constitutional order and the emergence of a new political order.

Historical Foundations and the Emergence
of the First Constitutional Order

The founding events of a political community are viewed rarely with unanimity. Nevertheless, in the case of Québec it is relatively easy to locate the important dates in which various interpretations are formed according to different political stands. We can identify, up to the 1960s, no less than four fundamental moments: (1) the Conquest of 1759-60 followed by the Surrender of 1763; (2) the Québec Act of 1774; (3) the Rebellions of 1837-1838 followed by the Act of Union in 1840 and; (4) the Confederation of 1867. Each of these moments marked the development of Québec's political culture in a notable manner. Indeed, contemporary authors often hark back to them or follow up on them, but rarely are they dismissed.

The great episodes of the Conquest and of the Surrender have frequently been reviewed in analyses centred on Québec-Canada relations. The clashing interpretations advanced respectively by the contentions of those in the *École de Montréal* and the *École de Québec* and, closer to us, in the production of the Radio-Canada televised series titled *Canada: A People's History*, or still further in the exchanges between Gérard Bouchard and John Saul[3] demonstrate the political consequences of targeting one or the other of these two events.

The Québec Act of 1774 constitutes a fundamental moment whose repercussions continue to this day. Some analysts have evoked the desire of Great Britain to prevent an extension to the former French and Catholic possession of its military conflicts with the Americans, who sought to emancipate themselves from their colonizers. Other analysts have advanced more nuanced interpretations, recalling with interest that the passage of the Québec Act would constitute the first imperial statute that recognized a colony's own formal constitution.[4]

In this context, those who identified themselves as *les Canadiens*, and their elites, found themselves with the recognition, on the one hand, of the right to exercise their faith and to use the French language, while on the other, to obtain the re-establishment of the seigneurial regime, the tithe and the use of common law. Indeed, the Québec Act represents an interpretive document whose importance for following generations cannot be ignored.

The relevance of the Québec Act on the legitimacy of Québec's demands within the Canadian federation is in many regards proportional to the significance of the Royal Proclamation of 1763 on the status of Aboriginal nations. At the very least, it probably served to incite the authors of the preliminary report of the Royal Commission on Aboriginal Peoples to establish, in 1995, parallels between the claims of these nations and those of the Québec nation within Canada as a whole.

The events surrounding the rebellions of Lower Canada as well as the Act of Union of 1840 marked the imagination of French Canadians at the time. Moreover, the emergence of republican and liberal ideas in Québec can also be attributed to this period. Nevertheless, the year 1840 does not represent a memorable year for French Canadians as it signified the forced merger of Upper and Lower Canada without the institution of responsible government; it was not until 1848 that this political victory was attained.

It was with the advent of the Union of the two Canadas that French Canadians turned resolutely towards the Church, which provided them with protection and marked the infancy stage of an agreed consociational formula.[5]

In founding the Canadian Confederation in 1867, or what can be designated as the first constitutional order, French and English Canadians agreed on the main tenets of a power-sharing formula. Despite periodic modifications, this constitutional order would continue until repatriation in 1981.

Three interpretations came to the fore during this period: the creation of Canada was interpreted either as an imperial statute, as an agreement between the founding provinces, or as a pact between English Canadians and French Canadians. In Québec, the interpretation that has dominated all debates is centered on dualism, which has given rise to a rich literature concerning constitutional matters. For example, the work of Judge Thomas-Jean-Jacques Loranger, at the start of the 1880s,[6] deserves attention to the extent that it established links to the Québec Act of 1774, and for providing interpretive boundaries with regard to Québec-Canada relations. The main premises of Judge Loranger are summarized in the preliminary report of the Royal Commission on Aboriginal Peoples in 1993:

1. The confederation of the British Provinces was the result of a compact entered into by the provinces and the United Kingdom.

2. The provinces entered into the federal Union with their corporate identity, former constitutions, and all their legislative powers intact. A portion of these powers was ceded to the federal Parliament, to exercise them in common interest of the provinces. The powers not ceded were retained by the provincial legislatures, which continued to act within their own sphere according to their former constitutions, under certain modifications of form established by the federal compact.

3. Far from having been conferred upon them by the federal government, the powers of the provinces are the residue of their former colonial powers. The federal government is the creation of the provinces, the result of their association and of their compact.[7]

Judge Loranger supported his contentions on the basis of continuity in constitutional matters, and reminds us that it is not permissible for political actors to ignore treaties, agreements, and conventions in the elaboration of constitutional reforms. The influence of interpretations advanced by Judge Loranger in the elaboration of Québec's constitutional positions can also be read between the lines in the report of the Royal Commission of Inquiry on Constitutional Problems, the Tremblay Report, which was released by the government of Québec in 1956. The Tremblay report emphasized the notions of provincial autonomy in fiscal and financial domains, coordination between the two orders of government, and the principle of subsidiarity. The report recommended that Québec, as a member-state of the Canadian confederation, is fully responsible for the development of its culture. The Tremblay report allowed for the actualization of the conceptual contentions of Judge Loranger in matters of provincial autonomy, while representing a major source of inspiration for the architects of the Quiet Revolution at a time where a vast program of reforms on the cultural, economic, and social levels were to be elaborated, with the aim of reducing the rift that was developing between Québec and Ontario in particular.

From the Quiet Revolution to Repatriation in 1982: A Period of Transition

The start of the 1960s was marked by an impressive political fervour in Québec: the arrival to power of the Liberals of Jean Lesage, the appearance of several third parties, state interventionism, the affirmation of civil society, the rise of the trade union movement and, to limit ourselves to these examples, the first expressions of the Front de Libération du Québec. Social and political actors sought to redress the structural inequities to which Québec had been subjected over the years and provided Quebecers with a context of choice that permitted their affirmation on cultural, political, social, and economic levels.

At the very beginning of the period, the government of Québec attempted to make alliances with the provincial capitals. Moreover, through the initiatives of Premier Jean Lesage, the provincial Premiers began to meet annually with a view to presenting a common front when confronted with unilateral actions by Ottawa in areas of competence that are exclusive to the provinces.

On the constitutional plane, and in response to Québec's demands, the minority Liberal government of Lester B. Pearson decided in 1963 to set up the Laurendeau-Dunton Commission on bilingualism and biculturalism, which provided real meaning to the principle of equality between the two founding peoples.[8] In this context of great fervour, the government of Québec, in concert with the other member-states of the federation, sought to elaborate propositions with the aim of arriving at negotiated agreements with the federal government. This had the particular effect of increasing the frequency of federal-provincial meetings, expanding the range of questions addressed at such encounters and promoting the creation of ministerial committees charged with studying disputed issues.

Subsequently, and inspired by the autonomist doctrine of Judge Loranger, Paul Gérin-Lajoie proposed the external extension of Québec's internal jurisdictions.[9] Québec invested in the international arena and began to establish relations with international organizations and foreign governments, provoking serious conflicts with Ottawa. The government of Québec recognized that foreign policy was a federal jurisdiction, yet argued for its right to act in this domain in cases that were relevant to its own exclusive fields. This approach was particularly effective from 1964-1966, a period in which Québec concluded several agreements related to education, youth, and cultural affairs (see the contribution of Louis Balthazar in this volume). Québec's initiatives, combined with efforts in concert with other provincial governments, served to increase the pressure for constitutional reform.

At the time, the establishment of an amending formula constituted a major problem that obstructed constitutional reform. During the Liberal tenure of Jean Lesage (1960-1966), two amending formulas were proposed in Québec, and then rejected. In 1961, Lesage refused the formula proposed by the federal Minister of Justice at the time, Davie Fulton, because the federal government refused to limit the powers that it assumed in 1949, powers that permitted the federal government to unilaterally amend the Constitution in fields of exclusive federal competence. Moreover, Ottawa refused to grant Québec a voice with regard to reforms to central institutions such as the monarchy, the Senate, and the Supreme Court.

In January 1966, the Fulton-Favreau formula, which at the outset was received favourably by all provincial Premiers at the federal-provincial conference of October 1964, would undergo a similar fate with Québec withdrawing its support. This formula would have required the approval of the federal government and all other provincial governments for provisions respecting the division of powers, the use of both official languages, denominational rights in education and representation in the House of Commons. Other provisions respecting the monarchy and Senate representation could be amended by Ottawa with the concurrence of two-thirds of the provinces comprising more than 50 per cent of the Canadian population. Upon reflection, an amending formula based on unanimity was opposed in Québec because it could threaten the possibility of obtaining intergovernmental agreements on culturally sensitive issues, such as language policy, and could discourage any transfer of powers from the federal to the provincial order. With the aim of providing the system with a measure of flexibility, Québec also envisaged a clause regarding delegation of powers that would permit member-states of the federation and Ottawa to delegate, respectively, and under precise conditions, given responsibilities. As it stood, the consent of four provinces and the federal Parliament was necessary, which in effect prevented any bilateral agreement between Québec and Ottawa. The principle of dualism had been supplanted.

The central issue for Québec, however, was not the amending formula, but rather the overhaul of the constitution and a new division of powers.[10] Faced with the prospect of a provincial election, Lesage could not consent to proposals that would run against growing nationalist and autonomist sentiments in the province. Lesage refused to consider repatriation or an amending formula unless this was combined with a clear definition of Québec's powers and responsibilities, as well as the protection of the French language and culture. He thus established the framework that would guide the demands by future Québec governments in discussions concerning constitutional reform.

Afraid of being outflanked by Daniel Johnson of the *Union Nationale* and pressured by the progressive wing within his party, Lesage abandoned any discourse on the equality of provinces in favour of a particular status for Québec. While Lesage was strengthening his autonomist discourse, he also sought to influence decisions of the federal government. In the 1966 Québec budget, the government went so far as to suggest that the province should participate directly in areas of exclusive federal jurisdiction, by participating in the development and execution of fiscal, monetary, and trade policies. The federal government rejected this proposition.

The Lesage government was resolute in pushing for reform, ready to risk an acrimonious relationship with Ottawa if this could enhance Québec's economic and political power and status. In 1964 the Québec government was granted control of its own public pension plan, which gave the province greater fiscal autonomy and allowed for new initiatives without authorization from Ottawa. The Québec pension plan constituted a major gain as it assisted in building the most impressive and durable public investment pool in Canada, the Caisse de dépot et placement, the gem of Québec's financial institutions. At the time, the federal government attempted unsuccessfully to convince other provinces to follow Québec's lead, so that the latter would not appear to have obtained de facto special status.

The Union Nationale defeated the Liberals in 1966 with the slogan "Equality or Independence" and would adopt the same approach with regard to federal-provincial relations, with a greater emphasis initially on nationalist discourse. By making reference to the binational character of Canada and by advancing a project based on distinct status, Premier Daniel Johnson conducted Québec to a new level. Johnson would later rely on his interpretation during the Confederation of Tomorrow Conference in the autumn of 1967, which was convened on the request of the Ontario Premier, John Robarts, who sought a solution to the Canadian malaise. Johnson wanted to obtain firm support from his colleagues, for a commitment recognizing

Québec's right to a particular responsibility that would permit Québec to ensure the promotion of French-Canadian culture.

The position adopted by Johnson, and subsequently Jean-Jacques Bertrand (1968-70), tended to concur with the *Report of the Royal Commission of Inquiry on Constitutional Problems* (the Tremblay Commission 1953-1956) that the division of powers and revenues between the provinces and federal government should be based on the Québec interpretation of the British North America Act (BNAA) of 1867. In this perspective, the Union Nationale demanded limits on federal government transfer payments to individuals through pan-Canadian social programs, and complete federal withdrawal if these were run on a shared-cost basis.

Pursuing his demand for constitutional reform, and benefiting from the momentum provided by the Royal Commission of Bilingualism and Biculturalism (the Laurendeau-Dunton Commission 1963-1969), Johnson envisaged a binational solution to Canada's constitutional problems. His proposal was founded on an interpretation of the BNAA as a pact between two founding peoples. The Union Nationale, under Maurice Duplessis, in power in Québec from 1936-1939 and from 1944-1959, had already attempted to protect the division of powers of 1867 from federal encroachment. Under Johnson, the party asked for additional powers to protect francophones within Québec and to some extent those living outside of the province. These modifications were seen to be commensurate with Québec's responsibilities as the primary protector of the French-speaking community in Canada.

Despite constitutional differences, several issues were resolved during the second half of the 1960s. For example, several deals were made with Ottawa on tax revenues, and an opting-out formula was implemented. In addition, Québec started to play an important role in *la francophonie*, while an informal agreement with the federal government allowed Québec to expand the small immigration bureau established during Lesage's mandate into a legitimate department. This departure from established practice paved the way for asymmetrical federalism.

The selection of Pierre Trudeau as leader of the federal Liberal Party in April 1968 and his subsequent election as Prime Minister of Canada in June of that year would change the stakes significantly. His project of constitutional reform lead to much wrangling with the various Québec governments that would follow and, finally, to the repatriation of the constitution in spite of unanimous disagreement by the parties represented in Québec's National Assembly.

Upon his arrival, Pierre Trudeau refused to accord to Québec anything that he was not ready to concede to other member-states of the federation. This did not prevent Johnson from defending the premise that programs such as family allowances, pensions, social assistance, health services, and manpower training were the sole responsibility of the provinces. For Johnson, it was clear that the distinct character of Québec warranted bilateral arrangements between Québec and Ottawa that were not contingent upon the federal government's relations with other provinces. The spending power of the federal government was perceived as having a negative effect on the maintenance of federalism since it did not respect a watertight division of powers between the two orders of government.

Under successive governments, Québec and Ottawa did reach more formal agreements that broadened the province's responsibilities in the areas of immigration and, to a lesser extent, international relations. It should be stressed, however, that neither Ottawa nor the other provinces agreed to constitutional entrenchment of Québec's rights in these domains, conceding only the possibility of making administrative arrangements that are nothing more than reversible deals.

During the 1970s, the Québec government continued its search for greater autonomy by urging that it be given additional powers and the necessary revenues for its exercise. It is in this context that Robert Bourassa, Premier of Québec from 1970-76 and from 1985-93, developed the objectives of profitable federalism, cultural sovereignty, and later, shared sovereignty. It must be noted that Bourassa's priority was not for the entrenchment of Québec's national aspirations in the Canadian Constitution; rather, he sought a revision of the federal system that would assign Québec the requisite powers and resources needed for an affirmation of the bicultural character of Canada. At the Victoria Conference in 1971, political analysts believed that the constitutional debate would be successfully resolved under Bourassa, but the nationalist opposition forces in Québec forced him to retreat, and the agreement was never ratified. The reason given for this reversal was the imprecision of the text, particularly Article 94A, which outlined responsibilities for pensions and other social programs. For Québec, 94A was said to be a test of the extent to which its constitutional partners were willing to push for a significant change in the sharing of powers. Moreover, there was intense political pressure in Québec regarding the proposed amending formula that would have given a veto to Québec, Ontario, to the Western provinces collectively, and one to the Eastern provinces. For Québec, this signalled a vision of Canada without regard for dualism. The package deal proposed by Ottawa failed to guarantee to Québec control over cultural and social policies.

Negotiations resumed in 1975 with the federal government's suggestion that the issue of the division of powers be set aside in favour of a simple patriation with an amending formula. This implied that any discussion of a new division of powers would be the subject of future multilateral and bilateral bargaining among Québec, the other provinces, and the federal government. Ottawa recognized that in modifying the federal sharing of powers, the protection and promotion of linguistic and cultural concerns were of primary interest to Québec, and this was presented at the time as the recognition of Québec's demand for "special status."[11]

In effect, the federal government did not want to give further ammunition to the Parti Québécois, which was rapidly gaining in popularity among the Québec electorate. Québec then made public that it was prepared to accept this approach provided that its linguistic and cultural concerns are entrenched in the Constitution.[12] In exchange for patriation, Bourassa asked that the following provisions be included in a new Constitution: the right for Québec to veto future constitutional amendments; control of policies in the fields of education and culture in the province; the right to opt out of federal programs with compensation; a more important role in immigration, especially aspects dealing with selection and integration of immigrants into Québec society; and limits of the federal government's declaratory and spending powers in areas of provincial jurisdiction.

The federal initiative was accompanied by a threat of unilateral patriation by Ottawa, without the consent of the provinces, prompting the Premier of Québec to call an early election in the fall of 1976. The PQ assumed power on 15 November 1976 with a program of sovereignty-association. Under René Lévesque, the PQ government was committed to acquiring full political sovereignty, accompanied by an economic association (later replaced by the notion of economic union) between Québec and the rest of Canada. The election of an autonomist government under Lévesque in Québec did not change the federal government's inclination to push for the patriation of the Constitution with an amending formula.

In the meantime, the Pepin-Roberts Task Force had received a mandate from the government of Pierre Trudeau to work towards "the elaboration of the means aimed at the reinforcement of Canadian unity."[13] In Pierre Trudeau's estimation, this entailed a centralization of powers to Ottawa. The conclusions of the Pepin-Roberts report rested on three elements: the existence of different regions, the predominance of two cultures, and equality of the two orders of government. The main thrust of the proposed changes was the institutionalization of asymmetrical federalism, which implies that all provinces are not equal, nor are they the same. While avoiding a *de jure* special status for Québec, Québec's special relationship with the rest of Canada was said to be *de facto*, recognized in the arrangements that had been offered to all provinces but in which Québec had been the only participant. The Québec Pension Plan is the most potent example. This recognition of special status and asymmetry was extended to language, with the contention that each province had the right to determine provincial language policy.

Major institutional innovations included proposals for reforming the Senate, an expanded Supreme Court, and the abolition of certain antiquated federal powers, such as the powers of disallowance and reservation. The task force proposed the replacement of the Senate by a Council of the Federation entirely composed of delegates nominated by the provinces. Moreover, seats based on proportional representation would be added to the House of Commons in order to obtain a more equitable representation of political parties. In the area of justice, expanding and dividing the Supreme Court into specialized "benches" designed to address deficiencies in the ability of the courts to rule in various jurisdictions was also among the proposals. Finally, concurrency was proposed for federal declaratory, spending, and emergency powers. In an attempt to reconcile western alienation and Québec nationalism, the task force tackled the issues of provincial autonomy, provincial control over language policy, representation of provincial interests in Ottawa, as well as the status of Québec within the federation.

Failing to deliver the report desired by Trudeau, the task force nevertheless permitted the federal authorities to gain precious time by giving the federal government the possibility of engaging itself simultaneously in the elaboration of its reform project, an initiative set aside during the Québec election in November 1976. Ottawa could then kill two birds with one stone. On the one hand, the political strategists let it be believed that reconciliation could be possible in response to the expectations of the member-states of the federation and, on the other, they were preparing their intended reply by elaborating Bill C-60: A Time for Action. The origins of a Plan A and Plan B approach were emerging.[14]

In 1978, Ottawa introduced Bill C-60, the Constitutional Amendment Bill, containing terms very similar to those of the 1971 Victoria formula. The Bill included intrastate modifications that would strengthen provincial representation at the federal level, as well as a Charter of Rights and Freedoms (which was conceived at the time as an "opt-in" arrangement for the provinces!). According to Bill C-60, these transformations would have involved replacing the Senate with a House of the Federation, with half of its proposed 118 members selected by provincial assemblies and the other half selected by the House of Commons. This would have been accompanied by an entrenched representation of Québec in the Supreme Court, with the right to name three judges. In addition, the ability of the House of the Federation to veto changes to language legislation could be reduced to a 60 day suspensive veto, but could be overturned with the support of two-thirds of the House of Commons.[15]

In a reference decision in 1979, the Supreme Court of Canada ruled that the Parliament of Canada was not empowered to modify itself in a manner that might affect the provinces. The Court argued that despite the power of amendment in Section 91(1), the House of the Federation, in substituting for the Senate, was affecting an institution that was of interest to the provinces.[16]

The Québec government showed no interest in this new initiative, as it was in the process of preparing its own White Paper, *Québec-Canada: A New Deal* (1979), which argued for the formation of "two communities" where nine provinces would reconstitute Canada and the tenth, that is Québec, would exist as a separate state, on a political level, but would remain tied to Canada in the form of a new economic union. From Québec's perspective, the sovereignty-association option had the advantage of dealing directly with the enduring issue of duality, whereas in the rest of the country it was perceived as ignoring the emerging equality of provinces principle, increasingly popular among less populated provinces outside central Canada.

In May 1979, Canada elected its first Conservative government since 1968. Prime Minister Joe Clark was more disposed than Trudeau towards an acceptance of decentralized federalism, expressed in the conception of Canada as a "community of communities," which was favourable to more harmonious Québec-Canada relations. At the time, Canada was experiencing both a debilitating economic recession and a continuing constitutional crisis. Despite the change in the federal position, the Québec government under René Lévesque remained committed to holding a referendum on sovereignty-association. Then, unexpectedly, the cards were re-shuffled. The Conservative minority government was forced to call an election and the Trudeau Liberals returned to power in February 1980 with a renewed desire to crush the "separatists" and demonstrated little interest in finding solutions to Québec's claims.

During the 1980 referendum campaign, Trudeau challenged Québec "independentists" and sent his Québec-based ministers to campaign for the "No" forces. The Trudeau Liberals had promised that defeat of the referendum would not be interpreted as an endorsement of the status quo, promising to elaborate policies that would respond to Québec's special needs and concerns. Many supporters of this option during the referendum campaign were made to believe that renewed federalism meant an official recognition of Québec as a distinct society/people, and that new powers commensurate with this position would be given to Québec. One will remember that federalists of different persuasions had rallied around Pierre Elliott Trudeau to defeat Québec's claim for sovereignty-association as a new option. Québec's federal MPs, in an ultimate attempt to convince Quebecers to vote against the PQ's proposal for independence, claimed that they were putting their seats on the line. This was generally believed to demonstrate the genuine desire of the federal government to accommodate Québec culturally and linguistically.

In 1981, the federal government repatriated the constitution without the consent of Québec. Instead of being granted special recognition, Québec was weakened by the federal order. The move was repudiated in Québec by both federalists and nationalists active on the provincial political scene, including those federalists who sided with Trudeau in May 1980. These federalists felt a sense of betrayal. Trudeau's victory turned sour as opinion leaders who once fought for the federalist cause (such as Claude Ryan, Robert Bourassa, and the business community at large) called for corrective measures to be implemented rapidly in order to keep Canada together.

This episode reveals that the federal government, contrary to what it had promised during the referendum campaign of May 1980, had interpreted the results

favouring the federalist option (40 per cent for the "yes" option) as an indication
that Quebecers desired to remain within the federation, rather than as a mandate
for its renewal. Ottawa's stance towards Québec became uncompromising since the
so-called "separatists" were deemed to be disorganized and demoralized. Trudeau
challenged provincialism and decentralization as outdated principles, and proposed
a centralist vision. The PQ was in disarray, the Québec Liberal Party had fought a
tough campaign against independence along with Ottawa, the Trudeau Liberals had
a majority government, the state of the economy was abysmal, and a neo-liberal
ideology was gaining support.

Trudeau lost no time after the referendum and planned a constitutional conference for September 1980. Afraid of a possible unilateral move by Ottawa if talks
failed, Québec was busy forging alliances with other provinces. The federal
government persisted by introducing, on 2 October 1980, a "Proposed Resolution
for Address to Her Majesty the Queen Respecting the Constitution of Canada."
Québec and seven other provinces—the Gang of Eight—opposed such action,
preparing reference cases in the Québec, Manitoba, and Newfoundland Courts of
Appeal that proved disappointing for the provincial forces. Ultimately, the case
reached the Supreme Court of Canada, which reached a majority decision. Richard
Simeon and Ian Robinson summarize the decision as follows:

> [I]t would be legal for Parliament to act without provincial consent,
> but that this would still be unconstitutional since it would breach an
> established convention of substantial provincial consent.... Provinces
> had been warned that if they continued to delay action, Ottawa might
> move. The only way out was to return to the intergovernmental table.
> But now there was a critical difference: the convention, said the Court,
> did not mean unanimity; it required only "substantial consent." Two
> provinces was clearly not "substantial consent," but one province
> could no longer stop the process. The groundwork for a settlement
> without Québec had been laid.[17]

Taking advantage of these circumstances, a constitutional conference was called
by Trudeau for November 1981. With the support of the Québec National Assembly and seven provincial Premiers (Ontario and New Brunswick excepted), Premier
Lévesque expressed opposition to the central government's plans to reform and
patriate the constitution unilaterally. Initially, and strategically, Lévesque agreed
to the principle of provincial equality. At the same time, he continued to oppose
patriation in the absence of agreement on an amending formula and a new division
of powers, demanded that Québec be recognized as a culturally and linguistically
distinct society, and asked for the responsibilities and resources that this implied.

In return for Québec's acceptance of the equality of provinces notion, the premiers accepted Québec's veto right.

Opposing any form of special status, Trudeau isolated Québec. On 5 November 1981, in the absence of Premier Lévesque, the other premiers agreed to patriation and the entrenchment of a Charter of Rights and Freedoms. With agreement came their preferred amending formula[18] and the right to opt-out of the secondary provisions of the Charter. The opting-out (or "notwithstanding") clause ensured the western premiers' support of the package deal. Québec was isolated, with no other course of action but to make use of the notwithstanding clause, which it did systematically until the election of the Québec Liberals in December 1985. The decision to patriate with an entrenched Charter of Rights and Freedoms proved to be a major assault on Québec's vision of federalism in an environment that was growing increasingly hostile to any protective measures. According to most centralist federalists, time would heal everything.[19]

This period of transition that began in the early 1960s with the firm desire to have Québec included as a fundamental element of the Canadian federation proceeds on a note of exclusion, isolation, and the refusal of recognition. During this time, the Canadian constitutional order has been reconsidered without Québec's demands being satisfied.

The Establishment of a New Constitutional Order: 1982 to the Present

The imposition of a new constitutional order in 1982 constitutes a break with continuity and disregards the dualist vision as a defining element of the Canadian federation. According to the political philosopher James Tully, the imposition of this new constitutional order has resulted in a situation in which Québec is not free within the Canadian federation for at least three reasons:

> 1. Other member states of the federation can impose constitutional amendments without its consent;

> 2. The content of the amending formula, introduced in 1982, renders it virtually impossible, in practice, to amend the Constitution so that Québec be recognized as a nation;

To these two reasons, Tully adds a third following the decision in August 1998 by the Supreme Court on the right of Québec to secede:

3. The Court maintains that phase two of the negotiations, initiated by the attainment of a clear majority in a referendum, subject to a clear question, must be framed in terms of the present amending formula. Therefore, due to the first reason mentioned above, Québec is not bound by this amending formula. Moreover, since Québec's right to initiate constitutional changes is impeded in practice, this phase of negotiations would conclude in an impasse and according to the Court itself, this injustice would legitimize Québec's position of claiming the right to secede unilaterally. Finally, every demand of recognition as a nation … implies as a corollary a demand for an amendment to the present amending formula.[20]

The fact that Québec is bound to the present amending formula, which it contests, implies in fact that its rights to propose constitutional changes are not recognized and that its sense of liberty has been unquestionably persecuted. A more in-depth discussion of the decision of the Supreme Court will be provided below.

The Constitution of 1982 has thus resulted in a reduction of democratic space by denying Québec a central place in the Canadian federation. This provided some motivation for the Conservatives of Brian Mulroney, following an election victory in September 1984, to identify a new path to repatriation and reintegrate Québec into the constitutional family with "honour and enthusiasm." Responding to this policy with friendly overtures, René Lévesque decided to re-enter the constitutional fray and spoke of the new situation as representing a "beau risque" for Québec.[21] In May 1985, Lévesque presented the new federal Prime Minister with a "Draft Agreement on the Constitution"[22] that embodied 22 claims made by Québec to settle the constitutional crisis.

These propositions would essentially be re-visited in the constitutional position adopted by Robert Bourassa upon his election victory in Québec in December 1985. The differences were more a question of degree than of kind. The *Péquiste* project, therefore, would serve as a point of departure for the Liberals in the negotiations that followed.[23] It must be noted that between 1981 and 1985, Lévesque, having lost the referendum in May 1980, negotiated from a position of weakness. This changed somewhat when Bourassa, a bona fide federalist, returned as Premier of Québec. The Québec Liberals limited their bottom-line demands to five, as a minimal condition to return to the negotiating table: (1) the explicit recognition of Québec as a distinct society; (2) increased power to Québec in immigration regarding recruitment, administration, and integration of new arrivals; (3) appointment of three Supreme Court judges with expertise in Québec civil law; (4) containment of the federal spending power, and; (5) a full veto for Québec on any new modifications to be made to the Canadian constitution.

The Meech Lake proposals (1987-1990) attempted to deal with most of these claims but failed due, on the one hand, to a lack of openness to difference on the part of the Canadian partners, and on the other, to a reform process (amending formula) that ignored Québec's view of Canadian dualism, as a principal founding partner of the Canadian federation. For Ottawa, the Meech Lake Accord reflected a constant preoccupation with uniformity as an operational principle of Canadian federalism, except for the distinct society clause. By providing all the other provinces that which had been granted to Québec, Ottawa could remove any impression of giving Québec a special status. In turn, the federal government would have obtained a major concession from Québec, as it was willing to recognize for the first time the federal spending power in spheres of exclusive provincial jurisdiction. In Québec, the federal spending power has always been viewed as a federal intrusion, and its acceptance by the Québec government lead to great disenchantment among autonomists and nationalists. In the rest of Canada, many observers believed that the distinct society clause would seriously weaken the federal government, for the reason that those provinces choosing not to participate in pan-Canadian programs would be afforded the possibility of opting-out with full financial compensation.

As the Meech Lake negotiations began, other interests organized with the aim of defeating Québec's vision of federalism. In the process, Québec's claims became secondary and were depicted as a threat to the rights of First Nations, the equality of provinces and the universality of social programs. The provincial elections of Manitoba, New Brunswick, and Newfoundland provided a platform for leaders to appeal to anti-Québec sentiments. This signalled the failure of the Meech Lake Accord.

Following the failure of the Meech Lake Accord in June 1990, the government of Québec no longer had a mandate to negotiate its reinsertion into the Canadian federation. This resulted in the Québec Liberal party's elaboration of a new policy platform (the Allaire Report) and convinced the Québec government to set up the Commission on the Political and Constitutional Future of Québec (the Bélanger-Campeau Commission). The mandate of this Commission was for a new definition of the political and constitutional arrangements that determined the status of Québec and its relations with other member-states of the federation. This constitutes a unique moment in Canadian history. A province, through its governing party and with the full backing of the official opposition, decided to assess the appropriateness of its continued association with the rest of the country of which it was a founding member, reviving the 1981 unanimity that had condemned unilateral patriation of the BNA Act without Québec's consent.

Following the tabling of the Bélanger-Campeau Report that recommended the setting up of two special National Assembly committees, Bill-150 was enacted to confirm such a proposal. The Québec government intended to maintain pressure on the other governments (provincial and federal) with these two public forums, by forcing a confrontation with the questions of renewed federalism and sovereignty on a daily basis. As a result, the Commission asked that a referendum on the future of Québec in Canada be held no later than 26 October 1992.

In an attempt to regain the initiative, on 24 September 1991, Ottawa released a discussion paper to propose, against all expectations, a restructured federation along the lines of a centralized economic model, and set up a joint Parliamentary Committee (Castonguay-Dobbie, and later Dobbie-Beaudoin) to once more examine the perennial issue of Québec's relations with the rest of Canada.

Contrary to all expectations, the federal government and the nine anglophone provinces reached a consensus on 7 July 1992. The essence of the deal was later confirmed in the 28 August 1992 Consensus Report on the Constitution (Charlottetown Accord). Far from recognizing Québec's distinct status in Canada, and proceeding towards a devolution of powers, the agreement proposed an increase of powers for the central government through the constitutionalization of its spending power, and the strengthening of federal institutions. Instead of transferring powers to the provinces, as has been demanded by Québec, the Charlottetown Accord proposed to make room for the provinces in the Senate and to consolidate the powers of the federal government to intervene in spheres of exclusive provincial jurisdiction. The Accord also included a "Canada clause" that gave equal weight to the distinct society clause, the equality of provinces principle, and the obligation for Canadians and their governments to promote Québec's anglophone minority. Moreover, a major section of the proposed accord dealt with Aboriginal rights to self-government.

The Accord was soundly defeated in Québec (56.7 per cent), as it was in Manitoba (61.6 per cent), in Saskatchewan (55.3 per cent), in Alberta (60.2 per cent), in British Columbia (68.3 per cent), in Nova Scotia (51.3 per cent) and in the Yukon (56.3 per cent). In addition, the Accord was rejected by Aboriginal communities throughout the country, to the great disappointment of the Chief of the Assembly of First Nations, Ovide Mercredi, whose leadership was shaken.

The defeat of the Charlottetown Accord constituted an unprecedented dismissal of the political class, as Canadians throughout the country said No to a package deal cobbled behind closed doors. Defeat also represented a major setback for Robert Bourassa who, according to his closest constitutional advisors, had "caved in" as he failed to defend Québec's traditional demands and political *acquis*. The Québec Premier did not secure even the five minimal conditions of the Meech Lake proposals that were to be met before Québec would agree to re-enter formal constitutional negotiations. In short, Québec had made no gains in the sharing of powers, and saw the centralization of power as being further ensconced, since the federal government could negotiate five-year reversible deals with individual provinces.

Moreover, Ottawa confirmed and potentially reinforced its capabilities of intervention in areas of exclusive provincial jurisdiction. It is in this context that the more nationalist wing of the Québec Liberal Party would leave the party to form, under the leadership of Jean Allaire and later Mario Dumont, the *Action Démocratique du Québec.*

The consequences of the failure of the Charlottetown Accord were major for the federal Conservatives in that, having almost achieved reform earlier in their mandate, they were virtually wiped off the map in the 25 October 1993 elections. Quebecers also voted in large numbers for the Bloc Québécois, as the party made impressive inroads by winning 54 of the 75 seats in Québec to form Her Majesty's Loyal Opposition in Ottawa. A nationalist party from Québec now occupied a strategic place within the House of Commons itself and could more effectively push for Québec's demands. The victory of the Parti Québécois in the 12 September 1994 election followed, and Jacques Parizeau, strengthened by the presence of the Bloc as an ally of Québec in Ottawa, pursued his intentions in favour of Québec sovereignty.

On the federal side, the governing party of Jean Chrétien proceeded, as though the national question in Québec was of interest to no one, to engage in a major reform project in the area of social programs. The best way to achieve this end was to significantly cut the lifeblood of the provinces, accomplished in February 1995 by the ratification of Bill C-76 that cut transfers to the provinces by a third, by six billion dollars over two years, in the field of health.[24]

It is in this context that a project of sovereignty, based on an economic and eventually a political partnership, was proposed as a solution to deal with the constitutional impasse in terms of Québec's position within the federation. The second referendum in 15 years was called on 30 October 1995, asking Quebecers to determine their political future. Unlike the outcome of the 1980 referendum, which saw the No forces gain nearly 60 per cent of the vote, this campaign resulted in 50.6 per cent for the No camp. Moreover, 49.4 per cent of Quebecers endorsed the option of sovereignty-partnership with a view to establishing a new political entity in Québec free to negotiate a new economic and political union with its partners.[25] A slim margin of 54,288 votes separated the two camps, and the referendum signalled somewhat of a victory for democracy, as 94 per cent of registered voters exercised their right to vote.

Reticent as always to any form of accommodation with regards to Québec, Prime Minister Chrétien preferred to maintain the constitutional status quo. In justifying such inertia, Chrétien referred to the notion that citizens were "fed up" with constitutional issues and that their immediate concerns related to more pressing matters of unemployment and the economy. With a certain urgency, and mostly to give the impression that it understood Québec's demands for political recognition, the Chrétien government adopted, by a simple statute, a resolution affirming the distinct character of Québec society within Canada, on December 11, 1995. Furthermore, on 2 February 1996, the federal government added a new obstacle to constitutional reform by superimposing a regional veto right to four territorial groups, consisting of Québec, Ontario, Western Canada, and the Atlantic provinces, onto the provisions already in the Canadian Constitution.[26] These veto rights are not guaranteed constitutionally, as they could be withdrawn following the adoption of a parliamentary statute.

In the same spirit, Ottawa and the Canadian provinces drafted the Calgary Declaration[27] on 14 February 1997, after public consultation among the Canadian population, and reiterated certain principles on which Canadian unity would be based. Having recognized the unique character of Québec society among a large array of conditions so as to undermine its significance, the signatories rejected all forms of asymmetrical federalism and agreed to prioritize one of the jurisdictions exclusive to the provinces, the performance of social programs. Moreover, they agreed that the declaration constitutes a framework for public consultation meant to reinforce the Canadian federation. The door was open for Ottawa to engage Canadians in a project for a social union, a project that had been in the works since the Charlottetown Accord.

The federal regime, notwithstanding a brief period of hesitation under the government of the federal Conservatives from 1984-1993, continued its assault on any form of provincial autonomy and chose to reinforce the new constitutional order of 1982 by establishing the rules of the game on its own. The re-election of a majority Liberal government in 1997, as well as in 2000, would contribute to making the task easier. The approach was simple: if the provinces did not collaborate in the direction desired by Ottawa, their transfers would be cut. The re-election of a sovereigntist majority government in Québec in 1998 did not put an end to the constitutional debates. Moreover, the fact that the provincial Liberals under the leadership of Jean Charest fell short of winning the 1998 election, yet still managed to garner more votes than the Parti Québécois, significantly limited the power of the governing party.

More recent years have been characterized by confrontations between Québec and the federal government. With a strong electoral victory in 1997, the Chrétien government engaged in a full frontal assault on Québec's right to secede. The responses obtained following the Reference case regarding the secession of Québec were not entirely expected by the federal government. Attempting to re-establish the principle of continuity in constitutional discourse, the Supreme Court recognized, as the very basis of the Canadian federation, four main principles: (1) federalism, (2) democracy, (3) constitutionalism and the primacy of law, and (4) the respect for minorities. The Supreme Court underlined, in Sections 84 and 85 of its ruling, that a constitutional modification could permit a province to secede. The

Court contends in paragraph 87 that "the results of a referendum have no direct role or legal effect in our constitutional scheme,

> [but] … it would confer legitimacy on the efforts of the government of Québec to initiate the Constitution's amendment process in order to secede by constitutional means."[28]

If the repatriation of the Constitution in 1982 undermined Québec's liberty of action, as James Tully contends, the Court Ruling allows for some corrective measures. Paragraph 88 constitutes the Gordian knot,

> The clear repudiation by the people of Québec of the existing constitutional order would confer legitimacy on demands for secession, and place an obligation on the other provinces and the federal government to acknowledge and respect that expression of democratic will by entering into negotiations and conducting them in accordance with the underlying constitutional principles …

The ruling of the Supreme Court allows for the possibility of relations between Québec and Canada to be more open, for the re-vitalization to some extent of the democratic foundations of the Canadian federation, and paves the way for a possible return to the principle of continuity. The Court stresses that the obligation to negotiate with Québec remains an inalienable right. In paragraph 92, the ruling contends, with some interest, that

> The rights of other provinces and the federal government cannot deny the right of the government of Québec to pursue secession, should a clear majority of the people of Québec choose that goal, so long as in doing so, Québec respects the rights of others.

Contrary to repatriation in 1982, which discredited the Supreme Court in the eyes of many Quebecers, the Reference Regarding the Secession of Québec has to some extent restored its credibility. James Tully concurs,

> The condition of liberty of a multinational society rests on the fact that its members remain free to initiate discussions and negotiations with regards to possible amending formulas to the structure of recognition in place and, as a corollary, the other members have the *obligation* to respond to those legitimate demands. A member that seeks recognition as a nation (in a form that is itself open to objection) is free to the

extent that the possibilities for discussions, negotiations and amendments are not impeded, in practice, by arbitrary constraints. The Constitution of a society that endures such obstructions can be likened to a
strait-jacket or a structure of domination. This situation of an absence
of liberty is revealed, in Canada, as much by the case of Québec as that
of the First Nations.[29]

What is the situation in Canada? Both the Aboriginal nations and the Québec
nation are confronted with situations of domination. The repatriation of the Constitution has led Québec into an era of subjection in terms of its political liberty and
the imposition of a new constitutional order.

Without delving deeply into the Clarity Bill (C-20), (see Chapter 7 Andrée
Lajoie in this volume), it is worth noting that we are under an imposition of arbitrary measures by the federal government. This law, to some extent, undercuts the
Ruling of the Supreme Court with regards to Québec's right to secede and under-
mines any desire for constitutional negotiations that Québec may want to pursue.

The re-election of the federal Liberals in the autumn of 2000 and the selection of
Bernard Landry to replace Lucien Bouchard as leader of the Québec government in
May 2001 did not bode well for any rapprochement between Québec and Canada in
the near future. Moreover, while Québec persists in demonstrating that Canadian
federalism is a façade, Ottawa continues to undermine the federal condition[30]
pertaining to the non-subordination of powers by substituting for them a set of
principles that do not take account of Canadian diversity, by imposing an increasing amount of constraining and homogenizing public policies, thus rendering any
significant reforms to the federation illusory. Truly helpful reforms would respond
to the fundamental expectations of Quebecers with regard to their diversity and
would affirm a legitimate context for real choice, which would be supported com-
prehensively by Quebecers.

Conclusion

The federal elections in autumn 2000 have not provided any reason for optimism
with regard to the re-establishment of constitutional peace in Canada. The Liberals
of Jean Chrétien, having succeeded in securing a majority government for the third
consecutive time, feel little urgency in proceeding towards constitutional modifications that would accommodate Québec's demands. It is, therefore, no great surprise
that the federal ministers reacted to the recent political program of the Québec Liberal Party, *Un projet pour le Québec. Affirmation, autonomie et leadership* (2001)
with a simple mention that this party did not exercise power in Québec, therefore it
did not merit any commentary.

The Canadian condition reduces Québec to merely a province like the others within the federation, which is far from corresponding to the image that Québec projects for itself here as well as on the international scene. Rupturing the founding constitutional order, Québec-Canada relations after repatriation in 1982 have entered a phase of non-recognition and the impoverishing of democratic practices. The ruling of the Supreme Court concerning Québec's right to secede served to widen the realm of the possible, only to be confined and limited by the federal government, which evidently sought to impede the holding of a fundamental debate on the future of the federation.

By constantly ignoring constitutional conventions and denying the existence of the Québec nation, the potential of the government to forge a symbol of identity and to mobilize politically remains doubtful. In short, the Canadian federal experience is not worth pursuing unless the member-states are free to adhere to the federation and all structures of domination are condemned.

Notes

1. The comments of Andrée Lajoie were very useful in the recasting of this text.

2. See the Commission sur le déséquilibre fiscal, *Pour un nouveau partage des moyens financiers au Canada* (Commission Séguin) (Québec: Bibliothèque nationale du Québec, 2002).

3. See Gérard Bouchard, "La vision siamoise de John Saul," *Le Devoir*, 15 and 17 Jan. 2000; John Saul, "Il n'y a pas de peuple conquis," *Le Devoir*, 22 and 24 Jan. 2000.

4. Hilda Neatby, *The Québec Act: Protest and Policy* (Scarborough: Prentice Hall, 1972); Philip Lawson, *The Imperial Challenge: Québec and Britain in the Age of the American Revolution* (Montréal: McGill-Queen's University Press, 1989).

5. Garth Stevenson, *Community Besieged: The Anglophone Minority and the Politics of Québec* (Montréal: McGill-Queen's University Press, 1999), ch. 2.

6. Thomas-Jean-Jacques Loranger, *Lettres sur l'interprétation de la constitution fédérale: première lettre* (Québec: Imprimerie A. Côté et Cie, 1883).

7. Royal Commission on Aboriginal Peoples (RCAP), *Partners in Confederation: Aboriginal Peoples, Self-Government and the Constitution* (Ottawa: Minister of Supply and Services, 1993), 22-23.

8. Every federal party has at one time or another in that decade recognized the concept of two founding peoples as a fundamental principle of the federation. This recognition, however, would vary in significance in the decades that followed.

9. The doctrine recognized and defended the right of provinces to negotiate agreements with international actors or organizations in their fields of jurisdiction.

10. Ironically, Québec accepted the principle of unanimity in 1980 in a last-ditch effort to block the repatriation project proposed by Ottawa.

11. Garth Stevenson, *Unfulfilled Union: Canadian Federalism and National Unity* (Toronto: Gage, 1982), 210.

12. Pierre Elliott Trudeau, "1976 Correspondence to all Provincial Premiers," in Peter Meekison, ed., *Canadian Federalism: Myth or Reality* (Toronto: Methuen, 1977), 140-67.

13. The Task Force on Canadian Unity, *Se retrouver. Observations et recommandations*, vol. 1 (Pepin-Robarts Report) (Ottawa: Official Editor, 1979), 143. Author's translation.

14. This consists of two approaches aimed at "resolving once and for all" the question of Québec: a conciliatory approach and a coercive one following the victory of the PQ in 1994 and the results obtained (nearly 50per cent of the votes) during the referendum in 1995. We can refer with much interest to the work of the jurist Daniel Turp, notably his work, *La nation bâillonnée: le plan B ou l'offensive d'Ottawa contre le Québec* (Montréal: VLB éditeur, 2000).

15. Douglas Verney, *Three Civilizations, Two Cultures, One State, Canada's Political Traditions* (Durham: Duke University Press, 1986), 367.

16. According to Douglas Verney, the Court supported its decision with the federal White Paper, published in 1965, which recognized the "role of the provinces, even for modifications touching questions that were not exclusive to jurisdictions of the provinces." Author's translation, Verney, *Three Civilizations*, 367.

17. Richard Simeon and Ian Robinson; *State, Society and the Development of Canadian Federalism* (Toronto: University of Toronto Press, 1990), 278.

18. The principal amending formula provided for constitutional changes to be undertaken with the support of seven provinces covering 50 per cent of the Canadian population. The reform of the amending formula was subject to unanimity. This situation was imposed on Québec, which from that moment on had to abide by rules adopted by others, losing all liberty of action in this area.

19. If one is to believe the events that surrounded the celebrations organized by the federal government to mark 20 years of repatriation, in April 2002, federal strategists have not yet regretted their actions, even though the referendum of October 1995 could potentially have represented a fateful moment for the country.

20. James Tully, "Liberté et dévoilement dans les sociétés plurinationales," *Globe*, 2, 2 (1999): 31-32. Author's translation. Also, for a larger analysis, see James Tully, "Introduction," in Alain-G. Gagnon and James Tully, eds., *Multinational Democracies* (Cambridge: Cambridge University Press, 2001) 1-33.

21. For a recent political analysis, see Michel Vastel, "La Charte a 20 ans: Des promesses plusieurs fois repudiées," *Le Soleil*, 17 April 2002, A-6.

22. This document was largely inspired by a document prepared by the Ministry of Intergovernmental Affairs during the first mandate of the PQ government. See *Les positions constitutionnelles du Québec sur le partage des pouvoirs (1960-76)* (Québec: Éditeur officiel du Québec, 1978). For document updated to March 2001, see <www.mce.gouv.qc.ca>.

23. Before arriving to power, the provincial Liberals had prepared a series of documents that discussed questions for which compromises would have to be negotiated. See *Une nouvelle constitution canadienne*, (1980), also known as the Livre Beige, *Un nouveau leadership pour le Québec*, (1983), and *Maîtriser l'avenir* (1985).

24. See Alain-G. Gagnon and Hugh Segal, "Introduction," in *The Canadian Social Union Without Quebec; 8 Critical Analyses* (Montréal: Institute for Research on Public Policy, 2000).

25. Alain-G. Gagnon and Guy Lachapelle, "Québec Confronts Canada: Two Competing Societal Projects Searching for Legitimacy," *Publius*, 26, 3, (1996): 177-91.

26. This indicated to specialists on the issue that the constitutional path had been closed. See Robert Dutrisac, "Une camisole de force," *Le Devoir*, 14 April 2002, G-7.

27. <http://www.ccu-cuc.ca/fran/dossiers/calgary.html>.

28. *Reference re Secession of Québec*, 2 S.C.R., 1998.

29. James Tully, "Liberté et dévoilement dans les sociétés plurinationales," 30. Author's translation.

30. Donald Smiley, *The Federal Condition in Canada* (Toronto: McGraw-Hill, 1987).

7

The Clarity Act in Its Context

ANDRÉE LAJOIE*

On 15 March 2000, the Parliament of Canada adopted An Act to give effect to the requirement for clarity as set out in the opinion of the Supreme Court of Canada in the *Québec Secession Reference*[1] (hereafter: *Clarity Act*). The text sets the procedure that should be followed and the criteria that the Parliament of Canada should use to decide if it has an obligation to negotiate, as established by the *Québec Secession Reference*[2] (hereafter: *Reference*) with a province that has decided to carry out its secession from Canada following a referendum. In particular, this law aims to prescribe the conditions and methods under which federal political actors could determine both the clarity of a referendum question pertaining to secession and the majority required to conclude that the consulted population is in favour of the idea.

To understand this legislation, which undoubtedly is unique in the world, we need to grasp the dual context from which it emerged. Indeed, Parliament invites such contextualization by the very title of its statute, which reads, in part: "to give effect to the requirement for clarity as set out in the opinion of the Supreme Court of Canada in the Québec Secession Reference." So, I will first analyze the relationship, ambiguous at best, between these two normative instruments before determining the larger context in which they both exist, the Canadian political conjuncture, where their role is strategic in the fight between Ottawa and Québec over sovereignty / secession.[3]

* Translated from French into English by Michael Szlamkowicz.

But from the start, especially for our foreign readership, we must recall the polit-ical antecedents during which these two amazing legal instruments were written. We must remember that this political chapter in our constitutional history began in 1995, with a referendum that proposed sovereignty-association to Quebecers, and was lost by an infinitesimal margin of 0.8 per cent of participants in a population where 93.5 per cent voted (50.4 per cent No to 49.6 per cent Yes). We know about the panic in the ROC,[4] and the fall in credibility of Prime Minister Jean Chrétien, who had remained passive during the referendum campaign, assuming that the results would be similar to those of 1980 (60 per cent No, 40 per cent Yes).

In reaction, the "federal political actors," as the Court would later call them, initiated "Plan B," which involved hardening their position towards Québec, in par-ticular by discrediting the unsettling results for the federalists of that referendum, as well of those of all referenda to come that were not based on a question and major-ity that in their opinion were not "clear." The Prime Minister kept repeating that he would not feel obligated to negotiate an association or partnership resulting from a Yes victory of 50 per cent +1 vote, while Minister of Intergovernmental Affairs, Stéphane Dion maintained that "Quebeckers would never renounce Canada in a clearly explained situation,"[5] making repeated references to a poll by sociologist Maurice Pinard, according to which many respondents believed that sovereignty implied maintaining political ties with Canada, while only 31 per cent of them would vote for sovereignty-association if it were not coupled with an economic association.[6]

The Ambiguous Relationship between the Secession Reference and the Clarity Act

It is in this context that the Canadian Justice Minister Allan Rock presented the following three questions to the Supreme Court in a reference formulated by decree on 30 September 1996.

1. Under the Constitution of Canada, can the National Assembly, legislature or government of Québec effect the secession of Québec from Canada unilaterally?

2. Does international law give the National Assembly, legislature or government of Québec the right to effect the secession of Québec from Canada unilaterally? In this regard, is there a right to self-determina-tion under international law that would give the National Assembly, legislature, or government of Québec the right to effect the secession of Québec from Canada unilaterally?

3. In the event of a conflict between domestic and international law on the right of the National Assembly, legislature, or government of Québec to effect the secession of Québec from Canada unilaterally, which would take precedence in Canada?

This Reference, therefore, aimed not only to declare the unconstitutionality under Canadian law, but the invalidity, under international law, of any Québec law that would propose a referendum on the sovereignty of Québec. Now, we have known for a long time (contrary to what legal positivists would still have us believe) that the courts, and more particularly the higher courts, when rendering decisions especially when they entail strong political implications—do not settle the conflicts by making a deductive ruling that applies a clear rule to hard facts. Instead, they construct their findings to give a result that is compatible with society's dominant, or majority, values.[7] Under these circumstances, the Court could not, in this debate, declare Québec, a non-dominant and minority audience, to be entirely right, especially since the judges undoubtedly, on a personal level, disagreed with its position on the question. But contrary to what one might have thought at first, the Court could not prove the federal Justice Minister right either, lest that would provoke secession. Therefore, the Court chose to give Ottawa its "negative support," by indicating to the federal government how far both of them could go together. By giving each half a loaf, as it did in the Constitutional Repatriation Reference,[8] that is, by attributing legality to Ottawa and legitimacy to Québec, the Court avoided both provoking secession and pulling the ground from beneath its own feet. For not only did the Court depend on Canada for its existence but, in a post-modern context, its legitimacy and the effectiveness of its pronouncements result not from its institutional authority, but from the coincidence of the values it endorses with those embraced by the judged.

This is, in my opinion, the most plausible explanation of the decision that confirmed the legitimacy of Québec's approach and the obligation of the Canadian authorities to negotiate when faced with a clear majority of Quebecers choosing secession, in response to a clear question. This judicial strategy succeeded, at least in the short term and, once made public, the *Reference* received unanimous approval—or just about—from its various audiences, if for patently different reasons.

If the legal status of the Reference and the skilled reasoning on which it is grounded served the institutional needs of the process superbly, it also subtly threw a line—or a trap, it all depends, and only time will tell—to the federal government, which did not miss the opportunity by adopting the *Clarity Act*. To grasp properly the ambiguous relationship between the latter and the *Reference*, one must look at the status and significance of the Reference, whose authors, not necessarily convinced of the usefulness of this political parade and barely inclined to participate in it, clearly wanted to let all responsibility lie with the political actors.

The Status and Scope of the Reference

The distinction between a *decision* by the Supreme Court in the framework of an appeal from a provincial Court of Appeals or from the Federal Court of Appeal, and an advisory *opinion* put forth in the framework of a reference, seems evident. But, as we shall see, evidence and clarity are elusive qualities. Indeed, there has always been confusion as to the effective scope of advisory opinions, which, though theoretically non-binding, are followed in practice in a large majority of cases.[9] In this context, the interview that Chief Justice Antonio Lamer, as he then was, gave to *Le Devoir* on the eve of his retirement,[10] assumes particular importance as evidence of the scope that the Court attributed to its own propositions. Reiterating what every first-year law student had already learned, he stated that advisory opinions rendered by the Supreme Court in a reference are nothing but opinions and are not enforceable decisions. Still, even if they are not legally bound to conform to the prescriptions of the Court for a democratic secession, Québec and Canada have an interest in respecting them in order to uphold their own respective legitimacy. Judge Lamer added further comments that have gone largely unnoticed: "the Court decided to give the responsibility for determining what represents both a clear majority and a clear question, in addition to the content of the negotiations, to the elected officials *and the international community*."[11] [Emphasis added.] We now need to analyze these conditions of legitimacy stated in the *Reference*.

The Conditions for Legitimacy Formulated by the Reference and their Effects

Two conditions set by the Court for the legitimacy of an eventual secession held everyone's attention: for Québec, a clear majority and question, and for Canada, the obligation to negotiate. A third condition passed virtually unnoticed: in an *obiter dictum*, the Court dismissed one of the methods that Parliament indeed no longer uses to impose its will on the provinces: the power of disallowance. All three are parts of the ideological context that resulted in the adoption of the *Clarity Act*.

Two Interrelated Conditions:
Clear Majority and Question, and the Obligation to Negotiate

As I have previously mentioned, the Reference gave each side half a loaf by granting Ottawa the two "no's" that it desired in response to its questions—unilateral secession is legal under neither Canadian nor international law—plus requirements for clarity, and to Québec the legitimacy of the referendum process and even that of a unilateral exit via an international route in the case of negotiations obstructed by federal and/or provincial authorities.

But the judges were very careful about defining "clarity," for the question and for the majority, and the grounds on which they chose to justify its imposition, like the correlative obligation to negotiate, are not without consequence for the subsequent exercise in which the federal authorities adopted the *Clarity Act.* Further, from the beginning the Court grounded the obligations for clarity and for the negotiations that it mutually imposed on Québec and Canada on the fact that secession constitutes in its opinion a modification of the constitution (84, 87, 88, 92, 104).[12] For the Court, secession is a particular case belonging to the category of constitutional modifications, and "the Constitution Act, 1982 gives expression to this principle, by conferring a right to initiate constitutional change on each participant in Confederation, and the existence of this right imposes a corresponding duty on the participants in Confederation to engage in constitutional discussions in order to acknowledge and address democratic expressions of a desire for change in other provinces (69)."

The obligation to negotiate is, therefore, not specific to the case of a referendum on a possible secession, but applies more widely to all initiatives of constitutional modification stemming from a participant in Confederation, as long as the process employed allows for an assurance to all parties of the respect and conciliation of rights guaranteed by the Constitution: "the existence of this right imposes a corresponding duty on the participants in Confederation to engage in constitutional discussions in order to acknowledge and address democratic expressions of a desire for change in other provinces (76)." In other words, a referendum on secession is a particular case of initiating a constitutional change, subject to conditions that the democratic principle imposes on such modifications (88). In this context the Court, applying this principle in this particular case, later stated the "clear question" and the "clear majority" as conditions of legitimacy in the particular process of constitutional modification that is a referendum of secession (84, 87), a process that will set in motion, as would similar initiatives of constitutional modification subject to the condition of democratic expression (76), the obligation to negotiate on the part of the other participants in confederation (87, 88).[13]

Therefore, we cannot draw from this ground any obligation to limit this imposition of negotiation to the case of secession: on the contrary, the rule is aimed at *any* constitutional modification, provided that the conditions of clarity are respected. But, as previously indicated, the question of knowing what is a clear majority and question remains unanswered, and the Court, leaving to the political authorities the responsibility of carrying it through, has been careful not to respond.

Indeed, in no paragraph where the Court refers to the "clear question" or to the "clear expression" have the judges either defined or clarified the meaning they intended to give to these expressions, or what eventual conditions the question should comply with in order to meet the expectations of clarity that it imposes as sufficient criteria of legitimacy to trigger the negotiating process involved in any constitutional modification. Admittedly, it consists of an "expression of democracy" (69, 87), but this *Reference* does not allow for further specification, especially taking into account the fact that the Court itself has previously given three separate meanings to the word "democracy" since 1984.[14]

Moreover, it expressly states that

> The Court has no supervisory role over the political aspects of constitutional negotiations. Equally, the initial impetus for negotiation, namely a clear majority on a clear question in favour of secession, is subject only to political evaluation, and properly so. A right and a corresponding duty to negotiate secession cannot be built on an alleged expression of democratic will if the expression of democratic will is itself fraught with ambiguities. Only the political actors would have the information and expertise to make the appropriate judgment as to the point at which, and the circumstances in which, those ambiguities are resolved one way or the other.

This affirmation, first appearing in the body of the text (100), is reiterated in its conclusion (153).

Therefore, for lack of finding the intended meanings of "clear question" in the *Reference,* we could, I believe, exclude at least two possible candidates, on the very basis of the requirement of clarity imposed by the Court. The first meaning we should exclude would be the one that expects a clear question to pertain only to secession, and to mention it specifically. The second would be one in which clarity has a single and univocal meaning. This second exclusion ensues equally from the requirement of clarity on any constitutional modification that the Court finds in democracy. Indeed, other constitutional modifications laid previously before the Court have never been commented on for their lack of clarity, though their wording was far from univocal.[15]

Beyond imposing this ambiguous condition linking the clarity of a question and of the majority to the obligation to negotiate, the Court has alluded indirectly to a third one, which received less attention from commentators, namely, the impossibility of using the power of disallowance, now obsolete in the Court's opinion.

A Third, Hidden Condition: The Obiter *on the Power of Disallowance*

Section 90 of The Constitutional Act, 1867 provided for the power of disallowance of provincial laws by the governor general. The Court, however, states, in an *obiter* formulated in paragraph 55 of the *Reference*, that soon after 1867, the underlying principle of federalism rapidly superseded this power, which numerous authors believe has been abandoned. There is little chance for the Court to retract this *obiter*, even if stated carefully. Neither is it likely that the federal government would revive a constitutional institution fallen into obsolescence by asking the Governor General — whose hesitation would be anything but minor — to exercise the power of disallowance to nullify a Québec law on a sovereignty referendum.

The Constraining Effects on Political Authorities

Nothing in the *Reference* imposed the obligation either on Parliament or on the government and out of the context of an actual referendum on secession, to select a meaning beforehand for the term "clarity" that the Court has refused to specify. On the contrary, the Court wrote, on two occasions rather than one (100, 153): "Only the political actors would have the information and expertise to make the appropriate judgment as to *the point at which, and the circumstances in which, those ambiguities are resolved* one way or the other."[16] [Emphasis added.]

It follows that if the political actors decide on such an exercise, they would have to do it by taking into account the constraints that the *Reference* has defined. The first of these constraints follows upon the confirmation by the Court of the obsolescence of the power of disallowance, which can no longer be directly exercised by the governor general as provided for in the *Constitution Act*, 1867. What seems even more certain is that Parliament cannot, without first going through the process of constitutional modification, transfer to itself the power of disallowance that the Constitution has attributed to the governor general.

The second constraint is more subtle and relates both to the explicit and implicit motives that brought the Court to refuse to clarify the meaning of the term "clarity." Not only could it not give a definition of "clear question" because, it believed, this task was not a matter within its competence, but because it was, in fact, a practically impossible exercise. It is in the context resulting both from these dual constraints and from the Canadian political conjuncture that one must analyze the *Clarity Act*.

The Clarity Act in the Dual Context of Dual Constraints Resulting from the Reference and from the Canadian Political Conjuncture

The effects of these constraints, interrelated to the point of being indissoluble in practice, are nevertheless analytically distinct in the sense that if those that are a result of the Reference materialized in the form taken by the federal authorities' intervention, the decision itself to intervene is that which the Canadian political conjuncture influenced.

The Constraints Resulting from the Reference

Under the constitutional circumstances that I have just mentioned, and particularly taking into account the obsolescence of the power of disallowance and the effects of the division of powers, once the decision was taken to put the *Reference* into effect by "clarifying 'clarity'" via legislative means, the federal Parliament obviously could not constrain the Québec National Assembly, which exercises its own legislative jurisdiction in a sovereign manner in accordance with the Canadian Constitution, and without the control of Canadian Parliament, which is sovereign only in its own jurisdiction. The federal authorities are well aware of this, which is why they have not attempted to control directly the legislative work of the Québec National Assembly, but rather to influence indirectly its members and their electorate.

In essence it is specifically for its own institutional needs[17] that Parliament gave itself the power to assess the clarity of a question and of a majority, providing for the federal political actors to decide under what conditions they believe their obligation to negotiate will be engaged by the process. This will be evaluated by the international community, as recalled by Chief Justice Lamer, but will have no effect on the legality of the Québec process whether it adopts a legislative route or not.

There is, therefore, no threat of disallowance in this case in the literal sense, though the *Clarity Act* would still achieve its purpose if it were to create enough confusion with respect to this subject to reassure the ROC by making Quebecers and other Canadians—of whom the majority are not constitutionalists but leave it to the media to inform them—believe that the federal Parliament could govern their political behaviour on this matter. The *Act* would achieve its purpose even without creating such confusion if the federal authorities, through its application, succeeded in intimidating the population by making it believe that they would not negotiate, a reasoning that seems already to have achieved at least some success considering the polls and the results of the last federal election.

The other constraint resulting from the *Reference* is no less serious for being more subtle, at least in the long term, though we are not clear if—and if so, how—the federal authorities have taken this into account. It relates to the impossibility of giving meaning to the term "clarity" outside the context in which the question will be asked. To get some understanding of this matter, one must consider the motives of the Court in not defining the term "clear question." It has explained some of these, while only implying others. Still more fundamental reasons could be invoked to support its choice in this matter.

The reasons the Court expressly put forth in refusing to specify what it meant by a "clear question" related to the restraint that it practises in the production of law. It drew a distinction between justiciable questions and the "political aspects of constitutional negotiations" (100), by referring the latter to the "political actors," not identified other than by the fact that they would dispose of "the information and expertise to make the appropriate judgment as to the point at which, and the circumstances in which, those ambiguities are resolved one way or the other" (100), "in the circumstances under which a future referendum vote may be taken" (153).

Despite the ambiguity—if not the absence—of criteria to distinguish "the relevant aspects of the Constitution" from "the political aspects of the constitutional negotiations" (100), the Court was perfectly justified, in my opinion, in refusing a leave to appeal decisions to which it cannot bring any valid clarification. For it not only cannot give a definition of "clear question" and "clear majority" because it believed this task was not within its constitutional competence, but because it is, in fact, a practically impossible exercise.[18]

Indeed, the meanings of words and statements are not objectively given, once and for all, but constructed according to the context in which they are used.[19] More specifically, the process of giving meaning does not occur unilaterally in a social vacuum, but rather within a community that the author addresses: the use of language implies dialogue. Thus, it is not only the author who determines the meaning of the discourse, but also those to whom the message is addressed. This is not to say that the reader of a text, or its audience, can attribute any meaning to it that he/she wishes. But it is up to this audience to choose it, within the interpretive margin at its disposal, in a given context.

Indeed, the limits imposed on the interpretation of a text come not only from its words, or even less from the author's intentions, but also from its compatibility with the common meaning it receives in its community's interpretive frame of reference.[20] This is particularly the case for legal texts that generally have the effect of constraining citizens or significantly modifying their situations.[21] The interpretive community will not permit the judges' interpretation to be incompatible with its major values and interests. This general principle holds true especially for texts having high social and political salience.

Stated differently, in the context of a referendum question, its degree of clarity is the concern of those who are asked the question: in this case, Quebecers. From the moment it is asked, and therefore from the time it is addressed to Quebecers, it is up to them to decide if they can understand it and are able to answer it, and no one else is able to decide that for them. There is no definition for clarity in context other than the one that suits them. So the meaning that others, to whom the question is not addressed, could give it, is not relevant.

In these circumstances, any forcibly simplistic attempt to impose a univocal meaning is both futile and, in the long run, doomed to fail. Some examples come to mind. The presence, in the eventual referendum question, of the terms "secession," "independence," or "country" appeared to be a guarantee of clarity to certain federalists. However, does "secession" exclude an ulterior ratification of a treaty? How can one maintain this without first refusing the negotiations that the *Reference* otherwise imposes? Since when can Parliament tie up its successors and prevent future constitutional modifications? What does "independence" refer to? For Stéphane Dion, then a professor of Political Science, this term was, in 1994, synonymous with "sovereignty," "secession," and "separation."[22] Could the expression not describe the actual relationship between Canada and the United States, in general, and within NAFTA, in particular? Finally, what is a "country": place of birth, region, territory? Larousse gives the three meanings, Vigneault adds "winter" to the definition, and the Basques have no illusions about the state-like character of the *Pays* Basque.

In addition, according to the *Reference*, it is not until the subsequent step, when the referendum is over, that the Canadian federal political actors as the "other participants in Confederation" will be brought to assess whether or not the expectations of clarity necessary for the process of the obligatory negotiation have been met. This is what the Court implicitly alludes to in referring this task to the political actors, unidentified other than by the fact that they would dispose of *"the information and expertise to make the appropriate judgment as to the point at which, and the circumstances in which, those ambiguities are resolved one way or the other"* (100), *"following the circumstances in which a referendum could be held in the future"* (153). By acting otherwise, by dictating their own conditions of clarity instead of respecting the collective position of Quebecers on the clarity of the question, the political actors in the ROC leave themselves open to criticism from the international community over their willingness to negotiate in good faith, as the Court itself has indicated (152, 154).

The Integration of these Constraints in the Canadian Political Conjuncture

In terms of the constraints that result from the *Reference*, nothing obliges the federal "political actors" to legislate in advance in order to give effect to the requirement for clarity as set out by the Court regarding an eventual referendum question. On the contrary, it is "to make the appropriate judgment as to the point at which, and the circumstances in which, those ambiguities are resolved one way or the other" that the Court welcomed the federal authorities, without even indicating the legal or political instruments that they should use to handle it. The choice made by the federal authorities for a legislative, preventive intervention through the *Clarity Act* in 1999 therefore was not dictated by the *Reference*, and its motivation and explanation must be found elsewhere. And if I am suggesting finding them in the Canadian political conjuncture, it is not only because of the form and scope of the *Clarity Act*, but also because the time chosen for bringing it to a vote, and the media hype that accompanied it, oriented attention both to the Canadian political conjuncture materialized in the confrontations between the Canadian federalists and the Québec nationalists, and to the more narrowly partisan conjuncture that prevailed within the federal Liberal Party from the moment this bill was presented.

Indeed, one cannot help but see that, conscious of not having the necessary authority to impose a decision of the federal Parliament on the Québec National Assembly, the drafters of this bill were careful not to do so and simply announced the conditions under which their obligation to negotiate would obtain. In other words, the only legal entity to which the *Clarity Act* applies, its official audience, is not the Québec National Assembly but the Parliament of Canada. Specifically, the legislative discourse is addressed to the Parliament in session at the time of an eventual referendum. But the subtext of this bill includes two implicit discourses: one, ideological, was addressed to the Québec electorate, and the other, partisan, is addressed to Paul Martin and his supporters within the federal Liberal Party.

The *Clarity Act* effectively indicates the criteria to which federal parliamentarians should refer in the case of a referendum on the secession of a province, to judge both the clarity of the question[23] and the adequacy of the majority.[24] If all Quebecers had read and understood the text themselves, they would have seen in these conditions that it was not addressed to their National Assembly.

But relayed by the media, specifically through interviews with federal politicians, it was perceived, in Québec as in the ROC, as constraining Québec's political authorities in the drafting of an eventual referendum question. And these constraints could easily appear imperative and legally binding to the ordinary citizen who does not make a living analyzing constitutional questions in general and the division of powers more particularly. And it is precisely on the ideological effects of this message that federal authorities were counting to arrive at the same practical result: to reassure the ROC by discouraging Québec from organizing a referendum asking a question of its choice, by persuading it that any question that would not meet the requirements of the *Clarity Act*, as well as an absolute majority of only 50 per cent +1 vote, would be illegal and unconstitutional.

But the time chosen by the Prime Minister to present this bill in a pre-election period and in the atmosphere then prevalent in the federal Liberal Party suggested that a second subtext was present in the bill. Indeed, this bill, already written in the style of what would later constitute Plan B, did not enjoy unanimity within the Government, or the Senate, or its advisers, or the Liberal Party, including minister Paul Martin, who rallied only later, in ministerial solidarity to this measure that he believed to be useless and certainly uselessly provocative to Quebecers.[25] But Prime Minister Chrétien, challenged from within his party by unofficial candidates to his succession, among them Paul Martin, held on to power, mainly with the goal of personally leading his party to a third mandate.[26] In these circumstances, he carried on despite this opposition and followed the advice of Stéphane Dion, using his control over the House to win the vote on the *Clarity Act* and to lock his opponent in a no-win situation. For once the bill was passed, Martin as party leader would be faced with three equally suicidal choices: not respecting the *Clarity Act* and putting himself at risk of impeachment; respecting it, thus alienating himself from Québec; or having it repealed by a new Parliament, and alienating himself from the ROC.

In response to this federal legislative intervention, the Québec National Assembly adopted the *Act respecting the exercise of the fundamental rights and prerogatives of the Québec people and the Québec State*,[27] which I will limit myself to contextualizing here by recalling its affirmation of the sovereignty of the Québec population and its consequences: the legitimacy of the Québec legislature and the exclusivity and range of its constitutionalized powers, specifically territorial and international, preceded by considerations based on facts that "political actors" should not have to be reminded of, in a country where the Supreme Court has affirmed it to be founded on principles that include, among others, democracy and the protection of minorities.

It is understandable that such federal initiatives of ideological disinformation would bring the Québec authorities to reiterate these indisputable truths. We can only deplore Parliament's and the National Assembly's use of legislation in what should have remained an exchange of ideas within the political debate. For this reduced the legislatures of the two orders of government to the level of mega-media and loudspeakers for political actors in a conflict that does not belong in these parliaments, which in a democracy are expected to limit themselves to producing legislative norms. Undoubtedly the Supreme Court did not foresee how right it would prove when, in the *Reference*, it called the federal authorities "political *actors*."

But in a climate where the political class suffers from a large legitimacy deficit, where citizens consult the courts more and more to settle conflicts of values that were once the prerogative of legislators, the latter cannot improve their image, nor that of Canadian democracy, by resorting to manoeuvres that do not relate to their mandate. And this situation is all the more dangerous since the role vis-à-vis supplicants that consequently befalls the Courts involves them in controversies that will only undermine their credibility. In leading these institutions astray, in perverting their specific functions for ideological purposes, it is democracy and politics as a whole that suffer, perhaps more profoundly and more definitively than the "political actors," busy playing sorcerer's apprentice, could ever imagine.

Notes

1. An Act to give effect to the requirement for clarity as set out in the opinion of the Supreme Court of Canada in the Québec Secession Reference, S.C. 2000, ch.26, coming from Bill C-20 (assented to 29 June 2000), 2nd session, 36th Parliament (Can.).

2. *Reference re Secession of Québec*, [1998] 2 S.C.R. 217.

3. This chapter draws on prior (but updated) analysis that I wrote on the Reference as well as on the Clarity Act: "La primauté du droit et la légitimité démocratique comme enjeux du *Renvoi sur la sécession du Québec*," *Politique et sociétés* 19 (2000): 31-42; "The double and inextricable role of the Supreme Court of Canada," *Canada Watch* 7 (1999): 14-15; "Le sens de l'expression 'question claire' dans le Renvoi relatif à la sécession du Québec," *Action Nationale* 40 (2000): 13-22; "How far can the Court go too far?" *Canada Watch, Special Issue: Supreme Court of Canada in 1997* (1998): 90-92.

4. "Rest of Canada," to use the expression by which Canadians other than Quebecers refer to themselves in the constitutional debate context.

5. Speech given on December 3, 1997, to the Cercle des journalistes de Montréal. See the web site of Québec's *Secrétariat aux affaires intergouvernementales:* www.mce.gouv.qc.ca/e/html/e0422002.html.

6. These data are analysed by the author in M. Pinard, "Les quatre phases du mouvement indépendantiste québécois," in M. Pinard, R. Bernier, and V. Lemieux, *Un combat inachevé* (Québec: Presses de l'Université du Québec), ch. 2, especially 38 and 46.

7. A. Lajoie, *Jugements de valeurs: le discours judiciaire et le droit* (Paris: Les Presses Universitaires de France, coll. "Les voies du droit," 1997.

8. *Reference re: Objection to a Resolution to amend the Constitution*, [1982] 2 S.C.R. 793.

9. For an analysis of the scope of such References, see *Reference*.

10. "Ottawa et Québec ne sont pas tenus de suivre l'avis de la Cour suprême sur la sécession," *Le Devoir*, 11 Jan. 2000, 1.

11. Ibid., 8 (our translation).

12. Numbers in brackets refer to the numbered paragraphs in *Reference*.

13. Of course, given the fact that the democratic principle surely predated its reaffirmation by the Court, one could wonder if that tribunal would be ready to invalidate the Canada Act, 1982, on the grounds that it contains expressions such as "free and democratic society," so unclear that the Court itself has attributed three different and mutually exclusive definitions to it since 1984, not to mention "Aboriginal rights," the meaning of which also does not seem to have been understood univocally by the interested parties.

14. A. Lajoie, R. Robin, S. Grammond, H. Quillinan, L. Rolland and A. Chitrit, "Les représentations de 'société libre et démocratique' à la Cour Dickson, la rhétorique dans le discours judiciaire canadien," *Osgoode Hall L.J.* 32 (1994): 295-391.

15. "Ottawa et Québec ne sont pas tenus...," *Le Devoir*, 11 Jan. 2001, 1.

16. Author's emphasis.

17. Not to mention the partisan interests of the federal liberals, which I analyze in the context of the Canadian conjuncture.

18. This however does not prevent the political actors from trying to influence the process, by pretending to define terms from an essentialist perspective.

19. E. Von Glaserfeld, "Introduction à un constructivisme radical," in P. Watzlawick, ed., *L'invention de la réalité — Comment savons-nous ce que nous croyons savoir?* (Paris: Éditions du Seuil, 1988).

20. S. Fish, *Respecter le sens commun*, coll. "Pensée juridique moderne," (Paris: L.G.D.J., 1995).

21. P. Ricoeur, "Le problème de la liberté de l'interprète en herméneutique générale et en herméneutique juridique," in P. Amseleck, ed., *Interprétation et droit* (Bruxelles/Aix-Marseilles: Éditions Émile Bruylant/Presses Universitaires d'Aix-Marseilles, 1995), 177-200; A. Lajoie, *Jugements de valeurs: le discours judiciaire et le droit.*

22. *La Presse*, 16 Dec. 1994, B3.

23. It must mention separation from Canada and "independance," but it should not include a mandate to negotiate nor offer any other possibility, especially not an agreement with Canada (s.1).

24. The percentage of votes cast, the percentage of admissible voters, and any other circumstance deemed relevant.

25. Not to mention the Senate, whose minority had to be transformed into a majority by last minute nominations, in order to help pass this bill: H. Young, "Le Projet de loi C-20," *Le Devoir*, 22 Apr. 2000, A3 and 20 June 2000, A2.

26. M. Cornellier "Congrès du P.C.: la question du leadership risque d'éclipser l'adoption de la Loi C-20," *Le Devoir*, 14 Mar. 2000, A3.

27. *An Act respecting the exercise of the fundamental rights and prerogatives of the Québec people and the Québec State*, S.Q. 2000, ch. 46.

8

Can Québec Neo-Corporatist Networks Withstand Canadian Federalism and Internationalization?

ÉRIC MONTPETIT*

In a North American context, Québec clearly distinguishes itself through the type of relationship the state maintains with civil society intermediary groups. These generally well-organized groups often enjoy a legal or implicit recognition that endows them with preferential participatory roles, along with the state, in policy development and implementation. Since the 1970s, European authors have employed the appellation of neo-corporatism[1] in order to distinguish this type of relationship between the state and intermediary groups from that of American pluralism and neo-pluralism.[2]

Nevertheless, the understanding of Québec neo-corporatism developed in this chapter rests on the policy network literature[3] and thus is distinct from European corporatism involving tripartite (trade union-employer-state) concertation over economic co-ordination.[4] We understand neo-corporatism as one form, among others, of policy networks that structure the relations between state and civil society during the formulation of public policy. More than other kinds of networks, neo-corporatist networks aim at developing public policies by institutionalizing a close relation between the state and a limited number of civil society actors. In contrast with traditional neo-corporatist studies that offer a global portrait of relations between state and civil society, the study of networks provides insights at the level of policy sectors. In other words, the network approach invites the investigator to

* Translated from French into English by Charmain Lévy.

be attentive to the possibility that within a given society, neo-corporatist networks and pluralist networks co-exist, albeit in different sectors.[5]

Consequently, an exhaustive analysis of Québec neo-corporatism would ideally call for a detailed study of public-policy networks responsible for the management of a large number of policy issues. Since undertaking such a study would require enormous resources, I rely on existing studies and it is therefore with caution that I offer a general overview of the evolution of state-civil society relations in Québec. In contrast to much of the policy network literature, I am less interested in the differences between sectors than in commonalities and evolution over time. Policy networks in Québec more and more frequently have adopted an inter-sectoral, neo-corporatist structure. Furthermore, until recently, neo-corporatism has evolved at the mercy of the balance of power in Québec society. However, I show that neo-corporatism is decreasingly influenced by Québec society and in return, more affected by external forces. Specifically, I argue that the combined effect of internationalization and the centralizing behaviour of the Canadian federal government could represent a not so negligible threat for Québec neo-corporatist networks.

These ideas are developed after a presentation of neo-corporatism in terms of public policy networks. This discussion is followed by a case study of agricultural policy development.

Neo-Corporatism and Public Policy Networks

The neo-corporatist and pluralist networks can be understood as the structuring of compromises between the span of formally represented ideas and the significance of the role granted to civil society during policy development. The vast and routine public consultations that characterize pluralist arrangements allow each and every individual and group who wishes to express its opinion to do it within official channels. However, these groups and individuals generally are reduced to advocacy because their numbers and the fragmentation of their ideas call for decisions to be made by governmental arbitration. In contrast, neo-corporatist networks allow intermediary groups to participate directly in the development of policies with decision-making being divided between the state and these groups. Naturally, to remain functional, such a structure can accommodate a limited number of actors and a range of ideas narrower than that commonly found within pluralist structures.[6]

Although we often limit ourselves to these distinctions between pluralist and neo-corporatist networks, the exact form of these arrangements, their success and their failures, diverges from one policy issue to another. Coleman insists on differences in the balance of power between the state and intermediary groups prevailing within networks to distinguish three types of neo-corporatist networks and three types of pluralist networks (Table 8.1).[7] In considering the temporal evolution of

TABLE 8.1

Typology of Public Policy Networks

STATE-CIVIL SOCIETY RELATIONS	PLURALIST NETWORKS	NEO-CORPORATIST NETWORKS
Balanced	Pressure Pluralism	Corporatism
Favours State	State-directed	State Corporatism
Favours Civil Society	Issue Network	Clientelism

Adapted from William D. Coleman, "Policy Communities and Policy Networks: Some Issues of Method," Paper presented during the Systems of Government Conference at the University of Pittsburgh in November 1997.

policy networks in Québec, these distinctions appear essential. In fact, the extent of the changes that a transformation from pluralism to neo-corporatism or vice-versa involves leads us to believe that this type of change is uncommon.[8] On the other hand, the transformation of a corporatist network into a clientelist network, that is, the transformation of a network that allows for the negotiation of policies into one that subordinates the state to the point of becoming dependent on a limited number of intermediary groups, appears to be more plausible.

According to Van Warden, what distinguishes neo-corporatism from pluralism is that the former always implies a relative delegation of authority towards civil society. While adhering to the idea that variations in the balance of power between the state and intermediary groups institute different kinds of neo-corporatism, Van Warden emphasizes the distinction between sectoral and inter-sectoral neo-corporatism. Whereas the first type of neo-corporatism often bestows a monopolistic status upon a particular group thereby depoliticizing policy development by simply legitimating the ideas of this group, inter-sectoral neo-corporatism requires dialogue and negotiation between several groups inasmuch as it deals with horizontal issues.[9] Indeed, as I argue below, the multiplication of horizontal issues could be responsible for a more or less general shift from sectoral to inter-sectoral neo-corporatism.[10]

If one acknowledges the possibility of inter-sectoral neo-corporatism, one must reject the idea that neo-corporatist networks inevitably install a reign of mainstream thought[11] that perpetuates the status quo and accepts that these networks can accommodate a plurality of ideas, some calling for important structural adjustments.[12] This understanding does not constitute the negation of the fact that arrangements of a pluralist nature are more open, but puts the alleged unenlightened and anti-democratic nature of neo-corporatist networks into perspective.[13] As the policy network literature suggests, the exact character of neo-corporatism varies according to the issue at stake and evolves over time.

Therefore, in theory, policy development in Québec can be under the rule of pluralist or neo-corporatist networks, depending on the specific issue at stake. However, networks are not static. According to well-established distinctions in policy network studies, they are susceptible to evolution over time, rarely between pluralism and neo-corporatism, but certainly within these categories. In the section that follows, I argue that from modest pluralism with a state-direction tendency during the Quiet Revolution, policy networks in several sectors in Québec adopted an inter-sectoral neo-corporatist form. Although encouraging in a context that values the shared management of public affairs between the state and civil society, neo-corporatist networks appear threatened by internationalization, as combined with the centralizing attitude of the federal government.

The Shift to Inter-Sectoral Neo-Corporatism

Traditional analyses of Québec neo-corporatism often concentrate on the large economic and social summits.[14] Even though they are fundamentally associated with the Parti Québécois,[15] since the 1970s several of these large conferences have brought together the government and leading intermediary groups of civil society in order to determine the foremost economic and social-policy orientations. Although these sessions are of interest, the network approach prompts the analyst to study rather the development of more precise policies than those orientations conceived during these events. In fact, the summit types of conferences are used more often to define a governmental agenda than to formulate precise policies.[16] When understood through the network approach, Québec neo-corporatism manifests itself more obviously at sectoral concertation meetings (in French, "tables de concertation"), which are numerous in Québec and institutionalized in a variety of ways. Less visible than the large summits, these sectoral concertation meetings are more concerned with precise issues, convening a more restricted range of intermediary groups around generally longer periods than the three- or four-day event of large conferences. In addition, the politicians assume only a monitoring role, leaving more room for civil servants who contribute substantially or fully participate in the deliberations, again depending on the issue. Although Québec policies are not formulated exclusively according to this concertation method, it is often followed regardless of which political party governs. Québec governments are inclined to reserve their arbitration only for special circumstances.[17]

Regarding one of the important economic summits of the 1976-1983 period, Brian Tanguay argues that the Québec institutional context did not favour the emergence of real neo-corporatist ties between the state and civil society. He argues that civil society was too fragmented, as much on the employers' as on the trade union side, and that the permanent secretary of socio-economic conferences granted an unduly substantial role to the state during the preparation of these conferences.[18] Although the summits of the 1990s invite us to review Tanguay's thesis, success is easier to attain at the sectoral level through concertation meetings than at large conferences. If Québec civil society, in global terms, appears to be fragmented, it is much less so at the sectoral level. In addition, the organization of concertation meetings is not the responsibility of a central agency, but of ministries accustomed to those groups active in their respective sectors. In a study of the Société québécoise du développement de la main d'œuvre, Rodney Haddow demonstrates that Québec possesses a favourable context for the establishment of neo-corporatist networks.[19] Montpetit produces a similar demonstration, by means of a study of an agri-environmental concertation meeting.[20]

In fact, if it is difficult for the Québec government to avoid the concertation-meetings method, it is because Québec civil society, at least within individual sectors, is solidly organized. I concur with Tanguay when he contends that the Conseil du patronat du Québec does not succeed in unifying the employers' discourse. Employers' associations within individual sectors, however, rarely are competing forces. Even the three large Québec trade unions—the Confédération des syndicats nationaux, the Fédération des travailleurs et des travailleuses du Québec and the Centrale des syndicats de l'enseignement du Québec—share, in a relatively harmonious way, the different sectors of economic activity. In addition, Québec is different from other Canadian provinces, in that it has an important number of sectors where regional and specialized groups are united thanks to so called peak associations.[21] The Fédération des femmes du Québec structures what is elsewhere in Canada considered a social movement often dependent on the spontaneity of the masses. The Union québécoise pour la protection de la nature presents a second example of such a structure, but in an entirely different sector: the environment. Last, the law bestows responsibilities on certain professions that demand an association possessing the attributes of a professional bureaucracy. The Fédération des médecins omnipraticiens du Québec and la Fédération des médecins specialistes du Québec, for example, both play official roles in the Medicare system.[22] As civil society contains such organizations in several sectors, the emergence of neo-corporatist networks that share the management of public affairs between state and civil society actors becomes plausible.

Although the network approach calls on us to take into consideration the differences among sectors of state activity, a series of studies allows us to observe the evolution of important tendencies in terms of state-civil society relations in Québec. Archibald argues that in the 1960s the state was not only "the issuing point in all social relationships," it also guided and reached individuals and groups "to such an extent that they were an integral part of the governmental apparatus." He adds that it is the state that "channelled individuals and groups that could decide either to remain uninfluenced or to integrate themselves into the decision making processes."[23] Archibald's thesis is controversial, but is based on convincing evidence that state development in the 1960s left a weak civil society. The state needed expertise and thus massively hired qualified personnel from civil society.[24] This certainly prompted the emergence of state-directed or state corporatist networks (see Table 8.1), depending on the exact consequences of state development on civil society for each sector. Where state development did leave a fragmented civil society, the latter played a marginal role in policy formulation in relation to state experts (state-directed network). Where fragmentation could be avoided, the state sometimes co-opted the leaders of weakened civil society associations to facilitate reaching previously decided goals (state corporatism).

One thing is clear, civil society regained its vitality at the beginning of the 1970s. Indeed, the 1970s connote the beginning of a confrontational relationship, common in pressure pluralist networks, between the labour movement and the Québec state.[25] It is partially in reaction to this type of pluralism that the Parti Québécois, which won the provincial elections in 1976, promised to institutionalize a genuine neo-corporatist relation between the state, trade unions and employers. This promise was ambitious because, as Tanguay emphasizes, the Québec institutional context is not auspicious for the establishment of such a macro-economic tripartite concertation mechanism. If the results were not those expected, this initiative still has contributed to the strengthening of civil society and to the embeddedness of some neo-corporatist networks at the sectoral level. Denis and Denis contend that Bourassa's return to power in 1985 did not end concertation between workers and the Québec state. They particularly emphasize that "it is difficult not to be surprised with the new participation of trade unions in initiatives of regional development in concertation with employers, the government and other economic partners."[26]

In the 1990s, neo-corporatist networks became decreasingly sectoral and thus increasingly inter-sectoral. On the one hand, observers claim that employers' groups and trade unions are interested in a wider range of issues. In fact, Denis and Denis comment on "the more frequent positioning of the trade union movement in coalition with representative organizations of employers around issues such as the environment, monetary policy, indigenous affairs, poverty, etc."[27] On the other hand, participation in policy development is expanded to a larger number of groups whose status varies. To illustrate, the Conférence au sommet de Québec in 1982 essentially accommodated well-established social organizations, among which we find the trade unions, the Conseil du partronat du Québec, co-operatives, and consumer associations.[28] In addition to welcoming traditional organizations, the economic summit in 1996 opened its doors to community organizations, to organizations that represent the para-public sector (i.e., Centres locaux de services sociaux et communautaires, the CLSCs) as well as to individual entrepreneurs. We shall see in the following section that this tendency is also observed in sectoral concertation meetings.

Three hypotheses can be advanced to explain the evolution of Québec neo-corporatist networks towards inter-sectoralism. First, the erosion of citizens' confidence in the traditional employer, trade union, and state elites encourages the expansion of concertation practices to groups that previously were left out, or to respected individuals. Among the neglected we find women's, ecological, youth, and senior citizens' groups, which are now more generally associated with the formulation of policies. Concurrently, several entrepreneurs enjoyed sufficient credibility for policy makers to consider as legitimate their participation, as individuals, in policy development.[29] Second, several problems previously dealt with in a sectoral manner are now considered horizontal issues, suitably the object of discussions within an increasing number of forums. The environment is the ultimate horizontal issue; that is to say, it should concern decision-makers in such diverse sectors as fisheries, agriculture, regional development, international policy, etc.[30] Horizontality, the logic goes, justifies the invitation of environmental groups to participate in more policy networks. Although the environment is the ultimate horizontal issue, problems of land use planning, transportation, commerce, health, etc. are often considered as belonging to this category of issues as well. Third, the period of budgetary austerity and reduction of services provided by the Québec government that began in the 1980s fostered the development of community organizations to the point that today we commonly speak of a social economy. Often dependent on favourable public policy, it is in the interest of these community organizations to become involved in policy development.

Despite their increasingly inter-sectoral nature, during the 1990s Québec neo-corporatist networks have been, surprisingly, the objects of recurrent criticisms.[31] We should be astonished with this situation because simultaneously in Western countries, the participation of civil society in the management of public affairs is being glorified through a discourse on governance. According to this discourse, the crisis of confidence in the state requires that the latter more stringently engage civil society in the formulation of public policy. The management of public affairs, it is argued, should no longer fall only within the competence of the state. The complementarities of state and intermediary groups' resources, according to a growing literature, carry a promising potential in terms of performance.[32] According to Pierre and Peters, "If they are to be successful in governing, democracies will have to devise means of accommodating more continuous forms of participation while still being able to supply the needed direction to society."[33] In short, the establishment of networks stringently associating civil society with policy development suggested by this discourse on governance closely resembles what is now common practice in Québec.

However, there is no consensus concerning the discourse on governance. Some see it as a way to legitimate the dismantling of the state.[34] Others, more cautious, consider governance, or the development of public policy networks, to be a political regulation mechanism that provides an alternative both to market and hierarchy. Like market and hierarchy, governance can entail certain difficulties, among which we find the indispensable maintenance of a relationship of mutual trust among actors.[35] In fact, Québec neo-corporatist networks are not always functional, some establishing a balance of power that does not inspire trust. No analyst, however, questions the importance of sharing responsibility between the state and civil society over policy development. Since Québec neo-corporatist networks allow for the institutionalization of this type of sharing better than any other form of network, abandoning them would seem a strange decision.

Nevertheless, the threat to Québec neo-corporatist networks comes not only from their critics. In fact, the context of internationalization, coupled with an apparent aspiration of the federal government to more directly serve citizens, may erode the ties that unite Québec state and civil society. Two opposing theses confront each other over the relationship between internationalization and Canadian federalism. The first one is optimistic and states that the federal and provincial governments perceive the integration of markets as a challenge that they must solve together. Having this common cause, the confrontation between the federal and provincial levels should transform into more co-operation.[36] The second, more pessimistic, asserts that the internationalization of policy issues that were previously domestic adds to the federal government's spending power to allow for more federal interventions in areas under provincial jurisdiction. Arguing that the principle of indivisibility of Canadian foreign affairs should have precedence over the constitutional responsibilities of the provinces, the federal government feels authorized to develop policies dealing with provincial issues when these are the objects of international discussions.[37] The refusal of the federal government to offer the Québec government a place at the Summit of the Americas adds credibility to this latter theory.

The desire of the federal government to become more directly visible to Canadians, and especially since the 1995 referendum to Québec citizens, adds to internationalization. In fact, what Donald Smiley has called executive federalism, that is, the negotiation of policies between members of the federal and provincial executives,[38] appears to be in the process of being replaced by more direct relationship between the federal state and Canadian civil society. In short, the development of federal policies would be less the product of inter-governmental negotiations and more the result of direct consultation with citizens. In a context of internationalization where the federal government further intervenes in areas of provincial jurisdiction, this trend marginalizes the Québec state. There is certainly a danger that interest groups lose interest in Québec neo-corporatist networks in favour of stronger ties with the federal state.

In the next section, I will attempt to illustrate these developments with an analysis of the agricultural sector, sectoral analyses being more adapted to the network approach. And the agricultural sector appears to be fertile ground for this kind of analysis. First, studies on the structure of relations between the state and civil society leave no doubt concerning the neo-corporatist nature of the networks that tie the Québec state and farmers.[39] Second, a domestic issue until the middle of the 1980s, agriculture has since become the object of intense international negotiations.

The Agricultural Neo-Corporatist Network

In 1972, the Bourassa government adopted the Loi des producteurs agricoles. This law contained three main provisions: first, it defined, in a precise fashion, what is a farmer; second, it required that only one association, endowed with given structural characteristics, be assigned to represent farmers; finally, it required that all Québec farmers participate in the financing of this association (Rand formula).[40] This law was requested by the Union des cultivateurs catholiques (UCC), which became the Union des producteurs agricoles (UPA) a few weeks before the adoption of the law. Fortunately, the structure of the UPA, a peak association comprising regional and specialized organizations, perfectly met the criteria defined in the law. Although the referendum required before the implementation of the Rand formula had mobilized important resources, the UPA had no difficulty fulfilling the legal obligations to become the official organization representing Québec farmers.

The agricultural neo-corporatist network precedes the adoption of this law, because the UCC was strongly tied to the Québec state during the Quiet Revolution. The law, nevertheless, solidified certain prerequisites of the institutionalization of a neo-corporatist sectoral network that does not place civil society in an unfavourable situation in relation to the state. First, the definition of a farmer in some ways outlines the boundary of the sector or, in other words, it defines the shape of the neo-corporatist network in such a way that the latter enjoys maximal cohesion. Second, the demand for a single representative association internally confines public policy debates—a situation that depoliticizes policy development.[41] However, the requirement to include the specialized and regional organizations within the peak association structure ensures the occurrence of internal debates. Third, the required contribution confers resources on the official association to acquire an expertise that allows it to surpass advocacy and participate directly in the development of public policy.

Further institutionalized, sectoral neo-corporatism in agriculture has certainly contributed to the consolidation and rapid development of some farm policies in the 1970s. Although a judicial framework to establish marketing arrangements for agricultural commodities has existed since 1956, the procedures were simplified after 1972, and arrangements quickly multiplied under the pressure exercised by UPA.[42] In 1975, the Québec government adopted a law outlining the general principles of income stabilization, an insurance against falling farm revenues administered jointly by the Ministry of Agriculture and UPA.[43] Québec is the only province that has its own income stabilization policy in agriculture.[44]

Before long, horizontal issues, requiring the UPA to discuss and negotiate policy development with civil society groups belonging to other sectors and with ministries other than that of agriculture, added to the sectoral issues. In other words, the dialogue and negotiation, typical of inter-sectoral, neo-corporatist networks, quickly politicized policy development in the agricultural sector. Regional development, agricultural zoning, and environment protection were among these horizontal issues that appeared on the political agenda of the 1970s.[45]

The inter-sectoral nature of the neo-corporatist agricultural network grew in importance at the beginning of the 1990s, thanks to the development of an industry wide approach (l'approche filière). This approach was officially introduced in 1992 at the Sommet sur l'agriculture québécoise and is based on the idea that concertation in the sector also should include actors on both sides of the farm gate. The industry-wide approach encourages the implementation of concertation meetings for each type of production. Although these groups have enough leeway to organize themselves as they see fit, they must include, as a minimum, representatives from the processing, production, and distribution industries as well as from the state. Their mandate consists in providing each commodity with a strategy to gain market shares. The follow-up of the proceedings of these meetings is guaranteed by a senior association, the Filière agro-alimentaire, composed of representatives from UPA, the Coopérative fédérée du Québec, the Association des manufacturiers de produits alimentaires du Québec, the Conseil canadien de la distribution alimentaire, the Association des détaillants en alimentation du Québec, the Corporation de développement agroalimentaire-forêt du Centre du Québec, and the agriculture ministry. The 25 industry-wide groups that presently exist are not all equally functional,[46] but are evidence of a will to expand the boundaries of the neo-corporatist agricultural network beyond those defined under the 1972 Loi sur les producteurs agricoles. The regional agri-food concertation tables are also a confirmation of this desire.

This change from sectoral to inter-sectoral practices also coincides with a relative erosion of the confidence in the UPA expressed by a number of farmers. In 1972, Québec agriculture still was predominantly family-run, but quickly found itself in the midst of a wave of restructuring around entrepreneurs who control input provision, breeding, processing, and distribution, especially in the hog and poultry sectors. Occasionally, these entrepreneurs did not hesitate to defy the UPA's authority over the agricultural sector, confrontations that the industry-wide approach now attempts to supersede with wider networking.

Canadian Federalism and the Internationalization of Agriculture

This dynamic of the Québec neo-corporatist network is no doubt affected, if not compromised, by the combined effect of Canadian federalism and of internationalization. Unencumbered by international trade discussions until 1986, agriculture was then integrated into the Uruguay Round of the General Agreement on Tariffs and Trade (GATT). After the creation of the World Trade Organization (WTO) in 1994, international attention focusing on agricultural trade was intensified until November 1999, the date of the famous Seattle meeting. These international events could constitute opportunities for the Canadian federal government to increase its influence in the agricultural sector. Even though agriculture is a shared jurisdiction according to the Canadian Constitution Act, it is, de facto, a very important area of responsibility for the provinces. In the past, the federal government has respected this fact, only more recently using its international prerogatives to increase its visibility in agriculture. A comparison, presented below, of the definition processes of Canadian trade positions in agriculture for the negotiations of the Uruguay Round and the Seattle ministerial meeting illustrates this change in attitude. This comparison also illustrates, in a convincing fashion, the transformation of the Québec neo-corporatist agricultural network that can be encouraged by the behaviour of the federal government, thanks to internationalization. This comparison is based on a series of confidential interviews with directly implicated individuals. These interviews were conducted in Québec and Ottawa during the winter of 2000.

Executive federalism was used in the 1980s to define the Canadian position on agricultural trade in regard to the Uruguay Round. That is, the Canadian position was essentially the product of inter-governmental negotiations. In brief, this position proposes the end of government subsidies believed to distort international agricultural markets, while maintaining the GATT's Article XI that protects the systems of supply management by permitting importation quotas. Some would call schismatic a position that attempts to reconcile the interests of cereal producers in the West and dairy farmers in the East. In any case, it was not easy to obtain the consent of the ministers from western Canada, who view the pan-Canadian distribution of dairy quotas as unfair, and those from eastern Canada, who demand a better share of agricultural subsidies.

Beyond the difficulty of reaching an agreement, what is astonishing is that the conservation of the GATT Article XI was an important element of the Canadian position. Indeed, at the end of the 1980s the climate was one of free trade as much in Québec as in Ottawa. The Progressive Conservative Party in Ottawa and the Parti liberal du Québec both were strongly in favour of free trade. In fact, the favourable inclination towards the GATT's Article XI in the Canadian position is essentially attributable to the neo-corporatist network that shapes the relations between the Québec state and the UPA. Several meetings between the UPA and the Québec government actually preceded the inter-governmental negotiations of the Canadian position.[47] A Québec civil servant emphasized the importance of these meetings arguing, "the relationship between the UPA and the Ministry of Agriculture was always strong and there was nothing that really occurred in terms of agricultural policy without the UPA being well informed." Creating difficulties in the way of state unilateralism, this neo-corporatist network served to inform the Québec government about farmers' concerns regarding supply management (they also made the UPA aware of the importance of free trade for certain activities). Thus armed with this basic information, the Québec government began negotiations with other provinces and with the federal government to define the agricultural trade position for the Uruguay Round. Nevertheless, the UPA, which did not completely trust executive federalism, did not neglect to pressure members of Parliament.[48]

Once the Uruguay Round had ended, and the protection offered by the GATT's Article XI had disappeared, despite Canada's position, the federal government's approach to international negotiations in agriculture was considerably modified: executive federalism was shelved, a decision which affected the Canadian position in view of the Seattle ministerial meeting. In fact, the government position for Seattle was less global, more segmented around particular issues. For example, an effort was made not to tie the export subsidy issue, one of the touchstones of the Canadian position at Seattle, to the issue of tariffs on imports replacing quotas as a mechanism to protect supply management. During the Uruguay Round, the federal negotiators also learned that a little flexibility in their position could influence the perception of an outcome otherwise easily perceived as a failure. The Canadian position was made possible thanks to the substitution of traditional mechanisms of executive federalism with more direct consultation between civil society and the federal state.

More precisely speaking, I do not contend that inter-governmental negotiations were altogether eliminated in favour of public consultations. Inter-governmental negotiations did indeed occur. However, it seems apparent that the relative importance of these negotiations has been reduced since the conclusion of the Uruguay Round in favour of more direct relations between the federal state and civil society. Already in 1988, in the middle of the Uruguay Round, the federal government felt the need to incorporate the recommendations of civil society actors on international trade. The Sectoral Advisory Groups on International Trade (SAGIT) were created to this end. The appointments to SAGIT are left to the discretion of the minister and the work of these committees takes place behind closed doors, a situation that raises important questions of representation and transparency. Nonetheless, one can plausibly suppose that this manner of functioning facilitates discussions compared to those occurring in inter-governmental forums and this even though in agriculture the main intermediary groups, including UPA, participate in the SAGIT. For example, a participant emphasized that Alberta's Cattlemen Association was not concerned with global issues such as the pan-Canadian distribution of dairy quotas, but provinces are. To avoid contentious global issues such as this, it is not surprising that the federal government gradually conceded more importance to these direct relations with civil society at the expense of inter-governmental negotiations. Naturally, this change in the attitude of the federal government made possible the more flexible and segmented negotiating position on agricultural trade.

Moreover, the relationship between the federal government and civil society after the Uruguay Round was not confined to SAGIT. After 1995, information and education meetings as well as consultation multiplied. Several federal civil servants have emphasized that the UPA is present and very active during these meetings. Naturally, these direct ties between the federal state and the UPA on international trade put into perspective those between the organization and the Québec state. During an interview, a UPA official confirmed that after the Uruguay Round the Québec state became a kind of insurance policy, an actor on whom the organization could eventually rely in case something goes wrong with the federal government. This situation is, to say the least, distant from the neo-corporatist relationship the UPA has maintained with the Québec government before and during the inter-governmental negotiation of the Canadian position for the Uruguay Round.[49]

In short, internationalization has provided an opportunity for the federal government to increase its importance in a sector where the provinces have exercised enormous responsibility. In the case of Québec, this situation has proportionately diminished the importance that farmers have traditionally accorded to their relations with the provincial state. In other words, the combined effect of internationalization and of the centralizing behaviour of Ottawa has undermined the agricultural neo-corporatist policy network that, since the Quiet Revolution, has exercised an important influence on the development of Québec's policies in this sector. Given these circumstances, we should not be surprised that one of the main internal criticisms of the industry-wide approach concerns the role of the Québec state, viewed by some as too substantial.[50] Under these circumstances, a drift of the neo-corporatist network towards clientelism is apprehensible.

Conclusion

In Québec, neo-corporatist networks often structure the relationship between the state and civil society, that is, policy development occurs through dialogues and negotiations between intermediary groups and the state. This indeed does not imply that the relation between the Québec state and civil society is monolithic; important differences may exist from one sector to another, especially in terms of the balance of power between actors and in inter-sectoral terms. Moreover, such differences also characterize the evolution of networks in time. Public policy networks in Québec, considered more sectoral and sometimes even state-directed during the Quiet Revolution, have evolved towards a better equilibrium in the balance of power between the state and civil society and have become more inter-sectoral. In several sectors, and especially in that of agriculture, neo-corporatist networks have become institutionalized.

Québec neo-corporatist networks are considered an institutional choice for sharing responsibilities for the management of public affairs between the state and civil society. Neo-corporatist networks accord a participant role to intermediary organizations in civil society, in contrast to pluralist networks that confine these organizations into an advocacy role. Neo-corporatist networks obviously have their shortcomings, notably the narrower range of ideas they can accommodate. I have argued nevertheless that neo-corporatism is an appropriate institutional choice in a context where governance appears to call for a greater participation of civil society in the management of public affairs.

One thing is certain, it should be up to Québec society to evaluate the benefits and the costs of neo-corporatist networks and to choose whether or not to preserve them. However, what this chapter illustrates is that the institutional choice of neo-corporatism decreasingly belongs to Québec society. As demonstrated in the analysis of the neo-corporatist agricultural network, internationalization combined with the centralizing attitude of Ottawa to destabilize the partnership that existed between the Québec state and intermediary groups. This may place before Québec society a form of governance that it has not chosen, and that may not even be desirable if it should take the form of clientelism, a disquieting situation in the agricultural sector.

Notes

The author would like to thank Alain-G. Gagnon and Paul André Comeau for their comments on the original version of this text.

1. Gerhard Lehmbruch and Philippe Schmitter, eds., *Patterns of Corporatist Policy-Making* (London: Sage, 1982).

2. On American pluralism see David R. Truman, *The Governmental Process: Political Interests and Public Opinion* (New York: Knopf, 1964). On neo-pluralism see Charles E. Lindblom, *Politics and Markets: The World's Political Economic Systems* (New York: Basic Books, 1977).

3. William D. Coleman and Grace Skogstad, eds., *Policy Communities and Public Policy in Canada: A Structural Approach* (Scarborough, ON: Copp Clark Pitman, 1990).

4. Brian A. Tanguay, "Concerted Action in Québec, 1976-1983: Dialogue of the Deaf," in Alain-G. Gagnon, *Québec: State and Society* (Agincourt: Methuen, 1984); Josée Lamoureux, "La concertation: perspectives théoriques sous l'angle du néo-corporatisme," Cahiers du CRISES no. 9607, 1996; Clinton Archibald, *Un Québec corporatiste?* (Hull: édition Asticou, 1983).

5. The number of ideal types of networks varies from one author to another.

6. On the distinction between neo-corporatism and pluralism see Lamoureux, "Concertation," 4-5.

7. William D. Coleman, "Policy Communities and Policy Networks: Some Issues of Method," paper presented at the Systems of Government Conference, University of Pittsburgh, November 1997.

8. This is what tends to confirm the research of Hugh Compston, "The End of National Policy Concertation? Western Europe Since the Single European Act," *Journal of European Public Policy* 5, 3 (1998): 507-26. However, this thesis is refuted by Wolfgang Streeck, "From National Corporatism to Transnational Pluralism: European Interest Politics and the Single Market," in Tiziano Treu, ed., *Participation in Public Policy-Making: The Role of Trade Unions and Employers' Associations* (Berlin: Walter de Gruyter, 1992), 97-126. A more nuanced position is presented by William D. Coleman and Anthony Perl, "Internationalized Policy Environments and Policy Network Analysis," *Political Studies* 47 (1999): 691-709.

9. Frans Van Waarden, "Dimensions and Types of Policy Networks," *European Journal of Political Research* 21 (1992): 29-52. Others use the concept of multipartite neo-corporatism rather than that of inter-sectoral neo-corporatism. See Éric Montpetit and William D. Coleman, "Policy Communities and Policy Divergence in Canada: Agro-Environmental Policy Development in Québec and Ontario," *Revue canadienne de science politique* 32, 4 (1999): 691-714.

10. Jacques Bourgault, ed., *L'Horizontalité*, edition publique (Québec: Presses de l'Université du Laval, 2002).

11. Translator's note: This is a rough translation of the concept *"pensée unique"* elaborated in the late 1990s by the editors and writers of the French monthly newspaper *Le Monde Diplomatique*.

12. This idea has been developed in Éric Montpetit, "Corporatisme québécois et performance des gouvernants: analyse comparative des politiques environnementales en agricultural," *Politique et Sociétés* 18, 3 (1999): 79-98. For a slightly different point of view see Hans Th. A. Bressers and Laurence J. O'Toole, Jr., "The Selection of Policy Instruments: a Network-based Perspective," *Journal of Public Policy* 18, 3 (1998): 213-39.

13. Henri Lamoureux, *Les dérives de la démocratie: questions à la société civile québécoise* (Montréal: VLB éditeur, 1999); Jean-Luc Migué, *Étatisme et Déclin du Québec: Bilan de la Révolution tranquille* (Montréal: Les Éditions Varia, 1998).

14. Tanguay, "Concerted Action in Québec, 1976-1983."

15. Archibald, *Un Québec corporatiste?*

16. Éric Montpetit, "Corporatisme québécois et Sommet du Québec et de la jeunesse," *Options politiques* 21, 5 (2000): 58-61.

17. The municipal amalgamation issue comes to mind.

18. Tanguay, "Concerted Action in Québec, 1976-1983."

19. Rodney Haddow, "Reforming Labour-Market Policy Governance: The Québec Experience," *Canadian Public Administration* 41, 3 (1998): 343-68. See also, Andrew F. Johnson, "Towards a Renewed Concertation in Québec: La Société québécoise de développement de la main-d'œuvre," in Andrew Sharpe and Rodney Haddow, *Social Partnership for Training: Canada's Experiment with Labour Force Development Boards* (Kingston: School of Policy Studies, 1997).

20. Éric Montpetit, "Corporatisme québécois et performance des gouvernants: analyse comparative des politiques environnementales en agricultural," *Politique et Sociétés* 18, 3 (1999): 79-98.

21. Rand Dyck, *Provincial Politics in Canada: Towards the Turn of the Century*, 3rd ed. (Scarborough, ON: Prentice Hall, 1996).

22. William D. Coleman, "Le nationalisme, les intermédiaires et l'intégration politique canadienne," *Politique et Sociétés* 28 (1995): 31-52.

23. Clinton Archibald, *Un Québec corporatiste?* (Hull: Édition Asticou, 1983), 181.

24. On the vitality of pre-Quiet Revolution civil society see Luc Turgeon, "La grande absente: La société civile au cœur des changements de la Révolution tranquille," *Globe: Revue internationale d'études québécoises* 2, 1 (1999): 35-56.

25. Roch Denis and Serge Denis, "L'action politique des syndicates québécois de la révolution tranquille à au'jourd'hui," in Alain-G. Gagnon, *Québec: État et société* (Montréal: Québec/Amérique, 1994), 161-62.

26. Denis and Denis, "L'action politique des syndicates," 173.

27. Ibid., 173.

28. Tanguay, "Concerted Action in Quebec, 1976-1983," 377.

29. At the 1996 Economic Summit, Lucien Bouchard invited personal guests, including Laurent Beaudoin, the Bombardier CEO. On this issue, see also Lamoureux, "Concertation," 5.

30. Mark Winfield, "The Ultimate Horizontal Issue: The Environmental Policy Experiences of Alberta and Ontario," *Canadian Journal of Political Science* 27 (1994): 129-52.

31. See Lamoureux, *Les dérives de la démocratie*; Migué, *Étatisme et déclin du Québec*.

32. Linda Weiss, *The Myth of the Powerless State* (Ithaca: Cornell University Press, 1998).

33. Jon Pierre and B. Guy Peters, *Governance, Politics and the State* (New York: St. Martin's Press, 2000), 4.

34. Bernard Cassen, "Le piège de la gouvernance," *Le Monde Diplomatique*, June 2001.

35. R.A.W. Rhodes, "The New Governance: Governing Without Government," *Political Studies* 44 (1996): 652-67.

36. Elizabeth Moore and Grace Skogstad, "Food for Thought: Food Inspection and Renewed Federalism," in Leslie A. Pal, ed., *How Ottawa Spends 1998-99/Balancing Act: the Post Deficit Mandate* (Toronto: Oxford University Press, 1998); Grace Skogstad, "Agricultural Policy," in G. Bruce Doern, Leslie A. Pal, and Brian W. Tomlin, eds., *Border Crossings: The Internationalization of Canadian Public Policy* (Toronto: Oxford University Press, 1996).

37. Ministère des Relations internationales, *Le Québec dans un ensemble international en mutation* (Québec: Gouvernement du Québec, 2001).

38. D.V. Smiley, *The Federal Condition in Canada* (Toronto: McGraw-Hill Ryerson, 1987).

39. Grace Skogstad, "The Farm Policy Community and Public Policy in Ontario and Québec," in Coleman and Skogstad, *Policy Communities and Public Policy in Canada*.

40. Jean-Pierre Kesteman in collaboration with Guy Boisclair and Jean-Marc Kirouac, *Histoire du syndicalisme agricole au Québec: UCC-UPA 1924-1984* (Montréal: Boréal Express, 1984), 270.

41. See Van Warden, "Dimensions and Types of Policy Networks."

42. Kesteman, *Histoire du syndicalisme agricole au Québec*, 289-90.

43. Ibid., 296-97.

44. However, this policy does not cover all commodities.

45. Kesteman, *Histoire du syndicalisme agricole au Québec*, 283; Montpetit, "Corporatisme québécois et performance des gouvernants"; Montpetit and Coleman, "Policy Communities and Policy Divergence in Canada."

46. Filière Agroalimentaire, *Bilan des Filières 1998* (Québec: ministère de l'Agricultural des Pêcheries et de l'Alimentation du Québec, 1999).

47. This conforms to the process of provincial participation in international trade negotiations described by Skogstad, "Agricultural Policy," 158.

48. Skogstad, "The Farm Policy Community," 83.

49. This contrasts with the process of provincial participation in international trade negotiations described by Skogstad, "Agricultural Policy," 158.

50. Filière Agroalimentaire, *Bilan des Filières*.

9

Managerial Innovation and the Québec Central Agencies

CHRISTIAN ROUILLARD*

Introduction

The managerial reform to which the Québec public sector has committed itself through its project "Pour de meilleurs services aux citoyens: un nouveau cadre de gestion pour la fonction publique" is not merely a managerial exercise in the reorganization of the state.[1] As in all important planned organizational changes, it, too, implies an inclination towards symbolic orientation and identity construction that goes beyond the quest for efficiency of providing services; that questions the ability of the state of Québec to intervene and regulate through the redefinition of its organizational resources, especially in view of its previous basis for legitimacy. This managerial innovation which was officially enacted by the Loi sur l'administration publique (adopted in May 2000), specifically allows for the modernization of the Québec administrative apparatus—considered the victim of the structural rigidity of the old bureaucracy—while ensuring the shift from a management based on respect for processes to a management based on results.

This shift leads us to the question of whether this new type of particularly ambitious managerial framework, accountable to the new public management, renders the Québec public administration—understood as a heterogeneous and complex set of institutions, organizations, activities, and people—redundant for purposes of managerial innovation. To what extent does this new managerial framework,

* Translated from French into English by Charmain Lévy.

clearly described in the Loi sur l'administration publique, modify the relationship between the Treasury Board and the public-sector organizations at which it is aimed (departments and financial organizations)? Beyond this, are the basic key elements that compose this new managerial framework placed in a perspective of differentiated governance?

In this chapter we will develop our argument across four distinct sections. The first presents the context and origins of this modernization project of the Québec administrative apparatus. The second part is based on a critical analysis of the principal elements of the new managerial framework in light of the questions that were presented in the Introduction. The third section continues the analysis while taking into account the strain between the horizontal pretension and the vertical sacralization that implicitly renews the new managerial framework. The last section attempts to reconcile observations on managerial innovation with those on governance, as it analyzes the converging and diverging elements as well as the complementarity between this administrative framework and differentiated governance.

To briefly summarize the argument in this chapter, the new managerial framework is neither distinctive nor progressive despite what some of its apologists may suggest. In addition, despite the assertions of new public management in terms of the decentralization and empowerment, it has not succeeded in modifying the traditional asymmetric relationship between the Treasury Board and the organizations at which the Loi sur l'administration publique was aimed. Furthermore, the internal contradictions of the new managerial framework are potential sources of perverse effects as much as they are factors that may reduce the collective participation on which is based all planned organizational change. In fact, I argue that as sensitive as it may appear, the balance between the new public management and governance is, on the contrary, shaky to say the least.

Context and Origins of the Modernization of the Québec State; or, The Need to Go Beyond the Weberian Administrative Environment

Despite repeated criticisms of the bureaucratic nature of the complex organizations that constitute Québec public administration—that more often than not are reduced to a simplistic caricature of the Weberian model—since the beginning of the 1980s it has been characterized by a manifest resolution to consent to a serious systematic change. This has been demonstrated, among other examples of structuring laws, by the adoption of the Loi sur la fonction publique in 1983 (which aimed at the accountability of employees, citizens' services, and the development of human resources), by the Loi sur l'imputabilité des sous-ministres et dirigeants d'organismes in 1994, and more recently, by the Loi sur l'administration publique that translated into a legislative framework the policy statement, "Pour de meilleurs services aux citoyens: un nouveau cadre de gestion pour la fonction publique," as well as internal and external deliberations that were integrated.

These various legislative initiatives rooted in the new public management movement were aimed at increasing the efficiency and efficacy of the Québec public sector and, hence, of performance through the pursuit of an increased external administrative accountability (1) of upper-level civil servants, (2) of a renewed participation and accountability of all civil servants, and (3) overstepping the traditional civic identity with one of clients, consumers, and taxpayers, all intricately merged with that of the citizen. Out of a concern to emphasize the quality of public services, this managerial reformism stresses that:

> [T]he chief mission of the state is to assure that citizens have access to and receive public services of the utmost quality within the best price range. The reform should lead to a modern administrative apparatus that is capable of adapting itself to challenges in the short and long term and that is focussed on the expectations and needs of diverse sectors of society.[2]

The contemporary Québec state is above all understood as a provider of public services, and thus, all references to its duty as a designer of policies are completely deleted. This more modern administrative apparatus appears to be quasi-reactionary because it is concerned about responding to societal expectations and needs, and as such it pursues a mysterious and still-undefined equilibrium between the cost and quality of a given service. The Québec reform project is supported by macro-economical and middle-level political contexts that refer to the integration of national economies, which is obviously tied to the increase in international commercial exchanges, to fiscal consolidation, and to opportunities created by recent developments in new information and communication technologies, needed to facilitate the integration of the Québec economy into the new global economy. As such, this reform project should give way to a new managerial framework, new laws, rules, regulations, and instructions that together would increase the institutional responsiveness of the Québec public administration.[3]

The Best Services for the Citizens: The Endless Search for the Congruence between Public and Private Management

The Loi sur l'administration publique, which is expected to lead the entire Québec public sector towards systematic modernization, favours, as a basis of the reform, management by results, which is elaborated along the following lines. The normative and regulative context in and through which the Québec public service proceeds would be alleviated. A diffusion supported by performance agreements and increased individual and organizational accountability would be created. Means of action and particular frameworks were retained.[4] More notably:

- a public engagement on quality of services by each department and organization;

- the creation of a strategic multi-year plan by each department and organization;

- the publication of a yearly expenditure management plan by each department and organization;

- the reformulation of each department and organization yearly report into a yearly management report;

- the reduction of monitoring activities previously performed by central agencies.

As may be implicitly suggested, management based strictly on results rests on narrowly defined goals, sufficiently specific to be measurable. According to this perspective traditional monitoring activities characteristic of the hierarchical Weberian model are inefficient and must make way for performance indicators in which the quantitative overrides the qualitative. The progressive reduction of traditional monitoring considered necessary until now to guarantee the legality and the congruence of managerial decisions and actions, have become factors of rigidity and obstruction, as much inhibitory to managers' empowerment and to the de-bureaucratization of departments and organizations. The implementation of the new managerial framework, which is a presumed source for empowering organizational and managerial intelligence, entirely depends on the creation of statistical instruments for output and performance evaluation. As innovative as this new managerial framework claims to be, we must acknowledge that it is based on a strictly positivist[5] conception of evaluation and monitoring activities. It is nevertheless a long-time victim of its high epistemological claims, as this policy statement seems implicitly to recognize in its own way:

> Experience demonstrates that it is not easy to define, for each administrative unit, sufficiently precise and measurable goals to serve the supervision and accountability frame. It is equally not easy to implement administration statistics that are required to measure whether goals have been reached or not. As long as these instruments have not

been implemented and have not been validated by the skew of experience, it would be presumptuous to speak of a management really led by results.[6]

Though it builds, overall, on a favourable interpretation of *The Next Steps* experience in the United Kingdom, this policy statement nevertheless recognizes that such a managerial framework, such an institutional change, cannot be carried out by a simple decree nor by mere voluntarism, and as such that a period of approximately five years is needed (half of what was required in the British experience) to allow for the complete and successful implementation of this managerial framework. The strategic actors central to this implementation are the parliamentarians, the minister, the deputy minister, the organization's leader, and of course, the public servants. As a sad irony, the only one who is absent is the citizen, he for whom and in the name of whom the first phase of the modernization of the Québec public sector is undertaken.

Supposedly empowered by the exceptional information found in the management report—more descriptive than the obsolete yearly report,—the parliamentarians' monitoring of senior public servants, which represents political power over administrative power, should increase through the implementation of the new managerial framework. While arguing that the constitutional principle of individual ministerial responsibility should be renewed, the minister should now approve the strategic plan of his administrative unit and conclude the performance and accountability agreements with the managers, as he should determine the management agreement of the aforementioned unit with the Treasury Board.

Although this new managerial framework is accountable to the new public management, which among other features crystallizes the dichotomy that opposes the political to the administrative, the latter seems to be immersed in relative confusion because, as the new ministerial responsibilities suggest—especially in terms of the negotiation of a management agreement and that of the performance and accountability agreement—the political actor (who is the minister in a British parliamentary system) becomes a managerial actor. This new managerial framework seems to distance itself from the famous call to managerial empowerment of the Glassco Commission, *Let the Managers Manage*.[7] This confusing, if not contradictory, rhetoric of the managerial framework implies the concomitant growth of political monitoring and managerial autonomy and is not intrinsic to Québec. It is rather an unclaimed, but perennial, characteristic of new public management obedience prescriptions implemented in many countries that have gone through administrative reforms.[8] In addition, without denying the customarily required competencies in ministers, one can question the capacity of the minister to appropriate such proto-managerial responsibilities. Contrary to what the new managerial framework is looking for, the absence of such a capacity can occur only through a decrease in political control over the administration, which is the only agent possessing the power that allows it to master these new political and managerial relationships.

Although he may be a pivotal actor of the progressive implementation of the new managerial framework, the deputy minister does not really take on new duties and responsibilities, other than to devote more of his time to monitoring and evaluation activities. We must once again emphasize that the deputy minister is a chief advisor to the minister, parallel to the current practice of the British institutional model, this time in regard to management agreements to be determined with the Treasury Board and with performance and accountability agreements with managers. In this manner, it is very difficult to decide upon an increase in the political control over the managerial one in so far as this new managerial framework creates new opportunities for a concrete exercise of the expertise of the deputy minister.

Even if we assume that in the end all this occurs entirely through the renewal of traditional power relationships between the minister and the deputy minister, we must admit that it is still impossible to put a stop to the growth of political monitoring.[9] Ultimately, we must recognize that the time the deputy minister and organization leader must sacrifice towards evaluation and monitoring activities are not part of a virtuous dynamic of organizational efficiency and efficacy growth, nor are they a factor of de-bureaucratization. Both of these activities are, of course, not part of the *raison d'être* of a department or organization, nor are they part of the provided services that the political statement precisely emphasizes. In other words, all organizational resources dedicated to evaluation and monitoring obviously are not dedicated to the primary mission of the department or organization, despite the specific or loose definition of that mission.

The public servants, considered the last pivotal actors of this administrative reform, are themselves subject to a preferential empowerment to increase the efficacy and efficiency of the entirety of departments and organizations. Thus,

> The government professionals and the civil servants become more accountable. They work towards clear goals expressed in terms of results. Since they are often at the front line of providing services, they are an important part of the definition as well as the application of quality goals.[10]

The new managerial framework tends, therefore, to combine high autonomy and individual emancipation that the new public-sector management attaches to the *sens de l'État* ("sense of statehood") of the so-called traditional public administration. All this occurs, while it avoids the practice of recurrent, vulgar mimicking (be it partially contextualized, from private-sector management), a snare with more serious negative effects that is not free from the latest management tendency or trend.[11] Even though this administrative reform is concerned with the distinctive, enduring elements of public-sector management,[12] it indiscriminately sanctions the recognition of individual performance on which so many managerial dialogues created for the private sector are based, naturally beginning with the one around quality management. There is no need to extensively affirm that this kind of performance recognition, more often than not accomplished by monetary recognition, disputes the validity of the Weberian bureaucracy principle of anonymity. As well, it implicitly subscribes to a quasi-competitive dynamic that aims to oppose individuals and organizations. This makes it even more difficult for inter-organizational coordination,[13] and further subsumes the *sens de l'État* to market logic. In the same manner that it pursues an elusive equilibrium between the cost and the quality of a public service, this administrative reform intends to solve an antinomy, in other words, to reconcile the best managerial techniques elaborated in the private sector with the specific context of the Québec public sector.

Rupture and Continuity: From Horizontal Pretensions to Vertical Sacralization

Perfectly adhering to the current debate around new public management, as illustrated in Table 9.1, the managerial framework aims at surpassing the traditional bureaucratic environment—more often than not reduced to its distorted effects—while favouring the same innovative dynamic, namely an emphasis on creativity and flexibility, empowerment, entrepreneurship, and, of course, on the organic metaphor that strives to be the preferred expression of this transition, a management of the third kind.[14] Even though it is concerned with increasing the responsiveness as well as the organizational and procedural flexibilities, the Québec project is based on a rigid and even determinist interpretation of organizational structures and processes. In other words, an organo-mechanist conception of political and administrative institutions, which is illustrated by the formal powers and characteristics of the Treasury Board that, as numerous as they are, remains full and whole. As for human resource management (HRM), a strategic element of public management, the Treasury Board has only, in terms of additional constraint, to involve departments and organizations in the elaboration of a managerial framework that limits their own HRM strategic and operational activities, thus favouring a consensual dynamic strongly marked by asymmetry.

Consequently, even though this project adheres to an increasing organizational autonomy, as much as to a managerial empowerment and accountability that reaches the entirety of public sector organizations, the traditional hierarchical relationship that links each of these to the Treasury Board remains intact. The latter can still, as it sees fit, "establish monitoring devices so as to guarantee the attainment of the

TABLE 9.1

The innovation dynamic of common constitutive elements of the political statement *Pour de meilleurs services aux citoyens: un nouveau cadre de gestion pour la fonction publique* and of new public management

Values	from prudence and stability to creativity and flexibility
Strategies	from centralization and homogeneity to decentralization and heterogeneity
Organizational metaphor	from the mechanical to the organic
Character of management	from paternalism to empowerment
Employee behaviour	from dependence to autonomy and entrepreneurship
Relationship dynamic between the individual and the organization	from careerism to contracting or from long-term to short-term (situational)
Locus of control and evaluation	from respecting the process to reaching results

application of the existing law and its goals."[15] The Treasury Board can, moreover, always establish instructions, prior to their approval by the government, pertaining to human resources, financial, material, and informational management that apply to the ensemble of organizations aimed at by the new managerial framework.[16] In other words, the prerogatives of the Treasury Board that are tied to the evaluation and monitoring of public organizations continue with this new managerial framework, as is often the case with administrative reforms and managerial innovations under the influence of new public management.[17] The Québec case would not be an exception to the rule, if it were not for the added emphasis on these long-held prerogatives. The transition from a management based on procedural conformity to a management based on results, inevitably increasing the preponderance of evaluation and monitoring activities, strengthens the solidly asymmetric character of the relationship between the Treasury Board and the public organizations in the Québec administrative apparatus.

Thus, the Treasury Board remains a preferential actor, unavoidable for the financial departments and organizations, considering the chief means of action and guidance specific to this new managerial framework. The pluriannual strategic plan of each financial department and organization must not only include the elements heeded by the organization, but also embrace all other elements considered essential by the Treasury Board.[18] In addition, the Treasury Board can itself determine the form, content, and period of each strategic plan, as it can also alone decide the frequency of its revisions.[19]

A similar prerogative also exists for accountability. The annual management report that must be prepared by each organization must also contain each element or information determined by the Treasury Board.[20] Insofar as one of the most distinctive elements of this new managerial framework is the transition of *a priori* control to *a posteriori* control, the possibility of participating in the elaboration of goals by which the organizations subsequently are evaluated is of utmost strategic importance. This last prerogative of the Treasury Board with regard to account-ability well illustrates the renewal of the traditional hierarchic relationship that ties it to departments and organizations targeted by this managerial framework. Far from being atypical, the weak nature of organizations vis-à-vis the power of the Treasury Board is congruent with the administrative reforms under the influence of the new public management. In fact,

> Given that the generic role of central agencies has not been diminished under NPM reforms even though some specific central agencies might have lost powers and functions, and that generally bureaucrats have been forced to be more responsive to political leadership, there should be little cause for concern that the progress of de-centralisation and devolution initiatives will weaken the central direction of government. Reform, in this respect at least, does not appear to lead to excessive pluralism or fragmentation in government as a whole.[21]

In addition, structural asymmetry not only persists under this new managerial framework, but also neglects to submit to this desire for modernization, to this concern about de-bureaucratization. Ironically, over the past 15 years the pivotal Treasury Board increased the number of its employees from 125 (in 1985) to 1,750 (in 1999).[22] We should add that this determinism is greatly reinforced by law as the preferred instrument of definition for this reform. The implementation of a law, in and by itself, is more rigid, constraining, and restrictive, thus less favourable to the creativity and flexibility that this project requires, than to implementation of a tar-geted innovation or even of a pilot project in any given administrative unit. Finally, even though it may be concerned about complying with a management of the third kind, this reform completely neglects the human dimension of the organization that is nevertheless at the heart of the spoken aims of this managerial style. It presents the principal actors as behaving in a mechanist and predictable manner as soon as they are bound by constitutive elements in the new managerial framework. Thus, we should perhaps no longer speak in an organo-mechanist metaphor, but rather simply of a mechanist one, evidently undesired and unacknowledged, to better illustrate the determinist nature of the project as well as to emphasize the distance between its rhetorical pretensions and its discursive content.

As suggested in the preceding paragraphs, this new managerial framework is less compliant to a dynamic of decentralization, even though the habitual discourse of managerial innovation under the influence of new public management[23] is towards an increase in the consensual dynamic specific to horizontal collaborations between complex organizations. We might consider this horizontal pretension more realist than a genuine exercise in decentralization because it is more modest, and especially more flexible and incremental. It is derived from the complexity of management and from the diversity of activities, both of which are increasing in complex public organizations. In fact, today the plurality of public-sector organizations affected by a sector of activities or given domain of intervention represents a new challenge to the efficient vertical management associated with traditional Weberian bureaucracy. Furthermore, the interdisciplinary problems linked to the elaboration of public policy and to program management delineates a further difficulty for this same vertical public management little concerned about horizontal collaboration, whether temporary or permanent. In a context where the logic of the strongly segmented bureaucratic empire on a vertical base seems ever more archaic and less favourable to a public management concerned about efficacy and efficiency, horizontal management—or, to better illustrate the interactional and political dimensions of this process: the horizontal collaborations—offer new perspectives in managerial innovation.

In short, these perspectives of managerial innovation through horizontal collaborations refer to the congruity of three factors: (1) interdependent strategic and/or operational elements among juridically distinct organizational units; (2) a structure of various levels in the middle of which are found the organizational units; (3) the absence of hierarchical authority exercised by an organizational unit or, in other words, a collegial decision-making process.[24] In light of the discussion above we must state that the new managerial framework only preserves among horizontal collaborations the pretension of consensus and consequently does not propose any structural change that might help the sustained implementation of this inter-organizational collegiality. In fact, insofar as the managerial innovations and the administrative reforms are created and diffused by the central agencies themselves, it is not surprising that the Treasury Board, contrary to the discourse of the new public management, does not cast off any of its traditional prerogatives. In addition, insofar as the required coordination of the entirety of public organizations is still accomplished only by the central agencies, and that we are dealing with a regal function, the vertical sacralization present in the new managerial framework is neither surprising nor inappropriate. The horizontal claim definitely is more doubt-ful and above all risks being the source of misconstrued effects.

In fact, the dithering of the new managerial framework in regard to the con-sensual dynamic specific to horizontal collaborations underestimates the potential for distorted effects and the undesirable consequences tied to the always partial and limited, but also very real exclusion that characterizes all application of negotiation and bargaining resolved by consensus. In other words, we must repeat that the horizontal pretension of the new managerial framework can be reached only as long as the structural asymmetry that persists alone allows for the Treasury Board to guarantee the coordination of the ensemble, that invariably creates expectations among individuals and groups at which it aims. As with all administrative reforms, as soon as these collective expectations are barely or not at all realized, they become as much factors that reduce the collective participation as factors that lead to the creation and extension of an organizational culture of disillusionment.[25] This last possibility has stronger consequences in that the organizational culture of disil-lusionment is a repetitive social process that is incremental but continuous. It also represents an important factor of inertia for all future horizontal experiences, the latter being in some way struck with a coefficient of lax participation. Repeated experiences of failure, especially the repeated exclusion of consensual decision-making, negatively influences the collective impression that the participant actors erect in this horizontal experience.[26]

Governance and New Public Management: Beyond a Shaky Equilibrium

The academic and empirical reflections on the renewal of functional structures and methods of the contemporary state extend broadly beyond simple managerial considerations. In the present case of the new managerial framework, beyond the pursuit of an equilibrium between the constitutive elements of so-called tradi-tional public administration and those tied to new public management, the issue of governance and its required symmetry with managerial innovation becomes unavoidable in a political context where the needs of collective participation in the decision-making process continue to grow and become more complex.

Even though, for the last few years, the notion of governance has undoubtedly enjoyed a high level of popularity, to the point that it has become a fashion trend among managers,[27] it remains a polysemous concept that can as easily refer to the discourse on the minimal state as to the one around new public management or even to that on autonomous inter-organizational networks.[28] Furthermore, in so far as the notion of governance can reach its assertion of conceptual distinction and originality only if it keeps its distance from these well known discourses, we must

TABLE 9.2

The key constitutive elements of the managerial framework
of the Québec state and of governance as a differentiated process

	MANAGERIAL FRAMEWORK	GOVERNANCE
Principal value	efficiency	democracy
Preferential structure	vertical	horizontal
Decision making	sibylline consensus	lax consensus
Control/evaluation locus	quantitative results	qualitative learnings
Accountability nature	polymorphy	diffused
Source of innovation	competition	collaboration
State legitimacy	weak/stable	relative/dynamic
Perspective	intraorganizational	inter-organizational
Domain of application	universal/timeless	contextual/periodic
Epistemological sensibility	positivist	post-structuralist

confer on it the meaning that is appropriate and permits it to better describe and explain the new and changing political and managerial realities.

Thus, governance is first and foremost understood as a dynamic process that pertains to diversification and the complicating of public policy networks built[29] by collective actors of the public, private, and third sectors—the third being the social economy. Even though its role ranges from central to peripheral, the state, as an ensemble of heterogeneous actors, remains the imminent collective actor in this dynamic process and for this reason: the preferential managerial innovations that transform its method of internal function directly influence its strategic capacity, that is, the form as well as the meaning of its participation in this process. The precision of their equilibrium, or at least of their complementarity, becomes explicit.

As suggested in Table 9.2, the equilibrium of key elements in the managerial framework of the Québec administrative apparatus with those of governance as a differentiated process indeed is not established, since the divergent elements remain numerous and fundamental. The possibilities for complementarity as such also are uncertain. Whereas the former emphasizes, through management based on results, efficiency as a cardinal value, the latter, concerned with increasing the participation of interested networks, stresses more the democratic character of the process. Despite the horizontal pretensions of the former, it sacralizes the hierarchical principle and verticality, while the latter achieves its claims of distinction through only a horizontal dynamic.

Decision-making, which is more complex, equally illustrates the distance, even antinomy between the two. While the managerial framework really only favours a sibylline consensus in so far as the possibilities of the participation of departments and organizations aimed at remains entirely defined, and as thus limited by the Treasury Board, the latter rests on a weak consensus, in the middle of which the state can exercise its dominance and beyond that avoid the break-down of the accountability of the political and managerial elite. Since it is based on the tacit reification of private-sector management, through its direct affiliation with new public management, the new managerial framework favours competition as a primary source of innovation, while governance and the loose consensus that characterizes it is contrarily based on collaboration.

Furthermore, while new public management wishes to present a solution to the reduced legitimacy of the state, by imitating managerial techniques belonging to big private companies, it participates in maintaining this reduced legitimacy more than finding a solution for it. Governance allows the state, in a relative and dynamic manner, to conserve and even to increase its legitimacy. Finally, this new managerial framework, dependent on new public management, distinguishes itself from governance through its pretensions of universality and timelessness, and equally through the implicit renewal of positivist orthodoxy on which, by definition, is founded management by results.

Finally, the new managerial framework, favoured for allowing for the modernization of the Québec administrative apparatus, as well as for increasing the collective participation of public servants—those who are managers as well as those who are not—cannot be considered a facilitator of the implementation, concomitant or subsequent, of a differentiated governance. On the contrary, the preceding argument suggests that its equilibrium is at the very least uneasy and that, for that reason, a more important and sustained consideration around the renewal of Québec governance implies a questioning of this new managerial framework.

Conclusion: A Critical Interpretation to Be Distinguished from an Apology for the Status Quo

In conclusion, while remaining critical of the new managerial framework, we should specifically emphasize that none of the precedent arguments is either a call to statism or to carelessness, nor that they are based on a complacent satisfaction with the managerial status quo of the Québec public administration. On the contrary, a certainty that a real reform project of Québec political and administrative institutions cannot be created from managerial models and precepts developed in a different environment (namely that of private companies) and more often than not in a competitive, oligopolistic situation, is subjacent to this critical argument. The managerial bias of these criticisms does not refer to a sacralization of the adverse effects of the traditional bureaucratic model, but agrees more with a radical change that occurs through the valorization of multiplicity of organizational identities and the rejection of the instrumental comprehension of organizational culture, still considered unique and belonging to high-level public servants by the preponderance of a fragmented rationality of cognitive, political, and emotional components.[30]

Even though bureaucracy alone certainly cannot be considered an organizational panacea, all the more because it is not a universal and timeless model of a so-called rational organization, but a heterogeneous complex and dynamic construction that, as a continuum, vacillates between its facilitating and coercive variant,[31] we must admit that Weber's model remains of contemporary interest for those who are concerned about upholding this fragile and uncertain, almost mysterious, but irreplaceable equilibrium between the pursuit for efficiency and the prosperity of democracy. We must above all also recognize that the second goal can be achieved only through the quest of the first one, and we must nevertheless accept that democracy is not in itself and by itself efficient. Despite the pretension of the ideological neutrality of efficiency as an organizational principle,[32] we must be attentive to the fact that this is merely a managerial value among several other possibilities and that by this reasoning, it neither can nor should be sublimated to the point of losing sight of the fundamental one that is democracy.

Notes

This chapter is a revision of the paper presented on 17-18 April 2001 at the Colloquium Québec: State and Society, a Study Program on Québec at McGill University in Montréal.

1. The president of the Treasury Board of the Québec government, the godfather of this managerial reform of the Québec state, strongly emphasizes to the contrary that the "operation does not aim at determining what the state should or should not do. It aims at correcting a highly restricted managerial framework that makes sure that the governmental machine is not always capable of efficiently and quickly responding to the needs of citizens" (Jacques Leonard quoted in Leduc, 1999).

2. *Pour de meilleurs services aux citoyens: un nouveau cadre de gestion pour la fonction publique*, Énoncé de politique sur la gestion gouvernementale (Québec: Conseil du trésor, 1999), iii.

3. Ibid., 1-14.

4. *Loi sur l'administration publique*, (Québec: Assemblée nationale du Québec, 2000), 10-16.

5. For an interesting, though at times demanding, discussion on the passing of positivism in public administration see David John Farmer, *The Language of Public Administration—Bureaucracy, Modernity, and Postmodernity* (Tuscaloosa, AL: U of Alabama P, 1995).

6. *Pour de meilleurs services aux citoyens*, 19.

7. *Rapport de la Commission royale d'enquête sur l'organisation du gouvernement (Glassco)*, (Ottawa: 1962). Centred on the organizational structures and processes, be it a management of the first kind, the Glassco Commission may be considered the apex, evidently itself imperfect, of managerial thought in the federal public sector. On this issue, as well as on those tied to management of the second and third kinds, see Mohamed Charih, "Le management du troisième type au gouvernement fédéral," in Roland Parenteau, ed., *Management public — Comprendre et gérer les institutions de l'État* (Sainte-Foy: Presses de l'Université du Québec, 1992), 115-28.

8. Christopher Pollitt, "Managerialism Revisited," in B. Guy Peters and Donald J. Savoie, eds., *Taking Stock — Assessing Public Sector Reforms* (Montréal and Kingston: McGill-Queen's University Press, 1998), 45-77.

9. Again, the Québec case is far from being the exception to the rule. For more details on the impact of the new public management on the relations of power between political and administrative elites, see James R. Mitchell and Sharon L. Sutherland, "Relations Between Politicians and Public Servants," in Mohamed Charih and Arthur Daniels, eds., *New Public Management and Public Administration in Canada / Nouveau management public et administration publique au Canada*, (Toronto: The Institute of Public Administration of Canada / L'Institut d'administration publique du Canada, 1997), 181-97.

10. *Pour de meilleurs services aux citoyens*, 26.

11. For more details on identity construction and managerial fashions see, among others, Timothy Clark and Graeme Salaman, "Telling Tales: Management Guru's Narratives and the Construction of Managerial Identity," *Journal of Management Studies* 35 (1998) and Jim Silver, "The Ideology of Excellence — Management and Neo-conservatism," *Studies in Political Economy* 24 (1987).

12. *Pour de meilleurs services aux citoyens*, 6.

13. Pollitt, "Managerialism Revisited," 66-69.

14. The expression that today is sacrilized in managerial studies was introduced to this milieu in the 1980s in the managerial best-seller by George Archier and Hervé Serieyx, *L'entreprise du 3e type* (Paris: Éditions du Seuil, 1984). Simply put, management of the third kind rejects the mechanist metaphor on which management of the first and the second kinds are based, both victims of their unwarranted emphasis on structures and processes. Management of the third kind stresses the primacy of individuals and groups and, in general, the human dimension of the organization. Having said that, the distinctiveness and originality of management of the third kind is too often overestimated. For more details, see Christian Rouillard, *Le syndrome du survivant et la fonction publique fédérale du Canada — une étude théorique à la lumière de la théorie critique et de la déconstruction derridienne*, doctoral thesis, (Ottawa: Carleton University, 1999).

15. *Loi sur l'administration publique*, article 75.

16. Ibid., article 74.

17. John Hart, "Central Agencies and Departments: Empowerment and Coordination," in B. Guy Peters and Donald J. Savoie, eds., *Taking Stock — Assessing Public Sector Reforms*, (Montréal and Kingston: McGill-Queen's University Press, 1998), 285-309.

18. *Loi sur l'administration publique*, article 9.6.

19. Ibid.

20. Ibid., article 24.3.

21. Hart, "Central Agencies and Departments," 304.

22. Roland Arpin, *La réforme administrative du Gouvernement québécois: entre pédagogie et autoritarisme*, paper presented at l'Institut de la gestion financière du Canada, 17 Nov. 1999.

23. Mohamed Charih and Lucie Rouillard, "The New Public Management," in Mohamed Charih and Arthur Daniels, eds., *New Public Management and Public Administration in Canada / Nouveau management public et administration publique au Canada*, (Toronto: The Institute of Public Administration of Canada / L'Institut d'administration publique du Canada, 1997), 27-45; Mohan Kaul, *An Outsider's Inside View: Management Reforms in Government — A Review of International Practices and Strategies*, (Ottawa: Commonwealth Association for Public Administration, 2000); Martin Minogue, Charles Polidano, and David Hulme, eds., *Beyond the New Public Management — Changing Ideas and Practices in Governance* (Cheltenham, UK: Edward Elgard, 1998).

24. Mark Sproule-Jones, "Horizontal Management — Implementing Programs across Interdependent Organizations," *Canadian Public Administration / Administration publique du Canada* 43 (2000): 92-109.

25. Organizational disabusement should be distinguished from organizational alienation and cynicism. Disenchantment rejects both the exclusively reactive nature of alienation and the explicit demonization of organizational cynicism, despite their common dimension of socio-psychological behaviour, or the possibility of being defeated, i.e., resolved, by a managerial exercise of planned symbolic supervision and manipulation. For more details, see Rouillard, *Le syndrome du survivant et la fonction publique fédérale du Canada*, 236-70.

26. In this sense, the idea of an organizational culture of disenchantment thus refers to a type of organizational legacy, to a residual perspective affecting not only horizontal management, but also all past projects of managerial innovation and organizational changes, those apparently successful, and those that were failures, as well as those that were anticipated but never carried out.

27. Among other examples of this hasty appropriation of the notion of governance in management discourse, see *Des résultats pour les Canadiens et les Canadiennes*, (Ottawa: Conseil du trésor du Canada, 2000); Ruth Hubbard, *Vers une saine gouvernance — la réforme réinventée* (Ottawa: Bureau du Conseil privé, 2000); as well as *Entrevue avec Monsieur Louis Bernard à son bureau de Montréal*, 26 Jan. 2001. Available at:<http://www.enap.uquebec.ca/Symposium/conf/bernard-fr.htm>; *Interview avec M. Ronald Bilodeau, Secrétaire associé du Cabinet et Sous-greffier du Conseil privé, gouvernement fédéral du Canada*, 12 Jan. 2001. Available at: <http://www.enap.uquebec.ca/Symposium/conf/bilodeau-fr.htm>.

28. R.A.W. Rhodes, "The New Governance — Governing Without Government," *Political Studies* 44 (1996): 652-67; G. Stoker, "Governance as Theory — Five Propositions," *International Social Science Journal* 155 (1998): 17-28.

29. These networks not only touch upon public policy development, but also their implementation and operational management.

30. Evidently, these details go beyond the purpose of this text and do not intend in anyway to explicate an alternative reform project or constitute elements of a progressive management framework. They aim more simply and maybe more humbly to avoid a trial by association or by intention, both being factors that avoid a real public debate on modernization of the Québec administrative apparatus.

31. For more information on this issue see Paul S. Adler and Bryan Borys, "Two Types of Bureaucracy — Enabling and Coercive," *Administrative Science Quarterly* 41 (1996): 61-89.

32. Herbert A.Simon, *Administration et processus de décision* (Paris: Economica, 1983).

10

State-Owned Enterprises in Québec: From Privatization to Globalization

LUC BERNIER AND FRANCIS GARON*

Introduction

State-owned enterprises have been part of Canada's economic landscape for nearly a century. State intervention in the economy, sporadic at the turn of the century, gradually expanded in scope; it also became more direct and sophisticated.[1]

In Québec, the development of state-owned enterprises occurred at the same time and along the same lines as in the other provinces.[2] What was different in Québec was that it built up the largest network of publicly owned corporations of any Canadian province, and they pursued nationalist ambitions.[3] After the oil crisis of the 1970s and the recessions of 1982 and 1992, however, successive governments gradually reversed course. Over the years, caught between globalization, budget pressures, technological change, and public disgruntlement with government administration, Western governments began seeking new ways to improve the management of public organizations, and Québec was no exception.[4]

Québec's state-owned enterprises were spawned by the Quiet Revolution. At the time, it was felt that all sectors of Québec's economy urgently needed to catch up to development elsewhere, an objective the publicly owned corporations were supposed to advance. They sprang from improvisation more than planning: for many

* Translated from French into English by Analogos.

199

years, efforts were directed towards creating the instruments, with little thought to developing a policy to govern them. That came only in the 1970s, and then in the 1980s came the trend towards privatization. Following the example of Great Britain, governments began privatizing on the grounds that publicly owned companies were necessarily less efficient than the private sector.

After much talk of privatization but little action, the government of Québec set a new course for its state-owned enterprises. They would be less involved in natural resources, more in finance. State-owned enterprises would have to adapt to new realities. For example, Hydro-Québec, the state-owned electric utility, would have to follow the North American trend towards energy deregulation. We shall trace the course of this history from 1960.

Research Methodology

The existing empirical research mainly covers the period 1960-96. It deals primarily with the nine of Québec's state-owned enterprises that have been required by the government to publish strategic plans since 1979: the Caisse de dépôt et placement du Québec, Société Générale de Financement (SGF), Société de Développement Industriel (SDI), Radio-Québec, Société québécoise d'exploitation minière (SOQUEM), Société québécoise d'initiatives pétrolières (SOQUIP), Société de recuperation, d'exploitation et de développement forestiers du Québec (REXFOR), Société québécoise d'initiatives agro-alimentaires (SOQUIA), and Sidérurgie québécoise (SIDBEC). In the late 1980s, we conducted 37 interviews with the executives of these corporations. Since that time, SIDBEC has been sold, Radio-Québec has been renamed Télé-Québec, the SDI has become Investissements Québec, and other corporations have been overhauled or downscaled. Along with Hydro-Québec, which has already been studied in detail (see Hafsi and Demers, 1989: Faucher and Bergeron, 1985), these were and remain the core of Québec's state-owned sector. To complement the interviews, we produced studies of their financial performance and strategic planning (Bernier et al., 1997).

First Generation of State-owned Enterprises in Québec

When Maurice Duplessis died in 1959, direct intervention in the economy by the Québec state was negligible in quantity and quality. The provincial civil service was small, poorly educated, and underpaid. Hydro-Québec was distributing electric power only in the Montréal area, Radio-Québec was a legal fiction that had existed on paper since 1944, and the Régie des Alcools owed more to the "ligues lacordaires" than to government planning. The subsequent Quiet Revolution saw the creation of many state-owned enterprises and massive direct state intervention in the economy, which would be scaled back in the 1980s.

In the wake of experiments with privatization elsewhere, particularly Great Britain, the Parti Québécois began privatizing some corporations in the early 1980s. At the time, public finances were in a shambles. After the Liberal election victory in 1985, the privatization drive picked up steam. A Cabinet minister, Pierre Fortier, was assigned to work full-time on the privatization portfolio. In 1988, he released a report that concluded the privatization efforts had been a resounding success and need not continue. So, from 1960 to the mid-1980s, Québec's state-owned enterprises may be said to have completed a full life cycle (aside from the privatization of some assets in 1994, on the eve of the general elections).

The mission of Québec's state-owned enterprises changed several times between their beginnings during the Quiet Revolution and the mid-1980s. During this period, numerous pieces of legislation affecting government-owned corporations were passed.[5] The criteria for assessing their efficiency also changed. Profit, an abstract notion for Québec's state-owned enterprises 20 years ago, became a priority, if not *the* priority. The corporations adapted to an environment that had turned hostile. From the baby steps of the 1960-1965 period to the wave of privatizations and rationalization of the 1980s, before the change in course of the 1990s, the corporations had first a co-operative relationship with the state, then a period of confrontation, then relative independence and finally a return to closer co-operation, although with some bumps along the road. These relations with the state, more than the corporations' efficiency, guaranteed their existence. To survive, state-owned corporations need to demonstrate their usefulness. Their efficiency is only one aspect of the demonstration; maintaining good relations with the government is also essential.

How Should We Study State-Owned Enterprises?

State-owned enterprises are supposed to pursue social objectives, which are less easily quantifiable than are economic targets, and these can hurt their bottom line. They play a role in the development and implementation of public policy. At the same time, they must post acceptable financial results. Proponents of privatization have statistics at the ready to prove that government-owned businesses are less efficient.[6] The other camp has its own statistics; it argues that the pro-privatization forces make dubious sampling choices and that the performance of state-owned corporations is attributable to other factors.[7]

State-owned enterprises are not the only organizations that pursue multiple objectives or difficult-to-measure objectives; so, too, do many public and private organizations that are only partially governed by the laws of the market, or not at all: universities, research centres, non-profit organizations, etc. More often than not, state-owned enterprises learn what they can and should do by doing it. They have at best a vague understanding at the outset of what is expected of them. The government apparatus is a perpetually moving machine with ill-defined and sometimes (often?) contradictory priorities. Typologies of possible objectives for state-owned enterprises may contain as many as 40 points. It is difficult to determine an order of priority for these objectives. Moreover, the objectives vary over time. A government-owned enterprise needs to stay attuned to its environment.

A public organization needs resources to survive, and it needs recognized legitimacy in order to be allocated those resources.[8] A publicly owned corporation must ensure that its legitimacy is not challenged by its environment, particularly by the government, which could decide to close it down or privatize it. A state-owned enterprise's legitimacy is secured through the institutionalization of its relations with the state.

The most elaborate model of relations between the state and government-owned corporations is the one developed by Hafsi.[9] For Hafsi, organizations are composed of two decision-making subsystems: a technological core (the organization's central operations) and a boundary subsystem, which handles relations with the environment. The boundary subsystem shields the technological core from environmental pressures. The technological core of a government-owned corporation dictates specific ways of doing things that political demands must not change if the corporation is to remain effective. To protect this technological core state-owned corporations seek to maintain their independence from the government.

Hafsi's model provides a structure for explaining the differences and contradictions between the studies of relations between the state and government-owned corporations that have been produced to date. These relations may be classified according to a three-stage cycle: co-operation, confrontation, independence. The initial, co-operative phase is marked by extensive informal communications; in this stage, the original objectives are shared by the government and corporate management. The initial state of concord is disrupted by four factors: the achievement of the original objectives, the development of the technological core, self-financing, and lack of consistency among the arms of the government apparatus.

The informal relationship of the beginning is gradually replaced by more institutionalized relations and state-owned enterprises strive to increase environmental predictability. They seek an institutional framework in order to limit informal intervention by government officials and politicians, and this can lead to confrontation. Statutory controls are put in place and state-owned enterprises gradually become independent, unless they have pressing financial needs. Télé Québec (previously Radio-Québec) still depends on the government for the bulk of its financing and will never be as independent as are profitable operations. It might be added that publicly owned corporations gradually create a client base or find partners for certain projects. Little by little, the founders are replaced by managers who did not know the early makeshift days.

What happens before and after this cycle? A state-owned corporation is not born of chaos. Nor is there any guarantee that it will remain independent forever. Hafsi's model explains what happens during a cycle; we must also consider how the cycle began and how the next cycle will begin. A distinction must be made between periods of creation and periods of institutional stabilization. The co-operation-confrontation-independence cycle describes what happens between two institutional crises. The full cycle includes both crises. During the first period of crisis, new state institutions emerge, which then go through the cycle described above until the second crisis prompts reconsideration. Institutional structures do not respond promptly and readily to transformations in the environment, domestic or international. Change is difficult; it happens in fits and starts, not slowly and surely.

In Québec, the first cycle lasted from the beginning of the Quiet Revolution into the 1980s. The privatization of some state-owned enterprises and subsidiaries at the beginning of the second cycle, around 1985, convinced the surviving corporations to co-operate with the government as they had at the beginning of the first cycle. These co-operative relations were premised on the assumption that management did not want the state-owned enterprise to be privatized. Aside from Air Canada, which did indeed want to be privatized, rare is the management team of a publicly owned company that desires privatization, if only because managers who keep their jobs after privatization are rarer still.

The difficulty for government is maintaining the climate of co-operation. In the second part of this section, we will describe how the government succeeded in doing so by keeping alive the threat of privatization after 1985. While state-owned enterprises did regain a measure of independence, the government kept the threat hanging over their heads by always having a possible privatization under study.

State-Owned Enterprises from 1960 to the 1980s

Québec's state-owned enterprises are engaged in a wide range of financial, commercial, and industrial activities. They operate in a wide variety of lines of business; forestry, mining, aluminum, television, tourism, venture capital. Sometimes they are in competition with the private sector, sometimes they co-operate, sometimes they supply the private sector with resources at advantageous prices. For example, Hydro-Québec performs the latter infrastructural function with the aim of attracting investment to Québec. Some state-owned enterprises regularly turn a profit, while others have racked up debts in the billions. While some have proven to be effective instruments of government intervention, others have resisted the governments that wanted to control them.

Although the Liberal government elected in 1985 had made noises about getting rid of state-owned enterprises, most survived the privatization drive intact.[10] As Table 10.1 shows, of the 10 companies considered for privatization in 1986, only the smallest, Madelipêche, was in fact sold off in its entirety. Raffinerie de sucre du Québec also was sold to be closed.

The case of Québec offers a unique framework for studying the development of publicly owned corporations during a cycle extending over the last 30 years. Most of Québec's state-owned enterprises were conceived of or created during what is commonly called the Quiet Revolution. The state was perceived as an instrument Québec could use to catch up. The main achievement of economic policy during this period was the emergence of state-owned enterprises.[11]

The Co-operation/Improvisation Phase

To understand the logic of the transformation process, we are well advised to look at the means used during this period to lengthen the arms of the state and at the nature of the expanding state apparatus, rather than of the stated objectives of each intervention.[12] It is difficult to discern a comprehensive economic policy. Rather, a series of sectoral policies addressed very specific and urgent needs. Often, Québec's state-owned enterprises were instruments of policies that were yet to be devised.[13] Given Québec's accumulated lag in many areas, decisions (be they improvised decisions) had to be made. In this sense, the creation of state-owned enterprises was a simple administrative response to complex needs. It insulated small teams of specialists from the pressures of private enterprise, the bureaucratic practices of government departments, and the vagaries of politics.

The policy statements that gave rise to the establishment of state-owned enterprises were seldom provided in that form to the corporations in question. For example, the forestry company Rexfor (short for Société de récupération, d'exploitation et de développement forestiers du Québec) does not have a copy of the Deschamps report that recommended its creation. With no fixed frame of reference, co-operation between the management of the state-owned enterprises, senior government officials, and politicians was crucial at the outset. In another example, the government of the day did not see fit to include any objectives in the charter of the Caisse de dépôt et placement, the government's pension fund manager. Almost 30 years later, they still refer to the speech Jean Lesage delivered in the National Assembly at the time. In an organization with so ill-defined a mission, objectives must be negotiated. So the Quiet Revolution was, for state-owned enterprises, a period of close collaboration with politicians and senior government officials.

The growth of government institutions proceeded chaotically. Let us take the example of Radio-Québec, whose legal existence dates back to the 1940s. It began

TABLE 10.1

State Enterprises

	1985	1988	1991	1995	2000
SGF	1 160	1 140	1 163	1 420	1 956[a*]
SOQUEM	272	124	110	68	
SOQUIA	58	87	130	117	
SOQUIP	437	166	193	254	
REXFOR	158	213	298	393	
SIDBEC	529	555	580	28	NSP[b]
SNA	256	93	70	28	NSP[c]
SQT (Québecair)	144	10	3	0.5	NSP[d]
SEPAQ	NSP	41	74	53	65
Radio Québec / Télé-Québec	48	48	51	54	43
SDI / I-Q	147	436	1 054	1 434	1 029
SDBJ	16	9	11	9	10
Hydro-Québec	27 129	31 659	36 684	46 271	56 785
Caisse de dépôt	22 502	29 918	36 245	52 547	88 263
Loto-Québec			98	302	643
INNOVATECH[c]	NSP	NSP	NSP	72	315
• Grand Montréal				62	242
• Québec Chaud.-Appalaches				5	58
• Sud du Québec				5	15
Société de financement agricole/ Régie des assurances agricoles Qc	18[e]	79[e]	60[e]	213	331
SAQ	172	212	220	196	372

a Since 1998, the activities of Soquip, Soquia, Soquem, and Rexfor are integrated in SGF.
b The Société québécoise des transports was abolished on December 18, 1997.
c Sidbec is now a State-owned enterprise without assets, and became Sidbec-Dosco
d The assets of the Société nationale de l'amiante have been privatized. Consequently, the SNA (3 remaining employees) only completes remaining pending transactions and liabilities.
e The Société de financement agricole has been created in 1993; the numbers are thus from the assets of the previous Régie des assurances agricoles du Québec.
* The numbers between parentheses are for the business year 1999 or 1999-2000 then the only ones available.

Sources: Gouvernement du Québec, 1988, Annual reports of Radio-Québec (1984-1988), Télé-Québec (1990-2000), Caisse dépôt (1990-2000), SEPAQ (1999-2000), SGF (1999), Investissement Québec (2000), SDBJ (1999), Hydro-Québec (1999), Loto-Québec (2000), Innovatech (2000), Régie des assurances agricoles du Québec et Société de financement agricole (1999-2000), SAQ (2000), États financiers du des entreprises du Gouvernement du Québec, 1990-1991, 1995-1996.

operating in 1969, several months before the creation of the Ministry of Communications, to which it reports. Its newly hired employees had to wait six months for their first pay cheques, as did workers at the agri-food company Soquia (short for Société québécoise d'initiatives agro-alimentaires). Similarly, Hydro-Québec and the oil company Soquip (short for Société québécoise d'initiatives pétrolières) had been meeting Québec's energy needs for over 15 years and 10 years, respectively, before the old Ministry of Lands and Forests, subsequently renamed the Ministry of Natural Resources, finally became the Ministry of Energy and Resources. In 1964, it was the Minister of Natural Resources who fielded questions in the National Assembly about the Sidérurgie québécoise (Sidbec), although the plans for a state-owned steel company were supposed to come under the authority of the Minister of Industry.

The apparent confusion may conceal a different logic. It has been suggested that in a weak state where government departments are beholden to big natural resource companies, publicly owned corporations may be created in a bid to form administrative islands with greater decision-making autonomy.[14] In Québec's case, the state's relative autonomy also guaranteed that economic growth would be driven in part by companies whose decision-making centres were located not in Toronto or New York but in Québec.

It has also been noted that in many cases the impetus for the establishment of state-owned enterprises in Québec came from civil servants with a business background.[15] Jacques Parizeau, Claude Castonguay, André Marier, and others convinced their ministers and the Premier to support their projects. They persuaded Jean Lesage and others that the Caisse de dépôt, the mining company Soquem (short for Société québécoise d'exploitation minière), Soquip, and Rexfor would be vital tools for development. The 1962 general election also played an important role in the process. The dominant issue was the nationalization of private electric utilities, an idea René Lévesque had sold to his colleagues.

The importance of the Quiet Revolution in this case is that state-owned enterprises still look to it for the foundations of their legitimacy.[16] Addresses such as Jean Lesage's 1965 speech at the assembly about the Caisse de dépôt provide the raison d'être for government-owned enterprises. The corporations have since adjusted their missions, to be sure, but it was in those early days that their organizational culture took shape. The Quiet Revolution remains the explanatory myth for both their creation and their economic nationalism, which has not waned.

A series of interviews was conducted with the executives of nine Québec state-owned enterprises in the late 1980s. The first question was "What were the milestones in your organization's history?" The answers began with the foundation of the corporations and referred to the Quiet Revolution, to which we shall return. Many of the executives went on to talk about opportunities their organization had seized. For example, the head of Rexfor discussed the sawmills and pulp and paper mills slated for closure by the private sector, which Rexfor had taken over and turned around. In the case of Soquem, the turning points were five discoveries of mineral deposits by the company. In the case of Soquip, there was the acquisition of an Alberta subsidiary. In some cases, the turning point was the arrival of a new President or a new management team;[17] in others, they spoke of the development of subsidiaries. They focused on their ability to take advantage of opportunities, not of their adherence to the strategic plans we discuss below.

Quest for Independence from Government

State-owned enterprises achieved independence in the 1970s. The informal relations of the first years were gradually replaced by policy statements more clearly setting out the objectives towards which the government wanted state intervention to be directed. The corporations became complex organizations. Where there had been one analyst responsible for relations with a state-owned enterprise, teams of analysts sprang up. The period also saw a tightening of administrative procedures.

During this period, the government of Québec produced and released its first integrated economic policy proposals. First, there was *Une Politique économique québécoise* in 1974 (known as the Vézina report), then *Bâtir le Québec* in 1979, and finally *Le Virage technologique* in 1982. Sectoral studies were replaced by a comprehensive vision. The role of state-owned enterprises, seen as indispensable in the first report, was overlooked in the second, and again became vital in the third.

The reports concluded that state-owned enterprises, most of which were up to cruising speed, needed better planning. The state-owned enterprises were becoming independent. They were generating earnings on a regular basis, though with uneven success, and acquiring recognized expertise in their lines of business. They could point to their track records to legitimate themselves to their environment: Soquem's five mineral discoveries, Rexfor's rescue of Tembec, the creation of Soquip Alberta, the Caisse de dépôt's performance, Hydro-Québec's successes, etc.

Also during the 1980s, the state-owned enterprises' missions were subjected to new scrutiny within the organizations as a result of the planning process; preparation of the required plans prompted discussion of how each organization's mission was to be interpreted. Then, say the state-owned enterprises' executives, in the talks on the strategic plans, they managed to negotiate their own survival with a privatization-prone government. Paradoxically, the strategic plans, which were supposed to reduce the corporations' manoeuvring room, actually increased it. First of all, they lessened the ambiguity in the environment by shielding publicly owned companies against the unpredictability of the various components of the state apparatus. More importantly still, the plans were and still are drafted by the corporations and then approved by the government: the planning process is conducted by the corporations.

At the same time, the charters of the state-owned enterprises were amended to include financial profitability as an objective. The corporations were, therefore, in a better position to resist government interference; they could use the strategic plan as a guide to action and invoke the need to turn a profit to escape government control. Acceptance of a government-owned corporation's development plan by the responsible ministry constitutes a big step towards the corporation's survival. And the government often agrees at the same time to investments that guarantee the company's expansion.

From Independence to Privatization

Privatization began timidly in the early 1980s but became the leitmotif of public policy when the Liberals took the reins of government in 1985. Over time, the independence of state-owned enterprises had increased as they became more self-sufficient financially. However, the 1982 recession undermined their self-sufficiency and spurred a spate of corporate reorganizations, which led to a general restructuring. For example, the Société générale de financement (SGF), launched in 1962, jettisoned its money-losing subsidiaries over the years, refocused its operations on specific areas, and was able to elude government control. The first state-owned enterprise spawned by the Quiet Revolution, the SGF, initially had an ill-defined role, which was subsequently clarified. To its first president, it was a business bank; to its first general manager, it was something of an industrial company.[18] It might be said that the other state-owned enterprises—Rexfor, the Société de Développement Industriel (SDI), which promotes industrial development, Soquia, Soquip, and Sidbec—were created to perform specific functions that the SGF itself could not carry out.

In 1982, the SGF proposed an ambitious expansion plan to the government that called for the administrative structures of two of its subsidiaries, Donohue and Domtar, to be integrated in order to produce a huge conglomerate. The SGF had reached the point of no return. Because of the limits of North American political culture, according to some managers, because of a lack of entrepreneurship, according to others, the government decided to pull back and make the SGF a catalyst rather than an operator.

What is surprising about this reconsideration of the role of state-owned enterprises is that, aside from financially struggling Sidbec, the loss of their legitimacy was not due to deterioration in their performance. For example, it was not until very late in the day that the government acknowledged that asbestos was not the industry of the future. In fact, in the 1980s the SGF was experiencing its best years, the Caisse de dépôt was in its heyday, and Rexfor, Soquem, Soquia, and Soquip all were running smoothly. In short, it was the environment that had changed. Legitimacy and economic performance are only tangentially related. For the first time, a Québec government was questioning the merits of publicly owned corporations. The government environment was becoming ambivalent for state-owned enterprises. The symbolic dimension was the most successful aspect of the rationalization process: the government had succeeded in reasserting its authority over the corporations.

Based on a study of the 500 largest companies outside the US,[19] Boardman and Vining have concluded that government-owned companies are less profitable than the private sector. They also found that mixed companies are less profitable than government-owned companies. But their sample of publicly owned companies was flawed. The privatization of government-owned corporations in Great Britain does not appear to have improved their financial performance. Productivity increased at the privatized companies as it did in all segments of the British economy during the same period. It would appear that the impact of ownership is mitigated by other factors, such as the development of the industrial sector.[20] Here as elsewhere, the decisive factor in financial performance is the existence of competition.

We have looked at the factors that may explain the financial performance of state-owned enterprises in Québec. Our analysis suggests that financial performance, the key consideration in comparisons between the public and private sectors, is influenced not only by ownership but also by the economic cycle, developments in the industry in which the firm operates, and the existence of monopoly power. Three other factors can also affect the financial performance of state-owned enterprises: the government of Québec's financial needs, the political party in power, and the political will to overhaul government policy on state-owned enterprises, particularly as concerns their independence and/or privatization. Finally, we looked at the entrepreneurship of corporate management. The results of this exploratory research suggest that the threat of privatization, the entrepreneurship of management and the line of business have an impact, as do the ideological leanings of the party in power and the government's financial needs. There is little justification for privatizing state-owned enterprises on grounds of economic rationality, which may explain why there has been more talk than action when it comes to selling them off.[21]

In this age of globalization, the tools available for implementing any economic policy are limited. The free-trade agreements and the GATT restrict the use of tariffs and subsidies. Government-owned corporations remain one of the few available instruments for camouflaging certain research costs and building international competitiveness. The research conducted by IREQ, a subsidiary of Hydro-Québec, is a case in point. The SDI's equity loans are another. In Canada, instruments of economic policy are divided between the federal and provincial governments. The federal government has exclusive jurisdiction over monetary policy and the two levels of government share jurisdiction over tax policy, subsidies, and regulation. Provincially owned enterprises are virtually the only companies that elude the authority of the federal government. Given their shrinking range of policy instruments, it is in the interest of provinces that have rationalized their investments to keep their state-owned enterprises.

Flexibility remains the major advantage of state-owned enterprises over other instruments of economic policy. Government-owned corporations can choose the private companies in which they want to invest, whereas subsidies must be distributed in accordance with established rules. Government-owned corporations can decide to invest in a given project, while the long decision-making chain in government ministries prevents them from responding in a timely manner. State-owned enterprises make it possible to carry out ad hoc interventions that would otherwise be impossible. We would like to think that the use of state-owned enterprises in recent years stems from better understanding of their advantages and disadvantages.

After Privatization

The dominant discourse about the privatization of state-owned enterprises, which prevailed up to the mid-90s, seems to have lost some of its sway. While a second massive wave of privatizations had been expected with the advent of the Free Trade Agreement and other international agreements that affected the capacity of states to intervene, there were in fact few privatizations in Québec. Despite the rise of neo-liberal rhetoric, the Liberals did not forge ahead, with the exception of a few pre-election privatizations such as Sidbec and Mont-Ste-Anne, one of Sepaq's main assets. When it was returned to power in 1994, the Parti Québécois intended to continue the process of privatizing state-owned enterprises, but with an added requirement to consult and to ensure that the government not lose money in the process.[22] More recently, during the last election campaign, Liberal leader Jean Charest called for the privatization of the SGF, a controversial plan that may well have cost him political support. The ADQ called for privatization of government agencies that had already been abolished by Bill 178. Successive governments were loath to seriously question the role of state-owned enterprises, a legacy of the Quiet Revolution.

In 1997, the Parti Québécois government charged a task force chaired by MNA Joseph Facal with examining the situation at 204 of the 207 governmental bodies, including a number of state-owned enterprises, Hydro-Québec, Loto-Québec, and the Caisse de dépôt et placement were not included in the terms of reference.

Among other things, the task force was mandated to examine the organizations' roles and functions, "and to maintain only those that are necessary for the government to properly perform its mission."[23] Given these terms of reference, it could be anticipated that major changes would be forthcoming and that they would entail a significant reduction in the number of government bodies.

As far as state-owned enterprises specifically were concerned, the task force made a number of recommendations, which tended towards integrating and/or merging companies, or abolishing them in cases where the corporation no longer served any useful purpose or was inoperative to all intents and purposes. The main recommendations included folding Soquem, Soquip, Soquia, and Rexfor into the SGF and merging the three organizations dedicated to agricultural development, namely the Société de financement agricole, the Régie des assurances agricoles and the Ministry of Agriculture's support program for agri-food businesses into a single corporation, to be called the Société de financement et d'assurances agricoles du Québec. The task force felt that Innovatech, a corporation dedicated to supporting hi-tech startups, had a valid mandate and should continue its operations, but should sell its stake in the projects it financed once they were capable of making it on their own. The task force recommended that the Société des alcools du Québec (SAQ), the provincial liquor board, not be privatized, given the substantial profits it generates for government coffers. The SDI was also considered to have a valid mandate; it was therefore recommended that it continue to be an instrument of government intervention. The task force recommended that the Société des établissements de plein air du Québec (SEPAQ) be maintained as part of the machinery of government, on the grounds that the state needed to play a role in recreational facilities, as it does in other countries. The Société nationale de l'amiante, the state-owned asbestos producer, was considered to be inoperative but had to be kept alive until the court cases against it were settled and it had paid its debts. The task force recommended that the Société de transport du Québec be closed down, since it had never been able to perform the role for which it had been created. Finally, the task force urged Télé-Québec to refocus its activities on its educational mission.

While the Facal report hardly revolutionized the realm of governmental organizations, it was still the most thorough study of state agencies and corporations of which we are aware in the last decade, as the Fortier report was in the 1980s. The Facal report reconsidered the appropriateness of state-owned enterprises and their operations from the point of view of complementarity, rationalization, and coordination. It has led to some changes but the real savings generated by rationalization as a result of the exercise will have to be analyzed in the longer term. Given the small scale of the changes, the savings may well prove to be slight.

Adapting to the New Financial Issues: Mergers/ Integration, Deregulation, Commercialization

It appeared likely that the impact of globalization in general and of international agreements in particular would lead to significant changes at Québec's state-owned enterprises, notably privatizations. Thus far, the preferred approach seems to have been mergers and/or the integration of business units in order to adapt them to the new economic and financial environment. What we have seen has been a rearrangement more than a fundamental transformation. The evidence to date is that, as a result, state-owned enterprises are enjoying more, not less, manoeuvring room to intervene in the economy.

Another effect of globalization is that the rationale for the existence of state-owned enterprises now revolves around the need for countries to have major players that can compete with or partner with major financial conglomerates. This trend can be observed in Québec, where more and more state-owned enterprises are trying to play in the financial big leagues, abandoning some of their traditional activities directed towards the local economy, such as financial support for Québec firms exclusively and the exploitation of natural resources. The government of Québec's recent actions tend in this direction and do not appear to diminish the role of state-owned enterprises.

In 1998, the operations of Soquia, Soquip, Soquem, and Rexfor were folded into the SGF, as recommended by the Facal report. SGF President Claude Blanchet would have liked to lay his hands on the SAQ and the Innovatech companies at the same time, but that wish was not granted by the government. However, the "new" SGF was allocated $2 billion in the 1998 budget—$400 million per year for five years. The objective was to generate $10 billion in investment over that period.

Also in 1998, Investissement-Québec was founded. It replaced the Société de développement industriel (SDI), which disappeared after nearly 30 years of activity. The workforces and portfolios of the SDI and Foreign Investment Directorate at the Ministry of Industry and Commerce were merged to create the new state-owned enterprise; its mandate is to boost investment in Québec and spur job creation. A subsidiary, Garantie Québec, was also created to finance small and medium-sized Québec businesses. As in the case of the SGF, the main change in the organization's mandate was directly related to the new economic environment. While the SDI's mandate had essentially consisted in financing businesses that could not meet the requirements of conventional lenders, Investissement Québec's mandate is to publicize Québec, attract investors and thereby create as many jobs as possible.[24]

More recently, the government has also gone ahead with plans to combine the programs of the Société de financement agricole and the Régie des assurances agricoles by creating Financière agricole du Québec, which was allocated a $300 million budget for 2001-2002. (This compares with slightly over $400 million in 2000-2001; does this mean the government is saving money, or simply that it is investing less?) Recent developments, therefore, demonstrate that Québec has chosen to merge and integrate state-owned enterprises, rather than privatize them.

Another important dimension of the recent development of state-owned enterprises, which relates to Hydro-Québec specifically, is the deregulation of energy industries in North America. This basic change in the industry's dynamics is leading to increased competition in electricity and gas markets. Hydro-Québec is keeping pace with the trend: for example, it has an interest in Noverco, the holding company that controls Gaz Métropolitain, and it is now operating as an electricity broker (one of the effects of deregulation has been to allow daily trading of electricity on power exchanges). Indeed, in 2000, Hydro-Québec's brokerage operations surpassed its electricity exports.[25] Hydro-Québec's expansion beyond its historic lines of business—electricity generation, transmission, and distribution—and its move into the brokerage market are leading some observers to view it as a privatized company even though there has been no change in ownership.

One of the objectives in Hydro's 2000-2004 strategic plan is to capitalize on the changes underway in the industry. The shift towards commercial operations, combined with the favourable business environment, yielded a net profit of slightly over $1 billion in 2000, half of which was turned over to the Québec government in the form of dividends. The amount of revenue Hydro pours into the public coffers may explain why there is less and less talk of privatizing the corporation. The only cloud, from a financial point of view, is subsidiary Hydro-Québec International, which Hydro President André Caillé acknowledges is off to "a very difficult start."[26] When it was created, its target was investments of $500 million per year, but it has made investments of only $300 million in two years.

We cannot discuss the commercialization of state-owned enterprises without mentioning the cases of the SAQ and Loto-Québec. Under President Gaétan Frigon, the SAQ's sales increased from $1.45 billion in 1998 to $1.86 billion in 2000 and some 800 jobs were created. A recent survey by Léger Marketing found the SAQ to be highly popular with Quebecers, ranking sixth on their list of "favourite companies." The pollster concluded that "the SAQ has successfully made the commercial shift." Frigon commented that "this ranking is all the more impressive in our view in view of the fact that we are a state-owned enterprise."[27] Meanwhile, Loto-Québec has expanded quickly, opening three government-owned casinos in 1993 and establishing a video lottery network. In 1999-2000, Loto-Québec returned dividends of more than $1.2 billion to the government.[28]

While the Caisse de dépôt et placement du Québec is more discreet about its operations, it is also plugging into the globalized economy. In 1997, its enabling legislation was amended to allow the Caisse to increase the equity portion of its portfolio to 70 per cent, giving it greater flexibility on international financial markets. In recent years, the Caisse has also established several specialized subsidiaries, such as Capital International, Sofinov, Capital Communication, and Montréal Mode, creating powerful financial vehicles to support business development in their respective fields. Once considered "Québec's sock drawer," the Caisse now has business offices in Warsaw, Milan, Hong Kong, Buenos Aires, and Brussels. It recently invested $125 million in Metro-Goldwyn-Mayer (MGM) in a bid to get in on the lucrative film production and distribution segment of the entertainment market.

At the same time, the push to adapt to the new economic and financial environment is also causing problems for Québec's state-owned enterprises. Globalization is breeding widespread discontent and complaints from pressure groups and the public about the growing lack of financial and economic transparency on the part of government-owned corporations and the state. Bill 116 and the debate on the Act Respecting Access to Documents Held by Public Bodies are two examples of the problems created by the need to adjust to the international environment.[29] Bill 116 substantially altered the powers of the Régie de l'énergie, created in 1996 to review Hydro-Québec's tariffs. The Bill removed electricity generation and exports from the Régie's authority; only transmission and distribution are still regulated. The government has therefore untied Hydro-Québec's hands so it can play by the rules of the North American market. Some observers believe the unstated intent of the legislation was to protect Hydro-Québec's position in the marketplace, an objective that could come into conflict with the Régie's mission of promoting sustainable development while taking economic, social, and environmental concerns into account. Others see a still graver issue, suggesting that the government of Québec is using its legislative power to amend an Act it finds inconvenient as a shareholder.[30] Either way, the end result is to remove a portion of Hydro-Québec's operations from the Régie's purview and therefore from public oversight.

The debate on the Act Respecting Access to Documents Held by Public Bodies raises essentially the same basic problem, i.e., the lack of transparency of state-owned enterprises and their subsidiaries. The proposed amendments will extend the Act's application to more public agencies, but not to subsidiaries of state-owned enterprises. Hydro-Québec subsidiaries, such as H-Q International and Nouveler, and the Société des loteries' subsidiaries, the Société des Casinos, will be able to continue their commercial and financial activities unperturbed. The reasoning is that subjecting these companies to the Act could compromise their ability to do business with private partners by forcing them to disclose any and all information about their plans and operations upon request. Recently, an entertainment company that had received $12 million from the SGF (which holds 49 per cent of its stock) and $11 million in loan guarantees from Investissement Québec claimed that it did not have to reveal the cost of three parties at its new offices because it is a "private sector" company. The Minister, Robert Perrault, justified the omission of subsidiaries of state-owned enterprises from his proposed amendments on the grounds that he had to "choose between two competing objectives, both of which are in the public interest," and that the subsidiaries' ability to pursue their economic development efforts had prevailed over the public's right to know.[31] These examples are indications of the tensions that can exist between the public interest and economic imperatives, bearing in mind that state-owned enterprises and their subsidiaries are financed from the public purse.

Most state-owned enterprises have expanded their operations beyond Québec's borders in recent years: Loto-Québec has entered the Chinese market through its private arm NTER; Hydro-Québec has landed contracts from Australia to Peru (not to mention the US); the Caisse de dépôt et placement is working with major foreign partners and has interests around the world; the SGF continues its overseas business development efforts. Despite the prevailing neo-liberal rhetoric, which advocates an end to all state intervention in the economy, Québec's state-owned corporations continue to grow and to play a vital role in the Québec economy. Their development shows that it is possible to play the globalization game without opting for privatization, which seemed improbable in the early 1990s.

Government-owned enterprises remain a flexible instrument of intervention, since it appears possible to adapt them to prevailing economic, legal, and ideological currents in the globalized environment. As we have seen, there have been some bumps on the road. It seems that the international rules that govern the business relations of state-owned enterprises with foreign countries are giving rise to legal frameworks at the local level that are increasingly flexible, not to say vague, in which political vision and economic issues (political, business, and legal considerations) are entwined in a complex dynamic. State-owned enterprises are being allowed to operate as private businesses, while simultaneously drawing on the government's deep pockets. This certainly explains some of the complaints from advocates of total transparency.

Despite all the political and legal pressures acting on them, which are not exactly transparent, state-owned enterprises continue, to different degrees, to pursue a social mission and promote Québec's economic development. It is clear that this consideration would fade in importance if their operations were entrusted exclusively to the private sector.

Conclusion

Québec's state-owned enterprises were born in the flush of improvisation known as the Quiet Revolution. The government wanted to act fast and it created organizations that were sheltered from political pressure. Creating the instrument was the end goal of the policy. Later, government belt-tightening gradually led to efforts to develop a comprehensive policy for publicly owned enterprises and to correct some of the more flagrant mistakes. For example, Sidbec was given the role it should have had from the outset. On the other hand, the ill-fated Société nationale de l'amiante was created. The privatization process began. The decision to privatize was made even though the situation in Québec was very different from that in Great Britain, which provided the rationale for the trend.

The next stage was trickier. The free trade agreements had reduced the number of policy instruments available to government. If the Government of Québec had decided to privatize its remaining corporations, it would basically have been left only with costly tax incentives as a means to promote job creation. State-owned enterprises were an important part of the Québec model. In our view, they have been part of the solution more than part of the problem. However, it must be recognized that Québec has a higher unemployment rate than the rest of North America, apart from the periphery. The Québec model has not delivered as much as hoped for during the Quiet Revolution. The process of adapting government-owned corporations to keep them in tune with changing realities in their industries must continue, and consideration could be given to privatizing some of them.

The literature on privatization tends to show that the private sector does a better job than government of distributing consumer goods. Should the government hold on to the SAQ, which is in a retail business? Would it be better to sell Hydro-Québec or keep it in the public sector? Can it be revamped so it can be successful in an industry undergoing profound change? The SGF, the Caisse de dépôt, and the other financial instruments must be able to more clearly demonstrate how they serve the common interest if they are to continue to exist. Commercial considerations alone cannot justify their existence.

Notes

1. Jeanne Kirk Laux and Maureen Appel Molot, *State Capitalism: Public Enterprise in Canada* (Ithaca: Cornell University Press, 1988).

2. Luc Bernier, "La création d'entreprises publiques," in Jean Crête, Louis M. Imbeau, and Guy Lachapelle, eds., *Politiques provinciales comparées* (Québec City: Presses de l'Université Laval, 1994), 315-33.

3. Ibid.

4. Mohamed Charih and Art Daniels, eds., *Nouveau management public et administration publique au Canada* (Toronto: Institute of Public Administration of Canada, 1997). Rod Dobell and Luc Bernier, "Citizen-Centered Governance: Implications for Intergovernmental Canada," in Robin Ford and David Zussman eds., *Alternative Service Delivery* (Toronto: Institute of Public Administration of Canada, 1997), 250-65.

5. Between 1961 and 1986, 69 bills making superficial or fundamental changes to the nine corporations studied here (including amendments to their original Charters) were passed. See also the note on methodology for an overview of the entire research project.

6. Anthony E. Boardman and Aidan R. Vining, "Ownership and Performance in Competitive Environments: A Comparison of the Performance of Private, Mixed, and State-owned Enterprises," *Journal of Law and Economics* 32 (1989): 1-33. Aidan Vining and Anthony E. Boardman, "Ownership Versus Competition: Efficiency in Public Enterprise," *Public Choice* 73 (1992): 205-39.

7. Yair Aharoni, *The Evolution and Management of State-owned Enterprises* (Cambridge, MA: Ballinger, 1986), 475. Luc Bernier, Patrick Petit, Michel G. Bédard, and André Forget, "La performance financière des sociétés d'État au Québec," in Marie-Michèle Guay, ed., *Performance et secteur public* (Sainte-Foy: PUQ, 1997), 97-113.

8. R. Richard Ritti and Jonathan H. Silver, "Early Processes of Institutionalization: The Dramaturgy of Exchange in Interorganizational Relations," *Administrative Science Quarterly* 31 (1986): 25-42.

9. Taïeb Hafsi et al., *Strategic Issues in State-Controlled Enterprises* (Greenwich, CT: JAI Press, 1989).

10. Gouvernement du Québec, Ministère des Finances, Cabinet du ministre délégué aux Finances et à la Privatisation, *Rapport d'étape, 1986-1988.*

11. Kenneth McRoberts, *Québec: Social Change and Political Crisis*, 3rd edition with postscript (Toronto: McClelland & Stewart, 1993).

12. Jean-Jacques Simard, "La longue marche des technocrates," *Recherches sociographiques* 18 (1977): 118-20.

13. Roland Parenteau, "Les Sociétés d'État : autonomie ou intégration," record of meeting of 8 May (Montréal: École des HEC, 1980).

14. Theda Skocpol, "Bringing the State Back In: Strategies of Analysis in Current Research," in P.B. Evans et al., eds., *Bringing the State Back In* (New York: Cambridge University Press, 1985).

15. Luc Bernier and Jean-Pierre Fortin, "L'entrepreneurship public dans les sociétés d'État au Québec," *Revue Organisation* 6 (1997): 13-23.

16. Luc Bernier, "La dynamique institutionnelle des entreprises publiques au Québec de 1960 à aujourd'hui," in *Politiques et management public* 7 (1989): 95-111.

17. Luc Bernier and Jean-Pierre Fortin, "L'entrepreneurship public dans les sociétés d'État au Québec," 13-23.

18. Luc Bernier, "La dynamique institutionnelle des entreprises publiques au Québec de 1960 à aujourd'hui," 95-111.

19. Anthony E. Boardman and Aidan R. Vining, "Ownership and Performance in Competitive Environments: A Comparison of the Performance of Private, Mixed, and State-owned Enterprises," *Journal of Law and Economics* 32 (1989): 1-33.

20. David Parker and Keith Hartley, "Do Changes in Organizational Status Affect Financial Performance?" *Strategic Management Journal* 12 (1991): 631-41.

21. Luc Bernier, Patrick Petit, Michel G. Bédard, and André Forget, "La performance financière des sociétés d'État au Québec," in Marie-Michèle Guay, ed., *Performance et secteur public* (Sainte-Foy: PUQ, 1997): 97-113.

22. "Daniel Paillé: pas de moratoires sur les privatisations," *Le Soleil*, 29 Oct. 1997, B16.

23. Gouvernement du Québec, Groupe de travail sur l'examen des organismes gouvernementaux—Rapport (Québec: Facal, 1997).

24. "Le Québec s'est donné des outils modernes de promotion," *Le Soleil*, 2 Sept. 1998, B4.

25. See "Hydro-Québec, une société plus rentable et pleine de projets," *Les Affaires*, 7 Apr. 2001, 11; "Hydro-Québec, courtier en énergie," *Le Devoir*, 15 Mar. 2001, B.

26. "Hydro-Québec International va rater sa cible," *La Presse*, 15 May 2000, A6.

27. "Sondage exclusif Léger Marketing sur la popularité et la notoriété de 134 entreprises," *Commerce*, 102, 3 (Mar. 2001): 22; "Plus personne ne parle de privatisation," *Le Soleil*, 2 Dec. 2000, A17.

28. "Loto-Québec rapporte gros au trésor public," *La Presse*, 22 July 2000, A20.

29. For more information on these controversies, see reports on Bill 116 in the Québec press during the spring and summer of 2000 and on the Act Respecting Access to Documents Held by Public Bodies in early 2001.

30. "Déréglementation de l'électricité: le véritable débat n'a pas eu lieu," *La Presse*, 9 June 2000, B3. See also "Les privilèges et le législateur," *Le Devoir*, June 2000, A6.

31. "Fonds publics et secrets d'État," *La Presse*, 3 Apr. 2001, A3; "Modification de la loi d'accès à l'information," *La Presse*, 11 May 2000, A1.

PART III
Political Parties and Social Movements

11

Sclerosis or A Clean Bill of Health?
Diagnosing Québec's Party System in the Twenty-First Century

A. BRIAN TANGUAY

Introduction

A great deal appears to have changed in Québec's party system since the collapse of the Meech Lake Accord in 1990. For one thing, all of the major players in the political game have been reshuffled: both the Québec Liberal Party (QLP) and the Parti Québécois (PQ) have had three leaders in the last decade. Jean Charest, Lucien Bouchard's former cabinet colleague in Brian Mulroney's federal Progressive Conservative government during the late 1980s, is now the leader of the Québec Liberals. He replaced Daniel Johnson, who had succeeded an ailing Robert Bourassa in 1994. Lucien Bouchard left the federal Conservative Party in 1990 to protest what he considered the watering down of the Meech Lake Accord (which had been diluted with the help of Jean Charest). He formed the Bloc Québécois and served as the initial leader of that "temporary" entity, only to move to provincial politics and replace Jacques Parizeau as leader of the PQ and premier of Québec in January 1996. In typically mercurial fashion, Bouchard resigned as PQ leader unexpectedly in early 2001, and was replaced by his Finance Minister, Bernard Landry.

Adding to this appearance of upheaval in Québec's party system is the fact that one minor party, the anglophone rights Equality Party, which won four seats in the 1989 provincial election, faded quickly from the political scene. A new minor party, the *Action démocratique du Québec* (ADQ), has emerged. It is led by the young, articulate and media-savvy Mario Dumont. In the 1994 provincial election, the ADQ managed to win 6.5 per cent of the popular vote, and it raised its share to almost 12 per cent in 1998. It won only one seat each time, however—that of the leader, Dumont.

On the other hand, it could be argued that nothing has fundamentally changed in Québec's party system since the late 1960s, when the PQ was created and began to eclipse the old Union Nationale as the primary vehicle of nationalism in the province. Partisan competition still centres on the unresolved question of Québec's constitutional status, as it did in the late 1960s and throughout the next decade. Three referenda have been held on this issue since 1980; in each case, the opponents of constitutional change emerged as victors. Lucien Bouchard promised to hold yet another referendum on sovereignty, but only at some unspecified time in the future when there was a likelihood that the PQ could win it, only when there were "winning conditions," in other words. Since assuming office in March 2001, Bernard Landry has given every indication that he does not harbour the Hamlet-like doubts of his predecessor, and that he will move forward aggressively in the planning of another referendum, should the PQ win the next provincial election (likely to be held in 2003). These recent shifts in the provincial party system are summarized in the next section of the chapter.

In the second section of the chapter, I examine various indicators of the health of Québec's two-party system. Is it fostering a dynamic clash of different world views, something that most Canadians are rarely or only accidentally offered by their party systems (provincial or federal)? Or are Québec's voters disengaged from politics and corrosively cynical about their politicians? By examining interest accommodation within the Parti Québécois, voter turnout in provincial elections, and citizens' financial contributions to the parties, we can get a picture of the complexity of Québec's party system today.

The Changing Configuration of Québec's Party System, 1970-2001

The existing party system in Québec took shape in the late 1960s, when the Parti Québécois was created out of the merger of dissident provincial Liberals, led by René Lévesque, with a small, right-wing separatist party, the *Ralliement national*. A second, much more radical separatist organization, the *Rassemblement pour l'indépendance national* (RIN) later disbanded, with many of its members joining the PQ. The new party married its nationalist project to a fairly radical—by North American standards, at any rate—social democratic world view, although the PQ eschewed formal organizational links with the trade unions, in contrast to the NDP in English Canada.

Beginning with the 1970 provincial election, the Union Nationale—which had governed the province from 1944 to 1960 and again from 1966 to 1970—gradually declined into electoral insignificance. Since the early 1970s, party competition in Québec has pitted the left-leaning, technocratic, *étatiste* and nationalist PQ against the centre-right, free-market and federalist Québec Liberal Party. Between them, the two major parties have won at least 85 per cent of the popular vote in every provincial election since 1973, the sole exception being the 1976 election which first brought the PQ to power (see Table 11.1). In that contest, anglophone voters, who have traditionally constituted the bedrock of Liberal Party support, deserted it in droves to protest against the Bourassa government's language legislation, Bill 22. Enough of them—just over 18 per cent of the electorate in total, many of them disaffected anglophones—voted for the Union Nationale to allow the PQ to win a solid majority of the seats in the contest (see Table 11.2). The UN's political resurrection was short-lived, however. Its leader at the time, Rodrigue Biron, eventually quit the party and joined the PQ (becoming a cabinet minister in the early 1980s); by the time the 1985 election was held, the UN was definitely dead.

It is possible to trace three different phases in the evolution of Québec's party system since 1970 (1970-80, 1981-93, 1994-present). The first phase was marked by the relentless build-up toward the first referendum on sovereignty-association, held in May 1980. Robert Bourassa, when he became premier, espoused the notion of "profitable federalism," the idea that the existing federal system could be shown to work in the best economic interests of the Québécois. His party's campaign slogan during the 1970 election was "Québec au travail" (Québec to Work). He promised to create 100,000 jobs during his first year in office, thereby demonstrating that Québec could enjoy economic prosperity within Canada, a prosperity that would be jeopardized if voters endorsed the radical experiment of separation. This plan almost immediately ran aground, however, as the young and inexperienced premier was forced to confront first the kidnapping crisis precipitated by the *Front de libération du Québec* in October 1970, then widespread public sector strikes in 1972 and again in 1976, massive work stoppages and labour strife on the James Bay construction site (1974), and finally the corruption and overspending that marred the 1976 Olympics in Montréal. Bourassa simply failed to deliver profitable federalism to the electorate, and the one formal attempt to reform the constitution while he was premier, at the Victoria Conference in 1971, foundered when Bourassa rescinded his government's initial agreement to Pierre Trudeau's proposals, in the face of intense nationalist pressure in the province.[1]

It was not only the Bourassa government's hated language law, Bill 22, and its economic mismanagement that propelled René Lévesque and the PQ to power in the 1976 election. Such a victory would have been wholly unthinkable had the PQ not softened its hard-line stance on separation. From 1970 until 1974, the PQ was

TABLE 11.1

Parties' Shares of the Popular Vote in Québec Provincial Elections, 1960-1998[a] (%)

PARTY	1960	1962	1966	1970	1973	1976	1981	1985	1989	1994	1998
QLP	51.4	56.4	47.3	45.4	54.7	33.8	46.1	56.0	50.0	44.4	43.6
PQ	-	-	-	23.0	30.2	41.4	49.3	38.7	40.2	44.8	42.9
UN	46.6	42.2	40.8	19.7	4.9	18.2	4.0	0.2	-	-	-
Crédit.[b]	-	-	-	11.2	9.9	4.6	-	-	-	-	-
ADQ	-	-	-	-	-	-	-	-	-	6.5	11.8
Equality[c]	-	-	-	-	-	-	-	-	4.7	0.3	0.3
Other	2.0	1.4	11.9[d]	0.7	0.3	2.0	0.7	5.1	5.2	4.1	1.4
Total	100.0	100.0	100.0	100.0	100.0	100.0	100.1	100.0	100.1	100.1	100.0

Figures may not add up to 100 because of rounding.

a   Shaded cells indicate party forming the government.
b   Ralliement Créditiste/Parti Créditiste.
c   Includes the Unity Party.
d   Ralliement Nationale won 3.2 per cent of the vote, Rassemblement pour l'indépendance nationale (RIN) took 5.6 per cent of the vote.

Source: [1960-1985] Québec, Bibliothèque de l'Assemblée nationale, *Statistiques électorales du Québec, 1867-1985*, compilées et présentées par Pierre Drouilly (Québec, 1986). [1989-1998] Québec, Directeur-général des élections, <http://www.dgeq.qc.ca/information/>.

wedded to the idea that a vote for the party was a vote for independence; in the event of a PQ election win (whether by absolute majority or not), the machinery of separation would be put in motion. As a number of scholars pointed out, and as some key party strategists realized, this position served to deter a great many voters from even considering the PQ as a possible option when they cast their ballots.[2] In 1974, at the urging of the party's chief constitutional strategist, Claude Morin, the PQ formally dissociated the act of voting for the party from support for separation. Instead, the PQ appealed to those voters dissatisfied with the Bourassa regime by promising to provide "good government" if elected, and to consult the electorate in a referendum on its sovereignty-association project sometime during its first mandate. This *étapiste* (literally, step-by-step) electoral strategy succeeded in breaking the unity of the anti-independence forces in the province and provided the PQ with a slim margin of victory over the Liberals (see Tables 11.1 and 11.2).

When the Parti Québécois took office in November 1976 it confronted a number of daunting problems. How could it mollify a frightened business community (skittish foreign investors, in particular), convince organized labour in the province

TABLE 11.2

Number of Seats by Party in Québec's National Assembly, 1960-1998

PARTY	1960	1962	1966	1970	1973	1976	1981	1985	1989	1994	1998
QLP	51	63	50	72	102	26	42	99	92	47	48
PQ				7	6	71	80	23	29	77	76
UN	43	31	56	17		11					
Crédit.[a]				12	2	1					
ADQ										1	1
Equality[b]									4		
Other	1	1	2			1					
Total	95	95	108	108	110	110	122	122	125	125	125

a   Ralliement Créditiste/Parti Créditiste.
b   Includes the Unity Party.

Source: [1960-1962] Québec, Bibliothèque de l'Assemblée nationale, *Statistiques électorales du Québec, 1867-1985*, compilées et présentées par Pierre Drouilly (Québec, 1986). [1966-1998] Québec, Directeur-général des élections, <http://www.dgeq.qc.ca/information/>.

of the reality of its rhetorical "favourable prejudice toward workers,"[3] defuse an explosive labour relations scene (strike rates in Québec during the Bourassa years had been among the highest in the western world), and cultivate the proper environment for the passage of the promised referendum on sovereignty-association, all at the same time?

Viewed from the vantage point of 2003, the accomplishments of the first Lévesque administration, confronting such diverse and at times mutually contradictory policy objectives, were quite impressive indeed. During its first year in power, the Parti Québécois introduced sweeping reforms of election finance legislation, with the objective of eliminating corruption and undue business influence on government. It revised the Labour Code, strengthening the financial base of trade unions (through the imposition of the Rand Formula),[4] prohibiting the use of replacement workers ("scabs") during legal strikes, and facilitating union certification in the province. It also nationalized part of the province's automobile insurance industry and purchased the American-owned Asbestos Corporation in an ultimately abortive attempt to create more manufacturing jobs in this important industry. These, along with the Charter of the French Language (Bill 101, adopted in 1977), were among the Lévesque government's more innovative and controversial measures.

TABLE 11.3

Referendum Results and Turnout in Québec, 1980-1995 (%)

	MAY 20, 1980[a]	OCTOBER 26, 1992[b]	OCTOBER 30, 1995[c]
Valid Votes	3,673,842	3,945,189	4,671,008
Rejected Ballots	65,012	87,832	86,501
Rejected Ballots, % of total	1.7	2.2	1.8
No[d]	59.6	56.7	50.6
Yes[d]	40.4	43.3	49.4
Turnout	85.6	82.8	93.5

a   Referendum question essentially asked voters to give the government a mandate to negotiate sovereignty-association.
b   Referendum question asked voters whether they agreed that the constitution of Canada should be renewed on the basis of the agreement [the Charlottetown Accord] negotiated on August 28, 1992.
c   Referendum question asked voters whether they agreed that "Québec should become sovereign after having made a formal offer to Canada for a new economic and political partnership."
d   As a percentage of valid votes cast.

Source: Québec, Directeur-général des élections, <http://www.dgeq.qc.ca/information>.

On 20 May 1980, the referendum was finally held, and the PQ suffered a stinging defeat. Almost 60 per cent of those voting rejected the PQ's watered-down proposal for a "mandate to negotiate sovereignty-association" (see Table 11.3). Surprisingly (at least for some observers), this referendum defeat was followed in April 1981 by the PQ's convincing election victory over the Liberals, then led by the former publisher of *Le Devoir*, Claude Ryan. In fact, as Tables 11.1 and 11.2 show, the PQ increased its margin of victory considerably over 1976, winning just under 50 per cent of the popular vote and 80 seats in the National Assembly — its best performance ever. This surprising victory was a testament to Lévesque's personal popularity, widespread satisfaction with his government's economic and social policies, as well as the somewhat feckless leadership of Claude Ryan. It may also have indicated a conscious desire on the part of many Québec voters to elect the party that they thought would do the best job of defending the province's interests against the federal Liberal government.

The 1981 election signalled the beginning of a new phase of party system evolution in the province, which would last until 1994. This was a time of missed opportunities on the constitutional front, as both the PQ and the Liberals — who won the

1985 provincial election under the renascent Robert Bourassa—made unsuccessful overtures to the federal Progressive Conservative government of Brian Mulroney to renew federalism. Immediately after the 1984 federal election, Lévesque uttered the Delphic remark that negotiating with the new government, and thereby postponing yet again the achievement of sovereignty-association, would involve a "noble risk." Within a couple of months of the Tory victory, Lévesque and the most important moderate in the PQ, Pierre-Marc Johnson, had completely repudiated the party convention's decision of 1982 to fight the next provincial election on sovereignty. This shift sparked a schism within the party, as the hard-line advocates of independence, the so-called *orthodoxes*, either renounced their party membership or resigned from the National Assembly altogether. More than a quarter of the PQ cabinet resigned, including such heavyweights as Jacques Parizeau, Camille Laurin, Jacques Léonard, and Denis Lazure.[5]

This rupture in the Parti Québécois was followed in short order by Lévesque's resignation from the leadership in 1985. He was succeeded by Pierre-Marc Johnson, who embraced the nebulous slogan of *national affirmation*. Because the PQ was defeated by the Liberals in the 1985 provincial election, however, Pierre-Marc Johnson had very little time in which to flesh out this concept. Johnson was eventually pushed out of the party leadership in an internal coup in late 1987 and replaced by the darling of the hard-line faction, Jacques Parizeau. Between 1987 and 1994, Parizeau succeeded in clarifying and simplifying the party's thinking on sovereignty: if the PQ returned to power, it promised to hold another referendum as soon as possible after its victory. Issues relating to economic partnership with English Canada, a common currency, and so on, would be sorted out *after* sovereignty had been proclaimed. As unlikely as the PQ's return to power appeared in the late 1980s—a time when many observers thought that Québec nationalism was a spent force—external circumstances quickly propelled the party back into electoral contention.

Robert Bourassa's second tenure as premier (1985-1994) was marred by his mishandling of the language and constitutional portfolios, which ultimately contributed to a dramatic surge in support for Québec independence in the early 1990s. The Liberals won a massive majority in the 1985 provincial election, taking 56 per cent of the popular vote and 99 seats out of 122 in the National Assembly (see Tables 11.1 and 11.2). During the campaign, Bourassa promised to relax some of the more irritating aspects of Bill 101 if his party was elected. The prohibition on the use of any language other than French in commercial signs was singled out as needlessly oppressive and unnecessary in a mature, civilized society. Public opinion, even among francophones, seemed to be receptive to bilingual commercial signs. However, since this provision of the Charter of the French Language had already been challenged as unconstitutional—an infringement of the freedom of expression guaranteed under the Charter of Rights and Freedoms—and the case was still before the Québec Court of Appeal, the Bourassa government decided to take no action until a decision had been rendered.

When the Québec Court of Appeal handed down its decision on 22 December 1986, ruling unanimously that the prohibition on bilingual commercial signs was unconstitutional, the Bourassa government appealed the decision again, to the Supreme Court of Canada. By waiting for two years while the Supreme Court deliberated, the Bourassa government effectively abdicated responsibility for language policy to an increasingly vocal minority opposed to any alteration of Bill 101. By the time the Supreme Court confirmed the lower court decisions on the unconstitutionality of this section of Bill 101, the widespread public support for relaxing some of the more intrusive aspects of the language law, which had existed only two years earlier, had by then evaporated.

Bourassa's attempted solution to the language crisis of 1988 was reminiscent of his earlier botched effort to defuse linguistic tensions in the province, Bill 22 (passed in 1974). Bill 178, hastily enacted in the wake of the Supreme Court decision, and passed with the help of the "notwithstanding clause" in the Charter of Rights and Freedoms, resembled Bill 22 in that both were compromises that failed abysmally to secure the support of either the militant francophone nationalists or the English community in the province. Bill 178, the so-called "inside/outside" law, permitted the use of English on signs inside a commercial establishment, but prohibited any language other than French on signs placed outside a store.

Despite the uproar caused by the inside/outside legislation, Bourassa and the Liberals won the 1989 provincial election quite handily, taking 50 per cent of the popular vote and 92 of the 125 seats in the National Assembly (see Tables 11.1 and 11.2). The Parti Québécois, fighting its first election with Jacques Parizeau as leader, nudged its share of the popular vote up from just under 39 per cent in 1985 to 40 per cent, taking 29 seats. A small English-rights organization, the Equality Party, managed to win almost five per cent of the popular vote in this election and took four seats in the predominantly anglophone ridings of west-end Montréal. This minor party slipped quickly and quietly into political oblivion, however, without leaving much of a mark on the legislature.

Bourassa's language policy played an important role in the unravelling of the Meech Lake Accord in June 1990. Many English-speaking Canadians detected in the legislation a simple desire for revenge, and wondered out loud why efforts at bilingualism should be made outside Québec when that province was implementing restrictive and seemingly vindictive measures against the minority language. To be sure, at least some of this outrage was purely hypocritical, given that English Canada's treatment of its francophone minorities has hardly been exemplary. Nonetheless, Bill 178, along with the closed and elitist process of bargaining that characterized the entire Meech Lake debacle, has to be considered one of the principal causes of the failure of the Accord.

The collapse of the Meech Lake Accord ushered in one of the strangest periods in Québec's political history. On 23 June 1990, the day the three-year limit for provincial ratification of the agreement expired, Robert Bourassa stood up in the National Assembly and declaimed: "No matter what anyone says or does, Québec has always been, is now and will always be a distinct society, free and capable of taking responsibility for its destiny and development."[6] This marked the beginning of a pronounced radicalization of the QLP's position on constitutional matters. This shift in Liberal Party policy paralleled a similar radicalization of public opinion, as support for Québec sovereignty spiked in the wake of the Meech Lake debacle.[7] In January 1991, the party's constitutional committee issued its position paper on Québec's future place in Confederation, the Allaire Report (named after the chairman of the committee, Jean Allaire). Affirming that Canada, "in its present form, can only lead ... to a constitutional, political, and even financial and economic impasse," the document called for the wholesale devolution of powers from Ottawa to the provinces.[8] The Liberals adopted the Allaire Report as party policy in March 1991, the same month in which the Bélanger-Campeau Commission issued its report calling on the Québec government to hold a referendum on sovereignty by October 1992 if it did not receive satisfactory constitutional proposals from the rest of Canada. These recommendations were enshrined in Bill 150, which was adopted in June 1991.

Was Robert Bourassa ever really committed to the idea of Québec sovereignty as a last resort, if constitutional reform failed? Or was his apparent support for the Allaire Report, the Bélanger-Campeau Commission's report, and Bill 150 simply an insincere means of buying time in order to allow the Mulroney government to come up with some minimally acceptable, face-saving reforms of the Constitution, which eventually took the shape of the Charlottetown Accord? Even those most closely involved in the constitutional reform process—like former Ontario premiers David Peterson and Bob Rae[9]—confess not to fully understand Bourassa's motives. Whether or not Bourassa was genuinely committed to each of the different constitutional options he endorsed between 1990 and 1992 may never be known for sure (unless he left a written account somewhere in his personal papers). What is certain, however, is that in August 1992, Bourassa persuaded most of his party—with the significant exceptions of Jean Allaire and Mario Dumont, then head of the QLP youth wing—to accept the Charlottetown Accord as a fundamental reform of the Canadian constitution. The October referendum would not be on sovereignty, after all, but on the package of proposals cobbled together by Joe Clark. Lisée writes that throughout this constitutional odyssey, Bourassa "swindled, abused and deceived. He ... lied to many people. He had shown pettiness towards his opponents, and he had played the partisan game when he should have acted the statesman. He had trampled on the dignity of his own office. It was not an edifying sight."[10]

On 26 October 1992, the referendum on the Charlottetown proposals was held, and almost 57 per cent of Québec's voters rejected the deal (see Table 11.3). Turnout in Québec—just under 83 per cent of the province's voters—was more than 10 percentage points higher than the average turnout in the remaining Canadian provinces. Québec joined Nova Scotia, Manitoba, Saskatchewan, Alberta, and British Columbia in voting against the Accord, but each region (like each individual voter, moreover) had its own reasons for finding the proposals inadequate. Most francophone Québecers felt that the Charlottetown Accord represented a significant step backward from the original Meech Lake deal; the implicit message they were sending Robert Bourassa was that he had not done a satisfactory job of defending the province's interests.[11]

This sorry episode closed the book on Robert Bourassa's lengthy and protean political career. It also marked the beginning of the most recent phase in party system development in Québec, one which featured a third referendum on the province's constitutional fate and a virtual standoff between the pro- and anti-sovereignist forces in the province. In the 1994 provincial election, the PQ and the QLP each took about 44 per cent of the vote, while the ADQ, which served as the vehicle for disaffected former Liberals and "soft nationalists"[12] like Jean Allaire and Mario Dumont, won 6.5 per cent of the vote. Because of the Liberals' huge majorities in the predominantly anglophone ridings of west-end Montréal, the dead heat in popular vote translated into a comfortable PQ majority (they won 77 seats out of the 125 in the National Assembly). True to his word, Premier Parizeau set about preparing for a third referendum immediately after his election win. Initially scheduled for the spring of 1995, the referendum was postponed until October of that year. As Table 3 suggests, the overwhelming turnout (93.5 per cent) and the closeness of the vote (the No side's margin of victory was a mere 54,000 votes out of some 4.7 million ballots cast), combined with the near absence of any sustained violence in the aftermath of the vote, indicate that the 1995 referendum was a remarkable watershed in Québec's—and Canada's—political history.

Much has been made of the so-called "Bouchard effect" during the referendum campaign—the surge in support for the Yes side that seemed to occur the moment Lucien Bouchard replaced Jacques Parizeau as the *de facto* head of the sovereignist forces on October 7. As Pierre Drouilly and others have noted, however, the turnaround in public opinion (the No side entered the campaign with about 50 to 55 per cent support, depending on the poll) began at least two weeks before Bouchard assumed the leadership of the Yes forces, although "évidemment l'arrivée de Lucien Bouchard n'a pu que consolider, et peut-être amplifier, cette remontée du OUI dans les sondages."[13] Drouilly's data show that the vote in 1995, not surprisingly, was polarized along linguistic lines: the higher the percentage of francophones in a given riding, the higher the support for sovereignty.[14] Anglophones and allophones voted massively for the No, as did the various aboriginal nations. The proportion of No votes among Aboriginals ranged from a low of 74.5 per cent among the Abenaki to a high of 98.9 per cent among the Micmac. As Drouilly observes, support for the Yes option was strongest among those first nations which, for historical and geographical reasons, have French as a second language (Montagnais, Hurons, and Abenaki).[15]

In total, Drouilly estimates that 60 per cent of the francophones in Québec voted for the Yes side. In addition to the language cleavage, there appeared to be a class bias to the vote, with the highest income regions in the province providing the strongest support for the No side. These linguistic and class bases of the federalist vote are what prompted Jacques Parizeau to make the infamous remark in his concession speech on the night of the referendum that the sovereignty project was defeated by "money and some ethnic votes" (*l'argent et des votes ethniques*). To Drouilly and others, this assertion may have been unstatesmanlike and "inopportune … [mais elle] exprime néanmoins dans une formule saisissante une vérité incontournable."[16] Drouilly even goes so far as to claim that the near unanimous vote of the minority anglophones and allophones in Québec frustrated the will of a clear majority of francophones in 1995, which represents their "systematic and stubborn rejection of francophone Québec."[17] Although Drouilly makes it clear that he believes sovereignists should continue to extend a welcome to their anglophone and allophone counterparts and try to "build a country together," his comments underscore the yawning gap in sensibilities between federalists and *indépendantistes* in the province. There is very little evidence to suggest that this gap has narrowed in the eight years since the 1995 referendum was held. Drouilly is, moreover, conveniently silent on the heterogeneous nature of the "clear francophone majority": not every voter in this 60 per cent of the francophone electorate was casting his or her vote for sovereignty. Many were simply voting strategically, to place a figurative "knife at the throat" of the ROC in order to initiate meaningful constitutional change of the federal system. Thus it is not at all clear that the 60 per cent of francophones who voted Yes in 1995 all shared the sovereignist dream of building a new (independent) country together.

No sooner were the referendum results announced on 30 October 1995, than Jacques Parizeau resigned as leader of the PQ and Premier of Québec. His successor was Lucien Bouchard, who was unopposed in his bid for the leadership and the premier's office. Two years after this change in party leadership, another occurred in the main opposition party, as Daniel Johnson Jr. was elbowed aside as leader of the Québec Liberal Party and replaced by Jean Charest. The manner of Johnson's removal—influential business groups within the QLP lobbied behind the scenes to have Jean Charest assume the party leadership, since opinion polls at the time indicated he was the one politician who seemed to stand a chance of defeating Lucien Bouchard and the PQ—underscores the extent to which backroom wheeling and dealing and intra-elite jockeying still play a prominent role in internal party politics, in Québec as elsewhere in Canada.[18]

The 1998 provincial election thus featured two former federal Conservative cabinet ministers running against each other as leaders of the federalist and sovereignist parties in Québec. The vote was a virtual replay of the 1994 outcome, with the PQ and the QLP taking almost equal, but slightly reduced shares of the popular vote (about 43 per cent). However, the PQ translated their votes more efficiently into seats in the National Assembly, winning 76 of 125 and forming a second consecutive majority government. The ADQ improved its performance quite markedly in 1998, taking almost 12 per cent of the vote but still sending only one *député*, Mario Dumont, to the National Assembly.

Since the 1995 referendum, the PQ government has been preoccupied with trimming public spending in order to eliminate the large budget deficit. As Premier, Lucien Bouchard was forced each year to square the budgetary circle, implementing major cutbacks in important areas of government spending (health, education, and welfare) while convincing his party's supporters in the public sector that a Liberal government would impose much deeper and bloodier cuts. Given the near impossibility of this task, Bouchard's performance was remarkably adept (and surprised many observers outside of Québec, who had predicted that Bouchard's political career would falter once he actually had to assume the responsibilities of power). He managed to mollify or at least neutralize the province's trade unions by carefully consulting them on key issues of public policy in a series of *tables de concertation*. According to James Iain Gow and André Guertin, the Bouchard government's overall policy direction—reduction in the size of government, rationalization of government ministries, and cutbacks in public spending—may well have been dictated by international and national trends, but it exhibited much greater concern for trade union opinion than any Liberal administration would conceivably have done.[19] For a variety of strategic reasons (fear of the Liberal alternative, support for the PQ's sovereignty project), the public sector unions were willing to make a leap of faith with Lucien Bouchard in the expectation of economic and constitutional payoffs down the road.

Just when it appeared that Lucien Bouchard had successfully negotiated the political tightrope imposed by the prevailing socio-economic circumstances of the late 1990s, he shocked the province by announcing in January 2001 that he was quitting the premier's office and politics altogether in order to return to private life. Bouchard's abrupt departure followed on the heels of the so-called Michaud Affair, which sparked a divisive internal debate in the PQ between hardliners and moderates. Yves Michaud, former Delegate-General of Québec in France (1979-84), had remarked to a radio journalist in early December 2000 that Jews feel that they are the only people to have suffered in the history of humanity. For some time, Michaud had been highly critical of the Bouchard government's laxity in defending the French language; in one op-ed piece in *Le Devoir*, Michaud had warned darkly that concessions to minority language groups in Québec amounted to a "linguistic Munich."[20] On 13 December 2000, Michaud appeared before the Estates-General on the Status of the French Language, excoriating the B'Nai Brith as an extremist, anti-Québec organization and complaining about "ethnic" (Jewish) voting against sovereignty in the Côte-St.-Luc region of Montréal. Bouchard quickly disavowed Michaud's comments and the National Assembly unanimously censured him on 14 December (the QLP introduced the motion of censure). Some of Michaud's supporters within the PQ complained of Bouchard's *duplessiste* tactics. On 10 January 2001, *Le Devoir* ran a full-page ad, purchased by some of Michaud's supporters, which condemned the National Assembly's censuring of a private citizen (Michaud), arguing that it had been a flagrant violation of freedom of expression. The next day, Bouchard announced his resignation.

In his resignation speech, Bouchard claimed that it was his inability to advance the sovereignty project, and not the Michaud Affair, that prompted his decision to quit politics. His efforts to kick-start the debate on the national question, he said, had been futile, and Québécois had remained "étonnamment impassibles devant les offensives fédérales comme l'union sociale, le programme de bourses millénaire, la création de chaires universitaires de recherche, l'adoption de la loi C-20 [the Clarity Bill] … En tout les cas, s'il y avait mécontentement, les résultats du dernier scrutin fédéral ne l'ont guère exprimé."[21] Nevertheless, Bouchard did state that he did not have the stomach for any more discussions about the nature of the Holocaust or the voting tendencies of Québec's various ethnic communities. He also affirmed that Michaud's remarks had harmed Québec's reputation on the international stage.

Bernard Landry replaced Bouchard as leader of the PQ and premier of Québec in March 2001. Like Bouchard, and Jacques Parizeau before him, Landry was unopposed for the leadership. Pauline Marois, the highly regarded Minister of Health and Social Services,[22] seemed poised to run against Bernard Landry for the leadership. Had she done so, it would have ensured a contest between competing economic visions, since Marois has long been associated with the social-democratic wing of the PQ and Landry with the more pragmatic or business-oriented faction. Marois ultimately decided not to run for the leadership, the apparent victim of a secret pact between Landry and another possible contender, the Minister of Education, François Legault. This means that the political party that was the first in Canada to adopt the universal membership vote (UMV) as the device for selecting its leader, has used the technique only once since 1985.[23]

Since assuming the leadership of the PQ, Landry has played to the hardliners in the party with a series of inflammatory comments about Canada and the federal system, the most notorious being his remark that Québec would not "sell itself on the street for some bits of red rag."[24] Landry's aggressive posturing may well have succeeded in energizing the PQ's rank-and-file for the upcoming provincial election, but it appears not to have had much of an impact on public opinion on the sovereignty issue. Survey data published by Léger and Léger indicate that support for sovereignty-association in Québec has averaged about 44 per cent over the last three years (1999-2001). Average annual support for the Yes option reached its peak in 1996 (51 per cent), and has declined slowly since then, stabilizing in the mid-40s, notwithstanding Landry's aggressive rhetoric.[25]

At the dawn of the twenty-first century, then, Québec's major parties appear to be suffering from a kind of programmatic sclerosis. Their continuing preoccupation with the unresolved national question, combined with their failure to articulate new and imaginative solutions to the problem, is sharply at odds with (and undoubtedly a contributing cause of) the constitutional fatigue that afflicts the province's voters almost as much as their counterparts in the rest of Canada.[26] Opinion poll after opinion poll in Québec has indicated that the electorate would prefer to postpone another referendum indefinitely, so that the provincial government can focus on more pressing concerns like unemployment and health care. One might expect this disconnect between parties and voters to lead to frustration in the electorate, heightened cynicism, and political disengagement. This has not entirely been the case, however, as I show in the next section of the chapter.

Québec's Two-Party System: Fostering Creative Politics or Limiting Choices?

In his magisterial investigation into the distribution of power in Canada, *Vertical Mosaic*, John Porter lamented the fact that Canadian party politics lacked an ideological dimension, one that revolved around issues of class in capitalist society. He argued that Canada was "one of the few major industrial societies in which the right and left polarization has become deflected into disputes over regionalism and national unity."[27] Referring specifically to the tendency of Canada's major parties to avoid hard issues, to try to be all things to all voters, Porter commented: "to obscure social divisions through brokerage politics is to remove from the political system that element of dialectic which is the source of creative politics."[28]

At first glance, it might appear that Québec's party system is the classic brokerage model, where all issues are refracted, and distorted, through the prism of sovereignty, where key issues of economic power take a back seat to the perennial question of independence, and where two broadly based parties vie for the support of the median voter. This is not the case, however, for several reasons. In the first place, the Parti Québécois, despite its undeniable deradicalization in the last 20 years—a process hastened by its tenure in power (1976-1985 and 1994 to the present) and the straitened economic circumstances in which it has had to govern—remains a complex coalition of competing social forces. It is also an organization that pays more than lip service to the notion of intra-party democracy. Its biennial conventions are almost always heated affairs in which the rank-and-file activists can force the party elites to modify or abandon their position on key issues, such as minority language rights or the need for an economic partnership with ROC after attaining sovereignty. The party program that issues from these conventions[29] thus embodies the "terms of a truce" between the different factions in the party, as is the case with the Labour Party in Great Britain.[30] More than most other provincial political parties in Canada, the PQ allows for interest accommodation *within* the party organization itself, thereby compensating somewhat for the limited choices offered to voters at election time.

This is not to say that all voters in Québec are perfectly happy with the system in place. The ADQ's modest success in the two most recent provincial elections is an indicator that a sizeable number of voters would like to see a third option between the PQ's sovereignty project and status quo federalism—which many voters clearly feel the QLP is powerless to alter. Nonetheless, the first-past-the-post electoral system discourages these voters—who may constitute as much as 20 per cent of the electorate[31]—from casting their ballots for their preferred option.[32]

Another group of increasingly disgruntled voters in Québec consists of the social democrats who really have no other credible political option at election time but the PQ. Yet increasingly, these voters find it difficult to support a party that they feel is more committed to mollifying international investors by trimming the provincial budget than it is to the notion of democratic equality. This widespread disillusionment among the PQ's left-wing supporters contributed to the party's shocking setback in the by-election in the riding of Mercier (in April 2001). While it is certainly true that by-elections do not provide solid grounds for generalizing about the state of the political system, there were a number of features of the race in Mercier that made it more than just a typical mid-term expression of discontent with the incumbent government. The riding of Mercier has a privileged place in *péquiste* mythology: it is the riding in which the poet-intellectual, Gérald Godin, defeated the Premier of the province, Robert Bourassa, in 1976. The PQ had held the riding since that election; in 1998, the *péquiste* candidate, Robert Perreault, had taken over 55 per cent of the vote. In the by-election, the Liberal candidate, Nathalie Rochefort, won the riding with just under 35 per cent of the vote. PQ support was split almost evenly between the officially endorsed candidate, Claudel Toussaint,[33] who received just under 29 per cent of the vote, and the representa-

FIGURE 11.1

Voter Turnout in Québec and the Other Provinces

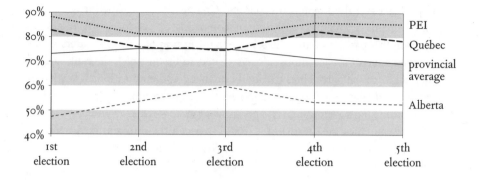

tive of the Rassemblement pour l'alternative progressiste (including the Greens, the NDP, the Communist Party, and the Parti de la démocratie socialiste), Paul Cliche. The latter, described in the mainstream media as an aging leftist warhorse, won 24 per cent of the vote. Turnout was a mere 41 per cent of registered voters, so one must be extremely cautious in making generalizations on the basis of this result. Nonetheless, Cliche's surprisingly strong showing underscores the level of disenchantment among the PQ's traditional social democratic supporters after years of cutbacks inflicted on the state infrastructure in order to achieve the Holy Grail of a balanced budget. This tension between social democracy and nationalism within the PQ ideology has existed, to a greater or lesser extent, since the party's creation in 1968. Indeed, it has provided party elites with a strategic lever to demobilize or neutralize opposition at key moments in the PQ's history.[34] Whether the PQ leadership can continue to mobilize the party's progressive supporters on the basis of their invocation of an independent, *social democratic* Québec will be a key to its success in the next provincial election and, should it win, in the referendum campaign that will inevitably follow.

While some groups of voters in Québec may rankle at the limited choices they are offered in provincial elections, this unhappiness does not appear to be spilling over into widespread disaffection from the political system as a whole. Figure 11.1 indicates that voter turnout in Québec in provincial elections[35] is much higher than in most of the other provinces. If we examine the five most recent elections in each of the provinces,[36] we can group them into three categories: those with very high turnout (Prince Edward Island at almost 84 per cent over the five elections, New Brunswick at 79 per cent, and Québec at 78.6 per cent), those with extremely low turnout (Alberta at 53.5 per cent and Ontario at 62 per cent), and the rest, with turnouts averaging between 70 and 77 per cent. For purposes of illustration, the

FIGURE 11.2

Number of Contributions (>$3,000, current dollars) to PQ and QLP, 1982-98

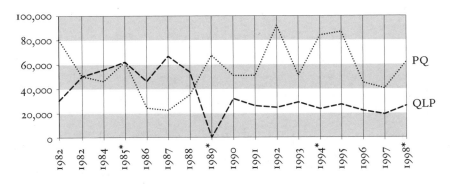

* election year

Source: Québec, Directeur-général des élections, *Rapport financiers, 1987-1998.*

figure uses Prince Edward Island as an example of a high-turnout province and Alberta as the low-turnout province. The average turnout for all 10 provinces is also calculated, and the data show that in three of the five most recent elections, Québec's voter turnout has been about 10 percentage points higher than the provincial average. Another interesting feature of the data in Figure 1 is that the three highest turnouts in recent Québec provincial elections occurred in 1981 (82.5 per cent), 1994 (81.7 per cent) and 1998 (78.3 per cent), precisely those elections won by the Parti Québécois. This suggests that the PQ's electoral success depends to a considerable degree on mobilizing its supporters, much more than is the case for the QLP.

Another indicator of the relative health of Québec's party system can be gleaned from the data on party finances contained in Figures 11.2 and 11.3. One of the most important policy innovations of the first PQ government of René Lévesque was the reform of the province's election financing law in 1977. Prior to the PQ victory, electoral politics in Québec had been characterized by rampant corruption, kickbacks, tollgating, and other forms of illicit fund-raising. In order to clean up the system and restore some integrity to party financing, the PQ government outlawed any form of corporate contribution, trade union or business, to a registered political party. Only individual citizens could make donations to parties, and the maximum allowable contribution was $1,000 (revised upward to $3,000 in 1985). This piece of legislation has helped transform both the PQ and the PLQ into mass membership parties, although, as the data in Figures 11.2 and 11.3 indicate, the PQ remains the party with the broader appeal. In 1998, both the PQ and the PLQ received roughly

FIGURE 11.3

Average Contribution in Current Dollars, PQ and QLP, 1982-99

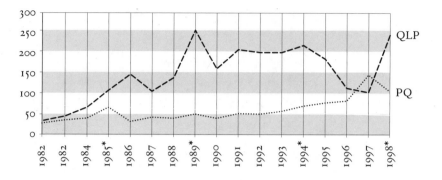

the same revenue from membership dues, individual contributions, and state subsidies—$6.6 million for the PQ, and $6.2 million for the PLQ—but the PQ received a large number (over 62,000) of relatively small donations (see Figure 11.2). The PLQ generally receives a much smaller number of larger contributions. Figure 11.2 underscores this relationship: in most years since 1982, the PQ has received far more contributions than the PLQ (in 1992, for instance, the ratio was four to one for the PQ, or some 80,000 contributions versus 20,000 for the PLQ). But the average size of the contribution to the PLQ is frequently three to four times bigger than that directed to the PQ ($216 versus $67 in 1994, for instance; see Figure 11.3).

Québec's electoral laws appear to do a much better job of fostering the participation of individual voters in the financing of political parties than does legislation in the other provinces or at the federal level. It is far from a perfect system, however, and there are some worrying signs that popular support for the parties may be declining. For one thing, state subsidies are playing a bigger role in party revenues than ever before. In 2000, the ADQ received fully 80 per cent of its revenues in the form of state reimbursements, while the proportion of the PQ's and QLP's revenues coming from state subsidies has ranged from 35 to 40 per cent in recent years.[37] For another, both of the major parties are relying increasingly on fewer, but larger, individual contributions for their revenues. Finally, the PQ's mode of financing has drifted, over time, towards that of the QLP, with greater reliance on "cocktails, dîners-bénéfices et autres activités partisanes avec prix d'entrée ..."[38] Party elites will be forced to pay attention to these trends if they are to head off any further demobilization of the electorate in Québec.

Conclusion

Much on the surface of Québec's party system has changed since the collapse of the Meech Lake Accord in June 1990. Each of the major parties has gone through two leadership changes in the last decade, and one minor party has disappeared, while another, which to now seems to be a one-man show (the personal vehicle of "Super Mario" Dumont), has emerged. Despite this apparent upheaval, the fundamental basis of Québec's party system—two-party competition centred on the still unresolved national question—has remained unaltered since the mid-1960s. At the dawn of the twenty-first century, Québec's voters wait for another—perhaps conclusive?—referendum on the sovereignty project, or, less likely, on some sweeping reform of the existing federal system. Until that time, significant changes in the pattern of party competition are unlikely to occur. Some voters may grumble at the apparent sclerosis of Québec's party system, but in comparative terms, their party system is healthier than most others in the country.

Notes

1. This episode is recounted by Alain-G. Gagnon, "Québec-Canada: Constitutional Developments, 1960-92," in Alain-G. Gagnon, ed., *Québec: State and Society*, 2nd. ed. (Scarborough, ON: Nelson, 1993), 100.

2. See the two seminal articles by Richard Hamilton and Maurice Pinard, "The Independence Issue and the Polarization of the Electorate: The 1973 Québec Election," *CJPS* 10, 2 (June 1977): 215-59 and "The Parti Québécois Comes to Power: An Analysis of the 1976 Québec Election," *CJPS* 11, 4 (Dec. 1978): 739-75.

3. In an interview shortly after the PQ victory, Lévesque claimed that his government "must maintain a favourable prejudice toward workers [*un préjugé favorable aux travailleurs*]." See René Lévesque, *La Passion du Québec* (Montréal: Éditions Québec/Amérique, 1978), 76.

4. The Rand Formula stipulates that "non-union employees in [a] bargaining unit must pay the union a sum equal to union fees as a condition of continuing employment. Non-union workers are not, however, required to join the union." Labour Canada, *Glossary of Industrial Relations Terms*, 3rd ed. (Ottawa: Minister of Supply and Services, 1984), 18. For a discussion of the PQ's labour legislation during its first term in office, see A. Brian Tanguay, "An Uneasy Alliance: The Parti Québécois and the Unions," in Jane Jenson and Rianne Mahon, eds., *The Challenge of Restructuring: North American Labor Movements Respond* (Philadelphia: Temple University Press, 1993), 154-79.

5. Graham Fraser, *PQ: René Lévesque and the Parti Québécois in Power.* (Toronto: Macmillan, 1984), 365.

6. Quoted in Jean-François Lisée, *The Trickster: Robert Bourassa and Québecers, 1990-1992*, abridged and translated by Robert Chodos, Simon Horn, and Wanda Taylor (Toronto: Lorimer, 1994), 7. This is a captivating insider's account of this period in Québec history. Lisée writes from the perspective of an embittered supporter of Québec sovereignty, for whom Robert Bourassa was nothing but a liar, a swindler, and a traitor.

7. Lisée provides survey data showing that support for "sovereignty-association" among Québec voters shot up from around 45 per cent in 1989 to over 60 per cent in mid-1990. The percentage of the electorate in favour of sovereignty-association remained in the high 50s until the PQ won the 1994 provincial election. See Lisée, *The Trickster*, 360.

8. Québec Liberal Party, Report of the Constitutional Committee, *A Québec Free to Choose* (28 Jan. 1991).

9. Both of whom were interviewed extensively by Lisée. In his interview with David Peterson, Lisée tells the former premier that he's trying to determine what Bourassa "really thought" while he was manoeuvring through the negotiations leading up to the Charlottetown Accord. Peterson's blunt response: "You'll never find out." This is included in the prologue to *The Trickster*.

10. Lisée, *The Trickster*, 127.

11. For a fuller discussion of the significance of the 1992 referendum, both for Québec and the rest of Canada, see Kenneth McRoberts and Patrick Monahan, eds., *The Charlottetown Accord, the Referendum, and the Future of Canada* (Toronto: University of Toronto Press, 1993). Appendix 3 contains complete voting results broken down by province.

12. This term is frequently used in the popular media to describe those Québécois who want far-reaching reform of the existing federal system but do not favour outright independence for the province.

13. Pierre Drouilly, "Le référendum du 30 octobre 1995: une analyse des résultats," in *L'Année politique au Québec, 1995-1996,* R. Boily, ed. (Montréal: Fides, 1997), 122.

14. The Pearson's correlation coefficient (Pearson's r) for these two variables (per cent francophone and per cent YES) in 1995 was .861 and even stronger when only the 40 ridings of the Montréal region were analyzed (.959). Similarly, there were strong correlations between the percentage of anglophones in a riding and the percentage NO (.795) and the percentage allophones and the NO vote (.650). See Drouilly, "Le référendum," Tables 5 and 6.

15. Drouilly, "Le référendum," 129.

16. Drouilly, "Le référendum," 132-33.

17. "Par ce vote unanime continuellement affirmé, les électeurs non francophones expriment plutôt un refus, le refus systématique et obstiné du Québec français." "Le référendum," 135.

18. Guy Lachapelle notes that a devastatingly critical article on the "leaderless" provincial Liberals appeared in the influential British weekly, *The Economist* in February, 1998. The article, according to Lachapelle, was undoubtedly "téléguidé ... par les milieux d'affaires québécois, [et] ne visait qu'à hâter le départ de Daniel Johnson au profit de Jean Charest." See Lachapelle's article, "Opinion publique: impasse constitutionnelle et réorientation du rôle des gouvernements," in Robert Boily, ed., *L'Année politique au Québec, 1997-1998,* (Montréal: Les Presses de l'Université de Montréal, 1999), 170.

19. James Iain Gow and André Guertin, "Les partis de gouvernement et l'administration publique: les convergences l'emportent," in Robert Boily, ed., *L'Année politique au Québec, 1997-1998,* (Montréal: Les Presses de l'Université de Montréal, 1999), 109.

20. Yves Michaud, "Réflexions d'avant-congrès," *Le Devoir,* 5 May 2000.

21. "Allocution à l'occasion de la démission du premier ministre du Québec," 11 Jan. 2001. Available at the Web site of the *Association internationale des études québécoises.*

22. When Bernard Landry assumed the leadership of the PQ, he appointed Marois Finance Minister and Deputy Premier.

23. For a discussion of the tactical reasons that propelled the PQ to adopt UMV in 1985, see Daniel Latouche, "Universal Democracy and Effective Leadership: Lessons from the Parti Québécois Experience," in R. Kenneth Carty, Lynda Erickson, and Donald E. Blake, eds. *Leaders and Parties in Canadian Politics: Experiences of the Provinces* (Toronto: Harcourt Brace Jovanovich, 1992), 174-202.

24. This remark was actually made before Landry officially became leader of the PQ, in January 2001, at a party caucus meeting. Landry's outburst was occasioned by the federal government's offer of an $18 million subsidy to the province for the renovation of the Aquarium de Québec. One of the strings attached to this money, however, was that the Canadian flag (the "bits of red rag" in question) be allowed to fly and bilingual signs be posted at the renovated site. This offer prompted Landry's somewhat crude imagery, which elicited the predictable outraged response in the rest of Canada.

25. The data are available at Léger and Léger's Web site: <http://www.leger-leger.qc.ca/français/set.html>. Sample size was generally close to 1000, and the surveys were conducted approximately 10 to 11 times each year. There is no information at the Web site about the wording of questions or margin of error.

26. For a perceptive commentary on the "sclerosis" of the Québec party system, see Chantal Hébert, "Sclérose et démission...," *Le Devoir*, 23 Jan. 2001 (Web version, therefore unpaginated). Hébert writes that Bouchard's resignation and the QLP's latest iteration of its constitutional strategy (which is yet another variation on the Meech Lake Accord) underscore the failure of Québec's political class to advance the national debate very much in the last 30 years.

27. John Porter, *The Vertical Mosaic* (Toronto: University of Toronto Press, 1965), 369.

28. Porter, *Vertical Mosaic*, 374.

29. The most recent program of the Parti Québécois is *Un pays pour le monde* (Montréal, 2000). It was adopted at the 14th biennial convention held in Montréal in May 2000.

30. Donald Savoie, in *Governing from the Centre: The Concentration of Power in Canadian Politics* (Toronto: University of Toronto Press, 1999), 77, contrasts British, and to a lesser extent Australian, political parties with those in Canada. In the former two countries, which also have a Westminster style of government (and thus in-built tendencies towards the concentration of power in the executive), parties "tend to debate and stake out policy positions.... In Canada, however, political parties are ... hardly effective vehicles for generating public policy debates, for staking out policy positions, or for providing a capacity to ensure their own competence once in office."

31. In the three years since the last provincial election, the ADQ has averaged 12.3 per cent (1999), 14.5 per cent (2000), and 16.5 per cent (2001) annual support in the Léger and Léger survey. In January 2001, fully 24 per cent of respondents indicated that they would vote for the ADQ if an election were held then.

32. A point made by Richard Nadeau and Éric Bélanger, "L'appui aux partis politiques québécois, 1989-1998," in Robert Boily, ed., *L'Année politique au Québec, 1997-1998* (Montréal: Les Presses de l'Université de Montréal, 1999), 206, 214.

33. Yves Michaud, the maverick hardliner who hastened Lucien Bouchard's departure from politics, initially indicated that he would seek the nomination. He withdrew after the storm of controversy created by his remarks to the Estates-General on the Status of the French Language. Claudel Toussaint, a member of Montréal's Haitian community, eventually won the nomination. But he, too, was the victim of controversy: during the campaign,

newspapers revealed that Toussaint had been charged with conjugal violence (a charge that had been dropped when his wife refused to testify against him).

34. As I argue in "Interest Aggregation in an Era of Political Change: A Study of Three Provincial Parties in Canada." Paper presented at the Workshop on "From Aggregation to Diffusion? Political Parties in an Individualistic Society," European Consortium for Political Research, Copenhagen, 14-19 Apr. 2000.

35. At the federal level, it is another matter: until recently, turnout in Québec has tended to be lower than the Canadian average. This has not been the case in the 1990s, however, and turnout in the 2000 federal election in Québec, while only 64 per cent, was the third-highest rate in the country, after New Brunswick and Prince Edward Island. For an analysis of federal turnout in Québec during the 2000 election, see Louis Massicotte and Édith Brochu, "Élections fédérales de novembre: coup de loupe sur un scrutin," *Le Devoir*, 26 Feb. 2001 (Édition internet). Available at the newspaper's website: <http://www.ledevoir.com/ago/2001a/mass260201.html>.

36. Official turnout figures for the 2001 election in British Columbia are not yet available, and thus the 1996 election was used as the most recent one.

37. Kathleen Lévesque, "80% de l'argent de l'ADQ provient de l'État," *Le Devoir*, 27 Apr. 2001 (Édition internet). Available at: <http://www.ledevoir.com/manchettes.html>.

38. Kathleen Lévesque, "Le financement des partis ... de moins en moins populaire," *Le Devoir*, 21 Feb. 2001 <http://www.ledevoir.com/que/2001a/fina210201.html>.

Bibliography

Drouilly, Pierre. 1997. "Le référendum du 30 octobre 1995: une analyse des résultats" in R. Boily, ed. *L'Année politique au Québec, 1995-1996*. Montréal: Fides 119-43.

Fraser, Graham. 1984. *PQ: René Lévesque and the Parti Québécois in Power*. (Toronto: Macmillan).

Gagnon, Alain-G. 1993. "Québec-Canada: Constitutional Developments, 1960-92," in Alain-G. Gagnon, ed., *Québec: State and Society*, 2nd ed. (Scarborough, ON: Nelson), 96-115.

Gow, James Iain, and André Guertin. 1999. "Les partis de gouvernement et l'administration publique: les convergences l'emportent," in Robert Boily, ed. *L'Année politique au Québec, 1997-1998*, (Montréal: Les Presses de l'Université de Montréal), 97-109.

Hamilton, Richard, and Maurice Pinard. 1977. "The Independence Issue and the Polarization of the Electorate: The 1973 Québec Election," *CJPS* 10, 2: 215-59.

Hamilton, Richard, and Maurice Pinard. 1978. "The Parti Québécois Comes to Power: An Analysis of the 1976 Québec Election," *CJPS* 11, 4: 739-75.

Hébert, Chantal. 2001. "Sclérose et démission...," *Le Devoir*, 23 Jan. Available at <http://www.ledevoir.com>.

Labour Canada. 1984. *Glossary of Industrial Relations Terms*, 3rd ed. (Ottawa: Minister of Supply and Services).

Lachapelle, Guy. 1999. "Opinion publique: impasse constitutionnelle et réorientation du rôle des gouvernements," in Robert Boily, ed. *L'Année politique au Québec, 1997-1998* (Montréal: Les Presses de l'Université de Montréal), 167-76.

Latouche, Daniel. "Universal Democracy and Effective Leadership: Lessons from the Parti Québécois Experience," in R. Kenneth Carty, Lynda Erickson, and Donald E. Blake, eds. *Leaders and Parties in Canadian Politics: Experiences of the Provinces* (Toronto: Harcourt Brace Jovanovich), 174-202.

Lévesque, René. 1978. *La Passion du Québec* (Montréal: Éditions Québec/Amérique).

Lévesque, Kathleen. 2001. "Le financement des partis … de moins en moins populaire," *Le Devoir*, 21 Feb. Available at <http://www.ledevoir.com/que/2001a/fina210201.html>.

Lévesque, Kathleen. 2001. "80% de l'argent de l'ADQ provient de l'État," *Le Devoir*, 27 Apr. Available at: <http://www.ledevoir.com/manchettes.html>.

Lisée, Jean-François. 1994. *The Trickster: Robert Bourassa and Québecers, 1990-1992*, abridged and trans. Robert Chodos, Simon Horn, and Wanda Taylor (Toronto: Lorimer).

Massicotte, Louis, and Édith Brochu. 2001. "Élections fédérales de novembre: coup de loupe sur un scrutin," *Le Devoir*, 26 Feb. <http://www.ledevoir.com/ago/2001a/mass260201.html>.

McRoberts, Kenneth, and Patrick Monahan, eds. 1993. *The Charlottetown Accord, the Referendum, and the Future of Canada.* (Toronto: University of Toronto Press).

Michaud, Yves. 2000. "Réflexions d'avant-congrès," *Le Devoir*, 5 May.

Nadeau, Richard, and Éric Bélanger. 1999. "L'appui aux partis politiques québécois, 1989-1998," in Robert Boily, ed., *L'Année politique au Québec, 1997-1998* (Montréal: Les Presses de l'Université de Montréal), 203-14.

Parti Québécois. 2000. *Un pays pour le monde*. Montréal.

Porter, John. 1965. *The Vertical Mosaic*. (Toronto: University of Toronto Press).

Québec Liberal Party. 1991. Report of the Constitutional Committee. *A Québec Free to Choose* (Montréal), 28 Jan.

Québec. Premier ministre. 2001. "Allocution à l'occasion de la démission du premier ministre du Québec," 11 Jan. Available at the Web site of the *Association internationale des études québécoises*: <http://www.aieq.qc.ca/bouchard.htm>.

Savoie, Donald. 1999. *Governing from the Centre: The Concentration of Power in Canadian Politics* (Toronto: University of Toronto Press).

Tanguay, A. Brian. 1993. "An Uneasy Alliance: The Parti Québécois and the Unions," in Jane Jenson and Rianne Mahon, eds., *The Challenge of Restructuring: North American Labor Movements Respond* (Philadelphia: Temple University Press), 154-79.

———. 2000. "Interest Aggregation in an Era of Political Change: A Study of Three Provincial Parties in Canada," paper presented at the Workshop on "From Aggregation to Diffusion? Political Parties in an Individualistic Society." European Consortium for Political Research, Copenhagen, 14-19 Apr.

12

Anti-Market Globalization Social Movements[1]

MARC LEMIRE[*]

In Québec, the rest of Canada, as well as in many other countries, the end of the twentieth century brought about a critical and open rise in awareness of the phenomenon of globalization. An opposition has developed on a world-wide scale, and is challenging what most people had, until recently, considered to be an inevitable, and essentially positive transformation. Rooted in many different local movements, this international opposition testifies to the concerns that groups and individuals of diverse origins and affiliations share, faced with the unfulfilled ambitions of the big actors in the economy, ambitions that are revealed through recently negotiated international economic agreements.[2] This opposition also reveals the concerns of populations in the North as well as in the South who are wary of the harmful consequences of globalized capitalism. Hence, we can distinguish a Left in the midst of rediscovering itself,[3] outside the structure of the political parties, whose capacities for integration and representation have been called into serious doubt. The Left that was becoming reserved, hesitant, even resigned in the face of the decisive advances of capitalism and the fall of communism, has come to express itself through a renewed discourse, new alliances, and modes of action, some of which have been reinvented.[4]

One of the fundamental characteristics of this opposition is that it has brought together a diverse array of activists such as feminists, environmentalists, peace activists, students, and anarchists, and united them in a single struggle.[5] There are also groups and individuals defending workers, consumers, and small busi-

* Translated from French into English by Marc Hanvelt.

245

nesses, or supporting human rights, social rights, and political rights. There has, therefore, been a new outbreak of social movements that has been combined with a radicalization of positions. It is also worth noting the convergence between "old" and "new" social movements that are awakening, meeting themselves, or discovering themselves around a set of issues that appear to them to be common to all, and in fact, that transcend their respective interests. This grouping of movements is defining itself around a set of affinity networks or a loose and latent solidarity the existence of which is, nevertheless, real. As was rightly noted by Alberto Melucci in his observations on contemporary movements, these networks appear in the most intense days during conflicts.[6]

In light of this convergence, it appears that a vast, complex, and diverse movement is emerging. My objective is to identify the elements that give it shape and singularity, without masking the differences of opinion that exist within it. Following from the work of Alain Touraine,[7] I will define a "social movement" as a set of more or less concerted, collective actions in which social actors engage with the goal of challenging a form of social domination and, through struggle, of establishing a new social order. In contrast with other forms of collective action, such as those led by partisan and simple interest groups, a social movement, particularly in the most developed form, that A. Touraine calls a "societal" movement, is characterized by "the fact that a category of actors enters into a conflict with an adversary over the management of the society's principal means of action upon itself."[8] Also, the group's struggle is necessarily political,[9] even though, these days, movements have tended to distance themselves from traditional political authorities and to abstain from seeking state power.[10]

In this chapter, I propose to study the numerous facets of the rise of this diverse and complex movement in the context of Québec. First, I will recount the principal moments that marked its emergence and discuss the different types of groups that were mobilized against the Multilateral Agreement on Investment (MAI) and the Millennium Round, as well as against the proposal to create the Free Trade Area of the Americas (FTAA). Second, I will describe the characteristics of the movement, emphasizing its modes of organization and the repertoire of actions it has used. Third, I will describe the elements of the movement's critique of globalization, as it currently exists. The critique leads to the view that this phenomenon is a system, process, and ideology of market globalization. In conclusion, I will underline certain implications of this movement for relations with the state and with the political world.

Overview of an International Mobilization

Criticisms of forms of domination transcend history, as is the case for the struggles that arise from those situations. Similarly, actions taken against government policies and interstate treaties are, in no way, new phenomena. Nevertheless, the characteristics of the international mobilization against neo-liberal economic globalization are sufficiently clear to permit us to situate it, according to its most visible demonstration in time and space.

One of the principal events leading to the appearance on the public scene of this international opposition appears to have been the disclosure over the Internet in the spring of 1997 of dealings that had been kept secret by 29 countries who had been engaged for two years in negotiations aimed at concluding the Multilateral Agreement on Investment, the MAI. Although other economic accords, notably the Free Trade Agreement (FTA) signed in 1988 by Canada and the United States, had raised the ire of groups and individuals, the sudden revelation of the existence of the MAI sparked a debate of a scope, vigour, and spontaneity such as had never before been seen in relation to negotiations of this sort.[11] In Canada, the opposition was stronger than that against the FTA.[12] Negotiated between 1995 and 1998 by the members of the Organization for Economic Co-operation and Development (OECD), formed essentially of rich countries such as Canada, the MAI was aborted shortly after France pulled out of the negotiations in face of, among other factors, the observed resistance to it.

Since then, the opposition to neo-liberal economic globalization has continued to confirm its place as a persistent and deep-rooted social force, as is attested to by the new mobilization against the FTAA. The opposition routinely makes its presence felt at the big international meetings of ministers and heads of state: Prague; Seattle; Milan; Melbourne; Seoul; Nice; Davos; Naples; Windsor, Ontario; Montréal; and Québec are a few of the places where, since the MAI, protesters have left their mark on the once-quiet meetings of the G-7, the OECD, the World Trade Organization (WTO), the International Monetary Fund (IMF), the Asia Pacific Economic Forum (APEC), and others. The images of altercations, sometimes violent, between protesters and police forces that are widely disseminated by the world medias contribute to the impression that this is a struggle to the death in which the stakes are related essentially to antagonistic conceptions of governance, and of the development of societies and their populations. In all of this, the MAI seems to have been the spark that ignited a latent opposition against this model, an opposition that had been, until this point, poorly articulated, and that had nothing as concrete as this proposed treaty against which to express its concerns and fundamental objections.

If this "nebula" or "constellation" of groups and of individuals appears to us to be deeply-rooted and persistent, certainly in the moments of greatest febrility or agitation it becomes palpable, and thus concrete in the eyes of the greatest number of people. So, a brief recounting of the events of recent years will permit us to appreciate the most tangible actions of this movement and to follow its evolution right up to the Summit of the Americas that was held in Québec City in April 2001.

The opposition to the MAI, which had won the support of the majority of the countries in the OECD as well as of certain countries in the third world,[13] manifested itself first in the public statements of associations and groups such as the Halifax Initiative, a coalition that was developed in the wake of the 1995 G-7 conference to demand a major reform of international financial institutions, and that counts amongst its members the Canadian Council of Catholic Bishops, the Canadian Council for International Co-operation, OXFAM-Canada, and the Sierra Club. Another example is *La Coalition québécoise pour la diversité culturelle* that brought together a dozen organizations to demand that arts and culture be excluded from trade negotiations. The largest coalition to denounce the MAI was the Council of Canadians which claims to represent some 100,000 people, notably, members of left-wing political parties such as the New Democratic Party (NDP), the Green Party, and the Communist Party.

Second, the opposition was expressed through more direct, more visible, and in some cases, more radical actions. In Québec, Operation SalAMI[14] gained media attention in May 1998 for organizing an act of civil disobedience in front of a downtown Montréal hotel where the 4th Montréal Conference on Economic Globalization was opening. The opening of the conference was delayed for several hours by a scattered group of 400 to 600 people from both anglophone and franco-phone neighbourhoods. Many of the participants had no experience in protests, had no culture of protest, and did not belong to any specific organizations. One hundred people from the group took part directly in a blockade of the entrance to the con-ference, an action that earned them criminal charges for mischief, hindering police, unlawful assembly, and breaking the peace. Operation SalAMI nonetheless received the support of some 1,500 supporters, including union organizations, which expressed their amazement at the group's capacity for mobilization. Politicians, such as Jacques Parizeau, the former premier of Québec, and Stéphane Tremblay, the federal MP for the Bloc Québécois, publicly recognized the pertinence of the group's opposition.

The third ministerial conference of the WTO, held in Seattle in December 1999, became the focus of further demonstrations and awareness-raising activities in Québec. The 135 member countries of the WTO had decided to begin a new round of trade negotiations at the conference, the Millennium Round, in order to further liberalize and integrate their economies. As with the MAI, this conference became the focus of an opposition movement that developed on a global scale.[15] More than 800 NGOs, from some 70 countries, met in the American city where the conference was taking place. The public demonstrations in Seattle, which attracted close to 50,000 people, disrupted the agenda of the conference, paralyzed the downtown core, led the police to adopt extremely severe measures (following the declaration of a state of emergency and a curfew for the duration of the conference), and contributed to the deadlock of the negotiations, which was also explained by other factors.[16]

Alongside the events in Seattle that garnered heavy media coverage, a week of education about the stakes of globalization was organized in Montréal by a coalition of associations and organizations that included the *Réseau québécois sur l'intégration continentale* (RQIC), which is itself made up of 20 groups (including Amnesty International, Peace and Development, The Québec Federation of Women, *Solidarité populaire du Québec*, The Rights and Freedoms League, academics, and unions), ATTAC-Québec (The Association for the Taxation of Financial Transactions for the Aid of Citizens), SalAMI, *Eau-Secours*,[17] and sociology students from UQAM. In Québec City, another coalition formed of students, and of social and humanitarian groups that included Alternatives, *les AmiEs de la Terre*, and the *Collectif masculin contre le sexisme*, held a rally that attracted between 200 and 300 people. Other demonstrations took place in the big cities of English Canada, including Toronto and Vancouver. The most original initiative was The Cross-Canada WTO Caravan which was supported by the big Canadian unions (the Postal Workers, Auto Workers, and Public Service Unions), by students associations, and by the Council of Canadians. A group of activists spent 22 days on board this caravan, travelling from Toronto to Vancouver, and then to Seattle. They stopped in 20 cities along the way, educating people about the stakes of the Seattle conference.

One year later, in October 2000, several hundred protesters gathered in the streets of Montréal, this time, on the occasion of the second meeting of the G-20. The G-20 is an international authority that was formed in 1999 by the G-7, who wanted the finance ministers of 19 countries and the European Union, as well as the governors of the IMF and the World Bank, to meet around the same table.[18] On the occasion of the meeting in Montréal, the protesters were organized, in particular, by a student association and a trade union, who presented this protest as a warm-up for the Summit of the Americas.

Leading to this event that took place in Québec City in 2001 was a buzz of activity among the groups and associations of activists in Québec. For the last few years, every international meeting had seemed to generate a similar turbulence in the locale directly affected. New coalitions were formed, and some continued to operate after the event had ended. One such example is the Halifax Initiative that was formed around the G-7 meeting that took place in 1995 in that Eastern Canadian city, and which continues to operate. In Québec, the opponents of neo-liberal economic globalization felt particularly called to action by an event during which

34 heads of state from the Americas and the Caribbean discussed the creation of a free-trade area of the Americas (FTAA) that would cover the entire hemisphere, with the exception of Cuba. This free-trade project was revived at the suggestion of the United States at the 1994 Miami Summit.

With an eye to the Summit of the Americas, numerous groups were formed in Montréal and Québec, as well as in Outaouais and other regions. Forums, workshops, and colloquiums were organized throughout the province, prompting several academics and university researchers to enter into the debate alongside these citizen groups. In the aftermath of the deadlock at the Seattle conference, 30 or so unions, left-wing political parties, humanitarian and environmental organizations, community groups, students associations, and neighbourhood committees came together to form the foundations of a large coalition called *Opération Québec Printemps* 2001 (OQP, 2001). This coalition took on the roles of putting into place the logistics for receiving the protesters who would come to Québec City, as well as of planning non-violent demonstrations around the event. OQP 2001 worked alongside other groups who, for reasons of practicality, strategy, history, or even, as we will see later on, ideology, decided to organize and recruit separately. Among these other groups, it is worth noting particularly the *Convergence des luttes anti-capitalistes* (CLAC), based in Montréal, and its counterpart in Québec City, the Comité d'Accueil du Sommet des Amériques (CASA). In contrast to OQP 2001, these groups recruited all of their members outside of institutions such as political parties and unions. Contrary to the policy of OQP 2001, they advocated a "diversity of tactics" to disrupt the summit, including, if necessary, violence. But just like OQP 2001, they were responsible for a large part of the mobilization, the awareness-raising, the receiving of protesters, and the organization of the logistics for the struggle.

The OQP 2001 coalition, SalAMI, and ATTAC-Québec, along with other groups such as RQIC and the Québec Nurses Federation (FIIQ), formed the Convergence table for the non-violent opposition. But each of the groups at the table maintained its complete autonomy with regards to the actions that it would undertake. So, while SalAMI emphasized peaceful civil disobedience and political pressure aimed at getting the texts that were being negotiated divulged to the public, ATTAC-Québec emphasized the education of the general public by offering, for example, conferences in local communities. For its part, RQIC devoted much of its time to arranging the "Peoples' Summit," a parallel summit that it organized in conjunction with Common Frontiers, its equivalent in English Canada, in the name of the Social Continental Alliance, an alliance that encompasses organizations throughout the entire hemisphere.

The majority of the groups and organizations maintained ties with organizations in other countries, such as Public Citizen, People for Fair Trade, Ruckus Society, and Direct Action Network in the United States, or *La Confédération Paysanne* and

Le Monde diplomatique in France. Organizations from diverse places felt called to action by the events in Québec, as is evidenced by the 50 or so activities that paralleled the April 2001 Summit in roughly 40 cities throughout the Americas. These activities included protests organized in Saõ Paulo, Brazil; along the Canada/US border in Maine, New York, and Vermont; and along the Mexico/US border around Tijuana and San Diego. We should also note the caravan of Rights Action, a humanitarian organization that planned stops in several Canadian and American cities as it travelled to Québec with activists from Honduras, Guatemala, and Chiapas in Mexico on board.

The result of all of this mobilization was an inexhaustible reservoir of networks of solidarity that gave rise to, sometimes unusual, coalitions, and to a multitude of more or less concerted group and individual initiatives. While the interrelations between each of the constituents of this whole are relatively difficult to retrace and describe, there can be no doubt, in light of the preceding, that a vast social movement has come into existence. As it is conceived by A. Melluci,[19] this movement first developed around pre-existing and scattered networks, which, by dividing and channelling themselves around a common cause, gained the public's attention and a certain visibility, and gave body and relative coherence to a veritable international opposition.

The Characteristics of a Movement

This stunning international mobilization, in which the youngest generations played a predominant role, has been described by certain people as the emergence of a "global civil society,"[20] of a "global opposition,"[21] of a "new internationalism,"[22] of a "civic internationalism outside of political parties,"[23] and of a "democratic movement."[24] The concept of a social movement, traditionally applied to the struggles of workers and unionists, then to the student demonstrations of May 1968, and later, to the struggles of the 1970s and 1980s for civil rights, the rights of women, peace, and the environment, is this time used to designate a mobilization the forms of which are as original as they are irregular.

The studies of Zsuzsa Hegedus[25] on the peace movements highlight certain dimensions of contemporary collective actions. According to her, the new social movements can be recognized by the following notable facts: they are assuming a much more global dimension, not limiting themselves to industrialized countries; they insist on the global nature of the stakes by linking them with domestic questions and by appealing to responsibility and solidarity; they attempt to free themselves from partisan strategies by largely ignoring traditional political structures and processes; they distance themselves from immediate and personal interests such as financial situation; and they favour expressive, pragmatic, planned, non-violent actions, such as civil disobedience. With the exception, in the present case that the modes of action appear to cover a larger spectrum, all of these aspects apply to the movement we are studying.

Three major characteristics appear particularly significant to its description. The first, to which I have just referred, is the international character of the struggle. The MAI, Millennium Round, and FTAA, all gave rise to an international mobilization, composed of the multitude of local, national, and international collective actions that were deployed. Although the attention of the media is often concentrated on the big events that take place in industrialized countries, these are only the most visible facets of an opposition that has developed, for several years, more deeply and more broadly in poor countries.[26] This opposition is incarnated, most notably, in recent movements such as those of indigenous equatorial peoples and of landless peasants in Brazil.

In the debates concerning international trade negotiations, we must underline the structural role played by a category of actors that was much more discreet before, and that is now seen, by some, as the symbol of an emerging international civil society, namely, the non-governmental organizations (NGOs).[27] NGOs such as Public Citizen, Friends of the Earth, and ATTAC were dominant figures in the opposition to the MAI and the Millennium Round, while more traditional activist organizations, such as unions and student associations, were also directly involved. Certain NGOs have the significant advantage of being active in more than one country, which permits them to synchronize the local actions that they lead or promote with struggles in which they are engaged elsewhere. The group ATTAC, for example, is active in France, Québec, Argentina, Brazil, Senegal, Portugal, Tunisia, Ireland, Belgium, and in Switzerland. The dispersion and the large number of bases from which these NGOs contribute to their struggles significantly augment the range and the power of their message, and at the same time, temper the severe inequality that has been created by international organizations that are as strong and as distant from the general public as are the WTO and the OECD.

The second characteristic of this mobilization, which also constitutes one of its strengths, lies in the flexibility and fluidity of its networks of solidarity. This characteristic appears, first, in the fluidity of its established links, that is to say, in the more or less solid and permanent character of the relations between groups and individuals involved in the struggle. A striking illustration of this appeared in the streets of Seattle where 15,000 members of the principal American union (AFL-CIO) agreed to protest alongside thousands of environmentalists, despite the traditional animosity that exists between the two groups in the United States. In this sense, the mobilization testifies to an identification with the conflict that transcends several traditional cleavages.

The flexibility and fluidity are observed also in the displacement of the struggle in time and in space. Therefore, the mobilization against the MAI, or those that came after, should be put in context with other, less recent, oppositions. Think of the oppositions that arose to the GATT accords, to the Uruguay Round of 1992 and 1993,[28] or to the North American Free Trade Agreement (NAFTA), which lead to the Zapatista uprising in Chiapas in 1994, which in turn, took the form of a movement rooted in several countries.[29] The recent mobilizations bring together other movements that are organized around closely related issues, such as the Québec March of "Bread and Roses" of 1995, and the World Women's March that was held in 2000 to protest poverty, exclusion, and violence.

The same phenomenon of flexibility and fluidity is observable in the evolution of individual and group participation in events such as Operation SalAMI. The idea for this operation came from a group of a half dozen activists associated with CANEVAS (Collectif d'actions non-violentes autonomes), which emerged from "Plan G," an act of civil disobedience led in November of 1997 by 300 protesters outside of a public service office in Québec City called Complex G. This action against the neo-liberal policies of the Québec government benefited from the feverishness that was overflowing from the student mobilization of the early 1990s, and from the struggle against the Canadian minister Lloyd Axworthy's reforms of unemployment insurance and social programs. A follow-up committee from "Plan G," worried by the possible signing of the MAI, made the operation SalAMI into its short-term project by aligning it with the days of action of the international network Peoples' Global Action. SalAMI later pursued its action by participating in, among other things, a much larger circle of influence, the Convergence committee for the non-violent opposition that was put into place for the Summit of the Americas.

Despite the explosion of forms, constituents and locations of collective action, we can observe a similarity between the organization and protest strategies among the new groups that are being formed, strategies that are clearly delineated from those of union movements, for example. This is the third important characteristic of the movement we are studying. First, concerning the organization plan, the new groups that are being formed—often on the initiative of more young activists—generally refuse to adopt formal, centralized, or hierarchical structures. On guard against advanced forms of institutionalization,[30] they generally define themselves around affinity groups and liaison committees. While certain members act in clear leadership roles, assuring continuity and cohesion, they generally seek to maintain a dynamic within the group that encourages initiatives coming from the activists themselves. This vision of organization, which is not always operationalized as harmoniously as it is conceived, appears to be directly linked with the values such as freedom of action and opinion, direct participation, equality, and the respect of differences, that are defended by the groups.

With regards to the strategic plans as well, the different struggles they have led demonstrate the existence of well-planned collective actions. This planning is coordinated with the calendars of the promoters of economic globalization, whose big meetings are closely followed by the active protesters. We are also witnessing an increase in the frequency of counter-summits—parallel conferences that offer a window for groups opposed to neo-liberal globalization, destroy the appearance of consensus, and contribute to the diffusion of alternative discourses throughout the media. The People's Summit that was held parallel with the Summit of the Americas is a fine example. But these counter-summits do not produce unanimity within the movement. Certain people denounce the financial participation of governmental organizations, as well as the predominance of institutionalized groups, such as unions, which are considered too willing to negotiate or compromise. Thus, the counter-summits are frowned upon by a group of opponents, more or less radical, who refuse all forms of framing, institutionalization, and uses of the struggle for political gain. Furthermore, the organization of structures for receiving, lodging, orienting, and planning for the stay of protesters from elsewhere, is growing in magnitude. These measures, to which a good part of the resources and the energy of the host group are devoted, attest to a certain professionalization of protest organization.

Still on the issue of strategy, the actions led against market globalization attest to the fact that a culture of non-violent protest, inspired particularly by the peace movements of the 1960s and 1970s has taken root. But real tensions exist throughout the movement on this subject. Certain coalitions or groups refuse to disavow more violent actions, in order to be able to respond to a radicalization of police, and sometimes military, crowd control methods, or to the radicalization of economic globalization itself. One of the most significant types of action remains civil disobedience (human chains, blockades, sit-ins). That is defined in protest circles, as a non-violent, planned, and openly announced action aimed at publicly defying the authorities in order to express opposition to a situation that is deemed unacceptable. Prior to carrying out this type of action, the organizers offer training in civil disobedience and in first aid, and education about the rights of those arrested. In the United States, for example, the Ruckus Society organizes an annual training camp for protesters. SalAMI did roughly the same thing in Québec. The host groups then plan the unfolding of the protest by studying the locations, by developing precise tactics for blockading the arteries to the sites, and by creating a centre for the supervision of affinity groups, which is often located in a strategic place and equipped with adequate means of communication.

The protesters are taking greater and greater advantage of new information and communication technologies. The Internet, in particular, has been added to the means of action and to the other resources at their disposal for giving form to the struggle and for enlarging the networks of solidarity. But in the opinion of some, it is also leading to the exclusion of those who do not have access to the Internet, because the groups making the greatest use of the Internet often neglect more traditional routes of communication, such as posters and telephone chains. Regardless, the use of the Internet was an important factor in the planning of the international mobilization against the MAI, the Millennium Round, and the FTAA. This communications network contributes to the sharing of expertise, to the development of a common discourse, as well as a common organization, and to the planning and public advertising of collective actions.[31] It also serves to put protest strategies into action. These include circulating petitions, pirating information, putting information on Web pages, and developing alternative electronic media that follow the news simultaneously with the protest. For the Summit of the Americas, the Centre for Alternative Media of Québec (CMAQ) was put into place. Just like Indymedia, which was created for the summit in Seattle, the CMAQ proposed a socially engaged treatment of the events.

The Shape of the Struggle

After having described the movement in its most visible manifestations, the central question becomes why such a mobilization emerged. In other words, which sufficiently serious problem or problems explain why citizens of diverse origins, interests, and values would feel themselves simultaneously drawn into the action, to the point of getting involved publicly. The answer to these questions can be found in the discourses of the different groups and of the individuals involved, to which we will now turn our attention.

Such an exercise brings us back to the multiple sources and the heterogeneous character of the movement, of which one of the principal causes of internal tension rests precisely on the identification of the common adversary or enemy. In effect, while some view neo-liberalism and the policies that flow from it as the enemy, others look to capitalism itself and challenge the entire system, not merely a part of it. For example, while the OQP 2001 coalition and most of the other members of the Convergence table focus on free trade and neo-liberalism, the ideological base of the Montréal coalition CLAC is anti-capitalist and opposed to reformism. They affirm that "regardless of the forms that it has taken throughout history (liberal, state, mercantile, neo-liberal, or even with a human face), capitalism will always be the domination of individuals by merchandise." This type of divergence of opinion has a direct impact on the relations maintained between the groups and individuals (more or less conflictual relations), and the means of action and opposition that they, respectively, employ (more or less radical means). These differences of opinion are also the subject of multiple debates and of incessant reflection at the heart of the movement, particularly among groups and individuals wishing to inject a greater degree of cohesion into it.

Despite this fundamental objection, and without wishing to assign a greater degree of cohesion to the movement than actually exists, three constants are apparent in the critiques most often expressed by the movement: first, globalization, as it is currently developing, poses a serious threat to the future of individuals, collectivities, and the places in which they live; second, the international trade agreements being negotiated today exacerbate and precipitate the problems being experienced; third, the legitimacy of the processes by which these agreements are negotiated is highly contestable from a democratic perspective. These are the three constants that we will now explore in order to better understand the central conflict that is at the heart of the movement.

A Struggle against Market Globalization and its Effects

While the French media and the public authorities often characterize those taking part in the movement as *anti-mondialiste* (a French epithet, which we choose to translate in this text by "anti-internationalist"), such an epithet seems inappropriate given that the activists view themselves as being citizens of the world, internationalists, or humanists. Their discourses make constant references to universal themes, such as liberty, justice, equality, solidarity, or the rights of individuals and peoples. For example, they reveal a manifest sensibility to international issues, such as poverty, war, the treatment of women and children, the situation of indigenous peoples, the lot of Third World countries, or the degradation of the environment, phenomena that are generally associated with issues of exploitation and the redistribution of wealth. A final declaration of the participants at the Peoples' Summit that was held in Santiago, Chile, states that "we are undertaking to unite across borders and all undistinguished sectors to oppose these particular interests, and to bring to the fore the interests of the vast majority of the inhabitants of this continent." The Québécois group CLAC "denounces imperialism, opposes patriarchy, and condemns all forms of exploitation and oppression." Clearly, therefore, rather than pertaining to globalization broadly conceived, the critique is directed at the particular type of globalization I am attempting to bring to light.

Internationalization (of the economy, of communications, or other forms) points to a practically inevitable tendency, which occurs first in the spatial-temporal realm. This tendency consists of "an increased mobility of goods, services, people, capital, and information in all of its forms."[32] The internationalization of economic trade is, therefore, a reality that is at least as old as the conquest of the continents by European merchants in the fifteenth century.[33] It is, however, passing through a period of unprecedented growth, sometimes called hypercapitalism,[34] in which neo-liberalism provides both the politico-economic reference and the policies for governance and development.[35] Specifically this form of globalization and its multiple effects on the economy, democracy, human existence, societal life, culture, and the environment is denounced by this social movement. In particular, it targets neo-liberal policies, such as deregulation, privatization of public sectors, and cutbacks in social programs.

This struggle, therefore, is not directed against the process of internationalization, but against other dimensions of globalization. The term globalization signifies both planetary and total. In other words, argues Jacques B. Gélinas, globalization expresses the tendency of global economic power, applied by technological and financial means, and by neo-liberal policies, to exercise "its hegemony over the entire planet, and throughout the entirety of the material, social, and cultural lives of women and men."[36] Faced with this phenomenon, the organizers of Operation SalAMI wrote in their May 1998 call for mobilization:

> Our resistance to the MAI is rooted in our fierce opposition to the fundamental tendencies of a patriarchy and a capitalism whose inhuman and murderous practices are, today, eating away at the last vital organs of the planet. We particularly denounce these systems for their continued domination and oppression of half of humanity (notably on the economic level) ... We proclaim our independence from monetarism, neo-liberal fundamentalism, and more simply, from the plain, cruel, and suicidal rules of a Monopoly game....

In the current phase of capitalist expansion, in which the objective is no longer to conquer countries but to conquer markets, almost everything is commercializable.[37] Commercial value is now assigned to such things as water, land, health, education, culture, knowledge, and even life (with the patenting of the human genome, for example). The appropriation of these spaces by the logic of the market signifies a very real transfer of human inheritance, of vital resources, and of public goods to those who control financial capital, in this case, transnational firms and their creditors. This transfer, very concretely, challenges the other logics of distribution of goods and resources that have prevailed until now, such as the logic of public service that has characterized the welfare state model since World War II.

A Struggle against Negotiated International Trade Agreements

As we have already seen, the opposition has often been led, up to this point, as a reaction against initiatives of the big actors of economic globalization, namely governments, international organizations, financial institutions, and transnational firms. The social forces that oppose the MAI, the Millennium Round, and the FTAA, are of the opinion that these projects will bring globalization to a level that will result in a dangerous degradation of the conditions of life for the populations of the Third World, as well as those of industrialized countries. All so-called social and environmental clauses are excluded from these negotiations. Several experts on globalization are of the opinion that the projects discussed today belong to a new generation of agreements that aim to eliminate the last barriers to commerce and the movement of capital among the markets in question in order to rewrite the rules to the advantage of investors.[38]

The North American Free Trade Agreement (NAFTA) that was signed by Canada, Mexico, and the United States in 1992, is often considered to be the archetype of this new generation of agreements to which the MAI (which in its turn, appears to be the prototype of the projects that succeeded it) belongs. NAFTA embodies two principal innovations. First, it permits corporations to bring a public complaint before a tribunal that, prior to this, would have adjudicated disputes only between states. Already, several foreign firms have made use of the dispute resolution mechanisms that are contained in the accord, which came into force in 1994, in order to bring complaints against Canada or Mexico, and sometimes win them, on the basis of the clauses pertaining to national treatment and anti-expropriation contained in Chapter 11 of NAFTA.[39]

Second, Chapter 10 of the accord allows for a process of negative economic integration, according to which liberalization applies to all services, except those that are expressly mentioned in the appendices and which are considered for periodic review.[40] Thus, the text of NAFTA delegates the power to pursue the negotiations of the terms of free trade, on a continuous basis, to a committee of bureaucrats. This represents a precedent that opens the door to a progressive liberalization of services, given the concessions that negotiators are likely to accept, faced with the constant pressure that will be exerted on them.

Although it was inspired by it, the MAI represents an ever more ambitious project than NAFTA because of the high level of legal protection it accords to transnational investors, the extraordinary obligations that were placed on the signatory states for the protection of foreign investors, and the expansion of the domains covered by the accord. While it established a series of rights and obligations, in a similar fashion as most international treaties, the MAI is fundamentally different because "the rights are reserved to international corporations and investors, while the governments assume all of the obligations."[41] Four elements of the original MAI text are revealing in this regard: the right of corporations to invest, without restrictions, where they wish (Articles 1.1 and 1.2); the right of compensation for policies (for example, relating to the environment and public health) which limit their profits (Articles 2.1 to 2.6); the right of compensation for civil troubles, revolutions, or states of emergency (Articles 3.1 and 3.2); and the obligation for states to afford the same treatment to foreign firms as they do to national firms (Chapter III).

According to Christian Deblock and Dorval Brunelle, this type of accord grants to international investors a new legal status, and by the same token, defines a new normative framework, which redraws the line between public and private spaces on national territory to the advantage of the latter.

> we see appearing four significant innovations: firstly, a greatly increased level of protection for the foreign investor and his investment which severely limits the right of expropriation; secondly, the forbidding of states to impose any performance obligations on investors; thirdly, the limitation of a state's power to intervene only in the spheres that are explicitly listed in the accord and included in the appendices; and, fourthly, the eventual imposition, at worst, of dispute resolution mechanisms whose rules and modes of operation would remain entirely outside of national law, which would create an insurmountable asymmetry between economic actors and other social actors.[42]

The launch of a new round of negotiations, the Millennium Round, forecast a return of the MAI negotiations, this time under the auspices of the WTO. The concern over the Millennium Round also related to the fact that 70 per cent of the countries on the planet, namely the 135 member countries of the international organization, were directly involved. The 1994 revisions of the Marrakesh Accord relating to agriculture, services, and industrial property were written into the initial program, but an impressive list of questions, regarding (among other things) investment and public markets, were added, similar to the MAI. Despite the absence of an official agenda, it was well known that no less than 160 sectors and subsectors of activity could become the subject of negotiation, including human and animal health, education, bulk water exports, culture, and agriculture. The very extended list of subjects on the table demonstrated the expansion of spheres sought after, and the willingness to commercialize "practically all human activities."[43]

The attention of opponents to globalization is now turning towards other projects, particularly towards the creation of a free-trade zone of the Americas (FTAA), which sometime before 2005 could create the largest common market in the world. For the three North American countries, which includes Canada, the objective is to extend NAFTA to the other countries of the Americas and to those Caribbean countries that are involved in the negotiations. The goal is also to tie together the different regional accords that have been negotiated in the past. Despite the secrecy surrounding the new negotiations, we know that this free-trade area must conform in every way to the requirements of the WTO, and that it must also include access to markets, protection for investments, liberalization of commerce in services, the opening of public sectors, the harmonization of agricultural and food-processing industries, and the putting into place of dispute resolution mechanisms and rules for compensation in the case of disputes.[44] A first draft of the chapter on investment, that was unveiled on the eve of the Summit of the Americas by an American NGO, and of which the authenticity was confirmed by the Canadian Minister of International Trade, seems to show that the FTAA could include certain principles of the MAI relating to the rights of investors and the obligations of the states.

The creation of a free-trade zone that would include so many domains and that would accord such extensive rights to corporations is seen, by members of the coalition OQP 2001, as treason against the citizens, because governments, as they write in their manifesto, "divert the collective wealth of the people in order to put it at the disposal of transnational corporations," they "voluntarily exacerbate an unhealthy competition between workers of different countries rather than creating an environment of solidarity," they block "equality between the sexes, because the dismantlement of public services and the deregulation of work inherent to these free trade agreements come at the price of the systematic and conscious exploitation of women," and they take a position "that supports a model of development that is already to blame for numerous environmental disasters."

In response to the FTAA, and to the other projects that preceded it prior to the MAI, an informed, coherent and well-argued counter-discourse has taken shape. "On this subject that is, nevertheless, very technical, the representative[s] of civil society appear to us to be perfectly well informed, and their critiques of the legal design, very well argued," observed the European delegate, C. Lalumière, in a report on the MAI that was commissioned by the French government.[45] In many different countries, the groups involved have articulated a very similar discourse that goes beyond particular and sectoral demands. This improvement of the discourse appears to be explained, first, by the willing efforts of certain NGOs to decode and make accessible the stakes and the contents of negotiated trade agreements to the greatest number of people; second, by the numerous exchanges of information that are possible on the international level because of the new telecommunication networks; and third, by the increased understanding and consciousness-raising of the dynamics and stakes of neo-liberal economic globalization.

A Struggle against the Legitimacy of the
Representatives at the Negotiating Table

The third recurring critique has a more immediate relevance in that it challenges the very legitimacy of the negotiation process for trade agreements as well as of the actors who take part in them. Of the three critiques we have identified, this is the one that receives the most attention from the general population, the media, and governments. The majority of the groups who appeared before the Commission of Institutions of the National Assembly in Québec, which studied certain political and socio-economic implications of the FTAA, denounced the "democratic deficit" that surrounds the negotiations for this agreement. Certain editorialists and columnists for major daily newspapers have also begun to do the same. While some of the critiques focus on the lack of information about the process, others attack its flaws. More precisely, four problems are raised.

The first problem relates to the secrecy that surrounds the negotiations. Since the shock caused by the secret negotiations of the MAI, this critique has remained a constant. Denouncing the closed nature of the FTAA negotiations, the Commission of Institutions of the National Assembly affirmed in the summary of its report: "We understand that we cannot effectively negotiate such a project in the public sphere. Nevertheless, what we cannot as clearly explain, is that neither the precise orientations, nor the state of advancement of the work is known."[46] The Convergence table, a coalition committed to non-violent struggle, sees the closed nature of the process as one of its principal failings, a failing that it must oppose by means of petitions, public declarations, ultimatums to the responsible authorities, and the threat of non-violent actions: "The clandestine negotiations have lasted too long. The right to know is fundamental in a democracy. We demand that you publish the entirety of the texts of the Free Trade Agreement of the Americas (FTAA) as they are at this stage of negotiations," wrote the members of the Convergence Table in a joint declaration.

The second problem is the legitimacy of the actors at the negotiating table, as well as of the institutions in which the agreements are negotiated, namely, the international economic organizations, which are seen as global executives coming to bypass the parliaments and states. The international economic organizations play a central role in the process of market globalization, while at the same time, they are charged with defining the rules of trade and investment through international agreements, supervising their application, and eventually, acting as arbitrators of the various parties' litigations. Therefore, they act as supranational powers and at the same time, as the vanguards and guardians of economic globalization. Despite their undeniably growing power, all demands for their accountability to the populations and to the governments concerned appear, for now, to have been ignored.

This is possibly because, considering themselves as mere representatives of governments, they would be limited to so-called technical and administrative functions. Many groups, including the RQIC, challenge the democratic character of these institutions and, thus, attack the legitimacy of the negotiations that are conducted in secrecy.

> ... if governments who negotiate agreements upon agreements are in reality 'democratically elected' governments ... the result is no less than our having an executive democracy, an expression which serves to designate the process by which these executives amass a whole range of prerogatives for which they give account neither to the population, nor to their own legislative powers.[47]

The third problem, resulting from the preceding, relates to the negligible power exercised by elected representatives in parliaments. Apart from a few ministers who are directly involved, parliamentarians are virtually always excluded, and generally do not gain access to the texts of the negotiations until the agreements have been concluded and signed by closed and small groups of executives. Many of the groups who appeared before the Commission of Institutions of the National Assembly underlined the fact that parliamentarians were not present "either before or after the negotiation process," while the Americas Business Forum achieved the status of an officially consulted group.[48] The commission suggests that the parliamentary "democratic deficit" is even greater in the case of Québec than in other provinces, given its position in the Canadian federation. The phenomenon, however, is generalized throughout the hemisphere, because the parliamentarians of the three Americas present at the Second General Assembly of the Parliamentarians' Conference of the Americas, held in Puerto Rico in July 2000, unanimously requested greater transparency, more information, and a greater degree of participation in the FTAA negotiations. In February 2001, the Bloc Québécois tabled, in vain, a motion supported by all of the opposition parties in the House of Commons that demanded access to the different texts for members of the legislative assembly and requested that a debate on the subject be held.

Finally, the fourth problem arising from the above observations concerns the absence of a meaningful debate in the media and political institutions on the issue of free trade and economic globalization. Refuting the discourse on the inevitability of the transformations underway, the OQP 2001 coalition affirms in its manifesto that "neo-liberal globalization is not a natural or disembodied phenomenon to which people and states must necessarily submit," but on the contrary, it "results from conscious policies put into place by financial and political elites, notably in the form of free trade agreements." This is why many groups have demanded that governments declare a moratorium, initiate a public debate, and eventually, hold a referendum in order to give a voice to everyone.

Yet, the federal election campaign that took place in the fall of 2000 already has demonstrated the absence of debate among the political parties on the stakes surrounding the negotiations of the FTAA. All have pronounced themselves in favour of the principles of free trade.[49] The same quasi-unconditional support is given by the political parties sitting in the National Assembly of Québec. Unanimity on the subject was particularly strong at the end of the 1980s when the Parti Québécois and the Parti Libéral du Québec, largely supported by the business community, publicly aligned themselves with the free trade policies of Brian Mulroney's Conservative federal government.[50] Since then, every government of Québec has, more or less, endorsed the federal position in favour of the basic principles of the MAI, Millennium Round, and the FTAA.[51] Again recently, the former premier of Québec, Lucien Bouchard, gave his unequivocal support to the creation of a free trade area of the Americas, while in Chile in May 2000: "It is a prospect that does not scare us. On the contrary, we welcome it wholeheartedly."[52] His successor to the title of premier, Bernard Landry, previously the Minister of Finance, has pronounced himself to be in favour of a common market with the United States since 1983.

The Meaning of the Movement

This appearance of social consensus the movement denounces and contradicts through its actions and its discourse. First, it opposes this contrived consensus through a resistance that takes shape in the choices and lifestyles both of individuals and of communities, as well as through the public meetings and demonstrations that it holds. Next, and even more clearly, the movement opposes this consensus through proposals for projects that it perceives to be credible, viable, and concrete. These projects include writing off the debts of poor countries, implementing the Tobin tax on financial speculation, eliminating tax havens, establishing a guaranteed annual income, and upholding the obligation to the "precautionary principle" in scientific and technological activities.[53] At the Peoples' Summit of the Americas, held in Chile in 1998 and in Québec in 2001, as well as at the Global Social Forum, held in January 2001 in Porto Alegre, in the south of Brazil, the work focused on alternative projects that the movement could propose in opposition to market globalization. The organizers of the Global Social Forum of Porto Alegre wanted to make this meeting the "anti-Davos of the South," explained one of its representatives, "a space that would allow us to advance towards a real global consensus, while accepting, with generosity and tolerance, the different ideas and conceptions that exist in each corner of the planet."[54]

The belief that the opposition movement manifests a rejection of change or a rejection of openness to the world appears to be erroneous. The question posed by the movement is not about the necessity of progress, but about the nature of that progress and the means by which it should be achieved. We can, however, ask ourselves whether the movement demonstrates a resistance to the ongoing process of globalization or, on the contrary, seeks to transform the very basis of the system. For certain experts, such as A. Touraine, a "societal" movement necessarily expresses a willingness to modify the system, to change the social order. In the present case, the two visions coexist in a more or less harmonious fashion, according to the circumstances and groups involved.

In effect, while certain groups view their actions primarily as acts of resistance, given that globalization threatens the ideal of a public, democratic, ecological space that must be preserved, others insist on its progressive dimension, because the very foundations of the system must be re-examined. In particular, this question divides the individuals and groups who are seeking a reversal of the tendency through reforms and reorganizations without re-examining the bases of the capitalist system, those who view a form of revolution as the only acceptable alternative, i.e., a quick and violent change to the current structures. The first camp is made up of such groups as unions, while the second includes such groups as militant anarchists. In itself, however, such a categorization is problematic, since, as we have seen, even those more moderate elements believe in the necessity of alternative solutions to the present economic globalization. The resistance to the ongoing process and the will for transformation often go hand in hand.

Finally, the three recurring critiques that we have identified in this section (critique of economic globalization, of international trade agreements, and of the negotiation process) permit us better to identify the central conflict that is at the heart of the struggle, better to explain what leads each of the social actors to take part in the movement. While these actors justify their opposition through arguments based on principles as varied as democracy, ecology, ethics, morals, and even anarchy,[55] all challenge the forms of rationalization, regulation, and domination that currently exist. In other words, all consider globalization to threaten or to affect individual and collective capacity for action and affirmation. This is what seems to be at the heart of the struggle led by this emerging movement, whose evolution is also conditioned by societies and political systems that are, themselves, in a process of profound transition. It is the search for liberty, self-fulfillment and taking charge of one's own destiny as humans, citizens, societies, or states that would be undermined by globalization. The reflections on the issues of identity developed for the study of new social movements are, in this respect, very instructive.[56] But as the researcher Zsuzsa Hegedus indicates well in her analysis of contemporary movements, not only are these movements desirous of autonomy and of fulfillment for individuals and social groups, but they are also the sign of an ethic of responsibility, in the sense that they testify to a strong collective will to resolve the problems that they deplore.[57] In this respect, the comments of the judge who heard the case of those who participated in operation SalAMI's civil disobedience in Montréal were very eloquent. After having delivered his verdict of guilty on the "criminal" charges, he recognized that he was facing people with well-developed "social consciences."

Conclusion

Against the "monolithic belief"[58] in the logic of globalization, the social movement that we have been studying is proposing alternative visions of regulation and the development of societies in which, through the reduction of external market and technological constraints, prevails the objective of allowing social actors to flourish and fulfill themselves. Therefore, it demands, without always expressing it in identical or specific terms, a commitment towards a real democracy that would be founded on the positive will to enhance the liberty and the equality of individuals and collectivities in respect of their differences and their environments.

In addition to contesting the inevitable and invincible character of globalization, the movement directly questions the modes of governance and representation that dominate the process. Therefore, the state, as the legitimate authority of regulation, is immediately called into question as are the limited possibilities it offers for exercising citizenship through participation. Furthermore, it must be seen that, if a majority of the opponents to globalization challenges the logic of an entire system (be it capitalism in its neo-liberal form, or capitalism in its essence), the political elites and the governments remain the primary targets of criticism (it is said) for having abdicated their duty to defend the common good and the social and political rights of the population in favour of a defence of the freedom of capital and the rights of investors. The emergence of this movement, therefore, illustrates in its own way the deficit of legitimacy suffered by the nation-state and its institutions, already weakened by the emergence of supra and intra-state actors and by internationalization, the multiplication and the intensification of flux in communications and in financial networks. Seen in this light, the critiques addressed by the movement appear ultimately an exhortation to overcome the citizenship crises of the state.

Given the diversity of proposals supported by those taking part in the movement, it is still difficult to identify a common social project, a vision of the world with which all of them identify. From a return to massive state intervention, to the complete dissolution of the state at the expense of management collectivities, from the humanization of the market through the integration of social and environmental norms into economic agreements, to a systematic rejection of all agreements of this type, various more or less radical ideas are defended and energetically debated.

Such debates are, at the very least, the sign of a veritable intellectual explosion on the Left. Also, there can be no doubt that we are witnessing throughout this plural and complex movement a new effervescence of ideas, an effervescence that confirms the forceful return of ideologies.

While multifaceted and fragmented, this social movement has already succeeded in promoting itself before the major actors of economic globalization, in making the media aware of secret trade negotiations, in modifying the agendas of some conferences, and in forcing these powerful actors to adopt a level of transparency and of relative openness. For the present, however, the principal victory of the movement seems to be having raised the awareness of the population to the multiple and sometimes indirect stakes of this global process. Through critiques of, for example, privatized health care, deforestation, bulk water sales, genetic engineering, and the exploitation of women and children, it has participated in a critical awakening of conscience regarding different stakes we associate with economic globalization. It remains to be seen how the movement will evolve and, in particular, which road the social imagination will take in formulating a credible alternative to globalization.

Notes

1. I would like to thank Claude Beauregard, Stéphane Thellen, and Luc Turgeon for their valuable comments.

2. Dorval Brunelle and Christian Deblock, "Les mouvements syndicaux et sociaux d'opposition à l'intégration économique par les marchés: de l'ALE à la ZLEA. Vers la constitution d'une Alliance sociale continentale, *Continentalisation (Cahier de recherche 99-1)*, GRIC, UQAM, Jan. 1999; Susan George, *L'Accord multilatéral sur l'investissement dans le contexte de la mondialisation économique et financière*, paper presented at the conference "Mondialisation et démocratie: les dangers de l'A.M.I," organized at the National Assembly, Paris, 4 Dec. 1997.

3. See, among others, Jacques Pelletier, "Radicaliser la pensée critique," *Possibles: "Sortir de la pensée unique,"* 24, 2-3 (2000): 5-10; Gabriel Gagnon, "Vers un nouvel imaginaire social," *Idem.*, 50-61.

4. Marc Lemire, "Mouvement social et mondialisation économique: de l'AMI au Cycle du millénaire," *Politique et Sociétés* 19, 1 (Summer 2000).

5. Anarchism, according to Atila Özer, is "the irregular collection of doctrines that endorse a social life, free from all coercive power, notably from that of the state, and that value the free development of men [and women]." *L'État* (Paris: Flammarion, 1998), 215.

6. Alberto Melucci, *Challenging Codes. Collective action in the information age* (Cambridge: Cambridge University Press, 1996).

7. Alain Touraine, *Pourrons-nous vivre ensemble? Égaux et différents* (Paris: Fayard, 1997).

8. Ibid., 132. (Translator's note: All quotations have been translated from the French unless otherwise indicated.)

9. Claus Offe, "Challenging the boundaries of institutional politics: social movements since the 1960s," in Charles S. Maier, ed., *Changing boundaries of the political:*

Essays on the evolving balance between the state and society, public and private in Europe (Cambridge: Cambridge University Press, 1987), 63-105.

10. Éric Neveu, *Sociologie des mouvements sociaux* (Paris: La Découverte, 1996), 67.

11. Catherine Lalumière, *Rapport sur l'Accord multilatéral sur l'investissement (AMI)* (Paris: Ministère de l'Économie, des Finances et de l'Industrie, Sept. 1998).

12. Lori M. Wallach, "La déclaration universelle des droits du capital," *Manière de voir (Le Monde diplomatique)* 42 (Nov.-Dec. 1998): 50-52.

13. François Chesnais, ed., et al., *Lumière sur l'A.M.I., Le test de Dracula*, Synthèse d'interventions, d'articles et de notes de travail émanant des membres de l'Observatoire de la mondialisation en collaboration avec L'Esprit frappeur et Le Monde diplomatique (Paris: L'Esprit frappeur, 1998). Demonstrations or awareness-raising activities have been observed in Japan, New Zealand, Turkey, Denmark, Norway, Belgium, the Netherlands, Switzerland, France, Germany, Italy, the United States, and Canada. India, Malaysia, and the Philippines were also among those represented in the international coalition against the MAI known as the "Citizens Forum," an organization formed of several hundred associations from Europe, North America, and the Third World.

14. Translator's note: SalAMI is a French play on words which combines the words "sal" (dirty), and "AMI" (friend, and also MAI) to form the word "salami," which is also a kind of sausage.

15. The largest demonstrations took place in Seattle, the host city. But there were also demonstrations elsewhere, such as those that took place in England, France, India, the Czech Republic, Brazil, Mexico, Italy, Germany, Switzerland, Belgium, Norway, and Canada.

16. BRIDGES, *Weekly Trade News Digest* 3, 48 (15 Dec. 1999).

17. Translator's note: Eau-Secours is a French play on words. "Au secours" is a call for help. In this case, "au" has been replaced with "eau" (water).

18. The member countries of the G-20 are South Africa, Germany, Saudi Arabia, Argentina, Australia, Brazil, Canada, China, South Korea, the United States, France, India, Indonesia, Italy, Japan, Mexico, Great Britain, Russia, Turkey, and the European Union. Also at the table are representatives of the IMF and the World Bank.

19. Alberto Melucci, *Challenging codes*.

20. Catherine Lalumière, *Rapport sur l'Accord*.

21. Ignacio Ramonet, "L'aurore," *Le Monde diplomatique* (Jan. 2000): 1.

22. Bernard Cassen, "Irréversible, la mondialisation?" *Le Monde diplomatique* (Jan. 2001): 4.

23. Edgar Morin, "Le XXIe siècle a commencé à Seattle," *Le Monde* (7 Dec. 1999).

24. Vandana Shiva, "The Historic Significance of Seattle," text put online by *WTO Watch* at: http://www.wtowatch.org/wtowatch/li...ric_Significance_of_Seattle_The.htm; Norman Solomon, "A pro-democracy movement," ZNET (26 Dec. 1999).

25. Zsuzsa Hegedus, "Social Movements and Social Change in Self-Creative Society: New Civil Initiatives in the International Arena," *International Sociology* 4, 1 (Mar. 1989): 19-36.

26. Jessica Woodroffe and Mark Ellis-Jones, "States of Unrest: Resistance to IMF Policies in Poor Countries," *World Development Movement Report* (Sept. 2000) [Rev. Jan. 2001].

27. Catherine Lalumière, *Rapport sur l'Accord*.

28. François Chesnais, ed., et al., *Lumière sur l'A.M.I.*

29. Brian Dominick, "Zapatisto, Anyone?" *Z magazine* (8 Aug. 2000).

30. On the institutionalization of social movements, see, among others, Pierre Hamel, Louis Maheu, and Jean-Guy Vaillancourt, "Repenser les défis institutionnels de l'action collective," *Politique et Sociétés* 19, 1 (2000): 3-25.

31. Christian De Brie, "Comment l'AMI fut mis en pièces," *Le Monde diplomatique* (Dec. 1999): 21; see also Éric George, *L'utilisation de l'Internet comme mode de participation à l'espace public dans le cadre de l'AMI et au sein d'ATTAC : Vers un renouveau de la démocratie à l'ère de l'omnimarchandisation du monde?*, Thèse de doctorat en sciences de la communication en co-tutelle France-Québec, Lyon: École Normale Supérieure de Lyon Lettres et sciences humaines; Montréal: Université du Québec à Montréal, 2001. For a critical analysis of electronic activism: Anne-Marie Gingras, *Médias et démocratie. Le grand malentendu* (Sainte-Foy: Presses de l'Université du Québec, 1999). An essay on the uses of the Internet by pressure groups and community groups is presented by A.-M. Gingras in "Internet et démocratie: quels usages pour quelle politique?" paper presented to the Congrès de la société française des sciences de l'information et de la communication (SFSIC), Grenoble, 15 Nov. 1996.

32. Pierre-Paul Proulx, "La mondialisation de l'économie et le rôle de l'État," in Sylvie Paquerot, ed., *L'État aux orties?* (Montréal: Écosociété, 1996), 234.

33. Jacques B. Gélinas, *La globalization du monde. Laisser faire ou faire?* (Montréal: Écosociété, 2000).

34. Jean-Guy Lacroix and Jacques-Alexandre Mascotto, *Manifeste pour l'humanité* (Montréal: Lanctôt Éditeur, 2000).

35. Gilles Dostaler, "De la domination de l'Économie au néolibéralisme," *Possibles: "Sortir de la pensée unique,"* 24, 2-3 (2000): 13-26.

36. Jacques B. Gélinas, *La globalization*, 41-42, 48-49.

37. This critique is addressed most notably by academics. In Québec, these include: Collectif étudiant UQÀM, *L'essor de nos vies. Parti pris pour la société et la justice* (Montréal: Lanctôt Éditeur et Société, 2000); Lacroix and Mascotto, *Manifeste pour.*; Christian Deblock and Dorval Brunelle, "Globalisation et nouveaux cadres normatifs. Le cas de l'Accord multilatéral sur l'investissement," *Continentalisation (Cahier de recherche 98-2)*, Groupe de recherche sur l'intégration continentale, May 1998.

38. See, for example, Dorval Brunelle, "Démocratie et privatisation dans les Amériques: de l'ALENA à la ZLEA, en passant par l'ACI," Mémoire du GRIC présenté à la Commission sur les institutions de l'Assemblée nationale, 22 Aug. 2000; Susan George, "À l'OMC, trois ans pour achever la mondialisation," *Le Monde diplomatique* (Jul. 1999): 8-9.

39. For example, the American firm Ethyl Corporation launched a $251 million suit against the Canadian government for "loss of anticipated profits" after the government banned a fuel additive called MMT because it was deemed to be harmful to public health. Rather than defending itself before the NAFTA tribunal, the government decided to beat a quick retreat and compensated the corporation. Also in Canada, the American firm United Parcel Service (UPS) launched a $230 million claim against the government for having unfairly privileged the Crown corporation Canada Post. Recently, the multinational Metalclad won its claim for "expropriation" against the Mexican government after the regional state of San Luis Potosi refused to allow the corporation to reopen a waste treatment plant that threatened to contaminate the local water reservoirs.

40. Jacques B. Gélinas, *La globalization*, 61.

41. Lori M. Wallach, "La declaration," 50.

42. Christian Deblock and Dorval Brunelle, "Globalisation et," 33.

43. Susan George, "À l'OMC, trois." 8.

44. For a critical analysis of the stakes of the FTAA, see Maude Barlow, *La Zone de libre échange des Amériques et la menace qu'elle constitue pour les programmes sociaux, la protection*

de l'environnement et la justice sociale au Canada et dans les Amériques, Ontario, Conseil des canadiens, Jan. 2001.

45. Catherine Lalumière, *Rapport sur l'Accord*.

46. Commission des institutions, *Le Québec et la Zone de libre-échange des Amériques: Effets politiques et socioéconomiques*, Assemblée nationale, Québec, Dec. 2000, 4.

47. Réseau québécois sur l'intégration continentale, "*La mondialisation de quoi, comment, pour qui?*" Document de référence, s.l., June 1999, 6. Also by the same author, see "*La Zone de libre-échange des Amériques et l'Alliance sociale continentale,*" s.l., Apr. 2000.

48. Commission des institutions, *Le Québec et La Zone de libre-échange*, 4.

49. François Normand, "Les enjeux négligés. Le Canada et la mondialisation," *Le Devoir*, 21 Nov. 2000, A6.

50. François Rocher, "Le Québec en Amérique du Nord: la stratégie continental," in Alain-G. Gagnon, ed., *Québec: État et Société* (Montréal: Québec/Amérique, 1994).

51. Beyond the Québec government's particular insistence on the exclusion of questions related to culture from the negotiations, the only real point of dispute relates to the Québec government's place at the negotiating table. Manifestly, this well-known duality between the two governments masks the real stakes that are revealed by the social movement.

52. Lucien Bouchard, "Allocution du premier ministre dans le cadre d'un déjeuner-conférence avec la collaboration de la SOFOFA (Sociedad de Fomento Fabril)," Santiago, Chile, 18 May 2000.

53. See, among others, René Passet, "Manifeste pour une économie à finalité humaine," *Le Monde diplomatique* (Feb. 2001): 14-15.

54. Information pamphlet of ATTAC, "Forum Social Mondial," 197, 29 (Dec. 2000).

55. On anarchy, see note 5.

56. See Louis Maheu, "Les nouveaux mouvements sociaux entre les voies de l'identité et les jeux du politique," in Louis Maheu and Arnaud Sales, *La recomposition du politique*, (Paris/Montréal: L'Harmattan/Les presses de l'Université de Montréal, 1991), 163-91; Will Kymlicka and Wayne J. Norman, "Return of the Citizen," *Ethics* 104 (1994): 352-81; Jürgen Habermas, "Struggles of Recognition in the Democratic Constitutional State," in Charles Taylor et al., *Multiculturalism, Examining the Politics of Recognition* (Princeton, NJ: Princeton University Press, 1994), 107-48; Alberto Melucci, "Individualisation et globalization," *Cahiers de recherche sociologique* 24 (1995): 185-207.

57. Zsuzsa Hegedus, "Social Movements."

58. Ignacio Ramonet first described the ideology of globalization in this way: "In contemporary democracies, more and more free citizens are feeling themselves to be caught by a sort of visquous doctrine that gradually envelops all rebel thought, inhibits it, troubles it, paralyses it, and finally extinguishes it. This doctrine is a monolithic belief, the only one authorized by an invisible, omnipresent opinion police.... What is this monolithic belief? The translation into ideological terms of the, seemingly universal, interests of a set of economic forces, in particular, those of international capital." See "La pensée unique," *Le Monde diplomatique* (Jan 1995): 1.

13

Labour Market Transformations and Labour Law: The Québec Labour Movement in Search of Renewed Growth

JEAN CHAREST*

Introduction

The twentieth century was a critical period for the labour movement, both in Québec and in most industrialized nations. Trade unions began essentially clandestine and went on to achieve social recognition in political and legal terms; they rose from marginality to being widely representative in many industries; they moved from a focus on the narrow representation of their members to a wider engagement with a range of social and economic issues. In short, the labour movement developed and adapted in response to the opportunities created by the economic and social transformations that occurred over the last century. However, the closing years of the century particularly, in Québec and the rest of Canada, were in many ways difficult ones for organized labour. Taken by itself, the relative decline in union density during the 1990s might be thought to support the thesis of convergence with the United States, a thesis that is strengthened in the context of globalization (or, rather, continental economic integration). In other words, as a result of the ineluctable pressure of the new rules of globalization, the Canadian labour movement seems to be experiencing, after a lag of several decades, the same decline as has occurred in the United States.

* Translated from French into English by Magee and Nguyen.

Without subscribing to this notion of convergence among national models, the argument made in this chapter is that it is nevertheless necessary to recognize that unions are confronted with a number of very significant problems. More particularly, we suggest that increases in unionization were tied to transformations of the labour market during two key moments of the twentieth century: the development of the manufacturing sector in the post-World War II period; and the development of the modern state, beginning in the 1960s. Both of these periods also saw changes in labour law that made possible an upsurge in union organizing. However, since the 1980s, the labour market has been undergoing a third transformation, one that entails the growth of employment in the private tertiary sector and an increase in non-standard employment. Confronted with these two phenomena, the labour movement is experiencing major difficulties, which have led it to support yet another recasting of labour law. To date, the political will to carry out this modernization has been lacking, and the union movement itself seems to have been unable to shape the nature of the proposed reforms. Is this simply the result of the labour movement's lack of political power? Or is it the repeated invoking of "globalization" by the state and employers that curtails organized labour's political influence? In any event, one thing seems certain: the current period could well mark a turning point in the history of organized labour in Québec and elsewhere, for it is labour's very place as a social actor that is in question.

Part 1 of this chapter offers a historical account of how union organizing was shaped by economic and labour market transformations, as well as by the institutional framework created by changes in labour law. Part 2 examines the more recent labour market transformations that have created difficulties for the labour movement, at least in terms of its ability to represent workers. Part 3 rounds out the analysis by examining the issue of labour law reform, particularly in the context of globalization. In the conclusion, we will identify a number of alternative scenarios for future union action.

Economic Transformation and Labour Law Change to the 1960s: The Origins and Growth of Modern Unionism

The labour movement's struggle for legal recognition and for the establishment of positive legal rights was a factor that continually marked its historical development. Before analyzing the contemporary situation, therefore it is important to understand the special importance of several critical moments in this struggle for recognition. Rather than trying to offer a complete analysis of the factors related to these labour movement struggles, a task already accomplished by other scholars,[1] the focus will be on the close relationship between certain contextual variables.

Even before the expansion of unionism after World War II, the importance of the political and institutional recognition of unionism can be seen by examining two early laws in Québec. First, in 1924, the Professional Syndicates Act allowed the legal recognition of unions and collective agreements. Then, in 1934, Québec adopted a law that remains unique in North America, the Act Respecting the Extension of Collective Labour Agreements (later renamed the Act Respecting Collective Agreement Decrees). The general thrust of this Act was to make it possible, by means of a government decree, to apply the major provisions of collective agreements negotiated by some unions and employers to all of the workers in a particular industry, usually within a particular region. More specifically, at the request of unions and employers in a particular industry, the government could decide that enough workers were already covered by negotiated employment conditions in that industry and in a particular region, and thus decree that the principal terms (notably, wages) should be a required minimum for all the firms in an industry, in one or several regions.[2] Clearly, one of the goals of this legislation was to eliminate the unacceptable competitive advantage of non-unionized firms vis-à-vis unionized firms. At the same time, however, the government was looking for a way to stop the downward spiral of wages during the Great Depression of the 1930s.

These first two legal and institutional foundations of unionism were critically important to the first wave of union growth in Québec. Indeed, put in perspective, union growth was subsequently relatively strong: from around 72,000 in 1931, union membership climbed to 158,000 by 1941 and then to 260,000 by 1946. As a result, union density in Québec grew from only 9 per cent to 21 per cent and then to 29 per cent between 1931 and 1946.[3] From less than one worker in 10, organized labour grew, in terms of representation, to almost one worker in three, and all in just 15 years.

Nevertheless, the legal foundations of what today remains the basic framework of labour relations in Québec was introduced in 1944 with the adoption of the Labour Relations Act. Inspired by the American Wagner Act (the National Labor Relations Act, adopted in 1935), this act established what Morin has called "the rule of the three units: the unit of place: the firm or one of its parts; the unit of person: one union at a time; the unit of time: a single collective agreement for a predetermined period of time."[4] It should be noted that, in the United States, the Wagner Act made it possible for organized labour to grow rapidly—from four million members in 1935 to nine million by 1940, and then to 15 million by 1950. In Québec, the adoption of the Labour Relations Act in a sense marginalized the effect of the decree system by opening the way to legally constituted unions at the level of the firm. The new Act corresponded, as it were, to the reality during the post-war economy of the labour market, i.e., large firms in the manufacturing sector with relatively stable, blue-collar work forces. Between 1946 and 1956, union membership grew by almost 100,000 (reaching 353,000 in 1956), although union density remained essentially static at 29 per cent.[5]

Until the 1960s, the rate of union density in Québec was largely the product of private-sector unionism. Indeed, union density was much higher in the private sector than in the public sector. However, with the development of the modern state and the parallel growth of employment in the public sector, it became crucial for the union movement to expand into this "new labour market." After numerous struggles and demands, the labour movement won amendments to labour legislation in 1964 that gave the right to strike and to bargain collectively to all public-sector workers (the Queen would, in the end, have to negotiate with her subjects, contrary to what Québec Premier Jean Lesage had claimed only a short time before). Because this new opening for the labour movement came at a time when union density in the private sector was beginning to decline, the rapid increase in public sector unionization meant that overall union density in Québec continued to grow.

From 1960 to 1970, largely because of public sector unionization, the number of union members doubled, reaching about 700,000. As a result, the unionization rate grew from close to 30 per cent to 39 per cent in just 10 years.[6] This was already 10 percentage points higher than the rate in the United States. The growth of public-sector employment and unionization continued, such that near the end of the 1980s the unionization rate in the private sector was still on the order of 30 per cent whereas the rate in the public sector had reached 80 per cent, for a weighted overall rate of 45 per cent in Québec, or 10 percentage points higher than in Canada as a whole and almost 30 points higher than in the United States (then at 16 per cent).

It is quite clear that the labour law amendments provided the impetus that was necessary for the Québec union movement to adapt to the changing labour market, drawing on the public sector to ensure that it continued to grow. Although organized labour in Québec sprang from private-sector unionization, as it did in the other industrialized nations, it can be said that the unionization of the public sector made it possible to reinvigorate the movement at a time when it was undergoing a certain stagnation—indeed, a relative decline—in the private sector.

The Growth of Tertiary and Non-Standard Employment: New Labour Market Segments Unfavourable to Unionization

After the expansion of the manufacturing sector and then the public sector, it came the turn of the private tertiary sector to generate a high percentage of the employment growth in the Québec economy, a shift that began in the early 1980s. This rapid transformation of the Québec labour market is illustrated by the fact that, between 1966 and 1995, employment declined at an average annual rate of

1.5 per cent in the primary sector, remained stable in the secondary sector (i.e., 0 per cent average annual change) and increased at an average annual rate of 2.4 per cent in the tertiary sector. Thus, the share of total employment accounted for by the primary sector dropped from 8.2 per cent to 3.5 per cent between 1966 and 1995, the share of the secondary sector declined from 35 per cent to 23 per cent and the share of the tertiary sector rose from 57 per cent to 73.5 per cent.[7] As we saw above, insofar as the union movement succeeded in penetrating the public sector, the gains that it achieved made it possible to offset the relative decline of employment in the secondary sector. However, beginning in the 1980s, the nature of employment growth in the tertiary sector changed significantly.

Indeed, subsectors like finance, insurance, and real estate services; business services and other services; retailing; and hotels and restaurants experienced strong rates of employment growth — 16 per cent in total between 1986 and 1995. Indeed, by 1995, these sectors accounted for one job in three in Québec, whereas in 1976 they had represented one in four. In contrast, in the public sector only the health and social services sector continued to grow up to the mid-1990s, while education increased slightly and public administration decreased slightly from 1986-1995.

The important point in terms of the impact on the union movement is that the subsectors of the tertiary sector, in which job growth was concentrated, were also the sectors where it was difficult to unionize, as the following data demonstrate. In 1997, union density was 17 per cent in retailing, 9.7 per cent in the finance, insurance, and real estate sector; 14.1 per cent in business services; 12.8 per cent in personnel, hotel and restaurant services; and 13.6 per cent in the miscellaneous services sector.[8] Together, these subsectors accounted for 45 per cent of the jobs in the tertiary sector and 35 per cent of all jobs in Québec. The average unionization rate in these sectors was only 14 per cent, which was much lower than in the tertiary sector as a whole (36.8 per cent) and than in Québec as a whole (40.3 per cent). Moreover, the rate of increase in unionization in these subsectors was extremely slow in the 1980s and 1990s (around 1.5 per cent between 1988 and 1997). In short, the tertiarization of the economy saw employment grow in subsectors where union density was relatively low and where it was growing very slowly.

In parallel with these transformations of the Québec economy, the well-known changes in the labour market must be identified in order to understand the serious difficulties facing unions. To begin with, we can take forms of employment as a first indicator of these changes. From 1976 to 1995, paid employment went from 91 per cent of all jobs in Québec to 86 per cent, whereas its counterpart, self-employment, grew from 9 per cent to 14 per cent. If we instead break down total employment between part-time paid employment, full-time paid employment, and self-employment, we find that part-time employment grew from 8 per cent to 15 per cent between 1976 and 1995, full-time employment declined from 83 per cent to 71 per cent during the same period, and self-employment rose from 9 per cent to 14 per cent. Government researchers who have studied this trend have projected that, at this rate, non-standard employment will surpass standard employment in the year 2017.[9] Even if this projection turns out to be wrong, these changes remain worrying from the point of view of unions considering that the rate of unionization among part-time employees in Québec was 29.6 per cent in 1999, representing a slight decline from the rate a few years earlier (30.2 per cent in 1993), compared to a unionization rate of 42 per cent among full-time employees.[10] As for self-employment, its very nature makes unionization virtually impossible. In sum, the labour movement's "traditional labour market," i.e., full-time paid employment, has shrunk considerably over the 1976-1995 period; and what are generally termed non-standard jobs (part-time jobs and self-employment) have increased to almost one job in three (or, more exactly, 29.3 per cent).

We can also examine the changing labour market from the perspective of firm size, which is another characteristic that is key to understanding some of the difficulties created by the tertiarization of the economy for unions. Between 1983 and 1997, the percentage of paid workers employed by establishments with less than 20 employees increased from 21.7 per cent to 24.7 per cent in Québec,[11] or one worker in four. (In firms employing five or fewer employees, the percentage went from 9.1 per cent to 10.4 per cent.) At the other extreme, the percentage of employees working in firms employing 500 or more workers decreased over the same period from 46.7 per cent to 40.5 per cent. One of the characteristics of jobs in small firms is their instability as compared to jobs in large firms (between three and four times more unstable in micro-enterprises—five or fewer employees—than in large firms, according to data from the ministère de l'Industrie et du Commerce du Québec).

It might be added that the private subsectors of the tertiary sector discussed above, in which unionization rates are low (retailing, finance, etc.) are composed primarily of small firms compared to the public sector, the primary sector and the secondary sector. Union organizing difficulties with small groups of workers and, even more so, with groups of workers whose employment is more unstable, means that it is difficult to introduce and sustain unionization among small groups of employees. Indeed, in 1999, the rate of unionization in small firms (fewer than 20 employees) in Québec was only 16.6 per cent, whereas it was 60.3 per cent in firms with 100 or more employees (and 66.3 per cent in firms with 500 and more).[12]

A final characteristic of the tertiarization and growing precariousness of the labour market that should be mentioned is the "generation" effect that these trends create for the union movement. Between 1976 and 1995, the number of jobs held by young people (15-24 years old) shrank and job duration decreased. Thus, between 1976 and 1995, total employment among young people declined more rapidly than the youth labour force (by 30 per cent versus by 29 per cent), full-time employment declined even more rapidly (minus 54 per cent) and part-time employment increased substantially (plus 110 per cent). In 1995, 48.3 per cent of young people worked part-time (14.6 per cent in 1976) compared to only 12-14 per cent of older workers.[13] As regards unionization of this age group, in 1999 union density was only 20.5 per cent among the 15-24 year-old age group in Québec. Lastly, the 15-24 year-old age group accounted for only 4.6 per cent of total union membership in Québec.

All of these transformations of the Québec economy and labour market had in many respects already begun to appear in the early 1980s. In addition, the example of union decline in the United States also prompted the Québec union movement to seek changes to labour legislation, the essentials of which had not been significantly modified (for the private sector at least) since the adoption of the initial framework in 1944, with the exception of the prohibition of the use of strikebreakers that was put into the law in 1977 and several other more minor changes regarding unionization. From the point of view of unions, the changes in the economy and labour market then occurring required new legislative provisions to bolster union organizing, especially in small and increasingly dispersed workplaces.

In the early 1980s, an important government commission was established and given the mandate of proposing an updating of labour legislation. Its final report was submitted in 1985. In terms of union demands, a key proposal was to be able to seek certification and engage in bargaining on a multi-employer basis in order to be able to bring together small groups of employees working closely together in the workplace but for different employers (e.g., in shopping centres or office buildings), which would make it possible to negotiate terms and conditions of employment for employees on a basis other than that of the single establishment as provided for in the 1944 Labour Code.[14] In the end, the Beaudry Commission (named after the judge who chaired the Commission), submitted a massive report that was almost totally ignored due to a change in government and also, no doubt, because unions did not have enough political power in a context where the ideas of economic and trade liberalization were beginning to take shape (i.e., privatization, the negotiation of the first free-trade agreement with the United States). In contrast with 1944 and 1964—periods during which the union movement had won legal provisions allowing it to extend its reach, first, into the then-dominant private sector (i.e., primary and secondary industries) and then into the public sector—the 1985 exercise ended in complete failure.

The economic and labour market transformations discussed above are not unique to Québec, and its labour movement is therefore struggling with problems that are essentially the same as those facing the labour movement in many industrialized nations. In his analysis of the European situation, Jelle Visser sketches a portrait of European unions that underlines the fundamental similarities to the situation that we have described for Québec.[15] His analysis identifies significant pressures on the representational capacity of the union movement, which is increasingly confined to the "traditional" segments of the work force, leaving young people, those in precarious jobs, and workers in the new economy unrepresented. His analysis also highlights organizational pressures on unions themselves, which are merging groups in order to make them economically viable in a context of smaller bargaining units and the need for new resources to organize the unorganized. All of this is leading to identity tensions within unions, the challenge being, in Visser's words, to "Preserve the Old and Organize the New."

The International Labour Office (ILO) has also conducted an analysis of a large group of industrialized and industrializing countries (70 in all) that generally arrives at the same findings: declining rates of unionization, economic changes, pressures of globalization, trade liberalization, lack of adaptation of labour laws and, indeed, lack of respect for fundamental union rights. Still, as the ILO stresses, "There is of course just as much need for representation, but traditional methods are unable to translate this need into practice."[16]

Despite the unfavourable changes in the economy and the labour market, Québec unions have been able to maintain an overall rate of unionization that remains significant (39.5 per cent in 1999). This relative success can be attributed to an operational capacity to penetrate certain segments of the labour market despite the obstacles, a capacity that stems from the Québec labour movement's relatively high level of organization (almost 75 per cent of union members are affiliated to one or another of the four union confederations[17]). This organizational capacity was further strengthened during the 1990s as a result of the restructuring of some federations and regional union bodies, which made it possible to combine resources (and even free up new resources) in order to tackle the growing difficulties of unionization on the labour market.

The proactive response of Québec unions to workplace and economic change (e.g., work organization, training of members, union democracy, participation in capital investment, participation in decision-making, new methods of negotiation, and lengthening of the duration of collective agreements) has often been cited to explain its dynamism and the level of union density,[18] although others have argued that there has been a loss in terms of identity.[19] But, overall, it remains the case that Québec unions are struggling with a series of economic changes that necessarily limit its capacity to respond to developments in the economy and labour market. In particular, unionism is increasingly confined to its traditional spheres (the primary and secondary private sector and the public tertiary sector), which, in simplified terms, means that it is sometimes characterized as "blue collar" (and also white collar for the public sector), "full-time" and "older." Is unionism, therefore, simply part of the "old economy"?

Globalization and the Modernization of Labour Law: Trying to Square the Circle?

Faced with the problems created by the transformations discussed above, the Québec labour movement successfully pressed the government to launch a new attempt to modernize its labour laws. Thus, more than 15 years after the fruitless exercise of the Beaudry Commission report, and more than 55 years after the adoption of the legal framework that is still essentially in place, the Québec labour movement is trying to obtain new legal tools that will allow it to cope with the new economy.

The union movement is not disguising its worries about the inadequacy of the means it currently has at its disposal to organize new segments of the labour force. Essentially, unions are calling for[20] a widening of the definition of employee so that they can organize the growing numbers of self-employed workers, many of whom are dependent on a single employer. This phenomenon is the result of new employer strategies aimed at enhancing flexibility in the management of labour costs and the employment relationship. The data presented earlier demonstrated the importance of this group of workers. Unions are also asking that this new definition of employee include first- and second-level managers in order to provide these latter groups with access to unions, as is the case in some other provinces and countries. Unions are asking, as well, for changes that will reduce the impact of subcontracting (another important element in employers' search for greater operational flexibility) on employees and unions. They are also demanding that multi-unit negotiation be allowed, which would make unionization and collective bargaining more effective in small workplaces. Here, too, we saw above that small firms have been growing in importance in recent decades. Finally, we should mention the union movement's demand to improve the administrative efficiency of the union certification process in order to reduce delays and the possibility of employer objections, which sometimes make joining a union a risky exercise, especially in workplaces where labour turnover is high (e.g., the largely unsuccessful attempts to unionize McDonalds restaurants in Québec).

In short, the union movement is asking for new tools that would enlarge its potential clientele, reduce the losses resulting from employer strategies, improve the certification process and allow for innovative forms of collective bargaining (by combining units). For their part, employers largely defend the status quo by invoking the environment of economic competition generated by globalization and the need to retain flexibility in the way they manage labour. At best, they admit that it is important to reduce certain administrative delays and to clarify the sections of the law relating to subcontracting (though in their case, the purpose is to allow greater recourse to it).[21]

The process of labour law revision began, nominally at least, in 1999 with formal consultations of employer and union associations, followed by a government statement tabled in 2000. From that point on, the government statement[22] left little hope for most of the union movement's demands, except for a possible widening of the definition of employee to include dependent, self-employed workers and some modifications in the administration of labour law. It is true that the statement referred to the inadequacy of labour laws in the face of economic transformations, stressing in particular the increase in self-employed workers, many of whom are dependent on a single employer, and mentioning the possible link between labour law and declining union density in Québec (from 46.4 per cent in 1993 to 40.0 per cent in 1998). However, on the one hand, the statement was careful to indicate that unions and employers "wish to remain free to control their own future" (p. 1), thereby suggesting that the government would not impose rules that were not desired by both actors. On the other hand—and, in our view, critically—the statement set out the principle that "changes made in the Labour Code must take into account the North-American context" (p. 1). In fact, the government has strongly supported free trade over the last several years and so it has conceded to the position of Québec employers that globalization of trade requires a degree of convergence between public policy in Québec and in other North American jurisdictions (especially in the rest of Canada and the United States), particularly in the area of labour law.

More precisely, the statement said that, because of the North American environment, it would be unrealistic to introduce, for example, unionization of managers or multi-employer certification in the absence of a "strong consensus" among the parties. Clearly, this reference to a strong consensus (*sic*), made necessary by the North American environment (read "globalization"), gives employers a de facto power advantage. All employers need to do to block a change is to oppose it, a situation that is hardly conducive to genuine debate. In fact, in order to lend the statement a "balanced" tone, the government even suggested that employers be given the new right (borrowed from the United States) to require that its offers at the negotiating table be put to a vote by a general union meeting.

The government statement was first followed by an initial bill tabled in 2000 and rejected as unacceptable by both unions and employers. The bill was then withdrawn and replaced with a new bill that was in the process of being adopted in June 2001. Although the substance of the new bill fell well short of the union movement's demands (in particular, there were no provisions for the unionization of managers or multi-employer bargaining), it was greeted differently by unions, whose initial unity around a common set of demands had given way to division.

The major argument of the largest union confederation, which supported the bill (which legitimized its adoption in the eyes of the government), was essentially that a realistic reading of the current environment of the union movement (i.e., of the economic, political, and social conjuncture) made a more substantial reform of labour law highly unlikely. After 15 years of fighting for labour law reform, to refuse to support the bill—the second in two years—would be to run the considerable risk that no changes would be made to the law at all. Indeed, it would have been possible for the government to claim that these failed attempts at reform were proof that nothing could be changed. The union movement's response to the new proposal was therefore deeply divided. Employers, for their part, were only mildly opposed, no doubt viewing the overall result as a victory of its claims that globalization narrows the government's margin to manoeuvre in the field of labour law.

The wide gap between the initial demands of the union movement and the final outcome raises an important question: Could the union movement have won more advantageous legislative changes, weakened as it was by a decline in union density over much of the previous decade and by an effective context of globalization in which Québec's two principal economic partners (Ontario and the United States) were anything but sympathetic to unions? And, relatedly, what will be the impact of this failure to achieve substantial changes in the union movement?

Conclusion: Possible Scenarios for Québec Unionism

Our analysis of the Québec union movement has been framed in terms of the parallel development of labour law and a number of major transformations of the economy and the labour market, so as to identify the impact of these changes on the development of unionism. This approach is open to the criticism that we have thereby neglected the effects of unionism on the growth of real wages, on standards of living, on social programs, on individual and collective rights, or, more generally, on social dynamics. In fact, we would be the first to recognize these major contributions of the union movement, in Québec and elsewhere. However, our reason for stressing the law and changes in the world of work is that it is clear that the Québec union movement would not have grown as significantly as it did over the last 50 and more years without the legislative advances that it won during its long struggle. Clearly, changes in the labour market since the 1980s are undermining unions' representation capacity and, in so doing, its capacity to engage in social action.

Changes to existing labour legislation could have revitalized this representation capacity, just as the labour laws of 1944 and the inclusion of the public sector in 1964 gave it a first and, then, a second boost. To conclude the chapter, this section outlines three scenarios for the labour movement as it searches for a way to spark a third wave of growth. The first of these scenarios is no longer in the cards because of the division of the union movement over the last bill proposed by the government. Nevertheless, it will be considered because it highlights certain conditions that, in our view, are essential to union action, and it also explains the relative failure of the union movement to achieve its demands.

Scenario 1:
Significant Labour Law Reforms and Revival of Union Organizing

The first scenario, embodied in the union movement's common demands formulated a number of years ago, envisages a genuine modernization of labour laws that would allow unions to make inroads among new groups in the labour force (i.e., private services, non-standard workers, and managers). Labour law reform would not automatically increase unionization rates, because unionizing and representing these new groups requires considerable effort and a capacity on the part of unions to innovate in order to reach new clients, to respond to their needs, and to include them in organizations dominated by traditional segments of unionized workers—or, as Visser put it, to "Preserve the Old and Organize the New." But, in this scenario, the union movement first had to win labour law reforms by doing battle with both the government and employers. This assumed, in particular, a joint strategy on the part of the various union confederations and a willingness to make it the most important union struggle for a long time. To succeed, it was necessary to convince current union members that defending the rights of unorganized workers was crucial to the very survival of the union movement as a whole. In short, to reach the "outsiders" it was first necessary to mobilize the "insiders" of the labour movement and, in addition, to adhere to a unified union strategy.

Yet, it must be recognized that, after a number of years of common demands, including a joint union platform developed in 1999, the labour movement fell short on both counts: it did not seek to mobilize its members in the battle; and it ended up showing the other parties that it was divided. This made the unified scenario of a long-desired, sweeping reform impossible.

Scenario 2:
A Strategy Focused on the Protection of Existing Union Rights

A second possible scenario assumes that the changes now being made to labour law will not provide unions with the much sought-after means to organize new segments of the labour force.[23] In this case, and taking for granted that the economic and labour market transformations discussed in Part 2 will be continuing (or will, at least, not be reversed), one possible union reaction is to focus on trying to protect its existing position in terms of union members and its capacity to improve their standards of living and working conditions. This is a defensive and protectionist strategy by unions that consider that this task is enough of a challenge, especially in the context of globalization.

In any event, this scenario could in fact make it possible to protect union members and to maintain the current level of unionization in particular industries. However, in view of the changing nature of employment and the growth of employment in industries and workplaces where unions are largely absent, the overall rate of unionization in Québec will inevitably fall. By how many percentage points? Possibly enough to affect the status the labour movement has enjoyed for several decades as a major social actor. Union density has already fallen below the 40 per cent mark for the first time in 20 years, and it could slide to 35 per cent very quickly, which would be its lowest level since the late 1960s. At these levels, Québec unionism would remain healthier than unionism in neighbouring jurisdictions, but its power to represent workers would be seen to be in decline by the other actors, including the other social actors traditionally allied to the union movement, who might try to play a larger role in representing workers. In such a defensive scenario, it is also possible that a climate of "every one for him- or herself" might exacerbate tensions among unions, thereby weakening the capacity of unions to act as a movement—an unpleasant scenario for the unions, to be sure, but one that is nevertheless possible, especially in light of the recent divisions that occurred when unions were faced with the most challenging exercise in solidarity that had confronted them for a long time.

Scenario 3:
A Diversified and Coordinated Strategy to Revive Unionism

The third scenario is, in fact, a hybrid of the first two scenarios. On the one hand, it accepts that the minor changes to labour legislation will not give unions easy access to new groups in the labour force. On the other hand, in contrast to the previous scenario, rather than focusing inward on the protection of its current members, unions would seek reinvigoration and expansion at two levels: union organizing and social action. As regards union organizing, this assumes that unions develop the capacity to use innovative and flexible forms of representing workers who are not yet unionized, as well as the injection of significant resources to try to organize these workers. In this respect, at least two complementary paths seem worth exploring: (1) the pooling of union expertise in the area of organization and innovation (including drawing on foreign experience); and (2) the assigning of particular industries or labour market segments to particular unions in order to avoid competition between organizations that have limited resources. In all of these cases, this scenario assumes a much higher degree of co-operation among unions than currently exists.

As for the need to revitalize social action, the union movement would have to get involved in the wider struggles that have always gone hand-in-hand with its development as an actor, both within and outside the firm. On this score, there is no shortage of causes, as evidenced by poverty, the deterioration of a number of social programs (e.g., Employment Insurance), and the impact of globalization. The union movement is already involved in these social and economic issues, but its involvement could be made more visible by linking it to its efforts to boost union organizing. In the absence of such a link, there is a risk that unions will rush blindly to join struggles that, albeit essential, are not central to unionism and that are in fact often the principal fields of action of other organizations that make up the social movement (the women's movement, youth groups, groups seeking to protect the rights of the disadvantaged, anti-globalization groups, etc.). Both of these forms of actions are mutually beneficial for the union movement, as its history in Québec and elsewhere demonstrates. This scenario puts the struggle for unionization and the fight for better working conditions back at the heart of union activity, but also promotes an inclusive social project that seeks economic and social improvement for everyone. In Québec, the union movement has often played a prominent role in advocating this kind of social project, sometimes even using a radical ideology. In this era of globalization and redefinition of collective issues, it is up to the union movement to return to the task of mobilizing, a task that inevitably will require it first to clarify the ideological framework of its action and the overall social project for which it wishes to work. The achievement of this third scenario will not be easy in the economic, political, and social environment of the various union confederations, but it is a plausible and stimulating scenario, both for the union movement itself and for democracy as a whole.

Notes

1. See Jacques Rouillard, *Histoire du syndicalisme québécois* (Montréal: Boréal, 1989); Bernard Dionne, *Le syndicalisme au Québec* (Montréal: Boréal, 1991); and CEQ-CSN, *Histoire du mouvement ouvrier au Québec (1825-1976)* (Montréal: CEQ-CSQ [co-publishers], 1979).

2. This law still exists in Québec, but the government recently engaged in a revision process that led to the abrogation of a number of decrees. In a detailed analysis of this process, we have identified a direct link between the context of trade globalization and this process of revision and abrogation. See Guylaine Vallée and Jean Charest, "Globalization and the Transformation of State Regulation of Labour: the Case of Recent Amendments to the Québec *Collective Agreement Decrees Act*," *International Journal of Comparative Labour Law and Industrial Relations* 17, 1 (2001): 79-91.

3. Rouillard, *Histoire du Syndicalisme*, 74, 201.

4. Fernand Morin, "La négociation collective selon le modèle de 1944 est-elle périmée?" in Colette Bernier et al., eds., *La négociation collective du travail, Adaptation ou disparition?* (Sainte-Foy: Les Presses de l'Université Laval, 1993), 15.

5. J. Rouillard, *Histoire du syndicalsime*, 201.

6. Gregor Murray and Pierre Verge, *La représentation syndicale. Visage juridique actuel et futur* (Sainte-Foy: Les Presses de l'Université Laval, 1999), 21.

7. Ministère de l'Industrie, du Commerce, de la Science et de la Technologie (MICST), *La tertiarisation de l'économie du Québec* (Québec: MICST, Direction de l'analyse de la conjoncture industrielle, 1996), 5-6.

8. Roger Shawl, "La présence syndicale au Québec en 1997," *Le Marché du travail* (Sept. 1998): 7.

9. Le Marché du travail. *L'évolution de l'emploi atypique au Québec* (Québec: Ministère du Travail, 1998), 20, 25.

10. Ernest B. Akyeampong, "Unionization—an update," *Perspectives on Labour and Income* (Ottawa: Statistics Canada, 2000), 49; G. Murray and P. Verge, *La représentation syndicale*, 26.

11. Ministère de l'Industrie et du Commerce (MIC), *L'évolution et la dynamique des emplois* (Québec: <www.mic.gouv.qc.ca>, 2000).

12. E. Akyeampong, "Unionization—an update," 51.

13. Le Marché du travail, *L'évolution de l'emploi*, 36-39.

14. In its final report, *Le Travail une responsabilité collective*, the Commission consultative sur le travail et la révison du Code du travail issued a recommendation regarding voluntary multi-employer certification and negotiation, but the recommendation was not acted upon by the government.

15. Jelle Visser, "European trade unions in the mid-1990s," *Industrial Relations Journal*, European annual review (1998): 113-30.

16. International Labour Office, *World Labour Report 1998-98: Industrial Relations, Democracy and Social Stability* (Geneva: ILO, 1998), 5.

17. The Fédération des travailleurs et travailleuses du Québec (FTQ), associated with the Canadian Labour Congress, accounted for 37 per cent of union members in Québec in 1997; the Confédération des syndicats nationaux (CSN) had 24 per cent; the Centrale des syndicats du Québec (CSQ), 10 per cent; and the Centrale des syndicats démocratiques (CSD), 4 per cent.

18. See, for example, Paul-André Lapointe and Paul R. Bélanger, "La participation du syndicalisme à la modernisation sociale des enterprises," in G. Murray et al., eds., *L'état des relations professionnelles. Traditions et perspectives de recherche* (Sainte-Foy: Les Presses de l'Université Laval, 1996), 284-310; Pierre Laliberté, "L'impact économique de l'action des fonds syndicaux de capital-risque: une étude de cas au Québec," *Revue internationale du Travail* 137, 1 (1998): 53-67; Christian Lévesque, Gregor Murray, and Stéphane Le Queux, "Transformations sociales et identités syndicales: l'institution syndicale à l'épreuve de la différenciation sociale contemporaine," *Sociologie et sociétés* 30, 2 (1998): 131-54; Reynald Bourque, "Coopération patronale-syndicale et réorganisation du travail," *Relations industrielles/Industrial Relations* 54, 1 (1999): 136-67.

19. Mona-Josée Gagnon, "La 'modernisation' du syndicalisme québécois ou la mise à l'épreuve d'une logique représentative," *Sociologie et sociétés* 30, 2 (1998): 213-30; Jean-Marc Piotte, "Post-scriptum aux deux sommets de 1996," *Du combat au partenariat. Interventions critiques sur le syndicalisme québécois* (Montréal: Éditions Nota bene, 1998), 257-69.

20. CEQ, CSD, CSN, FTQ, *Réforme du Code du travail. Demandes de la partie syndicale* (Montréal: Avis au Conseil consultatif du travail et de la main-d'œuvre, 1999).

21. See *Réflexions de la partie patronale sur la demande d'avis relatif aux améliorations des lois du travail* (Montréal: Avis au Conseil consultatif du travail et de la main-d'œuvre, 1999).

22. Ministère du Travail, *Pour un Code du travail renouvelé. Orientations ministérielles* (Québec: <www.travail.gouv.qc.ca>, 2000). For an English-language summary, see "For a renewed *Labour Code*" (<www.travail.gouv.qc.ca/renouv-code/English/sum_renewed.html>, 2001). Direct quotes are taken from this summary.

23. It should be mentioned that principal legislative changes in June 2001 seek to create a new decision-making body (the Commission des relations du travail). The most significant effect of this change for unions probably will be to make unionization more efficient by reducing the delays that used to be caused by employers' use of multiple appeals.

14

The Québec Women's Movement: Past and Present

CHANTAL MAILLÉ*

Introduction

To write about the history and current realities of the women's movement can seem to imply that the movement is unified, perfectly integrated, and operates on a single analysis with common positions. The reality of the women's movement is different. There are groups and individuals from all political tendencies, as well as non-organized elements and this is what makes it a subject of analysis that is capable of revealing the complexity of the social fabric of Québec society, as well as its pluralistic character.

When trying to identify characteristics that reveal the specificity of Québec, we must include the existence of an influential, highly structured and well-organized Québec-based women's movement; this in contrast to women in the rest of Canada, who are organized as a pan-Canadian movement, instead of on a province-by-province basis. The origins of change, over the past 40 years in Québec, consist of two sources: first, socio-political changes, or the dynamics of modernization, which facilitated modifications in the life trajectories of women. The second identifiable source of change is the establishment of the women's movement, which became an important participant in these transformations. This movement significantly shaped

* Translated from French into English by Lynda Lyness.

the socio-political dynamics of Québec society, and contributed to the broadening of political debates.

The women's movement played a preponderant role in the larger currents of social reform that have concerned women since the Quiet Revolution. It is formed by groups of feminists with greatly diverse practices, as attested to by certain radical 1970s groups, such as the *Front de libération des femmes* (FLF), who sought to raise the collective consciousness about the diverse forms of patriarchal oppression, as well as lobby groups such as the Association féminine d'éducation et d'action sociale (AFÉAS) and the Fédération des femmes du Québec (FFQ), two large women's organizations whose activities, from their inception, were oriented towards the promotion of women's economic equality. Add to this, service organizations and a network of women's centres, which are quite common even outside urban areas. These groups have set up and struggled to obtain financing for their operations, and have accomplished an enormous amount of work, drawing attention to critical problems such as violence in the family, the realities of immigrant and refugee women, integration into the labour force, and access to non-traditional occupations for women.

Women's groups occupy a relatively unique political position in Québec society. In fact, the women's movement constitutes an important space for women's political activism practised beyond the boundaries of traditional political institutions. The women's movement has been the most significant political actor representing the interests of women, and credit is owed to the sustained actions of the hundreds of women's groups that struggled for and obtained judicial reforms that ultimately benefited women as a group. Nevertheless, the women's movement has increasingly become integrated in the administration of public policy; principally, by being assigned, by the government, the role of managing women's interests, that is, channelling and expressing women's demands in acceptable terms for the government apparatus in exchange for a certain monopoly over the representation of women's interests.[1] As a result, on the one hand, women as a group are categorized and confined to a specific space of representation and, on the other hand, the women's movement is recognized as an authorized and legitimate representative of women in general.

The question becomes, how can we begin to evaluate the contribution of feminism to Québec society in the twentieth century? Diane Lamoureux contends that the feminist movement has played a decisive role in establishing democracy in Québec. Specifically, Lamoureux argues that the feminist movement has been consistently challenged to take advantage of democracy for women, despite its inherent limitations with regard to women. Thus, when considering the question of the constitutive exclusion of women, feminism demands democracy for women and, in the process, sheds light on the limits of the original concept of democracy, which was exclusionist.[2]

In this chapter, I will summarize the most important moments in the history of the women's movement in Québec, initially, by concentrating on the first half of the twentieth century, when the right to vote became a rallying point for the mobilization of the women's movement. This is followed by a description of the groups, actions and the manifestations included in the "second wave" of the women's movement. Finally, I reflect on the women's movement as a social movement and its connections to feminism, as well as the challenges and issues that it must confront. I focus on the multiple facets of the movement, that is, its diversity, since women from many different backgrounds are involved in the movement. Examples of this include, First Nations women's groups, the Montréal Council of Women, founded at the end of the nineteenth century, and Jewish women's groups, as well. In short, the women's movement in Québec endorsed expressions of women's diversity before the question of diversity became the high-stakes issue that it is today. Often, this point is neglected in the nomenclature; nevertheless, the women's movement, more than other social movements, is diverse, despite official recognition of certain groups as designated spokespersons for women; and this, to the detriment of a truly plural voice, which would be composed of diverse parts of the movement including those who are not members of organizations and those who may have different perspectives and points of view that are not being heard. The women's movement, as such, extends beyond those groups that emerged during the "second wave"; groups that articulated a liberal feminism that focused on demands addressed to the state. These groups constitute one of the most visible parts of the contemporary women's movement, which nevertheless cannot be reduced to a single component.[3] In fact, the women's movement consists of elements that include public figures, such as artists and authors, as well as women's studies programs, publications, publishing houses, art galleries; and resources, such as governmental agencies, which include the Secretariat à la condition féminine du gouvernement du Québec and the Conseil du Statut de la femme.

This being said, women's groups represent a central part of this canvas. These groups, whose numbers exceed one thousand,[4] "who, throughout the previous century, and particularly over the past twenty years, have established themselves throughout the Québec territory ... While their spheres of activity may vary greatly, all of these groups participate to achieve the same goal."[5]

A Movement Sustained by Militant Activists

Évelyne Tardy and André Bernard note the continuous commitment on the part of activists, despite such obstacles as financial uncertainties and the impossibility of long-term planning, since state funding is usually granted on an annual basis, as well as the tremendous needs in certain sectors, such as battered women's shelters, which are considerable undertakings. In addition, Tardy and Bernard observe that the greatest paradox is the persistence of militant action, despite the day-to-day difficulties that women's groups confront. In contrast to political and trade union militancy, they write, there is no crisis in terms of the activism of women's groups. Despite the many possible reasons to be discouraged, women do not concede. Notwithstanding the constant barrage of negative messages conveyed through the media and the *backlash* against feminism, its targets continue the struggle.[6] Thus, there is recognizable strength in terms of the mobilization of the women's movement despite, the term "feminism" being an object of criticism and questioning. The question then becomes, what are these criticisms? For many, the word "feminism" refers to the collective mobilization project of a specific generation of women whose project seems to belong to a bygone era; and for others, the current generation fails to comprehend the necessity of large-scale social movements and collective mobilizations, which can certainly influence the perception that young women have of activism in groups, established and sustained by their mothers' and grandmothers' generations. Certain women see this as a generational conflict between feminists: that is, the older generation refuses to think outside their narrow views expressed in terms that have been around for 30 years, while informing the younger generation that they are also victims, who should be concerned about losing acquired rights: whereas the younger generation wants to rethink the stakes from different perspectives, revise the past analysis, and do not accept collective action as a personal form of engagement, but prefer small-scale actions or actions taken at a personal level. Based on this analysis, one can oppose the feminist assumption that it is an intergenerational project, whose objectives, to be achieved, require several generations of women pursuing struggles that had begun long before.[7] Despite these criticisms, the women's movement in Québec has always been driven by the strength of numerous committed women, who devoted their energies and who based their ideas on this movement as a force for change.

In Québec, the women's movement has existed for over a century when considering its origins in the suffrage movement that demanded the right for women to vote. It was supported by the international women's movement, which simultaneously struggled to remove the most visible symbol of women's exclusion from citizenship, that is, the prohibition of women from voting. Let us not forget, the creation of an important Québec women's association, the Fédération nationale Saint-Jean Baptiste, in 1907, which operated during the first half of the twentieth century for women's political and legal emancipation,[8] although holding an ambiguous position on women's right to vote at the provincial level. Women in Québec obtained the right to vote in federal elections in 1918 and had to continue the struggle for the same right at the provincial level until 1940. This situation evoked a profound feeling of alienation. In her work on Québec women's access to the right to vote, Diane Lamoureux discusses the importance of the provincial vote for certain women's associations, such as the Ligue des droits de la femme, particularly since issues of concern to women, for example education, public health, work conditions and income, are provincial matters.[9] In this regard, the president of the FNSJB from 1912 to 1933, Marie Gérin-Lajoie, recognized the stakes that this vote represented for women. In one of her articles in favour of provincial suffrage, she describes the jurisdictional powers related to the provincial government and their strategic importance in women's lives. The FNSJB also established civic instruction courses in the 1920's that permitted women from Québec to vote with full knowledge and understanding of the facts in federal elections and also cut short arguments of opponents to women's suffrage, at the provincial level, who argued that women lacked competence and interest in politics.[10]

The mobilization of the women's movement around the issue of provincial suffrage unexpectedly led to the disintegration of the "first wave" of the women movement, once women in Québec obtained the right to vote. Interestingly, however, in 1965 on the twenty-fifth anniversary of women's suffrage at the provincial level in Québec, the founding of Fédération des femmes du Québec inaugurated the "second wave" of the women's movement. Then, one year later, a second nationally recognized organization, l'Association féminine d'éducation et d'action sociale emerged from an amalgamation of rural women's and farmers organizations. Both of these organizations situate themselves somewhere on the continuum of the two major streams of feminism from the beginning of the twentieth century. The FFQ supports the egalitarian ideology, and it's no surprise that such a group blossomed during the twenty-fifth anniversary of women obtaining the right to vote, nor that some founding members were also members of the suffragist movement. The AFÉAS on the other hand, stemmed from the "difference" and home economics stream, which swept through North America at the beginning of the century.[11]

Yet, in parallel to those who worked at all levels of government to obtain changes in the conditions of women's lives, a more radical branch of the women's movement began to take shape as witnessed by the short-lived existence of the Front de libération des femmes from 1969 to 1971; at the same time that Québec itself began to analyze questions of de-colonization and Marxism, which circulated within and were tied to demonstrations by the Front de libération du Québec (FLQ). The FLF organized "choc-actions," among other things concerning the exclusion of women jurors from trials, which eventually contributed to changes in the law regarding this issue, in 1971. As a group that asserted a radical political discourse, the FLF was also asked to take a position on the provincial elections of 1970. This event also brought about a profound debate within the group itself: the question, "Are we women first or Québecers first?" If one part of the FLF's activists, at that moment, chose to join the PQ's volunteers, others chose to participate in the campaign by making the political parties accountable, by questioning the candidates, and by protesting during electoral assemblies with signs that contained provocative slogans for that period of time, signs that demanded free daycare centres and free abortion.[12]

The Achievements of the Women's Movement

A significant number of women's groups have won recognition for their powerful influence upon Québec society. In this regard, Québec society has undergone an important set of transformations, which in large part, is due to the women's movement. The "second wave" of the women's movement emerged during a period of fluid cultural transformation, a period known as the Quiet Revolution, a time that

> is fundamentally expressed by a profound reorganization of the state's structures (creation of new ministries, the professionalization of the civil service, the attempt to create new structures of power, regionalization), the articulation of strategies including taking charge of services formally provided by the Church (education, health, etc.). At the same time, this partial rupture with traditionalism and Catholicism at the ideological level assisted with the process of modernization in terms of ideas and the secularization of Québec society. This did not occur without affecting women. The assuming of responsibility by the State, allowed demands to be directly addressed to the State itself; this explains in large part their legal aspect ... Finally, it is not surprising that in a society dominated by the logic of the market that equality for women equates to women becoming, both in theory and in practice, economic beings.[13]

Groups such as the FFQ and the AFÉAS strongly represent this stream of egalitarianism, at least throughout the 1970s. However, the "second wave" of the women's movement is also built around individuals that share a vision of women shaped by the feminist ideas of an impressive number of works about women's lives by authors such as Benoîte Groult, Marie Cardinal, Nicole Brossard, Louky Bersianik, and Marilyn French. Some publishing houses, such as *Remue-ménage*, have seen the day, and many women in the cultural and literary fields have disseminated a point of view centred on an analysis of the feminine universe. The establishment of the Powerhouse gallery in 1974, renamed La Centrale afterwards, established new prospects for women working in visual arts. This gallery devotes itself to presenting works of art created by women and to offering a space where women are free to experiment artistically. La Centrale supports the expression and establishment of multiple forms of artistic practice, feminism and inter-disciplinarity with the goal of representing the interests and the dynamism of it's continually changing community.[14] Québec universities followed that path by establishing women's studies programs, while offering a place for research projects to fill the immense knowledge gaps attributable to the previous absence of women as socially significant subjects for study. Thus, the "second wave" of the women's movement is not unified by a common analysis. In fact, many ideologies are both employed by and challenged by feminist groups: however, significant groups such as the FFQ and the AFÉAS can be defined as egalitarian, since they believe that the aim of feminist demands should be to give women the status and socio-economic conditions comparable to those of men. Here, the state plays a fundamental role in the adoption of legislation, which sanctions this form of equality. Briefly, in the egalitarian perspective, the concept of a revolution or women's values is not examined. However, the struggles for equality are numerous: labour discrimination, the absence of attention to maternity leave in the conditions of employment and the promotion of women, as well as stereotypic representations of women in the public domain, and the wage gap between women and men's traditional jobs.

If change is at the heart of action taken by the women's movement, then the state is the decisive link for these changes to occur: who else in Québec society can enforce legislation concerning discriminatory labour practices, parental leave and daycare? To this point, how can we evaluate the response of traditional political institutions to the demands of the feminist movement? We have to realize that a lot of improvements have been obtained on numerous issues. Since, the feminist movement in Québec is well organized, it forced the government to act and grant these improvements. These gains emerged in response to political pressure from the feminist movement and public support of their actions. However, it is difficult to evaluate the impact of each of the various components of the women's movement in this process of change, particularly when we consider that the Québec government created an advisory council on the status of women, that is, the Conseil du statut de la femme, in 1973 charged with the task of advising the government on questions concerning equality and the respect of women's rights as well as informing the people of Québec on these matters. As a conscientious observer of the status of women, the Conseil produces research and analysis that sheds light on the inequalities women encounter. It expresses opinions and makes recommendations concerning legislation, policies, and programs of concern to women. It is the sum of these components—including major collective mobilizations, such as the "Bread and Roses" March in 1995 and the World March of Women in the Year 2000—that provides the women's movement with a visibility that makes it an important force for change.

World March of Women in the Year 2000: A Turning Point

This event, initiated by the Fédération des femmes du Québec, marks a significant shift in the strategies and objectives of the women's movement: the aim, now, is to transnationalize and deterritorialize women's struggles and illustrate women's community of interests as well as the similarities in situations in the North and South. This strategy illustrates a major shift, that is, the opening-up to diversity and the recognition that women's realities are multiple. One of the organizers of the March explained how the consciousness of women's cultural diversity became an important issue for the March's activists:

> Out of concern to represent all women, we wanted indeed, to make our preoccupations the issues of women from ethnocultural communities. To do that, we had to think about the parameters of cultural diversity, to meet the 'others,' to listen to what they had to say, to understand what the conditions of their lives are and at the same time the similarities and differences with women from the majority, and to act in consequence. This has led us to really try to understand why women from certain minority groups, even if they found themselves more often than not confined to low-income ghettos, on unemployment and subjected to violence, discrimination and racism more that others, did not become involved in the women's movement.
>
> In part, the experience of managing ethno-cultural diversity, without it ever being officially brought to the fore, allowed us to tackle the intercultural challenges of organizing the *World March*. The particular demands of visible minority women, native women, immigrants, just to mention a few, are from our view point, tangible clues denoting the new solidarity emerging in the Québec feminist movement.[15]

For the activists who embarked upon this ambitious project, one of the most recent developments is the emergence of a transnational solidarity: "in terms of solidarity, the necessity of associating and working with women from around the world gave birth to a new feminist way of thinking and acting.... Solidarity is, needless to say, the basis for and the very heart of all actions taken by women's groups."[16]

Let us not forget that the World March of Women presented demands derived from two common themes, violence and poverty. Women's organizations from every country or region could establish their own list of demands based on these two themes. In Québec, the FFQ presented a very detailed list of 20 demands, primarily addressed to the government of Québec. These demands include increasing the minimum wage to a level that provides full-time workers with an income that surpasses the poverty line for an individual living alone. However, the government of Québec's response to the demands from the March was disappointing, since few commitments have been acted on and the minimum wage increased by a negligible 10 cents per hour. Nonetheless, in terms of the issue of violence, rape crisis centres have had consistent increases in funding, while women's shelters have had slight increases, and women's centres have received nothing. In addition, the government has agreed to undertake an awareness campaign. However, in terms of poverty, there have been no significant improvements.[17] Françoise David, the president of the Fédération des femmes du Québec at the time, noted in a report an obvious link between the policy choices of the Québec government and globalization:

> There is a reason that the government refuses to inject more money in social housing and increase social assistance benefits. The government is obsessed with the idea of a 'zero-deficit' and substantially reducing income tax. And who pays for this? People who need health care, children with learning difficulties in the education system and the poor.[18]

According to David, the international contacts made during the Women's March, confirmed the correlation between women's poverty and globalization; to produce more at a lower cost could have certain negative consequences, such as the creation of a low-waged workforce that most often consists of non-unionized women, who have no recourse against abusive employers.

Create a Feminist Party? Women and Politics

Confronted by the Québec government's blunt opposition to the demands from the Women's March, an alternative emerges to create a left-wing feminist party, which would be open to men, yet led by a core group of women.[19] Such a project should, nevertheless, consider the obstacles involved in elections that are based on a uninominal system in which third parties have less of chance to win seats, as opposed to a system of proportional representation, where the chances of electing small party representatives are more favourable. This new period of confrontation between feminists and traditional political institutions leads us to examine the symbolic function and the role of women in politics with respect to the Québec women's movement.

The entry of Québec women into politics is relatively recent. Let us not forget that the first woman to serve in the National Assembly was elected in 1961. The first women Quebecers to serve in the federal parliament did so in 1972. The percentage of women elected has grown considerably between 1980 and 1990, however there seems to be a ceiling of about 20 per cent. From the first generation of women who entered politics, few dedicated themselves to representing the interests of women or to becoming spokespersons for the women's movement. However, with the recent election of many women from the women's movement, we are witnessing the emergence of a new reality: that is, feminists, who are in politics to promote the interests of women. There is a significant qualitative distinction that emerges when comparing this generation with the first generation of elected women, who had no affiliation to the feminist movement. In this context, it seems that the women's movement has been the most important actor in terms of the representation of women's political interests; that is, the determining factor in the most significant victories for women, over the past 40 years, which include daycare, employment equity, abortion, to name just a few. These victories are mostly the result of the concerted efforts of feminist groups rather than the actions of elected women.[20] Nevertheless, a number of women's groups maintain connections with political representatives, and quite often act in collaboration with women in politics, such as Louise Harel, Minister of State for Municipal Affairs and the Greater Montréal Region (2001), who has also headed numerous other ministries including Sécurité du revenu as well as L'emploi et la solidarité. Harel's contacts with the women's movement stems from her involvement with issues such as poverty, among others.[21]

Globalization and the Women's Movement

Although concern was formulated relatively recently, the Québec women's movement, has become increasingly preoccupied by questions related to negotiations for a Free Trade Agreement of the Americas (FTAA) and the phenomenon of economic globalization. Let us not forget that Françoise David, the president of the FFQ, identified the connections between women, poverty, and globalization. The Conseil du statut de la femme, in a recent document, also argues that globalization is being built on the backs of women and suggests that Quebecers ought to think about the implications of globalization for women in Québec. For the CSF,

> women and children, particularly those living in developing countries, are often the first victims of a globalization that fails to integrate social development with economic objectives. In Québec, the state has contributed significantly to improving the condition of women's lives since 1960, whether through legislation directed towards equality, or by providing public services in education, health or social services. Even so, women have yet to reach equality in the economic and political spheres and continue to assume primary responsibility for childcare

and the care of individuals in both the private and public spheres. Women are aware that the employment and economic security situations of most women can be weakened by a retreat of the state and by a labour market driven by competitiveness or instability. In this context, it is increasingly relevant to try to understand the globalization phenomenon and to ask, whether the continental economic integration project will jeopardize women's advances, both here and elsewhere; what are the pitfalls that need to be avoided; as well as under what conditions will this project enhance the well-being of women.[22]

Yet another cause of concern related to the FTAA negotiations refers to the near absence of women in positions of authority participating in the current negotiation process. In this context, the question becomes, to what degree are the concerns of women being integrated into the negotiations? At the present moment, there is scant information regarding this matter. However, what is clear is the trepidation expressed by numerous women's organizations concerning the way that globalization is being accomplished, particularly with respect to women's equality, human and political rights, the fair distribution of wealth and resources, and environmental preservation.[23]

The Women's Movement and Questions of Identity

If the women's movement created openings at the legislative, social, and economic levels, it also participated in the debates on the political destiny of Québec. A significant segment of the women's movement has been strongly associated with Québec's identity project. This project, which has many faces, in part was also built by women, although in its contemporary form, its political agenda operates to the advantage of those who were its source, that is, essentially, French-speaking white males over the age of 50.

As previously noted, the Front de libération des femmes (FLF) utilized a discourse that linked women's emancipation to national emancipation, at the end of the 1960s. Let us not forget, that the FLF and the Parti Québécois were founded within months of each other. The FLF quickly distanced itself from this new political entity, for reasons explained by one of the founders of the FLF, Louise Toupin:

> It isn't necessary to go very far in the past … to try and understand why feminists quickly became disinterested by the Parti Québécois. The starting point of this disinterest began, from my point of view, during the 1970s: the PQ's nationalism had little or nothing to do with the national and social revolutionary projects that Québec militants

from that time, had in mind, including the FLF. The socialist and utopian ideas, which permeated the nationalism of the Left in its struggle against American imperialism and Anglo-Saxon colonialism, to use that period's terms, were foreign to the PQ.[24]

The historical importance of this group cannot be underestimated, since its short-lived existence nevertheless represents a decisive step in the history of Québec feminism. Patrice Leclerc asserts that the Québec feminist movement, during the period of nationalist affirmation, benefited from its political vocabulary. Leclerc contends that feminists and nationalists of that time shared similar characteristics, such as ancestry, class, and occupation. In addition, the demands were similar in that both rejected predefined roles based on sex or ethnic origin.

During the past few decades, the rise in neo-feminism paralleled the continued insertion of the women's movement in nationalist discourses. Micheline Dumont advanced the hypothesis that Québec women were at the heart of Québec's ideas about distinct society. In the early 1990s, Dumont wrote:

> Now that Québec is on the doorstep of fundamental decisions, political parties and pressure groups should not make the same error of forgetting that the distinct society exists because of women, as well. Separatists and federalists of all stripes can never forget that just before 1970, Québec's first feminist magazine, issued by the Front de libération des femmes (FLF), was named *Québécoises deboutte*! And if they follow current events, they should also know that the women of Québec are still standing.[25]

The affirmation of a nationalist dimension was still present in the feminism of the 1990's.[26] Certain women's groups, including the FFQ, have acted as beacons in this debate, taking strong positions when many other groups have stayed in the shadows. The positions of women, during Québec's first sovereignty referendum in 1980, have already been analyzed.[27] With reference to this event, there are memories of the Yvette assembly, that is women in the No camp; as well as the one organized to celebrate the fortieth anniversary of Québec women's right to vote, which transformed itself into a women's assembly for the Yes camp; there is also Regroupement des femmes québécoises pour l'indépendance, who proposed to set up a feminist and separatist platform. This group's executive suggested that women nullify their referendum vote by writing the term "women" on their ballot.[28]

The Meech Lake Accord period (1987-1990) marks another important moment in the mobilization of women around constitutional questions.[29] The accord was supported by many women's groups from Québec. However, the Native Women's

Association of Québec opposed the Accord and demanded that the Accord recognize the distinct character of First Nations peoples, and provide specific guaranties for Native women. The agreement was never ratified. Following this defeat, the government of Québec, led by Robert Bourassa's Liberals, set up the Bélanger-Campeau Commission on Québec's political and constitutional future. Eighteen women's groups and three interveners presented their positions.[30] The FFQ chose Québec sovereignty based on an analysis of politic studies that reveal that the sharing of powers between the two levels of governments often results in an inability to create coherent policies that respond to women's needs:

> From a feminist perspective, we understand the importance of autonomy and identity. Such issues have been and are still at the heart of women's struggles. If we want to elaborate and to form a feminist project for Québec society, a societal project for all, defined equally by women and men, a coherent project which addresses the needs and aspirations of Québecers, Québec needs to be in charge of its own development and providence.[31]

In 1992, the federal government proposed the Charlottetown Accord to the citizens of Canada and held a national referendum, which rejected the proposal by a margin of over 54 per cent in Canada (56 per cent in Québec). In Québec, the women's movement mobilized against the Charlottetown Accord, which culminated with a meeting at UQAM.[32] In English Canada, NAC also opposed the Charlottetown Accord.

In 1995, a second referendum on Québec sovereignty was held. Québec sovereigntists committed to attaining sovereignty based on a constitution written by women and men in equality, a promise that pushed women to support the project for a new Québec society.[33] It also seems that the female electorate did not remain indifferent to promises that favoured them, since the Yes option gained points between the beginning and the end of the 1995 referendum campaign with the assistance of women.[34] Prior to this referendum, the Québec government established a regional Commission on Québec's future, which held public hearings on sovereignty before Premier Jacques Parizeau adopted legislation on the issue of sovereignty in December 1994. A total of 16 regional commissions and one national commission listened to the positions presented by groups and individuals. More than 83 groups affiliated with the women's movement were heard.[35] The Fédération des femmes du Québec again favoured sovereignty, on a non-partisan basis, drawing parallels between the march toward women's autonomy, and Québec's approach to obtaining independence.[36] Its position is based on principles and values that should be integrated into the declaration of sovereignty, such as real equality between persons, men, women, Quebecers of all origins, social solidarity, and taxes based on the autonomy of people rather than on dependence. The group also insists upon the necessity of recognizing the First Nation's right to self-determination, in a similar manner to that of the Québec nation. It is essentially a position of principle. The group nevertheless wanted to take a non-partisan position: it's not a position in favour of the Parti Québécois, but a stand in support of the principle of sovereignty, which is judged to be more harmonious with a feminist vision of Québec society. Another underlying idea in the FFQ's position comes from the notion that "Small is Beautiful": "Because our project for a feminist society will be more readily accepted, from our viewpoint, by the birth of a nation. However, we are not affirming that it is an absolutely essential condition. We are simply saying that it is easier to obtain a socio-politic consensus in smaller units."[37] Nevertheless, the exercise has been quite perilous for the group. In the position adopted, as is often the case when pressure groups support a specific cause, any pretensions to representation become problematic. Affiliations to the traditional political scene are often very difficult for women's groups.

In addition, during the referendum campaign of 1995, the Regroupement des citoyennes pour la souveraineté was founded; this women's group aimed to promote sovereignty. At the same time, about 50 women from the group travelled around Québec by bus. The operation was called *opération porte-voix*. In an evaluation of the venture, Nicole Boudreau, spokesperson for the event discussed certain conclusions drawn from the experience. From her point of view, women are interested in the idea of sovereignty; they don't see it as an end in itself, but more as a way of improving their standard of living. The sovereignty supported by women includes the equality between the sexes, social programs, guarantees of fundamental freedoms, sustainable development with respect to the environment, and the redistribution of wealth. Finally, still from Nicole Boudreau's viewpoint, women are more sensitive to the sovereignty discourse when women present it and when it reflects their concerns. In the year after the referendum, the group organized an event called *De souveraineté et d'espoir*. In 1997, 250 women came together to debate the place of women in the history of the Québec nationalist movement. In 1999, the same group of women officially became the Regroupement des citoyennes pour la souveraineté and has members from all of Québec's regions. The group organized a series of events during the spring of 2000.

The involvement of women's groups on the question of Québec's constitutional politics confirms the representational function exercised by the women's movement. In spite of the small space accorded to the feminist agenda in official forums, women continue to struggle; many work behind the scenes to advance their cases, all the while ignoring the prevailing cynicism associated with traditional politics. Constitutional politics has become a rallying point for a number of women and women's groups, who perfectly understand its strategic importance for enhancing their own conditions. Women's groups also stake their positions outside identity considerations with arguments that are mostly based on the possibilities offered by one constitutional option over another, for the advancement of the groups' demands.

Conclusion

It must be said, that an important part of the Québec women's movement has mobilized through the organization of the Women's March. The two main objectives motivating this large-scale collective mobilization were: to provide the tools to struggle against violence and to end poverty. These goals are embedded in the continuity of egalitarian objectives pursued by the groups, which constitute organized feminism in Québec. Yet, this transnational struggle signifies an important change in the Québec women's movement; that is, its openness to diversity as well as its recognition that women's realities cannot be subsumed into one and only one truth. A new step in this direction occurred in June 2001 when the Fédération des femmes du Québec elected a new president: Vivian Barbot, a black woman of Haitian descent. In this regard, the women's movement became a significant indicator of openness to the diversity in Québec; and it is now women themselves who represent this diversity. Another important challenge that the women's movement is facing at this particular juncture is the passing of the torch to a new generation of women. As previously noted, the problems associated with this passing of the torch, include, for example, the prioritizing of demands and the choice of strategies to assert these demands. Many young feminists assert the right to see themselves as feminists without having to endorse the policies of previous generations of feminists; and beyond this, the possibility of expressing their own policies rather than being obliged to adhere to the policies defended by the women's movement since the 1970s.[38] This signifies a renewal from within that will allow the women's movement to continue to play a principal role in both Québec's political and social scenes.

Notes

1. Diane Lamoureux, *L'amère patrie, féminisme et nationalisme dans le Québec contemporain* (Montréal: Éditions du remue-ménage, 2001), 172.

2. Diane Lamoureux,. "La démocratie avec les femmes," *Globe* 3, 2 (2000): 23-24.

3. Chantal Maillé, "Féminisme et mouvement des femmes au Québec. Un bilan complexe," *Globe* 3, 2 (2000): 90.

4. According to statistics on the women's movement from the Conseil du Statut de la femme, the Québec Government's council on matters concerning women.

5. Femmes en tête. *De travail et d'espoir des groupes de femmes racontent le féminisme* (Montréal: Éditions du remue-ménage, 1990), 9.

6. Évelyne Tardy and André Bernard, *Militer au féminin* (Montréal: Éditions du remue-ménage, 1995), 19.

7. Chantal Maillé, "Féminisme et mouvement des femmes," 88.

8. For further information on this subject, see the description of the FNSJB's actions in the Clio Collectives', *L'histoire des femmes au Québec*, 2nd ed. (Montréal: Éditions du jour, 1992), 347.

9. See Diane Lamoureux, *Citoyennes? Femmes, droit de vote et démocratie* (Montréal: Éditions du remue-ménage, 1989) and Chantal Maillé, "Le vote des Québécoises aux élections fédérales et provinciales depuis 1921: une assiduité insoupçonnée," *Recherches féministes* 3, 1 (1990): 83-96.

10. See Yolande Cohen and Chantal Maillé, "Les cours d'instruction civique de la Fédération nationale Saint-Jean-Baptiste: Une voie d'accès à la citoyenneté politique pour les femmes du Québec," *Recherches féministes* 12, 2 (1999): 39-59.

11. Diane Lamoureux, *Fragments et collages, essai sur le féminisme québécois des années 70* (Montréal: Éditions du remue-ménage, 1986), 57.

12. Mentioned in Chantal Maillé, *Les Québécoises et la conquête du pouvoir politique* (Montréal: Éditions St-Martin, 1990), 90, from a thesis by Martine Lanctot. *Genèse et évolution du mouvement de libération des femmes à Montréal*, 1969-1979, masters thesis, History Department, UQAM, 1980.

13. Lamoureux, *Fragments et collages*, 82-83.

14. "La Centrale," in *Textura, l'artiste écrivant* (Montréal: Éditions du remue-ménage, 2000), 129.

15. Vivian Barbot, "La solidarité nouvelle et les nouvelles solidarités de la Marche mondiale des femmes en l'an 2000," *Recherches féministes* 13, 1 (2000): 20.

16. Ibid., 19.

17. Johanne Landry, "Une solidarité grandissante mais peu de gains à la suite de la marche des femmes, une entrevue avec Françoise David," *Le Devoir*, 8 Mar. 2001, E8.

18. Ibid.

19. Louise Leduc, "Oui à un parti féministe de gauche," *La Presse*, 7 Mar. 2001, B1.

20. See Chantal Maillé, "La problématique de la représentation politique des femmes: où en sommes-nous?" in *l'Égalité les moyens pour y arriver*, Conseil du statut de la femme, Québec government, 1991, 53-62.

21. According to the results of our inquiry on women's movements political strategies, researched and financed by SSHRC, see Chantal Maillé, "Féminisme et mouvement des femmes. Un bilan complexe."

22. Francine Lepage, *Les Québécoises, la mondialisation et la zone de libre-échange des Amériques, Une première réflexion*, Conseil du statut de la femmes, Québec government, 2000, 2.

23. Lepage, *Les Québécoises*, 8.

24. Louise Toupin, "Est-on d'abord femmes ou d'abord Québécoises? La liaison féministe-nationalisme à la naissance du néo-féminisme à Montréal: 1969-1971," communication presented at the 49th Congress of l'Institut d'histoire de l'Amérique française, Orford, 1996.

25. Micheline Dumont, "Les femmes entrent en politique," *Thérèse Casgrain* (Sainte-Foy: Presses de l'Université du Québec, 1993), 195.

26. See Micheline de Sève, "The Perspective of Québec Feminists," in Constance Backhouse and David H. Flaherty, eds., *Challenging Times, the Women's Movement in Canada and the United States* (Montréal and Kingston: McGill-Queen's University Press, 1992), 110-16.

27. See Chantal Maillé and Manon Tremblay, "Femmes et référendum: une force politique incontournable," in Guy Lachapelle et al., *L'impact référendaire* (Ste-Foy: Les Presses de L'Université du Québec, 1995), 347-73.

28. Danielle Couillard, *Féminisme et nationalisme, histoire d'une ambiguïté: 1976-1980,* masters thesis, Université de Montréal, 1987.

29. Barbara Roberts, *Beau fixe ou nuages à l'horizon? L'accord du lac Meech jugé par les groupes féministes du Québec et du Canada,* ICREF, 1989.

30. List of groups who have written a memorandum to the Bélanger-Campeau Commission: Assemblée des groupes de femmes d'intervention régionale, Association des femmes d'affaires, Centre pour femmes immigrantes de l'Estrie, Centre des femmes du Saguenay Lac-St-Jean-Chibougamau, Cercle des fermières du Québec, Comité d'action politique des femmes du P.Q., Conseil des femmes de Montréal, Conseil d'intervention pour l'Accès des femmes au travail, Conseil du statut de la femme, Fédération des femmes du Québec, Fédération nationale des femmes canadiennes-françaises, Concertaction Femmes Estrie, Ordre des infirmières et infirmiers du Québec, Regroupement des femmes de l'Abitibi-Témiscamingue, Regroupement des femmes de la Côte-Nord, Table de concertation des groupes de femmes de l'Est du Québec, Table de concertation Récif 02. The three contributors are: Diane Lamoureux, Micheline Dumont and Micheline Labelle.

31. Groupe de recherche, et d'enseignement multidisciplinaire féministe, Université Laval, *L'avenir politique et constitutionnel du Québec vu par les groupes de femmes,* Cahier 6, 1991.

32. Élaine Audet, "Les femmes absentes des négociations constitutionnelles. Une entente anti-démocratique," *L'Aut'Journal* 107 (1992): 1.

33. Micheline de Sève, "Les féministes québécoises et leur identité civique," in *Malaises identitaires, échanges féministes autour d'un Québec incertain* (Montréal: Éditions remue-ménage, 1999), 183.

34. Chantal Maillé and Manon Tremblay. "L'électorat féminin face aux options constitutionnelles: un groupe fragmenté," *Politique et sociétés* 17, 1-2 (1998): 121-49.

35. Conseil du statut de la femme. *Les femmes et les commissions sur l'avenir du Québec,* document prepared by Guylaine Bérubé and Lucie Desrochers, Government of Québec, 1995.

36. Fédération des femmes du Québec, *L'avenir du Québec sera féminin-pluriel,* memorandum presented to the Commission sur l'avenir du Québec, 1995.

37. FFQ, untitled document, 1995.

38. See Shandi Miller, "Lip Synching to the Beat of the Revolution," *Good Girl* 1 (Spring 2001): 23.

PART IV
Education, Language, and Immigration

15

Immigration, Pluralism, and Education

MARIE MC ANDREW*

Introduction

Throughout the last 30 years, the Québec school system—in particular, the traditionally homogeneous French-language sector—has been radically transformed by the impact of the ethnocultural diversification of its clientele. This evolution results from three major societal changes: the redefinition of linguistic relations due to the adoption of Bill 101 in 1977, the constant involvement of the Québec government in the selection and integration of immigrants and finally the opening of institutions and civil society to pluralism, reflected in the evolution of discourses, policies, and programs in this regard. Schools, therefore, were given a double mandate: on the one hand, hosting and integrating the children of the newly arrived immigrants and, on the other hand, preparing all future citizens to live together in a pluralist society. The challenges facing the Québec school system, as well as the debates regarding the measures most likely to address these challenges, are not unrelated to the experience of other Canadian provinces and of many countries that experience immigration. However, a major redefinition of the dynamic of ethnic relations characterizes the case of Québec, a peculiarity usually not experienced in societies where ethnic dominance is clear. The case of Québec can, in this respect, prove to be interesting both for assessing the strengths and weaknesses of a utilization of education to

* Translated from French into English by Érica Maraillet.

pursue social change, and for analyzing in a comparative light other societies with an ambiguous ethnic dominance, where the transformation of a majority/minority group with a defensive cultural identity is also on the agenda.[1]

In this article, which aims at a general overview of the question, we will first review the wider social context that characterized the period during which the transformation of the mandate given to the French-language schools of Québec occurred. Second, we will describe programs and interventions that have been undertaken to foster the integration of the new arrivals and the institutional adaptation to pluralism, focusing on recent debates. Finally, we will present an assessment of these actions through various indicators regarding the performance and mobility of students of immigrant origin; the linguistic uses in pluriethnic settings; the values, identities, and inter-ethnic relations among "the children of Bill 101," school/community relations; and the sharing of common schools. Throughout this analysis, we will attempt to determine the degree to which the mandate of transforming ethnic relations, given to the Québec school system 30 years ago, has been achieved. We will ask ourselves more particularly to what extent challenges experienced today are still specific to Québec or, on the contrary, are shared with other host societies.

The Wider Social Context and Its Impact on Schools

Before 1977, the Québec school system consisted of various ethnic "sub-systems" with almost no contact with one another.[2] The French-Canadian majority dominated the Franco-Catholic sector, the anglophone minority of British descent the anglo-Protestant sector, and the Catholic immigrants (first the Irish, then the Italians and Portuguese) the anglo-Catholic sector. As for non-Catholic immigrants (first, the Jewish community and later, the Greek Orthodox), they were evenly split between specific segregated schools of the anglo-Protestant sector[3] and private religious schools.

This situation was the result of various characteristics of the socio-linguistic and ethnic dynamic, which are discussed in other chapters of this volume, such as, for example, the anglophone economic and linguistic domination of the francophones, the closed identity and traditionalism of the latter, the importance of the clergy, and the weakness of the state at the institutional level, as well as the tendency of immigrants to integrate with the anglophone minority, both educationally and sociologically. The extent to which this choice of the immigrant population resulted from a conscious strategy for social mobility or from a certain rejection of what was different by the francophone population, is a matter of considerable debate.[4] However, it is clear that the attendance of English-language schools by students of immigrant origin was not defined as a social problem before the Quiet Revolution.

Indeed, each of the francophone, anglophone, and allophone groups seemed to be satisfied with the control of a relatively homogeneous sector.[5]

From the 1970s onwards, however, the schooling profile of students of immigrant origin became a major concern, primarily because of its possible impact on the demographic/linguistic situation in Québec and especially in Montréal. For, in the long run, the zero growth rate of the francophone population, combined with the linguistic integration of immigrants into the anglophone community, would have jeopardized the position of the francophone group in Québec and substantially limited its control of the only field it traditionally dominated, the political one.[6] Beyond this evident interest, the identity transformation of the French-Canadian group into "Québécois" and the redefinition of its ethnic and diasporic nationalism into a civic and territorial nationalism were also exerting an influence.[7] It was, indeed, acceptable—and even normal—that the French-Canadians' school would be attended only by the latter. However, a Québec state engaged in the process of nation-building could not easily accept the absence of some sort of common schooling for the various sectors of its population, even if the latter would still be limited by the historic rights of the anglophone minority and constitutional protections granted to Catholics and Protestants.

The battle that raged during the 1970s between the partisans of a "free choice" of language of instruction and the advocates of common schooling for immigrants and the francophone majority was tumultuous. It is not the purpose of this paper to expand on these events,[8] however, this battle was apparently settled by the adoption of Bill 101 in 1977. Indeed, the educational provisions of the Charte de la langue Française (Charter of the French Language)[9] established the attendance of French-language schools as the norm for all students, while preserving, through a series of exceptions[10] the educational institutional completeness of the anglophone community and that of immigrant groups who had already started their "anglicization."

It is, therefore, essentially on the relations between the francophone and newly arrived immigrant students that the impact of this legislation was felt.[11] Today, 95 per cent of the latter attend the French-language sector schools and, under the cumulative effect of the Bill, this is also the case for 78 per cent of allophones.[12] Moreover, on the Island of Montréal in 1998-99, 46.4 per cent of the school population within the French-language sector was of immigrant origin while 35.2 per cent of its schools had more than 50 per cent of this clientele.[13]

However, the ethnocultural diversity within the French-language sector is not due only to Bill 101's educational provisions. Indeed, from the end of the 1960s, the Québec government, more than any other Canadian province, had been determined to adopt a major role in the immigration field, which is constitutionally a shared jurisdiction between the federal and provincial governments.[14] Through a series of agreements, which culminated in 1990 with the Canada-Québec Agreement on Immigration, better known as the Gagnon-Tremblay-McDougall Agreement, Québec has gradually acquired the control of selected immigration (around 50 per cent of the total movement) and the exclusive responsibility of the linguistic and economic integration of newcomers.[15]

Québec's intervention in the immigration field, which bears many similarities to that of the Canadian state as a whole, is very different from the experience of European or South-American countries. It can be characterized by three elements. First of all, considering the potential economic consequences of the demographic decline and the ageing of the population, the aim is a gradual increase of entries which should eventually ensure that Québec receives 25 per cent of the total immigration to Canada.[16] Therefore, roughly 5,000 to 8,000 new immigrant students per year are integrated into the Québec school system.

Moreover, Québec's immigration policy is defined as a conciliation of various objectives: the recruitment of French-speaking immigrants, the contribution of immigration to economic development, the support for family reunification and the commitment to international solidarity. One of the consequences of such complexity is the high diversity of the school population regarding linguistic skills[17] and national origins,[18] which is a fairly common trend in North America and in Europe. This is also the case for social class, which is a characteristic more specific to Québec.[19] Indeed, the distribution of the immigrant population according to various indicators, such as the type of jobs they intend to occupy in Québec or their level of education, is largely similar, except for a slight bi-polarization at both ends, to that of the Québec-born population. This convergence can be explained by the importance (greater than in the rest of Canada) of the "independents" category within the total flux of immigration and by the historical inherited disadvantage of the francophone majority, educationally as much as economically, which is only partially dispelled even today. In the educational field, the consequence of this trend is that under-privileged neighbourhoods and schools and the immigrant clientele are not systematically integrated in the Greater Montréal area.[20]

Finally, unlike Canadian policy, the Québec immigration policy aims at permanent residency in the province. Citizenship, which obviously remains a federal prerogative, is obtained rapidly (three years), which can only enhance the already important political weight available to minorities, in society as well as in schools.[21]

Following this double process of establishing its majority status at the socio-linguistic level and of opening itself to immigration, the francophone community has had to define its normative position regarding the increased pluralism of public institutions and civil society. In this regard, the Québec position can be characterized as the search for a third path, between the Canadian multiculturalism, accused (wrongly in our opinion) of "essentializing" cultures and separating them from one another, and the French Jacobinism, which refuses to acknowledge intermediate identities between the state and the citizen and relegates diversity to the private sphere, rendering it hardly compatible with the North-American ideology of pluralism, which is widespread in Québec.[22] Although various models for reconciling diversity, social cohesion, and individual rights exist within civil society and public institutions,[23] if we limit ourselves to governmental discourse, more likely to be analyzed in a coherent manner, we can distinguish three phases. In the 1980s, in the wake of the Politique québécoise de développement culturel (Québec policy on cultural development)[24] and of Autant de façons d'être Québécois[25] (Quebecers, each and every one, the plan of action for cultural communities), the existence of a relatively homogeneous francophone culture, clearly distinct from that of other groups, was taken for granted; intercultural rapprochement between individuals from distinct groups was presumed and favoured. With l'Énoncé de politique en matière d'immigration et d'intégration (Vision: A policy statement on immigration and integration),[26] a more liberal perspective as well as a greater recognition of ethnic *métissage* as a consequence of the redefinition of ethnic relations in Québec, started to emerge. The concept of cultural communities was gradually replaced by the concept of Québécois from various origins, who were invited to balance their diverse criteria of belonging, both as individuals and as members of groups, in a civic space, essentially defined from a procedural perspective. Thus, for example, the third principle of the moral Contract proposed in the policy statement, recognizes the pluralistic character of Québec society "within the limits imposed by the respect for fundamental democratic values and the need for intergroup exchanges." This minimal aspect[27] criticized in the 1990s and characterized by various debates on the definition of an array of more substantive communal values, was named successively *public common culture, civic culture, societal culture*, and *common public space*.[28] This last paradigm, which is still dominant, is far from creating consensus. A testimony to this assertion, among others, is the reiterated postponement by the *Ministère des Relations avec les Citoyens et de l'Immigration* (Ministry of Relations with Citizens and of Immigration)[29] of the promised publication of a policy on civic relations, of which the last gasp has been the resounding failure of the minister Perreault during the public consultations he led in September 2000 on this subject.

In the educational milieu, it was not until 1998 that the Department of Education made public a Politique d'intégration scolaire et d'éducation interculturelle (School integration and intercultural education policy), in which the relation to diversity was clearly defined. In essence, even if this document is innovative regarding services for newcomers, when it comes to institutional adaptation to pluralism it shares the same paradigm as the policy statement of 1990. Indeed, even if the terminology has been adapted to current trends, the normative valorization of diversity is marked and the limits in this regard are noticeably the same: the protection of students' individual rights, the functionality of institutions, and the linguistic choices of Québec. However, it proposes to integrate all teaching and curricular and extracurricular activities, formerly carried under the label of *intercultural education*, under the wider rubric of *citizenship education within a pluralistic context*. As we will see later, the ins and outs of this last proposition remain difficult to evaluate.

Programs and Interventions

As is the case in most societies and school systems that face the challenge of immigrant integration,[30] the policies and programs implemented in Québec from the beginning of the 1970s were concerned mainly with the linguistic integration of newcomers or, to use McLeod typology,[31] interventions of a compensatory nature. A Bureau des Services aux communautés culturelles (service unit for cultural communities), was set up in 1969 by the Department of Education, while the Montréal Catholic Schools Commission was developing, on an experimental basis, the first *classes d'accueil* (welcoming classes).[32] Later, following the adoption of Bill 101, these classes multiplied and were generalized in metropolitan school boards. They consist of special full-time classes with a reduced student/teacher ratio, where immigrant students who have been in the country for less than five years[33] are initiated into everyday life in Québec and taught the basics of the French language and other school subjects until they are ready to be integrated into regular classes.[34] Moreover, an article that guaranteed universal access for immigrant clientele to some compensatory linguistic measures was added to the Public Education Act in 1988. Québec is, thus, the Canadian province where services of this nature are the most exhaustive. Finally, more recently, due to the linguistic diversification of the immigration stream, a linguistic support program, which follows students during the first two years of their integration into regular classes, was implemented in schools where the percentage of allophone students exceeds 25 per cent.

From an opposite perspective, other measures, taken as early as 1977, show that an awareness or respect for pluralism in public schools existed. For example, the *Livre Blanc sur la politique de la langue* (White Paper on Language Policy)[35] devoted ample attention to the promotion and teaching of other languages, and instigated the subsequent creation and implementation of a Heritage Language Program (*Le programme d'enseignement des langues d'origine*: PELO) in public schools.[36] But this vision of the impact of pluralism on the school system was a very limited one. It could be characterized, if we adopt again McLeod's typology, as "ethnic specific,"[37] or, in Bank's typology, as "additive multiculturalism."[38] Programs that aim at fostering respect for pluralism have only a marginal impact because they are limited to ethnic minority students, and leave unchanged the general functioning of schooling, notably its hidden curriculum.

Nevertheless, through the years we have witnessed a growing awareness of the multi-dimensionality of the adjustments needed to foster a social integration that would go further than mere linguistic integration or maintenance of heritage languages. This awareness has been sustained by the publication of various reports, research, and local policies since 1983.[39] Generally written from the perspective of an "intercultural rapprochement within a francophone society," these documents have brought about various ad hoc measures from the Department of Education of Québec and from the school boards of the Greater Montréal area more directly concerned with the integration of students of immigrant origin. Among others, several guidelines have been published to ensure the elimination of stereotypes in the teaching material; intercultural education objectives have been included in various programs; the teaching materials concerning these objectives have subsequently been developed, as well as in-service training programs and intercultural activities for teachers and principals. Special funds were also granted to pluriethnic schools to allow them, among other options, to hire liaison officers in order to develop relations between parents and the school at the elementary level, or between students at the secondary level. More recently, the Department has studied the issue of value conflicts in multi-ethnic school settings and has prepared a guide to support decision-making by school principals in these matters.[40] Moreover, even if the intercultural training of future teachers was left for a long time to the initiative of universities, it became a criterion for approval by the Department of Education of the new programs that were implemented in 1995.

Such an enumeration of governmental and local measures could give the impression that the Québec school system has definitely shifted towards a systemic adaptation to pluralism or that it now dominantly practices "multiculturalism as an integral part of the curriculum."[41] The actual situation is more complex. As in other contexts, various studies have, indeed, noted a hiatus between official policies and programs and their local interpretation and implementation. The latter is especially valid regarding the intercultural dimension.[42] The non-systematic character of both initial and in-service teacher-training has also been mentioned, while the persistence of an exclusionist collective "we" along with a certain "racialism" in the learning material, although revised, has been deplored.[43]

The recent debates, however, touch more on the services for newcomer students than on the institutional adaptation to pluralism. First, the 1998 *Policy* questioned the relevance of maintaining the exclusivity of the *classes d'accueil* as primary or principal places for the learning of French.[44] Among other issues challenged was the necessity of providing closed classes for those pre-school and early elementary students, who do not encounter particular problems. Moreover, we are still exploring, admittedly not always with success, various formulae that would allow a better response to the needs of under-educated students who are integrated into the school system during their adolescence, in particular by an increased use of their languages of origin. These propositions of the Department correspond to international tendencies regarding the learning of host languages, as well as the evolution of thought over the last 30 years, which renders less justifiable a rigid distinction between a *classe d'accueil*, responsible for the integration of newcomers, and a mainstream class, largely homogeneous. However, they have aroused great resistance from teachers' unions. The latter probably can be attributed equally to corporatist motives, as well as to pedagogical preoccupations concerning the school integration of newcomers or their linguistic integration over the long term.

Secondly, following the re-definition of ethnic boundaries within school settings, the future of Heritage-Language teaching is also debated.[45] Aiming essentially at second- or third-generation students at the elementary level, the Heritage Language program is not really adapted, on the one hand, to the crying needs of the under-educated, newly arrived, secondary students and, on the other hand, to the claims of parents (from all origins, including francophones), in favour of the learning of a third language at this level. Unless it gives way to the mobilization of some older established communities and maintains the program in its original form, the Department, and probably Québec society as well, is today at a crossroads. Either it redefines the teaching of Heritage Languages as a compensatory measure limited to "children at risk," or it turns it into an element of a larger strategy aimed at an increased pluralism within the population as a whole. Furthermore, even if this element has aroused less interest from the general public, the shift from intercultural education to citizenship education has raised some questions from school personnel or the more directly concerned groups.[46] Most have welcomed the proposition, first, to create a compulsory program of citizenship education associated with the teaching of history and, second, to promote this aim as a cross-curricular competence that needs to be acquired through all the disciplines and all activities at school. They saw in it an initiative that could contribute positively to the efforts already made regarding institutional adaptations to pluralism. This proposition is also in line with the general evolution of intercultural education in Québec, as elsewhere, where the issues of a common educational framework within which pluralism can blossom and the negotiation of value conflicts have become more and more central. However, various concerns remain. Some fear the interpretation of this change of direction by teachers—that citizenship education could sometimes mask the return of cultural assimilationism or, at least, an insensitivity to diversity. For others, the association of the compulsory program with the teaching of history reinforces the feeling that it is also the allegiance to the specific trajectory of the francophone community that is aimed for. However, the legitimacy of this fear needs to be evaluated, keeping in mind the pluralist redefinition that has occurred in the teaching of history in Québec, which should be more pronounced in the new programs.[47]

Assessment

After some 30 years of Québec interventions aimed at the transformation of eth-nolinguistic relations, it is possible to formulate a first assessment of the strengths and weaknesses regarding the schooling of immigrants and the preparation of all students to live in a pluralist society. In this matter, we can classify, on a continuum running from maximal success to relative failure, the performance and educational mobility of the clientele of immigrant origin; the mastery of French by allophone students; and their linguistic uses, identity redefinition, and inter-ethnic relations among the "children of Bill 101"; school/community relations; and, finally, the extent to which the clientele from various origins share common schools. In all cases, the gains and limits can be linked—partially and in varying degrees—to Québec's social or educational specificity, but can also depend on dynamics com-mon to all Western societies hosting immigrants.

Thus, it is clear that 25 years after the adoption of Bill 101, and despite all the fears it had generated in various groups, the relative educational advantage of the immigrant groups when they were part of the anglophone sector was not signifi-cantly altered by their enrolment in the francophone sector. For a long time,[48] the allophone population has had to have an equivalent or slightly superior success rate on ministerial exams in comparison to the francophone students, in the English sec-tor as in the French sector, although the results are a little weaker when the students are taught in French. Moreover, the clientele of immigrant origin continue to have a rate of secondary qualification slightly superior to the average and are more likely to pursue studies at CÉGEP and university.

These positive results must be interpreted in the light of the educational deficit of the francophones at the dawn of the Quiet Revolution, which still persists today. The impact of the characteristics of the selection policy described above also oper-ates strongly in this matter, even if, as in other contexts, immigrant groups have a tendency to succeed slightly better than their class composition would predict and this, more particularly in disadvantaged milieus.[49]

This positive assessment is, however, to be qualified for some more recently arrived groups, in particular the clients who have had little or no schooling in their country of origin and arrived in Québec during their adolescence. Moreover, the very method by which the Department gathers the data related to performance and educational mobility reflects a certain anachronism. Indeed, apart from a few minor improvements in this matter, language still serves as a basis for comparison between students.

This choice has the effect of rendering *invisible*, so to speak, *visible minorities*, precisely the groups more likely to encounter problems. Among others, this is the case of anglophone Caribbean students and of a not-negligible number of Haitian students who are reluctant to claim Creole as their mother tongue. Nevertheless, rumours within schools and communities tend to validate the hypothesis that, nowadays, educational failure in Québec more often touches racialized groups, rather than linguistic groups, a tendency common to many immigration destination countries.[50] It is, therefore, high time that the Department recognizes this change of paradigm, as much in its monitoring of immigrant clients as in its definition of the actions to benefit them.

If the performance and the educational mobility of the students of immigrant origin seem to depend as much on socio-economic factors as on educational factors, the results, all in all remarkable, regarding the mastery of French and the promotion of its use by the allophone clientele, clearly demonstrate the importance of institutional efforts and staff commitment. Regarding the linguistic competence particularly of newcomers, a series of longitudinal studies[51] have illustrated the very favourable profile of students who attended *classes d'accueil* throughout their higher schooling, while the results of allophone students, as the tests of French as the language of instruction revealed, are almost equivalent to that of the francophones.[52] Faced with these largely positive results, the perceptions of the observers appear more mixed. Various qualitative studies[53] have, indeed, shown that the latter have a tendency to over-evaluate the problems of linguistic competence of allophones or, according to the preferred interpretation, to identify weaknesses that the sole ministerial exams cannot detect. However, during the last few years, the theme of the weakness of the mastery of French by allophone students has tended to die away within the professional and public discourse, allowing the concerns over their linguistic uses to emerge as dominant.

In a context where the attendance of a French-language school is mandatory, it can be assumed that immigrant parents and students invest a maximum of effort to master the French language and succeed at ministerial exams, in a strategy of social mobility. Therefore, their choice of a language of communication in informal contexts appears, in the eyes of the francophones who are the most preoccupied by the demographic and linguistic situation, as the ultimate indicator of their subsequent integration.[54] This issue has been the object of a few educational conflicts, widely publicized, in Québec as well as in English Canada, sometimes generating the perception that Bill 101 has been a Trojan Horse, that is to say, that instead of ensuring the francization of immigrants, it has contributed to the anglicizing of the pluriethnic milieus.[55] Yet, Hensler and Beauchesne's study[56] had shown that the French language was already, in 1987, widely the common language in the pluriethnic schools in Montréal, even if English dominated in some schools where the neighbourhood was anglophone or the clientele included an important percentage of previously anglicized groups.

A more recent study,[57] which combines the analysis of the perceptions of school personnel and students with the structured and systematic observation of informal exchanges between students in 20 elementary and secondary schools, confirms and accentuates these positive results. The French language, which occupies 60 to 100 per cent of situations of informal exchanges, dominates in all schools. Heritage languages, predictably, are limited to intragroup communication. As for the English language, it achieves a certain common language status, while being limited to global exchanges, in only two schools, where the presence of the "old stock" anglophones (having freely chosen to enrol in a French-language school) or of a long-time anglicized clientele is important. Furthermore, data from interviews carried out with secondary students show that a valorization of the French language and the importance of its use enjoy a wide consensus. However, positions in favour of pluralingualism are normative within all of the youth, francophones as well as allophones, with the exception of the disadvantaged francophone group, which clearly presents a more traditional profile of exclusive attachment to the French language. Of course, these results cannot be extrapolated to the whole society. Because of the still important status of English as the language for media and work, it is plausible that the use of French by "the children of Bill 101" in their life outside school might be less dominant. Nevertheless, this study, unlike others that are based on reported uses by respondents,[58] is far from indicating a resistance from youth of immigrant origin to the "francization" efforts of the host society, a situation largely contrasting with the polarization and the tensions that surrounded the adoption of Bill 101 25 years ago.

The extent to which this sharing of French as a common language has allowed the emergence of a new pluralist generation, bringing together harmoniously the second-generation francophones (called "old stock" Quebecers in the past), the francophones of immigrant origin and allophones, is, however, more open to debate. This is also the case for the relationships of schools that still are largely dominated by the francophone majority, with parents, and with the pluriethnic milieu. Indeed, although major steps have been taken in the last 30 years, it is clear that important gaps remain. Some seem specific to the incomplete character of the pluralist transformation of Québec and others, closely linked to the international context.

Thus, a survey[59] carried out among about 2,800 Montréal youngsters in their last year of secondary education in 1995 showed that they largely shared the same values, which could be characterized as those of liberal individualism and democratic egalitarianism. As in other contexts they identified themselves, first and foremost, as "young" and took the same critical distance regarding their parents' values, particularly in the field of inter-ethnic relations. According to respondents, inter-group relations in the school setting are highly positive, the choice of friends resting mostly on their personal characteristics. Moreover, the study has shown a high sense of belonging to the Québec society among the students of immigrant origin, which was not correlated with their degree of identification with their specific community.[60] Despite these globally positive tendencies, it would be naïve to ignore the possible influence of social desirability on their responses here, as well as in other surveys. Throughout the world, the persistence of ethnic markers in the definition of conflicts surrounding the educational or social space, is generalized even when the objective differences between groups are decreasing.[61] Indeed, in the Québec educational setting, other studies[62] using qualitative interview methodologies in smaller groups or ethnographic observations, have shown the resilience of the us/them cleavage among the "children of Bill 101." Nevertheless, although larger political issues continue to play a certain role in it, the criteria of differentiation appear to be undergoing mutation. Indeed, when one compares the studies of the 1980s with those of the end of the 1990s, language seems gradually to lose its salience to be replaced by "race" or religion, indicating here again a *normalization* of the Québec situation.

In this matter, it is obvious that during the 1990s the conflicts, as much between the students as with the parents, have widely touched the Muslim community. The Québec school system, although remaining mostly the fief of a French-Canadian staff,[63] has been relatively well able to adapt to cultural diversity. The latter is widely considered as enriching, even if in the case of disadvantaged immigrant groups, compensatory approaches still retain their popularity. In any case, for many parents of immigrant origin, the attitude of schools here is clearly more open than that of the institutions in their country of origin. Even if an attentive observer can sometimes discern within it a certain amount of ethnocentrism or paternalism, in general these parents said they were satisfied.[64]

Religious diversity has proved to be more difficult to negotiate, particularly in the case of Islam, which separates less clearly the private from the public than do modern versions of the other great religions. The Québec school system has thus experienced a certain number of publicized conflicts concerning some demands for adaptation of the norms and school regulations. The most notable has been the hijab crisis, which aroused a large public debate throughout the autumn of 1995 and winter of 1996.[65] The debate concerned, among other issues, the importance of respecting religious pluralism when faced with other fundamental values, such as equality between the sexes, perceived by some, mostly women, as being challenged by the symbolic meaning of the Islamic veil. This controversy, which has been described exhaustively elsewhere, has created two disparate coalitions, holding no close link with ethnic allegiance. Those promoting tolerance for the wearing of the *hijab* included many human rights associations from the majority community, the leadership of unions, professional associations and feminist groups and some spokespersons of the Muslim community, generally of the older establishment. The opponents to any accommodation included recent immigrant groups from Muslim countries where fundamentalism thrives, grassroots feminists, some teachers nostalgic for "genuine integration," and left-wing groups taking advantage of the crisis to call for the complete secularization of the system.[66]

The fact that most other school conflicts that received media attention during the last 10 years in Québec concerned the Muslim community, such as the hysteria that has surrounded the proposition of the teaching of the Koran in a suburban school board,[67] or the only known resistance to the implementation of a Heritage Language program, which concerned the teaching of Arabic at the Sainte-Croix school board,[68] is not unrelated to the world context where the anti-Muslim stereotypes are dominant. However, in a more general way, the attitudes of francophone teachers, regarding the recognition of diversity in their daily practices, seem to be influenced by a set of factors among which the specificity of their past experience as a dominated group in Québec and in Canada is not without influence. The latter is often positive but sometimes also, paradoxically, sometimes negative.[69] Québec teachers are a group who collectively benefited from the modernization of the 1960s and linguistic normalization in the 1970s. They show an attachment to the separation of Church from the state and to equality between the sexes, that is especially strong because these achievements can still be considered fragile in the Québec context. Furthermore, the degree to which they are willing to accommodate cultural and, especially, linguistic pluralism seems proportional to their sense of security regarding their identity. Although a majority of teachers adopt a professional position linked to their evaluation of students' needs and to their acknowledgement of the importance of co-operating with the parents, a minority of the teachers, opposed to taking into account diversity, clearly articulate their arguments in socio-political terms.

A final field where conclusions are mixed concerns the extent to which students of all origins today share the same schools. As seen above, we have come a long way in this matter in Québec, where ethnicity and school structures had for a long time coincided. Moreover, the objectives of rapprochement and redefinition of identity and attitudes through common schooling was only implicit in Bill 101. However, the important debates that took place later on the effects of the concentration of immigrants in certain schools, show a strong consensus for common schooling.[70] In this matter, two contradictory tendencies have held an uneasy equilibrium. On the one side, 30 years of Québec interventionism strongly contributed to reducing the traditional intercommunity isolation that prevailed at the educational level. The main turning points of this movement were, first, the adoption of Bill 101 and, more recently, in 1998, the abolition of religious school boards and the establishment of new linguistic school boards. This reform created roughly two types of schools: those of French-language, the first real public schools in Québec's history, and those of English-language, thence linked to the maintenance of both the culture and the identity of a community that defines itself more and more as a minority. In the French sector, one of the consequences of the reform, in the middle-term, will be to direct many students of immigrant origin who formerly attended a Protestant school towards schools where the francophone population is, if not the majority, at least important.[71] Nevertheless, this dynamic is counteracted by a set of deep-rooted tendencies, specific to Québec or generalized to all Western societies, which tend to make common schooling an exception rather than a rule.

On the one hand, indeed, the exceptionally high metropolitan concentration of immigration in Québec must be pointed out.[72] This concentration limits the rather positive assessment described above to the sole metropolitan region, which raises important questions regarding the hiatus that could be created with the rest of Québec, which is much less pluralistic and needs no redefinition of its collective identity. Moreover, it creates a situation where an immigrant population of 46 per cent in a French-language school in Montréal, today represents a balanced and normal distribution. Therefore, it is more than likely that some schools will emerge principally or almost exclusively constituted of students of immigrant origin. On the other hand, as in all other metropolises of the world, various phenomena contribute to school segregation, among them: the concentration of immigrants in certain areas; the policies allocating services aimed at them, always theoretically directed to the whole neighbourhood of schools but *de facto* often towards specific schools; and the popularity of private schools, which concern mostly francophones and, to a lesser extent, some of the more affluent groups of immigrant origin.[73]

Until the mid-1990s the greatest positive impact was that of Bill 101 on the reduction of school segregation. While in 1969, the very great majority of allophone students (89 per cent) had hardly any contact with the Québec-born francophones, in 1993-1994, 46 per cent of the clientele of immigrant origin on the Island of Montréal was enrolled in schools where they represented less than 50 per cent of the population.[74] Moreover, one must consider that even in schools with an immigrant population between 50 and 75 per cent, contact with second-generation (or earlier) francophone students is not impossible, the latter often being the most important group demographically, representing more than 60 per cent of the clientele. However, in the last few years, the increase in immigration combined with the factors described above, has had the effect of steadily decreasing common schooling. In 1999-2000, only 40 per cent of students of immigrant origin were enrolled in a school with a francophone majority and, even if schools with an important francophone minority are included, the difference is still not very great. Indeed, in the last 10 years schools with a very high concentration of students of immigrant origin have grown rapidly.[75]

Of course, given the significant performance and the educational mobility of students of immigrant origin, it is difficult to define this issue as a major preoccupation in Québec. Studies have shown that the impact of ethnic concentration on linguistic uses or social integration is less marked than some would claim.[76] Moreover, given that the population of immigrant origin experiences a relatively rapid intergenerational social and residential mobility, the phenomenon of ghetto schools, in a strict sense, is not known in Québec.

If one believes that schooling has a major role in the development of attitudes and of inter-ethnic relations, it is difficult to envision how it could be limited to the transmission of normative ideals and to the teaching of explicit curricula, especially when one considers the importance that sociologists and anthropologists are ascribing to the "hidden agenda" of schools. At the same time, it is clear that, without a motivation linked to equal opportunities, and given the extremely limited impact of all attempts put forward in other countries to ensure a more balanced distribution of school clienteles,[77] it is unlikely that the Québec government will choose to intervene on this issue. It seems, therefore, that despite their undeniable impact, we may now have reached the limits of social engineering approaches.

Notes

1. S. Dunn, "L'éducation dans une société divisée: le cas de l'Irlande du Nord," in M. Mc Andrew and F. Gagnon, eds., *Relations ethniques et éducation dans les sociétés divisées, Québec, Irlande du Nord, Catalogne et Belgique* (Montréal/Paris: L'Harmattan, 2000), 111-26. A. Medoune and M. Lavalée, "Le système scolaire en Belgique: clivages et pratiques," in Mc Andrew and Gagnon, eds., *Relations ethniques*, 147-69. M. Mc Andrew, "Conclusion, comparabilité des expériences décrites et perspectives de collaboration," in Mc Andrew and Gagnon, eds, *Relations ethniques*, 225-41. L.S. Rasero et al., "Éducation et ethnicité: le cas catalan," in Mc Andrew and Gagnon, eds., *Relations ethniques*, 127-47.

2. M. Laferrière, "L'éducation des enfants des groupes minoritaires au Québec. De la définition des problèmes par les groupes eux-mêmes à l'intervention de l'État," *Sociologie et société* 15, 2 (1983): 117-32. M.D. Behiels, "The Commission des écoles catholiques de Montréal and the Neo-Canadian question: 1943-1963," *Canadian Ethnic Studies/Études ethniques au Canada* 18, 1 (1986). Mc Andrew and Proulx, "Éducation et ethnicité au Québec: un portrait d'ensemble," in Mc Andrew and Gagnon, eds., *Relations ethniques*.

3. A sector in which, until the 1960s, they were considered as being accepted "as a matter of grace" in the words of a famous judgement at the beginning of the century.

4. R. Cappon, *Conflit entre les Néo-Canadiens et les francophones de Montréal* (Québec: Université Laval, CIRB, 1975). G. Deschamps and A. Laperrière, "Les fondements sociaux des types d'insertion culturelle observés chez les Néo-Québécois et l'utilisation politique des cultures ethniques," *Actes du Colloque sur la souveraineté du Québec: aspects politiques, économiques et culturels*, Association canadienne des sociologues et anthropologues de langue française, 1978.

5. It should be noted in this matter, that despite widespread perceptions, until the mid-1960s, white Protestants had not been obliged to share their schools with a diversified ethnocultural population, massively concentrated in the anglo-Catholic sector or in Protestant schools situated in disadvantaged areas. On the contrary, various studies have shown

that franco-Catholic schools were less homogeneous, at least paradoxically until 1945, than the stereotyped perception that prevails today.

6. J. Henripin, *L'immigration et le déséquilibre linguistique*, Main d'oeuvre et Immigration Canada, 1974. L. Dion, "French as an adopted language in Québec," in J. Mallea, ed., *Québec's Language Policies: Background and Responses* (Québec: CIRB, 1977).

7. D. Juteau, "The production of the québécois nation," *Humbolt Journal of Social Relations* 19, 2 (1993): 79-108. D. Juteau, "Du dualisme canadien au pluralisme Québécois," in Mc Andrew and Gagnon, eds., *Relations ethniques*, 13-26

8. J. Mallea, *Québec's Language Policies: Background and Responses* (Québec: CIRB, 1977). M. Plourde, *La politique linguistique du Québec 1977-1987* (Montréal: IQRC, 1988).

9. Gouvernement du Québec, *Charte de la langue française*, Title I, Chap. VIII, approved 26 Aug. 1977 (Québec: Éditeur Officiel, 1977).

10. The latter concerns the children already enrolled in English-language schools at the time of the adoption of the Bill, their brothers and sisters as well as those whose parents have had their primary education in English in Québec and, more recently, in Canada, following different judgements from the Supreme Court. Free choice also extends to children of the First Nations, the handicapped, and those whose parents are residing temporarily in Québec.

11. It also played a role in the decline of the school population attending the English-language schools, an issue raised in Brian Young's article. The latter, indeed, is reduced to the demographic weight of both the anglophone community and of groups anglicized in the past (around 10 per cent of the total school clientele).

12. Ministère de l'Éducation du Québec (MEQ), *Une école d'avenir. Intégration scolaire et éducation interculturelle* (Québec: Gouvernement du Québec, 1998).

13. M. Mc Andrew and M. Jodoin, *L'immigration à Montréal au milieu des années 90: Volet éducation* (Québec: Immigration et métropoles, 1999).

14. Ministère des Communautés culturelles et de l'Immigration (MCCI), *Au Québec pour bâtir ensemble*. Énoncé de politique en matière d'immigration et d'intégration (Québec: Direction des communications, 1990). M. Gagné and C. Chamberland, "L'évolution des politiques d'intégration et d'immigration au Québec," in M. Mc Andrew, A.C. Decouflé, and C. Ciceri, eds., *Les politiques d'immigration et d'intégration au Canada et en France: analyses comparées et perspectives de recherche* (Paris, Ottawa: Ministère de l'Emploi et de la solidarité, Conseil de recherche en sciences humaines du Canada, 1999), 71-90.

15. Immigration, in Canada as much as in Québec, is composed of three categories: the independents (workers and investors) from which a selection is made; the family category, which can only be defined in a more or less broad manner, but is not subject to selection per se; and the refugees, who can be targeted according to various priorities but whose recognition is the prerogative of a sovereign country signatory of the Geneva Convention.

16. Canada is today the country that receives, in relation to its total population, the greatest annual percentage of immigrants (250,000 for a total population of 30 million, that is, nearly 0.8 per cent). In the case of Québec (with some 35,000 immigrants on average for a population of seven million) it is 0.5 per cent of its total population with a possible objective of 0.75 per cent per year, which is still a high immigration rate, even when compared with that of traditional countries of destination for immigration such as the US and New Zealand.

17. Recall that despite the biased perception sometimes spread by the media in English Canada, the knowledge of French is not an eliminatory criterion on the Québec selection grid. Thus, the percentage of people having immigrated to Québec during the last 10 years

who did not know French beforehand is more than 60 per cent (Ministère des Relations avec les Citoyens et de l'Immigration, *Le Québec en mouvement: statistiques sur l'immigration* (Québec: MRCI, 1997).

18. Those from non-traditional sources, which is to say, neither North America nor Europe, represent today more than 80 per cent of the total flux, while they accounted for only 20 per cent in 1961. The part of non-European languages also has increased within the migratory flux (Québec: MRCI, 1997).

19. MCCI, *Profil de la population immigrée recensée au Québec en 1986* (Québec: Direction des communications, 1990).

20. Conseil scolaire de l'île de Montréal, *Les enfants des milieux défavorisés et ceux des communautés culturelles*, Mémoire au ministre de l'Éducation sur la situation des écoles des commissions scolaires de l'île de Montréal, Feb. 1991. M. Mc Andrew and M. Ledoux, "La concentration ethnique dans les écoles de langue française de l'île de Montréal: un portrait statistique," *Cahiers québécois de démographie* 24, 2 (1995): 343-70.

21. We remind our foreign readers that Québec, like the rest of Canada, shares the North-American model of elected school authorities.

22. M. Mc Andrew, "Multiculturalisme canadien et interculturalisme québécois: mythes et réalités," in M. Mc Andrew, R. Toussaint, and O. Galatanu, eds., *Actes du 20e colloque de l'AFEC—Pluralisme et éducation: politiques et pratiques au Canada, en Europe et dans les pays du Sud. L'apport de l'éducation comparée*, Montréal 10-13 May 1994, (1995), 33-51. D. Helly, *Le Québec face à la pluralité culturelle 1977-1994. Bilan documentaire* (Ste-Foy: PUL, 1996). D. Juteau, M. Mc Andrew, and L. Pietrantonio, "Multiculturalism à la Canadian and intégration à la québécoise. Transcending their limits," in R. Bauböck and J. Rundell, eds., *Blurred Boundaries: Migration, Ethnicity, Citizenship* (Ashgate: European Centre Vienna, 1998), 95-110.

23. M. Mc Andrew, M. Jacquet, and C. Ciceri, "La prise en compte de la diversité culturelle et religieuse dans les normes et pratiques de gestion des établissements scolaires: une étude exploratoire dans cinq provinces canadiennes," *Revue des sciences de l' éducation* 22, 1 (1997): 209-32. M. Mc Andrew, M. Lavallée, and D. Helly, "Citoyenneté et redéfinition des politiques publiques de gestion de la diversité: la position des organismes non gouvernementaux québécois," *Recherches sociographiques* 41, 1, (2000): 271-98.

24. Gouvernement du Québec, *La Politique québécoise de développement culturel* (Québec: Éditeur officiel, 1978).

25. Gouvernement du Québec. *Autant de façons d'être Québécois* (Québec: Éditeur officiel, 1984).

26. MCCI, *Profil de de la population immigrée.*

27. In other words the "thin culture" is clearly preferred to the "thick culture." See, among others, W. Kymlicka, *Multicultural Citizenship* (Oxford: Clarendon Press, 1995).

28. Conseil supérieur de l'éducation (CSE), *Pour un accueil et une intégration réussis des élèves des communautés culturelles*. Avis au ministre de l'Éducation et ministre de l'Enseignement Supérieur et des Sciences (Québec: CSE, 1993). G. Bourgeault, F. Gagnon, M. Mc Andrew, and M. Pagé, "L'espace de la diversité culturelle et religieuse à l'école dans une démocratie de tradition libérale," *Revue européenne des migrations internationales* 11, 3 (1995): 79-103. Conseil des communautés culturelles et de l'immigration, *Un Québec pour tous ses citoyens*. Avis presenté au Ministre (1997). M. Pagé and F. Gagnon, *Les approches de la citoyenneté dans six démocraties libérales* (Ottawa: Ministère du Patrimoine canadien, 1999).

29. Reflecting the evolution described above, the Ministère des Communautés culturelles et de l'immigration changed its name in 1997. Conserving its vertical role of selection and

integration of newcomers, it now covers a set of horizontal mandates including various criteria of exclusion and belonging, among which ethnocultural diversity occupies only a limited space.

30. J.A. Banks, "Race, ethnicité et scolarisation aux États-Unis: bilan et perspectives," in F. Ouellet, ed., *Pluralism et école* (Québec: IQRC, 1988), 157-86. J. Lynch, "Le développement de l'enseignement multiculturel au Royaume-Uni," in F. Ouellet, ed., *Pluralisme et école*, 137-56. K.A. Moodley, "L'éducation multiculturelle au Canada: des espoirs aux réalités," in Ouellet, ed., *Pluralisme et école*, 187-222. M. Abdallah-Pretceille, *Quelle école pour quelle intégration?* (Paris: Hachette, 1992).

31. K.A. McLeod, "Multiculturalism and multicultural policy and practice," in CSSE, ed., *Education and Canadian Multiculturalism: Some Problems and Some Solutions* (1981).

32. MEQ. *L'École québécoise et les communautés culturelles*, Committee Report, G. Latif, ed. (Québec: MEQ, 1988). M. Messier, *Les modèles de services réservés aux élèves nouveaux arrivants: une études comparée entre Montréal et Toronto* (Montréal: Université de Montréal: Immigration et métropoles, 1997).

33. Allophone students born in Canada or those who arrived more than five years ago, but who do not have a sufficient mastery of the French language, also have access to special classes, whose organizational modalities are, however, somewhat less generous.

34. Theoretically, at any time of the year, but in fact, following the resistance of teachers, generally after 10 months or even more.

35. Gouvernement du Québec, *La politique québécoise de la langue française au Québec* (Québec: Éditeur officiel, 1977).

36. This is a regular educational program developed and financed by the Québec government that was offered in 1996-1997, in 14 languages, to some 7,000 students, for two and one-half hours per week, often outside the school timetable. Since 1988, it is also accessible, under certain conditions, to children who do not speak the target language, in order to foster intercultural awareness within the majority. See M. Mc Andrew, *L'enseignement des langues d'origine à l'école publique au Québec et en Ontario: politiques et enjeux* (Montréal: Université de Montréal, 1992). M. Mc Andrew and C. Ciceri, "Immigration, diversity and multilingual education: The Canadian example," *Zeitschrift für internationale erziehungs — und sozialwissenschaftliche Forschung* 15, 2 (1998).

37. K.A. McLeod, *Multiculturalism*.

38. J.A. Banks, "Race, ethnicité, et scolarisation," 157-86.

39. Conseil supérieur de l'éducation (CSE), *L'éducation interculturelle*. Avis au ministre de l'Éducation (Québec: CSE, 1983). *Les défis éducatifs de la pluralité* (Québec: CSE, 1987). CSE, 1993. Commission des écoles catholiques de Montréal, *Politiques de services aux élèves des communautés culturelles fréquentant les écoles françaises de la CECM* (Montréal: Service des études, 1984). MEQ, *L'école québécoise et les communautés culturelles*. Chancy report (Québec: Direction des communications, 1985). Conseil de la langue francaise CCLE, *Vivre la diversité en français. Le défi de l'école française à clientèle pluriethnique*. Notes and Documents, 64. (Québec: CLF, 1987) *Réfléchir ensemble sur l'école française pluriethnique*. Notes and Documents, 63. (Québec, Protestant School Board of the Greater Montréal, 1987). *A Multicultural/Multiracial Approach to Education in the Schools of the PSBGM* (Montréal: Commission scolaire Ste-Croix, 1988). *Politique d'éducation interculturelle: but, principes, objectifs* (Ville St-Laurent: Services éducatifs, 1989).

40. MEQ, *La prise en compte de la diversité religieuse et culturelle en milieu scolaire: un module de formation à l'intention des gestionnaires* (Montréal: Direction des services aux communautés culturelles, 1994).

41. J.A. Banks, *Multiethnic Education. Theory and Practice*, 2nd ed. (Boston: Allyn and Bacon, 1988).

42. J. Hohl, *Singulier/Pluriel* (Québec: CSIM, 1991). W. Cummings-Potvin, C. Lessard, and M. Mc Andrew, "L'adaptation de l'institution scolaire québécoise à la pluriethnicité: continuité et rupture face aux discours officiels," *Revue des sciences de l'éducation* 20, 4 (1994): 679-96.

43. J. Berthelot, *Apprendre à vivre ensemble, immigration, société et éducation* (Montréal: CEQ and the Éditions St-Martin, 1991). D. Blondin, "Les deux espèces humaines ou l'impossibilité de la communication interculturelle entre les races," in Ouellet, ed., *Pluralisme et l'école*, 485-510. M. Mc Andrew, "La lutte au racisme et à l'ethnocentrisme dans le materiel didactique: problématique et interventions québécoises dans le domaine," *Le racisme et l'éducation: perspectives et expériences diverses* (Ottawa: Canadian Teachers' Federation, 1992), 49-60.

44. M. Messier, *Les modèles de services*. MEQ, *Une école d'avenir*. M. Mc Andrew, *Intégration des immigrants et diversité ethnoculturelle à l'école de demain: le débat québécois dans une perspective comparative* (Montréal: Presses de l'Université de Montréal, 2001).

45. MEQ, *Une école d'avenir*. M. Mc Andrew and C. Ciceri, "Immigration, diversity and multilingual education: The Canadian example," *Zeitschrift für internationale erziehungs — und sozialwissenschaftliche Forschung* 15, 2 (1998).

46. MEQ, *L'école tout un programme*. (Québec: Gouvernement du Québec, 1997). C. Tessier and M. Mc Andrew, "L'éducation à la citoyenneté," in C. Goyer and S. Laurin, eds., *Entre culture, compétence et contenu: la formation fondamentale un espace à redéfinir* (Montréal: Éditions Logiques, 2001). M. Mc Andrew, *Intégration des immigrants*, 2001.

47. Ministère de l'Éducation du Québec, *Se souvenir et devenir*. Report of the workgroup on the teaching of history (Lacoursière) (Québec, Gouvernement du Québec, 1994).

48. C. St-Germain, *La progression des élèves au secondaire et au collégial selon la langue maternelle. Évolution de 1976 à 1982* (Québec: MEQ, 1988). Conseil des communautés culturelles et de l'immigration, *Le rendement scolaire des élèves des communautés culturelles*, annotated bibliography (1990). Ministère de l'Éducation du Québec, *Performance des élèves aux épreuves ministérielles en langue française et en langue anglaise selon leur origine linguistique* (Québec: Direction de la recherche, Feb. 1994). MEQ, *Réalités linguistiques et réussite scolaire au Québec*, working paper, Québec, Direction de la recherche, Apr. 1997.

49. H. Van Dromme (Ruimy), L. Van Dromme, and P. Liamchin, "Bilan d'une expérience d'évaluation des élèves de l'accueil," *Québec français* 83 (1991): 69-71.

50. One can see there is a certain *normalisation* of the determinants for educational failure in Québec, as much as an unacceptable situation can be considered as "normal."

51. G. Pelletier and M. Crespo, *Le jeune immigrant dans le système scolaire*. A socio-educational study of students coming out of the *classes d'accueil* of the Commission des écoles catholiques de Montréal. Report subsidized by MEQ, 1979. D. Maisonneuve, *Le cheminement scolaire des élèves ayant séjourné en classe d'accueil* (Québec: MEQ, Direction générale de la recherche et du développement, 1987). MEQ, *Le point sur les services d'accueil et de francisation de l'école publique québécoise. Pratiques actuelles et résultats des élèves* (Montréal: Direction de la coordination des réseaux, Direction des services aux communautés culturelles, 1996).

52. In this matter, it is interesting to note that a comparison of the results of various groups on these tests does not corroborate the hypothesis, sometimes popular within the educational setting or wider public, that difficulties are related to the linguistic distance between the target language and French. In fact, Chinese-speakers are on top of the list

while Spanish-speakers and Creole-speakers are much more disadvantaged. Thus, here, as in other fields, the ethnicization, typical to the North American discourse, should be avoided while reintroducing the "social class" variable that our French colleagues have the reverse tendency to use too exclusively.

53. CLF, *Vive la diversité en français.* MEQ, *Une école d'avenir,* J. Berthelot (1991).

54. Gouvernement du Québec, *Exposé de la situation* (Québec: Commission des États généraux sur l'éducation, 1996). M. Mc Andrew and M. Jacquet, "Le discours public des acteurs du monde de l'éducation sur l'immigration et l'intégration des élèves des minorités," *Recherches sociographiques* 37 (1996): 1-41.

55. The data concerning the free choice of a French-language or English-language CÉGEP for students of immigrant origin schooled in French at the secondary level is also scrutinized by nationalists. In this field, also, as in that of linguistic uses, despite a few recent setbacks, the data are more positive than general perceptions (see MEQ, *La situation linguistique dans le secteur de l'éducation en 1997-1998.* Bulletin statistique de l'éducation 10 (Mar. 1999).

56. H. Hensler and A. Beauchesne, *L'école française à clientèle pluriethnique de l'île de Montréal,* Dossiers du Conseil de la langue française 25 (Québec: Les Publications du Québec, 1987).

57. M. Mc Andrew, C. Veltman, F. Lemire, and J. Rossell, *Concentration ethnique et usages linguistiques en milieu scolaire* (Université de Montréal: Immigration et métropoles, 1999). M. Mc Andrew, M. Pagé, F. Lemire, and J. Rossell, "L'aptitude au français des élèves montréalais d'origine immigrée: impact de la densité ethnique de l'école, du taux de francisation associé à la langue maternelle et de l'ancienneté d'implantation," *Cahiers québécois de démographie* 29, 1 (2000): 89-118.

58. C. Veltman and S. Paré, *L'enquête de 1993 sur la pratique linguistique des immigrants* (Montréal: UQAM, Département des études urbaines et touristiques, 1995). M. Mc Andrew et al., *Cahiers québécois de démographie* 24, 2 (1995): 343-70.

59. M. Jodoin, M. Mc Andrew, and M. Pagé, *Le vécu scolaire et social des élèves scolarisés dans les écoles secondaires de langue française de l'île de Montréal: une analyse comparative,* GREAPE, Centre for Ethnic Studies, Université de Montréal, Research report tabled to the ministère des Relations avec les Citoyens et de l'immigration du Québec, 1997.

60. Thus, the study does not corroborate, nor reject, the multicultural hypothesis that a strong ethnic identity contributes to the sense of belonging to the new society, nor the assimilationist hypothesis that conceives these two phenomena in a subtractive dynamic (see M. Pagé, M. Jodoin, and M. Mc Andrew, "Pluralism et style d'acculturation d'adolescents néo-Québécois," *Revue québécoise de psychologie* 19, 3 [1998]).

61. D. Juteau, *L'ethnicité et ses frontières* (Montréal: Presses de l'Université de Montréal, 2000).

62. A. Laperrière et al., "De l'indifférenciation à l'évitement," in F. Ouellet and M. Pagé, eds., *Pluriethnicité, éducation et société* (Québec: IQRC, 1991), 543-62. A. Laperrière et al., "L'émergence d'une nouvelle génération cosmopolite?" *Revue internationale d'action communautaire* 31, 71 (1994): 171-84. A. Laperrière and P. Dumont, *Le vécu démocratique des jeunes dans deux écoles secondaires montréalaises à haute et faible densité ethnique* (Montréal: Université de Montréal, GREAPE, 2000).

63. This is a tendency that should wither as the "children of Bill 101" choose teaching careers, in a context of high demand due to massive retirements since the mid-1990s and to the advent of equal-opportunity programs aiming at a more balanced ethnocultural representation within the school staff.

64. Rather, the personnel regret the difficulty of involving parents of immigrant origin in the formal school structures. Such a lack of interest is often shared by parents of the francophone community where an only limited elite becomes involved. However, both groups participate in a fairly equivalent way in activities affecting their children or of a social character (see M. Mc Andrew, *Les relations École/communautés en milieu pluriethnique montréalais* [Montréal: Conseil scolaire de l'île de Montréal, 1988]). J. Hohl, "Les relations enseignantes-parents en milieu pluriethnique: de quelques malentendus et de leurs clarifications," *PRISME* 3, 3 (1993): 396-409. MEQ, *Parents-Partenaires. Répertoire de projets et de pratiques favorisant la participation des parents en milieu scolaire multiethnique*, Cahier no 9, Éducation interculturelle, Direction des services aux communautés culturelles (1995).

65. M. Mc Andrew and M. Pagé, "Entre démagogie et démocratie: le débat sur le hijab au Québec," *Collectif interculturel* 2, 2 (1996): 151-67. C. Ciceri, *Le foulard Islamique à l'école publique: analyse comparée du débat dans la presse française et québécoise francophone (1994-1995)*, working paper. Immigration et métropoles, 1999.

66. In this matter, the extremely reductionist analysis of this issue carried out by the anglophone media outside Québec is to be deplored. Rather than having to acknowledge the fact that the French-language school system was sharing the international controversies regarding the balance to be found between the public space and the individual rights on the one hand, and religious and cultural diversity on the other, it chose to present the case as another proof of the hypotheses that tribalism would still be the dominant mode of ethnic relations in Québec. This should not come as a surprise when one knows the tendency of the anglophone media to ethnicize, and even to demonize the entire nationalist movement, and, by extension, the francophone population in Québec. See Cisco and Gagné, "Le Québec vu par le Canada anglais," *Voir* (18-24 June 1998) and M. Potvin (in collaboration with M. Mc Andrew), "Les dérapages racistes à l'égard du Québec au Canada anglais depuis 1995," *Politique et Sociétés* 18, 2 (1999): 101-32.

67. J.P. Proulx, "La prise en compte de la diversité religieuse à l'école québécoise: une tentative avortée, l'enseignement coranique à l'école publique," in M. Mc Andrew, O. Galatanu, R. Toussaint (in collaboration with C. Ciceri), eds., *Pluralisme et éducation: politiques et pratiques au Canada, en Europe et dans les pays du sud. L'apport de l'éducation comparée* (Montréal: Les publications de la Faculté des sciences de l'éducation/Paris, Association francophone d'éducation comparée 1 [1995]: 251-66).

68. M. Mc Andrew, *Models of common schooling*.

69. J. Hohl, "Le choc culturel de connaissance et de communication interculturelle," in M. Mc Andrew, ed., *Repères*, special issue, Le pluralisme éthnique en éducation: une perspective québécoise (Faculté des sciences de l'éducation: Université de Montréal, 1994). J. Hohl, "Résistance à la diversité culturelle au sein des institutions scolaires," in M. Pagé, M. Mc Andrew, and F. Gagnon, eds., *Citoyenneté, pluralisme et éducation* (Montréal: L'Harmattan, 1994). J. Hohl, 1996. J. Hohl and M. Normand, "Enseigner en milieu pluriethnique dans une societé divisée," in M. Mc Andrew and F. Gagnon, eds., *Citoyenneté, pluralisme et éducation*, 168-81.

70. CSE, *L'éducation interculturelle*, Gouvernement du Québec, Mc Andrew and Jacquet, "Le discours public des acteurs," 37, 1-41.

71. J.P. Proulx, "Restructuration scolaire: la concurrence des valeurs religieuses et linguistiques," in L. Corriveau and M. Saint-Martin, eds., *Transformation des enjeux démocratiques en éducation* (Montréal: Éditions Logiques, 1998), 165-203. Mc Andrew and Proulx, "Éducation et ethnicité."

72. While almost 90 per cent of the immigrant population in Québec settles in the Greater Montréal area, this ratio is only 65 per cent in Toronto in relation to the entirety of Ontario and 70 per cent in Vancouver, here again in relation to the entirety of British Columbia.

73. M. Mc Andrew and M. Ledoux, *Identification et analyse des facteurs socio-écologiques et scolaires influençant la dynamique de la concentration ethnique dans les écoles de langue française de l'île de Montréal*, Rapport soumis à la Direction des Études et de la Recherche, MAIICC, 1996. M. Mc Andrew and M. Ledoux, "Identification et évaluation de l'impact relatif des facteurs influençant la dynamique de la concentration ethnique dans les écoles de langue française de l'île de Montréal," *Revue canadienne des sciences régionales* 20, 1-2 (1998): 195-216.

74. Mc Andrew and Ledoux, *Identification et analyse des facteurs socio-écologiques*, 343-70.

75. Mc Andrew and Jodoin, *L'immigration à Montréal*.

76. M. Mc Andrew, M. Pagé, M. Jodoin, and F. Lemire, "Densité ethnique et intégration sociale des élèves d'origine immigrante au Québec," *Études ethniques au Canada/ Canadian Ethnic Studies* 31, 1 (1999): 5-25. M. Mc Andrew, C. Veltman, J. Rossell, and F. Lemire, "Les usages linguistiques en milieu scolaire pluriethnique à Montréal: situation actuelle et déterminants institutionnels," *Revue des sciences de l'éducation* 27, 1 (2001): 105-26.

77. M. Mc Andrew, *Models of common schooling*, 333-45. 1996. M. Mc Andrew and F. Lemire, "La concentration ethnique dans les écoles de langue française de l'île de Montréal: que pouvons-nous apprendre de la recherche americaine sur le busing," *Éducation canadienne et internationale* 27, 2 (1999): 1-24.

16

English-Speaking Québec: A Political History

GARTH STEVENSON

Québec has always been a predominantly francophone society, and in recent years there has been a growing tendency to define its identity in terms of the French language, the predominance of which is the most obvious difference between Québec and the rest of North America. Nonetheless, Québec has for more than two centuries included a substantial minority of anglophones, and the situation of this minority within Québec has been a political issue for most of that time: witness Lord Durham's celebrated comment in 1839: "I found two nations warring in the bosom of a single state."[1]

Unlike some other minorities, for example the Acadians of the Maritime provinces, Québec anglophones are not a separate ethnic group sharing common origins and a distinct culture. Over the years anglophone Québec, like the anglophone population of the rest of Canada, has grown increasingly diverse. Even in 1867 it included English, Scottish, and Irish elements that were quite distinct. The majority of the Irish and some of the other anglophones were Catholic, while the remainder of the anglophone population was Protestant. In subsequent years, a substantial Jewish community, tracing its origins mainly to eastern Europe, was added to the anglophone population, along with a variety of other persons, some of whom, but by no means all, could be fitted into the traditional categories of Catholic and Protestant.

Today anglophone Québec includes people with a variety of ethnic, religious, and racial origins, some of them recently arrived in Québec and some with roots that extend back for many generations. Québec anglophones also vary in socio-economic status; only a small minority resemble the stereotype, still widely accepted among francophones, of the affluent anglophone business or professional person who resides in a mansion in Westmount, Hampstead, or the Town of Mount Royal. A final source of differentiation is geography. The rather large anglophone community of Montréal and the small and scattered anglophone minorities in the different regions of southern, western, and eastern Québec have their own distinct characteristics, problems and points of view. In short, there is no such thing as a typical Québec anglophone. The only attribute that all of them share is one that most other North Americans take for granted: the use of English as their primary language. In Québec, and only in Québec, this cannot be taken for granted, because it sets them apart from most of their fellow-citizens.

Measuring the size of the anglophone population in Québec is not as simple as it might seem. The Canadian census records the answers to a number of questions relating to language, including mother tongue (a category first used in 1921), language spoken at home (first used in 1971), and first official language spoken (first used in 1991). As an added complication, it allows multiple answers such as "English and French" or "English and Italian" to any of these questions. Another category used by Statistics Canada in recent years is "official language minority," which includes all Québec residents whose first official language spoken is English, plus half of those whose first official language spoken is "both English and French." By this definition, the anglophone community comprised 925,835 persons in 1996, or 13.1 per cent of Québec's population. Well over half of Québec's official language minority (560,810 persons) lived in the urban community of Montréal, where they comprised 32.1 per cent of the population.

If "anglophone" is defined to mean only those of English mother tongue, the percentages in 1996 were much smaller: 9.4 per cent in Québec as a whole and 19.9 per cent in the Montréal urban community, indicating that the anglophone community has absorbed many persons who originally spoke a different language. The "mother tongue" percentages have declined steadily, as greater economic opportunities elsewhere, recently reinforced by political anxieties about Québec, have caused many anglophones to leave the province and have discouraged anglophones in other provinces from going there. The most rapid decline was between 1976 and 1981, when Québec residents of English mother tongue fell in absolute numbers by 94,570, and as a percentage from 12.8 to 11.0. The anglophone community has tried to compensate for such losses by absorbing allophone immigrants into the official language minority, but Québec legislation directing immigrant children into French schools is deliberately designed to prevent this.

Québec anglophones have grown accustomed, in recent years, to complaints from some francophones that the English language is too widely used in Québec, that French has not yet established itself as the common language of the province, or even that French is in danger of becoming a minority language in Montréal. Such concerns are sometimes used as arguments to justify administrative or legal restrictions on the use of English or on the autonomy of English-language institutions. Occasionally, a francophone will suggest that "Québec should be made as French as Ontario is English," a transformation that would be difficult, since the official language minority in Ontario comprises less than 5 per cent of Ontario's population.

Such comments seem bizarre to Québec anglophones, many of whom believe that their own language is in danger of disappearing from Québec and that English, rather than French, needs protection. At the time of Confederation, persons of English mother tongue comprised about 22 per cent of Québec's population. Nine rural counties, as well as the city of Sherbrooke, had anglophone majorities.[2] Even a century after Confederation, anglophones controlled most of Québec's economy, apart from agriculture, as well as a network of educational, medical, and social institutions that operated entirely in English and were largely independent of control by the state. In those days, anglophones were a secure and privileged minority, thousands of whom lived comfortably in Québec while never speaking (and rarely hearing) a word of French. Contrasting these facts with their present situation, most anglophones have difficulty understanding why many francophones still feel insecure about the status of the French language in Québec.

A survey of Québec anglophone attitudes, conducted by the Missisquoi Institute in the spring of 2000, identified some of the community's concerns at that time.[3] Asked to name the most important problem facing the community, 20 per cent of the respondents cited the need for "equal rights for anglophones," 10 per cent noted the shortage of services in English, 9 per cent named the possibility of Québec sovereignty, 7 per cent stated the lack of communication with francophones, and 6 per cent pointed to the restrictions on English-language commercial signs. When asked to rate issues on a list as "extremely important," 41 per cent selected access to health and social services in English and 29 per cent, access to government services in English. Only 29 per cent were convinced that the anglophone community had "effective and strong leadership," while 49 per cent believed that it did not. Fifty-six per cent were unable to name an organization or group "most dedicated to serving the interests of the anglophone community."[4]

Although Québec anglophones often are annoyed when francophones describe them as "the best-treated minority in the world," it is fair to say that they are not really suffering and that their community is unlikely ever to disappear from Québec. On the other hand, their complaints are more intelligible when viewed in the light of their history, particularly the changes that have occurred in their situation over the last four decades, a subject to be considered below.

Anglophone Québec before the Quiet Revolution

Anglophones began to arrive in Québec almost immediately after the British took possession of the colony. A generation later, Loyalists fleeing the newly independent United States were added to the original anglophone population. Immigration from England, Scotland, and Ireland followed in the nineteenth century. Many anglophones settled in the two major cities, Québec City and Montréal, but the largest concentration for many years was in the area south of the St. Lawrence and east of the Richelieu known as the Eastern Townships, which had attracted few French settlers before the Conquest, and which remained predominantly anglophone until after Confederation. Other important anglophone communities developed in the Ottawa Valley and the Gaspé Peninsula. Anglophone merchants took control of finance and external trade soon after the Conquest, and as Québec industrialized, the new industries were largely dominated by anglophone capital as well.

The union of Upper and Lower Canada by the British Parliament in 1841 made Québec anglophones part of an anglophone majority in the united provinces and gave them the political balance of power between their fellow-anglophones in Canada West (Ontario) and their francophone compatriots in Canada East (Québec). A colonial statute in 1846 provided them with an autonomous Protestant school system, operating entirely in English. Subsequently, English-language schools were established within the Catholic system to accommodate Irish immigrants.

Confederation initially was not welcomed by most Québec anglophones, particularly the Protestants, because it would place them, for the first time, under the jurisdiction of a mainly francophone provincial government. To reassure them, the British North America Act of 1867 included a guarantee of official bilingualism within Québec (Section 133), entrenchment of the separate Protestant school system (Section 93), and provisions to ensure their continuing representation in both houses of the Québec legislature, as well as the Canadian Senate. More significant, perhaps, than these formal safeguards were the economic power of the anglophone elite and their position as part of the anglophone majority in Canada as a whole.

Despite their initial misgivings about it, and despite a gradual decline in their percentage of Québec's population, anglophones flourished in the newly autonomous province of Québec. For a century after Confederation, Québec was governed through an informal but effective system of intercultural elite accommodation. Arend Lijphart, a political scientist who has devoted his career to studying such systems, refers to them as "consociational democracies." According to Lijphart, these systems are able to combine deep cultural diversity with democratic stability by following four principles: political leaders from the various cultural communities participate in the executive government, the government delegates extensive control over their own affairs to the communities, benefits are allocated proportionally between communities, and each community can veto decisions that would threaten its fundamental interests.[5]

These principles describe the way Québec was governed until at least the 1960s. There were always anglophone ministers in the Executive Council of Québec, and, until 1944, the Provincial Treasurer (since 1951 called the Minister of Finance) was almost always an anglophone. Anglophones also played a significant part in the municipal government of Montréal, which operated in both languages and maintained a tradition of alternating anglophone and francophone mayors until 1930. The anglophone community controlled its own schools, universities, hospitals, social services, and cultural institutions with almost no interference by the Québec government, even though the constitution placed such matters under provincial jurisdiction. Anglophones received at least their fair share, if not more, of the benefits distributed by the provincial government. No Québec government attempted to undermine fundamental anglophone interests such as the status of the English language, the almost complete autonomy of the Protestant school system, the existence of unilingual anglophone suburbs around Montréal, or the fact that provincial borrowing was handled by anglophone financial institutions. Certainly, none challenged anglophone economic power, which reinforced anglophone political power and gave unilingual anglophones significantly higher incomes, on the average, than their francophone compatriots.

Knowing that the provincial government would not threaten their interests, particularly with an anglophone minister in charge of Québec's finances, Québec anglophones, at least those in urban areas, could ignore that government most of the time. (Rural anglophones, who worked on farms or in the forest industry, were more affected by provincial policies.) The federal government, with its jurisdiction over banking, railways, tariffs, and immigration, was considered more important.

One reason these arrangements lasted as long as they did was that they suited the preferences of the Catholic Church as well as those of the anglophones. (In fact, all of the consociational regimes identified by Lijphart and other political scientists are in countries that are largely, but not entirely, Catholic.) In particular, the delegation of most of the province's responsibilities for social policy to autonomous cultural communities could be considered an application of the principle of "subsidiarity" recommended by Pope Pius XI in the encyclical *Quadrigesimo Anno*: "It is an injustice and at the same time a grave evil and a disturbance of right order to transfer to the larger and higher collectivity functions which can be performed and provided for by lesser and subordinate bodies."[6] By delegating its authority, Québec ensured that the Catholic Church, rather than the state, would control the education, health care, and social services provided to the Catholic part of the population. The Church was content that the Protestant and Jewish minorities were free to make their own arrangements independently, since it shared their desire for autonomy from the state.

Social Change and the Decline of Segmentation

By the end of World War II the conditions that had facilitated these arrangements were increasingly fragile, and the long post-war government of Maurice Duplessis, who abandoned the practice of choosing an anglophone as provincial treasurer, can be seen in retrospect as a period of transition. John A. Macdonald's National Policy was in decline and Canada was changing from an east-west economy, which traded with Britain through the port of Montréal, into a northern economic region of the United States. Toronto replaced Montréal as the economic and financial centre of Canada, undermining the importance of Montréal's anglophone business elite and encouraging many Québec anglophones to pursue their business or professional careers in Ontario and further west.

Within Québec, many francophones were beginning to resent the economic power and wealth of an anglophone business elite whose privileges no longer seemed to be justified by their performance, now that Québec, under their leadership, was visibly deteriorating in relation to Ontario. The same could be said for the privileges of the Catholic Church, whose schools, hospitals, and other institutions were increasingly dependent on government subsidies and whose educational system was viewed by growing numbers of critics as old-fashioned, elitist, and unsuited to the needs of a modern society.

Change became the order of the day after Duplessis died in September 1959. Most anglophones welcomed the reforms introduced by the Liberal government of Jean Lesage, between 1960 and 1966, partly because they seemed to make Québec more similar to the rest of North America and partly because Duplessis' anti-conscription agitation during World War II had caused most anglophones to support the Liberals ever since. However, the Quiet Revolution, as it was called, reduced the power of the Catholic Church and created a bureaucratic state that would eventually undermine anglophone autonomy.[7] It also stimulated expectations that could not be fulfilled without challenging Anglophone economic power and the status of the English language, not to mention the authority of the federal state.

The impact of change on the anglophones was gradual at first. The new merit-based bureaucracy probably included fewer anglophones, proportionately, than its patronage-ridden predecessor, but anglophones had never cared much for provincial jobs, given their greater opportunities in Ottawa and the private sector. The Office de la langue française, established in 1961, was initially preoccupied with improving the quality of French, not with restricting the use of English. The nationalization of mainly anglophone-controlled electric power companies in 1963 troubled some anglophones, but most excused it on the grounds that electricity was a special case and that Ontario had done the same thing half a century earlier. Bill 60, which established a Ministry of Education in 1964, maintained the autonomy of the Protestant system; a common curriculum was not imposed until 17 years later under the Parti Québécois. The takeover of social services by the province did not occur until 1971, by which time it was overshadowed by more dramatic events.

Anglophone unhappiness increased, however, after the Lesage government suffered electoral defeat in 1966. Two minor parties committed to an independent Québec contested that election, while the victorious Union Nationale advocated a radically decentralized federalism. In the following year, the Québec Liberal Party split and its most popular ex-minister, René Lévesque, became the leader of the independence movement, known after October 1968 as the Parti Québécois. Anglophones became increasingly preoccupied with the possibility that Québec might cease to be a Canadian province.

The Politicization of Language and the End of Consociational Politics

Even more disturbing to anglophones, at least in the short term, was the emergence of a movement to curtail the use of English in Québec, particularly in the schools. This movement was stimulated by anxieties about immigration and the rapid decline in the francophone birth rate during the 1960s, as well as by the fact that language was replacing religion as the touchstone of Québec's *pure laine* (white-as-wool) identity. Neither development had much to do with anglophones, but they and their schools soon became the targets of resentment.

Non-Catholic immigrant children in Québec, including those who were Jewish or Greek Orthodox, had always attended Protestant schools, which operated entirely in English. Catholic immigrant children had sometimes been educated in English and sometimes in French, since the Catholic school boards operated schools in both languages. Italians, who became the largest immigrant group in the 1950s, traditionally had leaned towards French, but they, too, began to prefer English schools, which would give their children access to jobs throughout North America.[8] As a result, enrolment grew faster in the English Catholic sector of education than in either the Protestant or the French sector. Combined with the declining francophone birth rate and federal control over immigration, this trend caused some francophones to fear that Montréal would again become a predominantly anglophone city, as it had been for a brief period after the Irish immigration a century earlier. Some Québec nationalists began to advocate measures to curtail enrollment in English schools, or even to eliminate English education altogether.

In 1968, a nationalist campaign to force Italian children into French schools in the largely Italian Montréal suburb of St. Léonard led to a major confrontation. The nervous Union Nationale government responded by appointing the Gendron Royal Commission to study the position of the French language. It also adopted Bill 63, which allowed "freedom of choice" between English and French schools for all Québec parents. The bill was intended to reassure the Italians and the anglophones and was in harmony with Catholic doctrine that the family should take priority over the state. It outraged linguistic nationalists, most of whom cared little about Catholic doctrine. They feared that not only immigrants but many francophones would view Bill 63 as a green light to educate their children in English. The Union Nationale was overwhelmingly defeated in the next election.

The new Liberal government of Robert Bourassa received the report of the Gendron Commission in 1972.[9] The report was a well-researched and fair-minded assessment of Québec's linguistic situation, which included a long list of recommendations, but the Liberals ignored it until after their next election campaign, during which they hardly mentioned the subject of language. Then, having won an overwhelming majority, they introduced Bill 22, the Official Language Act, in 1974. This Act followed the Gendron recommendations by making French the official language of Québec, while retaining English as a second language, and by requiring members of certain professions to demonstrate competence in the official language. However, the business-oriented Liberals soft-pedalled Gendron's recommendation to encourage the use of French in the private sector. Instead, they introduced a provision that Gendron had not recommended, requiring immigrant children to receive their education in French unless they could pass a test in English.

Anglophones reacted with shock and outrage, signing petitions and denouncing the government at mass meetings in the west end of Montréal. From their standpoint, Bill 22 violated the consociational principle that the anglophone community should have a veto over legislation affecting its fundamental interests. They had not even been given the opportunity to discuss or consider such legislation during the election campaign. The fact that it came from the Liberal Party, which anglophones had supported consistently and overwhelmingly since 1939, added insult to injury. Immigrants were particularly offended by the English-language tests for allophone children, which they viewed as discriminatory. Anglophones also felt threatened, because their community and its institutions relied on the tacit understanding that most immigrants, or their children, would become anglophones.[10] Two Liberals from ethnically mixed ridings, one of whom was John Ciaccia, the first Italian-born parliamentarian in the party's history, voted against Bill 22 in the National Assembly. Bourassa's three anglophone ministers, who publicly supported the bill, lost much of their credibility. Two of them retired before the next election, since their chances of being renominated in their mainly anglophone ridings were very slim.

(The one who was re-elected, Dr. Victor Goldbloom, later served in the 1990s as Canada's Commissioner of Official Languages.)

Yet Bill 22 was only the beginning of attacks by Québec governments on the status of English. In 1976, the Parti Québécois was elected to office after promising to hold a referendum on sovereignty-association during its first mandate. The election of the new government was alarming in itself to anglophones, but worse was to follow. In 1977, the government introduced Bill 101, the Charter of the French Language, as a successor to the Official Language Act.

The new law was almost twice as long as its predecessor. It declared that Québec would no longer be bound by Section 133 of the British North America Act, which provided for bilingualism in Québec's legislature and courts. Municipalities, which under Bill 22 could use both languages if their population was at least 10 per cent anglophone, could henceforth do so only if a majority of their population had a mother tongue other than French. All businesses with more than 50 employees would be required to demonstrate that French was the main language of the workplace. Commercial signs were required to be in French only, or else fines would be imposed on their owners. Access to English schools was restricted so narrowly that an anglophone family moving to Québec from another part of Canada would have to educate its children in French, as would all immigrants. Enrollment in English-language schools declined by almost half in the next decade as a result of this measure.[11]

The Supreme Court of Canada soon declared what should already have been obvious: Québec was still bound by Section 133.[12] In a later decision, it used the Canadian Charter of Rights and Freedoms (incorporated in the constitution in 1982) to require giving anglophone Canadians from other provinces (although not immigrants) access to English schools.[13] A third Supreme Court decision ruled that prohibiting English on commercial signs violated the constitutional right to freedom of expression, guaranteed by Québec's own Charter of Human Rights and Freedoms, as well as by the Canadian Charter, although the law was justified in requiring the use of French.[14]

The last decision produced another serious confrontation between Québec and its anglophone minority, even though the Liberals, again led by Robert Bourassa, had returned to office. During the election campaign of 1985, Bourassa had promised to allow bilingual signs. However, in response to the Supreme Court's decision, he introduced Bill 178, which used the notwithstanding clauses in the Canadian and Québec Charters to continue the ban on bilingual signs. (An exception was made for indoor signs if the English text was less prominent than the French.) This time, three anglophone ministers, Richard French, Clifford Lincoln, and Herbert Marx, resigned from Bourassa's government. (John Ciaccia, now a minister, did not resign despite his vote against Bill 22 in 1974.) The resignations did the government little damage, however, and it was returned at the next election. Consociational democracy was dead and buried in Québec; in fact, its demise can be dated back to 1974, when Bill 22 was adopted.

The Anglophone Community Mobilizes

During the heyday of consociational politics, Québec anglophones made little effort to mobilize for political action. As long as the English language seemed secure, there was no sense of an "anglophone community" strong enough to overcome the cleavages of religion, ethnicity, and geography. In addition, anglophones had relied on their community's economic elite and on their spokesmen in the Québec government and legislature to protect their interests. Bill 22 revealed the limitations of this strategy, but it took the community by surprise and there was little or no time to mobilize against it. The election of the Parti Québécois, which in 1976 had no anglophone members in either the Executive Council or the National Assembly, finally provoked some Anglophones to pursue a different strategy.

One obvious alternative was to form interest groups. The first of these, the Freedom of Choice movement, had already appeared in response to Bill 22. Two that appeared soon after the 1976 election were Participation-Québec, a group of young professionals who promoted dialogue between anglophones and francophones, and Positive Action, a more establishment-oriented group, which tried to discourage anglophones from leaving the province. In 1977, the federal government, which already subsidized francophone groups in other provinces, offered funds to anglophones in Québec. This offer contributed to the formation of the Council of Québec Minorities (CQM). It included a number of ethnic associations, the most important of which represented the Greek, Italian, and Jewish communities. Regional anglophone groups also appeared, the oldest and largest of which was the Townshippers' Association, founded in 1979, while the most militant was the Chateauguay Valley English-Speaking People's Association (CVESPA).

When the Parti Québécois won a second mandate in April 1981, the need for a permanent lobbying organization to represent Québec anglophones became more obvious. Furthermore, it was hoped that a single inclusive group, like those representing official language minorities in the other provinces, would receive a larger federal subsidy than a collection of small groups. Both motives contributed to the formation of the Coalition of English-Speaking Quebecers, which signed up several thousand members in the winter of 1981-82. In May 1982 it changed its name to Alliance Québec (AQ) and held a founding convention. Most of the regional groups affiliated with AQ, while the CQM, Participation-Québec, and Positive Action ceased to exist. The first two presidents of AQ, Eric Maldoff and Michael Goldbloom (the son of Victor Goldbloom), had been prominent members of Participation-Québec.

For the next six years, AQ was reasonably successful. It achieved the feat of attracting a sharply increased federal subsidy, at the same time as it established a fruitful dialogue with the sovereignist government of Québec. Its lobbying contributed to Bill 57 (1983), which inserted in the preamble of the Charter of the French Language a pledge of respect for the institutions of the anglophone community, allowed such institutions to make more use of English in their communications, and exempted those who graduated from a Québec high school in 1986 or later from the French language tests required to enter certain professions. When the Liberals returned to office in 1985, AQ continued its lobbying. It was rewarded in 1986 with Bill 142, which guaranteed anglophones access to health care and social services in their own language. These victories suggested that AQ's moderate and non-partisan approach, which accepted the legitimacy of Québec nationalism and the need for some measures to protect the French language, was more useful to the community than the more confrontational approach of groups like Freedom of Choice.

From this point onwards, however, AQ's fortunes began to decline. Many members failed to maintain their memberships after the Parti Québécois lost office, apparently believing that AQ was no longer necessary. After 1987, AQ, like the anglophone community more generally, was divided by disagreements over the Mulroney government's constitutional proposals, known as the Meech Lake Accord. Many of AQ's prominent personalities were active in an organization called The Friends of Meech Lake, while most of the rank and file probably agreed with former Prime Minister Pierre Trudeau, who campaigned effectively against the proposals.

The greatest blow to AQ, however, was Bill 178, which seemed to discredit its moderate approach and gave credence to anglophones who argued for a more confrontational stance against Québec nationalism. Critics argued that by taking a middle-of-the-road position on questions of language policy, AQ ensured that the eventual compromise adopted by the government was always detrimental to anglophone interests.[15] Two new political parties, the Equality Party and the Unity Party, were formed in response to Bill 178. Their supporters, who included some members of AQ, openly derided the moderate leadership of AQ, or "Compliance Québec" as some of them called it. To make matters worse, a fire destroyed the AQ office in Montréal a few days after Bill 178 was adopted. AQ's president, Royal Orr, was absurdly accused in certain French-language media of setting the fire himself to win sympathy for anglophones. He sued the media for libel but the episode took its toll on the organization.

Robert Keaton, a CÉGEP teacher and former municipal politician, who was president from 1989 to 1993, worked hard to revive AQ's reputation. Under his leadership AQ helped the Bourassa government to draft Bill 86, which replaced Bill 178 and allowed bilingual advertising on outdoor signs. However, he faced repeated challenges to his leadership from the more militant and francophobic element among the members.

From 1994 onwards, with the Parti Québécois back in office, AQ had to compete with rival groups that considered AQ too moderate. These included the Special Committee for Canadian Unity, which recommended partitioning Québec if Québec voted for sovereignty, and the Québec Political Action Committee, founded by Howard Galganov, which conducted demonstrations at stores that refused to display signs in English. The increasing signs of anger and frustration in the anglophone community led Premier Lucien Bouchard, in March 1996, to deliver a conciliatory speech in English at the Centaur Theatre, an important anglophone cultural institution in Montréal. The speech was welcomed by most of those who were invited to hear it, a hand-picked group of moderate anglophone community leaders, but received a cool or hostile reception from many, perhaps most, of the anglophones who were not invited.

The militant faction gained control of AQ in 1998, when William Johnson, a controversial journalist sometimes known as "Pit Bill" and the author of two hostile books about Québec nationalism, defeated the establishment's candidate by the narrow margin of eight votes to become president. Several affiliated groups, including the Townshippers, severed their ties with AQ. The moderates who objected to Johnson's leadership formed a rival organization known as Coalition Québec. The federal subsidy to Québec's official language minority was again divided among several groups, as it had been before AQ existed. Johnson decided not to seek re-election in 2000 and was replaced by Anthony Housefather, a young lawyer and municipal politician from the affluent and predominantly Jewish suburb of Hampstead.

Anglophones and Political Parties

Since 1939, anglophones usually have supported the Québec Liberal Party, which has been perceived as less nationalist than either of its main rivals, the Union Nationale, before 1970, or the Parti Québécois subsequently. In doing so they give credence to the observation by political scientist Vincent Lemieux that the Liberals are less firmly rooted in the civil society of francophone Québec, but more closely linked to the world outside Québec than their opponents.[16]

Admittedly, the Union Nationale retained a significant rural anglophone vote throughout the Duplessis era, although it was unpopular with Montréal anglophones. The Parti Québécois, with its commitment to sovereignty, has no realistic hope of winning substantial support from anglophones, although it has made serious overtures to them and usually manages to find a few anglophone candidates.

In the 1962 election, a number of independent anglophone candidates campaigned against the nationalization of electricity and in 1966 some anglophones formed a

Conservative Party, which ran a few candidates on a platform hostile to the Quiet Revolution. Support for these initiatives was insignificant. Anglophones abandoned the Liberals in large numbers only in 1976 and in 1989, the elections that followed Bill 22 and Bill 178, respectively. Both elections demonstrated that the Liberals, and specifically Robert Bourassa, could not take anglophones for granted, but it is not clear that anglophones gained anything of substance by proving this to be so.

In 1976 the Union Nationale, which had been shut out in the previous election, revived its fortunes by emphasizing "Freedom of Choice" between English and French schools. It elected 16 members, mostly in ridings with substantial non-francophone minorities, and gave several other ridings to the Parti Québécois by splitting the federalist vote. In the six Montréal Island ridings with substantial anglophone majorities, the Union Nationale vote increased to 30 times its level in the previous election: from 1,763 votes to 53,032.[17] Dr. William Shaw, in Pointe Claire (the riding with the second-highest percentage of anglophones in Québec), was the first Union Nationale candidate in 40 years to win a predominantly anglophone Montréal riding. However, he left the party within two years, when it proved less committed to bilingualism than he had expected.

Those anglophones who were disillusioned with the Liberals, but unwilling to support the right-wing Union Nationale, had another option in 1976. A group of moderately left-wing federalists formed a predominantly anglophone party called the Democratic Alliance. It ran 13 candidates on Montréal Island under the leadership of Robert Keaton, who later became president of Alliance Québec. None came close to being elected and the party soon disintegrated. Keaton later told an interviewer that he regretted having formed the party.[18]

The adoption of Bill 178 led to the formation of two anglophone protest parties in 1989. The Unity Party, which grew out of CVESPA, was organized only in rural areas, a fatal handicap for an anglophone party, since only one rural riding came close to having a majority of anglophone voters. The Equality Party, which concentrated most of its efforts in Montréal, was more successful. It won four seats at the expense of the Liberals, including the ridings previously represented by Richard French and Herbert Marx. AQ's acting president, Peter Blaikie, had publicly urged anglophones not to vote for the Liberals. A post-election analysis suggested that the Equality Party won 70 per cent of the anglophone vote where it ran candidates, doing particularly well among Jewish voters.[19] However, the loss of four anglophone seats did not prevent the Liberals from winning the election.

Robert Libman, the young leader (and founder) of the Equality Party, was an articulate and effective anglophone spokesman, but he had difficulty controlling his three colleagues in the National Assembly, all of whom were considerably older than he was. The most unruly of them, Richard Holden, was expelled from the party in 1991 and, somewhat ironically, joined the Parti Québécois a year later.

Although the Equality Party was critical of AQ, it shared with that organization the problem of conflict between a relatively moderate elite, which included all four of the elected members, and a more militant and francophobic element at the grassroots. The influence of the latter increased as more moderate members failed to renew their memberships. Libman's support for the Charlottetown Accord, the successor to Meech Lake, precipitated an attempt to remove him from the leadership. By 1993, the militants, led by CÉGEP teacher Keith Henderson, had taken over the party. Libman resigned, to sit as an independent, as did Gordon Atkinson, leaving Neil Cameron as the only Equality Party MNA. In the next election, anglophone voters gave almost unanimous support to the Liberals, who lost anyway. The Liberal defeat in 1994, like the Liberal victory in 1989, demonstrated that the anglophone vote has little impact on Québec elections, since it is concentrated in a few ridings. However, it can be decisive in referenda, where riding boundaries are irrelevant. This was demonstrated in October 1995.

The Prospects for Anglophone Québec

As it enters the twenty-first century, anglophone Québec faces an uncertain future. The days when Montréal anglophones controlled the Québec economy (and much of the Canadian economy) are long gone, leaving few career opportunities within Québec for those who are not completely fluent in French. As a result, Québec attracts few anglophone migrants from other provinces or from English-speaking countries, and large numbers of young anglophones leave Québec as soon as they have completed their education, if not sooner. It has even been suggested that English-language education, which the community has fought so hard to maintain, is contributing to its demise, since it trains Québec anglophones for jobs outside of Québec rather than for jobs within it.[20]

Although the exodus is, or should be, the main concern, there are other sources of anxiety. Québec's constitutional future remains unsettled, and federal power over the province has weakened. Immigrants are now selected by Québec, rather than by the federal government. Francophone immigrants are preferred and other immigrants are strongly encouraged to adopt French as their new language. Labour training has also been transferred from federal to provincial control, creating concerns about its availability in English. Access to health and social services in English, although guaranteed by Québec law, is attacked by elements within the Parti Québécois, who argue that it conflicts with the right of francophones in those fields to work in their own language. Municipal amalgamations have eliminated most of the predominantly anglophone municipalities, including all of those on Montréal Island, although the amalgamation will give anglophone voters far more influence in Montréal itself. Bill 171, introduced at the same time as the amalgamation measure, provides that municipalities or boroughs can be granted bilingual status only if a majority of their population is of English (rather than merely non-French) mother tongue.

On the other hand, the anglophone community has adapted quite well to the changes in Québec since 1960. Those who could not adapt have left and those who remain, particularly the younger generation, are more resilient and feel more comfortable in contemporary Québec. While only 36.7 per cent of Québec anglophones could speak French in 1971, 61.7 per cent could do so in 1996. The percentage of allophones who could speak *both* English and French, as well as their original language, increased over the same period from 33.1 per cent to 46.7 per cent.[21] Social interaction between anglophones and francophones is far greater in quantity and quality than it was a generation ago, and for many of the younger generation the old linguistic barriers and conflicts are almost irrelevant. Intermarriage between anglophones and francophones is increasingly common, and residential segregation has decreased.[22] Although most still think of themselves as Canadians first and foremost, Québec anglophones have more in common with other Quebecers, and less in common with other Canadians, than many of them realize.

With the virtual disappearance of the economic disparities between the two groups, most francophones today have little or no hostility towards the anglophone community. A poll conducted in January 2001 indicated that 83 per cent of Québec francophones described their personal relations with anglophones as at least fairly good. Almost as many favoured allowing bilingual signs, access to health care in English, and even freedom for all parents to send their children to English schools. Yet the same poll indicated that 61 per cent still believe the French language to be in danger.[23] The paradox and the tragedy of the anglophone minority in Québec is that many francophones still view it as a threat, rather than as an opportunity, even though it is no longer powerful enough or numerous enough to threaten francophone interests in any way.[24] Regardless of how weak the minority becomes, some francophones continue to feel insecure because the francophone birth rate is very low and because the English language dominates the global economy, American mass culture, and the Internet. Québec's anglophone minority is made the scapegoat for these unwanted circumstances, even though it did not cause them and can do nothing to change them. Until that paradox is resolved, if it ever can be, some tension between Québec's two main language communities will persist.

Notes

1. *The Report of the Earl of Durham, Her Majesty's High Commissioner and Governor General of British North America* (London: Methuen, 1902), 8.

2. Richard Joy, *Languages in Conflict: The Canadian Experience* (Toronto: McClelland & Stewart), 1972), 28 (map), 97-102.

3. Hubert Bauch, "Institute sheds light on Québec anglos," *The Gazette* (Montréal), 20 Jan. 2001.

4. Sue Montgomery, "Health is top Anglo concern," *The Gazette* (Montréal), 17 Jan. 2001.

5. Arend Lijphart, "Self-Determination versus Pre-Determination of Ethnic Minorities in Power-Sharing Systems," in Will Kymlicka, ed., *The Rights of Minority Cultures* (New York: Oxford University Press, 1995).

6. William J. Gibbons, ed., *Seven Great Encyclicals* (Glen Rock, NJ: Paulist Press, 1963), 147.

7. Sheila Arnopoulos and Dominique Clift, *The English Fact in Québec* (Montréal and Kingston: McGill-Queen's University Press, 1984), 95-108.

8. Marc V. Levine, *The Reconquest of Montréal: Language Policy and Social Change in a Bilingual City* (Philadelphia: Temple University Press, 1990), 56-57.

9. *The Position of the French Language in Québec*, vols. 1-3 (Québec: l'Editeur officiel du Québec, 1972).

10. Hubert Guindon, *Québec Society: Tradition, Modernity and Nationhood* (Toronto: University of Toronto Press, 1988), 85.

11. Jack Jedwab, *English in Montréal: A Layman's Look at the Current Situation* (Montréal: Editions Images, 1996), 86.

12. *A.G. Québec v. Blaikie* [1979] 2 S.C.R. 1016.

13. *A.G. Québec v. Association of Protestant School Boards* [1984] 2 S.C.R. 66.

14. *Québec v. Ford et al.* [1988] 2 S.C.R. 712.

15. Robert Libman, *Riding the Rapids: The White-Water Rise and Fall of Québec's Anglo Protest* (Montréal: Robert Davies Publishing, 1995), 33-35.

16. Vincent Lemieux, *Le Parti libéral du Québec* (Sainte-Foy: Les Presses de l'Université Laval, 1993), 200-03.

17. André Bernard, *Québec: élections 1976* (Montréal: Hurtubise, 1976), 136.

18. Garth Stevenson, *Community Besieged: The Anglophone Minority and the Politics of Québec* (Montréal and Kingston: McGill-Queen's University Press, 1999), 156.

19. Pierre Drouilly, "Le succès des partis Égalité et Unité," *Le Devoir* (Montréal), 4 Oct. 1989.

20. Norman Spector, "Language of lost opportunity," *Globe and Mail* (Toronto), 21 Mar. 2001; Stevenson, *Community Besieged*, 304-05.

21. Stevenson, *Community Besieged*, 305.

22. Alexander Norris, "What is an anglophone?", *The Gazette* (Montréal), 24 Mar. 2001.

23. Allison Hanes, "Two solitudes mingling more," *The Gazette* (Montréal), 14 Feb. 2001.

24. Reed Scowen, *A Different Vision: The English in Québec in the 1990s* (Don Mills, Maxwell Macmillan, 1991), 143-49.

17

Language and Cultural Insecurity

ELISABETH GIDENGIL, ANDRÉ BLAIS,
RICHARD NADEAU, AND NEIL NEVITTE

Raymond Breton has described the continuing evolution of Québec nationalism from an ethnic to a civic form of nationalism, likening it to a similar (and similarly incomplete) evolution in English-speaking Canada that began half a century earlier.[1] The task has been doubly difficult in Québec because "le Québec doit ... livrer deux combats à la fois: celui de l'affirmation nationale et celui de l'affirmation pluraliste."[2] In the process, the "narrow vision that equates the nation with ethnicity"[3] has become merely one endpoint defining a continuum of positions.[4] Yet, some critics continue to perpetuate a stereotype of Québec francophones as ethnocentric at best and xenophobic at worst. These critics have been able to point to a series of studies conducted in the 1970s and 1980s that indicated that Québec francophones held less positive views than other Canadians towards immigration and toward ethnic and cultural diversity in general.[5] Those differences were typically attributed to a greater sense of cultural insecurity among Québec francophones, given a declining birth rate and the tendency of immigrants to assimilate to the province's anglophone minority. However, much has changed since these studies were conducted. Québec has been gaining increasing control over immigration to the province, the proportion of French-speaking immigrants has been rising, and language legislation has encouraged the integration of newcomers into the French-speaking milieu. One consequence may be that immigration is no longer perceived as posing such a threat.

Studies of attitudes towards Aboriginal peoples in the 1970s and 1980s revealed a quite different pattern: Québec francophones were *more* sympathetic than other Canadians to the plight and aspirations of Canada's Aboriginal peoples.[6] This, too, was linked to the fact of being a cultural minority, but now a shared history of resisting assimilation and a shared experience of subordinate status were seen as making for empathy. Again, though, much has changed. The claims of Aboriginal peoples have been forcing the dominant white majority in both Québec and Canada at large "to decide the extent to which they are really prepared to go to accommodate difference: what price are they willing to pay for the recognition of otherness?"[7] And events in the early 1990s have made this question especially pertinent for Québec francophones. One consequence may be that Aboriginal peoples have come to be perceived as more of a threat.

Meanwhile, members of the dominant English-speaking majority have had their own cultural insecurities to contend with. The most salient source of cultural insecurity outside Québec has been the United States. As Sylvia Bashevkin notes, "Virtually all English-Canadian nationalists maintain that American corporate penetration endangers Canadian sovereignty."[8] While conventional wisdom held that Québec francophones do not share this concern, Bashevkin showed that Québec francophones were actually quite supportive of measures designed to control US direct investment in Canada, and Québec nationalists were *more* supportive than members of the francophone and anglophone publics alike. However, her survey data came from the late 1970s, a decade before the advent of the Canada-US Free Trade Agreement. Bipartisan support within Québec for that agreement suggests that Québec francophones may indeed perceive continentalism to be less of a threat to their cultural distinctiveness?[9]

Clearly it is time to re-examine orientations to all three potential sources of cultural insecurity. In this chapter, we compare the attitudes of Québec francophones with those of anglophones in English-speaking Canada toward immigrants, Aboriginal peoples, and continentalism.[10] Our data are taken from the Canadian Election Studies, conducted at the time of the 1988, 1993, 1997, and 2000 federal elections and the 1992 referendum on the Charlottetown Accord. A succession of momentous events form the backdrop to these studies: the failure of two constitutional accords, the implementation of two comprehensive trade agreements, a referendum on sovereignty that came very close to victory, and a violent confrontation with Québec's Mohawks.

Immigrants and Ethnic and Racial Minorities

Another momentous event—Canada's adoption of an official policy of multiculturalism in 1971—prompted the landmark study of multiculturalism and ethnic attitudes in Canada in 1974. Based on this survey, John Berry and his colleagues concluded that "French Canadians evidenced a profile of attitudes which can be described as ethnocentric, and this pattern was more pronounced for French Canadians than for any other Canadian ethnic group."[11] They characterized this as a "chilling factor in an otherwise favourable climate for immigration."[12] Subsequent studies confirmed that Québec francophones held less favourable attitudes on issues relating to immigration, multiculturalism, and ethnic diversity in general.[13] So, too, did a partial replication of the survey conducted in 1991.[14]

Two explanations typically are offered for these findings. Berry and his colleagues pointed to the perceived threat to the survival of the French language, a threat made all the more real by a declining birth rate in Québec and the propensity of newcomers to integrate into Québec's English-speaking community.[15] Indeed, they concluded that, "a pattern of ethnocentric attitudes ... would seem only reasonable under the circumstances."[16] Subsequent studies have taken up this theme.[17] Denis Bolduc and Pierre Fortin have provided the most systematic test of this notion that ethnocentric attitudes are linked to the sense of cultural threat.[18] They were able to confirm that concerns about the future of the French language were responsible for the differences they observed in the attitudes of Québec francophones and Québec anglophones towards immigration and multiculturalism.

The second explanation focuses on the impact of the introduction of official multiculturalism in Canada. There is a perception that, "official multiculturalism trivializes ... the identity and particularistic claims of Québec."[19] Leslie Laczko takes the explanation a step further: "Multiculturalism is seen as all the more dangerous because many of the groups being granted symbolic collective rights are viewed as by and large assimilated into the larger Anglophone community across Canada."[20] It should hardly surprise us, then, that Québec francophones proved to be less positive about ethnic diversity, in general, and multiculturalism, in particular.

That was the picture in the 1970s and 1980s, but there have been a number of important changes in Québec that might have caused a shift in opinion in recent years.[21] First, Québec has gained an increasing degree of control over immigration. Second, there has been a concerted move to legislate what Breton termed "Franco-conformity."[22] This move began in the 1970s, with the enactment of Bill 22, and then Bill 101, but it was in the 1990s that the impact of this legislation (and, specifically, its requirements with respect to schooling) on first-generation Quebecers became apparent. Third, beginning in 1990, the Québec government has made strenuous efforts to raise the proportion of immigrants from French-speaking countries. It is against this background that Bourhis and Laczko alike have asked whether the ethnic attitudes of Québec francophones have changed.[23] Laczko concludes that, "defensive minority reflexes are ... still evident," but his data are drawn from a 1991 survey and, thus, predate the policy initiatives of the 1990s.[24]

FIGURE 17.1

Percentage Wanting to Admit Fewer Immigrants

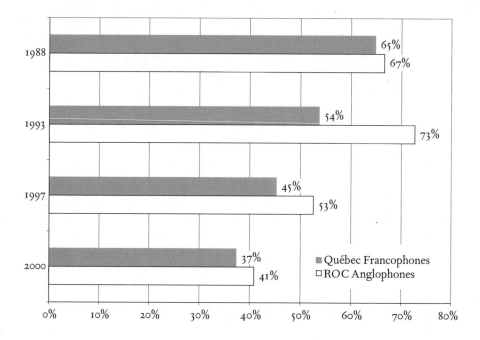

If we look at simple measures of likes and dislikes, or affect, responses to recent Canadian election studies seem to support the conventional image of Québec francophones as harbouring less positive feelings towards ethnic minorities than anglophones outside Québec. The wording of the questions has changed across time and so has the target group, but the gap between francophones in Québec and anglophones outside Québec has persisted. In 1988, the target group was "ethnic minorities" and the average score (on a scale from 0 to 100) was 60 for francophones in Québec, compared with 65 for anglophones in the rest of Canada. In 1992, respondents were asked about "immigrants" and the mean scores dropped to 53 for Québec francophones, versus 64 for anglophones outside Québec. The target group changed to "racial minorities" in 1993 and 1997, and the mean scores were 63 and 53, respectively, for Québec francophones, compared with 68 and 61 for the other language group.[25] Regardless of the wording or the target group, Québec francophones responded less positively than English-speakers in the rest of Canada. It bears emphasis, though, that their mean scores were always positive (a score of 50 represents neutral affect). Clearly, we can reject the notion that Québec francophones typically have negative feelings about immigrants or ethnic and racial minorities.

FIGURE 17.2

Views about Immigrants (percentage agreeing with the statement)

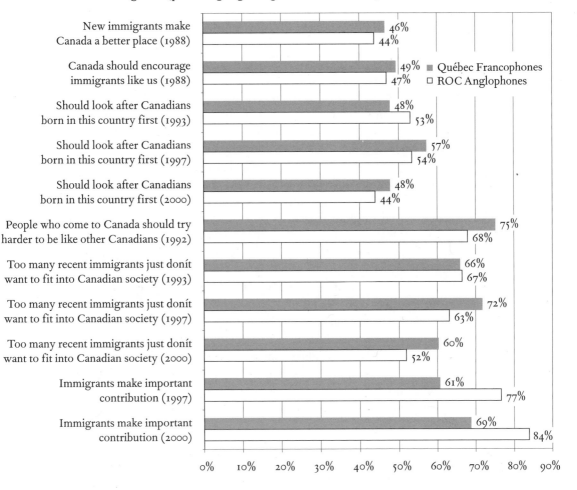

Similarly, the entrenched image of Québec francophones as being less open to immigration is not supported by the survey data. Since 1988, the Canadian election studies have been asking respondents whether Canada should admit more immigrants or fewer immigrants. It is clear from the responses that francophones in Québec are no more opposed to immigration than English-speakers in other parts of Canada (see Figure 17.1). On the contrary, in both 1993 and 1997, Québec francophones were significantly *less* likely to favour a reduction in the number of immigrants admitted. It is also clear that *both* language groups have become progressively more open to immigration since 1988.[26]

Francophones in Québec and anglophones in the rest of Canada respond quite similarly when asked whether new immigrants make Canada a better place, whether Canada should encourage immigrants "like us," or whether foreign-born Canadians should take second place to those who are Canadian-born (see Figure 17.2). On all of these questions, opinion tends to be more or less evenly divided in both groups. The picture changes, though, when the questions relate to how well immigrants fit in. Now there are signs that Québec francophones do have less positive views. They were more likely to say that immigrants should try harder to be like other Canadians and (except in 1993) they were more likely to agree that recent immigrants do not want to fit in. They were also much less likely to agree that immigrants make an important contribution.

There are signs of a hardening of opinion between 1993 and 1997. It is tempting to attribute this to the aftermath of the 1995 referendum and the perception that "the ethnics" deprived the Yes side of victory. It turns out, though, that committed sovereignists and steadfast federalists held very similar views in 1997 on whether immigrants make an important contribution and whether recent immigrants try to fit in. They differed only on the question of giving priority to the Canadian-born, and those who strongly *favoured* sovereignty were less likely to agree with what is tantamount to discrimination against "new Canadians" (54 per cent).

More important than views about sovereignty are perceptions of a threat to the future of the French language in Québec.[27] In 2000, 66 per cent of those who considered the future of French to be in jeopardy thought that immigrants do not try to adapt to their new surroundings, compared with 54 per cent of those who were more sanguine. This difference may not be huge, but it is sufficient to explain most of the difference between francophones in Québec and anglophones in the rest of Canada. Control for linguistic insecurity and the difference between the two groups is reduced to a mere two points.

It bears emphasis that there was a noticeable softening of attitudes towards immigrants on the part of Québec francophones between 1997 and 2000. A similar trend was apparent among English-speakers in the rest of the country. What makes the shift in opinion on the part of Québec francophones especially interesting is that it occurred despite an apparent increase in linguistic insecurity over the same period.[28] It is not that linguistic insecurity mattered less in 2000, but, rather, that the shift in opinion was just as apparent among those who were fearful for the future of French.

They may continue to be less sanguine about the extent to which newcomers try to adapt, but, in 2000, fully two-thirds of Québec francophones agreed that immigrants make an important contribution. And when the focus shifts from immigrants to racial minorities, there are indications that Québec francophones are *more* accepting of ethnic and racial diversity than English-speaking Canadians outside

FIGURE 17.3

Percentage Wanting to do More for Racial Minorities

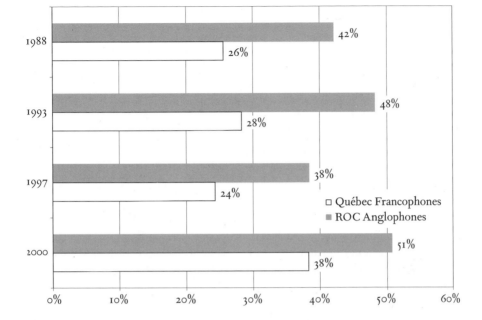

Québec. Québec francophones are significantly more likely to say that more should be done for racial minorities (see Figure 17.3).[29] In 1988, the question asked about "ethnic minorities," and it is plausible that some Québec francophones interpreted this term to include their own community. However, the difference persisted when the wording was changed to "racial minorities" in 1993, so it cannot be attributed simply to self-interest.

The difference also persisted when respondents were asked about concrete measures to benefit members of racial minorities. The 2000 Canadian election study asked respondents whether they favoured or opposed requiring political parties to have more members of racial minorities as candidates, to remedy the numerical underrepresentation of racial minorities in the House of Commons. Fifty-four per cent of Québec francophones were in favour, compared with only 41 per cent of the other language group. A similar number of Québec francophones (53 per cent) responded affirmatively when asked about action to remedy the lack of women MPs in the House of Commons. This is telling, because the questions were not being posed to the same respondents. One random half-sample was asked about racial minorities and a second random half-sample was asked about women, so we can rule out any strain to consistency motivating these responses.[30] This suggests that

Québec francophones may be more sympathetic to minorities in general, reflecting perhaps their own experience of being a minority within Canada.

Aboriginal Peoples

A similar explanation was advanced when studies of attitudes towards Aboriginal peoples in the 1970s and 1980s revealed that Québec francophones were *more* sympathetic than English Canadians to the plight and aspirations of Canada's Aboriginal peoples.[31] Laczko, for example, suggests that this reflected "a sense of shared collective minority status within the Canadian state."[32] Not only has there been a common experience of subordinate status, but the claims of Québec francophones and Aboriginal peoples alike have been couched in the language of collective rights and have had a territorial basis.[33] We could add a shared history of resistance to assimilation and concern for the survival of their cultural distinctiveness as additional sources of Québec francophones' greater sympathy for Aboriginal peoples.

Much has changed, though, since the 1970s. Laczko himself points to the deterioration of relations between Québec francophones and Québec's Aboriginal peoples.[34] These tensions came to a head in 1990 with two events. The first was the role of Elijah Harper in the collapse of the Meech Lake Accord. His vote in the Manitoba Legislature led to the perception among some Québec francophones that "Native people as a group were ... the ones who, in collusion with a hostile English Canada, had killed the constitutional agreement" that would have recognized Québec as a distinct society and brought Québec back into the Canadian constitution.[35] This was followed in the summer by the violent standoff at Oka, just outside Montréal. The Oka crisis was precipitated by a dispute over land for a golf course. The resulting confrontation pitted Mohawk protesters against both the provincial police force and the Canadian armed forces. In addition to the death of a police officer, a major bridge linking Montréal to the South Shore was blockaded for several weeks.

Laczko speculates that these tensions may have wrought a shift in the climate of opinion on Aboriginal peoples among Québec francophones. He notes a 1994 poll finding that showed that more than half of Québec francophones were under the impression that Aboriginals living on Québec reserves enjoyed a higher standard of living than other Quebecers, a perception quite at odds with the realities of reserve life. He concludes that opinion on Aboriginal rights is presenting "a more ambiguous picture" than heretofore, though he cautions that the hardening of opinion on the part of Québec francophones might represent a temporary aberration rather than the beginning of a trend.[36]

There is reason, though, for greater pessimism on this score. There are deeper structural sources of deterioration in relations with Québec's Aboriginal peoples. As Salée notes, Aboriginal claims pose a much more fundamental challenge to

FIGURE 17.4

Feelings about Aboriginal Peoples (mean scores on a 0 to 100 scale)

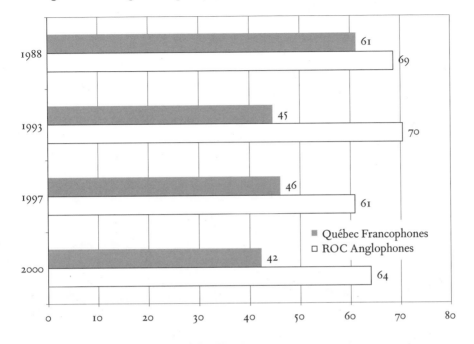

Québec identity than do Québec's "cultural communities." Where immigrant minorities seek to share in existing power structures, the claims of Québec's Aboriginal peoples ultimately imply autonomous power structures. Moreover, Québec francophones and Aboriginal peoples across Canada have become, in a very real sense rivals as "recognition seekers within the Canadian polity."[37] To many Québec francophones, this is the legacy of official multiculturalism and the Charter. Each, in turn, undermined the "hierarchy of identities" implicit in the notion of two founding nations.[38] Even more fundamentally, though, Aboriginal claims threaten Québec's territorial integrity. For Salée, it is precisely the territorial component of Aboriginal claims that makes them so problematic for Québec: "The Aboriginal question challenges Québec francophones in a most brutal fashion.... The Québec identity comes with a profound sense of belonging to the territory traditionally recognized by cartographers. Many believe that to carve up this territory would be tantamount to carving up the identity of Québecers."[39]

There has, indeed been a decline in sympathy on the part of Québec francophones for the conditions and aspirations of Canada's Aboriginal peoples. When asked to rate their reactions to Aboriginal peoples in the 1988 Canadian Election Study, francophones in Québec provided less favourable ratings than anglophones outside

FIGURE 17.5

Views about Aboriginal peoples (percentage agreeing)

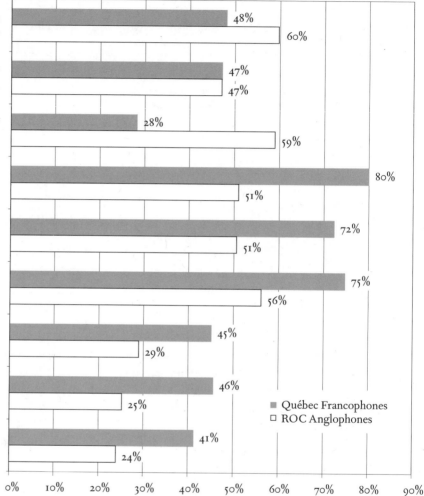

Québec, but their average rating was still clearly favourable (see Figure 17.4). The picture changes quite dramatically by the time of the 1993 Canadian Election Study. On the one hand, the gap between the mean ratings of the two language groups has widened to 25 points on a 0 to 100 scale and, on the other hand, the ratings of Québec francophones are now clearly unfavourable on average. What we are seeing is the imprint on Québec public opinion of the failure of the Meech Lake Accord and the Oka crisis in the summer of 1990. These legacies endure. There is no sign of warmer feelings on the part of Québec francophones in 2000. Moreover, this hardening of feelings is largely confined to *francophones* in Québec.[40] The mean ratings of Québec *anglophones* are as favourable as those of their counterparts in the rest of the country.

There is a similar trend in views about the conditions of Aboriginal peoples (see Figure 17.5). In 1988, Québec francophones were as likely as not to think that more should be done for Aboriginal peoples and they were, actually, less likely to believe that Aboriginal peoples should be completely assimilated.[41] Again, the three most recent Canadian Election Studies provide a starkly different portrait of the climate of opinion among Québec francophones. By 1992, English-speakers in the rest of Canada were twice as likely as Québec francophones to respond that more should be done for Aboriginal peoples. Meanwhile, Québec francophones were much more likely to think that Aboriginal peoples could be as well off as other Canadians if they just made more effort, and they were more likely to believe that Aboriginal peoples are in fact better off than other Canadians. Not surprisingly, Québec francophones also were more likely to say that the federal government should cut spending for Aboriginal peoples. These differences show little sign of abating in the most recent study.

Sovereignists are, if anything, a little more sympathetic towards Aboriginal peoples. In 2000, for example, the strongest sovereignists rated Aboriginal peoples a little more positively on average (45 per cent) than committed federalists (40 per cent) did, and they were not quite as inclined (74 per cent) as their opponents (81 per cent) to believe that Aboriginals needed to try harder. However, the larger fact remains that strong federalists and sovereignists alike tend to harbour more negative feelings than English-speaking Canadians in the rest of Canada (and in Québec). This is understandable in light of Pierre Martin's observation that, "In a way, the distinct situation of Québec in North America makes almost every franco-phone Québecker, to some degree, a 'nationalist.'"[42] And Aboriginal claims cut to the heart of the nationalist project, however defined.

Interestingly, the gap between francophones in Québec and anglophones outside Québec narrows when we turn from views about the conditions of Aboriginal peoples to perceptions about their rights (see Figure 17.6). It is clear that opinions relating to Aboriginal rights depend very much on the phrasing of the question: the vaguer the principle at stake, the more positive the opinion within both language groups. This is a typical finding of surveys on tolerance and civil liberties as well: the more grounded the situation, the less favourable opinion becomes.[43] In the 1988 Canadian Election Study, respondents were asked whether native peoples should be able to have a large amount of self-government "as long as their system of government conforms with principles of Canadian democracy" or "no matter what system of government they adopt." "Neither" was also a possible response option.

FIGURE 17.6

Views about Aboriginal Rights (percentage agreeing)

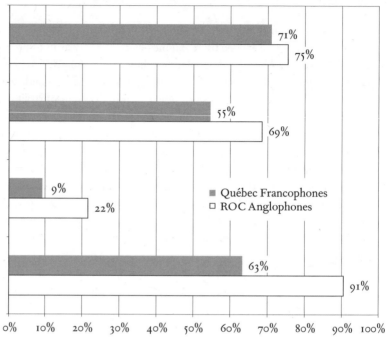

Francophones in Québec were actually more likely (14 per cent) than anglophones in the rest of the country (6 per cent) to respond "no matter what" and they were almost as open to the notion of a large amount of self-government provided it was in conformity with Canadian norms. The 1992 study on the referendum on the Charlottetown Accord asked respondents whether they agreed or disagreed with "recognizing the right of Canada's Aboriginal peoples to govern themselves." In the wake of the Oka crisis, Québec francophones proved to be less accommodating on this question. Interestingly, though, the gap between the two language groups is not as wide as Figures 17.4 and 17.5 might have led us to expect. And when the implications of self-government are spelled out, as they were in the 1993 study, both groups are much less open to the idea of self-government. However, even when the implications are spelled out, the gap remains.

Perhaps the most interesting result in Figure 17.6 is the relatively high proportion of Québec francophones who agreed in 1997 that Aboriginal communities have the *right* to remain part of Canada if Québec separates. Almost two out of three Québec francophones recognized such a right. And even among those who were very favourable to Québec sovereignty, nearly half (48 per cent) agreed with the proposition. This is remarkable, given that "territorial reappropriation ... can only be seen as a frontal assault against the Québec identity, whose subconscious foundation is intimately tied to a geography considered as inalienable and untouchable."[44] Should commitment to this right actually be put to the test, of course, opinion might well be different. Nonetheless, the willingness of two in three Québec francophones to recognize this right in the abstract can only reinforce Salée's observation that, "It would be incorrect, and intellectually dishonest, to conclude that the absence of the will to satisfy completely Aboriginal identity claims demonstrates the narrowness and intolerance of the Québec blueprint for identity."[45]

Continentalism

Explanations of why Québec francophones appear to hold more negative views on immigration and multiculturalism have typically pointed to the importance of linguistic insecurity. We have shown that concerns about the future of the French language are indeed an important factor in explaining Québec francophones' opinions about immigrants' efforts to fit in. This emphasis on the perceived threat to the French language poses a puzzle: if Québec francophones are so fearful for the future of their language, why did both provincial political parties come out in favour of a comprehensive free trade agreement with the United States? If Québec francophones feel culturally threatened by the immigrant presence in their midst, why are they not even more fearful of opening up Québec to the influence of the vast English-speaking neighbour to the south? The Canada-US Free Trade Agreement (FTA) and then the North American Free Trade Agreement (NAFTA) will surely "maintain if not accentuate the presence of English on the Québec economic and cultural market."[46] The contrast with Canada outside Québec is striking: for many English-Canadian nationalists, these agreements posed a fundamental threat to Canada's identity, if not to Canadian sovereignty itself. It is all the more puzzling given the fact that "conventional theories of international political economy would lead one to predict that Québec should have resisted free trade."[47] In linking nationalism and protectionism, Martin explains, these theories imply that "free-trade nationalism" is "a contradiction in terms."[48] He concludes, though, that "Québec did not endorse free trade *in spite* of its nationalism; it endorsed free trade *because* of its nationalism."[49]

Bashevkin was the first to examine empirically whether Québec nationalism is characterized by "an unavoidable tilt toward continentalism."[50] The notion was plausible, she argued, because closer Québec-US relations would serve as "a political and entrepreneurial counterweight to English Canada."[51] Moreover, Québec needed more US investment to ensure economic growth. However, when she examined views on foreign investment controls in Canada,[52] she found little support for the notion that Québec nationalists are continentalist. In fact, Québec nationalists proved to be more supportive of the proposed measures than Québec francophones, in general, *and* non-Quebecers, in general.

Bashevkin's data were taken from a survey conducted in 1979, 10 years before the ratification of the FTA. It is quite possible that Québec nationalists have become more continentalist in the wake of the shift to continental free trade. This is Martin's thesis.[53] He argues persuasively that FTA was strategically important to sovereignists and moderate nationalists alike. Free trade with the United States offered moderate nationalists the hope of "more economic autonomy, while preserving the political security of federalism" *and* undercutting the need for secession.[54] Meanwhile, the institutionalization of trade liberalization offered sovereignists a way not only of reducing Québec's dependence on Canadian markets, but also of easing the transition to independence and its attendant costs.

It turns out that Québec francophones *in general* are more continentalist than English-speaking Canadians in the rest of the country. This parallels Neil Nevitte's finding, based on the 1991 World Values Survey, that Québec francophones were more likely than non-Quebecers to support doing away with borders between Canada and the United States.[55] Since 1988, the Canadian Election Studies have asked respondents whether Canada's ties with the United States should be closer or more distant. In every survey, Québec francophones have been more likely to respond that ties should be closer (see Figure 17.7). The gap was widest in 1988, when the Canada-US Free Trade Agreement dominated the election agenda, and in 1993, when the North American Free Trade Agreement had been negotiated. In both years, the gap was 20 percentage points or more. Not surprisingly, the gap has narrowed in the two recent elections. After all, the two trade agreements have institutionalized the closer ties that many Québec francophones wanted. Nonetheless, a gap persists: Québec francophones are more likely to want even closer ties.

Interestingly, the gap is smaller when we look at support for the trade agreements themselves (see Figure 17.8). Québec francophones were more likely to support the FTA in 1988 (and to remain supportive in 1993) and NAFTA in 1993, but English-speakers outside Québec were more supportive of both agreements than we might anticipate on the basis of Figure 17.1. It turns out, the latter's views about ties with the US were more strongly related to their support or opposition to the FTA in 1988 (tau=.50) than they were among Québec francophones (tau=.30). On the one hand, compared with English-speakers outside Québec (84 per cent), Québec francophones who wanted closer ties in the abstract were less likely (71 per cent) to come out in favour of the concrete agreement. On the other hand, Québec francophones who resisted closer ties were much more willing (35 per cent) than English-speakers in other parts of Canada who felt the same way (16 per cent) to

FIGURE 17.7

Percentage Wanting Closer Ties with the US

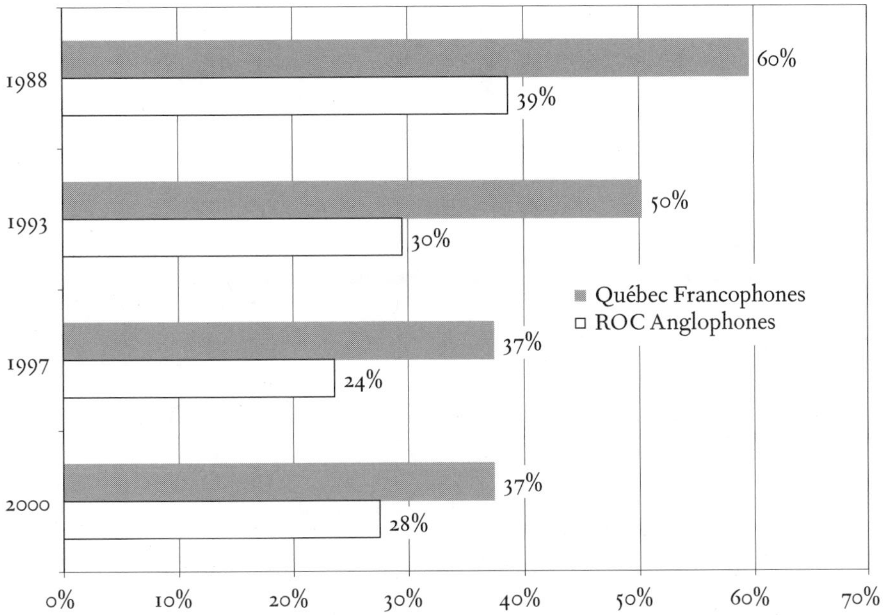

support the FTA. One possible explanation is that opinion about the FTA was less polarized in Québec because both the Parti Québécois and the provincial Liberal party supported the agreement.

This explanation gains credence when we look at the strength of support and opposition to the FTA. Opinion about the agreement was much more polarized outside Québec in 1988. Among supporters, 34 per cent of English-speakers outside Québec felt strongly, compared with only 25 per cent of Québec francophones. Even more tellingly, 51 per cent of opponents outside Québec felt strongly, compared with only 21 per cent of their Québec francophone counterparts. Support for NAFTA was much more lukewarm among Québec francophones (10 per cent) and English-speakers in the rest of the country (18 per cent) alike, but NAFTA's opponents within the latter group were significantly more likely to feel strongly (56 per cent) than their francophone counterparts in Québec (26 per cent). Continentalism, it appears, is much less of an axis of conflict among Québec francophones than it is beyond Québec's borders.

There were three aspects of trade and investment relations with the United States that really differentiated the opinions of Québec francophones (see Figure 17.9). First, they were much more likely to believe that more US investment was

FIGURE 17.8

Support for FTA and NAFTA

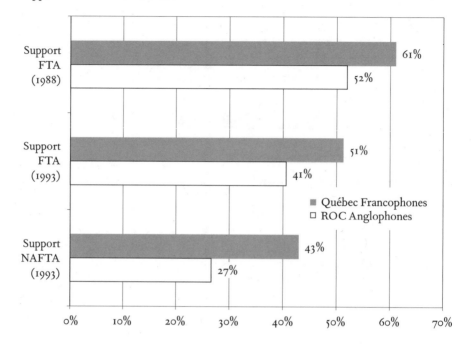

necessary. While we cannot tell from the survey data, this could plausibly be because Québec francophones see US capital as "a convenient and less ideologically troubling source of development."[56] Second, Québec francophones were much less concerned that the FTA would compromise control over key industries or pose a threat to social programs. Among English-speakers outside Québec (and within Québec), concern on both fronts was higher. These differences are not simply a function of the gap in support for the FTA. The two communities were much closer when it came to fears about job loss, on the one hand, and the perceived need for a larger market and a hedge against US protectionism, on the other (see Figure 17.9).

By 1993, however, the gaps had widened on these questions. Just over half (53 per cent) of Québec francophones believed that unemployment had gone up because of the FTA, compared with three-quarters of those in the other language group (74 per cent). A similar gap appeared (58 per cent versus 73 per cent) when it came to the view that NAFTA would cause unemployment to go higher still. Meanwhile, Québec francophones (54 per cent) and especially English-speakers outside Québec (41 per cent) were much less persuaded that NAFTA was necessary to maintain Canada's position in the US market. Not surprisingly, support for the FTA had dropped by 1993, and support for NAFTA was lower still.

FIGURE 17.9

Views about FTA and US Investment in 1988 (% agreeing)

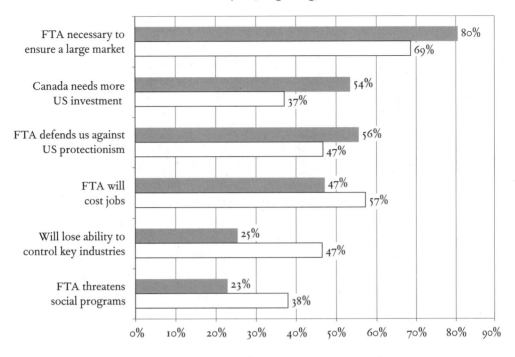

Since then, the unemployment rate has dropped and by 1997, a majority of Québec francophones (71 per cent) and English-speakers in the rest of Canada (62 per cent) alike agreed that free trade has been a good thing for Canada. By 2000, these figures had risen slightly to 75 per cent among Québec francophones and remained at 62 per cent in the other language group.

Clearly, though, for all the changes in opinion wrought by the advent of comprehensive trade agreements with the United States and by the upturn in the job situation, Québec francophones remain more continentalist at the beginning of the twenty-first century than non-Quebecers. The question remains: "Why?" We can rule out at least three plausible explanations. One possibility is that Québec francophones are simply more open to liberalized trade in general. However, when asked in 1997, Québec francophones were actually more likely (85 per cent) than English-speakers outside Québec (69 per cent) to agree that more should be done to protect Canadian business. They were also slightly less likely (58 per cent) to agree that international trade creates jobs, compared with 64 per cent in the other language group. Continentalism, then, is not simply another manifestation of a more open attitude towards the liberalization of trade on a global scale. In fact, Québec francophones' views both on the need for protection and whether international trade creates jobs are virtually unrelated to their opinions about closer ties with the United States (tau of .04 and .03, respectively). Among English-speakers outside Québec, on the other hand, there is a closer link, at least with respect to international trade (tau of .19).

A second possible explanation for why Québec francophones are more continentalist is that they simply feel more warmly about the United States. However, when respondents in 1988 were asked how they felt about Americans on a 0 to 100 scale, there was little difference between the mean ratings provided by Québec francophones (58 per cent) and English-speakers in the rest of Canada (60 per cent). The same was true when respondents were asked a similar question about the United States in 1997 (except that the mean scores were a little lower at 56 per cent and 58 per cent, respectively). Meanwhile, in both 1993 and 2000, Québec francophones actually rated the United States significantly lower on average (53 per cent in 1993 and 49 per cent in 2000) than did the other language group (60 per cent in 1993 and 58 per cent in 2000).

Finally, we find no support for the argument that sovereignists are more continentalist than federalists. Indeed, like Bashevkin, we find that sovereignists are actually *less* continentalist than federalists.[57] In both 1988 and 2000, we compared the views of those who were very favourable to sovereignty with those who were very opposed. In both years, the strongest sovereignists were less supportive (48 per cent in 1988 and 28 per cent in 2000) of closer ties with the United States than the staunchest federalists (59 per cent in 1988 and 49 per cent in 2000).

On the other hand, strong sovereignists *were* more likely (74 per cent) to support FTA than strong federalists (63 per cent) in 1988. How can we resolve this apparent contradiction? Martin has argued convincingly that sovereignists see free trade agreements as a way of "reducing the economic risks of sovereignty … [through] the combination of open markets, which favour the natural north-south flow of economic transactions, and strengthened international institutions, which reduce the risks of open trade for a smaller political unit."[58] This thesis suggests that it is the institutionalization of ties that enhanced the appeal of the FTA to sovereignists. Sovereignists may be more cautious when it comes to endorsing closer ties *without* the accompanying institutional safeguards. A second possibility is partisanship. Strong federalists were more likely to identify with the federal Liberal Party than with the Conservative government that had negotiated the agreement. Finally, for sovereignists, support for the free trade agreements likely has an important strategic component. These agreements make it easier to "sell" sovereignty: if Québec has guaranteed access to the North American market, the argument goes, it does not need Canada.

We are still left with the puzzle of why Québec francophones are more continentalist overall than non-Quebecers. Our data point to one possible answer and that is the language barrier. We cannot test this possibility directly, but it is revealing that perceptions of a threat to the future of the French language were unrelated to views about closer ties with the United States. This contrasts with the pattern we observed for opinions about immigrants. The absence of a similar relationship with continentalism strongly suggests that Québec francophones may not share the fears of cultural assimilation that have often characterized views about the United States among English-speakers in the rest of Canada.

Discussion

Reviewing the findings of earlier studies of the attitudes of Québec francophones, Laczko observed that, "during the 1970s Francophones were apparently *more* sympathetic than Anglophones were to Indian [*sic*] affairs, and *less* sympathetic than Anglophones to immigration and the ethnic diversity that it has produced."[9] This picture no longer holds. Québec francophones are now *less* sympathetic than English-speakers outside Québec to the conditions and aspirations of Canada's Aboriginal peoples (though tellingly the gap narrows when concrete proposals are under discussion). And while we cannot claim that Québec francophones have become *more* sympathetic than non-Quebecers to immigration and ethnic diversity, the picture that emerges from our analysis of Canadian Election Study data is much more mixed than it once was. Certainly, any global generalization about ethnocentrism is unwarranted. Québec francophones' views about immigration are little different from those of the other language group and they are actually more open to racial diversity. This is significant, given the changing complexion of immigrant flows. Where Québec francophones do appear less positive is in their views on the integration of immigrants, but here, too, there is a softening of attitudes, even among those who are fearful for the future of the French language.

The perception of threat has been a thread running through discussions of Québec francophones' attitudes towards immigration and ethnic diversity since the 1970s. This only serves to underline the contrast in orientations towards the United States. Québec francophones clearly are more open to closer ties with the United States than are English-speakers outside Québec. Far from perceiving a threat to their language and culture, Québec francophones seem to see the language as a barrier to assimilation. The contrast with the cultural insecurity of English-Canadian nationalists vis-à-vis the United States is striking. It is interesting, though, that the continentalist division between Québec francophones and non-Quebecers has narrowed considerably since the "free trade election" of 1988.

What can we say about the future trajectories of opinion? If the key to Québec francophones' views of immigrants is their perceived threat to the future of French, then it will take a reduction in the perception of threat for those views to become more positive. The policy initiatives of the 1990s were designed to encourage more French-speaking immigrants to come to Québec and to facilitate the integration of those who arrived with no knowledge of the language. To the extent that those policies are successful, the climate of opinion may well improve. Set against that, however, are the realities of a French-speaking enclave that constitutes a mere 2 per cent of the North American population and a globalized culture that places a premium on the ability to speak English.

It is harder to be sanguine about shifts in opinion about Aboriginal peoples. The threat that Aboriginal claims pose are of a quite different order of magnitude. They are not simply a matter of integrating to one, rather than the other, linguistic community, but challenge the very conception of Québec identity. In fact, given the context of Aboriginal claims, what is perhaps surprising is that the gap between Québec francophones and English-speakers outside Québec (who have yet to experience their own "Oka crisis") is not a good deal wider. That it is not should give pause to those who still subscribe to the old stereotypes of Québec francophones as xenophobic and ethnocentric.

Notes

The authors wish to acknowledge the financial support of the Social Sciences and Humanities Research Council of Canada under its Major Collaborative Research Initiatives program. The authors would also like to thank Delton Daigle for his research assistance and Alain Noel for his comments on a preliminary version of this chapter.

1. Raymond Breton, "From Ethnic to Civic Nationalism: English Canada and Québec," *Ethnic and Racial Studies* 11 (1988): 85-102.

2. France Giroux, "Le nouveau contrat national est-il possible dans une démocratie pluraliste? Examen comparatif des situations française, canadienne et québécoise," *Politique et sociétés* 16 (1997): 147.

3. Gérard Boismenu, "Perspectives on Québec-Canada relations in the 1990s: Is the Reconciliation of Ethnicity, Nationality and Citizenship Possible?" *Canadian Review of Studies in Nationalism* 3 (1996): 101.

4. Gérard Bouchard, "La nation au singulier et au pluriel: L'avenir de la culture nationale comme 'paradigme' de la société québécoise," *Cahiers de recherche sociologique* 25 (1995): 79-99; Gilles Bourque and Jules Duchastel, "Pour une identité canadienne postnationale, la souveraineté partagée et la pluralité des cultures politiques," *Cahiers de recherche sociologique* 25 (1995): 17-58; M. Labelle, "Immigration, culture et question nationale," *Cahiers de recherche sociologique* 4 (1990): 143-51; Daniel Latouche, "Le pluralisme ethnique et l'agenda public au Québec," *Revue Internationale d'action Communautaire* 21 (1989): 11-26.

5. John W. Berry, Rudolf Kalin, and Donald M. Taylor, *Multiculturalism and Ethnic Attitudes in Canada* (Ottawa: Supply and Services Canada, 1976); Ronald D. Lambert and J. Curtis, "The French and English Canadian Language Communities and Multicultural Attitudes," *Canadian Ethnic Studies* 16 (1982): 30-46; Ronald D. Lambert and J. Curtis, "Opposition to Multiculturalism among Québécois and English-Canadians," *Canadian Review of Sociology and Anthropology* 20 (1983): 193-206; Paul F. Sniderman, David Northrup, Joseph Fletcher, Peter Russell, and Philip E. Tetlock, "Psychological and Cultural Foundations of Prejudice: The Case of Anti-Semitism in Québec," *Canadian Review of Sociology and Anthropology* 30 (1993): 242-70.

6. Leslie S. Laczko, *Pluralism and Inequality*; J. Rick Ponting and Roger Gibbins, "The Reactions of English Canadians and French Québécois to Native Indian Protest," *Canadian Review of Sociology and Anthropology* 18 (1981): 222-38.

7. Daniel Salée, "Identities in Conflict: The Aboriginal Question and the Politics of Recognition in Québec," *Ethnic and Racial Studies* 18 (1995): 280.

8. Sylvia Bashevkin, "Solitudes in Collision? Pan-Canadian and Québec Nationalist Attitudes in the Late 1970s," *Comparative Political Studies* 23 (1990): 9.

9. Bashevkin, "Solitudes in Collision?" 10.

10. Two language groups are defined in terms both of first language learned and still understood and of language usually spoken at home. Given the focus on attitudes towards immigrants and immigration, people born outside Canada are not included.

11. Berry, Kalin, and Taylor, *Multiculturalism and Ethnic Attitudes*, 217.

12. Ibid., 88.

13. Lambert and Curtis, "The French and English Canadian Language Communities" and "Opposition to Multiculturalism," Leslie S. Laczko, *Pluralism and Inequality in Québec* (Toronto: University of Toronto Press, 1995).

14. John W. Berry and Rudolf Kalin, "Multicultural and Ethnic Attitudes in Canada: An Overview of the 1991 National Survey," *Canadian Journal of Behavioural Science* 27 (1995): 301-20; Rudolf Kalin and John W. Berry, "Ethnic and Multicultural Attitudes," in John W. Berry and Jean Laponce, eds., *Ethnicity and Culture in Canada: The Research Landscape* (Toronto: University of Toronto Press, 1994).

15. Berry, Kalin, and Taylor, *Multiculturalism and Ethnic Attitudes*. The authors also emphasized the importance of processes of social comparison whereby feelings of relative deprivation vis-à-vis English Canadians fostered a strong sense of "ingroup solidarity, awareness of own ingroup identity, tightness of group boundaries and ethnocentrism." 220.

16. Ibid.

17. Berry and Kalin, "Multiculturalism and Ethnic Attitudes"; Richard Y. Bourhis, "Ethnic and Language Attitudes in Québec," in John W. Berry and Jean Laponce, eds., *Ethnicity and Culture in Canada: The Research Landscape* (Toronto: University of Toronto Press, 1994); Laczko, *Pluralism and Inequality*; Lambert and Curtis, "Opposition to Multiculturalism," 1995; Joseph O'Shea, "Individual versus Collective Rights in Québec," in Leo Driedger and Shiva S. Halli, eds., *Race and Racism: Canada's Challenge* (Montréal and Kingston: McGill-Queen's University Press, 2000).

18. Denis Bolduc and Pierre Fortin, "Les francophones sont-ils plus 'xénophobes' que les anglophones au Québec? Une analyse quantitative exploratoire," *Canadian Ethnic Studies* 22 (1990): 54-77.

19. Salée, "Identities in Conflict," 300.

20. *Pluralism and Inequality*, 166.

21. See Bourhis, "Ethnic and Language Attitudes."

22. "From Ethnic to Civic Nationalism."

23. Bourhis, "Ethnic and Language Attitudes"; and Laczko, *Pluralism and Inequality*.

24. *Pluralism and Inequality*, 167.

25. The question was not asked in the 2000 Canadian election study. The gaps persist, even when we restrict the definition of English-speakers outside Québec to those with English, Irish, Scots, or Welsh ancestry.

26. It is possible that some of the apparent change is an artifact of a change in question wording. In 1988 and 1993, "stay the same" was not an explicit response option. However, the percentage responding "fewer" continued to decline after the inclusion of "stay the same" among the response options in 1997.

27. The two sets of attitudes are, of course, related: 34 per cent of Québec francophones who perceived a threat were very favourable to sovereignty, compared with 16 per cent of those who did not perceive a threat.

28. Sixty per cent of Québec francophones in the 2000 study responded that they perceived a threat to the future of their language, up from 54 per cent in 1997.

29. This is true of sovereignists and federalists alike. Interestingly, some of the earlier studies of ethnic and multicultural attitudes also found that Québec francophones were more tolerant of racial diversity than anglo-celtic respondents (Lambert and Curtis, 1983), suggesting that our conclusions are not bound to the particular questions asked in the Canadian Election Studies, but reflect a more enduring orientation.

30. English speaking people in the rest of the country were even less supportive (30 per cent) of action on behalf of women than they were on behalf of racial minorities.

31. Laczko, *Pluralism and Inequality*; J. Rick Ponting and Roger Gibbins, "The Reactions of English Canadians and French Québécois to Native Indian Protest," *Canadian Review of Sociology and Anthropology* 18 (1981): 222-38.

32. Laczko, *Pluralism and Inequality*, 165; see also Sylvie Vincent, "La révélation d'une force politique: les Autochtones," in G. Daigle, ed., *Le Québec en jeu: Comprendre les grands défis* (Montréal: Les Presses de l'Université de Montréal, 1992), 749-90.

33. Laczko, *Pluralism and Inequality*, 161-62.

34. Ibid.

35. Ibid., 164.

36 Ibid.

37. Salée, "Identities in Conflict," 277.

38. Ibid., 301.

39. Ibid., 295.

40. Higher education is typically associated with greater tolerance (see, for example, Herbert McClosky and Alida Brill, *Dimensions of Tolerance: What Americans Believe About Civil Liberties* [New York: Russell Sage, 1983]), but the hardening of feeling among Québec francophones is evident at every education level. In 2000, for example, mean ratings of Aboriginal peoples ranged from 41 per cent among those who did not complete high school to 48 per cent among university graduates.

41. The 1988 Canadian Election Study used the term "native peoples" in English. Since 1993, the terminology has been "Aboriginal peoples." In French, the term "Autochtones" has been used throughout, so we can rule out the possibility that the changes in the climate of opinion between 1988 and 1993 are an artifact of differences in question wording.

42. Pierre Martin, "When Nationalism Meets Continentalism: The Politics of Free Trade in Québec," *Journal of Federal and Regional Studies* 5 (1995): 14.

43. James L. Gibson, "Pluralistic Intolerance in America," *American Politics Quarterly* 14 (1986): 269-93; McClosky and Brill, *Dimensions of Tolerance.*

44. Salée, "Identities in Conflict," 302.

45. Ibid., 304.

46. Bourhis, "Ethnic and Language Attitudes," 337.

47. Martin, "When Nationalism Meets Continentalism," 2.

48. Ibid., 1.

49. Ibid., 2.

50. "Solitudes in Collision?" 10.

51. Ibid., 6.

52. Her data came from the 1979 Social Change in Canada survey.

53. "When Nationalism Meets Continentalism."

54. Ibid., 13.

55. Neil Nevitte, "Toward A North American Community? Canada, the United States and Mexico," in Donald Berry, ed., *Bringing Values Back In: Value Change and North American Integration* (Boulder, CO: Westview Press, 1995), 185-209.

56. Bashevkin, "Solitudes in Collision?"

57. Ibid.

58. "When Nationalism Meets Continentalism," 20.

59. *Pluralism and Inequality*, 165.

18

Interculturalism: Expanding the Boundaries of Citizenship

ALAIN-G. GAGNON AND RAFFAELE IACOVINO

Introduction

This chapter addresses the impact of polyethnicity on political communities by focusing specifically on the symbolic aspect of citizenship—the markers of a country's self-identification through which citizens are said to exhibit a sense of social cohesion and allegiance for effective democratic participation in a given polity.[1] What are the symbolic "anchors" that frame and define sentiments of belonging in a democratic polity? How do we evaluate such criteria in light of the challenge of polyethnicity? Such questions will be explored through a comparative conceptual assessment of the Canadian policy of multiculturalism and Québec's model of interculturalism. Both of these liberal political communities have responded to the challenge of polyethnicity by formulating models of integration that go beyond the idea of "benign neglect" in cultural matters. A comparison of two distinct approaches may serve to elucidate some of the issues and challenges confronting culturally heterogeneous liberal democracies more generally.

Citizenship extends further into the realms of formal representation (electoral systems, representation) and issues related to social entitlements (the relationship between the state, the market, and society). Indeed, citizenship involves multiple mechanisms, practical and symbolic, of social and political inclusion. This chapter does not claim to cover the issue of citizenship exhaustively, but merely attempts to address an increasingly salient aspect of citizenship that has gained prominence in political communities of liberal democratic states. This heightened awareness may be due in part to migration and the subsequent growth of identity politics, incomplete nation-building projects, or, in the case of small nations such as Québec, the quest for recognition as a host society in its own right—its affirmation as a "global society." In short, the aspect of citizenship discussed here relates to sentiments of belonging and solidarity. This chapter will proceed, in the first section, to unpack the concept of multiculturalism as a theoretical paradigm, and attempt to develop normative criteria with which to evaluate current models of cultural pluralism in Canada and Québec. The second section will offer a conceptualization of Québec's model of interculturalism, and the third section will assess the models in light of their functions as concurrent nation-building strategies. Regardless of strict definitions, multiculturalism, or the "politics of difference," constitutes a response to the late twentieth-century phenomenon that has been called the "age of migration," inviting countries to redefine the rules of political life.[2]

Multicultural versus Homogeneous Citizenship

According to Christian Joppke, multiculturalism is an intellectual movement premised around the concepts of equality and emancipation. Its appeal lies in the defence of particularistic, mostly ascriptively defined group identities that reject Western universalism as the basis for allegiance to a given collectivity. Western universalism in this view is seen as "falsely homogenizing and a smokescreen for power."[3] As such, multiculturalism implies the salience of multiple cultures coexisting within a limited state-bounded territory, rejecting the modern Jacobin view of the nation-state and the homogenization of identities. The key issue is that such "cultural communities" are said to regulate not only specific aspects, but the entire life conduct and sources of meaning of the individual. Joppke summarizes:

> Defenders of multiculturalism have argued that the exercise of individual rights and liberties depends on full and unimpeded membership in a respected and flourishing cultural group. But the tension between liberalism and multiculturalism is real, as the latter is based on the ontological primacy of the group over the individual and, if necessary, takes into the bargain the suppression of individual claims.[4]

This approach views assimilation or acculturation as a violation of the integrity or dignity of the individual, whose cultural habits should be recognized fully as an integral element of a person's identity. Any stifling of particular cultural expressions, by way of the symbolic construction of a larger socio-cultural identity, limits the individual's capacity for self-realization, thus negating the liberal-democratic ideal that individuals, as members of the larger society, be given the means by which to explore their own life chances and directions. Ascriptive aspects of identity—particular cultural sources of meaning—are said to act as prerequisites to self-realization. Stripping such sources of meaning in the name of universal markers of identity, in the construction of a mononational (Jacobin) identity that is meant to provide common purpose, denies the individual the empowerment to determine the direction of his/her life through participation in the affairs of society. Iris Marion Young argues that if one conceptualizes such cultural differences as "relationally constituted structural differentiations," then the supposed link between citizenship and the common good is upheld, because,

> It becomes clear that socially situated interests, proposals, claims and expressions of experience are often an important resource for democratic discussion and decision-making. Such situated knowledges can both pluralize and relativize hegemonic discourses, and offer otherwise unspoken knowledge to contribute to wise decisions.[5]

The polemic between universal and particular bases of allegiance thus demarcates the contours of the debate. The idea of multiculturalism can be embedded in a wider area of post-national consciousness—some say post modern, or "identity politics"—as an attack on the assimilation implied by nation-states with the aim of attaching a sense of common purpose to citizenship status.[6]

The sentiments associated with equal citizenship status have long been regarded by liberal theorists as integral to democratic political communities—for fostering the civic-spiritedness, mutual trust, and allegiance required for meaningful self-government, self-realization, and political stability. Kymlicka notes that the classical liberal response to polyethnicity has been to develop common (undifferentiated) bases of citizenship in a universal vein. In this view, the integrative function of citizenship requires that cultural differences be treated with "benign neglect," in order to forge a shared civic identity, regardless of collective, or group-based, identity differences. Iris Marion Young notes that proponents of such arguments view any particular demands based on sociological "differences" as detrimental to the functioning of democracy, due to the contention that citizens concern themselves less with the common good and more with their own group-based, or "special," interests.[7] Kymlicka summarizes this view, thus:

> Citizenship is by definition a matter of treating people as individuals with equal rights under the law.... [If it is group differentiated], nothing will bind the various groups in society together, and prevent the spread of mutual mistrust or conflict. If citizenship is differentiated, it

no longer provides a shared experience or common status. Citizenship would yet be another force for disunity, rather than a way of cultivating unity in the face of increasing social diversity. Citizenship should be a forum where people transcend their differences, and think about the common good of all citizens.[8]

In short, culture, like religion, should be left to the private sphere and should not concern the state. The only way for a democracy to flourish is for the political community to be predicated on universal bases of belonging that are "civic" and amenable to identification across cultures.

For defenders of multiculturalism, however, the notion of "benign neglect" is in itself infused with cultural meaning. It simply represents a preservation of the status quo in many previously homogeneous nation-states. State inactivity, thus, reflects a failure to adapt to dynamic, polyethnic realities in society. Minority cultures are rendered unequal participants and second-class citizens if their sources of meaning are neglected in the public realm. As such, the ideal of equality cannot be achieved if citizens are forced to conform to a "civic" denial of identity, a renewed self-definition for individual citizens. Isajiw notes that the force of multiculturalism arises out of a particular sentiment in which citizen dignity is tied to the collective dignity of one's ethnic community. Multiculturalism represents a set of values whereby the recognition of identity needs is linked to the instrumental power of members of ethnic communities.[9] Charles Taylor explains,

> The demand for recognition in [the politics of multiculturalism] is given urgency by the supposed links between recognition and identity…. The thesis is that our identity is partly shaped by recognition or its absence, often by misrecognition of others, and so a person or group of people can suffer real damage, real distortion, if the people or society around them mirror back to them a confining or demeaning or contemptible picture of themselves. Nonrecognition or misrecognition can be a form of oppression, imprisoning someone in a false, distorted or reduced mode of being.[10]

The recognition of cultural pluralism by the state is a call for increased citizen empowerment. How can citizens in a polyethnic society equally be empowered to share and participate in the affairs of the polity, without sacrificing self-fulfilling "modes of being"? How have states adapted to such challenges?

The theoretical contours outlined above reveal that normative evaluations of integration rest on two broad considerations. The first is that full citizenship status requires that all cultural identities be allowed to participate equally in democratic life, without the need to tone down conceptions of identity to the level of the individual. Empowerment implies that citizens are permitted to maintain their cultural differences when affecting the affairs of the polity through democratic participation. This implies some acceptance that policy outcomes will reflect some groups' differentiated initiatives by the central state. The second concerns the salience of unity in any society. Here, the key element is a sense of common purpose in public matters, in order that deliberation is not confined to pockets of self-contained, fragmented collectivities in juxtaposition. These two broad poles are at issue in any model of integration and subsequent conceptualizations of citizenship status. In short, a balance must be struck between the *equal empowerment of group identities* as active constituents of the larger political community and the need for a *common ground for dialogue*, for the purposes of unity—a *centre* that also serves as a marker of identity in the larger society and denotes a pole of allegiance for all citizens.

"Interculturalism": Québec's Model of Cultural Pluralism

Québec's persistent attempts to establish itself as a "host society" can be traced back to the Quiet Revolution, the increased activity of the state in many dimensions of the lives of Quebecers, and can be qualified as a project gradually to construct Québec citizenship. Otherwise stated, the idea of Québec citizenship cannot be divorced from the larger issue of Québec's national affirmation in the face of pan-Canadian attempts at nation-building. In constructing its own model for integration, Québec has, in effect, formulated a response to the Canadian policy of multiculturalism—a position that affirms the primacy of the Québec state in the areas of politics and identity, and challenges the reductionist notion that Québec is a monolithic ethnic group. The treatment of diversity, when placed in a larger historical context, can be seen as but one of the many areas of contention between opposing visions regarding Canada's constituent political communities, or national groupings. Kymlicka highlights this progression towards a formal Québec citizenship,

> The notion of a distinctly Québécois citizenship has seen a spectacular progression. In the space of a lifetime, the dominant identification of Québecers has been profoundly transformed. From Canadians, they became French-Canadians, then Franco-Québécois and finally, Québécois.... These transformations cannot be interpreted as a simple evolution of a sort of sentiment of belonging to the tribe. Rather, they represent a continuing progression of Québécois identity, in which its foundations have passed from non-citizenship to citizenship.[11]

Historically, the main impetus for the increasing salience of the discourse on Québec citizenship has been language—the idea of the French language being the primary vehicle for the preservation and flourishing of Québécois identity. Language was indeed the precursor to concerns over immigration and integration. With an alarming decline in the birth rate in Québec, state actors became concerned with the tendency of allophones to gravitate linguistically towards the anglophone community. Immigration and integration became inextricably tied to the fate of the Québec nation. With a Ministry of Immigration in place since 1968, the Québec government was very active in almost all aspects of immigration except recruitment and reception.[12] Some of its activities included an employment search service for newly arrived immigrants, support for community groups with the aim of adaptation, and the funding of cultural and linguistic heritage programs, including the translation of literature into French, in the hopes of building bridges between the allophone and francophone communities. From 1969 to 1979-80, the Ministry's budget grew from 2.8 to 20 million dollars. The Québec government took a wide range of measures in the areas of language acquisition and cultural adaptation, the initial steps towards a more fully articulated model of integration. Indeed, as a response to critics who view the legal imposition of French on individuals as an affront to liberal principles of individual rights over society, Joseph Carens turns to this participatory aspect of the model to defend the liberal democratic merits of the Québec model. In his words,

> The duty to learn French is intimately connected to the duty to contribute and to participate in society, which is connected, on this account, to fundamental democratic principles. Learning French is, among other things, a necessary means to participation in society so that if one can defend the duty to participate, and I think one can, one can defend the duty to learn French.[13]

As Michael Behiels argues, however, many such positive (as perceived by allophones[14]) measures were overshadowed by more controversial language legislation, which began with the Liberal Government's Official Language Law (Bill 22) in 1974, in which Québec was formally declared a unilingual French society, and later culminated in the Charter of the French Language (Bill 101) in 1977, under René Lévesque's Parti Québécois Government. This was seen by many as a hardline approach, out of line with the bridge-building measures in progress, and was generally rejected by allophones and anglophones.[15] With the adoption of the Charter, the PQ government affirmed the vision of a linguistically unilingual and ethnically pluralistic political community in Québec, a vision that nourished subsequent models of integration to this day. As early as 1981, the Québec model began taking shape, with a publication entitled *Autant de façons d'être Québécois.*[16] The essence of the publication was that unlike Canadian multiculturalism, Québec integration would stress the idea of "convergence." This will be elaborated below. Of significance here is the fact that the Québec model explicitly challenged the Canadian variant as a primary basis for citizenship. The jurisdictional battles of the Quiet Revolution and the linguistic conflicts of the 1970s culminated in a fully articulated discourse centred on citizenship in Québec. As such, it can no longer be disputed that Québec constitutes a host society whose model of integration ought to be emulated by other liberal democracies.

Québec has adopted as its official position a discourse of interculturalism to address its polyethnic composition. This view contends that the incorporation of immigrants or minority cultures into the larger political community is a reciprocal endeavour—a "moral contract"—between the host society and the particular cultural group, with the aim of establishing a forum for the empowerment of all citizens—"a common public culture."[17] The "moral contract" is summed as follows:

> a society in which French is the common language of public life

> a democratic society where participation and the contribution of everyone is expected and encouraged

> a pluralist society open to multiple contributions within the limits imposed by the respect for fundamental democratic values, and the necessity of inter-community exchange.[18] (Author's translation.)

The Government of Québec describes the general thrust of this model:

> The "moral contract" affirms that, in its options for society, it follows that rights and responsibilities apply as much to immigrants, on the one hand, as to the receiving society itself (including Québécois of cultural communities already integrated or on their way to being integrated) and its institutions, on the other hand. Being a Québécois means being engaged in fact in Québec's choices for society. For the immigrant established in Québec, adopting Québec as an adopted land, an engagement is required as from all other citizens, to respect these choices of society. It is the simultaneous existence of complementary rights and obligations attributed to all parties—and to engage in solidarity in relationships of reciprocal obligation—which justifies the vocabulary of "moral contract" to designate the general environment governing such relations with the aim of fully integrating immigrants.[19]

The common public culture in this view does not consist solely of the juridical sphere—it is not a procedural definition based on formal individual rights. Instead, the basic tenets of the "moral contract" are such that the established "modes of being" in economic, political, and socio-cultural realms are to be respected as markers of identification and citizenship status, with the institutions of democratic participation acting as a point of convergence for groups of specific collective identities, in order that all may share equally in democratic life. Carens highlights this feature of the model:

> Immigrants can be full members of Québec's society even if they look and act differently from the substantial segment of the population whose ancestors inhabited Québec and even if they do not in any way alter their own customs and cultural patterns with respect to work and play, diet and dress, sleep and sex, celebration and mourning, so long as they act within the confines of the law.[20]

In establishing a model based on the convergence of collective identity, the French language is to serve as the common language of public life: this is seen as an essential condition for the cohesion of Québec society. Indeed, the French language constitutes the basis for Québec's self-definition as a political community. In this view, language is not conceptualized as an individual right. Rocher et al. elaborate:

> In Québec ... the French language is presented as a "center of convergence" for diverse groups which can nevertheless maintain and let their specificity flourish. While the Canadian policy allows the privilege of an individualist approach to culture, Québec's policy states clearly the need to recognize French as a collective good that requires protection and encouragement.[21]

The contours of "public life" are somewhat ambiguous—indeed, what constitutes a "public exchange" is not often clear. As a general rule, the confines of public space are not relegated solely to the activities of the state, but encompass 'the public space of social interaction' as well. For example, students may, as a matter of individual right, communicate in any language they wish on the playground of a francophone school. However, language use in the classroom is considered public space. More examples of what constitutes 'private interaction' are relations with family members, friends, colleagues, or anyone involved in the social circle of the individual in question, in which the choice of language use is of a consensual nature. Again, in the words of Rocher et al.:

It must be emphasized that valuing French as the common language does not imply in itself the abandonment of a language of origin, for two reasons. The first is related to the democratic nature of society that must respect individual choices. The second is a question of utility: the development of languages of origin is considered an economic, social and cultural asset. It must be stressed that a fundamental distinction exists between the status of French as a common language of public life and that of the other languages.[22]

Thus, an emphasis on the proficient use of the French language is taken as a minimal condition of the exercise of common citizenship—as an instrument of democracy. To quote Giroux,

It is of importance that the French language is taken first and foremost as a condition of the exercise of citizen rights; the modern nation cannot claim to be a forum for discussion and decision-making without the existence of a community of language.[23]

Moreover, the host society expects, as a matter of obligation, that members of minority groups fully integrate into the larger community, with the expectation that all citizens are to contribute and participate in the social fabric of the common public culture. As a democratic community, this implies that once citizenship is attained, all members are equally encouraged to "participate in defining the general direction of society."[24]

With regard to the eventuality of conflict arising between individuals or groups, the method of resolution must correspond to democratic norms. This point is important because it highlights a perspective fundamentally different from an emphasis on procedural legal channels. The Québec model stresses that, in the initial manifestation of conflict, deliberative measures such as mediation, compromise, and direct negotiation are preferred, leaving as much initiative and autonomy as possible to the parties in question. Legalistic measures and the recourse to specified rights are to be an option of last resort. In other words, this model values deliberation, mutual understanding, and, generally, dialogue as fundamental characteristics of democratic life, in the realm of civil society, and is instrumental in the aim of fostering a cohesive and participatory conception of citizenship.

The treatment of difference in this model does not imply a society built on the juxtaposition of ethnic groupings, in a "mosaic"; nor does it reduce citizenship status simply to procedural safeguards from state intrusion through the codification of fundamental individual rights, and the assimilation of particular identities to universal principles.[25] The Québec model of cultural pluralism operates fundamentally in the tradition of parliamentary democracy—with an emphasis on deliberation and representation. Pagé summarizes,

> In conceptualizing a common civic space, common civic norms constitute the basis for social cohesion. The norms transcend particular ethnic cultures and are broad enough to govern the actions of a society consisting of individuals belonging to a plurality of ethnic groups. *These norms are established by democratic institutions, which are capable of accounting for pluralism in seeking always, through decisions arrived at by democratic voting, as large as possible a consensual base, which does not limit itself only to the majority ethnic group or an ensemble of minority groups.*[26]

Within the framework of basic principles—a commitment to the peaceful resolution of conflict, a Charter of Rights and Freedoms, in order to provide legal recourse for the protection of individual and group rights, equality between the sexes, a secular state, and equality and universality of citizen access to social provisions (e.g., healthcare)[27]—interculturalism attempts to strike a balance between individual rights and cultural relativism by emphasizing a "fusion of horizons," through dialogue and consensus. Through the participation and discourse of all groups in the public sphere, the goal of this approach is to achieve the largest possible consensus regarding the limits and possibilities of the expression of collective differences based on identity, weighed against the requirements of social cohesion and individual rights in a common public context. The recognition of cultural differences is assumed in such a view and the sources of meaning accrued from cultural identity are acknowledged as an explicit feature of citizen empowerment, yet an obligation is placed on all parties to contribute to the basic tenets of a common public culture.

In the final analysis, the recognition of minority cultures is built into the model; the "moral contract" is an integrative principle whereby ethno-cultural groups are given the empowerment to contribute, in a common language, and to make their mark on the basic principles of the common public culture. Difference is recognized within the limits of societal cohesion and political community, not as a *fundamental starting point* for common identification and unity.

Concurrent Nation-Building Strategies

Public/civic policies cannot be assessed without a clear understanding of political processes related to the strategy of nation-building. This qualification is particularly salient in the Canadian case, where the precarious nature of pan-Canadian identity has traditionally been, in itself, somewhat of a "national symbol" (*sic*), due to the persistent existential question in Québec. Indeed, as will be shown below, policy-makers at the federal level, charged with defining the bases of belonging to Canada, have not only faced the challenges associated with the incorporation of diverse cultural identities, but have been confronted with a national minority with established political institutions within a well-circumscribed territory. This fact represents a qualitatively different challenge confronting Canada in comparison to that of the United States. As Joppke makes clear, each society's actual response to immigration and polyethnicity does not stem merely from an abstract model that is subsequently applied to the real world,

> The concrete meaning of multiculturalism and its linkage to immigration differs significantly across these societies. These differences are conditioned by distinct traditions of nationhood, the specific historical contexts in which immigration has taken place, and the existing immigration regimes.[28]

As such, the case of Québec, although formally a province of Canada, nevertheless merits independent consideration, as the Québec state has negotiated extensive authority over immigration. Moreover, Québec constitutes a distinct political community with a well-defined collective cultural project that includes the integration of immigrants into that project. Canada's other provinces, by contrast, have been content to leave this policy area in the hands of the federal government. In short, Québec should be viewed as a host society in its own right, with its own historical and cultural development, its own sense of nationhood, and a distinct discourse with regard to the general orientations and choices of society.

There are, indeed, political imperatives at work in such policy outcomes. This chapter has attempted to clarify the meaning of the term "multiculturalism"—distinguishing between its use as a general label for an emerging tradition in political thought and the actual policy bearing its name in Canada—in order to alleviate the ambiguities surrounding the concept. An assessment of Canadian multiculturalism cannot forego the fact that, in the final analysis, it is a policy and not an "ontological" principle devoid of contingencies. The ideal of multiculturalism must not be confused with the Canadian policy, as this is prone to stifling debate concerning the value of the policy in framing citizenship status.

Returning to the normative backdrop for evaluating integration as developed above, it is clear that the Canadian strategy was related both to the goal of unity and to the fostering of citizen dignity through the recognition of particular cultural affiliations. First, it seeks to achieve unity through a pan-Canadian nation-building project that emphasizes the primacy of individual rights in a constitutional Charter of Rights and a choice of language use, between French or English, across the country. Superimposed on individual rights is the official recognition equally of all constituent cultures. Such recognition, however, is largely a symbolic concession—the fabrication of an identity marker based on the voluntary adherence to particular cultural allegiances. In Weinfeld's words,

> In the absence of any consensus on the substance of Canadian identity or culture, multiculturalism fills a void, defining Canadian culture in terms of the legitimate ancestral cultures which are the legacy of every Canadian: defining the whole through the sum of its parts.[29]

It was hoped that by forging a common identity throughout the country based on the "sum of its parts," the identity marker for unity could be universal—the equal recognition of all cultures, within a regime governed by individual rights and bilingualism. In this way, adherence to particular cultural attachments could be voluntary for all *individuals*, while at the same time claiming to "empower" citizens of minority cultures through reductionist means—Canada's symbolic order was to be based on the negation of any particular cultural definition. Bourque and Duchastel argue that the Canadian response, by conceptualizing citizenship in such terms, has in effect altered social relations to the point of damaging the exercise of democracy. The Canadian political community, in this sense, is predicated on the judicialization of social interactions, to the detriment of the deliberative aspects of representative democracy. The idea of public space for citizen participation, reflection, and deliberation within the political community is reduced to a narrow forum of rights-bearers. Deliberative assemblies give way to the "legalization" of social relations, preventing parliaments from being responsible for organizing social life and, ultimately, preventing citizens from identifying with others in the political community.[30]

According to Kymlicka, the final outcome of Canadian multiculturalism as a symbol for identification is analogous to the United States in its failure to differentiate between national minorities and polyethnic communities. The fundamental difference between the two is that the former strives for self-determination while the latter seek inclusion. Canada's policy fails to address this distinction—multiculturalism becomes a mechanism by which to quell legitimate national aspirations—thus, it fundamentally shares with the US model a certain homogenizing, or universalizing of identity, albeit through cultural relativism. Kymlicka argues that the American reluctance to recognize minority nations is a direct result of its assimilationist model, a fear that such recognition will trickle down to polyethnic communities and, thus, undermine the bases for unity.[31] Canada's policy stems from similar fears. However, Canada's response was to elevate the status of cultural groups to the same level as that of national minorities. Both are universal, both are bound by nation-building projects that stress unity, and both fail in any significant way to recognize territorially defined, group-differentiated rights as a federal principle.[32]

As such, the Canadian response was not predicated on a genuine commitment to the "ideology of multiculturalism" as a pillar upon which to frame citizenship status. The goal was unity, in the face of a national minority challenge. Québec's national identity was placed, constitutionally, alongside every other minority culture as a basis for identification.[33] In Giroux's words,

> The partial recognition of ancestral rights reveals, *a contrario*, a refusal to recognize the Québec nation.... As such, demands by national minorities, those of cultural communities, and those of the majority group are being considered without explicitly accounting for the definitive criteria of legitimacy attributed to a nation which allow[s] for a viable and effective democratic order.... In effect, without valid criteria for inclusion and exclusion, all demands become acceptable; thus it becomes possible to pit group demands against one another and to transform pluralism into a zero-sum game.[34]

In Taylor's terms, multiculturalism, as such, fails to appreciate the "deep diversity" in Canada, in which difference can be recognized on tiered levels in view of particular groupings' political aspirations and historical/territorial/linguistic realities. In adopting a strategy for unity similar to the American approach—uniformity from coast to coast based on universal principles—the Canadian policy, in effect, failed to recognize that national minorities, as opposed to polyethnic communities, seek to provide a "centre" for identification, their own pole of allegiance necessary for unity and common purpose. In other words, national identity in Québec assumes a self-determining project for society. The community of reference for all citizens under the banner of multiculturalism, however, is Canada. Bourque et al. summarize,

> This ideology ... defines itself in relation to the territorial state: it circumscribes a community of belonging to the state within a country—Canada. It thus privileges, clearly, national dimensions of the production of the community, even though the discourse struggles to find a coherent representation of the Canadian nation. This Canadian nationalism finds its full significance in its opposition to the "counter-nationalisms" of Québec and the Aboriginals.[35]

The arguments put forth above are predicated on the notion that Canada's similarity to the United States flows from the assumption that equality stems from an emphasis on the individual and on what characteristics such individuals share with others across the country. The Canadian Constitution protects individuals from collective intrusions. It can be argued that the failure to achieve unity and common purpose is not inherent in the model of multiculturalism adopted. Rather, disunity is a product of federal dynamics—Canada cannot claim the status of a single and unified host society. One can assess the policy independent of the Québec question, which may largely explain the motivation for the policy but not its actual effects as a model for integration. If we disregard the variable of multinationality in Canada, has multiculturalism been successful in integrating immigrants and ethnic groups? Indeed, if we begin with the assumption that Canada constitutes a single political community, or host society, we can proceed to evaluate the success of multicultural-ism without considering disunity in terms of the fragmentation of "national alle-giance." Thus unity can be conceptualized as the extent to which minority groups feel as though they belong to a single community called Canada, and actually participate in the general affairs of the larger society.

As a response to critics who view multiculturalism as a divisive force in Canada, Will Kymlicka provides some empirical data that demonstrates the success of multiculturalism in terms of the integration of minority cultures.[36] Indeed, the line of criticism in this chapter does not challenge the integrative success of the policy. The claim is that, due to the imperatives of nation-building and for the purposes of unity in the face of the Québec question, Canada chose to adopt a "lowest com-mon denominator" formula that rejected the recognition of culture as an aspect of belonging altogether. Again, Trudeau's "just society" is predicated on the notion that any emotive attachment to a polity is destructive and backward, and that progress requires an emphasis on reason, which is universal, to serve as a guiding principle in any citizenship regime. If we look closely at Kymlicka's indicators for integration, however, it may be argued, that although integration has been rather successful, it came at the expense of the recognition and preservation of minority cultures—which, in the final analysis, is the defining feature of ideological multi-culturalism.

The Canadian model operates along the primacy of individual rights in a consti-tutional Charter of Rights, with an interpretive clause for the recognition of diverse cultural affiliations. The interpretive clause is the only element of differentiation from American assimilation. There is no democratic imperative for the recogni-tion of diverse minority cultures other than a legal/procedural provision that may be invoked if the minority group in question chooses to do so. This is a pivotal conceptual distinction between the Canadian and Québec models and it stems from the nature of the expectations of democracy itself. The fact that Canadian identi-ty—the way citizens relate to each other and to the state in determining societal preferences—is predicated on such terms implies that there is no public culture on which minority cultures can make their mark. Multiculturalism in Canada does not reflect the recognition of diverse cultures; rather, to be blunt, it refers to the denial of culture altogether in defining the limits and confines of public space. Public space is based on individual participation via a bill of rights. To return to Kymlicka's assessment on the success of Canadian multiculturalism in terms of integration, we note a dearth of evidence regarding the extent to which minority cultures feel as though they have been able to persist in living according to the sources of meaning garnered by their cultural affiliations. In his defence, this undertaking would require a large-scale empirical study, and the fact that he was able successfully to operationalize "integration" merits credit, as it deepens the conceptual discourse surrounding these models of integration. However, the success of minority groups within indicators such as "naturalization rates," "political participation," including the institutional avenues of participation; "official language competence"; "intermarriage rates," and lack of territorial enclaves of cultural groups[37] are addressed to those critics who view multiculturalism as divisive to the forging of a strong Canadian identity. They do not speak explicitly for the preservation and flourishing of minority cultures within the political community—the capacity of such groups to participate in and affect the public affairs of the country without shedding their particular group identities. The debate itself takes place outside of the imperatives of ideological multiculturalism. In other words, these criteria may very well be addressing a regime committed to assimilation.

The virtue of Québec's model of interculturalism is that it strikes a balance between the requirements of unity—an identity basis—and the recognition of minority cultures. Québec's model of integration is not assimilatory as that of the US, nor does it conceptually fall into cultural relativism and fragmentation in its commitment to cultural pluralism. The idea of empowerment, as it pertains to marginalized ethno-cultural groups, is such that integration is a necessary prerequisite to full participation in the construction of a "common public culture" as an identity centre. Identification with and participation through a variety of cultures is not ruled out as a basis for citizenship status, yet the possibility of enclosure and ghettoization is discouraged because the recognition of particular cultural identities is de facto the *recognition of the right and obligation to participate* in the polity, not the recognition of culture as existing in self-contained communities, in a vacuum of space and time. In other words, recognition is an *outcome* of participation; it is in contributing to the development of a common public culture, to larger consensual bases of allegiance and identification, without a rejection of the established symbolic order offered by Québec society as it has evolved historically, that members of minority cultural groups can make a difference regarding their status as citizens. In this sense, the unity and solidarity sought by any model of citizenship is viewed as a process, to be constructed by the various parties involved through exchange and dialogue, rather than a model that offers a pre-existing blueprint of recognition.

Interculturalism, as a model for addressing polyethnicity, represents a forum for citizen empowerment, not retrenchment. From the initial premise that a national culture consists of a "daily plebiscite," in Renan's conceptualization, the Québec model rests on the idea that the common public culture be inclusive of all groups in its changing and evolutionary fabric. Jeremy Webber has located this dynamic aspect of a national identity in the idea that communities are forged through public debates in a common language through time. Shared values, in themselves, do not provide the sense of allegiance necessary for a national community to thrive. Indeed, disagreements about the major orientations of society are perhaps emblematic of a healthy political community, because they demonstrate that people are concerned with the state of the community. The democratic quality of a constantly changing political community lies precisely in the idea that citizens are able to identify with and make an impact on the current streams of public debate in society—and this requires that citizens interact within the framework of a common vernacular.[38] In short, Carens states it succinctly, "In integrating immigrants, Québec is transforming not only their identity but its own as well."[39] As such, the French language is not meant to define a static culture into which immigrants and cultural minorities are expected to "melt." Rather, French is the conduit through which the disagreements, contentions, and conflicts inherent in a culturally diverse society can be aired in a situation of normal politics. In the end, participation implies some degree of political conflict. The political community is based on a shared language, and challenges to the prevailing tenets of the "national culture" are not viewed as threatening, but are encouraged as a normal and healthy effect of democratic deliberation.

Conclusion

Two general considerations are pertinent in assessing the models presented as they apply to polyethnicity and democratic citizenship. First, the model must consider unity as a basis for democratic stability—which provides a shared sentiment, a common ground for dialogue. In other words, a pole of allegiance, which acts as a centre of convergence for identity, is required for active participation in a democratic polity. Second, the recognition of difference and a respect for the sources of meaning of minority cultures is an integral element of the equality of citizenship status—of citizen dignity or empowerment. In traditional liberal thought, such goals are incompatible. The involvement of group-differentiated recognition is said to mitigate the former ideal, in which equality emanates from shared adherence to universal principles and culture is treated with "benign neglect" in the public sphere. Recognizing cultural distinctions shatters such unity and renders citizens unequal.

This discussion is not meant as a radical argument for post-national identity politics; indeed, the normative merits of unity in any given state have been explicitly acknowledged. Nor is it meant to prescribe a formula for unity in a specifically federal context. It seeks to demonstrate the merits of interculturalism as an alternative model for integration, and to show that Canadian multiculturalism has been and continues to be a product of nation-building efforts rather than a genuine commitment to the main tenets of ideological multiculturalism. In other words, it is an element of a political strategy by the central state to forge a strong commitment, by its citizens, to Canada as a single and unified political community. Canadian multiculturalism should not be viewed as an example of the emerging ideology of multiculturalism and its implications for the redefinition of the legitimacy of nation-states in the case of polyethnic societies. The main tenets of Canadian citizenship are not very different from those of the United States. Indeed, the place of culture in Canadian conceptions of citizenship is liberal—it is about building a nation based on universal principles. A model of cultural pluralism along the lines of Québec interculturalism makes a more serious effort to balance the prerogatives of unity with the preservation and flourishing of minority cultures. The enduring problem confronting the Québec model, one that would have to be taken into account in any future attempts at empirical verification, is the idea of competing interpretations of citizenship by those targeted for integration in the first place. As Labelle and Levy have demonstrated in interviews with leaders of ethnocultural groups, there is continuing ambivalence with regard to the legitimacy of the Québec model in the eyes of ethnocultural groups.[40]

The Québec model is unlike the others, in that it is embedded in a larger project for national affirmation. The fact that it can be included legitimately as a model for integration demonstrates at the very least the strides that Québec has made in the area of citizenship, and perhaps such conceptual overviews can spark some interest in more empirically-based research in the future. Whether or not such research can be undertaken in a context of competing models of citizenship within a single territory should not undermine efforts to include conceptually the model of interculturalism in debates about recognition and integration in liberal democracies.

Notes

1. Will Kymlicka and Wayne Norman note that citizens' perceptions about their political communities, their sense of belonging and level of commitment, has become an increasingly salient concern for contemporary political theorists, and that this is due partly to the challenge of integrating minority groups in established liberal democracies. In their words, "the health and stability of a modern democracy depends, not only on the justice

of its institutions, but also on the qualities and attitudes of its citizens: e.g., their sense of identity, and how they view potentially competing forms of national, regional, ethnic, or religious identities; their ability to tolerate and work together with others who are different from themselves; their desire to participate in the political process in order to promote the public good and hold political authorities accountable; ... Without citizens who possess these qualities, the ability of liberal societies to function successfully progressively diminishes." Will Kymlicka and Wayne Norman, eds., *Citizenship in Diverse Societies* (Oxford: Oxford University Press, 2000), 6.

2. Will Kymlicka, *Multicultural Citizenship: A Liberal Theory of Minority Rights* (Oxford: Clarendon Press, 1995), 193.

3. Christian Joppke, "Multiculturalism and Immigration: A Comparison of the United States, Germany and Great Britain," *Theory and Society* 25 (1996): 449.

4. Ibid., 452.

5. Iris Marion Young, *Inclusion and Democracy* (Oxford: Oxford University Press, 2000), 7.

6. For more on multiculturalism's challenge to liberal models of citizenship, see Andrea Semprini, *Le multiculturalisme* (Paris: Presses universitaires de France, 1997).

7. Iris Marion Young, *Inclusion and Democracy*. See in particular Chapter 3, where Young (p. 83) offers a review of arguments that "construct group specific justice claims as an assertion of group identity, and argue that the claims endanger democratic communication because they only divide the polity into selfish interest groups."

8. Kymlicka, *Multicultural Citizenship*, 174-75.

9. W.W. Isajiw, "Social Evolution and the Values of Multiculturalism," paper presented at the Ninth Biennial Conference of the Canadian Ethnic Studies Association, Edmonton, Alberta, October 14-17 1981, cited in Evelyn Kallen, "Multiculturalism: Ideology, Policy and Reality," *Journal of Canadian Studies* 17, 1 (Spring 1982): 52.

10. Charles Taylor, "The Politics of Recognition," in Amy Gutmann, ed., *Multiculturalism: Examining the Politics of Recognition* (Princeton, NJ: Princeton University Press, 1994), 25.

11. Will Kymlicka, *Théories récentes sur la citoyenneté* (Ottawa: Multiculturalism and Citizenship, Canada, 1992), 40, quoted in Micheline Labelle, *Immigration et diversité ethnoculturelle: Les politiques québécoises*, Cahiers du Programme d'études sur le Québec de l'Université McGill, 13 Sept. 1998, 13. Authors' translation.

12. The Couture-Cullen Agreement, signed in 1978, however, would grant extensive powers in recruitment and reception to the Québec Government.

13. Joseph H. Carens, *Culture, Citizenship and Community: A Contextual Exploration of Justice and Evenhandedness* (Oxford: Oxford University Press, 2000), 128.

14. Allophones are defined as members of Québec society that are neither English (anglophone) or French (francophone) in origin. It is a significant grouping with regard to any discussion of citizenship, in that they are, in large part, targets of integration for the host society.

15. Michael D. Behiels, *Québec and the Question of Immigration: From Ethnocentrism to Ethnic Pluralism, 1900-1958* (Ottawa: Canadian Historical Association, 1991).

16. Marcel Gilbert, *Autant de façons d'être Québécois. Plan d'action à l'intention des communautés culturelles* (Québec: Ministry of Communications, Direction générale des publications gouvernementales, 1981).

17. For more on the conceptualization of the principles of the "common public culture" as it is understood in Québec see Julien Harvey, "Culture publique, intégration et pluralisme," in *Relations* (Oct. 1991); and Gary Caldwell, "Immigration et la nécessité d'une culture publique commune," in *L'Action Nationale* 78, 8 (Oct. 1988).

18. Gouvernement du Québec, *Au Québec pour bâtir ensemble. Énoncé de politique en matière d'immigration et d'intégration* (Québec: Ministère des Communautés culturelles et de l'Immigration du Québec, Direction des communications, 1990), 15.

19. Gouvernement du Québec, Conseil des relations interculturelles; "Culture publique commune et cohésion sociale: le contrat moral d'intégration des immigrants dans un Québec francophone, démocratique et pluraliste," in *Gérer la diversité dans un Québec francophone, démocratique et pluraliste: principes de fond et de procédure pour guider la recherche d'accommodements raisonnables* (1994), 11. Authors' translation.

20. Joseph H. Carens, *Culture, Citizenship and Community*, 131.

21. François Rocher, Guy Rocher, and Micheline Labelle, "Pluriethnicité, citoyenneté et intégration: de la souveraineté pour lever les obstacles et les ambiguïtés," in *Cahiers de recherche sociologique* 25 (1995): 221.

22. Rocher et al., "Pluriethnicité," 225. Authors' translation.

23. France Giroux, "Le nouveau contrat national est-il possible dans une démocratie pluraliste? Examen comparatif des situations française, canadienne et québécoise," *Politique et Sociétés* 16, 3 (1997): 137. Authors' translation.

24. Gouvernement du Québec, *Au Québec*, 13. Authors' translation.

25. Julien Harvey, "Culture publique, intégration et pluralisme," *Relations* (Oct. 1991), 239: "Intégration dit contact culturel intermédiaire entre l'assimilation et la juxtaposition, tenant compte des deux cultures en contact et constituant une nouvelle synthèse et une nouvelle dynamique."

26. Michel Pagé, "Intégration, identité ethnique et cohésion sociale," in Fernand Ouellet and Michel Pagé, eds., *Pluriethnicité et société: construire un espace commun* (Québec: Institut québécois de recherche sur la culture (IQRC), 1991), 146-47. (Authors' translation, emphasis.)

27. Gouvernement du Québec, *La gestion de la diversité et l'accommodement raisonnable* (Montréal: Ministère des Communautés Culturelles et de l'Immigration, 1993), quoted in Rocher et al., "Pluriethnicité," 225.

28. Joppke, *Multiculturalism and Immigration*, 454. Joppke compares Germany, Great Britain and the United States.

29. Morton Weinfeld, "Myth and Reality in the Canadian Mosaic: 'Affective Ethnicity,'" *Canadian Ethnic Studies* 13 (1981): 94.

30. Gilles Bourque and Jules Duchastel, "Multiculturalisme, pluralisme et communauté politique: le Canada et le Québec," in Mikhaël Elbaz and Denise Helly eds., *Mondialisation, Citoyenneté et Multiculturalisme* (Sainte-Foy, Les Presses de L'Université Laval, 2000).

31. Will Kymlicka, "Ethnicity in the USA," in Montserrat Guibernau and John Rex, eds., *The Ethnicity Reader: Nationalism, Multiculturalism and Migration* (Cambridge: Polity Press, 1997), 240. See also Bourque and Duchastel (2000), *Multiculturalism* 159, where the authors argue that Canadian multiculturalism is in large part a product of the refusal to allow the country be defined in multinational terms. The Canadian political community was, thus, in itself founded on this negation of multinationality precisely because of the perceived imperative to negate Québec's place as a "national minority."

32. For more on the distinction between national minorities and polyethnic communities in the framing of citizenship status, see Gilles Paquet, "Political Philosophy of Multicul-

turalism," in J.W. Berry and J.A. Laponce eds., *Ethnicity and Culture in Canada* (Toronto: University of Toronto Press, 1994).

33. For more on the idea that official multiculturalism represents a wholesale redefinition of Canada's constitutional order in terms of collective identity references, see Fernand Dumont, "La fin d'un malentendu historique," in *Raisons Communes* (Montréal: Éditions du Boréal, 1995), 33-48; and Gilles Bourque and Jules Duchastel, "La représentation de la communauté," in *L'identité fragmentée* (Montréal: Éditions Fides,1996), 29-51.

34. France Giroux, "Le nouveau contrat national est-il possible dans une démocratie pluraliste? Examen comparatif des situations française, canadienne et québécoise," *Politique et Sociétés* 16, 3 (1997): 141. Authors' translation.

35. Gilles Bourque, Jules Duchastel, and Victor Armony, "De l'universalisme au particularisme: droits et citoyenneté," in Josiane Ayoub, Bjarne Melkevik, and Pierre Robert eds., *L'Amour des Lois* (Sainte-Foy/Paris: Presses de l'Université Laval/l'Harmattan, 1996), 240.

36. Kymlicka's work is mainly directed towards the contentions of Neil Bisoondath. Bisoondath argues that, in the Canadian model, minority cultures are recognized, a priori, in a vacuum of space and time, which tends towards ghettoization and fragmentation in terms of allegiance to a larger polity. Bisoondath argues this point forcefully, labelling the phenomenon "cultural apartheid." The contention here is that multiculturalism, in effect, defines culture provisionally—in a static sense—and prohibits full social interactivity. In other words, the dynamic nature of cultural sources of meaning are neglected, resulting in the stagnant "folklorization" or "commodification" of cultural production, reducing culture to "a thing that can be displayed, performed, admired, bought, sold or forgotten ... [it is] a devaluation of culture, its reduction to bauble and kitsch." As such, neither unity nor the dignity the citizen accrues from cultural recognition is achieved here. This is the result of recognizing cultures in juxtaposition, without any expectation that such cultures may contribute to the overall direction of the larger society in an evolutionary interplay of ideas. The substantive elements of minority cultures, their bases of meaning, are virtually predetermined and unchanging, disregarding the very real effects of displacement into a new context. See Will Kymlicka, *Finding Our Way: Rethinking Ethnocultural Relations in Canada* (Toronto: Oxford University Press, 1998); and Neil Bisoondath, *Selling Illusions: The Cult of Multiculturalism in Canada* (Toronto: Penguin Books, 1994), 83.

37. Kymlicka, *Finding Our Way*, 17-19.

38. Jeremy Webber, *Reimagining Canada: Language, Culture, Community and the Canadian Constitution* (Montréal and Kingston: McGill-Queen's University Press, 1994). See in particular Chapter 6, "Language, Culture and Political Community," 183-229.

39. Carens, *Culture, Citizenship, and Community*, 133.

40. Labelle, *Immigration et diversité ethnoculturelle*, 14.

PART V

Territoriality, Globalization, and International Relations

19

Stateless Nations or Regional States?
Territory and Power in a Globalizing World

MICHAEL KEATING

Beyond the Nation-State

Recent years have seen a vigorous debate about the past, future, and present of the nation-state and about the emergence of new forms of order above, below, and alongside it. For some, the nation-state remains the fundamental unit of political and social order; for others, it is fading away; while others again argue that it is being transformed. The problem is that the nation-state is itself such a complex concept. Some observers put the emphasis on the "nation" part of the expression to claim that, given the plurality of most states, the expression is a misnomer. Others put the emphasis on the "state" part, using the expression as a synonym for a sovereign actor in world politics. It is probably most useful not as a description of a state of affairs, but as an ideal type of political order, with which we can compare regimes past, present, and future. Taken in this way, the key features of the nation-state are its internal and external sovereignty and its ability, within its territorial borders, to contain a range of social, political, economic, and cultural systems. Nation-states have often defined national cultures, in the process making a nation out of the state. They have defined the citizenry, who are the only ones endowed with full civil and political rights, and who comprise the *demos* underlying democracy. They create, define, and sustain political institutions, including systems of representation and accountability. Finally, they define and regulate a series of functional systems, in the economy, social integration, and other forms of regulation. These are, in the ideal type, linked to each other so that social solidarity is sustained by a common identity and common norms. This in turn facilitates the production of public goods and handles the externalities that could otherwise hamper economic development. Social bargains and compromises are mediated by the state, and underpinned by a common national sentiment.

To the extent that nation-states did function this way, they are being transformed by powerful forces for change, from above, from below, and laterally. Transnational integration is shifting the locus of many decisions and, although in most cases the new fora are meeting places of states, in this context individual states lose their autonomy. Political and functional reasons have at the same time led many states to decentralize, establishing or strengthening regional levels of government. Privatization and deregulation have eroded the capacity of the state in the face of the market, a trend facilitated by transnational capital flows and the strategies of large corporations. Social and cultural pluralism has reduced the state's ability to shape identities, norms, and minority cultures. State cultures are challenged by the rise of "global" (which may in fact be the US) culture and the renaissance of local and regional cultures. Individualism has eroded the old instinctive loyalties and generally the state has experienced an ideological demystification. Functional systems are escaping the boundaries of the state and reconstituting at transnational, sub-state levels, or in non-spatial forms. This is most obviously so in the economy, where transnational effects have reduced the ability of states to manage their own spatial economies; to those who say that these "globalizing" trends have occurred before, a hundred years ago, we can answer that then, too, they had radical effects on the territorial economics and politics of states.

The result has been described as the "end of territory"[1] or even the "end of democracy"[2] but what these French authors really seem to be referring to is the end of the old nation-state monopoly in defining territory. This is by no means the end of territory, since, along with certain trends to deterritorialization, we are seeing forms of reterritorialization, impelled by functional and political forces. At the same time as the phenomenon of global capital flows, trade, and the global corporation have captured attention, observers have noticed a new importance for territory in economic change and development. Despite instant communications, local languages and cultures are increasingly territorialized, since most communication is face-to-face and maintaining minority language and culture requires control of territory-based institutions (Québec, Flanders, and Catalonia are examples here).

So, we are witnessing a complex process of restructuring in which functional systems, identities, and the institutions of the state coincide ever less perfectly. This poses a series of problems for functional capacity and efficacy, for democratic legitimacy, and for the ability to strike positive-sum social bargains combining economic development with social integration and the conservation and development of vulnerable cultures. There are a number of responses to this. One is a form of hyper-individualism in which the individual becomes the sole unit of analysis, and the market the sole form of social regulation. Margaret Thatcher's famous comment that "there is no such thing as society" comes close to this, although Thatcher herself appeared well aware of the need to maintain a strong law-and-order state in order to contain the social fallout from such a prescription. More broadly, it is widely recognized that capitalism itself cannot flourish without a series of public goods, and that markets depend on a complex mix of competition and co-operation. Other responses privilege economic restructuring at global and local levels, and insist that politics and society must adapt. Ohmae's globalist phantasia[3] presents a world of dynamic "regional" economies engaged in global competition, with government and social distribution issues dismissed as mere obstacles to the attainment of the productivist Utopia.[4] The nation-state, he predicts, is on the way out, to be replaced by these "regional states," which are, in fact, less states than local productive systems.

Another response is institutional restructuring, at the transnational and sub-state levels, in order to improve functional capacity and democratic performance. The problem here is that there does not appear to be any level now that can perform all the necessary tasks at the same time. So, the European Union has been a success in promoting market integration and across a number of other policy fields, but it suffers from a lack of democratic legitimization and participation. For the last 50 years, the process has been legitimated almost entirely by its results. Decentralization to lower levels may also improve functional efficiency, as well as enhancing democratic performances, but if this goes so far as setting up new states at a smaller spatial scale than the old ones, it risks losing influence over functional processes taking place at higher levels. Instead, we must face up to a world in which functional systems, identity formation, and institutionalization take place at multiple levels.

Nationalist and regionalist parties within consolidated states are generally well aware of this phenomenon. Few of them aspire to be a nation-state in the classical sense; rather, they are seeking a capacity for self-government within the emerging transnational order. Specifically, most of the stateless nationality movements in Europe and North America have embraced free trade and transnational integration; they do not want to assume responsibility for their own defence and security; and they generally support strong transnational institutions. This debate is familiar in Québec, where for decades people have argued over various formulas for sovereignty, sovereignty-association, sovereignty with partnership, sovereignty within the supposedly integrating Americas, or asymmetrical federalism. The same is true of Europe, where Catalan nationalists are divided into those who overtly disown any ambition to independent statehood (*Convergència i Unió*) and those who believe in independence, but only when the old model of the state has given way to a united Europe of the Peoples (*Esquerra Republicana de Catalunya*). Scottish nationalists are more united on independence, but they are also pro European integration, with one sector wanting a Europe so closely integrated as largely to supersede the old state system. The same is true in the Basque Country. It is sometimes said that these movements, because of the modesty of their aims, are not true nationalisms; or that they are cunningly disguising their real aim, which is to achieve sovereign statehood. This reflects the statist obsession in social science, and the unwillingness or inability to see that there may be perfectly good reasons for nations to adopt forms of political autonomy and seek powers that make them less than fully-fledged states. What is lacking, however, is a new formula to capture this new form of order.

Looking for Concepts

To appreciate the transformation of the nation-state and the rise of new forms of social and political regulation, we need to place it in historic perspective, looking at its history and its prospective long-term futures. The nation-state can then be seen as historically contingent, one outcome out of many possible ones, and with multiple possible futures. Sweeping away the teleology that has so often dominated state historiography, we can reveal other, competing traditions of political authority, which may have lost out in the state consolidation of the nineteenth and twentieth centuries, but which never died out completely. Often these alternative traditions are based on notions of divided and diffuse authority, of pact and negotiation, rather than the principle of the sovereign and autonomous state. It is no accident that, at a time when the state is being demystified and its capacity to impose unity and authority is being challenged, these older traditions should be refurbished. Yet, while this reveals a different form of order, we are handicapped in describing and analyzing it by the incubus of the state, which has moulded the social sciences so powerfully and even dictated the vocabulary of authority. So it seems that all the terms we have available for the alternative forms of order refer to the state in some shape or form, normally by describing a state lacking in some of the classical features. The impression can be given that we are talking of a state of a second-class type. Georg Jellinek, writing in the nineteenth century, identified the "fragment of state," a political unit that had some of the qualities of statehood but lacked others.[5] The concept is a powerful one and could well describe cases that Jellinek did not mention, such as Scotland, with its distinct civil society and law or, indeed, Québec. Yet the phrase "fragment of state" appears so disparaging that it is difficult to imagine any national or regional movement embracing it willingly. Some historians write of Catalonia, between the union of the Crowns and the abolition of Catalonia's own institutions in 1714, as an imperfect or incomplete state, not to suggest that it was missing something, but merely to indicate that it did not assume all the powers and prerogatives of the nation-state.[6] Another formula was that Catalonia was an incomplete state, but a state all the same.[7] Carens similarly writes of the institutional incompleteness of nations in multinational states.[8]

Observers surveying the new complexity are similarly lost for a term that sums it all up in the way the nation-state (albeit briefly) seemed to do. It has become fashionable to label it "multi-level governance," but this term is so vague as to obscure more than it reveals, providing no guidance as to the design of functional systems or the nature of the democratic challenge. As a depoliticized concept drawn from organizational theory and rational-actor approaches, it divorces organizations as units of analysis from their social context. This imports an insidious conservative bias into the analysis, since we no longer have the old social categories and collectivities and can bring in issues of social solidarity or cultural protection and development only in the form of actor preferences. Nor is it clear whether multi-level governance is a general comment on the state of the world, or a tool of analysis enabling us to differentiate between some situations and others.

Another recent contender is the regional state, a territorial unit with its own capacity for self-government, but without the full panoply of sovereign powers. This has emerged as a functionally driven analysis of territorial restructuring around issues of economic development in a competitive global economy. At the centre of this analysis is a new focus on place as a factor in economic growth. While neo-classical regional development models saw place only as location—that is, as distance from markets, labour, or raw materials—the new approaches give it a social content.[9] In the literature on economic sociology[10] and on the social construction of the market "place,"[11] in this broader meaning, becomes a factor of production. Another key term is "social capital,"[12] by which is meant patterns of social relationships and trust that permit a balance of co-operation and competition, allowing the production of public goods and long-term collective investment[13] and overcoming the division between individual short-term rationality and long-term collective interest, which is one of the abiding problems of market capitalism. "Traded dependency," in which complementary industries can reduce their costs, has often been used to define economic regions. The new approaches add "untraded interdependency"[14] arising from the proximity of innovators and entrepreneurs and the dense pattern of informal exchanges and general milieu that this encourages. These allow for the production of regional public goods, for a longer-term approach to development and for forms of reciprocity based on trust. This associational economy[15] represents a distinct form of productive organization different from individualistic capitalism, blending co-operation and competition in complex ways. Another central idea is that of the learning region[16] in which innovation is self-sustaining and success, by fostering trust and co-operation, lays the ground for future success. Many observers have also noted a change in production technologies and systems of innovation, such that the old idea of comparative advantage—under which every region had a place in the national and international division of labour, and which underlay traditional regional policy—has given way to absolute or competitive advantage.[17]

In response to these economic, technological, political, and intellectual changes, regional development policy has been refocused. It now tends to be more decentralized, whether to the regional or the local level where the capacity for horizontal integration and knowledge of problems is greatest. There is a strong emphasis on institution-building, with a new emphasis on strategic planning. A widespread belief holds that regional-level institutions are necessary to help build networks of co-operation and partnership. Policy places less emphasis now on physical infrastructure and more on human resources development. Training policies have been widely decentralized to complement other instruments of intervention and education often has been tied into economic policy in a more direct way than before. Also, we see a strong emphasis on research, development, and technology transfer. Much effort is put into forming networks and linkages among firms and between them and universities, research centres, and governments to foster the untraded interdependencies typical of successful regions. There is less emphasis on synoptic planning or large-scale intervention and more on "steering" and selective intervention to remedy market failures. While governments tend to be wary of trying to pick winners, they focus on the need to determine the region's niche in the global economy and to foster clusters of industries that can exploit this best and sustain each other. Industry itself is defined more widely, to include traded services as well as manufacturing. Small firms and endogenous development are especially targeted, although the promotion of inward investment is still important.

While there is widespread agreement that there have been big changes, there is no consensus on what these are, how they have come about, or what determines which regions have the requisite qualities to compete in the new order. Since the qualities of individual places are the key factor, it may be that there is no "model" at all.[18] Doubts have been expressed about the tendency to generalize from a few successful cases or a partial view of reality, and even about a certain collusion between academics and practitioners to promote the new paradigm.[19] Criticisms have also been voiced about the implication in the new paradigm that regions are in competition, with the inevitable consequence of inequality.[20] This has led to a reification of the region as a unit of production, the attribution to it of a unitary interest and a form of neo-mercantilist politics in which regions are portrayed as pitched in zero-sum competition to survive in global markets. Yet, this emphasis on the imperative to compete in the global economy may be as much an ideological interpretation as a matter of reality, legitimating neo-liberal policies or social discipline.

Whatever are the merits of this new paradigm in explaining the new geography of economic production, it is another matter altogether to extrapolate from it to politics or to construct a whole model of society around it. After all, we know from the experience of European integration that functional economic change and politics are very different things; nevertheless, the term "regional state" is used to straddle both. Ohmae uses the term, without ever really defining it, to refer approvingly to a neo-liberal order in which functional systems defined by global economic competition will replace political order altogether.[21] Courchene's adaptation of the regional-state model[22] is more sophisticated and explicitly brings in issues of institutional change and public policy, but remains largely embedded within a political economy framework, referring to the capacity of a region to reposition itself within the new global economic order. It is difficult to see that the term "state" adds here to the conception of a region as defined by the recent regionalist literature,[23] especially as we are not talking of states in any sense that a political scientist or constitutional lawyer would recognize.

Beyond the Regional State

A stateless nation is clearly more than a regional system of production so that these functionalist versions of the regional state, even apart from the criticisms of the model itself, can capture only a part of the reality. Nations also are based on shared identity and a normative order.[24] Culture and language are important constitutive elements. There is also the question of social solidarity and integration, an important function of the nation-state but largely neglected, as we have seen, by the regional state literature. At a normative level, we need to see the region as a space for democratic deliberation and decision. In the narrow neo-liberal view, economic competitiveness is the only factor that matters and identity, culture, and social solidarity must be subordinated to this. Michael Porter dismisses both traditional social democracy and more recent "Third Way" formulas as distractions from the reality.[25] Since, as he claims, all regions can succeed, there is no trade-off to be made between social solidarity and competitiveness; he does not even mention culture. Ohmae believes that the prosperity generated by the competitive "regional state" will make people so happy that they will forget identity worries, even in places like Northern Ireland.[26]

More serious analyses argue that in the new transnational order of culture, identity and social solidarity can enhance competitiveness, producing a new social equilibrium to replace that of the old nation-state. Since the new models of regional production systems depend heavily on shared values, trust, and co-operation, it is argued that regions with a strong historic identity may have a competitive advantage. This underpins the initiative of the Foundation Europe of the Cultures,[27] founded by the government of Flanders to promote the concept of cultural regions as a contribution to economic growth and the adaptation of the concept by the Flemish employers' organization.[28] There are some theoretical reasons to believe that culture and language can strengthen competitiveness and that the old modernist assumption that associated minority cultures with backwardness and pitched tradition against progress certainly must be revised. Traditional languages and cultures may be revalorized and their symbolic status changed to associate them with progress. Catalan has always retained a rather high status and is spoken widely among the middle and professional classes, but in other regions there is a diglossia in which the local language is used in familiar contexts or in the rural areas, while the state language is used for high-status communication and in business. In Québec, French used to have second-class status within the world of business and changing this was one of the tasks of the Quiet Revolution. In Galicia, Wales, and the Basque Country, language policies have sought to raise the status of the local language and extend its social range. There are, however, limits to the success of linguistic normalization. It is relatively easy to extend the use of the language in the education system, where government has wide powers in provision and regulation. Matters are more difficult in the area of the economy and especially in private business, given the need to insert the region into state-wide and global networks functioning in state languages and above all in English. Catalonia has adopted an ambitious three-language policy with the aim of making its educated population fluent in Catalan, Spanish, and a foreign language, usually English or French. Some argue that only by achieving the levels of multilingualism found in small nation-states like Norway, the Netherlands or, more recently, Slovenia can the local and the global be reconciled.

It may also be that small nations, endowed with their own social institutions, may be able to respond more flexibly to external challenges and adapt to global market conditions, again like the smaller nation-states.[29] Québec's quasi-corporatist arrangements, described, no doubt with some exaggeration, as "Québec Inc." have been widely cited in this regard.[30] More recently, Ireland's economic success has been credited to its system of social concertation. Yet, again, we have to be cautious about generalizing from the model. Regional-level corporatism or milder forms of concertation require representative bodies at the regional level, capable of delivering the consent of their members, and a government able to deliver a range of policies across the fields of taxation, spending, and regulation as its part of the bargain. It also requires a strong sense of common identity transcending class divisions, which nationality might supply. Business organizations have generally shown increasing reluctance to be drawn into these sorts of bargains, whether at national or regional level, especially as they have internationalized. It is not that business does not appreciate the need for the public goods produced by regional governments;

on the contrary they have often been strongly in favour of regionalized forms of policy delivery. They are not generally willing, however, to enter into wider social partnerships or to welcome the introduction of social or cultural considerations into the regional development agenda. They have, therefore, preferred limited sectoral partnerships, or development agencies with a narrowly defined goal focused on competitiveness.

There have also been efforts to link social solidarity to the new regionalist paradigm. On general theoretical grounds it is argued that poverty is a burden to regional competitiveness and that a healthy and well-educated workforce is essential to prosperity. Proponents of the new economic regionalism often distinguish between a "low road" in which regions seek to compete through low wages and deregulation, and a "high road" in which they aim to get into higher value-added sectors and market segments. The latter is a high-cost option, involving large public investments but, it is argued, these pay off in the end. Governments have often sought to bridge the gap between policies for development and policies for social inclusion by emphasizing instruments that can do both—notably in education, training, and human capital generally. Cooke and Morgan present their version of the new regionalism, the "associational economy," as both more economically efficient and more socially just than the neo-liberal alternative.[31] Again, there is great force in these arguments, but they do not necessarily follow from the emergence of the new economic regionalism and the degree of social integration achieved depends in each case on a host of specific factors.

In the case of stateless nations, it is often claimed that they are inherently more solidaristic. In so far as this is part of the propaganda of nationalists seeking to legitimize their project, we can be sceptical. Too often it is based on stereotypes or wishful thinking. Surveys tend to show a convergence of values across states and nations, with social solidarity remaining strong in the face of neo-liberal pressures in most places. The link between nationality and social solidarity may, however, be present less as a result of inherent social virtues, than because of political competition and institutional factors. Since the nation is a collectivity, nationalists and nation-builders are likely to stress solidarity as a means of reinforcing the collective identity. Appealing broadly across the social spectrum, they are likely to avoid divisive class issues, although some nationalist parties have more of a class profile than others. It may also be that territory can replace class as the basis for social solidarity as a result of social and political change, although evidence for this is as yet sporadic. So it is perhaps not surprising that stateless, nationalist parties in North America and western Europe range ideologically from social democracy to Christian democracy, with a scattering of extreme left and extreme right versions (the Vlaams Blok). It may be possible to build a version of the regional state within a stateless nation incorporating a strong social dimension, but again this is not something that can be assumed. Italy's Lega

Nord, combining what most people would see as a thoroughly contrived nationalism with a populist neo-liberal economic program, shows that these values can be mixed and matched in different ways.

Institutions and Opportunities

Regions and stateless nations can, therefore, constitute themselves as systems of action and social regulation without transforming themselves into states, but the model will vary from one case to another. Governing institutions clearly are important, with powers broadly enough defined to permit creativity in policy and flexibility in program design. With the main powers of macroeconomic regulation remaining at the state level, and lacking their own currencies, their room for manoeuvring in economic policy is restricted. On the other hand, with the emphasis shifting to supply-side measures and the role of public goods in promoting competitiveness, they may have some key powers at their disposal. Powers over social policy are also important in order to address issues of social solidarity, and to engage in policy trade-offs among social and economic objectives. This suggests a decentralizing of welfare state functions to match regions' increasing economic role, but within a broad framework of standards, so as to prevent a "race to the bottom." Canadian social union proposals and the European Union's social chapter are a step in this direction, however weak in practice.

Institutions are also important in civil society, sharing the same boundaries as government institutions. In this way, social dialogue and structured participation in policy-making can take place. While regional corporatism might be too ambitious a goal and, in any case, too rigid a way of thinking about policy, concertation at the regional level would be possible. Broadening participation by groups and institutions in civil society will serve to broaden the policy agenda, which might otherwise be monopolized by issues of economic competitiveness, narrowly defined in a form of constraining corporatism.

Next, there is the need for an external support system. State restructuring and global economic change have in many ways reduced the dependence of regions on state policies and protection, and placed them in a more direct relationship to the market and transnational regimes.[32] This, in the regional state paradigm, is presented as a form of liberation, but it can mean equally new forms of dependency. This issue is particularly acute in North America where free trade has reduced the protective capacity of the state, leaving regions in more direct competition. Québec has generally embraced this challenge, while Ontario for a long time was more reluctant. European regions and stateless nations also are exposed to market competition, but they possess an overarching order in the form of the European Union with its own regulatory powers. Over the years, regions have sought, with varying degrees of success, to gain access to European levels of decision-making, to gain resources, and to influence policy. Europe also facilitates regional autonomy by externalizing matters formerly in the purview of the nation-state, notably competition laws, the currency, and, increasingly, human rights and security.

The conception of the region as a democratic space is subordinated in Ohmae's regional-state model to the imperative of competition, which allows no choice of policies and imposes a single logic. This is no more than a piece of ideological mystification, but the emphasis on regional competitiveness has often led to a closure of democratic debate and to a privileged role for the business community in policy-making. Here again, stateless nations may have an advantage, given the sense of common identity and the possibilities this offers for a broader debate. For this to happen, it is important that the development project be subject to political debate and open to a wide range of social interests. We have no guarantee, however, that these spaces of democratic deliberation will correspond to the functional spaces being defined by the new economic trends. So, the region or stateless nation cannot replicate the old role of the nation-state in trying to bring within the same boundaries, functional systems, identities, and institutions. Democratic spaces are reconstituting themselves at multiple levels. Rather than subordinating politics to functional logic, in the manner of Ohmae and others, or constricting functional systems to politically defined units, in the manner of classical nationalists, we may just have to accept this disjuncture. In this new context, self-government for a region or stateless nation is less a matter of autonomy in the traditional sense, and more a matter of policy capacity: the ability to frame and carry through a project of economic, social, and cultural development. Nobody is any longer independent in the classic sense, but some places are equipped better than others to manage the new patterns of interdependency.

Notes

1. Bertrand Badie, *La fin des territoires. Essai sur le désordre international et sur l'utilité sociale du respect* (Paris: Fayard, 1995).

2. Jean-Marie Guéhenno, *Fin de la démocratie* (Paris: Flammarion, 1993).

3. Kenichi Ohmae, *The End of the Nation State: The Rise of Regional Economies* (New York: The Free Press, 1995); Ohmae, "How to Invite Prosperity from the Global Economy into a Region," in Allen Scott, ed., *Global City Regions* (Oxford: Oxford University Press, 2001).

4. It is a comment on this sort of breathless techno-determinism that Ohmae (2001) dwell on regarding the extraordinary expansion of the value of high technology industries, which he sees as a permanent transformation of the economy, but that the delays of academic publishing are such that the piece appeared when the NASDAQ had gone into its tail-spin. Kenichi Ohmae, *The End of the Nation State*; Ohmae, "How to Invite Prosperity from the Global Economy into a Region."

5. Georg Jellinek, *Fragmentos de Estado*, translation of *Über Staatsfragmente* (Madrid: Civitas, 1981).

6. Salvadò Albareda and Pere Ribes Gifre, *Història de la Catalunya moderna* (Barcelona: Edicions de la Universitat Oberta de Catalunya, 1999).

7. Nùria Sales, *Els sigles de la decadència*, Vol. IV of *Història de la Catalunya* (Barcelona: Edicions 62, 1989).

8. Joseph Carens, *Culture, Citizenship and Community. A Contextual Exploration of Justice as Evenhandedness* (Oxford: Oxford University Press, 2000).

9. John Agnew, *Place and Politics. The Geographical Mediation of State and Society* (London: Allen and Unwin, 1987).

10. R. Swedberg, "Introduction," in R. Swedberg, ed., *Explorations in Economic Geography* (New York: Russel Sage Foundation, 1993).

11. Arnaldo Bagnasco, and Carlo Trigilia, *La construction sociale du marché. Le défi de la troisième Italie* (Cachan: Éditions de l'École Normale Supérieur de Cachan, 1993).

12. James Coleman, "Social Capital in the Creation of Human Capital," *American Journal of Sociology* 94 Supplement (1988): S95-S120; Robert Putnam, *Making Democracy Work. Civic Institutions in Modern Italy* (Princeton, NJ: Princeton University Press, 1993).

13. Charles F. Sabel, "Studied Trust: Building New Forms of Cooperation in a Volatile Economy," in R. Swedberg, ed., *Explorations in Economic Geography* (New York: Russel Sage Foundation, 1993).

14. Thomas Courchene, "Celebrating Flexibility: An Interpretative Essay on the Evolution of Canadian Federalism," C.D. Howe Institute, Benefactors Lecture, 1994, Montréal, 1995; Michael Storper, "The Resurgence of Regional Economies, 10 Years Later," *European Urban and Regional Studies* 2, 3; Kevin Morgan "The Learning Region. Institutions, Innovation and Regional Renewal," Papers in Planning Research, no. 157 (Cardiff: Department of City and Regional Planning, University of Wales College of Cardiff, 1995).

15. Philip Cooke and Kevin Morgan, *The Associational Economy. Firms, Regions, and Innovation* (Oxford: Oxford University Press, 1998).

16. Morgan, "The Learning Region."

17. Allen Scott, *Regions and the World Economy. The Coming Shape of Global Production, Competition, and Political Order* (Oxford: Oxford University Press, 1998).

18. Michael Storper, *The Regional World. Territorial Development in a Global Economy* (New York and London: Guildford, 1997).

19. John Lovering, "Theory Led by Policy: The Inadequacies of the 'New Regionalism,'" *International Journal of Urban and Regional Research* 23, 2 (1999): 379-95.

20. Mick Dunford, "Winners and Losers: The New Map of Economic Inequality in the European Union," *European Urban and Regional Studies* 1 (1994): 95-114.

21. Ohmae, *The End of the Nation State.*

22. Thomas Courchene, *A State of Minds. Toward a Human Capital Future for Canadians* (Montréal: Institute for Research in Public Policy, 2001); Thomas Courchene, in Allan Scott, ed., *Global City Regions* (Oxford: Oxford University Press, 2001).

23. Michael Keating, *The New Regionalism in Western Europe. Territorial Restructuring and Political Change* (Aldershot: Edward Elgar, 1998).

24. Ohmae, "How to Invite Prosperity from the Global Economy into a Region," (2001), writes, "Fortunately we do not need to waste time on redefining the term 'nation-state' on behalf of the UN. The real economy is moving ahead, with a new reality of 'city-regions'

and 'city-states.' Therefore, while the term 'nation-states' has potential to cause inconvenience, we are not inconvenienced." Unfortunately, I have no idea what this means.

25. Michael Porter, in Allen Scott, ed., *Global City Regions* (Oxford: Oxford University Press, 2001).

26. Ohmae, *The End of the Nation State*; Ohmae, "How to Invite Prosperity from the Global Economy into a Region."

27. Foundation Europe of the Cultures, *Towards a Europe of the Cultures. Target 2002* (Brussels: Foundation Europe of the Cultures, 1996).

28. Vlaams Economisch Verbond, *Open Region—Forward-Looking* (Antwerp: Vlaams Economisch Verbond, 1999).

29. Peter Katzenstein, *Small States in World Markets. Industrial Policy in Europe* (Ithaca: Cornell University Press, 1985).

30. Daniel Latouche, "La stratégie québécoise dans le nouvel ordre économique et politique internationale," Commission sur l'avenir politique et constitutionel du Québec, *Document du travail, 4* (Québec: Government of Québec, 1991).

31. Cooke and Morgan, *The Associational Economy*.

32. Keating, *The New Regionalism in Western Europe*.

20

Québec in the Americas: From the FTA to the FTAA

FRANÇOIS ROCHER*

Québec cannot disregard its multifaceted fate as part of North America. Its complexity is reflected not only in the commercial and economic links that exist between Québec and its partners, namely the other provinces and the United States, but also in the politics that influence the nature and depth of these links. The question that arises is to what degree Québec has been facing up to the requirements of continental integration in light of the challenges that the future will present. If Québec must pursue close relationships with its continental partners, it has through different periods done so in various ways. Thus, the federal system and the political forces within Québec have determined the way in which Québec historically has apprehended its continental integration. From an unenthusiastic acceptance of the constraints imposed by this reality, Québec has recently sought to revisit its defining features.

When factoring in the issues presented to Québec by the continental reality, four questions arise that are addressed in this chapter. First, what is the extent of Québec's integration within the continent? This question hinges on the structure of the economic relationship that binds Québec and its continental partners. Reading between the lines, it is not only a matter of assessing the importance of commercial links, but also of taking stock of the constraints inherent in them. Second, what are the structural aspects that determine the nature of Québec's integration in the continental economy? In other words, the economic development of Québec is

* Translated from French into English by Norman Meyer.

characterized by a dual dependence, one on Canada, and the other on American markets whose importance cannot be underestimated. This phenomenon limits the political choices historically available to Québec. Third, in what political manner have the various provincial governments of Québec, notably since World War II, managed the strengthening of continental ties and have they integrated this reality into their strategy for economic development? There may be many answers to these questions and some of them contradictory. Last, how can we evaluate, in terms of socio-political relationships, Québec's adherence to the federal strategy that led to the adoption of the Canada-US Free Trade Agreement (FTA) and later on the North American Free Trade Agreement (NAFTA)?

Panoramic View of Québec Trade

Québec's economy, like Canada's, is fundamentally open. Thanks, in part, to the outstanding performance of the American economy, total exports from 1992 to 1998 increased 70 per cent to 107 billion dollars. Québec's international exports increased an average of 13.3 per cent a year, placing Québec among the provincial leaders, while interprovincial exports increased only 3.6 per cent over the same period. While external trade accounted for 40 per cent of GDP in 1992, it accounted for 55 per cent in 1998.[1] Interprovincial and foreign trade each account for a significant portion of Québec's GDP. Québec has one of the highest ratios of external trade relative to GDP of any market economy. Discussing Québec's role within the Americas cannot be limited solely to its relationship with the United States. We must consider the economic links that unite Québec to the Canadian market, links that affect the manner in which Québec can envision control over its economic future. The purpose here is to demonstrate the scope of integration of Québec's economy into the overall American economy and to show its strengths and weaknesses. These weaknesses have helped to shape the constraints Québec encounters in its relationships with the rest of Canada and other countries in the Americas.

In the past decades, trade has evolved in a global context marked, on the one hand, by the globalization of national economies and, on the other, by rapid technological change that has compelled these same economies to improve their competitiveness. Québec cannot dissociate itself from this process and due to its proximity to the US (like the rest of Canada), its room to manoeuvre is limited. The value of international exports from Québec in 1998 amounted to approximately 69 billion dollars. This represents an astonishing increase in less than a decade, given that in 1991 the value of international exports was 26 billion dollars. However, the percentage of Canadian international trade for which Québec accounts is less than it was. In 1968, international exports from Québec accounted for 22.5 per cent of all Canadian exports; this decreased to 18.9 per cent by 1997. Similarly, Québec exports to the US represented only 16 per cent of Canadian exports in 1997 versus 27 per cent in 1965. This means that while Québec's economy is relatively open, it is also vulnerable.

Several elements must be considered in order to obtain an accurate picture of trade in Québec. More and more, Québec's trade is with the US. In 1980, the US received 58 per cent of Québec's exports; by 1991, this number had increased to 73.5 per cent and by 1998 to 83.6 per cent. Conversely, exports to Latin America decreased from 2.4 per cent in 1990 to 1.9 per cent in 1998. The range of products making up Québec's exports is narrower than that of the rest of Canada. Five principal industrial groups make up almost 64 per cent of total international exports. It is to be noted that, in 1998, exports from Québec were concentrated in four products groups: transportation products (17.3 per cent), electronics (15 per cent), primary mining products (12.3 per cent), and paper and related products (12.1 per cent).[2] This strong concentration of trade in a few industries must not stop us from remembering that, in 1997, Québec had more than 7,000 different businesses involved in exporting to the US, making up 22.5 per cent of the Canadian total. These businesses accounted for 18.9 per cent of all Canadian exports.[3] In other respects, products bound for export have become more diversified, in spite of the fact that products from primary natural resource industries remain very important. The notion that Québec exports only raw materials and imports all of its finished products does not do justice to the complexity of its economic reality.

The economic relationship between Canada and the US has been characterized by an atypical phenomenon among industrialized countries, namely the importance of intra-corporate trade. By the end of the 1970s, almost 60 per cent of Canadian exports were of this type. Similarly, in 1978, 72 per cent of Canadian exports were carried out by subsidiaries of foreign corporations.[4] By 1990, the share of foreign corporations carrying out intra-corporate exporting to the US remained almost unchanged at 71 per cent. These businesses operated primarily in the chemical industry, textiles, electronics, and, most importantly, in the transportation sector. Québec's economic reality, in the early 1980s, differed little from Canada's with regard to exports: 40 per cent of Québec exports were the result of intra-corporate trade.[5] However, this phenomenon was most evident in Ontario, where 53 per cent of all business revenues were done by non-Native businesses. In Québec the percentage was only 17 per cent. During the 1990s, subsidiaries of companies based most notably in the US, but also in Great Britain, Japan, and Germany, and constituting only 2 per cent of exporting corporations, accounted for 44 per cent of all exports from Canada (without mentioning that they also accounted for 25-30 per cent of domestic trade). To summarize, foreign companies are principally based in Ontario, at the expense of the other provinces and Québec, in particular.[6]

Even as Québec exports to the US gradually increase in value, it is important to remember that the Québec economy traditionally has been linked to and, to a large extent, been dependent on the Canadian market. It is not surprising that the province that accounts for the bulk of Québec's interprovincial trade is Ontario. In 1998, Ontario accounted for nearly 60 per cent of Québec's interprovincial exports and almost 75 per cent of its interprovincial imports. In absolute terms, interprovincial exports to all provinces grew to 38 billion dollars by 1998, an average annual increase of 3.6 per cent from 1992.

In light of these facts, we can state that, with regard to the "continental" market, in the broader sense of the term, Québec has experienced a reversal of trends. Whereas Québec used to depend more on the other provinces than on the US for trade, during the 1990s, the situation reversed itself. The FTA and NAFTA have contributed in significant measure to the increase in trade between Canada and the US to the detriment of interprovincial trade.[7]

The continental market largely determines the structure of exports and it would be difficult to underestimate Québec's dependence on Canadian and American markets. Québec's international imports, largely of American origin, have increased concurrently with its international exports (9.5 per cent between 1992 and 1998). In another respect, three quarters of interprovincial imports were from Ontario, reaching 51 billion dollars in 1998.[8]

In summary, the level of interdependence between Québec's economy and that of the rest of North America is very high. Given the asymmetry of economies it is even possible to speak of a two-dimensional relationship of interdependence. First, interprovincial trade constitutes a non-negligible portion of Québec's economic reality. However, given the increased depth of Québec's foreign economic relations, Québec's dependence on the Canadian marketplace has been greatly mitigated. Moreover, Québec's trade relations with the US have greatly developed, most notably in the area of exports. This reality not only demonstrates an outward-looking Québec economy, but also its dependence on its principal trading partners. As a result, Québec is particularly vulnerable to economic slowdowns that may occur in the US, particularly with regard to the fluctuation in the demand for raw materials. This illustrates Québec's economic vulnerability to cyclical changes that may occur with its chief trading partner.

Political Strategies and Continental Realities

Even though the dependence of Québec's economy on the continental market is a long-established reality, its governments have only recently sought to take this into account when developing their economic strategies.

The government of Maurice Duplessis and the Union Nationale largely shaped post World War II economic policy. In reality, Duplessis followed the policies adopted by his predecessors.[9] The philosophy of the time was simple: the state must limit its direct intervention in the economy, while at the same time furthering its growth through the maintenance of favourable social and material conditions. This position inspired government policies throughout the 1950s. These policies encouraged foreign investment by making major land concessions so as to stimulate the exploitation of natural resources. The emphasis of foreign companies (typically American) on the natural resources exploitation sector was expected to bring about the growth of the manufacturing sector. Thus, this economic strategy drew from a cumulative model where direct foreign investment acted as the primary force in Québec's economic development. This can be explained by the structural conditions of the Québec economy that existed at the time: a restricted domestic market and home-based financial institutions too weak to support needed significant domestic investment. The available course of action then was to turn to the North American market to obtain the necessary economic stimuli for industrialization and job creation. The economic integration of the Québec economy into that of North America was the result not only of the economic liberalism put forth under Duplessis, but also of the strong endorsement of his government, which saw in this a means to ensure the conversion of Québec's economy. It was with this goal in mind that the government of the time actively sought American investment, as much for the manufacturing sector as for the natural resources sector. We can say that Québec eagerly accepted its dependence on the United States.[10]

The coming to power of the Québec Liberal Party in 1960 marked the start of the Quiet Revolution. Even if the integration of the economy into the North American marketplace was not the key purpose of the many reforms that were adopted at the time, nevertheless, they had an impact on the manner in which Québec was to position itself vis-à-vis its primary trading partner. On the one hand, Québec's economy presented traits akin to those of underdeveloped nations' economies. According to Gaudet, "the province lacked the coherent and well-integrated inter-industry trade structure vital to any well-developed economy."[11] On the other hand, taking into account the extent of the weakness of francophone Quebecers' socio-economic status contrasted with the dominance exerted by the English-speaking establishment on big industry, finance, and commerce, the Québec government sought less to develop trade than to help create a francophone establishment. In addition, in response to the previous willingness to welcome American investment, forces within the new government challenged, in the name of nationalism, the over-exploitation of Québec's natural resources and pressed for state intervention in that sector.

In response to foreign domination of the Québec economy, the intervention of the state appeared to be an effective method of limiting this massive foreign presence, to help francophones rise to positions of power and influence, and, ultimately, to strengthen the foundations of a francophone establishment. The new political elite would thus create a network of public institutions (Hydro-Québec, la Société générale de financement, la Caisse de dépôt et de placement, etc.) wherein members of the new francophone middle class would have access to technical and executive positions. The state sought primarily to support small and medium-size businesses, mostly in the hands of francophones.[12] This was a conscious effort to take hold of an economy largely under the control of English-Canadian and foreign capital.[13] The nationalization of electricity, proposed by the Liberal Party of Québec in 1962, fitted perfectly within Québec's economic self-emancipation process. The collective appropriation of such an important natural resource was a landmark moment in the "decolonization" of the economy. It is important to remember, however, that the nationalization of electricity covered only production and distribution. Remaining under private control was the production of hydroelectricity, by industry, for use within their own production activities. Thus, Québec did not seize full control of hydroelectric resources, leaving some enterprises (typically of the monopolistic sort under foreign control, such as Alcan) to manage their own hydroelectric dams. The electricity produced by these enterprises represented 30 per cent of Québec's total production.[14] In another respect, in order to limit Québec's vulnerability to foreign control, several Crown corporations were created to become the pivots of the government's economic strategy and to promote the socio-economic status of francophones.[15]

Reconciling the need to obtain foreign investment with the will to promote a greater integration of these new investments within Québec's economy presented a real challenge. As a matter of fact, by the policies implemented over the decades that followed, the Québec Government continued to try and further the increase of both foreign investment and domestic control over the economy. In other words, successive governments attempted to demonstrate that Québec nationalism could accommodate an economy broadly open to foreign investment. Québec has always refused to attribute blame for all its economic woes to foreign investors. However, it insisted that economic development could not rest solely on the capacity to attract foreign investment.

In contrast to the economic nationalism that manifested itself in Canada, visible notably in the Gordon Report (1958), the Watkins Report (1968), and the Gray Report (1972), the Québec Government was more preoccupied with the need to exert influence over its economy than to use its legislative powers to limit the nature and importance of American investment penetration on Québec soil.[16] Accordingly, the Québec Government's reaction to the law creating the Foreign Investment

Review Agency stressed the lack of attention given by the federal government to the regional development dimensions of such an initiative. In addition, the Québec government was concerned that the criteria adopted would help reinforce the existing industrial structure to the detriment of Québec's efforts to modify its own industrial base and stimulate local business interests to participate in this process. In fact, Québec's opposition to this federal initiative reflected a difference in priorities in the direction of an increase in foreign investment rather than in a limiting of it. Québec's position with respect to foreign investment goes back to the very framework of the Québec economy. Thus, foreign investment continues to be perceived as essential to maintaining the pace of economic growth and in order to increase its room to manoeuvre with respect to English Canada. All the governments that succeeded Jean Lesage have followed this course of action. As a matter of fact, Mr. Bourassa's Liberal government of 1970-76 displayed an even greater openness towards foreign investment.

The Parti Québécois (PQ) Government published two economic policy statements, the first in 1979 and the second in 1982, which spelled out the foundation of its industrial strategy. One of the main thrusts of the government was the promotion of domestic investment, particularly in the primary and advanced technology sectors. Directly in line with economic nationalism were the objectives of increasing the share of domestic capital in certain key sectors (telecommunications, transportation, finance, and the steel industry) and increasing Québec's export capacity.[17] Nevertheless, the natural resource and hydroelectric sectors constituted the two principal foundations of this strategy. Thus, the government's intention of increasing the domestic share in the ownership structure clearly targeted the natural resources sector. However, even though government policy sought to increase local entrepreneurship, nowhere was it mentioned that this should be pursued to the detriment of foreign investment. The intention was to seek the integration of foreign-owned subsidiaries and to increase the Québec content of goods and the access of Québec's firms to the purchasing and investment networks of multinational corporations.[18] However, as Bonin noted, "nowhere in Québec's industrial policy has the contribution expected from foreign-owned firms or from foreign relations in general been clearly stated," even adding that "the absence of an international perspective is noticeable in both documents."[19]

Though state interventionism was directed towards all sectors, it had its greatest effect on the natural resources sector. In fact, in the last 20 years, francophone capital increased most in the areas of forestry and mining. Foreign control of employment in forestry decreased from 37.7 per cent in 1978 to zero per cent in 1987, and from 64.9 per cent to 24.6 per cent in the mining sector for the same time period.[20] This exceptional growth in the influence exerted by francophones is largely attributable to the policies put in place in the 1960s that sought to develop the infrastructures needed to exploit Québec's natural resources more fully. Québec created a number of Crown corporations in many economic sectors, not the least of which was financing. They include—English translations being here unofficial—the Québec Mining and Exploration Corporation (SOQUEM—the Société québécoise d'exploration minière), the Québec Petroleum Initiatives Corporation (SOQUIP—the Société québécoise d'initiatives pétrolières), the Forestry Recovery and Exploitation Corporation (REXFOR—the Société de récupération et d'exploration forestière), the Québec Steel Production Corporation (SIDBEC—the Sidérurgie du Québec), and the James Bay Development Corporation (SDBJ—the Société de développement de la Baie-James). These numerous Crown corporations allowed Québec better control of the exploitation of its natural resources. The preferred market towards which to channel these resources remains the United States, but their domestic exploitation no longer depends on strategies elaborated beyond the border. Incidentally, the Québec government has traditionally proven to be much more interventionist than Ontario with regard to the exploitation of their respective natural resources.

The overall governmental strategy has been more one of ensuring that francophones acquire greater power within the Québec economy than one of diminishing its dependence on the American market. The growth in the number of jobs under francophone control can be attributed to the acquisition of foreign businesses by the state (the purchase of the Asbestos Corporation and other asbestos mines by francophones and the takeover of Domtar by the Caisse de dépôt) and by other corporations (paper company acquisitions by Cascades), or the expansion of certain firms (Noranda, Cambior).

Québec's management of its dependence on the continental economy was accomplished in other ways. The Québec Government has opened numerous "delegations" in the United States, notably in New York, Boston, Chicago, Los Angeles, and Atlanta. A primary mission of these delegations consists in promoting trade, looking for new technologies that might benefit Québec, and being on the lookout for investors interested in Québec. Moreover, these delegations also provide technical assistance to Québec businesspeople wishing to gain access to the American market.[21] These Québec initiatives were responses to complaints from francophone business interests that the federal government was not doing enough to assist in American market penetration, particularly when Québec producers were in competition with those of other Canadian provinces.[22]

Although it was thought by some that the opening of Québec's economy to foreign influences represented a hindrance to self-directed economic development,[23] the concern brought to bear on the development of trade relations between Québec and the United States emphasized the benefits of a continental framework, in contrast to the constraints imposed by the traditional Canadian policy favouring east-west trade. Thus, in 1983, the PQ Minister of Foreign Trade, Bernard Landry, declared himself in favour of a common market between Québec and the United States. The arguments put forth stemmed from the desire to lower the cost of imports by reducing tariffs and to bring about greater integration between the two markets, which in turn would translate into a greater integration of production processes.[24] But the Americans rejected the offer, alleging that they would rather negotiate with all of Canada and, therefore, the federal government rather than with a provincial government.[25] Given the impossibility of striking a deal directly with the American government, supporting the Mulroney government's free trade initiative seemed like a viable alternative to many Québec nationalists.

Within Québec, the free trade debate has always been linked to the question of the nature of the economic relations between Québec and the rest of Canada. Two problems were raised: on the one hand, the development of greater north-south trade implies a reappraisal of the traditional east-west trade axis; on the other hand, the negotiations have to fit within the dynamics imposed by the Canadian constitutional framework. It may seem surprising to link the constitutional question to the debate over free trade, but one must realize that the federal government saw a necessary link between the elimination of interprovincial trade barriers, which increase the fragmentation of Canada's industrial structure, and the introduction of free trade. Evidently, the problems specific to Québec's economy have traditionally led its governments to seek a greater measure of freedom in implementing policies developed at the federal level, as well as the respecting of the existing division of constitutional powers. With some nuances, the positions presented by the Parti Québécois and the Québec Liberal Party, before the Royal Commission on the Economic Union and Development Prospects for Canada (commonly known as the Macdonald Commission), were similar; in the course of the hearings both dealt with these two issues.

The Parti Québécois, in its brief tabled with the Macdonald Commission during the course of its hearings, stressed the need for the Québec government to have complete control over manpower, education, and professional development policies to compensate for the imbalance resulting from the lesser degree of mobility of its population.[26] In this way, the Québec strategy conflicted, in part, with the Canadian approach that favours worker-availability-based manpower mobility. Québec's strategy would rather create jobs within the province to restore balance to the job market. It was from this perspective that the Parti Québécois pushed for the decentralization of power. Two years later, Québec's Premier, Pierre-Marc Johnson, reiterated Québec's support of the federal free trade initiative under certain conditions. In particular, he asked that Québec take part in the negotiations, that the transition measures be developed jointly by the federal government and all provinces, that the federal government abide by the Constitution so that Québec would consider itself bound with respect to matters within Québec's areas of jurisdiction only insofar as it would have consented, and, finally, that certain sectors be given special consideration (for example, agriculture, textiles, clothing, and shoe manufacturing).[27]

The agreement in principle of such Québec nationalists as Parizeau or Landry with a free trade policy supports an approach that wants to strengthen economic ties with the United States without there being a relinquishing of power by the Québec government in favour of the federal government. The "péquistes" are taking a strategic gamble that in the long term a free trade agreement could benefit their project of political sovereignty for Québec. The protectionist measures of the *National Policy* are the ones that make for east-west trade over the more natural north-south inflow and outflow of trade. The logic behind the "péquiste" strategy is that a re-establishment of the more natural north-south trade lines could result in a weakening of Canada's economic foundation, allowing Québec eventually to disengage more easily.[28] The reconfiguration of the Canadian economic space could prove favourable at length to the sovereignty project and reduce related transition costs. In this manner of thinking, there is not necessarily any contradiction between the espousal of free trade principles and the principles propounded by Québec nationalists.[29]

While the Parti Québécois' argumentation hinges on the centralization-decentralization dichotomy, the Québec Liberal Party's (QLP) position concentrates more on making proposals that guarantee a common Canadian market. However, in order to achieve this, the QLP rejects the introduction of new constitutional rules limiting the powers of provincial governments.[30] Thus, the QLP rules out that the Québec Government should part with any of the economic levers essential to its development. However, the QLP has not always been in favour of free trade. While Robert Bourassa was head of the opposition, he voiced concerns about a closer economic union with the United States possibly transforming into a political union and then a monetary one. However, in light of the matters forming part of the negotiations themselves, Mr. Bourassa softened his stance. Taking into account that what was essentially being negotiated was a more open market, on a sector-by-sector basis that excluded culture, and that there was even a transition period, free trade would not lead to a political association.[31] Moreover, the QLP considered that an agreement liberalizing trade would help improve and guarantee the access of Québec's production to the American market. Finally, a Liberal government would not strive for economic integration to the extent of having the federal government play a determining role in the mapping out of economic intervention strategies by the Québec government.

Once in power, the QLP maintained this stance. The conditions set out by the Liberal Party government remained, by and large, the ones that had been put forward and adopted by the previous government, with the exception of the request for provincial participation at the negotiating table. Québec's position regarding free trade set limits to continental integration since it rested on three elements: first, respect for the constitutional framework and for Québec's legislative jurisdictions; second, the need to preserve for the government a sufficient measure of latitude in strengthening its industrial fabric and its technological base, having specifically in mind the most vulnerable small and medium-size businesses; and last, the absolute necessity of allowing for transition periods and support programs designed to help certain sectors affected by the new framework.[32] A similar position was put forward by the Québec government with regard to NAFTA.[33]

The need to establish a transition period of adequate duration followed from recognition of the disparity between the member economies and of the fact that Canada has traditionally experienced a higher level of protection. On the other hand, when the Québec government speaks of the need to enjoy a sufficient measure of latitude, it refers to its ability to influence market mechanisms, notably with business support and regional development programs. The possibility of maintaining such activities required that the Canadian government attempt to negotiate grandfathering clauses so that governments would be able to continue to support economic development, with programs having improved criteria of accessibility. This power to intervene was not to translate into a clause allowing the American government to abuse the recourse to protection measures.[34]

The Liberal government's assessment of the Canadian-American free trade agreement's content was very positive. This was due to the fact that the sharing of legislative and constitutional jurisdictions was not affected by the Agreement and that the legislative changes needed to be effected by the provinces to follow suit were rather limited. Moreover, considering the provisions of the Agreement as drafted, the Québec government argued that none of these entailed changes in the areas of social policies, communications, language, and culture. The government could, therefore, claim to have conserved all of the latitude it had in reaching its objectives of modernization and economic development.[35]

The free trade option has managed to rally the support of both major provincial political parties and of a significant portion of the business community. The support of a large majority of Québec's employers for the continental strategy reflected the new maturity acquired by francophone capital translating itself into the needed structural affirmation. In this spirit, Québec's business class aligned itself behind the Mulroney-Reagan agreement on trade during the federal election campaign of 1988. Thus, in response to the negative advertising put forth by Québec's trade union federations, the business class created the Regroupement pour le libre-échange (Free Trade Support Network) and financed a competing publicity campaign in favour of free trade. Nonetheless, the debates held by large employer associations illustrate the complexity of the issue. Taking into account the structural problems affecting the Québec economy, it is not surprising to see that businesses operating in "fragile" sectors pressured the major employer organizations to qualify their support appropriately.

Because leading public figures campaigned to have more open markets, some saw this as evidence of total support on the part of Quebecers.[36] Even if it is true that Quebecers appeared more open to the idea of free trade than were the other Canadians when bilateral negotiations began (in Québec, 58 per cent were in support to 35 per cent against versus 46 per cent in support to 50 per cent against in Canada as a whole, and in Ontario 36 per cent in support to 60 per cent),[37] nevertheless a significant opposition movement to free trade developed in Québec, led mainly by the large trade union federations. This movement used essentially the arguments advanced elsewhere in Canada by those opposed to free trade. There was, notably, a denunciation of the concessions that the Americans demanded, these being viewed as so many ways of reducing the power of governments (federal and provincial), to replace it with an industrial development borne by free market forces alone, and of constraining any government intervention intended to steer or direct the evolution of economic activity.[38] Those opposed to free trade believed that Québec would no longer be able to use industrial adjustment measures (such as public purchasing programs, the provision of low-rate electricity, export markets promotion and development programs, subsidies in support of industrial activities, and sector-specific modernization programs). Québec had the most to lose since it had developed a coherent and focused policy to respond to structural weaknesses in its economy. There was concern over the future of social programs and cultural industries that would not be able to withstand the expectations of an overwhelmingly powerful America. In short, opponents of free trade considered that it was an option to be equated with a return to market forces alone as the regulating economic and social mechanism. They would rather have had multilateral liberalization and improved rules of trade under the GATT. In addition, they called upon governments to adopt a strategy of economic development that would strengthen the industrial structure and of improved productivity in order to face the coming globalization of national economies.

The deepening of continental economic links entered a second phase with the inclusion of Mexico in the free trade agreement. Canada's participation in this new agreement rested essentially on tactical reasons aimed fundamentally at not losing the benefits obtained through the FTA. Dorval Brunelle noted that the principal areas of innovation in the North American Free Trade Agreement (NAFTA) lay in the provisions regarding the public institutions both of the provinces and of the states to investments (notably in the area of the patriation of profits and benefits), and to compensation, in the case of expropriation, in which case businesses could resort to a dispute resolution mechanism.[39]

The Québec government wanted to comply with the provisions of these agreements that fell under its jurisdiction by adopting in 1996 the Agreement on Internal Trade Implementation Act (AIT). By and large, be it Liberal or PQ, the free trade approach of the Québec government remained unchanged. Conversely, in 1997, in order to ensure that internal trade was not more constrained than international trade, the Québec government signed the AIT. The Agreement on Internal Trade draws on principles—as well as terms and conditions—that characterize international commercial treaties (the World Trade Agreement and NAFTA). Meant essentially to guarantee the free flow of goods, services, people, and capital, the Agreement hinges on general rules of mutual non-discrimination, the right of entry and exit, the absence of barriers, legitimate objectives, conciliation, and transparency. The AIT creates obligations in the areas of government purchases and of manpower and capital mobility, and sets guidelines on the rationalization and harmonization of regulations and standards for transport and consumer protection. Under the AIT, an Internal Trade Committee, composed of ministerial level representatives was formed. Its primary function is to determine the areas and time frame of future elimination of trade barriers negotiations. In the case of dispute, a special, impartial panel can be established. In case of disagreement, retaliatory measures may be taken. Nonetheless, exceptions are allowed when the preservation of law and public safety is at issue or when issues arise of health, protection of plants and animals, consumers, workers and groups benefiting from affirmative action policies. Overall, even as the Agreement results from a process of interprovincial co-operation, the combined effect of the numerous exceptions and of the dispute resolution mechanism make for a continuation, to a large extent, of the status quo and is less constraining than the international trade agreements ratified by the federal government. In a different respect, the AIT did not help in reducing the pressures in favour of a greater intervention on the part of the federal government, an intervention that the federal government could pursue unilaterally.

With the 1994 Summit of the Americas in Miami the question of continental integration entered a new phase. At the initiative of President Clinton, the heads of state of the Americas (with the exception of Cuba), met with the goal of negotiating a plan of action aimed at increasing economic integration and achieving by 2005 a Free Trade Area of the Americas (FTAA) that would extend from Terra Del Fuego to Baffin Island. The philosophy behind this initiative feeds on the mercantile belief that economic growth and the fight against poverty is conceivable only in terms of open markets. A simplistic political science notion (apparently shared by the Canadian government) has it that the opening of markets can only strengthen democracy (Why then exclude Cuba?), bring about a greater participation in public life (hard to fathom, given the secrecy surrounding the negotiations), and entail greater access to education and health care. The negotiations were carried on by nine sectoral groups: access to markets; capital investment; services; public markets; agriculture and agri-food; dispute resolution; intellectual property; subsidies, anti-dumping and compensation rights; and competition policy.[40]

Since the constraints imposed by international trade agreements directly affect infra-national political entities, Québec's National Assembly felt it appropriate to convene, in 1997, the Parliamentary Confederation of the Americas. Not only were representatives of the 35 countries of the Americas invited (initially Cuba was included but then excluded in the negotiation process meant to lead to the creation of the FTAA), but the Conference also was open to all infra-national governments (provinces and states) of the six federations of the Americas and also to the representatives of the five supranational parliaments (the Latin American Parliament, the Andean Parliament, the Central American Parliament, the Parliamentary Assembly of the Caribbean Community, and the Joint Parliamentary Commission of MERCOSUR). This meeting promoted the realization that, although the agreements are ratified by state entities, they directly affect the capacity of all other "loci" of power and result not only in the concentration of power in the hands of the political executives but affect the distribution of powers to suit the objectives of central governments, while putting at issue the principle of accountability as representative democracies know it.[41] This aspect is problematic, insofar as the institutional measures giving effect to the agreements seek not only to liberalize trade by gradually eliminating tariff and non-tariff trade barriers, but to liberalize all economic sectors of goods, services, and investment.[42] In this regard, the institutional structure (committees and task forces) is host both to governmental representatives and to representatives of the private sector.

The issue of how to harmonize the policies of the different signatory states is raised inevitably by the proliferation of international trade. Such is also the case when it comes to implementing the agreements' provisions in political environments where sovereignty is being shared, as is supposed to be the case in federal systems. When governments ratify an agreement, they are acting as unitary political entities even though actualization of the agreements involves infra-national political entities. Thus, when the federal government commits itself at the international level in areas under provincial jurisdiction, it must negotiate terms and conditions of implementation with the provinces. Agreements are binding on provincial governments when they legislate or issue an order sanctioning the agreement's terms falling under their jurisdiction. As the Québec National Assembly's Institutional Commission (*Commission des institutions de l'Assemblée nationale*) notes in one of its papers, no formal mechanism exists that defines the roles and participation of provincial governments in trade negotiations, so the actual manner in which they are carried out depends on the relations between the federal government and the provinces. The federal government obviously consults with the provinces at the annual meetings of provincial trade ministers and deputy ministers or at meetings that gather officials, but no formal overarching mechanism exists to encompass these talks.

In view of the complexity of the issues discussed during these international meetings (one need only think of public purchasing policies), the federal government is increasingly seeing itself negotiating over matters that fall in areas of provincial jurisdiction and then finding itself more or less compelled, by virtue of the "federal clause," to ensure that provincial governments give effect to the provisions endorsed as part of these agreements.[43] Obviously, the provinces enjoy a certain measure of latitude insofar as they may refuse to sanction the terms of these agreements, though this depends in large part on a provincial common front, which, as recent history has shown us repeatedly, invariably disintegrates in favour of the federal government. With a certain clear-mindedness the consultation document tabled by the Québec government notes that, "in the case of division between provinces, the federal government has, in fact, full latitude and the provinces none."[44]

It remains extremely difficult, if not impossible, to assess fully the fallout from North American free trade. Trade with Mexico has not increased by any significant measure. Québec continues to direct its exports largely and even increasingly to the United States. However, Québec exports have increased most in sectors where trade has been liberalized and in high-value-added sectors (office automation and telecommunications). In the more traditional sectors (natural resources, food products, textiles, clothing, and furniture), growth has been faster than before the adoption of free trade. For Louis Balthazar and Alfred Hero, "Québec's particular expectations in regard to free trade agreements have in large part been met ... the opening of American markets was like a breath of fresh air and provided a significant stimulus."[45] The exceptional performance of the American economy throughout the 1990s and the marked lowering in the value of the Canadian dollar likely had a greater effect on that phenomenon than did the adoption of free trade. Such an adoption of free trade may have "civilized" continental trade practices by shielding Canadian producers from the traditional US protectionist reflex when its industries are declining or experiencing a low level of productivity. However, the soft wood lumber dispute, demonstrates that the arbitration mechanisms can be circumvented when American economic interests are at stake by turning, then, to bilateral agreements, where the weaker player — Canada, in this case — is forced to make concessions.

In other respects, the promises of increased job creation that were at the heart of the pro free trade rhetoric of the 1980s have not been met. Employment decreased 15 per cent in sectors unaffected by free trade and 8 per cent in those sectors directly affected. Brunelle concludes that the direct and indirect effects of the agreements have been disastrous in terms of job creation.[46]

This rather pessimistic assessment of the actual fallout from free trade did not stop the major Québec trade federations from declaring themselves in favour of greater economic ties throughout the continent. During public consultations held by the National Assembly's Institutional Commission in September and October of 2000, the CSN (Confédération des syndicats nationaux—Federation of National Trade Unions) and the FTQ (*Fédération des travailleurs du Québec*—Workers Federation of Québec) did not oppose the furthering of economic integration within the FTAA. Instead, they asked that social concerns be given greater importance in future negotiations. They reminded the Commission that economic rights should not take precedence over human rights. Referring to the gap between rich and poor countries, the unions noted that parallel agreements, dealing in particular with the rights of workers and the protection to the environment, did not suffice to correct the negative impact of free trade inasmuch as breaches entail no economic sanctions, their only effect being that failure to respect these rights would be known publicly. The trade federations proposed, therefore, to set up social protection mechanisms in all member countries of the FTAA. They also called for the creation of an employer-financed compensation fund to ensure professional development and retraining for victims of lay-offs resulting from trade liberalization. For its part, the CSN denounced the fact that trade agreements take away the latitude of governments and influence their priorities that may be established and worried over the privatization of public services.

As was the case in the free trade debate of the 1980s, employers have continued to support the FTAA. Noting that both the Canada-US trade agreement and NAFTA had had positive economic results, specifically when it comes to the creation of high tech businesses, increased exports, and access to import products, the possibility of liberalizing trade with other countries in the Americas raised the possibility of increasing exports to countries with strong population growth. Also, it was believed that such openness would decrease Québec's economic dependence on the US market, while improving the social conditions and democratic processes of a large number of countries in the Southern Hemisphere. The linkage at the root of such reasoning is fairly simple: an FTAA would increase production, employment, the demand for goods and services, and revenues—all in all a growth in wealth that could only benefit governments, whose tax revenues would increase accordingly. The Québec Association of Manufacturers and Exporters (QAME) also pointed out that such an agreement would replace the existing uncertainty with a clear set of legal rules and offer the possibility of having recourse to fairer dispute mechanisms. With regard to the concerns expressed by unions and social and environmental groups, QAME did not believe in the efficiency of a constraining framework of government and private sector practices, but rather, invited the participants to favour awareness and education processes. However, their concerns over social standards stem from an economic and utilitarian approach. During their presentation to the Institutional Commission, the AMEQ representative stated the following: "We believe in the need to include social and environmental protection clauses. At the moment, Québec businesses already conform to numerous environmental and social standards. It would, therefore, be in their interest to ensure that international competitors also have to meet equivalent environmental and social standards in various fields." He cautioned, however, that such standards could be used unjustly, disguised as non-tariff trade barriers.

Nonetheless, if the adoption of a pro free trade strategy on the part of the Québec government can be explained in part on the basis of adhesion to prevailing neo-mercantile theses, it also has inspired an emerging discourse within Québec's sovereignty movement. Globalization has become the significant word added to the array of reasons used to justify Québec's support for sovereignty. The Bloc Québécois (BQ), less encumbered by the constraints of governing than the PQ, developed a document on globalization that relates primarily to the World Trade Organization (WTO) and omits entirely the continental dimension. Nonetheless, the logic presented in the BQ document can be extended to the integration of Québec into the Americas. It mentioned that Canada is made to forgo a portion of its sovereignty in favour of supranational organizations and that, in order to retain a strong degree of sovereignty, it wants to centralize its powers, finding a balance between what can be accepted externally and what must be ceded internally. The reasoning is as follows: in order to compensate for loss of sovereignty under international trade agreements, the federal government eats away at the exclusive powers of provinces. The federal government legitimizes its action on the pretext of an obligation to ensure that the provinces adopt policies that conform to the standards applicable under the trade agreements. The BQ has come to the conclusion that the choice for Québec is between holding onto powers that are more and more shared with the federal government (powers that are of less and less consequence) or of achieving its own sovereignty by "following the path of least resistance for the economy—the United States and the Americas, the path of least resistance for cultural specificity—France and 'francophonie,'—and by opening up new horizons."[47]

For its part, the PQ makes its agreement to free trade and, more specifically, its support for the FTAA dependent on the extent to which such a process is consistent with two basic principles: the respect for human rights and for the diversity of languages and cultures (this element being closely connected to the need to retain the power of governments to legislate, to act, and to intervene). While giving unrestricted support to the unions with regard to social rights and the need for trade agreements to refer to international charters, help economic development, and facilitate cultural and scientific co-operation, the PQ cannot remain silent when Québec is deprived of access to negotiations and hopes that all parliamentarians be fully involved in this process. Considering the implications of free trade for the political sovereignty of Canada, and, by extension, of Québec, and the constraints it will impose on government intervention, Brunelle and Deblock have stressed that this continental strategy is in conflict with the nationalist theses rooted in government intervention.[48] The failure of the government intervention system put in place since the Quiet Revolution would explain this change, in part. This is to say that the continental option reflects a reconfiguration of the nationalism of the 1960s and 1970s that rested on public intervention in the economy, the society, and culture. The public perception of the government's role and of mechanisms of social regulation has been markedly influenced by Québec's agreement to free trade. Brunelle concluded:

> In instituting pan-economism as the ultimate way of rationalizing and sanctioning individual and social behavior, this new political economy now dominates the definition of social programs, education, and the purchasing policies of each and all public organizations. And so it is that provincial governments are having to forgo their historic prerogatives in matters of political economy to be supportive instead, in the wake of the commitments made by Canada during the previous G-7 meeting, and with a pleasing unanimity this time throughout the country over the so called "zero deficit" policy regardless of the costs in social terms and, more particularly, in terms of an increase in the level of poverty.[49]

Conclusion

Québec has always sought to account for its economic position in the continent. It had to do so within a political framework that created regional disparity and shaped the development of Québec's industrial structure, one in which the importance of the problem sectors has been a historical feature. In doing so, this continental integration features a series of factors that work at limiting possible political options in order to minimize unwanted effects. The continental market largely determines the structure of Québec's exports. Québec is one of the most important provincial exporters to the Canadian market, though this has diminished during the 1990s. On the other hand, Québec's exports to the United States have largely been limited to a few key sectors, while US imports show a much greater diversity. This underlines the vulnerability of Québec's export base to the tremors that may occur with its principal trading partner. This fragility is greater since Québec deals largely with neighbouring American states who themselves are confronting a marginalization problem from the gradual move to the West of the major centres of economic growth. Furthermore, the relative importance of English Canadian and American control of the Québec economy and the need to attract foreign investment for large scale public projects has limited the latitude available to a Québec government wishing to minimize the dependence of the Québec economy on the continental market. The choice of reducing Québec's economic dependence has never been put in terms of that between a self-sufficient closed economy or an open economy.

Two attitudes characterize the strategy adopted by Québec governments with regard to continental integration. The first, adopted by Duplessis and his predecessors, was to encourage foreign investors indiscriminately and with a minimum of constraints. This option was ingrained within the ideas of classic liberalism concerning state interventionism. The second, which appeared with the start of the Quiet Revolution and was supported by successive governments, sought less to limit Québec's economic dependence on the continental market than to ensure that francophone capital would play an important role in this process. In other words, the goal was not one of wholesale changes to Québec's economic and industrial fabric, though this objective has been raised from time to time under the term of "the technological hard curve" (*le virage technologique*), but rather one of improving the socio-economic state of francophones by way of an interventionist government that would seek to soften the negative effects resulting from structural weaknesses endemic to Québec's economy. In the end, francophone capital has succeeded only mildly over the last decades in modifying Québec's industrial structure and the problems that it must face.

The fact that Québec was a full-fledged supporter of the federal free trade strategy appears paradoxical, at first glance. This apparent paradox results from the dual economic and political dynamic accompanying this movement. From an economic standpoint, the deepening of continental trade strengthens ties along a north-south axis, at the expense of an east-west one. This trend, present before the signing of the Canada-US Free Trade Agreement, can only continue to grow. The trend helps to lessen the age-old dependence of Québec's economy on the Canadian market by diversifying its trade structure. In this sense, it feeds a desire for greater autonomy that is shared by a large number of Quebecers and promoted by the two major political parties. At the political level, however, free trade can eventually reduce the Québec government's latitude by subjecting it to new rules of conduct decreed under the various trade agreements or to their interpretation by new multilateral bodies. It also reinforces the power of the federal government to present itself as the defining authority for Canadian trade policy. The logic of free trade can do away with this paradox only if it comes in the wake of the quest for a greater measure of political autonomy for Québec. Reduced dependence on the Canadian marketplace takes its full meaning from an increase of the Québec government's power to intervene. Moreover, it demonstrates the optical illusion represented by the growth in the control of francophone capital on Québec's economy. This new reality has fed a strong attitude on the part of Québec's business class, proud of its successes and convinced that tomorrow's achievements will be equally gratifying. Thus, Québec is seeking to establish economic links with the rest of Canada similar to those it has with the United States.

Finally, Québec is not seeking to break the dependence resulting from its continental integration. Instead, it proposes to revisit its terms and conditions to adjust them in favour of Québec's capital rather than English Canada's. In that process, the Québec government has played an important role. Taking into account the weaknesses of the Québec economy and the foundations of francophone capital, the business community will continue to call for government support, preferably under terms with which it agrees.

Notes

1. Canada, Statistique Canada, *Le commerce interprovincial et international au Canada 1992-1998* (Cat. No. 15-546-XIF, 2000), 67.

2. Québec, Assemblée nationale, *Document de consultation. Le Québec et la Zone de libre-échange des Amériques: Effets politiques et socio-économiques* (Commission des institutions, June 2000), 39.

3. Canada, Statistique Canada, *Profil des exportateurs canadiens 1993-1997* (Cat. No. 65-506-XIF, 2000), 30-31.

4. B. Perron, "Les contraintes dans les relations entre le Québec et les États-Unis," *Politique* 7 (Hiver 1985): 19-20; B. Bonin, "US-Québec Economic Relations, Some Interactions Between Trade and Investment," in A.O. Hero Jr. and M. Daneau, eds., *Problems and Opportunities in US-Québec Relations* (Boulder and London: Westview Press, 1984), 22-23.

5. P. Martin, *When Nationalism Meets Continentalism: The Politics of Free Trade in Québec* (Xeroxed document, November 1993), 6.

6. Canada, Industry Canada, *Intrafirm Trade of Canadian-Based Foreign Transnational Companies* (Working Paper number 26, December 1998), 6.

7. J.F. Helliwell, F.C. Lee, and M. Hans, *Effects of the Canada-US FTA on Interprovincial Trade* (Xeroxed document, 1999).

8. Statistique Canada, *Le commerce interprovincial et international au Canada 1992-1998*, 70.

9. Y. Roby, *Les Québécois et les investissements américains, 1918-1929* (Québec: Presses de l'Université Laval, 1976).

10. G. Boismenu, *Le duplessisme* (Montréal: Presses de l'Université de Montréal, 1981), 125.

11. G. Gaudet, "Forces Underlying the Evolution of Natural Resource Policies in Québec," in C.E. Beigie and A.O. Hero, eds., *Natural Resources in US-Canadian Relations, vol. I, The Evolution of Policies and Issues* (Boulder, CO: Westview Press, 1980), 251.

12. R. Pelletier, *Partis politiques et société québécoise. De Duplessis à Bourassa 1944-1970* (Montréal: Québec-Amérique, 1989), 202-03.

13. A. Raynauld, *La propriété des entreprises au Québec, les années 1960* (Montréal: Presses de l'Université de Montréal, 1974), 81.

14. D. Brunelle, *La désillusion tranquille* (Montréal: Éditions Hurtubise HMH, 1976), 145.

15. M.B. Montcalm and A.-G. Gagnon, "Québec in the Continental Economy," in A.-G. Gagnon and J.P. Bickerton, eds., *Canadian Politics: An Introduction to the Discipline* (Peterborough, ON: Broadview Press, 1990), 352.

16. Gaudet, "Forces Underlying the Evolution of Natural Resource Policies in Québec," 243-54.

17. M. Romulus and C. Deblock, "État, politique et développement industriel du Québec," in *Interventions économiques* 14/15 (Spring 1985): 202-03.

18. Ibid., 203.

19. Bonin, "US-Québec Economic Relations, Some Interactions Between Trade and Investment," 33-34.

20. F. Vaillancourt and J. Carpentier, *Le contrôle de l'économie du Québec, la place des francophones en 1987 et son évolution depuis 1961* (Québec: Office de la langue française, 1989), 53.

21. Québec, Report by the Ministre délégué aux PME 1987, *The State of Small and Medium-Sized Business in Québec* (Québec: Éditeur officiel, 1988), 188-90.

22. L. Balthazar, "Québec's Policies Toward the United States," in A.O. Hero Jr. and M. Daneau, eds, *Problems and Opportunities in US-Québec Relations* (Boulder and London: Westview Press, 1984), 223.

23. R. Parenteau, "L'expérience de la planification au Québec (1960-1969)," *Actualité économique* 45, 4 (Jan.-Mar. 1970): 679-96.

24. B. Perron, "Les contraintes dans les relations entre le Québec et les États-Unis," *Politique* 7 (Winter 1985): 24.

25. Balthazar, "Québec's Policies Toward the United States," 220.

26. Parti Québécois, *Mémoire présenté à la Commission d'enquête sur l'union économique canadienne* (Conseil exécutif national, Xeroxed document, Dec. 1983), 28-30.

27. Canada, Conférence annuelle des premiers ministres sur l'économie, *Compte rendu textuel* (Ottawa: Secrétariat des conférences intergouvernementales canadiennes, 1985), 41-42.

28. F. Rocher, "Fédéralisme et libre-échange, vers une restructuration centralisée de l'État canadien," in C. Deblock and M. Couture, eds., *Un marché, deux sociétés?, 1ere partie* (Montréal: ACFAS, 1987), 151-68.

29. Martin, *When Nationalism Meets Continentalism.*

30. R. Bourassa, *Mémoire présenté par le Parti libéral du Québec devant la Commission sur l'union économique* (Xeroxed document, Feb. 1984), 21-22.

31. J. Blouin, *Le libre-échange vraiment libre?* (Québec: Institut québécois de recherche sur la culture, 1986), 101.

32. Gouvernement du Québec, *La libéralisation des échanges avec les États-Unis. Une perspective québécoise* (Québec: Xeroxed document, Apr. 1987), 83-85.

33. Gouvernement du Québec, *Québec and the North American Free Trade Agreement* (Québec: Éditeur officiel, 1993), 14-17.

34. Ibid., 70-74.

35. Gouvernement du Québec, *Éléments de l'Accord entre le Canada et les États-Unis, analyse dans une perspective québécoise* (Québec: s.n., 1987), 25.

36. P. Resnick, *Lettre à un ami québécois* (Montréal: Boréal, 1990).

37. Martin, *When Nationalism Meets Continentalism,* 4.

38. Coalition québécoise d'opposition au libre-échange, CEQ, CSN, FTQ, UPA, *Danger libre-échange* (Québec: la Coalition, 1987), 15-22; P. Bakvis, "Free Trade in North America: Divergent Perspectives Between Québec and English Canada," *Québec Studies* 16 (Spring/Summer 1993).

39. D. Brunelle, *L'ALENA cinq ans après: un bilan critique* (Département de sociologie et de science politique, Université du Québec à Montréal, Groupe de recherche sur l'intégration continentale, cahier de recherche 2000-04, Apr. 2000), 7.

40. Assemblée nationale, *Document de consultation. Le Québec et la Zone de libre-échange des Amériques: Effets politiques et socio-économiques*, 7.

41. Brunelle, *L'ALENA cinq ans après: un bilan critique*, 18-19.

42. D. Brunelle, R. Sarrarin and C. Deblock, *Libre-échange et gouvernance: le Canada et la politique de continentalisation* (Département de sociologie et de science politique, Université du Québec à Montréal, Groupe de recherche sur l'intégration continentale, Cahier de recherche 01-01, Jan. 2001), 23.

43. Assemblée nationale, *Document de consultation. Le Québec et la Zone de libre-échange des Amériques: Effets politiques et socio-économiques*, 29-32.

44. Ibid., 32.

45. L. Balthazar and A.O. Hero, *Le Québec dans l'espace américain* (Montréal: Éditions Québec Amérique, 1999), 176-77.

46. Brunelle, *L'ALENA cinq ans après: un bilan critique*, 11.

47. Bloc québécois, *Faire notre place dans le monde* (Document de travail du Chantier de réflexion sur la mondialisation présenté au Bloc québécois à l'occasion de son Conseil général des 17 et 18 avril 1999 à Rivière-du-Loup), 17.

48. D. Brunelle and C. Deblock, *Le libre-échange par défaut* (Montréal: VLB Éditeur, 1989), 131-32.

49. Brunelle, *L'ALENA cinq ans après: un bilan critique*, 12. Trans. Meyer.

21

Nationalism and Competitiveness: Can Québec Win if Quebecers Lose?

PETER GRAEFE

The assumption commonly made when discussing the economics of nationalism in Québec is that nationalism reduces economic competitiveness. Many argue that Quebecers' desire to exert greater control over the economy has encouraged extensive state intervention, which has in turn distorted the efficient functioning of the free market, fattening the bureaucrats while reducing wealth generation.[1] Language legislation and the uncertainty about Québec's constitutional future also are held responsible for the flight of head offices and skilled personnel to Ontario (and beyond), and for maintaining an unfavourable investment climate. While it is undeniable that nationalist economic impulses have led to *some* inefficient state intervention, and that constitutional uncertainty has had *some* negative effects on firms' investment decisions, these arguments are not broadly persuasive. At most, uncertainty accelerated the difficult restructuring of the Québec economy in the face of the shift in continental economic activity to the southwest, and the reorganization of the modern service industries on a linguistic basis.[2] The free market alternative embraced by these critiques is also questionable, given the persistence of high unemployment, low wages, and regional inequalities in the extended period of *laissez-faire* market liberalism predating the Quiet Revolution.[3] As Jacques Beauchemin states, "I do not know what amnesia can lead to forgetting that market regulation in Duplessis' Québec led to a housing crisis, precarious incomes, insufficient health care and restricted access to education."[4]

More recently, a number of researchers have suggested that minority nationalist economic strategies are, in fact, highly compatible with global economic competitiveness. As the hollowing out of the national state shifts responsibilities for governing economic development to subnational or regional scales, territorially concentrated minority nations find the opportunity to take the lead in fostering economic growth. Moreover, as forms of economic development that provide good jobs with good pay come increasingly to depend on intangible and extra-economic inputs (such as trust, tacit knowledge, learning, social cohesion, and social capital), nationalism stands to reinforce competitiveness, since its shared cultural and institutional basis helps provide precisely these inputs. At the same time, economic success based on such an inclusive development model should further strengthen minority nationalism by ensuring that all members of the nation benefit and come to see the nation as the natural economic community. In short, it is possible to imagine a virtuous circle whereby minority nationalism underpins an innovative and competitive economy, and the very success of that economy benefits all members of the minority nation. In the second section of the paper I will underline how Québec's economic policies follow this general recipe, and provide a tentative assessment of the extent to which they have been successful.

Despite this rosy portrait, the subtitle of the paper addresses a troubling question: Does the virtuous circle hold? Indeed, a number of relevant political and economic limitations to progressive competitiveness threaten to prevent this desirable upward spiral. If the internationally competitive sectors are unwilling or unable to redistribute their gains to the rest of Québec society, rising inequality may threaten the supportive culture of trust, knowledge, co-operation, and social capital. More pointedly, the nationalist coalition itself may be fractured: rather than strengthening the national community through an inclusive model of economic development, the strategy may starkly divide society instead into winners and losers.

Nationalism and Competitiveness

Before developing the arguments for linking minority nationalism and competitiveness, it is useful to define these terms. I follow Michael Keating in my use of the term "minority nationalism" to refer to a national group within a broader nation-state that seeks wider forms of self-rule, self-expression, and recognition, although not necessarily the full accoutrements of sovereign statehood.[5] These nationalisms, like those of their broader nation-states, can be considered social constructions. Minority nationalist movements manipulate the cultural, political, economic, and social dimensions of regional and national identity in order to form them into a coherent appeal.[6] Nationalism seeks to gather individuals together on the basis of a shared national identity, while overcoming or downplaying other bases of division, such as class or gender. The defining of minority nationalist identity is, thus, an act of power, integrating a variety of conflicting groups unequally into that identity, and assigning different roles and positions based on their relative influence and strength.

Competitiveness is another contentious issue, particularly as different definitions of competitiveness (e.g., *static* and *dynamic* competitiveness) have been developed in the literature. The definition adopted here is borrowed from Coates, who defines "structural competitiveness" as "the ability of national economies to provide high and growing per capita incomes while exposed to foreign competition."[7] Although this definition is biased, because it excludes economic strategies in which firms in the national economy compete on the basis of low wages or devaluations of the national currency, it provides the basis for the mobilization of social actors around the goal of "competitiveness," because it promises income gains for the national population. This underlines the importance of distinguishing competitiveness as a *strategy* that can mobilize a coalition of actors on the *promise* of gains for all, from the actual *achievement* of such gains. In fact, to anticipate my conclusion, these strategies may frequently fail to keep their promise.

But how is it that these two disparate concepts, one that deals with communities of belonging and the other evaluating economic performance, come to be linked? The answer lies in two interconnected issues. The first is a reordering of the scales of state economic policy that favours the regional level. The second is the change in the bases of competition at the regional level.

The reordering of the spatial scales of economic and political activity since the mid-1970s makes an important contribution to the linking of nationalism and competitiveness. Two general tendencies are at work here, namely the decline of the nation-state and the concomitant rise of the region. It has become a cliché to note that the nation-state is being hollowed out, its powers passed upward to supranational institutions, downward to regional and local governments, and outward to the market. The post-World War II coincidence of national borders with national economic spaces, national citizenship, and national identity was upset in the process. This opened new spaces of state regulation and identity formation.[8] In the post-war era, the willingness of nation-states to take responsibility for regulating the economy, promoting development, and building the welfare state solidified national ties of universal citizenship. By naming citizens and extending their rights, nation-states changed the map of identities by elevating national identity over transnational or local ones.[9] Regional anti-disparity policies followed a similar logic of national integration, by seeking to equalize living standards across the territory.[10]

However, as capital mobility and trade flows have increased, nation-states have had to deal with the rising cost of social provision, decreasing revenues, and reduced regulatory effectiveness. This has placed nation-building projects on hold.[11] The push to compete internationally also involves a shift in state priorities, with governments supporting the most dynamic and competitive regions and sectors at the expense of underdeveloped territories or peripheries.[12] The retrenchment of the welfare and regional policies that supported the territorial integration of the nation-state provides an opening to minority nations to assert themselves. However, seizing this opening requires succeeding where the nation-state failed, namely, on the terrain of development. Success on this terrain promises the minority nation greater control of its economic destiny and increasing economic and policy autonomy from its broader nation-state. Success will also strengthen citizens' attachment to the minority nation as the legitimate community in which to plan social and economic development.

This is where the second element, the changing bases of competition at the regional level, comes into play. The political hollowing out of the nation-state involves a regional dimension, as the regional and local governments become key sites for crafting strategies of international competitiveness. The dominant advantage attributed to the regional state is its capacity to foster and nurture an innovative and learning economy. In the face of globalization's competitive pressures, the maintenance of well-paid, secure jobs is linked to quality, innovation, and productivity. Culture and institutions are assigned major roles in ensuring continued productivity gains, both by closing off the possibility of competing on low wages (hence, forcing firms to compete on innovation and quality) and by providing an environment conducive to the constant innovation and product differentiation required to fill high-end market niches. Included in this environment are non-market institutions, which are felt to play central roles in economic success (or failure). For instance, the density and character of associational life becomes of central importance, because in its networks and relationships trust is nurtured, tacit information is shared, and learning emerges.[13] Implicit in these strategies is the need to maintain social cohesion and relative income equality, since exclusion and inequality risk splintering social exchanges and networks, thus undermining their innovative and economic potential.

In this sort of economy, the state's role increasingly involves mobilizing the knowledge and power resources of influential non-government actors and stakeholders, and of steering them towards its economic development objectives. The regional state is better placed than the nation-state to play this role, since it is closer to the milieu and its actors, and shares a national identity. As well, the shift in economic policy from macroeconomic management to supply-side measures encouraging flexibility and innovation (e.g., labour market policy, technology policy), also favours the capabilities of subnational governments.[14]

National states are felt to be too distant and heavy-handed to steer these forms of economic coordination. By contrast, regions "represent authentic communities of interest, define meaningful flows of economic activity and are advantaged by true synergies and linkages among economic actors." They provide "a system of collective order based on microconstitutional regulation conditioned by trust, reliability, exchange and cooperative interaction."[15] The region is, therefore, the ideal locale for competitiveness strategies, since it can provide the closer interdependencies that economic actors need to overcome barriers to co-operation in learning and innovation.[16] These interdependencies are further cemented by the effects of proximity, as local business associations, banks, civil servants, governments, and unions can set tax, research, education, and infrastructure policies through more concertational fora, making them more efficient and effective.[17]

Nationalism and Regional Economic Strategies

It is important to note the complex interaction between nationalism and these regional strategies. On the one hand, nationalism provides a societal culture with some collectivist traits, which are important elements in building an environment of reflexive learning, or a culture rich in social capital. The nation can play a role that working-class power may play in other contexts, by promoting positive-sum solutions to economic coordination and adjustment problems.[18] Nationalism, likewise, provides a series of shared meanings, codes, and symbols that make sense of the world and that can aid, thereby, in mediating the nation's involvement in the world economy.[19] It can also play a role in building democratic alternatives to neo-liberalism because it protects the idea of a shared public space for political debate, above and beyond particularities of class, race, or gender.[20] This is of particular importance, since the polity retains a key role in smoothing institutional change.[21]

More fundamentally, since minority nationalisms have developed outside the centralized state, a high degree of organization in civil society has been required. They are able often to draw on governing institutions, networks, and partnerships formed outside the state. Nationalist economic strategies usually are spearheaded by coalitions of political, economic, and social actors, who temper the growth imperative, in the realization that social solidarity must be assured for future competitive success and national cohesion.[22]

On the other hand, progressive competitive strategies are attractive to nationalist movements, because they promise more inclusive forms of development and, thus, help foster the image that the national community does not reproduce the inequalities of class society. Conversely, where development is highly unequal, nationalist movements risk losing strength to class-based organizations, and are likely to spend their energies smoothing out internal divisions, rather than in mobilization towards shared ends.[23] Successful regional strategies are, therefore, likely to strengthen loyalty to minority national identities, and to strengthen the political and cultural position of these nations within their larger state. Even if regional strategies fail to deliver inclusive development, their discourse and ideology of intense inter-regional competition, where failure to compete is linked to underdevelopment and social disintegration, encourages a broadly-based "buy-in." By posing the development issue as one of the survival of the minority nation as a whole, politicians can build new social alliances beyond their usual base, and can often convince labour to sign on as a junior partner in the pursuit of the shared goal of competitiveness.[24]

Keating argues that regional identities (including minority nationalist ones) and economic competitiveness can exist in a virtuous circle. In this scenario, "social integration is assured and marginalization avoided. Culture and identity are safeguarded. The environment is conserved. These serve to create social capital and public goods, which, in turn, favour economic growth."[25] This virtuous circle is nevertheless premised on an inclusive form of development, and is by no means an easy and automatic creation. It is also possible for minority nations to fall into a vicious circle where "the region is subject to the disintegrating effects of the international market. Growth is narrowly defined and socially divisive. Cultural identity is destroyed or fragmented," which in turn leads to dependency and low social capital formation.[26] The challenge for minority nations in this view is to provide the basis for sparking the virtuous circle, while avoiding the vicious one.

Québec's Economic Development Policies

Québec provides an interesting case for assessing the interplay of regional competitiveness strategies and nationalism. Latouche has argued that Québec has moved to the limits of what a regional state can do in terms of mobilizing "all elements of Québec society around an industrial strategy that builds on a thick network of associations and on a strategic leadership role for the regional state."[27] Québec is particularly well-equipped with the factors raised by Cooke et al. that transform "regionalization" into the political and cultural expression of "regionalism." Québec firms are able to draw on a well-structured set of indigenous financial institutions, while the provincial government has significant budgetary autonomy (raising corporate and personal income taxes, and determining spending on healthcare, education, social assistance, infrastructure, and investment promotion) and plays a key role in structuring the soft infrastructure of universities and research institutes.[28] The fact that Québec controls these levers, which often are beyond the budgetary or constitutional capacity of minority nations, makes it a critical case for demonstrating the extent to which minority nationalism and regional competitiveness strategies are mutually reinforcing. If any minority nation is likely to ride a regional strategy to success, Québec is a good bet.

Building the Québec Model

The modern Québec nationalist movement is generally portrayed as a post-1960 phenomenon. The victory of the Québec Liberal Party (QLP) in 1960 marked a break with the conservative strain of nationalism, with its classical liberal conceptions of economy and society. The QLP was given to a more aggressive brand of nationalism and to the proactive use of the state for economic and social ends. State activity expanded considerably in the 1960s as Québec adopted the accoutrements of the North American post-war compromise: the welfare state; increased public wealth generation; and union recognition in terms of "responsible unionism" and decentralized collective bargaining. The parallel development of the welfare state and the upward surge of wages through public-sector collective bargaining completed the model of development and spread economic benefits widely, albeit while incurring large public debts.[29]

While these elements were in keeping with developments across the industrialized West, the national question added three particularities. First, a central aim of this activity was to strengthen the position of indigenous, francophone capital relative to that of the traditional anglophone business elite. The post-war repertoire of state intervention, such as infrastructure megaprojects, the creation of domestic financial institutions, and strategic Crown corporations thus took on a particular flavour by seeking to heighten the economic control exercised by members of the minority nation. Second, the expansion of the state and of these instruments of economic intervention had the explicit goals of opening the professional and managerial ranks of the economy to francophones, and of shifting the language of the workplace towards that of the majority.[30] The use of the Québec state to promote the interests of francophone capital and the francophone new middle class, in turn, accelerated the territorialization of French-Canadian nationalism around the Québec state, giving rise to a properly Québec nationalism.[31] Finally, the collective nature of the project of creating an economic space controlled by the minority nation also implied giving a greater role to the union and co-operative movements in state-building than elsewhere.[32]

By the late 1960s, the neo-nationalist movement behind the QLP had fractured along the lines of nationalist ideology, with the QLP coming to represent elements seeking greater autonomy for Québec within the Canadian federation, and the newly formed Parti Québécois (PQ) representing elements seeking some form of "sovereignty-association" with the rest of Canada. Although the QLP drew on close links with business, and the PQ was drawn to the unions and a more social democratic platform, a bipartisan consensus existed on questions of the state's role in the economy.[33]

By the early 1970s, it had become clear to state planners that an economic policy based on increasing aggregate demand through state spending, and of developing Crown corporations and financial institutions, could not modernize and upgrade an industrial structure based on resource exports and technologically stagnant, labour-intensive industry. As early as 1974, an internal document raised the need for a new industrial strategy, and suggested an approach based on supporting innovative firms and specialized producers. This perspective was taken up publicly by the PQ after their election in 1976. This period was marked by a sustained effort to launch an industrial strategy that urged firms to increase innovation, productivity, quality, and niche specialization. The government sought to aid this transition with tax and spending measures that encouraged research and development, managerial upgrading, information-sharing between firms in the same sector, marketing, and export promotion. By the early 1980s, the government's policies encouraged the growth of leading sectors, such as high technology, electronics, and biotechnology.[34] Overall, these policies represented an opening to less hierarchical and state-directed forms of economic planning, as well as a strategic shift away from mass production towards innovation and specialization.[35]

These industrial policies complemented the PQ's attempt to foster collaboration between business and labour, in the hope of improving economic performance (or at least the investment climate), and of strengthening a shared national project cutting across class lines. Efforts to this end bore little immediate fruit. The "economic and social council" proposed by the late 1970s industrial policy never saw the light of day, and attempts to replicate elements of European corporatist practices through more than 20 socio-economic conferences (including three "grand summits") limped along, hampered by the weak organization of business interests and the labour movement's scepticism.[36] The short-lived sectoral council tables set up at the urging of the Fédération des travailleurs et travailleuses du Québec (FTQ) proved unable to overcome the suspicions of a business community that was increasingly hostile to the PQ government.[37] The PQ's tenure, nevertheless, provided evidence of a shift in the political economy underlying the national project, with the embrace of supply-side state intervention and associative forms of economic governance.

The QLP's return to power in 1985 threatened these efforts at building the province's innovative milieu, as the party appeared set to break with the post-1960s bipartisan consensus and to pursue neo-liberal policies of deregulation, privatization, and welfare state retrenchment. This stance reflected the confidence of Québec's business community that they could compete effectively and provide benefits to society, if only the government would get out of the way. Nevertheless, the QLP quickly backed away from this approach for at least three reasons. First, despite the party's virulent neo-liberal discourse, the Premier himself was committed to a high technology policy. His "liberal vision" focused on the entrepreneur, who was argued to need a range of state-provided infrastructure and supports, albeit in a context of low taxes and deregulation.[38] Second, ill-considered diversification in the late 1980s and the severe recession starting in 1990 chastened Québec capital and reignited an interest in policies to aid industrial modernization and work reorganization. A reading of the pre-budget briefs of the Conseil du Patronat (Québec's most influential business lobby) reveals a shift around 1990-91. The blunt calls for massive spending cuts are softened (without disappearing), while issues of state support for training and research come to the fore.[39] Finally, assigning entrepreneurs the task of advancing the nation proved difficult when the latter's neo-liberalism openly disparaged the nation-building efforts of the preceding quarter century. When constitutional conflicts sparked a resurgence of sovereignist sentiment, the QLP had little choice but to embrace a more inclusive nationalist coalition[40] that provided a strategic opening for a renewal of a high-end supply-side strategy in the early 1990s.

This time, party policy was phrased in the language of "clusters," language chosen specifically for its ability to mobilize a broad range of social actors.[41] Aimed at five "competitive" clusters (i.e., aerospace, metal- and mineral-processing, pharmaceuticals, information technologies and products, and electrical energy production/distribution), as well as nine "strategic clusters" showing strong growth potential, the policy encouraged the adoption of best practices in training, research and development, innovation, design, labour relations, quality, and export marketing.[42] The new plan also returned to the theme of social partnership, playing on the major union federations' willingness to support an offensive restructuring of work organization and technology in return for employment guarantees. This time, however, partnership would focus less on the peak level than on the challenges facing individual firms.[43]

This policy represented a further step away from state-directed development and towards an associative form of economic planning. By insisting on both cross-class partnerships and intra-industry co-operation, the policy portrayed economic development as a collective and shared project.[44] The documents surrounding the policy exhorted all citizens to pitch in for success: "the task of improving the competitiveness of our economy can only be fulfilled by a co-operative and joint effort by government, industry and the labour force";[45] "[the action plan] is based on a collective effort, which draws on the contribution of the individual and of the association, of the firm and of the regions, social organizations and cultural milieus, in a fruitful spirit of partnership";[46] "all decision-makers and participants in the domain of economic development admit that solidarity and cohesion are essential for the development of a small economy in a changing world."[47]

The post-1994 Parti Québécois government has maintained this general approach of promoting more associative forms of economic coordination, of providing extensive supply-side support, and of calling upon all actors to pull together for the sake of Québec's economic renewal. This was perhaps most clearly articulated at the two major summits organized by the government in 1996 in order to gain a wide consensus on the elimination of the deficit and on Québec's broad social and economic objectives. For instance, la Société québécoise de développement de la main-d'œuvre, a tripartite body that, at the time, controlled Québec's training policy, prepared a paper for the second summit calling for "a collective effort on all fronts" to combat unemployment.[48] Similarly, the discussion paper prepared to orient the participants at the first summit declared that "the government convokes all socio-economic partners and, more generally, all Quebecers to renew the social pact."[49]

Positive Returns

To date, this strategy seems to have strengthened Québec nationalism. The mobilization of economic actors around the cluster strategy and the legitimacy granted to the 1996 summit processes (as compared to the wariness of both the unions and business to the summitry and concerted action under the first PQ government) indicates that Québec is seen as a highly relevant space for organizing economic activity. The willingness of the union movement to sign on to a competitiveness strategy and to tie its fate to the competitive success of firms located in Québec is likewise suggestive of a national identity trumping a class identity.[50] Jean-Marc Piotte describes this subsuming of class identities when he notes the presence of a dominant language of "partnership, served in a nationalist sauce, in whose name union leaders call their troops to ally with the Québec State ... and organized business in order to take on globalization, to combat foreign competitors on the international scene."[51]

This strategy also seems to have paid some dividends in terms of modernizing Québec's industrial structure. The Québec economy has become far more export oriented, with international exports growing 7.9 per cent between 1989 and 1996. These exports, and manufacturing shipments, more generally, have moved at the margin from labour and resource intensive industries to capital and technologically intensive industry.[52] Québec is also breaking away from Canadian norms in terms of research and development spending and technological adoption. Research and development as a share of GDP grew from 1.41 per cent in 1985 to 2.0 per cent in 1995 (as compared to the Canadian average of 1.63 per cent). The number of firms active in research doubled between 1990 and 1995, and the adoption of general applied technologies has more than doubled since 1989.[53] Latouche's study of science and technology policies provides similar results, although he underlines the concentration of over half of research and development expenditures in just 10 firms, and of 81 per cent of total expenditures in the top 50 firms.[54] These elements may help explain how Québec increased its productivity rate from 86 per cent of Ontario's rate in 1960 to 93 per cent in 1999.[55]

One can also speak of changes in the economic culture, in terms of more co-operative labour-management relations, the *rapprochement* of financial institutions and local capitalists, and greater inter-firm collaboration. This should not be exaggerated, however, since this is in comparison with the North American reality of a diffuse organization of labour and business interests and of limited ties between banks and businesses. While few would deny that Québec's economic culture is distinct within North America, from a European perspective, it remains distinctly North American.[56] It is nevertheless possible to look at these various indicators and argue that choosing a region-based competitiveness strategy has paid off in terms of solidifying the economic space congruent with the borders of the minority nation.

Will the Virtuous Circle be Unbroken?

Despite these evident successes, the 1995 Women's March Against Poverty placed a very different assessment on the table. The portrait of Québec provided in the demands of the marchers was not one of social co-operation leading to a modern, competitive economy and rising standards of living. It was, instead, one of rampant poverty, precarious work, dead-end work placements for social assistance recipients, low minimum wages and substandard work conditions, and inadequate social housing.[57] The widespread popular support for the March, in turn, underlined that this portrait was not exaggerated.

Indeed, an examination of Québec's labour market performance reveals the extent to which success in nurturing high-end economic activities has had little impact on the broader labour market. Between 1976 and 1996, the unemployment rate averaged 11 per cent, which was higher than all OECD countries except Ireland and Spain.[58] It took six straight years of growth before the rate fell below 10 per cent in 1998. Continued growth has brought the rate down to 8 per cent (as of December 2000), albeit with one of Canada's lowest labour force participation rates (63 per cent). For those who have jobs, the quality of work is still at issue. Between 1976 and 1995, paid work grew by only 19 per cent, compared with a 100 per cent increase in self-employment. Full-time paid work grew by 19 per cent compared with a 126 per cent growth in part-time work. This has led to an increased polarization of working time, as the decrease in the percentage of people working 35-40 hours a week (8.7 percentage points) mirrored the increase in people working 1-29 hours (8.1 percentage points). The share of the labour force in non-standard work (part-time, temporary, self-employed, multiple jobholders) reached between 29 per cent and 36 per cent of total employment by the mid-1990s.[59] While the effect of the current expansion remains to be seen, incomes stagnated or even declined over the previous business cycle.[60]

Given these labour force trends, it is not surprising to find that Québec is Canada's poverty hotbed. The 1996 census revealed that 23.4 per cent of Québec's population living in private households had low incomes in 1995, up from 19.4 per cent in 1990.[61] This rate, which is the highest for any Canadian province, is linked to high rates of urban poverty. Québec boasts six out of the top seven cities in terms of poverty rates, with Montréal and Québec City at the top of the list at 41.2 per cent and 34.7 per cent respectively (up from 33.3 per cent and 29.3 per cent in 1990).[62] Moving up the scale from individual cities to census metropolitan areas, one notes that the absolute size of the poor population in metropolitan Montréal was larger than that for metropolitan Toronto, even though Toronto's population was roughly 30 per cent larger. The generalization of poverty is remarkable, not only as it extends down Québec's urban chain, but also in its pervasiveness in the Montréal census metropolitan area. Even when the three largest cities (Montréal, Longueuil, and Laval) are removed from this area's figures, the incidence of low income for the remainder of the metropolitan areas was 20.6 per cent. Nowhere else in Canada, outside Québec, does this "remainder" category exceed 16 per cent.[63] While some gains have been made in upgrading the economic structure, particularly around the "new economy" centred in Montréal, the benefits do not seem to have spread within that metropolitan area, let alone province-wide.

In this context, it would seem propitious to demand that the businesses profiting from their more competitive footing be called upon to help counter these trends through paying higher wages, or underwriting better social provisions through higher taxes. However, despite the promise of competitiveness leading to higher profits, Québec's economic policy documents have never ceased to underline that maintaining competitiveness requires lower taxes, less regulation, and, indeed, lower minimum wages and public-sector salaries.[64]

The unsettling labour market statistics do not mean that Québec's economic development strategy is the cause of widespread unemployment and poverty, but they suggest that it has done little to solve these problems. Competitiveness, as a strategy, may not have given rise to structural competitiveness, with its high and rising incomes. This is not entirely surprising given the growing body of research that questions whether progressive competitiveness is a realistic goal for most (or any) countries.[65] If competitiveness policies cannot deliver high and rising incomes, the virtuous circle risks being broken as inequalities and exclusion fracture the nation along class lines.

Squaring the Circle

These strains in the virtuous circle present a long-term challenge to a nationalism premised on competitiveness, since the economic sacrifices made do not remedy high rates of unemployment and poverty. The Québec government and its administrative apparatus are, thus, faced with the unenviable position of attempting to broaden the inclusiveness of economic development without too greatly upsetting the existing set of cross-class alliances. Efforts, to date, along these lines have given limited success, in part, due to the fact that business has refused to make meaningful concessions on the grounds that they would impede competitiveness.

This dynamic was at work during the 1996 summits. Québec's labour federations had been calling for a summit in order to confront the widespread unemployment and poverty lingering from the early 1990s recession. In the run-up to the March 1996 Summit, it became clear that the government had had to make major concessions in order to bring business to the table. The question of deficit reduction would take centre stage, putting off the jobs issue until the fall, and centring debate on whether the budget would be balanced in two years or three. The March summit gave rise to deficit-reduction commitments that were treated as binding by the government. The same cannot be said of the jobs question debated at the October Summit. The agreement to make job creation a priority did not give rise to firm and binding commitments by the private sector. The government emphasized, instead, the continued need to increase firms' ability to compete by cutting regulations (including some language provisions).[66] While the labour leadership treated this commitment as a major victory, the fact that such experienced negotiators were so badly outmanoeuvred pointed up the extent to which the language of partnership was one-sided in its demands.[67] Labour's patience with co-operation and partnership is sorely tested, as elements facilitating its survival, such as changes to the labour code to assist organizing efforts in the new labour force, have been shelved by the government in the face of business disapproval.[68] The unions remain nationalist, but some elements within the labour movement are attempting to link the national question to a more substantive project of social change.[69]

Another example of the government's attempt to maintain a national consensus behind the competitiveness strategy concerns the development of the social economy or third sector. The political "father" of Québec's cluster strategy, Gérald Tremblay, has argued that jobs need to be created in this sector, since job creation in the competitive sectors is unlikely to be sufficient to absorb all the unemployed.[70] The call to use this sector to shore up social cohesion by creating work and meeting social needs represents an opening to the demands of the women's movement and the community movement. These movements believe in investing resources in the not-for-profit sector in order to consolidate precarious and unpaid work in socially valuable activities, and in order to increase the communities' capacities for planning their economic and social development. While the government has sold its policies in this area in terms of contributing to social cohesion, the programs have spent small sums on discreet problems and sectors, rather than creating a coherent response to exclusion and underdevelopment.[71] Within these programs, the neo-liberal logic of using non-profit organizations as an inexpensive alternative to welfare state services, while far from uncontested, seems to hold the upper hand on the expansive vision of community empowerment.[72] As with the summits, the state is attempting to shore up a sense of national solidarity, but the need to keep costs down for the business community renders the exercise futile.

Conclusion and Prospects

I have considered arguments about the interplay of nationalism and economic competitiveness against the backdrop of Québec's experience, noting that the adoption of such competitiveness policies, reinforced by a discourse of cross-class national partnership, coincides with an uneven economic and social performance. While a number of economic indicators have improved, incomes have stagnated and labour market conditions remain weak.

This raises questions about the ability of the discourse of competitiveness to maintain the extraordinary coalition behind Québec's regional economic strategies. Having said as much, it is hard to discern what political economy might underpin a nationalist project capable of displacing the existing one. It is likewise hard to make out which social forces might bear such an alternative project. The union movement has long linked the achievement of sovereignty to social progress, but the correlates of what that progress would entail are much less clear. The unconditional support that the unions gave to the sovereignty-partnership project in the 1995 Summit effectively precluded debate on what would change in a sovereign Québec. Despite having formulated a renewed full-employment strategy, based on reduced hours of work, new forms of work organization, and the development of the social economy, the CSN signed on to the decisions of the 1996 Summit on the Economy and Employment, which made few strides in that direction.[73] Having invested so heavily in concerted action and workplace partnerships as a proactive response to industrial restructuring, the unions seem to have lost the ability to formulate an independent agenda, although there are signs of disquiet on the margins.[74] Opportunities for change may be greater in the women's movement and the community movement as they give form to the idea of a social economy that develops the democratic capacity of communities to plan their own economic and social development.

For the moment, however, the central actors in Québec society are willing to leave the major decisions about economic development to the profit-driven decisions of private capital. The ideology of competitiveness has an uncanny ability to mobilize across class divisions, particularly with its promise of national affirmation and enrichment as the pay-off for throwing all of society's energies and solidarity behind its businesses. Yet, as this paper has argued, competitiveness may be a false god that can maintain a broad national consensus for only so long. This is not to say that Québec nationalism will be irrevocably caught on the horns of this dilemma, but it is to say that there are very significant limits to the virtuous interaction of nationalism and competitiveness. On the one hand, the exclusions resulting from the failure to realize a progressive competitiveness lessen national consensus and national confidence. On the other hand, increased dissension within the nation will make it difficult to employ nationalism as a non-market economic good. It would seem that another economic model is needed for the benefit of both citizens' well-being and for national cohesion. In the long run, the Québec nation cannot win if Quebecers continue to lose.

Notes

1. For popular accounts, see for instance Brian Lee Crowley and Michel Kelly-Gagnon, "The economic jig is up, Mr. Landry," *Globe and Mail*, 19 Mar. 2001, A11; Konrad Yakabuski, "Sugar Daddy: Québec's investment in a snack-cake maker signals a resurgence of economic nationalism," *Report on Business Magazine*, Dec. (1999). The most convincing and best documented presentation of this argument has been made by Michael Smith, "L'impact de Québec Inc., répartition de revenus et efficacité économique," *Sociologie et Sociétés* 26, 2 (1994).

2. Alain-G. Gagnon and Mary Beth Montcalm, *Québec: Beyond the Quiet Revolution* (Scarborough: Nelson, 1990), ch. 1-2; Mario Polèse, "La thèse du déclin économique de Montréal, revue et corrigée," *L'Actualité économique* 66 (1990): 133-46.

3. See for instance Alain Noël, "Politics in a High Unemployment Society," in Alain-G. Gagnon, ed., *Québec: State and Society*, 2nd ed. (Scarborough: Nelson, 1993). John McCallum has traced how market mechanisms left Québec with fewer tools for subsequent economic modernization in *Unequal Beginnings: Agriculture and Economic Development in Québec and Ontario until 1870* (Toronto: University of Toronto Press, 1980).

4. Jacques Beauchemin, "La Révolution tranquille: Le temps de désenchantement," in Y. Bélanger, R. Comeau, and C. Métivier, eds., *La Révolution tranquille 40 ans plus tard: un bilan* (Montréal: VLB Éditeur, 2000), 96.

5. Keating, *Les défis du nationalisme moderne: Québec, Catalogne, Écosse* (Montréal: Presses de l'Université de Montréal, 1997), 35.

6. Michael Keating, "The Political Economy of Regionalism," in Michael Keating and John Laughlin, eds., *The Political Economy of Regionalism* (London: Frank Cass, 1997), 24.

7. David Coates, *Models of Capitalism: Growth and Stagnation in the Modern Era* (Cambridge: Polity Press, 2000), 16.

8. Bob Jessop, "The Crisis of the National Spatio-Temporal Fix and the Tendential Ecological Dominance of Globalizing Capitalism," *International Journal of Urban and Regional Research* 24, 2 (2000): 337-39, 352; Ramesh Mishra, *Globalization and the Welfare*

State (Cheltenham: Edward Elgar, 1999), 12-14; Jane Jenson, "Mapping, naming and remembering: globalization at the end of the twentieth century," *Review of International Political Economy* 2, 1 (1995): 101-04.

9. Jenson, "Mapping," 100.

10. Michael Keating, *The New Regionalism in Western Europe: Territorial Restructuring and Political Change* (Cheltenham: Edward Elgar, 1998), 47-51.

11. Jenson, "Mapping," 103-04; David Brown, "Why is the nation-state so vulnerable to ethnic nationalism," *Nations and Nationalism* 4, 1 (1998): 9.

12. Michael Keating, *The New Regionalism*, 73; Thomas Hueglin, "Better Small and Beautiful than Big and Ugly? Regionalism, Capitalism and the Postindustrial State," *International Political Science Review* 10, 3 (1989): 210.

13. Joel Rogers and Wolfgang Streeck, "Productive Solidarities: Economic Strategy and Left Politics," in David Miliband, ed., *Reinventing the Left* (Cambridge: Polity Press, 1994), 135-38; Ash Amin, "Beyond Associative Democracy," *New Political Economy* 1, 3 (1996): 315-16; J. Rogers Hollingsworth and Wolfgang Streeck, "Countries and Sectors: Concluding Remarks on Performance, Convergence and Competitiveness," in J. Rogers Hollingsworth, Philippe Schmitter, and Wolfgang Streeck, eds., *Governing Capitalist Economies* (Oxford: Oxford University Press, 1994), 280-83.

14. Bob Jessop, "Towards a Schumpeterian Workfare State? Preliminary Remarks on Post-Fordist Political Economy," *Studies in Political Economy* 40 (Spring 1993); Bob Jessop, "Capitalism and its future: remarks on regulation, government and governance," *Review of International Political Economy* 4, 3 (1997): 572-75; Bob Jessop, "The Changing Governance of Welfare: Recent Trends in its Primary Functions, Scale and Modes of Coordination," *Social Policy and Administration* 33, 4 (1999): 354-56.

15. Philip Cooke, "Introduction: Origins of the concept," in Hans-Joachim Braczyk, Philip Cooke, and Martin Heidenreich, eds., *Regional Innovation Systems: The role of governances in a globalized world* (London: UCL Press, 1998), 15-16; see also J. Rogers Hollingsworth and Robert Boyer, "Coordination of Economic Actors and Social Systems of Production," in J. Rogers Hollingsworth and Robert Boyer, eds., *Contemporary Capitalism: The Embeddedness of Institutions* (Cambridge: Cambridge University Press, 1997), 25-27.

16. Michael Storper, *The Regional World* (London: Guilford Press, 1997), 18-20; Hans-Joachim Braczyk and Martin Heidenreich, "Regional governance structures in a globalized world," in Hans-Joachim Braczyk, Philip Cooke, and Martin Heidenreich, eds., *Regional Innovation Systems: The role of governances in a globalized world* (London: UCL Press, 1999), 435.

17. Robert Boyer and J. Rogers Hollingsworth, "From National Embeddedness to Spatial and Institutional Nestedness," in J. Rogers Hollingsworth and Robert Boyer, eds., *Contemporary Capitalism: The Embeddedness of Institutions* (Cambridge: Cambridge University Press, 1997), 465.

18. Erik Olin Wright, "Working-Class Power, Capitalist-Class Interests, and Class Compromise," *American Journal of Sociology* 105, 4 (2000): 959-60. Michael Keating has noted the need to distinguish the respective roles of *nationalism* and *nationality* in this sort of explanation. I have not been able to figure out how to do so yet. To the extent that nationalism constructs and modifies the sense of nationality, this distinction may not matter greatly.

19. Daniel Latouche, "'Québec, see under Canada', Québec Nationalism in the New Global Age," in Alain-G. Gagnon, ed., *Québec: State and Society* (Scarborough: Nelson, 1993).

20. Gilles Bourque and Jules Duchastel, *L'identité fragmentée* (Montréal: Fides, 1996); Keating, *Les défis du nationalisme moderne*, 81-82.

21. Boyer and Hollingsworth, "From National Embeddedness," 441.

22. Michael Keating, *Territorial Politics in Europe: a Zero-Sum Game? The New Regionalism. Territorial Politics and Political Restructuring in Western Europe* (Florence: European University Institute, 1998), 9-14.

23. This holds in instances where the minority nation has a significant role in determining economic policies. Where these policies are in fact largely set by the competing national group, inequality may in fact serve nationalist mobilization. This clearly was the case in Québec before 1960, where development policies that favoured the English elite (and American capital) at the expense of the francophone majority served as a useful target for building a counter-nationalism. See McRoberts, *Québec: Social Change and Political Crisis*, 3rd ed. (Toronto: McClelland & Stewart, 1988), ch. 4-6; Yves Bélanger, *Québec inc.: L'entreprise québécoise à la croisée des chemins* (Montréal: Hurtubise, 1998), 96-101.

24. Keating, *Territorial Politics in Europe*, 5-6.

25. Keating, "The Political Economy of Regionalism," 32.

26. Keating, "The Political Economy of Regionalism," 32.

27. Daniel Latouche, "Do regions make a difference?" 322.

28. Cooke, Uranga and Etxebarria, "Regional Systems of innovation," 1574-77; Latouche, "Do regions make a difference?"

29. See McRoberts, *Québec*, ch. 5-6; Bélanger, *Québec inc.*, ch. 5.

30. Marc Levine, *The Reconquest of Montréal* (Philadelphia: Temple University Press, 1990).

31. Gilles Bourque, "La Révolution tranquille entre les velléités de l'oubli et les impératifs de la mémoire," in Bélanger, Comeau, and Métivier, eds., *La Révolution tranquille 40 ans plus tard*, 114.

32. Gilles L. Bourque, *Le modèle québécois de développement: de l'émergence au renouvellement* (Sainte-Foy: Presses de l'Université du Québec, 2000), 41.

33. Pierre Martin, "When Nationalism Meets Continentalism: The Politics of Free Trade in Québec," in Keating and Laughlin, eds. *The Political Economy of Regionalism*, 247-48.

34. The key government reports are Ministère de l'industrie et du commerce, *Une politique économique québécoise* (Québec, Ministère de l'industrie et du commerce); Ministre d'État au développement économique, *Bâtir le Québec* (Québec: Éditeur officiel du Québec, 1979); Ministre de développement économique, *Le virage technologique* (Québec: Ministère des communications, 1982).

35. Bourque, *Le modèle québécois*, 50-51.

36. A. Brian Tanguay, "Concerted Action in Québec, 1976-1983: Dialogue of the Deaf," in Alain-G. Gagnon, ed., *Québec: State and Society* (Toronto: Methuen, 1984), 370-76.

37. Bourque, *Le modèle québécois*, 56.

38. Robert Bourassa, *Le défi technologique* (Montréal: Québec/Amérique, 1985), ch. 4.

39. Compare Conseil du Patronat du Québec, *Les priorités budgétaires 1990-91 à l'aube d'un nouveau mandat politique* (Montréal: CPQ, March 1990) with preceding years of *Les priorités budgétaires*.

40. Bélanger, *Québec inc.*, ch. 6; Peter Graefe, "The High Value-Added-Low Wage Model: Progressive Competitiveness in Québec from Bourassa to Bouchard," *Studies in Political Economy* 61 (Spring 2000): 9-10.

41. Jacques Brin d'Amour, "La stratégie industrielle du gouvernement du Québec: rétrospectives et perspectives," in Charles Carrier, ed., *Pour une gestion efficace de l'économie* (Montréal: Association des économistes québécois, 1992), 80-83.

42. See Ministère de l'Industrie, du commerce et de la technologie, *Industrial Clusters* (Québec: MICT, 1993), 4-6, 9.

43. Pierrette Gagné and Michel Lefèvre, *L'entreprise à valeur ajoutée: Le modèle québécois* (Montréal: Publis-Relais, 1993), 59.

44. Bourque, *Le modèle québécois*, 135-38.

45. Ministère de l'industrie, du commerce et de la technologie, *La Stratégie industrielle du Québec "Le Point"* (Québec: Gouvernement du Québec, 10 Mar. 1994), 1.

46. Ministère de l'industrie, du commerce et de la technologie, *Ensemble vers la réussite: Mesures pour le soutien de l'économie et la création d'emplois* (Québec: MICT, 1991), 5.

47. Gagné and Lefèvre, *L'entreprise à valeur ajoutée*, 76.

48. Société québécoise de développement de la main-d'oeuvre, *Une stratégie québécoise pour l'économie et l'emploi* (Montréal: SQDM, October 24 1996), 1.

49. Conférence sur le devenir social et économique du Québec, *Un Québec de responsabilité et de solidarité* (March 1996), 5.

50. This acceptance is made most clearly in the report of the Conseil Consultatif du travail et de la main-d'oeuvre, which was signed by Québec's three largest union federations and the Conseil du Patronat. See *Document de réflexion sur une nouvelle organisation du travail* (Québec: Conseil Consultatif, 1997).

51. Jean-Marc Piotte, "Du combat au partenariat," in Yves Bélanger and Robert Comeau, *La CSN: 75 ans d'action syndicale et sociale* (Sainte-Foy: Presses de l'Université du Québec, 1998), 195.

52. Ministère des finances, *Québec objectif emploi: Vers une économie d'avant garde. Une stratégie de développement économique* (Québec: Ministère des Finances, 1998), 18-19, 23. Capital and resource intensive industries dropped from 55 per cent of manufacturing shipments in 1975 to 49 per cent in 1997. By contrast, capital and technology intensive industries grew from 19.6 per cent to 29.9 per cent. In terms of exports, equipment goods grew from 33 per cent of exports in 1984 to 40 per cent in 1996. Québec's share of Canada's manufactured exports rose from 18.7 per cent to 20 per cent over this period. See Bourque, *Le modèle québécois*, 181.

53. Ministère des finances, *Québec objectif emploi*, 20.

54. Latouche, "Do regions make a difference?" 339.

55. Pierre Fortin, "La Révolution tranquille et le virage économique du Québec," in Bélanger, Comeau, and Métivier, eds., *La Révolution tranquille 40 ans plus tard*, 168-69.

56. This point is elaborated in Graefe, "The High Value-Added, Low-Wage Model," 20-21.

57. Françoise David and Louise Marcoux, *Du pain et des roses: cahier des revendications et guide d'animation* (Montréal: Marche des femmes contre la pauvreté, Feb. 1995).

58. Chantier sur l'économie et l'emploi, *La Relance de l'emploi au Québec: Agir dans la compétivité et la solidarité* (N.p.: Sommet sur l'économie et l'emploi, Oct. 1996), 10.

59. These figures are drawn from *Le Marché du travail* 19:5 supplement (1998): 17, 22, 87-88; Statistics Canada, *Labour Force Annual Averages* (various years, cat. no. 71-529, 71-220); Statistics Canada, *Labour Force Update* (Summer 1997, cat. no. 71-005), Table 25; Statistics Canada, *Labour Force Information* (December 2000, cat. no. 71-001), Table 8.

60. Average total income per family unit (1991$) stood at 37,827 in 1981 and $36,967 in 1991. Between 1990 and 1995, which includes a severe recession, average family income fell 5.3 per cent and average household income fell 7.4 per cent. (Gouvernement du Québec,

Le Québec Statistique (Québec: Éditeur officiel, 1995), 230-31; Statistics Canada, cat. no. 93F0029XDB96008 and 93F0029XDB96009.

61. Statistics Canada, *Incidence of Low Income among Populations Living in Private Households.* <http://www.statcan.ca/english/pgda/people/families/famil6oa.htm>.

62. Kevin K. Lee, *Urban Poverty In Canada: A Statistical Profile* (Ottawa: Canadian Council for Social Development, April 2000), 14, 82.

63. Lee, *Urban Poverty*, 9, 15.

64. Ministère d'État au développement économique, *Bâtir le Québec*, 120-22; Ministère des Finances, *Québec: objectif emploi*, 82-84, 92.

65. The political critiques of progressive competitive strategies generally stress the difficulty of extracting concessions from business and forcing it to share its economic power, particularly as capital mobility tilts bargaining power further in its favour. In such a context, business interests will be happy to receive state incentives and promises of labour co-operation, while making few binding commitments in return (see Neil Bradford, "Prospects for Associative Governance: Lessons from Ontario, Canada," *Politics and Society* 24 [1998]: 564; Keating, *The New Regionalism*, 149-51). The economic critiques raise two issues. First, the ability to pay high wages and maintain good jobs is conditional on maintaining a sufficient performance gap with respect to low-cost mass producers (through innovation, product customization, superior quality etc.) so as to limit competition and raise profits. However, there is some evidence that mass producers are taking advantage of accelerated technological diffusion in order to mass produce products with a modest degree of customizability, and thus reduce the performance gap. This brings wage costs back into play, and pushes even high-end producers to hold the line on wage and tax costs (see Jody Knauss, "Modular Mass Production: High Performance on the Low Road," *Politics and Society* 26 [1998]: 289-92). Second, these strategies are based on a macroeconomic fallacy of composition, since the neo-mercantilistic export-orientation means economic success can only come at the expense of other economies, at the expense of depressing aggregate demand in the world economy. This should further strengthen cost competition, particularly with respect to labour cost. Greg Albo has sketched out how this turns "progressive competitiveness" into "competitive austerity" ("A World Market of Opportunities? Capitalist Obstacles and Left Economic Policy?" in Leo Panitch [ed.] *The Socialist Register 1997* [Halifax: Fernwood, 1997]). For a more detailed discussion of these arguments, and a tentative application to the Québec case, see Graefe, "The High-Value Added, Low-Wage Model," 19-23.

66. Chantier sur l'économie et l'emploi, *La relance*, 16, 18, 89.

67. Jean-Marc Piotte, *Du Combat au Partenariat: Interventions critiques sur le syndicalisme québécois* (Montréal: Nota Bene, 1998), 260-68.

68. Jean Charest, Gilles Trudeau and Diane Veilleux, "La Modernisation du code du travail du Québec: Perspectives et Enjeux," *Effectif* 2, 2 (1999): 25, 31.

69. See for instance Conseil Central du Montréal Métropolitain, *Question nationale et stratégie syndicale* (1998?) <http:www.ccmm-csn.qc.ca/publications/positions/qnationale.html>.

70. Gérald Tremblay in F. Youssofzaï, *Les Contrats Sociaux» du MICT: Une voie de modernisation des entreprises?* (Montréal: CRISES, 1996), 35-36.

71. Martine D'Amours, *Procès d'institutionalisation de l'économie sociale au Canada* (Montréal: CRISES/LAREPPS, Jan. 2000).

72. Peter Graefe, "Whose social economy? Debating new state practices in Québec," *Critical Social Policy* 21, 1 (2001).

73. Sharing work time was explicitly rejected on the grounds that it would hurt the economy's competitiveness. See Chantier sur l'économie et l'emploi, *La relance*, 76.

74. Piotte, *Du Combat*, 268; Conseil central du Montréal métropolitain, "Bilan de la participation de la CSN au sommet socio-économique," 1997, <http://www.total.net/~ccmm2/sommet.html>.

22

Québec's International Relations

LOUIS BALTHAZAR*

Among non-sovereign States, Québec is without contest the one that operates the most extensive network of international representation. Due to its six general delegations, five delegations, six offices, nine branches and four non-delegation specialized services,[1] it is situated at the top of approximately 350 federated political entities that exercise a jurisdiction over a given territory within a sovereign state. Its influence extends to five continents and to about 20 countries.

This international activity did not begin yesterday. Québec has, in effect, dispatched temporary immigration officers to various countries since the early years of Canadian Confederation. It delegated its first agent-general, Hector Fabre, to Paris in 1882 and delegations were created subsequently in the United Kingdom and in Belgium. In 1940, a law regarding agents-general foreshadowed representation in several countries for the purposes of external trade and tourism—and an office was created in New York.[2]

In the beginning of the 1960s, within the setting of the Quiet Revolution, Québec's international relations began to take on the magnitude that they assume today. This chapter will draw attention to the origins of this spectacular development and to the definition of the international status that resulted; it will proceed then to examine the American dimensions of Québec's policies, their extension to Europe and elsewhere in the world, and finally, to the administrative aspects of such policies.

* Translated from French into English by Raffaele Iacovino.

The Origins of Developments in the 1960s

Four factors initiated the new international activity of the 1960s. Foremost among these factors is the actual setting of the Quiet Revolution. The well-documented change of government in Québec served to stimulate the exploration of new policy avenues. Contrary to conventional wisdom, however, it was not Québec's Liberal Party (PLQ) that initiated the project of launching an embassy in Paris in its electoral program. Rather, it was the Union Nationale under the leadership of Antonio Barrette that included this point among its commitments, albeit without much prioritization. The visit of French President de Gaulle in the winter of 1960 also played a role. For its part, the PLQ had engaged, in creating a Ministry of Cultural Affairs, which was to be headed by Georges-Émile Lapalme. It was then, after a more or less planned meeting between Lapalme and André Malraux in the late summer of 1960, that a decision was made to open a Québec office in the French capital and subsequently to set in motion a process of international expansion.[3]

The events of the Quiet Revolution are not negligible in their contribution to the establishment of Québec's international relations. For example, the nationalization of all the electric power-producing companies in 1962 necessitated an appeal for American capital in order to finance the operation, and consequently, it served to reinforce Québec's presence in the financial centres of the United States. The reform of the education system and the creation of a Commission of Inquiry inevitably caused an opening towards the outside world and led to missions in France and other francophone countries. Its new affirmation of autonomy within the Canadian federation pushed Québec to demand a renewal of its jurisdictions and, naturally, their extension to the international level. Québec could not affirm itself as a distinct society, as "the political expression of French-Canada," a phrase often used by Jean Lesage, or further as a national state, without attempting to project this image outside its borders.

A second factor favourable to the boom in international relations resides in the general climate of the international scene during that era. This point must be underscored: Québec's Quiet Revolution would not have been pursued with so much success had it not been placed in an international framework. During the first years of the 1960s, many ideas began to be questioned throughout the world. In the United States, a new administration under John F. Kennedy intended to inject a new dynamism into American diplomacy. In France, the return to power of General Charles de Gaulle signalled a renewed French impetus and the projection of an image of modernity. European integration was in full progress. Even within the Catholic Church, a renewed climate emerged under the framework of the Vatican II Council. In the Third World, decolonization was in full force, prompting the emergence of several states that had no experience with independence and international presence.

A new definition of international relations was already clearly in development during this period. Foreign relations could no longer be restricted to the role of diplomats due to the proliferation of transnational relations that escaped the control of governments. Increasingly, a growing number of fields of government intervention were already proving that they could not function without accounting for the international context. One could no longer think of the economy, labour relations, education, the environment, culture, and many other fields that had previously belonged to the domestic realm without considering other regions of the world, and even engaging in dialogue with foreign countries. American specialists have created an expression to describe such questions that straddle the frontiers of internal and external politics: "intermestic" politics. In essence, the phenomenon has been characterized by Thomas A. Levy as "the internationalization of internal politics and the internalization of international relations."[4] This phenomenon accounts for several non-sovereign federated states endeavouring to establish diverse relations with other political entities beyond their borders, either to promote their exports, to attract capital, or to stimulate cultural and other exchanges. As such, other Canadian provinces, undoubtedly more discreetly than Québec and without demands for international status, followed by opening offices in the United States, Europe, and Asia. It must be emphasized that Canadian tradition lends itself fairly well to these kinds of incursions on the part of the provinces. This is the third factor that favours the international emancipation of Québec.

The Canadian constitution makes no explicit mention of foreign politics and with good cause. At the moment of its inception, Canada was still a colony with its autonomy limited by imperial authority in matters of international relations. The Dominion did not conclude a treaty without the presence of representatives from London until 1923. It waited until 1927 before it commissioned a diplomatic delegation outside of the Empire, and only in 1931 did the Dominion obtain complete sovereignty by the Statute of Westminster.

Although it enjoyed great success after World War II, Canadian diplomacy was still relatively young and fragile. In Québec, around 1960, critics of Canadian foreign policy pointed to the fact that it had not taken sufficient account of its francophone population, as Canadian diplomats were trained within the framework of British traditions and few among them could express themselves adequately in French. Also contested was the legitimacy of Canadian international activities in matters of provincial jurisdiction, and consequently, demands for a formal role for the provincial government emerged.

This situation came to a dramatic turn when the few francophone Quebecers who had managed to secure a place within the Canadian Foreign Service became divided among themselves as to the attitude to adopt to the new international pretensions of the government of Québec. A minority openly deplored their situation within Canadian diplomacy and some offered their services to the Québec state. The most notable among them, Jean Chapdelaine, former ambassador to Brazil, Sweden, and Egypt, who became in 1965 Québec's Delegate General in Paris, a post that he was to occupy for more than 10 years.

On the other hand, other francophone diplomats wanted to stay in Ottawa to reap the fruits of their efforts, with the intention of providing a more bilingual and representative character to Canadian foreign policy. Among this group, the most illustrious within the Ministry at the time was Marcel Cadieux. After a bitter battle with Québec officials who, in some ways, pulled the carpet from under the feet of their courageous francophone counterparts and tended to delegitimize their role, he eventually rose to the summit of the Ministry by becoming Deputy Secretary of State between 1964 and 1970, a critical period of tension between Ottawa and Québec in matters of international relations. These persistent antagonisms between brothers in arms exacerbated such tensions, as could be readily observed.

While Québec explored the potential for profit from a badly defined legal situation, and from a Canadian federal system that at times seemed rather flexible and conducive to decentralization, it also aroused a certain hardening on the part of representatives of the federal government, who had become touchy and determined to reinforce the role of Ottawa in foreign policy. From Lester B. Pearson (1963-68) to Pierre Trudeau (1968-79; 1980-84), a clear change of direction took place, in the sense of a new affirmation of and a new rigidity towards Québec on the part of the central government of Canada. The arduous struggle of Québec for an international status was to be subjected to serious obstacles.

Finally, the fourth and perhaps most important factor, according to some analysts, is the particular role played by France. As noted above, General de Gaulle, having been returned to power in Paris in 1958, visited Canada in 1960. He was received in Québec and formed the impression of a vibrant and dynamic francophonie. According to the observations of Georges-Émile Lapalme, de Gaulle immediately gave instructions to his Minister of Culture, André Malraux, to establish links with Québec.[5] We can assert, therefore, that the opening of the Québec Office in Paris in 1961 was largely initiated and prepared for at the highest levels of the French political hierarchy. Following this, France was to follow the evolution of the Quiet Revolution in Québec. For instance, as soon as the Québec Ministry of Education was created, in the spring of 1964, the first person to pay a personal visit to the new Minister, Paul Gérin-Lajoie, was the ambassador of France to Canada, Raymond Bousquet.[6] This would result in an agreement between Québec and France in matters of education, signed in 1965, prior to Ottawa's intervention to include this relationship in a framework-agreement. The Gérin-Lajoie doctrine was to come about on the heels of this event.

Later on, it was the same head of the French state who, after having received with great ceremony Premiers Lesage and Johnson at L'Élysée and conferring a special diplomatic status on Québec, solemnly turned up in Québec, took the route of the Chemin du Roy, spanning the length of the North Shore of the St. Lawrence, and launched a message of emancipation from the balcony of Montréal's City Hall on 24 July 1967: "Vive le Québec! Vive le Québec libre!"

It was, again, France that persuaded Gabon to invite Québec, with the exclusion of the Canadian government, to an international conference on education for francophone countries, in 1968. Finally, France played an unequivocal role in Québec's acquisition of an international status within *la francophonie*.

This fourth factor, likewise, contained a contingent feature. In effect, just as Canada was not the same with the rise of Pierre Trudeau to power, France no longer demonstrated the same sustained ardour in the promotion of Québec after the departure of Charles de Gaulle. The first two factors, the national consciousness of Québec and the rise of paradiplomacy are, without a doubt, those that maintain the continuity of Québec's diplomacy and that continue to legitimize its manifestations. Nevertheless, the international status of Québec was obtained and sustained in the triangular context of relations with Ottawa and Paris, as was clearly apparent in 1965, in the legitimizing statement of Québec's international presence, with two accords that entrenched this presence by conferring a particular status, and with persistent efforts to maintain this status through the years.

The International Status of Québec

It was Paul Gérin-Lajoie who first stated in an explicit and, in some ways, definitive manner the reasons that legitimized the international role of the Québec state. His speech, delivered before the consular corps of Montréal on 12 April 1965, has become somewhat of a permanent doctrine for the government of Québec. By virtue of this doctrine, extension of external jurisdictions by a Canadian province is the responsibility of this province, to the same degree as its internal aspects. The government charged with executing an international agreement must negotiate and sign the agreement on its own.

> There is no reason, claimed Gérin-Lajoie ... that the fact of executing an international convention should be dissociated with the signing of this convention. They represent two steps that are essentially one single operation. Moreover, it is also not acceptable that the federal

state be empowered to exercise a sort of monitoring and control of the opportunities available to Québec in its international relations.[7]

The federal government reacted swiftly to this position by declaring that Québec's intentions were in fact, inadmissible, due to the indivisibility of the sovereignty of the Canadian state. The federal government conceded that provinces could be associated with negotiations that might lead to treaties and that they could be responsible for their execution. However, it stringently affirmed Ottawa's exclusive jurisdiction in matters of foreign relations. The Minister of External Affairs, Paul Martin, submitted a declaration written on 29 April 1965:

> Canada possesses a single international personality within the community of nations. There is no doubt that only the Canadian government holds the power or the right to conclude treaties with other countries....[8]

Afterwards, when Québec received an exclusive invitation by Gabon to participate in an international conference on education, the federal government reacted firmly by breaking diplomatic relations with the state that dared treat Québec like an autonomous international actor and by publishing two brochures that established the unique jurisdiction of the Canadian state in matters relating to international conferences, treaties, and other diplomatic instances.[9]

More than 35 years later, this question is yet to be resolved. Québec continues to affirm its right to international extension of its constitutional jurisdictions, notably in a law passed by the National Assembly in December 2000, on "the exercise of the fundamental rights and prerogatives of the Québec people and the state of Québec." The triennial plan for 2001-04 of Québec's Ministry of International Relations continues to refer to the Gérin-Lajoie doctrine as the fundamental expression of its international legitimacy.[10]

For its part, the Canadian government never ceased to assert its primacy in the area of diplomacy, more or less tolerating an international presence for Québec while intending always to keep it under tight scrutiny and supervision. With the exception of its participation at the aforementioned conference in Libreville, Gabon in 1968, Québec has never attempted a cavalier approach to go it alone and ignore Canadian policies. As such, none of Québec's external delegations was established without the consent of Ottawa. The federal government makes a strong point of asserting its discretionary powers when it comes to giving out visas to Québec civil servants, necessary for residence in foreign countries, and in demanding recognition from the large majority of foreign states as the sole valid representative body of all Canadian citizens, including Quebecers.

Québec has thus been forced to take into account Canadian reactions to its intentions on the international scene. In other words, if France has, to a large extent, contributed to carving out a particular place for Québec within *la francophonie*, it could not have occurred without the consent of the federal government. The international status of Québec was achieved only through a compromise.

The Agence de coopération culturelle et technique (ACCT)—The Agency for Cultural and Technical Co-operation, was created in Niamey in April 1970, at France's instigation, as a permanent international institution meant to stimulate the efforts of entirely or partially francophone countries. This was undertaken in order to promote an increase in the use of the French language in various exchanges in matters of culture and education, and to encourage co-operation between these countries. From the beginning, it was unthinkable that Québec would not take part. It was also unthinkable that Canada would not play a leading role. The Gabon affair was resolved fairly quickly and to Canada's satisfaction, as the small African state soon recognized its error in its mistaken appreciation for the major financial reward resulting from co-operation with Canada. General de Gaulle, for his part, could no longer permit himself to be audacious after his setback in May 1968, and he would soon abandon his post—in March 1969. His friend, Premier Johnson, passed away in September 1968 and Pierre Trudeau was confirmed as Canada's prime minister by an electoral victory in June of the same year. Robert Bourassa took power in Québec in April 1970 with a mandate that did not emphasize great international ambitions. The political triangle of Pompidou-Trudeau-Bourassa was much less favourable to an international breakthrough for Québec than that of de Gaulle-Pearson-Johnson.

In this context Trudeau believed he was breaking down Québec's ambitions by imposing a unique Canadian presence in the ACCT. Thus, it took much perseverance on the part of Québec bureaucrats and their Parisian counterparts to come to compromises that would determine the modalities of Québec's presence and to give its government, albeit within a Canadian delegation, a formal role and international status. This was attained by virtue of an accord between Québec and Ottawa, on 1 October 1971, and culminated in the adoption of Article 3.3 of the Agency's Charter:

> With the full respect of the sovereignty and jurisdictions of member-states, all governments can be admitted as participants in the institutions, the activities and the programs of the Agency, subject to the approval of the member-state that is responsible for the territory on which the participating government exercises its authority and according to the modalities convened between this government and the government of the member-state.[11]

The international position of Québec thus remains largely circumscribed by its status as a Canadian member-state and, as such, it lacks the capacity to operate fully without at least a minimal co-operation between the governments of Québec and Ottawa. This co-operation has been manifested both at international meetings and in Québec's foreign activities. It has sometimes proven to be difficult, and at other times totally non-existent, as in the issue of the Summit of Francophone Countries under Trudeau. This project had been conceived in the 1960s by Senegal's President, Léopold Senghor. It received the support of the prime minister of Canada, who saw the occasion as uniquely propitious for Canada to be present in an organization of sovereign states in which global objectives were to be placed above the jurisdictions of one province. Once again, due to France, a francophonie that would have excluded Québec was not created.[12]

Only in the 1980s with the advent of a Conservative government led by Brian Mulroney, in a climate of reconciliation between Ottawa and Québec, was a compromise achieved, permitting Summits that involved heads of states and heads of governments of francophonie. Essentially, all that was required was to revive the 1971 formula and adding pertinent clauses that did not challenge nor alter the jurisdictions of Québec. As such, by virtue of an agreement reached on 7 November 1985, between the governments of Brian Mulroney and Pierre-Marc Johnson, the following rule was to apply to the development of Summits of francophonie:

> On questions related to the global political situation, the Premier of Québec is present and may act as an interested observer. On questions related to the global economic situation, the Premier of Québec may, after consultation and with the formal approval of the Prime Minister of Canada, intervene on questions which are of interest to Québec … With regards to the second part, the government of Québec may participate entirely in debates and activities, according to the modalities and the practices agreed upon by *l'Agence de coopération culturelle et technique* (ACCT).[13]

The atmosphere of reconciliation did not outlive the Mulroney government. The Liberal Party of Canada returned to power in 1993 and Trudeau's policies, aimed at limiting the external actions of Québec, would resurface under the government of Jean Chrétien. These policies applied equally both to federalist and to Parti Québécois (PQ) governments, although federal opposition was much stronger towards a sovereignist Québec government.

In its White Paper of 1995 on foreign policy, the Canadian government outlined its objectives as though Canada were not really a federation. In no part of the document are provincial prerogatives and jurisdictions (notably in the area of education) mentioned were it only in the execution of international agreements concluded by Canada. Provinces are mentioned as only one aspect, among others, of Canadian society[14] and not as one of the two levels of the government of the country, as established in the Canadian constitution. It even goes so far as to allude to "our educational system"[15] without any reference to the diverse provincial systems of the country. Three objectives of the Canadian policies are outlined: the promotion of prosperity and employment, the protection of our security within a stable global framework, and the projection of Canadian values and culture.

It is this third objective that has troubled Québec governments. It is expressed among others in this manner: "The celebration of Canadian culture and the promotion of Canadian cultural and educational industries, so that they can continue to compete at home and abroad, are central tenets of Canadian policy."[16] In its strategic plan of 2001-04, the Ministry of International Relations of Québec disputed the validity of this formulation. After having confirmed that Québec voluntarily adheres to the first two objectives of the Canadian government with the full respect of exclusive federal jurisdictions, Québec officials wrote that: "the formulation of this objective in matters of education, culture and identity, has by no means been drafted with the consent of the Government of Québec, even though these areas are, first and foremost, among its jurisdictions."[17] The document continues on a positive note, however, by confirming that in practice, the Québec Ministry joins its voice to that of the Canadian government in the promotion of cultural diversity.

The federal ministry sometimes defends its pretension of exclusivity on the international scene by arguing that it must promote Canadian unity externally and, thus, must oppose everything that interferes with that. As such, it accuses the PQ government of engaging in the promotion of Québec sovereignty outside of its borders. The validity of this accusation is doubtful, with the exception of the brief pre-referendum period of 1994-95, under the leadership of Jacques Parizeau. Following that period—most notably during the Bouchard years (1996-2001)—the Québec government sought to reassure its partners, as had been the case under René Lévesque, rather than to win them over to the cause. Indeed, in the strategic plan of 2001 there is no mention of the sovereignty option.

Québec's international status was bolstered by the new importance accorded to paradiplomacy, which is to say, the practice of diplomacy undertaken outside of the confines of a sovereign authority, particularly by non-sovereign states. It is no longer rare that such states, whether or not as members of federations, manifest themselves at the international level through official representatives and by the completion of agreements with other sovereign or non-sovereign states. Some of these actors, like the Belgian communities and regions, and the Swiss cantons, even have the international status of their jurisdictions recognized by their constitutions. Others, like certain Spanish regions (Catalonia, Basque Country), German *länder* (Bavaria, and others) have established relations in some areas of the world. Québec's status has been strengthened by the presence of these new partners. Québec must content itself with this type of limited status without any official character in its diplomacy on the American continent, where its interests are becoming increasingly important.

The American Dimension

The most important, pressing, and immediate relation for Québec is that which must be maintained with its giant neighbour, the United States. This is an undeniable reality. Not only is the US a superpower that any international actor cannot ignore, it is also the only state (with the exception of the Canadian provinces) with which Québec shares a border, and this border is becoming more and more porous. Through it economic exchanges have reached, in 2001, close to 86 per cent of Québec's total international trade, and American culture and institutions affect all of Québec society most profoundly. This is a reality that Quebecers have often sought to ignore or at least to neglect. For historic and cultural reasons related to the particular identity and character of francophone Québec, a greater insistence has been laid on the bonds that unite Québec society with France and *la francophonie*. This has been and will no doubt continue to be essential to the security and development of Québec. This aspect remains important on an international scale, given the significance of France as a launching pad for Québec's diplomacy. What is less acceptable is that the *Americanness* of Québec has sometimes been neglected—that is to say, the inevitable insertion of Québec into the geographic tissue of America.

Québec's relations in North America, notably with the United States, have, nevertheless, become multiple, diverse, and intense. Paradoxically, in a state where the central government recognizes no real partner other than the Canadian government, Québec representatives have been able to engage in significant levels of diplomacy, often more subtly than the official Canadian diplomats. The latter have been forced to struggle constantly against the tendency of Americans to ignore their northern neighbours—to take them for granted—even at the highest levels, and to view them almost as if they were a part of the same country. This applies to Québec, as well, although Quebecers often appear more "foreign" and "bizarre" to American eyes, particularly when its distinct culture is actively promoted. In a country where the acquisition of a foreign language is not prevalent, the affirmation in Québec of an official language other than English is not easily appreciated, despite the enormous progress of the Spanish language in several states. Therefore, Québec representatives have made use of Canadian diplomatic institutions, while promoting Québec as a distinct society and defending the interests, as well as the products, of this society to the Americans.

As mentioned, Québec had established by 1940 a modest office in New York for commercial and tourist purposes. This office was later upgraded to a General Delegation in 1962, in order to favour the opening of Québec to the world, particularly in the context of the nationalization of private electric companies that necessitated an appeal for American capital. Indeed, it was not believed necessary to extend this presence to other regions for several years. When extension was undertaken, it was due to an old desire to service French America beyond Québec's borders. Premier Lesage intended to deliver a Québec message to New England cousins and to renew relations with distant Louisiana. First in Lafayette, but also in Chicago, other representations were established in 1969. Economic imperatives quickly won the day over cultural preoccupations as delegations were established in Boston, Los Angeles, and Dallas by 1970.

Premier Robert Bourassa also took an interest in the United States, as expected, as a result of the priority his government placed on economic development, notably in the gigantic project of James Bay, which for the most part relied on the interests of American financiers and electricity importers. It was René Lévesque, however, who would launch *Operation Amérique*, an endeavour to intensify the presence of Québec in the United States and to signal a *rapprochement* with American interlocutors. Since World War II in which he worked as a journalist covering American forces, Lévesque had maintained a predilection for the United States. Moreover, from the outset of his leadership of the PQ government, Lévesque believed in and felt it imperative to declare frankly his project of independence for Québec in American economic circles. His speech to the Economic Club in New York in January 1977 did not attain its desired effect. He succeeded only in arousing more concern among American elites as to the intentions of his government. It was in the wake of this setback that Opération Amérique was launched in 1978, which consisted in increasing all sorts of contacts with Americans by means of ministerial visits, invitations to journalists, and cultural and other manifestations in territories served by these delegations. This no longer meant persuading them of the soundness of the PQ option, which henceforth appeared an unrealistic task, but rather to reassure the Americans as to the effects of actions planned by the government. The intention was to demonstrate the fundamentally peaceful character of Québec society, its openness towards market economies, the dynamism of its institutions and a firm commitment to appeal to democracy for any important changes. This campaign resulted in some success, as Washington maintained a non-interventionist stance towards the referendum of 1980.

During these years President Jimmy Carter formulated what has been called the *mantra* of American policy towards the Québec sovereignty movement: (1) The United States expresses a clear preference for the preservation of Canadian unity; (2) it nevertheless does not intervene in the debate surrounding this question in

Canada, leaving Canadians with the task of resolving their internal problems; (3) The United States respects the will of Canadians to express themselves in a democratic verdict. (Special care is taken not to specify to what extent they would respect the democratic will of Quebecers in the process of a referendum.) The government of Québec was satisfied with this approach as it assured a significant amount of discretion on the part of the Americans. Nonetheless, during that time period, many American friends of Canada as well as those in Canadian circles with close ties to the Americans, attempted to exert pressure with the aim of stimulating an American intervention, hoping to influence the Québec population. In Washington, such pressure tactics were resisted due to the belief that an intervention might prove a counterproductive.

The government of Québec has enjoyed much less success in its attempt to establish a political presence in Washington. It was able, although with much difficulty, to create a Tourism Office in 1978, albeit devoid of any political ambitions. Indeed, Ottawa continued firmly to oppose a province's representation in the American capital by asserting the necessary indivisibility of Canadian diplomacy in the complex universe of American national institutions, where major interests for all of Canada are at stake. By refusing to grant visas and in winning over the power of the American executive to its cause, the Canadian government was successful in limiting Québec's presence at tourism promotion functions and in setting up a discreet monitoring on the part of the councillor for national affairs of the General Delegation of New York.

After the referendum defeat, Opération Amérique was upheld, not any more for the purpose of reassuring Americans about the sovereignty project, as this was no longer on the agenda, but to attract investments, especially in the difficult circumstances surrounding the recession of 1982. The period witnessed Jacques-Yvan Morin, for example, as the Minister of Intergovernmental Affairs (MIA) during the short period between the resignation of Claude Morin and the ministerial reorganization of 1983-84, travelling through American capitals with a rather benevolent message for the economic and political leaders of our neighbouring country, and manifesting a new Québec sensitivity to North American insertion. Subsequently, Bernard Landry, having been Minister of International Trade and then of International Relations, wasted no time in strengthening American links in economic matters, having somewhat foreseen the advent of free trade.

The return to power of Bourassa at the end of 1985 did not signal a break in this campaign of economic overtures. The Liberal government supported the Free Trade Agreement of 1988 with enthusiasm, with the support of the Official Opposition. Moreover, Minister of International Affairs John Ciaccia (1988-94) travelled regularly to the United States, seeking to rectify misinformation circulating about Québec, most notably in the area of Aboriginal relations.

The government of Jacques Parizeau, for its part, delivered a sort of Opération Amérique in view of the referendum of 1995, but with less restraint and subtlety than René Lévesque and Claude Morin. On the American side, the so-called neutrality professed in 1980 was attenuated to make room for more specific intervention in favour of Canadian unity.

Lucien Bouchard, once in power, applied himself to an approach that stressed reassurance, as at the end of the 1960s, and placed much emphasis on cultivating the image of a Québec that is dynamic and fundamentally committed to intense economic exchange with the United States. The links between the premier and his counterparts, state governors, were strengthened.[18]

Once again, in 2001, Québec sought to undertake an intense cultural campaign with the United States, particularly in New York.[19] Opération Amérique, having proven rather fruitful, thus became a permanent enterprise. The opening of American markets due to the Free Trade Agreement contributed spectacularly to an increase in commercial exchanges with the United States. Québec also created a network of sympathizers by encouraging, during the 1980s, the creation of an association of Québec studies, the American Council for Québec Studies, and by proliferating its support to various francophone or francophile intermediaries—for example, French language professors working in the United States.

The delegations that had been shut down abruptly in 1996 in Boston, Chicago, and Los Angeles (for very questionable economic reasons), all were reopened during 2000-01. Moreover, a new office was created in Miami, due to the city's pan-American ties. The Office of Tourism in Washington remained similar to what it had been in 1978. Québec's limited political functions continue to operate from the general delegation in New York.

It must be noted that, throughout, these years, Washington maintained a diplomatic post in the Québec capital. In spite of the fact that the United States did not want any other sovereign partner than the Canadian state, it nonetheless conceived a discreet political relationship with Québec. The consulate general of Québec City has no other function, since current consular interests are sufficiently served by only five other general consulates in Canada as a whole (Halifax, Montréal, Toronto, Calgary, and Vancouver). Thus, no other than a political reason can justify a second diplomatic presence in the province of Québec. According to a Consul General in 1991, American diplomats posted in Québec City are "the eyes and ears of Washington," demonstrating a desire to sustain, in an unofficial capacity, particular links with Québec.

In short, despite the absence of official political recognition, American-Québec relations have nevertheless been very complex over the years. If Québec enjoys little presence in Washington, it is compensated by an ever-increasing role in regional institutions like the annual Conference of New England Governors and

Eastern Canadian Premiers and the Council of Great Lakes Governors, as well as the Great Lakes Commission. Québec is also an associate member of the Council of State Governments and it has shown much interest in the activities of the National Governors Association.

Moreover, the government of Québec monitors very closely any economic developments that may affect its population, especially when the US Congress attempts to impose restrictions on Canadian exports in defiance of the North-American Free Trade Agreement (NAFTA). The inclusion of Mexico in this accord, as well as the project to create a free trade area across the Americas (FTA), has contributed to bolstering Québec's relations with Latin American countries.

As of 1979, with the help of a more conciliatory conservative federal government under Joe Clark, a general delegation was opened in Mexico City and a delegation in Caracas. An immigration office had already existed within the Canadian Embassy in Buenos Aires since 1977. Québec's interests during this time period were mainly concerned with cultural affinities and with the fact that many immigrants from these regions were drawn to Québec. Furthermore, Canada was already present in the Organization of American States (OAS) in an observer capacity. Later, after Canada gained membership in the OAS in 1989, and especially since the beginning of NAFTA in 1994, as well as because of a free trade accord between Canada and Chile in 1997, economic exchanges with these countries grew considerably and are expected to increase if the FTA comes into effect in 2005.

In 2000, the Décennie québécoise des Amériques was launched in an attempt to make a breakthrough, particularly in Mexico, but also in other countries of the hemisphere, like Argentina, where Québec has a delegation, in Chile, which has a Québec branch that could be upgraded, and in Brazil, where Québec expects representation fairly soon.

Another development was the Office Québec-Amérique pour la jeunesse, modelled after the Office franco-québécois, an institution that has contributed significantly to communications with France. Moreover, Québec has introduced the learning of a third language into its educational system, of which most students doubtless will choose Spanish.

Many in Québec circles favour increased linkages with Latin-America. Although the FTA project has provoked much concern and opposition, it is remarkable that, despite the large protest movement surrounding the April 2001 Summit in Québec City, the Summit unfolded in an atmosphere of *rapprochement* and solidarity between the peoples of the two American continents.

Québec's Americanness, is thus, a *fait accompli* for the Québec Ministry of International Relations. Other aspects of diplomacy, however, have not been neglected. France, la francophonie, Europe, Asia, and the Middle East constitute continuing poles of interest and activity.

European and Other Dimensions

France

To begin with, France and la francophonie continue to act as the major axes of Québec's international relations apart from the Americas. As stated above, it was the relationship with France that has permitted Québec to play a major role in the multilateral institutions of la francophonie. The general delegation in Paris remains the most important of its kind in Québec's international network. Furthermore, Québec also maintains a delegation for francophone and multilateral affairs in Paris.

During the 1970s, a decade of consolidation for Québec's international relations,[20] even after the departure of de Gaulle, relations with France never ceased to intensify. The government of Robert Bourassa (1970-76), although federalist, applied itself to protecting its gains within la francophonie and to sustaining its particularly tight links with France. In his obsession with the uncertain concept of "cultural sovereignty," Bourassa sought to strengthen the bonds with France, as was evident in his elaborate accords with Prime Minister Chirac in 1974.[21]

Later on, René Lévesque also was anxious in his own way to consolidate Québec's particular relationship with France. He was received with great ceremony by President Valéry Giscard d'Estaing and was made *Grand Officier de la Légion d'honneur* in 1977. The President then made a commitment to support Québec "regardless of the road you decide to follow." They also mutually agreed that the French prime minister and the Québec premier would visit one another alternately once per year.[22]

This scenario, established as early as the 1960s, was never officially called into question, although it has been slightly disturbed. The relationship with France, due to the strength of the various bilateral institutions that gave rise to it, has always been of primary importance to Québec. During the period of Liberal government between 1985 and 1994, however, France-Québec relations lost some of their lustre, with official visits less frequent between the respective leaders. The tradition of annual meetings between the premier and prime minister waned, for several more or less legitimate reasons. The Minister of International Affairs, John Ciaccia, for example, seemed much less inclined to travel to France.

In 1994, with the ascension of a francophile premier who was devoted to the cause of Québec's independence, relations with France regained their significance. Jacques Parizeau made his way to Paris a few months after his election and actively sought support for the cause of sovereignty. He obtained it from the President of the French National Assembly at the time, Philippe Séguin, and even, in a rather more subdued manner, from Jacques Chirac, who would later win the Presidential

Elections in March of 1995. Valéry Giscard d'Estaing's commitment would be echoed some 18 years later.[23]

Since the referendum defeat, the ardour had seemingly subsided. Nothing significant was modified in the arsenal of diverse exchanges that had been institutionalized. Moreover, nothing indicated that France would call into question, in some manner, its unconditional support for the international status of Québec. What nevertheless did transpire was an effort by President Chirac to solidify more prominent links with Jean Chrétien than with Lucien Bouchard or Bernard Landry. As for the Prime Minister, Lionel Jospin, it can be plausibly stated that he wanted nothing to do with friendships that were primarily cultivated by the Gaullists. During a visit to Canada in 1998, he seemed to be more fascinated by Canadian multiculturalism than by Québec identity, although he did end up recognizing the virtues of Québec's own interculturalism.

In spite of everything, the fact that the links have already been formed and societies are so close to one another has resulted in France remaining by far Québec's major partner, and continues to be the primary channel of Québec's international influence. One need only take into account that approximately 500,000 French citizens visit Québec each year, that Québec artists are now recognized more than ever in *l'Hexagone*, and that a large number of French businesses are concentrated in Québec, more than anywhere else in North America.[24] Specific contacts are also frequent in ministerial circles, particularly in areas of culture and education.

La francophonie is the most significant sphere of Québec's multilateral activities. To the extent that there now exists a veritable international organization of French-speaking countries with its own general secretariat, Québec has jealously guarded its status of participant government, and has pursued policies contingent on the evolution of circumstances, for example, the promotion of cultural diversity and the affirmation of democratic principles in a context of accelerated globalization. This activity continues to proceed within the framework of the France-Canada-Québec triangle, in an atmosphere that is sometimes harmonious, sometimes difficult, and influenced by antagonism existing within the Canadian federation.

Other European Countries

Québec has demonstrated a growing interest in Europe, particularly in the evolution of the institutions of the European Union, which many Quebecers consider a viable model for the sharing of sovereignty. The government of Québec does not yet enjoy direct access to European institutions where more and more decisions that concern particular European states are taking place. Several accords have been concluded between Canada and the European Union. Québec has insisted that the federal government "recognize the importance of accepting Québec's contributions in the development of these accords, which is not the case presently," according to the Québec Ministry of International Relations.[25]

Among European countries, the United Kingdom occupies a place of utmost importance for Québec, due to historical ties sustained for more than two hundred years. It was the British Parliament that initially recognized the specificity of Québec in 1774 and served to inspire Québec's parliamentary government since its inception in 1792. Québec culture, for reasons of a long colonial history and the origins of an important component of the Québec population, is infused with British traditions. Following Paris, London is without a doubt the European capital to which Quebecers find themselves most connected. The United Kingdom is also an important economic partner, following only the United States. All of these reasons, with the addition of the particular attention that Québec pays to the evolution of the status of Scotland and Wales, have conferred to the general delegation of Québec in London a rather special function.

Belgium also enjoys a privileged relationship with Québec, which had established a general delegation there at the start of the 1960s. Strong multilateral and multi-sectoral relations have been pursued with the two large communities of Belgium, Wallonia-Brussels, and Flanders. The *Québec-Wallonie-Bruxelles* youth agency organizes more than 800 internships annually. Moreover, Belgium offers Québec a model of decentralization in the areas of international relations by guaranteeing the right of its component communities to sign international treaties pertaining to their particular jurisdictions.

Germany, particularly since its rise to prominence in Europe in terms of power and population since reunification, is also a pole of attraction for Québec's international relations. Germany's economic dynamism makes a partnership with this country as prestigious as with the United Kingdom and France, a considerable source of investment, and a destination for Québec's products. Québec has long been represented in Dusseldorf, at the heart of the Rhineland industrial zone. Since 1989, however, Bavaria has emerged as a point of interest. Accords have been concluded with this Land, which guards its autonomy and is proud of its economic prosperity. Indeed, Québec has established an office in Munich.

Italy is also considered to be a significant economic power by Québec. It is a country of origin for many Quebecers, where multiple bonds have been established due to cultural affinities and the shared tradition of the Catholic Church. At the present time, Québec holds only one cultural agency, in Rome.

Spain has caused a particular interest since admittance into the European Union and above all since its Autonomous Regions have been granted an expansion of their jurisdictions, fashioned after Québec in the Canadian federation. Links with Catalonia have developed considerably during the last decade of the twentieth century. Québec has established an office in Barcelona.

Elsewhere in the world, with the exception of the privileged relations with member countries of la francophonie and in matters of immigration, Québec's relations rest mainly on economic matters. In Asia, Québec, like others, is attracted to the dazzling economic evolution in certain countries, even though this evolution has encountered a serious slowdown at the end of the century. Québec has kept a general delegation in Tokyo since 1973, taking into account the considerable economic force of Japan and the attractive potential of Japanese investments in Québec. Tokyo is also a prestigious cultural capital of Asia and an area of exchange in the domain of education. China, due to its spectacular economic opening during the last few decades, has also been a target interest on the part of Québec. Several visits have been organized and offices were set up in Beijing and Shanghai. Québec has also established branches in other Asian countries, in Seoul, Manila, Kuala Lumpur, and Hanoi.

In Africa and the Middle East, exchanges have been conditioned by the presence in la francophonie of certain countries in these regions, and by economic interests, especially in the countries of Northern Africa and in South Africa. Another factor has been a number of communities emanating from these countries in Québec.

As demonstrated above, this is a rather extensive network of foreign relations for a non-sovereign state of modest size. Given some uncertainties and inevitable trials throughout this complex undertaking, the administration of Québec's international relations has sometimes been erratic. It has been particularly difficult to integrate all foreign operations within one single agency.

The Hazards of Administration

It may be useful at first to outline the evolution of the administration of international relations within the Québec state and then to assess the diversity of the formal expressions of these relations.

To begin with, a rather revealing fact of the uncertain and "adventurous" character of the development of international relations during the 1960s must be highlighted. These relations did not stem from a formal ministry until 1967. Since relations had been strictly economic in the past, the first offices of Québec in foreign countries were placed under the responsibility of the Ministry of Industry and Commerce. It was nevertheless the Ministry of Education that signed Québec's first important agreement in 1965, in effect initiating a doctrine of legitimizing Québec's new international efforts. That same year, Québec signed another agreement, with France, yet this time by the Ministry of Cultural Affairs. Recall in this regard that at the outset of the opening of an office of Québec in Paris, the creation of this ministry by George-Émile Lapalme and his meeting with André Malraux took place. Finally, the Ministry of Federal-Provincial Affairs, created in 1961, was the most actively engaged in international relations. Its deputy-minister, Claude Morin, would later figure, with Paul Gérin-Lajoie, as the co-signatory to the agreement of 1965.[26]

The Ministry of Intergovernmental Affairs was created on 12 April 1967 by Premier Daniel Johnson with the intention of conferring a certain unity on Québec's international relations policy. The attempt remained only partially successful, however, as the ministries already engaged in external affairs did not abandon their responsibilities. Moreover, for about 15 years the new ministry managed both external affairs and federal-provincial relations, two rather different portfolios despite the evident links that frequently bring them in contact.

In 1974 another important step was taken in the effort to consolidate the administration of international relations. Robert Bourassa, concerned about efficiency in governmental organization, solidified the establishment of the Ministry of Intergovernmental Affairs by integrating the international programs of other ministries. The Law on the Ministry of Intergovernmental Affairs continues to constitute the basis for the present Ministry of International Relations. This is made explicit in the strategic plan of 2001-04, reminding us that this law, updated several times since 1974, "decrees that the Ministry of International Relations has the mandate to plan, organize and to direct the external actions of the government, as well as to coordinate the activities, in Québec, of its ministries and organizations in matters of international relations."[27]

This intention to grant a central role to the Ministry reveals a certain maturity of Québec policies in matters of international relations. All the ministries of external affairs of the major industrialized countries seek to impose their appropriation of the international aspects of policies, especially in an era where the line between internal and external politics is increasingly open to interpretation. In effect, the majority of sector-related ministries of modern governments, aware of the international ramifications of their policies, have exhibited an inclination to institute their own external service, to the extent that a ministry responsible for international affairs of a state tends to lose some control, at the expense of the very cohesiveness of the international actions of the state. In Québec in the 1960s, at least five ministries sought aggressively to support programs that were aimed externally: education, culture, social affairs, industry and commerce, and immigration. The first three had their programs integrated with the Ministry of Intergovernmental Affairs in 1975, following the law of 1974. The other two followed suit in 1977, under the Lévesque government. In this period "the Ministry of Intergovernmental Affairs established its ascension within the governmental apparatus. In a word, it became an essential hub of Québec's international activities."[28]

The administrative structures, however, remain basically uncertain and often misleading. Shiro Noda, a scholar who has researched extensively the organization of Québec's international relations during the 1970s, reminds us that, "the mechanical and impersonal arrangement characterizing the organization of government demonstrates an eminently human reality, inspired by considerations other than simple concerns about administrative efficiency."[29] Luc Bernier, who wrote on Québec's international politics from a perspective of public administration, concurs with this assessment, claiming, in a more peremptory manner, that "if indeed there has been an institutionalization of Québec's external relations, it was mostly the result of favourable circumstances, of chance, and of reversal of fortunes rather than a planned process...."[30]

Everything points to an "eminently human reality" as the basis for the administrative reforms undertaken in 1983. A new ministry devoted to international trade was created. On its own terms, this decision was not easily justifiable. It may very well be legitimate to separate the functions of international trade in a large country like Japan, for example, which instituted its famous MITI, but it is difficult to understand why it was necessary to institute two centres of decision-making on foreign policy in a small non-sovereign state like Québec. Even the Canadian Ministry of International Trade, created in the same time period, is integrated within the structures of the Ministry of Foreign Affairs. It seems as though the pressure exerted by the talented minister of state for economic development, Bernard Landry, was an essential factor in the decision to divide the functions of the Ministry of Intergovernmental Affairs.

The following year, in 1984, federal-provincial affairs were separated from international affairs, an action that was much more justifiable. The result was a Ministry of International Relations with a considerably reduced mandate. In this period of economic recession and declining state intervention, this reduction did not help to contribute to the morale of the Ministry's bureaucrats. Extracting the economic aspects of a foreign policy, which had widened considerably, hardly left a glowing prospect to the new, essentially political, ministry. Cultural activities, diminished by budgetary reductions, were not sufficient to lend lustre to the new Ministry of International Relations. Nevertheless, it must be noted that the assignment of one person to the helm of the two new ministries (External Trade and International Relations) did contribute to reuniting these two separate mandates.

The Liberals assumed power in December 1985. This time, two ministers were assigned to the respective international ministries. Since the PLQ of Robert Bourassa considered economic policy to be a priority, and justified the international presence of Québec in terms of investments and job creation, the division appeared more futile than ever. As a consequence, in 1988 a decision was taken once again to reshuffle the administration. A new ministry that reunited external trade with international relations was created. The ministry was named "International Affairs," with an emphasis on the strict economic sense of the word "affairs" (business rather than affairs).

One might think that a tradition of a high international presence was finished. This was reinforced by the fact that the new office was headed by individuals with little calling for diplomacy, like Paul Gobeil, who came straight out of the business community, and John Ciaccia, who seemed to respect entirely the federal government's drive to reign in external politics. However, these two ministers soon embraced their office and did not even try to reduce Québec's representation abroad. John Ciaccia, the Minister of International Affairs from 1989 to 1994, travelled more than any of his predecessors over all continents seeking first and foremost to press for Québec's economic interests, but also taking the opportunity to plead for Québec's position in the Canadian Federation and its distinct cultural character.

Two important reports were issued during the years of Liberal government. The first evaluated representation channels abroad out of a concern for efficiency, return, and a better assessment of strategic targets. The report submitted in 1988 did not include recommendations for radical change in areas of representation. It limited itself to suggesting the relocation of a few offices or delegations and placed an emphasis, quite vehemently, on the strengthening of the so-called politics of public interest (*affaires publiques*), that is the sponsorship of Québec internationally and the correction of any distortions in its image if needed.[31] This was followed by a political statement issued in 1991, in the same vein as the one delivered by the PQ government in 1985.[32] In contrast to the latter, the former tries to distinguish the need for international business policies, in a world of growing interdependence, from foreign policy, which, in line with federalist orthodoxy, is left to the federal government.

It did not follow, however, that Québec should decrease its activities. On the contrary, a number of targets for foreign intervention were elucidated in the areas of economy, culture, language and communication, science and technology, human resources, social affairs and the environment, diplomatic expansion, and even intergovernmental and institutional affairs. This document, the lengthiest produced by any Québec government in matters of international relations, developed a policy based on partnerships and an integrated approach. It did not, in any way, seek to decrease Québec's presence in the four corners of the world.[33]

The apparent discontinuities have been less important than the continuities during the years of the Liberal government, as had been the case in the preceding decade. It can even be said that combining economic functions with cultural ones created fortunate results. Luc Bernier writes, "it is possible that ... strategic planning efforts have in the final analysis been especially useful for the exercise that they represented. In discussing ways in which to join the cultural and commercial missions, the Ministry of International Affairs managed to secure its role."[34]

The return of the PQ to power in 1994, under the leadership of Jacques Parizeau, in a pre-referendum context, signalled an administrative reorganization.

Bernard Landry returned to head the merged ministry to which was added the responsibility over Immigration and Cultural Communities. For the most part, the administration was not changed drastically. A year and a half later, with the arrival of Lucien Bouchard in January 1996, the Ministry reverted to operating under the same logic of separating commercial functions from the rest, again for personal reasons. Bernard Landry was brought to the head of all economic ministries, including that of Industry, Commerce, Science and Technology, which would include the function of international trade. A new Ministry of International Relations was created. History repeats itself, as the coordination between economic and political activities is still uncertain.

In the 2001-04 Strategic Plan, however, great emphasis was placed on the integration and management of the Ministry of International Relations. Regarding integration in particular, greater cohesiveness of Québec's international action through the Directorate of Interministerial relations and sectoral action (created in 1999) is stressed:

> Civil servants who are posted abroad by Sectoral ministries such as Industry and Commerce, or organizations such as Investment Québec, are all under the authority of the chief of staff, who oversees the coherence of general activities for Québec on its territory.[35]

Is this a pious hope? Maybe not, again due to the character of those involved. The strong personality of Louise Beaudoin, Minister of International Relations since 1998 (who was already present during the consolidation of the Ministry during the 1970s), combined with the fact that Bernard Landry became premier, creates the hope that there will be improvements in the link between economic functions and Québec's international activities. However, the fact remains that the ministerial "cultures" of civil servants are very different from one ministry to the other. Those involved in matters of international trade often have disdain for purely diplomatic activities or protocols, while individuals engaged in political activities or public affairs may overlook the economic aspects of issues. This is another situation that warrants improvements in coordination.

As one can see, the administration of Québec's international relations has witnessed a number of changes. The Ministry was renamed on five occasions over a period of 15 years. This is often for a small state. However, one should take notice of the remarkable continuity in the desire of different administrations to open relations to the world under varying circumstances and different conceptions of how this opening should be undertaken. Moreover, throughout the eras, the modalities of Québec's foreign policy have diversified. It is important, therefore, to examine the expansion of such activities.

The Gérin-Lajoie doctrine justifies Québec's international activities as an inevitable extension of its jurisdictions on the international level. These jurisdictions are obvious mostly at the level of education, language, and culture. As a consequence, Québec's international policy was first formulated in these areas. However, it was soon realized that Québec's own interests extended to other levels. First and foremost, to the economic level where it was possible to persuade the population of Québec to accept the further expenses that international dealing entails. It is also in this area that interdependence was always felt. Later on, due to modernization and a drastic fall in the birth rate, an immigration portfolio was wanted. To promote Québec, improve its image and increase information was also desired in a world where information was becoming a valuable asset. Finally, Québec's modest size and the growth of multilateral organizations across the world meant that what was true for Canada became true for Québec. International activity could only be pursued within the framework of co-operation and participation in multilateral forums.

Over the years, economic issues were attributed more and more weight. Robert Bourassa has demonstrated concern for this area, notwithstanding the considerable interest his government had for other issues such as communication and so-called cultural sovereignty. As for the PQ government of René Lévesque, it increased the economic aspect of international relations, contrary to what some might have expected, to the point that intervention in areas of trade and economic growth in the pre-referendum period exceeded that of the Bourassa years.[36]

The priority given to the economy grew even further in the following periods. First, the Parti Québécois focused on economic issues and the stimulation of private enterprise following the loss of the 1980 referendum and the constitutional setback of 1981-82, in an environment affected by the worst recession since the 1930s. The party was even accused of having lost its social democratic aspirations. Under these circumstances Jacques-Yvan Morin was travelling in the United States seeking investors and Bernard Landry was inaugurating the new Ministry of International Trade. The PQ remained committed to major issues of international policy, as is shown by its 1985 statement. However, its concern for economic issues was becoming a major part of its international activities. This concern became even more important with Robert Bourassa's return, when other aspects of international relations were willingly pushed aside. The Liberal government's policies of international affairs were focused on the economy. This became very clear with the 1991 statement and the many travels undertaken by Ministers Gobeil and Ciaccia.

Despite his concern, first and foremost, for Québec's independence, Jacques Parizeau had nonetheless shown some interest towards international economic issues. Being an economist by profession, he could not ignore these issues when it came to undertaking the big turn that he was hoping for. It should be noted once more that the then Minister of International Affairs, Bernard Landry, shared the same concerns.

Finally, Lucien Bouchard's focus on the poor state of public finances led him to limit Québec's international activities to their simplest expression by replacing many delegations and offices with basic economic branches and primarily economic missions.

Québec's international relations could thus be characterized as the perpetual rediscovery of the economy by each succeeding government. It was periodically decided that economic issues should be given weight, leaving one under the false impression that this had never been done before.

Such was not the case for immigration, which had not received much attention in the past. It is only by the late 1960s that the importance of a ministry dealing with this issue was recognized. Later on, Québec managed to conclude agreements with the federal government with the aim of playing a greater role on this level. The Andras-Bienvenue agreements under Bourassa and Cullen-Couture under Lévesque have gradually enabled Québec to influence the flow of immigration to its territory. The Ministry of Intergovernmental Affairs has never been able to gain autonomy in its area of intervention, but its responsibilities increased. Immigration consultants were appointed to most Québec delegations. Services were integrated with Canadian embassies in locations where Québec was not represented. Immigration had thus become for Québec a major area of intervention at the international level during the 1970s.

This issue inevitably gained importance in the following periods. The competency of Québec in the areas of selection, reception and integration of immigrants was part of the minimal conditions demanded by Québec in view of the constitutional Accord of Meech Lake. Although the Accord failed, the articles concerning immigration were incorporated in a federal-provincial agreement of 1991, the Gagnon-Tremblay-McDougall agreement.

All governments of the past 20 years have concentrated on this issue. Among other things, they sought to recruit as many French-speaking immigrants as possible, and new immigration services were opened in various Canadian embassies, notably in Hong Kong, Vienna, Beirut, and Rabat.

Information is another issue of growing importance. Public affairs programs were set up during Opération Amérique in 1978. It was becoming increasingly necessary to use various means to raise the level of knowledge about Québec. The distribution of news bulletins, as well as organized trips for journalists and influential individuals, can be traced to this period. It was gradually understood that trying to attract investment and to market products were useless efforts if people did not know Québec and were hardly able to place it on a map.

It has been stated time and again that the role of information has increased exponentially during the last years of the twentieth century, with the use of tools such as the Internet that make communication across the globe all the more possible. The Ministry of International Relations adopted a web site to distribute information about Québec. The web site contains, among other things, newspaper and magazine articles written in French and translated into English, and then into other languages.

Québec's policy regarding public affairs has gone through highs and lows. It was sometimes neglected and even considered somewhat superfluous. Despite variations in the degree of importance given to public affairs, overall progress was still recorded in this area with remarkable results. The strategic plan of 2001 provides an assessment: "There are more than 2000 specialists in universities and research centers who are interested in Québec. Their work sometimes has a considerable impact in their respective areas and contributes to the knowledge and appreciation of Québec."[37] An international association of Québec studies, founded in 1997 through the sponsorship of the Ministry, is now able to function autonomously in line with academic norms. The association has been able to recruit hundreds of members in many different countries.

The Strategic Plan still points to the lack of information about Québec internationally. The information often is distorted due to the reliance on data in English emanating from Toronto or Ottawa where most foreign correspondents are situated. This was already noted 20 years ago by an American commentator.[38] Québec's diplomatic agents must try harder than others to diffuse positive information about the economic, political, and cultural reality of Québec. The International Relations Ministry set in place programs to invite foreign journalists and notable individuals to that end.

Finally, Québec's international relations had to be extended to multilateral organizations. This appeared to be a necessity as Québec's international status was at the heart of ACCT. Soon after, a directorate of international co-operation was created within the Ministry of International Affairs. Québec sought to make its voice heard in the growing number of forums that dealt with issues relevant to its constitutional competency. This did not lead to immediate or conclusive results, in part due to the federal government's inflexibility on the issue.

Though Québec is not a member of organizations such as the United Nations' Education, Science, and Cultural Organization (UNESCO) or the Organization for Economic Co-operation and Development (OECD), it did establish relations with some member countries through the channels of la francophonie. However, the fact that Québec cannot in any way participate in the decision-making process at UNESCO, despite being a province entirely responsible for its education and in large part for the evolution of a culture, is highly problematic. It should nonetheless be noted that Québec City has for a number of years housed UNESCO's secretariat of world heritage cities.

Québec has still managed to become a member of multilateral international organizations that do not deal with sovereign states, like the Conference of New England Governors and Eastern Canadian Premiers and others that were recently established to gather a number of federal states and/or autonomous regions.

Québec has also sought to gain recognition as an autonomous actor on the issue of cultural diversity, which it ardently promotes in North America and other regions, most notably through the organization of French-speaking nations. Québec is able to work in parallel with the federal government on this issue because both governments seek to dissociate the economic aspects of trade liberalization from its cultural aspects. There is no reason to believe that this cannot lead to an increase in the ability of Québec to affirm its distinct culture and gain a voice in Canadian delegations. Logically, Canada cannot stress the uniqueness of Anglo-Canadian culture without accepting the cultural specificity of Québec. It is, therefore, regrettable that artificial conflicts have been created and maintained on this issue, as they have in others.

Conclusion

The international relations of Québec have developed throughout the past 40 or so years with remarkable continuity. Of the factors that have stimulated the development of these relations during the 1960s, two have stable attributes and are more legitimate than ever—the context of an international system in which diplomacy no longer remains the exclusive preserve of sovereign states, and the resolve of Quebecers to constitute a distinct society, a particular political entity with specific external as well as internal interests. The two others, stemming from features of the Canadian federation and the role of France, are specific to a given time period. Canada has undergone much change since then. It increasingly affirms itself as a nation-state and much less as a federation. France no longer plays the same role with regard to Québec but continues to represent an essential and privileged partner.

Québec's international status is still assured within la francophonie, which has become a stable international organization, even though the Canadian government frequently attempts, in an indirect way, to undermine this status. Despite these obstacles, Québec's network of international representation continues to extend to various points of the globe, primarily in the American continent but also in more distant parts of the world.

The administration of international relations within the government of Québec has endured trials, difficulties, and hesitations. It is seriously limited by the absence of an external service, but it has nevertheless accomplished an impressive diversification of functions related to international influence. The record is quite positive.

Notes

1. "The general DELEGATION OF QUÉBEC is a representation ... led by a general delegate of Québec. The latter is appointed by the government (Decree of the Council of Ministers), by a commission under the seal, in all countries of designation, to represent on the indicated territory, Québec in all sectors of activity that are within the constitutional jurisdiction of Québec....

"The DELEGATION OF QUÉBEC is a representation ... led by a delegate of Québec. The latter is appointed by the government (Decree of the council of Ministers) to represent, on the designated territory, all of the sectors attributed to Québec ...

"The OFFICE OF QUÉBEC is an establishment ... under the responsibility of a director and a member of the Québec public service, who is appointed by the Minister of International Relations and acts as a representative of the Minister....

"A BRANCH is established in a foreign country in order to provide at that location the services of the government of Québec, in one or several determined fields. The administration may demand that it render certain services to particular individuals or groups from Québec. The branch is directed by a resident of the country and does not employ bureaucrats from Québec. It has no function of representation.

"SPECIALIZED SERVICES, in domains such as the economy, culture and immigration, can be located within or outside of delegations."

Ministry of International Relations, *Le Québec dans un ensemble international en mutation. Plan stratégique 2001-2004* (Québec, Government of Québec, 6). Author's translation. See also the Web site of the Ministry of International Relations: <www.mri.gouv.qc.ca>.

2. Ministry of International Relations, *Guide de la pratique des relations internationales* (Québec: Government of Québec, 2000), 5-10.

3. Georges-Émile Lapalme, *Le paradis du pouvoir (mémoires, t. III)* (Montréal: Leméac, 1973), 47.

4. Thomas Allen Levy, "Le rôle des provinces," in Paul Painchaud, ed., *Le Canada et le Québec sur la scène internationale*, Québec Centre québécois de relations internationales (Sainte-Foy: Les Presses de l'Université du Québec), 144. Author's translation.

5. Lapalme, *Le paradis du pouvoir*, 47.

6. Paul Gérin-Lajoie, *Combats d'un révolutionnaire tranquille* (Montréal: Centre éducatif et culturel, 1989), 322ff.

7. Cited by Claude Morin, *L'art de l'impossible. La diplomatie québécoise depuis 1960* (Montréal: Boréal, 1987), 28. Author's translation.

8. Cited by Claude Morin, *L'art de l'impossible*, 29. Author's translation.

9. Secretary of State for External Affairs, *Federalism and International Relations*, Ottawa, Queen's Printer, 1968; Secretary of State for External Affairs, *Federalism and International Conferences on Education* (Ottawa: Queen's Printer, 1968).

10. Ministry of International Relations, *Le Québec dans un ensemble international en mutation*, 21.

11. Quoted by Morin, *L'art de l'impossible*, 227. Author's translation.

12. See Frédéric Bastien, *Relations particulières. La France au Québec après de Gaulle* (Montréal: Boréal, 2000).

13. Cited by Morin, *L'art de l'impossible*, 457.

14. *Canada in the World: Government Statement* (Ottawa: Canada Communication Group Publishing, 1995), 38.

15. Ibid., 11.

16. Ibid., 39.

17. Ministry of International Relations, *Le Québec dans un ensemble international en mutation*, 23.

18. Louis Balthazar and Alfred O. Hero, Jr., *Le Québec dans l'espace américain* (Montréal: Québec Amérique, collection "Débats," 1999), 311-12.

19. A series of Québec-sponsored cultural events were supposed to take place in New York. It was abruptly interrupted by the tragic events of September 11.

20. See Shiro Noda, *Entre l'indépendance et le fédéralisme. 1970-1980. La décennie marquante des relations internationales du Québec* (Sainte-Foy: Les Presses de l'Université Laval, 2001).

21. Ibid., 65-68.

22. Ibid., 187-93. Author's translation; see also Bastien, 152-54.

23. Bastien, *Relations particulières*, 329-33.

24. It must be noted, however, that commerce with France amounts to 1 per cent of Québec's international trade.

25. Ministry of International Relations, *Le Québec dans un ensemble international en mutation*, 40. Author's translation.

26. Noda, *Entre l'indepenance et le fédéralisme*, 20.

27. Ministry of International Relations, *Le Québec dans un ensemble international en mutation*, 1. Author's translation.

28. Noda, *Entre l'indépendance et le fédéralisme*, 194. Author's translation.

29. Ibid., 207.

30. Luc Bernier, *De Paris à Washington. La politique internationale du Québec* (Québec: Les Presses de l'Université du Québec, 1996), 19-20. Author's translation.

31. Ministry of International Affairs, *Évaluation du réseau de représentation du Québec à l'étranger*. Rapport synthèse, Marcel Bergeron (Québec: Government of Québec, 1988).

32. Ministry of International Relations, *Le Québec dans le monde ou le défi de l'interdépendance* (Québec: Government of Québec, 1985).

33. Ministry of International Affairs, *Le Québec et l'interdépendance. Le monde pour horizon. Éléments d'une politique d'affaires internationales* (Québec: Government of Québec, 1991).

34. Bernier, *De Paris à Washington*, 127.

35. Ministry of International Relations, *Le Québec dans un ensemble international en mutation*, 57.

36. Louis Balthazar, Louis Bélanger and Gordon Mace, eds., *Trente ans de politique extérieure du Québec, 1960-1990* (Québec: Centre québécois de relations internationales, Le Septentrion, 1993), 70.

37. Ministry of International Relations, *Le Québec dans un ensemble international en mutation*, 51.

38. Stephen Banker, "How America Sees Québec," in Alfred O. Hero, Jr. and Marcel Daneau, eds., *Problems and Opportunities in US-Québec Relations* (Boulder, CO: Westview Press, 1984), 181.

Contributors

LOUIS BALTHAZAR is Emeritus Professor in the Department of Political Science at Laval University and adjunct professor in the Department of Political Science at the Université du Québec à Montréal. He is the co-author with Alfred O. Hero, Jr., of *Le Québec dans l'espace américain* (1999) and is the co-editor, with Louis Bélanger and Gordon Mace, of *Trente ans de politique extérieure du Québec, 1960-1990* (1993).

JACQUES BEAUCHEMIN is Professor of Sociology at the Université du Québec à Montréal. He specializes in political sociology and is the author of *L'histoire en trop. La mauvaise conscience des souverainistes québécois* (2002). He has published, in collaboration with Gilles Bourque and Jules Duchastel, *La société libérale duplessiste*.

LUC BERNIER is Professor at the École nationale d'administration publique (ÉNAP). He has published, in collaboration with Evan H. Potter, *Business Planning in Canadian Public Administration* (2001) and with Guy Lachapelle and Pierre Tremblay, *Le processus budgétaire au Québec* (1999).

ANDRÉ BLAIS is Professor in the Department of Political Science and holds the Canada Research Chair in Electoral Studies. Among his recent publications are *To Vote or Not to Vote? The Merits and Limits of Rational Choice Theory* (2000) and, in collaboration with Elisabeth Gidengil, Richard Nadeau, and Neil Nevitte, *Anatomy of a Liberal Victory: Making Sense of the 2000 Canadian Election* (2002).

JEAN CHAREST is Professor at the École de Relations industrielles, Université de Montréal since 1997. He has published extensively in the areas of manpower training, industrial relations, and labour organizations.

ALAIN-G. GAGNON is Professor in the Department of Political Science at the Université du Québec à Montréal where he holds the Canada Research Chair in Québec and Canadian Studies. He is also the coordinator of the Research Group on Plurinational Societies. His most recent publications include, *Ties That Bind: Parties and Voters in Canada*, co-authored with James Bickerton and Patrick Smith (1999); *The Canadian Social Union Without Québec* (2000), co-edited with Hugh Segal; *Multinational Democracies*, co-edited with James Tully (2001); and *Repères en mutation*, co-edited with Jocelyn Maclure (2001).

FRANCOIS GARON is a Ph.D. candidate at the École nationale d'administration publique (ÉNAP). His research deals with the consultative process in Canada and France, especially in the field of biotechnologies.

ELISABETH GIDENGIL is Professor in the Department of Political Science at McGill University. She specializes in the study of voting behaviour, public opinion, gender, and the media. She has been a member of the 1993, 1997, and 2000 Canadian Election Study teams. She is a co-author of *Anatomy of a Liberal Victory: Making Sense of the 2000 Canadian Election* (2002), *Unsteady State: The 1997 Canadian Election* (2000), and *The Challenge of Direct Democracy* (1996).

PETER GRAEFE is Assistant Professor in the Department of Political Science at McMaster University. His main areas of expertise include economic development and social economy. His publications include articles in *Policy & Politics*, *Critical Social Policy*, *Studies in Political Economy*, as well as *Lien social et Politiques*.

RAFFAELE IACOVINO is a Ph.D. candidate at McGill University. His research focuses on Canadian politics, Québec-Canada relations, and citizenship. In 2003, he has published in collaboration with Alain-G. Gagnon "Framing Citizenship Status in an Age of Polyethnicity," in Harvey Lazar and Hamish Telford, eds., *The Transformation of Canadian Political Culture and the State of the Federation*, and "Strengthening Regional Responsiveness and Democracy in Canada," in David Stewart and Paul Thomas, eds., *The Changing Nature of Democracy and Federalism in Canada*.

DIMITRIOS KARMIS is Assistant Professor of Political Science at the University of Ottawa. He works in the fields of political theory, comparative politics, and Canadian politics. His research focuses on the normative dimensions of federalism, identity politics, language policy, citizenship education, and democracy in diverse societies. His publications include articles in *Ethnic and Racial Studies*, the *Canadian Journal of Political Science*, and *Politique et Sociétés*. He is currently working on two books entitled *Between Nationalism and Cosmopolitanism: Reassessing the Potential of Normative Theories of Federalism in the Modern World* and, as co-editor with Wayne Norman, *Theories of Federalism*.

MICHAEL KEATING is Professor of Regional Studies at the European University Institute of Florence and Professor of Scottish Politics at the University of Aberdeen. He has published abundantly on the subjects of local and regional politics and on nationalism. He is the author of *Plurinational Democracy: Stateless Nations in a Post-Sovereignty Era* (2001), *Nations Against the State: The New Politics of Nationalism in Quebec, Catalonia and Scotland* (2001).

ANDRÉE LAJOIE is Professor in the Law Faculty at the Université de Montréal where she is a member of the Centre de recherche en droit public. Recently her work has been on legal theory (pluralism as well as hermeneutics) especially in relation to minority rights and production of a legal corpus. Her publications include *Quand les minorités font la Loi* (2002) and *Jugements de valeurs: le discours judiciaire et le droit* (1997).

MARC LEMIRE holds a Ph.D. from the Department of Political Science at the Université du Québec à Montréal. His principal areas of interest are political participation, social movements, public health services, and social computerization. He is the author of "Globalization, Information Society and Social Movement," to appear in Peter Saunders, ed., *Citizenship and Participation in the Information Age*.

JOCELYN MACLURE is completing a post-doctoral fellowship in Political Science at the University of Toronto. His research interests centre on democracy and the integration of societies in an era marked by the pluralism of values and cultural diversity. He has published, in the *Débats* series, *Récits identitaires: Le Québec à l'épreuve du pluralisme* (2000). The English version of this book has been published by McGill-Queen's University Press. He has co-edited, with Alain-G. Gagnon, *Repères en mutation: Identité et citoyenneté dans le Québec contemporain* (2001).

CHANTAL MAILLÉ is Associate Professor at the Institute Simone de Beauvoir, Concordia University. She is Vice-présidente of the Conseil du statut de la femme du Québec. She is the author of several books among which *Cherchez la femme: trente ans de débats constitutionnels au Québec* (2002), and co-author with Diane

Lamoureux and Micheline de Sève of *Malaises identitaires, échanges féministes sur un Québec incertain* (1999).

MARIE MC ANDREW is Professor in the Departement d'études en éducation et d'administration de l'éducation of the Université de Montréal and Director of Immigration et métropoles of the Centre de recherche interuniversitaire de Montréal sur l'immigration, l'intégration et la dynamique urbaine. She is the author of *Immigration et diversité à l'école: le débat québécois dans une perspective comparative* (2001).

ÉRIC MONTPETIT is Assistant Professor in the Department of Political Science at the Université de Montréal. He specializes in democratic legitimacy in the field of biotechnologies in Canada. Recently he has published in *Governance, Journal of European Public Policy, Canadian Journal of Political Science*, and *Politique et Sociétés*. His work has also been published in *World Politics* and *Globe*.

RICHARD NADEAU is Professor in the Department of Political Science at the Université de Montréal. He has been a member of the Canadian Election Study teams. His fields of research include electoral behaviour and public opinion in Western democracies. He has published extensively in the *Canadian Journal of Political Science* and the *American Journal of Political Science*. He is the co-author (with André Blais, Elisabeth Gidengil, and Neil Nevitte) of *Unsteady State: The 1997 Canadian Election* (2000) and *Political Value Change in Western Democracies* (1998).

NEIL NEVITTE is Professor of Political Science at the University of Toronto. His work concentrates on public opinion and electoral behaviour. He has been a member of the Canadian Election Study teams as well as the principal researcher of World Values Poll for Canada. He is the editor of *Value Change and Governance* (2002) and the co-author (with André Blais, Elisabeth Gidengil, and Richard Nadeau) of *Unsteady State: The 1997 Canadian Election* (2000) and *Political Value Change in Western Democracies* (1998).

FRANÇOIS ROCHER is Professor at Carleton University in Ottawa where he is the Director of the School of Canadian Studies, as well as teaching in the Department of Political Science. He has served as President of the Société québécoise de science politique (2001-02) and co-director of the Canadian Journal of Political Science (1996-99). His research centres on Canadian federalism, citizenship, and interethnic relations in Canada. He is a member of the Research Group on Plurinational Societies (RGPS) and the Centre for Research on Immigration, Ethnicity and Citizenship (CRIEC). He has published, in collaboration with Miriam Smith, *New*

Trends in Canadian Federalism, 2nd ed. (2003), as well as *Bilan québécoise du fédéralisme canadien* (1992).

CHRISTIAN ROUILLARD is Assistant Professor at the École nationale d'administration publique (ÉNAP) since 1999 where he teaches public management. He specializes in the study of power structures in complex public organizations, with a specific focus on public management and innovation.

GARTH STEVENSON is Professor in the Department of Political Science at Brock University. His main fields of research are Canadian federalism, minority politics, and Québec politics more generally. He is the author of *Community Besieged: the Anglophone Minority and the Politics of Québec* (1999).

DANIEL SALÉE is Professor of Political Science and Director of the School of Community and Public Affairs at Concordia University. He is a member of the Centre for Research on Immigration, Ethnicity and Citizenship (CRIEC). He specializes in social relations in Québec and Canada. His recent studies focus on inter-ethnic relations within Québec, the national question, and citizenship in Canada and Québec.

BRIAN TANGUAY is Associate Professor of Political Science and a former coordinator of the Canadian Studies program at Wilfrid Laurier University. He is the co-editor (with Alain-G. Gagnon) of *Canadian Parties in Transition* (1990, 1996) and has published articles on the political activities of interest groups and social movements for the Royal Commission on Electoral Reform and Party Financing, the *International Journal of Canadian Studies*, and *Canadian Public Administration*. He is currently conducting research on electoral reform in liberal democracies and on the evolving division of labour between political parties and organized interests.

LUC TURGEON is a doctoral candidate in the Department of Political Science at the University of Toronto. His research looks principally at the relations between the state and society in Canada and in Great Britain, public policy of economic development, and theories of constitutionalism and federalism. He has published articles in *Globe*, *Revue internationale d'études québécoises* and the *Journal of Commonwealth and Comparative Politics* and has forthcoming chapters in edited books on Québec politics, democratic consolidation, and transnational democracy.

Index